# Never Forget Your Name

# NEVER FORGET YOUR NAME

## The Children of Auschwitz

Alwin Meyer

*Translated by Nick Somers*

polity

Originally published in German as *Vergiss deinen Namen nicht. Die Kinder von Auschwitz* by
Alwin Meyer
© Steidl Verlag, Göttingen 2015

This English edition © Polity Press, 2022

The translation of this work was funded by Geisteswissenschaften International – Translation
Funding for Work in the Humanities and Social Sciences from Germany, a joint initiative of
the Fritz Thyssen Foundation, the German Federal Foreign Office, the collecting society VG
WORT and the Börsenverein des Deutschen Buchhandels (German Publishers & Booksellers
Association).

The publishers gratefully acknowledge Catriona Corke's contribution to the English translation.

Polity Press
65 Bridge Street
Cambridge CB2 1UR, UK

Polity Press
101 Station Landing
Suite 300
Medford, MA 02155, USA

ISBN-13: 978-1-5095-4550-6

A catalogue record for this book is available from the British Library.

Library of Congress Control Number: 2021941498

Typeset in 11.5 on 14 Adobe Garamond
by Fakenham Prepress Solutions, Fakenham, Norfolk NR21 8NL
Printed and bound in Great Britain by TJ Books Ltd, Padstow, Cornwall

The publisher has used its best endeavours to ensure that the URLs for external websites referred
to in this book are correct and active at the time of going to press. However, the publisher has
no responsibility for the websites and can make no guarantee that a site will remain live or that
the content is or will remain appropriate.

Every effort has been made to trace all copyright holders, but if any have been overlooked the
publisher will be pleased to include any necessary credits in any subsequent reprint or edition.

For further information on Polity, visit our website:
politybooks.com

This book is dedicated to Janek (Jack) Mandelbaum, without whose generosity the English translation would not have been possible. Having survived five Nazi concentration camps and the murder of his parents, sister and brother during the Holocaust, he has spent the last seventy-five years educating people about this dark period of history. His contribution to the publication of this book is part of that noble effort.

# Contents

# *Preface*

Children in Auschwitz: the darkest spot on an ocean of suffering, criminality and death with a thousand faces – humiliation; contempt; harassment; persecution; fanatical racism; transports; lice; rats; diseases; epidemics; beatings; Mengele; experiments; smoking crematorium chimneys; abominable stench; starvation; selections; brutal separation from mothers, fathers, sisters, brothers, grandmothers, grandfathers, aunts, uncles and friends; gas ...

In 1940, a first camp by the name of Auschwitz, later to be known as the Main Camp or Auschwitz I, was erected by the Nazis on the outskirts of the Polish town of Oświęcim (65 kilometres west of Kraków). The first transport of Polish inmates arrived from German-occupied Poland in mid-1940. In 1941, the Nazis planned and built the killing centre (extermination camp) Auschwitz-Birkenau, also known as Auschwitz II, on the site of the destroyed village of Brzezinka.

From March 1942, Jewish children and their families were transported to Auschwitz from almost all German-occupied countries, for the sole reason that they were Jews. There were already a large number of Jewish boys and girls in the first transports to Auschwitz from Slovakia. Well over 200,000 children were to follow, and almost all of them were murdered.

The Auschwitz complex consisted of forty-eight concentration and extermination camps. Auschwitz-Birkenau has become the unmatched symbol of contempt for humanity, and a unique synonym for the mass murder of European Jewry. It was the site of the largest killing centre conceived, built and operated by the Germans, and played a central role in the Nazi 'Final Solution',[1] the systematic extermination of Europe's Jewish inhabitants.

By far the largest group of children deported to Auschwitz were thus Jewish girls and boys (see also pages xi and xii). Most of them were transported with their families in packed, closed and sealed freight cars, mercilessly exposed to the summer heat and freezing winters. They had to relieve themselves in buckets that were soon full. Because the wagons were so packed, many couldn't even reach the buckets in time and the floors were swimming in urine and excrement. The stench was overwhelming. In many cases, the deportees had little or nothing to eat or drink. Although especially the small children begged constantly for water, their entreaties went unheard. Many – particularly infants, young children and elderly persons – died during the journeys, which often lasted for days.

The Jews were deliberately kept in the dark about the real intentions of the Nazis. Before the deportations, they were told that they were being resettled in labour camps in the East, where they could start a new life.

The opposite was true. The Jewish children, women and men were destined to be murdered. They were 'welcomed at the ramp in Auschwitz with the bellowed order: "Everyone out! Leave your luggage where it is!"' The few people who were initially kept alive never again saw the possessions they had been allowed to bring with them.

Selections began sporadically from April 1942, and then regularly from July of that year. They were carried out on the railway ramp, usually by SS doctors but also by pharmacists, medical orderlies and dentists. Young, healthy and strong women and men whom they considered 'fit for work' were temporarily allowed to live and were separated from the old and invalid, pregnant women and children. Germans randomly classed around 80 per cent of the Jews – often also entire transports – as 'unfit for work', particularly during the deportations to the Auschwitz-Birkenau killing centre of 438,000 Hungarian Jewish children, women and men from May 1944. These people were marched under guard or transported in trucks by the SS to one of the crematoria, where they were ordered to undress. Under the pretext that they were to be showered, the SS herded them into the gas chambers disguised to look like showers. The poisonous gas Zyklon B was then introduced, and those inside suffered an agonizing death by suffocation. It took 10 to 20 minutes for them all to die.

Small children in Auschwitz were almost all killed on arrival. If a mother was carrying her child during the initial selection, they were both gassed, however healthy and 'fit for work' the young mother might be. This was irrelevant. Pregnant woman also suffered a terrible fate in Auschwitz. They were 'automatically' killed by phenolin injection, gassed or beaten to death. This applied initially to Jewish and non-Jewish women alike. Pregnant women from other concentration camps were also transferred to Auschwitz exclusively to be gassed.

A stay of execution was granted only to those condemned to heavy physical slave labour inside and outside the camp. These men and women were physically and psychologically exploited in road building, agriculture or industrial and armaments factories, in which inmates from the satellite camps in particular were forced into slave labour.

Sometimes children aged between 13 and 15 were also 'selected for work' and allowed to live, usually only for a short time. For example, a large group of children and juveniles were assigned to the 'Rollwagen-Kommando', where they pulled heavy carts in place of horses, transporting blankets, wood or the ashes of incinerated children, women and men from the crematoria. They were highly mobile and had plenty of opportunity to see the atrocities taking place in the camp.

Some sets of twins up to the age of 16 were also kept alive for a time. SS doctor Mengele exploited and misused both Jewish and Sinti and Roma twins for pseudo-medical experiments. They were selected, measured, X-rayed, infected with viruses or had their eyes cauterized, and then killed, dissected and burned.

Throughout the five years of its existence – from the first to the last – however, the main purpose and primary aim of the killing centre was extermination. All other aims by the Nazis – such as exploitation of the children, women and men as slave labourers, or the criminal, so-called 'medical', experiments by SS doctors – were of secondary importance.

The children and juveniles transferred temporarily to the camp soon became acquainted with the reality of Auschwitz. They didn't know whether they would still be alive from one day to the next. No one could foresee how the same situation would be dealt with by the SS the next day, the next hour or the next minute. Any act could mean immediate death. Apart from extermination, nothing in Auschwitz was predictable. The children were permanently confronted with death and knew that they had to be on their guard at all times.

*

• More than 1.3 million people were deported to Auschwitz between 1940 and 1945. Among them were at least 1.1 million Jews. They came from Hungary, Poland, France, the Netherlands, Greece, Czechoslovakia,

Belgium, Romania, the Soviet Union (especially Byelorussia, Ukraine and Russia), Yugoslavia, Italy, Norway, Luxembourg, Lithuania, Latvia, Austria, Germany and elsewhere.[2]

- The Auschwitz complex consisted of three main units. The Main Camp, Auschwitz I, held up to 20,000 people. The killing centre Birkenau, or Auschwitz II, was the largest unit of the camp complex, containing as many as 90,000 children, women and men. Birkenau was divided into ten sections separated by electrified barbed-wire fences. For example, there was the Women's Camp, the Theresienstadt Family Camp, the Men's Camp and the Gypsy Family Camp, where Sinti and Roma were interned. In Auschwitz III (Monowitz), IG Farbenindustrie AG (headquarters Frankfurt am Main) employed Auschwitz concentration camp inmates as slave labour to make synthetic rubber ('Buna') and fuel. There were also forty-five satellite camps of various sizes, such as Blechhammer, Kattowitz or Rajsko.[3]

- At least 1 million Jewish babies, children, juveniles, women and men, mostly in Auschwitz-Birkenau, were starved to death, killed by injections into the heart, murdered in criminal pseudo-medical experiments, shot, beaten to death or gassed.[4]

- Between 70,000 and 75,000 non-Jewish Poles, 21,000 Roma and Sinti, 14,000 Soviet prisoners of war and 10–15,000 non-Jewish inmates speaking many languages were murdered in Auschwitz.[5]

- At least 232,000 infants, children and adolescents between the ages of 1 day and 17 years inclusive were deported to Auschwitz, including 216,300 Jews and 11,000 Roma and Sinti; 3,120 were non-Jewish Poles, 1,140 were Byelorussians, Russians and Ukrainians, from other nations.[6]

- On 27 January 1945, only about 750 children and youths aged under 18 years were liberated; only 521 boys and girls aged 14 and under,[7] including around 60 new-born babies, were still alive, and several of them died shortly afterwards.[8]

\*

Very few of the children deported to Auschwitz remained alive. To some extent, the survival of every child was an anomaly unforeseen by the Nazis, a type of resistance to the only fate that Germans had planned for the children – namely, extermination. Very many of the children and juveniles in this book are fully aware that their survival was a matter of pure luck.

In some cases, comradeship and solidarity among the camp inmates helped them to stay alive. For example, some women relate how their pregnancy remained undetected because of the starvation rations in the camp, enabling them to give birth in secret. Once the child was born, it had practically no chance of survival. SS doctors, medical orderlies and their assistants took the mother and child and killed them. Sometimes, however, the mother managed, with the aid of other women inmates, to hide and feed her baby for a while. This was particularly true of the infants born in the last weeks and days before Auschwitz-Birkenau was liberated.[9]

Others are convinced that they survived through their belief in God. Otto Klein, who, at the age of 11, was claimed with his twin brother Ferenc by Mengele for pseudo-medical experiments, for example, never dared to doubt in God. 'That would have been the end. Deep down in my heart, I always remained a Jew. No one and nothing could beat that out of me. Not even Auschwitz.'

For the few children who were liberated, the pain is always there: before breakfast, during the day, in the evening, at night. The memory of mothers, fathers, sisters, brothers, the grandparents, girlfriends, boyfriends, aunts and uncles, killed in the camps. For a lifetime and beyond, the pain is ever present, not only in their lives but also in those of their own children and grandchildren.

Even if the number tattooed on the forearm, thigh or buttocks is often the only outward sign that they were in Auschwitz, they bear the traces of suffering on their bodies and in their souls.

The older liberated children of Auschwitz talk about their happy childhoods at home, about school, life in a Jewish community, the relationship between Jewish and non-Jewish children, the arrival of the Germans, the growing apprehension, the refugees, the chaos prior to deportation, the end of playing, the transport in cattle wagons, the arrival in Auschwitz, the mortal fear.

The children remember the gnawing hunger; the experiments carried out on them; the cold that pierced to the bone; the constant selections by the SS; the fear that their number would be called out; the longing for their parents, a good meal, an eiderdown, warmth. They were torn between despair and hope. They wanted to see their mothers and fathers, brothers and sisters again. They wanted to go home. They wanted their old and happy lives back. They wanted to be able to be children again.

Only a few survived Auschwitz and the other camps where they were interned. The children rescued from the camps were just skin and bone. The people caring for them feared that they would not live. They looked like skeletons, with bite wounds from the dogs, bodies covered in sores, eyes stuck together with pus; for a long time, anything they ate went in one end and straight out the other; they had tuberculosis, pneumonia and encephalitis.

Some had no idea where they were from. Practically all of them were orphans. The smaller children in particular were marked by their life in the camp. They spoke a mixture of languages. For a long time, the girls and boys lived in fear that something – particularly food and clothing – would be snatched away from them. Hiding food was part of their survival strategy. They defended it with their lives, because in the camp even the smallest possession had had inestimable value. Every small piece of bread meant survival for one or two days or more. Even spoiled food was not thrown away. When adults who had not been in the camp suggested this, they would look at them incredulously and think to themselves: 'You have no idea what life is really like!'

The small children were incapable of playing. When they were presented with playthings, they gave them a cursory glance or threw them away. They didn't know what they were or what to do with them. These children had first to learn how to play. They were irritable and mistrustful. Dogs, rats and uniforms caused indescribable anxiety. When someone left them, some of the smaller children assumed they were dead. Others couldn't believe at first that people could die of natural causes.

The children of Auschwitz were free, but how could they live after what they had been through? It took them years of painstaking work to learn to see life from a perspective other than that of the camp. They had to learn to survive the camp emotionally. They had to learn to be young again so as to be able to grow old like others.

As they grew older, those children of Auschwitz were increasingly motivated to find out where they came from. In searching for their parents, the number tattooed on their arm often helped, because their numbers were tattooed at the same time – first the mother, then the daughter with serial numbers from the Women's Camp; or the father, then the son, from the Men's Camp.

Only a few were reunited, years later, with their parents. They were soon conflicted as to who their real mothers and fathers were. In the experience of the author of this book, the answer was always the adoptive parents. They went back to the place where they had experienced most warmth in their lives. For the biological parents, this was a bitter disappointment, losing a son or a daughter for a second time. The others never stopped asking whether their families had been killed in the gas chambers, or had perhaps survived somewhere. They continued to look for their parents, siblings, grandparents and friends – at least in their dreams.

Those who survived Auschwitz as children or juveniles continued to wonder whether their families had really died in the gas chambers. They would come across newspaper articles reporting on the return of people thought dead. Hope made it possible for them to continue living. It was just a dream that they would wake from. Then everything would be fine again. But no one came back.

The survivors' children and grandchildren can sense how their parents and grandparents suffer. They often know much more than their parents and grandparents think – despite their having done everything possible to protect them from the consequences of Auschwitz.

The children of Auschwitz had to show supreme resolve to make their way in the world. They sought and found new lives, went to school, studied, married, had children, pursued careers and created new homes. But as they got older and no longer had to concern themselves as much with their own families, the memories of Auschwitz returned with a vengeance. Every day, every hour, the pain is there: the memory of their mothers, fathers, brothers and sisters, all murdered. Many can still remember them quite clearly. How they would love to hear their voices again. How they would love once again to speak to their parents and siblings, or to hug them.

The ancestors and descendants of the children of Auschwitz who tell their stories in this book lived and live among us in Będzin, Békéscsaba, Berlin, Bilky, Budapest, Csepel, Czaniec, Davos, Delvin, Dimona, El Paso, Esslingen, Frankfurt am Main, Gdynia, Geneva, Givat Haviva, Haifa, Hajdúböszörmény, Hartford, Herzliya, Hronov, Jerusalem,

Kansas City, Kaunas, Konstanz, Kraków, Kutná Hora, London, Los Angeles, Lubin, Miskolc, Montreal, Mukachevo, Naples, New York, Odolice, Orsha, Oslo, Ostrava, Paris, Prague, Providence, Sárospatak, Thessaloniki, Topol'čany, Toronto, Turany nad Ondavou, Veľký Meder, Vienna, Vilnius, Vitebsk, Warsaw, Yad Hanna, Yalta, Yenakiieve, Zabrze, Zurich.

When the persecutions by Nazi Germany began throughout Europe, the children of Auschwitz featured in this book were babies, toddlers and children up to 14 years old. When they were forced to work as slaves or were interned for the first time in ghettos or camps, they were all children. When they were transported to Auschwitz-Birkenau, four were juveniles, none of the others older than 15. Four of the children were born in Auschwitz.

The children of Auschwitz interviewed for this book are among the very last survivors. Herbert Adler, Yehuda Bacon, Halina Birenbaum, Robert Büchler, Gábor Hirsch, Lydia Holznerová, Krzysztof J., Otto Klein, Kola Klimczyk, Josif Konvoj, Eduard Kornfeld, Heinz Salvator Kounio, Géza Kozma, Ewa Krcz-Siezka, Vera Kriegel, Dagmar Lieblová, Dasha Lewin, Channa Loewenstein, Israel Loewenstein, Mirjam M., Jack Mandelbaum, Angela Orosz-Richt, Lidia Rydzikowska, Olga Solomon, Jiří Steiner, William Wermuth, Barbara Wesołowska and other children of Auschwitz were willing to tell the story of their survival, and life afterwards.

The life stories of the children of Auschwitz are based above all on numerous lengthy interviews with them, their families and friends. This book could never have been written without the willingness of the children of Auschwitz to provide information, without their hospitality, their openness and their trust. It is their book first and foremost. It contains the life stories of people who know more than others what life means.

# Acknowledgements

This book could not have been written without the cooperation and willingness to provide information of the following:

Herbert Adler, Frankfurt am Main, Germany
Yehuda Bacon, Jerusalem, Israel
Halina Birenbaum, Herzliya, Israel
Robert Büchler, Lahavot Haviva, Israel
Gábor Hirsch, Esslingen, Switzerland
Lydia Holznerová, Prague, Czech Republic
Krzysztof J., Poland and Germany
Otto Klein, Geneva, Switzerland
Kola Klimczyk, Kraków, Poland
Josif Konvoj, Vilnius, Lithuania
Eduard Kornfeld, Zurich, Switzerland
Heinz Salvator Kounio, Thessaloniki, Greece
Géza Kozma, Budapest, Hungary
Ewa Krcz-Siezka, Poland
Vera Kriegel, Dimona, Israel
Dasha Lewin, Los Angeles, USA
Dagmar Lieblová, Prague, Czech Republic
Channa Loewenstein, Yad Hanna, Israel
Israel Loewenstein, Yad Hanna, Israel
Mirjam M., Tel Aviv, Israel
Jack Mandelbaum, Naples, FL, USA
Angela Orosz-Richt, Montreal, Canada
Hanka Paszko, Katowice, Poland
Anna Polshchikova, Yalta, Ukraine
Lidia Rydzikowska-Maksymowicz, Kraków, Poland
Adolph Smajovich-Goldenberg, Bilky, Ukraine
Olga Solomon, Haifa, Israel

ACKNOWLEDGEMENTS

Maury Špíra Lewin, Los Angeles, USA
Jiří Steiner, Prague, Czech Republic
William Wermuth, Konstanz, Germany
Barbara Wesołowska, Będzin, Poland

I give them my thanks for their trust and hospitality.

I was first inspired to investigate the lives of the children of Auschwitz
by Tadeusz Szymański (Oświęcim, Poland) in 1972. I am particularly
grateful to him for setting up initial contacts and providing advice and
documents.

The following offered information and indispensable assistance in putting
this book together:

Benton Arnovitz, Washington DC, USA / Jochen August, Berlin,
Germany, and Oświęcim, Poland / Auschwitz-Birkenau Memorial
and Museum, Oświęcim, Poland / Leah Bacon, Jerusalem, Israel /
Edmund Benter, Gdynia, Poland / Jörn Böhme, Berlin, Germany /
Esther Büchler, Lahavot Haviva, Israel / Catriona Corke, Cambridge,
UK / Neithard Dahlen, Butzbach, Germany / Neil de Cort, Cambridge,
UK / Sabine Dille, Berlin, Germany / Fred Frenkel, Munich, Germany /
Daniel Frisch, Göttingen, Germany / Goethe-Insitut, Munich / Ulla
Gorges, Berlin, Germany / Elise Heslinga, Cambridge, UK / Christoph
Heubner, Berlin, Germany / Margrit Hirsch, Esslingen, Switzerland /
Chaim Schlomo Hoffman, Mukachevo, Ukraine / Anne Huhn, Berlin,
Germany / International Tracing Service, Bad Arolsen, Germany /
Stanisława Iwaszko, Kęty, Poland / Tadeusz Iwaszko, Oświęcim and Kęty,
Poland / Tobijas Jafetas, Vilnius, Lithuania / Věra Jilková-Holznerová,
Prague, Czech Republic / Miroslav Kárný, Prague, Czech Republic /
Adam Klimczyk, Jawiczowice, Poland / Dorota Klimczyk, Kraków,
Poland / Emilia Klimczyk, Jawiczowice, Poland / Ewa Klimczyk,
Kraków, Poland / Richard Kornfeld, Los Angeles, USA / Ruth
Kornfeld, Zurich, Switzerland / Zoltan Kozma, Budapest, Hungary /
Helena Kubica, Oświęcim, Poland / Erich Kulka, Jerusalem, Israel /
Konrad Kwiet, Sydney, Australia / Richard Levinsohn, Ben Shemen,
Israel / Petr Liebl, Prague, Czech Republic / Dietrich Lückoff, Berlin,

Germany / Mark Mandelbaum, Naples, FL / Rita McLeod, Saskatoon, Canada / Jan Menkens, Göttingen, Germany / Alan Meyer, Cloppenburg, Germany / Janna Meyer, Paris, France / Moreshet Archives, Givat Haviva, Israel / Leigh Mueller, Cambridge, UK / Musée de l'Holocauste, Montreal, Canada / Simon Pare, Im Dörfli, Switzerland / Jadwiga Pindeska-Lech, Oświęcim, Poland / Wojciech Płosa, Oświęcim, Poland / Karl-Klaus Rabe, Göttingen / Bronisława Rydzikowska, Czaniec, Poland / Aryeh Simon, Tel Aviv, Israel / Maryna Smajovich-Goldenberg, Bilky, Ukraine / Nick Somers, Vienna, Austria / Gerhard Steidl, Göttingen / Ewa Steinerová, Prague, Czech Republic / Irena Szymańska, Oświęcim, Poland / John Thompson, Cambridge, UK / United States Holocaust Memorial Museum, Washington DC, USA / George Weisz, Sydney, Australia / Yad Vashem Memorial, Jerusalem, Israel

# *Life Before*

HEINZ SALVATOR KOUNIO enjoyed his life as a young boy. He loved his parents, his sister Erika, who was a year older than him, and his grandparents. Of course, there were things he didn't like so much: the disputes with boys in the neighbourhood or with classmates in the school yard. But in retrospect they were trivial.

Thessaloniki – also known as Saloniki, Salonika (Judeo-Spanish), Selanik (Turkish) or Solun (Bulgarian/Macedonian/Serbian) – the second-largest city in Greece, where he lived, fascinated him and promised a good life for a Jewish boy. Until he was 11.[1]

At the age of just 24, his father Salvator Kounio had opened a small photo supply shop. That was in 1924. He sold photographic paper and cameras to the many street photographers in Thessaloniki. He obtained his goods from Germany. At the same time, he and his brother exported sheepskins in the opposite direction. He bought them untreated from the farmers in and around Thessaloniki. The skins were then dried and transported by road or sea to Germany. Heinz's father and brother were very hardworking and were soon well respected far and wide, not only in Thessaloniki but also in Germany. Their customer base grew rapidly.

Every year Heinz's father visited the photography fair in Leipzig, which was part of the Leipzig industrial fair. There he found out about new products and placed orders for photographic paper, cameras and accessories for the whole year. On one of his business trips, he met the 'self-assured, obstinate and intelligent' Helene Löwy (known as Hella). The 18-year-old was a fifth-semester medical student in Leipzig. The two fell in love at first sight. They wanted to get married. Hella was determined to abandon her studies to go with Salvator Kounio to Greece.

The young woman's parents lived in Karlsbad (Karlovy Vary) in multi-ethnic Czechoslovakia. Her father, Ernst Löwy, was a well-known

1

architect and engineer; her mother Theresa, 'a beautiful and educated Viennese woman'.

The Jewish inhabitants of Karlsbad have a turbulent history. For around 350 years, they were not allowed to reside permanently there. Only during the spa season from 1 May to 30 September were Jews permitted to stay and do business there. Afterwards, they had to leave again.[2]

Many Jews had moved since the mid sixteenth century to the surrounding villages, from where they could reach Karlsbad on foot to sell their goods. They were thus able to quickly improve their impoverished situation.

A large number of Jews living and working in Karlsbad during the spa season came from Lichtenstadt (Hroznětín). *Die Juden und Judengemeinden Böhmens in Vergangenheit und Gegenwart* [The Jews and Jewish Communities of Bohemia in the Past and Present] by Hugo Gold, editor-in-chief of the Brno magazine *Jüdische Volksstimme*, and published in Brno and Prague in 1934, says of this period:

> We do not know whether individual Jews lived in those cities before 1568. But after that time a larger Jewish community was gradually established ... in the town of Lichtenstadt, just two hours' walk from Karlsbad. It has an ancient Jewish cemetery and an old synagogue. According to legend it is 1,000 years old, which is naturally a great exaggeration. But it is nevertheless a few centuries old, as the oldest gravestones reveal.[3]

Over the centuries, the Jews living in the villages near Karlsbad attempted in vain to be allowed to reside permanently in the spa town. Their efforts were not to come to fruition until the mid nineteenth century: a Jewish cemetery was laid out in 1868, and the Great Synagogue was officially dedicated on 4 September 1877.

The Jewish community of Karlsbad grew rapidly: in 1910, there were around 1,600 Jews living there, and by 1931 their number had grown to 2,650, representing 11 per cent of the total population.[4]

Back to the year 1924 and Salvator Kounio and Hella Löwy's desire to get married: 'Neither family', says Heinz Kounio, 'was keen on the marriage plans.' The Löwys asked: 'Where do you intend to go? Saloniki? To the south? You will be a long way from the vibrant cultural life!' And the Kounios said of the north: 'Where does she come from? Karlsbad? The people there have no culture!'

The young couple finally had their way and got married in Karlsbad in 1925. Beforehand, with the help of his parents, Salvator Kounio had had a nice two-storey house built for himself and his young wife right by the sea in Thessaloniki. 'She should be made to feel at home' in this part of Europe, which was completely foreign to her.

In fact, Hella Kounio's new home could look back on an old and vibrant Jewish culture dating back more than twenty centuries. It is thought that the first Jewish families settled in Thessaloniki around 140 BCE. The community received a decisive boost from 1492 onwards with the arrival of 15,000 to 20,000 Jews who had been expelled first from Spain, where Jews had lived for more than 2,100 years,[5] then a year later from Sicily and Italy, which was ruled by the Spaniards, and then in 1497 from Portugal. At the time, Thessaloniki was part of the Ottoman Empire, which welcomed the Jews with open arms and also guaranteed them freedom of religion.[6]

The situation remained unchanged for centuries afterwards. The *Baseler Nachrichten* reported in 1903: 'The Jews, who manage their affairs independently and in complete freedom, are staunch supporters of the Turkish government. They know that no other power offers the same freedom as they now enjoy under the sign of the crescent.'[7]

Among the Jewish refugees from 1492 were important and knowledgeable academics, writers, artisans, merchants and Talmudists – students and experts in the Talmud, the primary source of Jewish religious law.

This massive new impetus brought about a radical change in Thessaloniki. The Jewish refugees introduced novel methods of working. Many artisanal businesses were established – silk mills, goldsmiths' studios, tanneries and, above all, weaving mills, where a large number of new immigrants found work. The conveniently located port became a hub for trade with the Balkans and a centre of European Jewish scholarship.[8]

Thessaloniki held a great fascination for students from all over the world. The Talmud Torah school founded in 1520 was both a cultural centre supported by the Jewish community and a school of higher education for trainee rabbis.[9] It was to produce celebrated doctors, writers and rabbis.[10]

Over the centuries, other schools and institutes, such as a trade school, boys' school, girls' school and apprentice training school were established. The Jewish cultural magazine *Ost und West* wrote in January 1907: 'Saloniki has a well-established apprenticeship system. There is none of the frequently insurmountable difficulty found elsewhere in finding a decent master for the young trainees. Most of the master craftsmen in Saloniki are Jews.'[11]

This development, the spread of modern teaching and training establishments in Thessaloniki, was mainly due to the Alliance israélite universelle, founded by French Jews in Paris in 1860. In Thessaloniki by 1914, around 10,000 students had graduated from the Alliance's educational institutions.[12]

Many synagogues existed for centuries in the city. Their names give an indication of the places where the inhabitants had arrived from: Aragon, Kalabrya, Katalan, Kastilia, Lisbon, Majorca, Puglia, Sicilia,[13] to cite just a few. During the heyday of Judaism, there were around forty synagogues and prayer houses in Thessaloniki.[14]

'Of all the synagogues that of "Arragon" seemed the most picturesque. It is large, and the Alememar [bimah or raised area in the centre of the synagogue where the Torah is read] is a lofty dais at the extreme west end, gallery high. The Ark is also highly placed, and many elders sit on either side on a somewhat lower platform.'[15]

These lines were written in the late nineteenth century by Elkan Nathan Adler, son of the chief rabbi of England, who called himself a 'travelling scholar' and visited Jews in many countries between 1888 and 1914.[16]

'"Italia" was more striking', wrote Adler, who visited Thessaloniki in autumn 1898, 'for the synagogue is but half-built, the floor not yet bricked in, and the galleries of rough lathes, and yet the women climbed up the giddy steps of the scaffolding, and the hall was full of worshippers.' In practically all of the synagogues in the city there was a two-hour break between *musaf* (midday prayer) and *mincha* (afternoon prayer), when some worshippers took a siesta. Many went to the coffeehouses, full of people, who neither smoked nor drank. During the services, the streets were deserted.[17]

The journalist Esriel Carlebach, born in Leipzig and later living in Israel, who visited Jewish communities in Europe and beyond, wrote in the early 1930s, about Thessaloniki, that booksellers there offered collections of prayers everywhere for the holidays. But each one recommended a different version. 'Saloniki had thirty-three synagogues with thirty-three different rites, and a member of a Castilian family would never dare to call to God with Andalusian poems and songs.'[18]

The Jewish inhabitants formed separate synagogue communities based on their places of origin. They were extensively autonomous and even had their own (limited) jurisdiction. They also administered the districts they lived in, with delegates elected to represent the communities, who met regularly, consulted and adopted decisions on affairs concerning them.[19] And the first Jewish printing works was established as early as 1506. Hundreds of publications appeared, and Thessaloniki became 'the centre of printing in the Near East'.[20] The first Jewish newspaper – also the first newspaper in the city – *El Lunar,* was launched in 1865. It was followed by *La Época*[21] in 1875, and *El Avenir*[22] in 1897. Between 1865 and 1925, seventy-three newspapers were published in Thessaloniki, thirty-five in Judeo-Spanish, twenty-five in Turkish, eight in Greek and five in French.[23]

Thessaloniki became the 'Jerusalem of the Balkans', the 'Mother of Israel' or the 'Mother of Jerusalem', as the poet Samuel Usque – who was born in Portugal, fled to Italy and later lived in Safed, Palestine – described the city during a visit in the mid sixteenth century:[24]

> Saloniki is a devout city. The Jews from Europe and other areas where they are persecuted and expelled find shelter in the shade of this city and are as warmly welcomed by it as if it were our venerable mother Jerusalem itself. The surrounding countryside is irrigated by many rivers. Its vegetation is lush and nowhere are their more beautiful trees. Their fruit is excellent.[25]

According to official Turkish sources, in 1519 over 50 per cent of the population of Thessaloniki were Jews: 15,715 children, women and men, compared with 6,870 Muslims and 6,635 Christians. The situation had barely changed by the end of the nineteenth century, when there were over 70,000 Jews in the city – again, half of the population.[26]

Thessaloniki's privileged position in international trade gradually declined as a result of the transformation of the world economy. The burgeoning transatlantic economy, particularly the rise of the Netherlands and England, shifted the traditional balance.[27] It was not until the second half of the nineteenth century that the revival of trade relations with the Mediterranean ports of western Europe helped the city to flourish again.[28]

At this time, Jews were present in all professions. There were 40 Jewish chemists, 30 lawyers, 45 doctors and dentists, 150 fishermen, 500 waggoneers and carters, 220 self-employed artisans, 100 domestics, 3 engineers, 10 journalists, 2,000 waiters, 8,000 retailers and wholesalers, 60 colliers, 2,000 porters, 300 teachers, 250 butchers, 600 boatmen and 50 carpenters. There were also several Jewish businesses: a brewery, nine flour mills, twelve soap factories, thirty weaving mills and a brickworks.[29]

At the end of October 1912, during the First Balkan War waged by Bulgaria, Greece, Montenegro and Serbia against the Ottoman Empire, Thessaloniki became part of Greece,[30] bringing many Greeks to the city as a result.[31]

In August 1917, the city was extensively destroyed in a huge conflagration. The Jewish districts were particularly hard hit. Around 50,000 Jews became homeless. The Greek government promised to compensate them for their losses, but the Jews were not allowed to return to certain parts of the city. This prompted many Jews to leave Thessaloniki. They emigrated to Alexandria (Egypt), Great Britain, France, Italy and the USA.[32]

After the Greco-Turkish War (1919–22), an exchange of populations was agreed. A large number of Greeks living in Anatolia in Turkey were forced to move to Thessaloniki. In return, the Muslim inhabitants had to leave the city.[33] As a result of all these events, within a few years the Jewish population became a minority.[34] According to the first Greek population census of 1913, 61,439 of the 157,889 inhabitants were Jews.[35] By the early 1930s, Jewish children, women and men made up only around 20 per cent of the population.[36] One contributing factor was a law promulgated in the early 1920s prohibiting the inhabitants of Thessaloniki from working on Sundays, prompting a further Jewish emigration.[37] For several centuries previously, the Jews had not worked on Saturdays: during Shabbat, no ships were unloaded and no stores were open.[38] This was still the case in 1898: 'All the boatmen of the port are Jews, and on Saturdays no steamer can load or discharge cargo.'[39]

For over 400 years, the language brought from Spain remained the lingua franca of the persecuted Jews who had fled to Thessaloniki. Anyone visiting the city between 1500 and the early twentieth century who sat down, closed their eyes and listened to the people talking could imagine they were in a Spanish city. For many generations, the city was mostly Spanish-speaking and Jewish. The Greek Christians, Slavs and Muslims in Thessaloniki also spoke Spanish and conducted their daily business in it.[40]

'There are people and lifestyles that are rightly called Sephardic, which means Spanish',[41] wrote the journalist Esriel Carlebach around 1930. He continued: 'When two Sephardim met, they spoke Spanish; when two families married, the ceremony was performed according to the rites of Seville and Cordoba; when they built a house there was a patio in the centre surrounded by a small number of cool rooms with mosaic floors, grated windows and Moorish paintings.'[42]

The Jewish version of Spanish spoken in Thessaloniki was sprinkled with terms and phrases from Hebrew, but also from Portuguese, and, in the last decades of the nineteenth and early decades of the twentieth centuries, also from Turkish, Italian and – particularly during this time – French. These influences blended over the centuries in Thessaloniki to produce an autonomous language of particular beauty, known as Judeo-Spanish, Spaniolish or Ladino, although the latter refers not to the vernacular Judeo-Spanish but to the liturgical language: 'Ladino is used to introduce worshippers to the Hebrew original in a manner that is not genuine Spanish but rather a ... hispanicized Hebrew.'[43] 'Indeed, the amount of Ladino introduced into the service was quite astonishing', wrote the travelling scholar Elkan Nathan Adler in the late nineteenth century. 'Most of the Techinnoth, Confessions and Selichoth were in the vernacular, and the Reader seemed really moved as he held forth in that language.'[44]

From the second half of the nineteenth century, French became increasingly the language of 'culture and elites ... on account of the economic western orientation', but the vast majority of Jewish inhabitants continued principally or exclusively to use Judeo-Spanish as their everyday language.[45]

Myriam Kounio, Heinz and Erica's grandmother, also spoke almost exclusively 'Spaniolish', as the language was called in the family. For that reason, the children, although they could also speak it a little, were not able to communicate very well with her. At home, the younger family members and their grandfather, Moshe Kounio, spoke Greek. With their mother, Heinz and Erica spoke her native language, German. Thus, the children grew up with 'two and a half languages'.[46] 'We were not a strictly religious family', says Heinz Kounio. They went to the synagogue 'of course' on Shabbat and all major holidays. And on those days, he and his sister didn't go to school. 'But we were an open-minded family interested in culture. Books, theatre and concert visits were part of our lives.'

Heinz and his sister attended the Greek school from Year 1. 'But we also had classes in Jewish schools. And religious instruction took place in the Jewish community. In the holidays we went to Karlsbad. It was fantastic there. Where my grandparents lived there was a lake of around 1 hectare in size. We often took a boat out. We went on walks a lot, and the forests there were marvellous.' They strolled through Karlsbad, a well-known spa, with their grandparents, who looked forward impatiently to the children's visit every summer. They drank the water – at a temperature of 42 to 73 degrees – from the healing springs, and the highpoint of their excursions was a visit to the expensive cake shop at Hotel Pupp. 'It was a completely different world from Saloniki. But just as nice. The weeks flew by. I have a very fond memory of those times.'

In Thessaloniki, they also spent every free minute outdoors. 'We played a lot. Our friends were the neighbourhood children – also non-Jewish children, although several Jewish families lived in our street. Most of my friends were Christian. But there were also four Jewish boys I got on well with.'

Their house was right next to the sea. 'It was a fantastic district. As soon as the weather allowed, my sister and I spent the entire day on the beach or in the water.' They had a small white rowing boat, which they used extensively.

Even as a small boy, Heinz had a great passion – namely, fishing. He would get up early and prepare the bait, a well-kneaded mixture of bread and cheese, and then sit with his fishing rod for hours, above all catching mullet, of which there are around eighty varieties worldwide. And with his sister Erika he caught crabs, which their mother cooked. 'A delicious special treat.'

Heinz still recalls the 'chamalis' or porters:[47] 'They were almost all Jews.' They carried the goods unloaded in the port of Thessaloniki to the city and the nearby mountain villages in horse-drawn carts, or pulled them in elongated handcarts on the narrow mountain roads.

> The chamalis were very strong and could carry over 100 kg on their backs up to the third or fourth floor of the houses. And when they came down from the mountains and ran down the streets at great speed with the handcarts, they made a lot of noise and shouted: 'Watch out! Get out the way!' The carts had a bell that rang constantly. And when they came to a crossroads, everyone stopped. They always had priority. The chamalis were very well known and a typical feature of Saloniki at the time.

The hardworking Jewish dockers in the port of the picturesque city on the Thermaic Gulf were also famous. The Viennese newspaper *Die Stimme – Jüdische Zeitung* reported on 20 November 1934: 'Aba Houchi, member of the board of the Histadrut ha-Ovdim [labour federation] of Haifa, arrived in Saloniki to choose 100 to 150 Jewish dockers for immediate resettlement in Palestine. These dockers will work mostly in the port of Haifa but also in Jaffa. There are already 300 Jewish dockers' families from Saloniki living in Palestine.'[48]

Heinz Kounio: 'If you get into a taxi in Haifa today and ask to hear a Greek song, the driver will put one on for you. Many of these taxi drivers are descendants of those first dockers from Thessaloniki.'

In spite of the recurrent expulsion, persecution and pogroms,[49] there was Jewish life everywhere in Europe. The creativity and work of Jewish researchers, industrialists, painters, doctors, musicians, politicians and writers had a far-reaching impact in many countries. In large parts of Europe, they were and are part of the history not only of the Jewish people but also, for example, of the people of Austria, Belarus, Belgium, Bulgaria, the Czech Republic, Denmark, Estonia, France, Germany, Greece, Hungary, Italy, Latvia, Lithuania, Luxembourg, the Netherlands, Norway, Poland, Portugal, Russia, Slovakia, Switzerland and Ukraine.

Before the Nazi era, there were few cities in Europe, large or small, which did not have Jewish children, women and men living in them, often for several hundred years, in some cities and regions for over 1,000 or 2,000 years. Well over 30,000 localities in Europe had Jewish inhabitants.[50]

DÁŠA FRIEDOVÁ spent the first years of her life with her parents, Otto and Kát'a Fried, and her sister Sylva, three years older than her, in the small Czech village of Odolice. It was around 40 kilometres north-east of the German border. The parents owned a large farm with 360 hectares of land. The village had around 150 inhabitants, Czechs and Germans. The Frieds were the only Jews.

When the neighbours slaughtered a pig, they gave some to the Frieds. 'We did the same. We gave them grain or whatever our neighbours and friends needed. This was the way we were, and the Germans living in the village were not excluded.' The Frieds did not keep kosher. 'We cooked and ate just about everything.' They regarded themselves as Czech but still celebrated Pesach, recalling the exodus from Egypt, and Purim, commemorating the rescue of the Persian Jews. These were large family gatherings. But they also celebrated Easter and Christmas with their Christian friends and employees.

Dáša and Sylva's closest friends were the daughters of her father's employees who worked on the farm. 'We played together every day and were good friends.' Dáša and Sylva went to the village school like the other children. The school consisted of two rooms, one for the smaller children up to Year 3, and the other for the older girls and boys. 'We were the only Jewish children in the school and village, but it was not an issue. We never felt any antisemitism, not even from the German children.'

The Fried family travelled regularly to Most, a short drive from Odolice. The town was a trading hub and centre of the large brown-coal field in north-western Bohemia. In 1930, Most had a population of around 28,000, including 662 Jews. The history of the Jewish community dated back to the fourteenth century, and since 1872–3 it had had its own synagogue, which was destroyed by the Nazis in 1938.[51] The old Jewish cemetery survives to this day as the last relic of the Jewish citizens of Most.

In the 1930s, the Frieds travelled to Most to do their shopping, visit the theatre or spend their Sundays in the park of the nearby spa resort Bílina. Jews had been documented in Bílina since the fifteenth century.

The Jewish cemetery was laid out in 1891 and a synagogue was dedicated four years later. In the early 1930s, the rabbi of Bílina, A. H. Teller, noted: '[The Jewish community] has 120 souls and around 50 taxpayers. The community has a temple and cemetery in good condition. May the community be allowed to continue in future to work for the benefit of Judaism through the peaceful collaboration with all members.'[52]

The main attraction for the Fried family was the public mineral spring in the park. 'My father played cards and my mother chatted with other women. Sylva and I played with our governesses or with other children whom we met by chance in the park.'

On the major holidays, the family went to the Moorish-style Jubilee Synagogue,[53] built in 1905–6, Prague's largest Jewish prayer house on Jeruzalémská, among other things to meet up with their relatives. The parents also took their children to the Jewish cemetery in Prague, where they placed small stones on the gravestones in memory of the deceased. 'Visitors to a cemetery always left a stone. It's a Jewish tradition all over the world.' The family travelled once a week to the capital, 80 kilometres away. 'We had lots of relatives in Prague – aunts, uncles and cousins. We were all very close and enjoyed each other's company. It was always a great family occasion.'

'I have only good memories of the first nine years of my childhood. It was a nice, happy time.'

GÁBOR HIRSCH The 'King of Trains' – more precisely, one of the routes of the Orient Express – passed from the 1920s through the town of Békéscsaba in south-eastern Hungary.[54] Even as a boy, Gábor Hirsch was fascinated by it, imagining the adventure, glamour and unknown worlds associated with this special train.

Gábor's father János owned an electrical supply and radio shop in Békéscsaba, which he had opened around 1925 with his uncle Ferenc. The uncle emigrated a few years later to Egypt, after which János ran the business on his own. His wife Ella was one of the sales assistants. In its heyday, the business had between ten and fifteen trainees.[55]

Békéscsaba had a population of around 50,000 at the time, of whom some 2,500, or perhaps 3,000, were Jews, like the Hirsch family.[56] The Jewish community of Békéscsaba dates back to the end of the eighteenth century. The oldest gravestone in the Jewish cemetery of the Neolog (reform) community is of Jakob Singer, who died in 1821. A monument in the town park commemorates the victims of a cholera epidemic of 1825, including eleven Jews. According to Gábor Hirsch's research, there were two independent religious Jewish communities in Békéscsaba after 1883: the orthodox, and the liberal – or Neolog – community, which the Hirsch family belonged to. The first synagogue was built in 1850, and a second one for the orthodox community was built in 1894.[57] The two synagogues faced one another on either side of Luther Street.

Gábor's Austrian nanny was called Hildegard. She was around 25 years old and he got on well with her. His mother wanted him to learn languages. 'She believed it was important. That's why we had Hildegard.' From 1933, Gábor attended a private German-language kindergarten, and in 1936 he started at the Neolog community's Jewish elementary school. 'There were only three boys and thirteen girls in my class, two of whom were not Jewish.'

The Hirsch family were so-called 'three-day Jews'. They celebrated the High Holidays: Rosh Hashanah, the Jewish new year, at the end of the summer, marking the start of autumn; then, ten days later, Yom Kippur, the Day of Atonement at the end of forty days of repentance.

In 1940, Gábor switched to the Evangelical Rudolf-Gymnasium. There were fifty-four boys and girls in his class, including four Jewish pupils, 'more than usual for the time'. While the non-Jewish children had religious instruction, they were allowed to play in the school yard. 'We had religion classes at other times in the Jewish community rooms.' One of his teachers was the rabbi Jakob Silberfeld, who was murdered in Auschwitz in the summer of 1944.[58]

And, 'naturally', Shabbat, the weekly day of rest from Friday to Saturday evening, was particularly important for the Hirsch family. 'On Friday evening, we lit the candles and ate the Shabbat bread, the braided poppyseed loaf.'

On Saturday morning, however, Gábor went to school, which was held on six days a week. On Saturday afternoon, he attended the service in the synagogue in preparation for his barmitzvah, the religious coming of age of young boys when they turn 13. Some non-Jewish boys made occasional reproaches to Gábor: 'If you're a Jew, you must like the English.' One was the son of a doctor. After the war, 'this boy, of all people' attended an English grammar school and 'later went to the USA'.

## Dagmar Fantlová

> Kutná Hora is a typical Czech town. There was a German man living in our building. He came from somewhere near the border. Later, he proved to be a Nazi. Before, he had lived there without attracting notice.

> My father was a doctor, and my mother a housewife. I had a younger sister called Rita. We lived peacefully in Kutná Hora until 1939.

These were the first sentences that Dagmar Lieblová (*née* Fantlová) related about herself.

The town, founded in the twelfth century as a miners' settlement, became very wealthy towards the end of the thirteenth century on account of its silver mines. The famous Prague groschen were minted there at the time.[59]

For a long time, Jews were not allowed to live in the old central Bohemian town. On 30 July 1526, the mayor and elders of Kutná Hora adopted a decision: 'The Jews may not stay in Kuttenberg [Kutná Hora] except on market days or if they have to appear in court. Non-observance of this regulation will be subject to a fine of 5 schock groschen.'[60] A bill or clearance called a 'bolette' had to be acquired beforehand.[61] It remained that way for several centuries.[62] Almost without interruption since the early fourteenth century, however, there had been a large Jewish community in the neighbouring town of Kolin,[63] where many Jews who did business in Kutná Hora lived.[64] The old Jewish cemetery in Kolin, with over 2,500 graves, has survived to this day. The oldest legible gravestone dates from 1492.[65] The seventeenth-century baroque synagogue is also still standing.[66]

Jews were not allowed to settle permanently in Kutná Hora until the second half of the nineteenth century. In 1871, the first Jewish religious association was constituted, with fourteen members. A good twenty years later, there were 159 Jews in the town, and by 1910 their number had grown to 206. An imposing synagogue had been built eight years earlier. There was no Jewish cemetery in Kutná Hora, and the autonomous community buried its dead in the cemeteries in Malešov, Zbraslavice and Kolin. The Jewish inhabitants lived above all from commerce, or owned businesses making consumer items. There was a textile factory, the Teller sugar factory and the Strakosch shoe factory.[67]

Like most of the Jews in Kutná Hora, the Fantl family regarded themselves first and foremost as Czech. They 'naturally' celebrated the main holidays and went to the synagogue. On Shabbat, Dagmar was allowed to go to school. 'I wasn't supposed to do any homework. My grandmother didn't want me to, but my father always said: "No, the children have to do their homework on Saturdays."'

The Fantls celebrated Christmas.

> It was a major family celebration. Relatives came to our house. We also had visitors at Easter and Pesach. We bought matzo, unleavened bread, and baked cakes ourselves. My mother would prepare little packages as presents for various acquaintances. That's how it was in those days in a town like Kutná Hora. The Jewish and Christian holidays were mixed up. And during the Nazi era people said in surprise: 'Dr Fantl is a Jew? We didn't know.'

In 1932, when Dagmar's younger sister Rita was born, the family bought a nice large house with several apartments. On the ground floor was Julius Fantl's surgery. In the new house there was also a Sudeten German lodger called Zotter. 'He worked in a small shoe factory owned by a Jew.'

Dagmar's maternal grandparents moved into the house in 1935. They brought their old housekeeper Františka Holická with them. She had been with the family since the 1920s and was affectionately referred to as Fany, Aunt Fany or Fanynka.

Dagmar started learning German when she was 8. Her parents and grandparents knew German 'of course', but it was never spoken at home. 'It was customary to learn languages.' Two years later, Dagmar started learning English. 'My German wasn't particularly good at the time. And my grandmother always went on about it.'

JÜRGEN LOEWENSTEIN AND WOLFGANG WERMUTH are real Berlin boys – or at least they were once. They never met.

Jürgen grew up in the Scheunenviertel district of Berlin. Now in the Mitte district, not far from the television tower, it was originally outside the city walls. There were stalls, sheds and barns, where Berlin farmers stored hay and straw. This is how the district got its name ['Scheune' is German for 'barn'], which it retained long after the barns had disappeared. From the late nineteenth century, it was often the first port of call for Jews fleeing the pogroms in eastern Europe. The colloquial language was Yiddish.[68]

Jürgen lived in highly impoverished circumstances. His mother Paula was divorced and worked writing addresses on envelopes in which advertisements were sent out. She later married Walter Loewenstein, who worked as a chemist in the perfume section of a large department store. They sublet an apartment at Oranienburger Strasse 87. The building still stands today.

As a boy, Jürgen lived with his grandparents Berthold and Agathe Sochaczewer at Gipsstrasse 18, then Kaiserstrasse 43. When the Nazis evicted them from this apartment,[69] they moved to Grenadierstrasse 4a (now Almstadtstrasse 49) in the Scheunenviertel in the centre of Berlin.

Grenadierstrasse was inhabited above all by Jews from Poland. Most of them were small tradesmen, tailors or shoemakers. There were small rooms everywhere which served as synagogues. The people dressed differently from us and spoke Yiddish, which I barely understood. The Jews in the Scheunenviertel were unimaginably poor. People at the time said that the Jews were to blame for everything and that all Jews were rich. This was in blatant contradiction to the social situation in which my family and others lived in the Scheunenviertel.

'The Wuthe toy shop', says Jürgen Löwenstein, 'was at Gipsstrasse 18, the Loser und Wolf cigar shop on the corner of Rosenthaler Strasse.' The Bio cinema was on Hackescher Markt. You had to climb a stairway. There was a cinema called the Imperial in Hackesche Höfe, the Babylon near Bülowplatz (now Rosa-Luxemburg-Strasse 30), the Imperial at the former U-Bahn Schönhauser Tor (now Rosa-Luxemburg-Platz), three others in Münz- and Memhardstrasse, and two in Neue Schönhauser Strasse. He also vividly recalls the Lehmann lending library in Kaiserstrasse and the WILPA (Wilhelm Pappelbaum) ice cream shop 'on the left-hand side of Rosenthaler Strasse at the beginning of Hackesche Höfe'.

In 1923, under the pseudonym Linke Poot, the doctor and writer Alfred Döblin described the street where Jürgen Loewenstein lived from

1938 in a newspaper article entitled 'Östlich um den Alexanderplatz' [To the East on Alexanderplatz]: 'Left (into) Grenadierstrasse. The street is always busy. The Damm is full of people, coming in and out of old twisted houses.... The few shops have Hebrew inscriptions; I see first names, Schaja, Uscher, Chanaine. In the display windows a Jewish play is advertised: "Jüdele der Blinde, five acts by Joseph Lateiner". Jewish butchers, craftsmen's workshops, bookshops.'[70]

Jürgen attended an Evangelical kindergarten, then the Jewish boys' school at Kaiserstrasse 29/30 (now Jacobystrasse) and the Jewish middle school at Grosse Hamburger Strasse 27, still standing and now the site of the Jewish Moses Mendelsohn secondary school.

Wolfgang Wermuth's father Siegmund was born in Lübben in the Spreewald. The 'Jewish street' in this town was first recorded in the annals in 1525. After being expelled several times in previous centuries, in the mid nineteenth century a few Jewish families were allowed to settle permanently in Lübben. The community had a small synagogue with a schoolroom, a mikvah – the ritual bath for spiritual and bodily cleansing before Shabbat – and a cemetery outside the town. The synagogue was burnt down by the Nazis in November 1938, the Jewish cemetery destroyed and the gravestones used for road-building.[71]

Wolf Wermuth, Wolfgang's grandfather, was buried in the Jewish cemetery in Weissensee, Berlin. This important Jewish site was ceremoniously opened on 9 September 1880 – 4 Tishri 5641 according to the Jewish calendar. Today, it is the largest Jewish cemetery in Europe. Major artists, scientists, doctors and industrialists are buried there: Micha Josef Bin Gorion (writer), Samuel Fischer (bookseller and publisher), Adolf Jandorf (founder in 1907 of KaDeWe, the largest German department store), Lina Morgenstern (social worker and writer), Ferdinand Strassmann (head of the Berlin health service) and Lesser Ury (painter and graphic artist).[72]

Wolfgang Wermuth's mother was from Berlin. His maternal grandfather arrived from Poland in 1892, and around 1910 became a 'privileged honorary citizen with German nationality because he was supplier of timepieces to the imperial court'.

His grandmother came from Altenkirchen in the Westerwald, where her family had lived for around 300 years. Her ancestors were thus among the earliest Jews to live there. The first are said to have settled in Altenkirchen at the end of the sixteenth century. In 1852, there were eighty-six Jews living there, and the highest population was reached in 1908 with 260 Jews. Here, too, the synagogue was burned to the ground in the night of 9–10 November 1938, Jewish houses and businesses were demolished, and some years later all of the remaining Jewish inhabitants deported.[73]

Wolfgang Wermuth's father Siegmund was co-owner of an antiques business in Berlin and had a share in a silent movie theatre 'which was unfortunately put out of business in 1928 by talkies'. This was a great blow for the Wermuths since it meant a considerable reduction in the family's income. They had to give up the apartment at Duisburger Strasse 13 and move to Sybelstrasse 29 in Charlottenburg. Both buildings are still standing.

There were twelve large synagogues in Berlin in the 1920s, with an average of 2,000 seats, as well as over seventy smaller Jewish prayer houses. At the time, Berlin had more synagogues than any other city in Europe.[74] Over the centuries, it had developed into the hub of Jewish life in Germany. From the first mention of Jewish traders in a certificate authorizing the guild of wool weavers at the end of the twelfth century,[75] it became one of the most important centres of Jewish architects, scholars, writers, composers, painters, politicians and scientists on our planet.

Many innovations in the first three decades of the twentieth century were due to Berlin Jews: Max Reinhardt with his theatre productions; Arnold Schönberg with his twelve-tone music; Max Liebermann with his paintings and illustrations; Alfred Döblin with his novel *Berlin Alexanderplatz*; Theodor Wolff as editor-in-chief of the *Berliner Tagesblatt* with its articles criticizing Germany's war policy during the First World War; and Paul Ehrlich, Nobel Prize-winner in Medicine and co-founder of modern chemotherapy.[76]

In 1933, there were 160,000 Jews living in Berlin, out of a total of almost 500,000 in the whole of Germany. A good 50 per cent of the Jewish population lived in one of the ten largest German cities with over 100,000 inhabitants. The others lived and worked in other cities and, to a lesser extent, in small towns, villages and rural districts.[77] Jewish women and men worked in mid-1933 in Germany in trade and transport (61.3 per cent), handicrafts and industry (23.1 per cent), public service and professions (12.5 per cent), farming and forestry (1.7 per cent) and domestic service (1.4 per cent).[78]

The Wermuth family participated in the life of the Jewish community, going to the synagogue and observing the holidays.

> My mother was very liberal, more than my father, who came from an orthodox family. Shabbat was a day of rest, but that didn't mean there was no work. We observed the High Holidays and the minor festivals. We acknowledged the religion, but it didn't play a dominant role in daily life. We were aware of our identity and never denied it.

JANEK (MANELA) MANDELBAUM Ships from all over the world docked in the port. Sailors of all skin colours could be seen in the streets. Lots of languages could be heard. The international flair was part of his life from early childhood. Janek Mandelbaum lived in the Polish port of Gdynia with his father Majloch, his mother Cyrla (*née* Testyler), his sister Ita, who was three years older, and his brother Jakob, five years younger. In the 1930s, Gdynia was a large city with over 100,000 inhabitants. The family also looked forward to the frequent visits to the nearby Free City of Danzig/Gdańsk, a partially autonomous and independent free city with Polish harbour rights under the protection of the League of Nations.

Majloch Mandelbaum was co-owner of the Ocean fish conserve factory, which offered employment to a large number of workers. Business flourished and the products were sold throughout Europe. 'We weren't rich, but we were comfortably off.' This enabled them to live in one of the better parts of Gdynia. The 110-square-metre apartment was comparatively big for the time, and had large windows. The family occupied an entire floor.

The beach was 10 minutes away, and Cyrla Mandelbaum often spent entire summer days there with the children. Janek's father joined them during his lunch break: 'He would often buy us hand-made waffles filled with sweet cream. They tasted fantastic.' A 'pretty young woman' came every day by tram to look after the household. Janek got on well with her and liked to tease her. 'In spite of the home help, my mother liked to cook. We were all particularly fond of her turnovers with jam filling.'

Janek had nice clothes and – memorably – leather boots, which he liked to wear whenever the weather permitted. 'My mother dressed smartly. She was a good-looking woman with dark eyes and long shiny hair. My father was relatively light-skinned. My brother Jakob and my sister Ita took after my mother and had dark eyes and a dark skin. I had fair hair as a boy and took more after my father.'

As there was no Jewish school in Gdynia, Janek went 'where everyone went, the Catholic state school'.

As in all classrooms, there was a picture of the Polish president Ignacy Mościcki hanging on the left-hand wall and a portrait of the prime minister, General Józef Piłsudski, on the right. On the back wall, there was a crucifix in plain view during the lessons. Every morning the first class was religious instruction with a prayer service. We called it 'catechism'. The two or three Jewish pupils in my class didn't have to attend religious instruction lessons, but we usually went anyway. We didn't want to draw attention to ourselves, and besides all our friends went. We didn't think about it much. I soon knew more about Catholicism than Judaism.

The Mandelbaums celebrated the major festivals such as Pesach, the eight-day commemoration of the exodus from Egypt, and ate matzo, the bread made with water and grain but without leavening. 'I also recall that we got new clothes for the holidays. My mother took me to the shirt- and shoe-makers and to the tailor to be fitted for a new suit. In those days we didn't by anything off the peg, because the quality was not normally good enough.'

There was no synagogue in Gdynia, just two prayer houses. The community had no rabbi but a cantor, who led the prayers:[79] 'As far as I can recall, most of the Jewish families living there were moderately religious. They met for the holidays and prayed together, for which in our faith a rabbi is not required.'

The first Jewish inhabitants of Gdynia moved into the present-day district of Chylonia in 1876. According to the second Polish population census, there were eighty-four Jews in the city in December 1931, of whom twenty-three put Yiddish, and one Hebrew, as their mother tongue. The records state that there were sixty-five permanently resident Jewish children, women and men. The other nineteen were presumably temporary residents. The Polish government decided in the 1920s to develop Gdynia as a port and gateway to the world. As the work progressed, the city became increasingly attractive for Jewish families. By around 1935, there were already 700 Jews living in this Baltic city, and by the end of 1938 around 4,500.[80]

Janek had lots of interests and enjoyed sports. One day his father gave him a bicycle. He trained on Skwer Kościuszki. This square had a street on each side leading directly to the Baltic Sea. It is still one of the most popular places for the people of Gdynia. Cycling became Janek's great passion. He took part in school races. 'Once I even came third.' In winter, he preferred ice skating at Kamienna Góra, the stone mountain. This small hill close to the beach also gave its name to the smallest district of Gdynia, with magnificent villas on its slopes. 'I loved to skate there. It was very cold in winter right next to the sea. We also played ice hockey. I often used to take my little brother Jakob with me. He loved sports as much as I did. And when there was snow or ice on the paths and roads, we slid down the hill on wooden boards.'

As far as he can recall, neither he nor the other Jewish children suffered from antisemitism. Janek and his classmates and friends didn't care who was 'Jewish or Catholic or whatever else'. He would play football in the summer or hang around the harbour area with friends, always ready for a new adventure. 'For example, we would jump into the harbour and swim alongside the ships.' This was forbidden, of course, and also dangerous, because they could have been crushed by the ships' hulls. His parents knew nothing about this. 'Yes, I was a lad ready to get into all kinds of mischief.'

'It was great the way the boys played together and looked out for one another.' He never felt, or was made to feel, any different from the non-Jewish children. One indication of how Polish they felt was the fact that Janek's family almost always spoke Polish at home. 'I didn't know any other language.' His parents still spoke Yiddish to each other and with friends and relatives. Majloch and Cyrla Mandelbaum came from large families. Janek's father had four sisters and three brothers, and his mother had nine sisters and brothers, including two sets of twins.

Many Poles living inland – including the Mandelbaums' relatives – would visit the port cities during the holidays. Janek got on particularly well with Uncle Sigmund, his father's youngest brother. 'And don't forget Hinda, my mother's youngest sister. She was cultured, very good-looking, fashionably dressed and had lots of admirers in Gdynia.' She once stayed with them for a whole year. 'We all got on well with one another. My parents loved each other and we loved them. I can't remember any major arguments. Without exaggeration, I would say that we had a good and interesting life.'

JIŘÍ AND ZDENĚK STEINER The children's German nanny was called Trude, and she was very fond of Jiří and Zdeněk Steiner. The twins were almost inseparable. 'We were always fighting but loved each other a lot.' Their father Pavel ran a wholesale business with a partner in Prague. Fabrics were purchased and delivered to businesses throughout the country. Their mother Jana sometimes took the orders.

The Steiners lived in the Žižkov district, not far from the city centre, in a large modern apartment. The family was well established and was part of the liberal Jewish community. 'But we celebrated all the holidays and went to the synagogue on Saturday mornings.'

The origins of the Prague Jewish community date back to the tenth century. Its Jewish scholars enjoy a legendary reputation. For example, the renown of Rabbi Judah Loew ben Bezalel (born probably in Posen (Poznań) around 1520 and died in Prague in 1609) extended over centuries.[81] Rabbi Loew, as he was referred to for short, devised a fundamental reform of the Jewish school system. He suggested that the main principle of the learning process was the logical progression from simple to complex content. He was interested above all in understanding the material. His tomb states that he wrote fifteen books, addressing fundamental questions of human existence – the philosophy of religion, teaching, ethics. He was a great thinker, far ahead of his time, whose writings were notable for 'a worldview characterized by intense humanity'.[82]

Rabbi Loew's grave, along with that of many other leading figures in the Jewish community, is to be found in the Old Jewish Cemetery, possibly the most famous Jewish cemetery in Europe. The graves and the inscriptions on them tell the history of Prague's Jewish community between the fifteenth and eighteenth centuries. During this time, more than 100,000 Jews were buried there. As space was limited and the

Talmud states that graves are inviolable, a layer of earth was placed over the old graves in order to bury more people. In total, the Old Jewish Cemetery consists of twelve layers. With every layer of earth, the old gravestones were planted higher and higher, next to the new ones.[83] In this way, a cemetery with a unique atmosphere was formed over the centuries.

'Yes, these old gravestones speak a powerful language', wrote Abraham Stein, a rabbi from Radnice (Radnitz), around 25 kilometres north-east of Plzeň (Pilsen), in the early twentieth century:

> They tell of tongues of flame from the terrible suffering and martyrdom of previous centuries, of the Jewish persecutions and mass murders and of the slaughter by Christian fanatics and zealots ... of innocent people for the glory of God.
>
> If the graves opened, if the earth gave forth its stony treasures, the world would be amazed at the precious items – not glittering and magnificent objects and clothing, not Pompeian antiquities made of gold, silver and marble, but invaluable scientific material for the cultural history of Judaism.[84]

From the thirteenth century, and for several centuries thereafter, there was a Jewish district in Prague called Josefov.[85] The Jewish town hall – something that no other Jewish community in the Diaspora had – was mentioned for the first time in 1541. It was the residence of the mayor of the Jewish district and the headquarters of the Jewish self-administration, the meeting place of the Council of Elders and for jurisdiction on Jewish affairs.[86]

In 1522, there were 600 Jews living in Prague. By 1930, the number had risen to a good 35,000.[87] When the Nazis came to power in Germany on 30 January 1933, many refugees went to Prague, to be joined later by Jews from Austria and Sudetenland, increasing the Jewish population to around 56,000.[88]

The Steiner family knew some of them. 'I remember a German woman', said Jiří Steiner decades later, 'who got on very well with my mother. She married one of my father's business colleagues.'

In September 1935, the twins started school. At the time, the news filtering through to Prague from Germany was becoming more and more unsettling. Jiří Steiner recalls one situation in particular: 'We were at home and the radio was on. Hitler was speaking at a party rally to great applause. My mother started to cry and my father said: "It's terrible! What will happen to us now?"'

Even before the Germans occupied Sudetenland on 1 October 1938, many people had left. 'An uncle of mine was one of them.' He came to Prague and lived for a time with the Steiners before fleeing to Brazil.

CHANNA (HANNA) MARKOWICZ Before the First World War, the small town in the Carpathians was part of Hungary and then the former Czechoslovakia, before being annexed by Hungary in 1939, From the Second World War until 1991, it belonged to the former Soviet Union and then afterwards to Ukraine. The town in question is Irshava[89] in the extreme west of present-day Ukraine, where the Markowicz family lived. They spoke Yiddish at home. 'When they didn't want us to understand them', says Channa, her parents, Awraham and Zseni Markowicz (*née* Schwarz), spoke Hungarian, reason enough for her and her four brothers – Schmuel, Jakov, Herschel and Josel – to learn that language.

The two elder brothers attended the Czech middle school in Irshava. Lessons were in Czech and German. 'We had a teacher who came to our house to help them learn German.' Channa learned with them. She herself went to the Russian school, where the lessons were in Russian and Czech.

The family owned land and forest. 'We children also helped working in the field. We did so because we liked it, not because we had to.' Wood was chopped in the forest and exported, also to Germany. In 1930, there were 102,542 Jews living in the part of the Carpathians belonging to Czechoslovakia.[90] This was equivalent to around 15 per cent of the total population.[91] In Irshava, Jews made up 30 to 40 per cent of the inhabitants.[92] The Jewish community had two synagogues, a cemetery and a Jewish primary school.[93] In 1768, there were only two Jewish families there. By 1941, there were around 1,350 Jewish inhabitants. Many were businessmen or craftsmen, but there were also three Jewish doctors and three lawyers.[94]

The Markowicz family kept kosher and observed the Jewish holidays. Channa describes them as religious but not orthodox. Her father wore 'modern clothing'. The family was invited every Christmas by a Christian family. Her father usually went with the children to the party, her mother not always. 'She didn't like it so much.' In return, the Christian neighbours visited the Markowicz family on Jewish holidays.

'I didn't initially experience any antisemitism. There were arguments in school, but they had nothing to do with antisemitism. At least I can't remember any. I had both Russian and Jewish friends. That was not uncommon.'

EDUARD KORNFELD was born in the western Slovakian town Veľký Meder (Hungarian: Nagymegyer), 70 kilometres from Bratislava and 20 from the Hungarian border. It had a population of around 5,000, with some 100 Jewish families, about 530 people.[95]

The first Jews settled in Veľký Meder in the mid eighteenth century. The Jewish community grew steadily. In 1869, there were 217 Jews in the town, by 1919 there were 416, and in 1941 the town had 522 Jewish inhabitants, around 12 per cent of the total population. They were businessmen or craftsmen.[96]

There was a large synagogue in Veľký Meder, a Jewish cemetery, the Beit Hamidrash school near the synagogue, and a mikvah.

The Jewish primary school had around 100 pupils, with two teachers for eight years in two classrooms. The 'little school' was for Years 1 to 3, and the 'big school' was for the other five. While the 'little school' teacher was occupied for half an hour with the youngest pupils, the other two years had to write or do arithmetic. The classes rotated on this principle every 30 minutes. The same system operated in the 'big school': Years 4 and 5 formed one group, and Years 6 to 8 the other.[97]

When Eduard was 2 years old, the family moved to Bratislava, where Simon Kornfeld opened a flourishing linen goods shop. They lived in a large apartment. 'The Danube was just a stone's throw away.'

Bratislava at the time was the centre of orthodox Judaism. In the mid thirteenth century, it already had a sizeable Jewish community.[98] In the mid fourteenth century, there were probably several hundred Jews living in the city. They had a synagogue, a cemetery and their own jurisdiction.

There were expulsions in the fourteenth and fifteenth centuries, but from 1800 the number of Jewish inhabitants rose steadily, from 2,000 to 15,000 around 1930, 12 per cent of the total population. The Great

Synagogue was built in 1864, and many other institutions were created, such as the Jewish hospital, boys' and girls' orphanages, and the Jewish old people's home. In the early twentieth century, there were several hundred businesses owned by Jews, who exerted an influence on both public and economic life in the city.[99]

Even today, countless pilgrims come to visit the grave of the orthodox rabbi, teacher and writer Chatam Sofer (1763–1839), born Moses Schreiber in Frankfurt am Main. He was principal of the rabbinical school in Bratislava, which became a centre of Jewish scholarship of international renown.[100]

The Kornfeld family was 'very religious'. 'We went to the synagogue not only on the holidays but also on Shabbat. Anything else would have been unthinkable.' They respected Shabbat as the weekly day of rest ordered by the Torah. It begins on Friday evening when the first three stars are visible in the sky or when it is no longer possible to distinguish between a white and a black thread, and ends on Saturday evening. 'During this time, no fires could be lit or lights switched on, and no food could be prepared.' On the other hand, the Kornfelds wore modern clothes and didn't have payot (sidelocks). 'Bratislava was more of a western city, just 80 kilometres from Vienna.'

From the age of 6, Eduard attended a religious Jewish, but German-speaking, school. 'We had only a few compulsory lessons in Slovakian.' At the time, there were over sixty Jewish primary schools in Slovakia. Half of the schools taught in Slovakian, twenty-five in Hungarian, and six in German.[101]

The Kornfeld family had little contact with non-Jewish families. 'We had a good and friendly relationship with our closest neighbours.' Otherwise, they barely met non-Jews. 'We simply felt most comfortable among Jews.'

Eduard had a Hungarian nanny, enabling him to learn Hungarian as well as Slovakian and German, 'which soon turned out to be a valuable advantage'.

He liked to play football and a wooden spinning top game with other children. 'A piece of wood was sharpened to a point and made to "dance" with a kind of whip. Each person had four or five goes. The one who span the piece of wood furthest was the winner.' A certain amount of skill and practice was required, 'but then it would work'.

In winter, there was a 'special hill' that was highly popular. 'I loved to go sledding there.' He couldn't get enough of it.

'But my untroubled childhood didn't last long.'

FERENC AND OTTO KLEIN were born in 1932 in the eastern Hungarian town of Hajdúböszörmény. Their sister Ágnes was born two years earlier in August 1930.

Their father, Salomon Klein, was a hardworking businessman. He owned a wood and coal yard and a small roof tile factory. He was actually a rabbi 'but didn't practise'. 'I only discovered that after the war.' Their mother Lilly was a housewife and looked after the children's upbringing. The family had their own house in the centre of the town. There was no ghetto. 'The population was mixed.' The Kleins were respected citizens of the town.

Around 1920, Hajdúböszörmény had a population of some 28,000, including about 1,000 Jews. The history of the Jewish community began in the early nineteenth century, and the synagogue was built in 1863.[102]

The family valued Jewish rites, customs and traditions, 'as it should be'. They kept a kosher household. Every Friday evening and Saturday, Salomon Klein went with the twins to the synagogue. The women only went on the High Holidays. 'That's how it was in Hungary at the time.' Salomon and Lilly Klein spoke fluent Hungarian, Yiddish and German. 'We children only spoke Hungarian. Our mother could also speak Slovakian.' Her family had moved, around 1920, from Slovakia to Miskolc in northern Hungary.

From 1939, Otto and Ferenc attended the Jewish primary school in Hajdúböszörmény. In the afternoon, they both went to Talmud Torah school. There was a group of pupils in the neighbouring Christian school who made antisemitic comments. 'They would fight us when we were coming home.' The Jewish children didn't put up with that for long and fought back. 'Then they left us alone.'

'There was not a lot of antisemitism, but we boys had few non-Jewish friends. Somehow, that didn't work.'

Their father's brothers and sisters lived in Debrecen, the second-largest city in Hungary, 20 kilometres from Hajdúböszörmény. It was the largest industrial and trading centre in the region. There were 9,142 Jews living in the city in 1941, 7 per cent of the total population.[103]

'We enjoyed being with relatives from Debrecen. Everyone got on well.' The boys also enjoyed going to Miskolc, two hours' drive from Hajdúböszörmény, where their mother's family lived. 'There was a small spa resort nearby where we would go swimming during the holidays.'

Miskolc, at the centre of northern Hungary, is the country's third-largest city. The first Jewish families settled there in the late eighteenth century. In 1941, there were 10,428 Jews in Miskolc, around 14 per cent of the total population.[104]

Otto and Ferenc liked to spend their free time at their father's work in Hajdúböszörmény. They loved to play hide-and-seek on the large site. Sometimes, the adults could be persuaded to look for them. 'They would look for an hour, but they could never find us.' In the end, they had to leave a clue somewhere on the site. Only then were they found.

'We had a good time playing together.' They also played in the small brickworks. 'When there was no one there, we would make roof tiles for fun. That was a fantastic game.'

Until his death in summer 2014, Otto Klein retained only good memories of the first years of his life. 'We were a respected family. My parents loved each other and the children. We had a nice, happy life.'

YEHUDA BACON was born in the 'city of black diamonds', known far and wide for centuries as a city with large coal reserves – a mining and iron and steel city. It was Moravská Ostrava (Mährisch Ostrau), today part of Ostrava. The city is in the north-west of the Czech Republic, at the tripoint junction of Poland, Slovakia and the Czech Republic.

In the nineteenth century, it was one of the cities where Jews were not allowed to settle. Some skirted the prohibition by living outside the city, on the other side of the Oder in Poland. Jewish families managed to settle in Ostrava gradually from 1792, and more so after 1848. Brown coal was discovered in the mid eighteenth century, and industrialization made the city increasingly attractive for Jewish immigrants. They were strongly represented in economic life and commerce, as entrepreneurs and in the professions.

A Jewish school was established first of all, then, ten years later, a two-class and then four-class state primary school. By the end of the nineteenth century, the school had a good 300 pupils. In 1872, a plot was acquired for a cemetery, and four years later for a synagogue. On 15

September 1879, the new house of prayer was officially opened. Within fifty years, a total of six synagogues were built.[105]

The historian Hugo Gold wrote of the dedication of the first synagogue: 'This ceremonial act took place before a crowd of thousands, and the beautiful, truly uplifting ceremony presented to the people of Ostrava a dignified testimony to tolerance, of which the population of some other cities could be rightfully envious.'[106]

In 1900, the Ostrava Jewish community celebrated its twenty-fifth anniversary. It had been built up from nothing. The rabbi recalled in his ceremonial speech:

> It is easy to build up from something that already exists, to work where there is already something. It is easy to enlarge on what you already have, but it is difficult to build and plant where the ground is completely barren, where there are no traditions. To adapt the words of the poet: 'Woe to you that you are not a grandson!' That's how it was in Mährisch-Ostrau as well. There used to be no Jews living in this city, there were no institutions or memories, nothing to connect to, everything had to be built up from scratch.[107]

But the Jewish community grew quickly. In 1929, it had 10,000 members living in thirteen localities in and around Ostrava.[108]

Yehuda Bacon was born on 28 July 1929 in Ostrava. Hanna (Channah) and Rella, his sisters, were six and five years older than him, respectively. Their father, Isidor Bacon, was a hardworking manufacturer and businessman. He owned a leather factory with his brother Baruch. Their mother Ethel was a housewife who looked after the children's upbringing. The Bacon family was religious. Yehuda had religious instruction. Shabbat, the weekly day of rest from Friday to Saturday evening, was of 'great importance' for the family. 'The candles were lit on Friday evening at dusk, the Shabbat bread eaten and a festive meal prepared.'

Jews were commonplace in Ostrava. Relations between Jews and non-Jews were relatively good. 'I didn't experience any antisemitism at first. We lived a completely "normal" life.'

ROBERT (YEHOSHUA) BÜCHLER was born on 1 January 1929 in Topol'čany in western Slovakia, 110 kilometres from Bratislava, a town with a population of 12,000. Around 1 in 5 inhabitants was Jewish, like the Büchlers.

Some 70 per cent of the population worked in agriculture. Robert's father Josef, however, came from a commercial family, selling hand-made suits, shirts and work clothing at markets. He was the only one of thirteen siblings to have attended secondary school. He wanted to study at university but was conscripted into the Austrian army during the First World War. In 1918 he obtained a position as a *Prokurist* (authorized signatory) in Produktiva, a farm trading company in Topol'čany. Here he met the office clerk Terezia Weinberger, his future wife.

> My father's ancestors had lived for around 200 years in the city. My mother came from a small village called Oslany, 30 kilometres away.
>
> Our grandmother had stalls on the market square in Topol'čany and in the surrounding villages. It was a real family business. Of my grandparents' thirteen children, five were tailors like my grandfather. Everything they sold was hand-made.
>
> When I was a little older, I helped with sales. It was a great treat for me and I loved doing it.

There were Jewish merchants in Topol'čany already in the fourteenth century. The first synagogue was built in 1780. Five years earlier, the first Jewish cemetery was dedicated. It was one of the oldest in Slovakia. The Jewish population grew steadily and, in 1828, 561 of the population of 2,500 were Jews.

In 1895, a dream harboured by the Jewish community came true with the start of construction of the Great Synagogue. It was completed five years later. Hundreds of guests from all over the country, representatives of the communities, rabbis and the Jews of the city attended the opening. Thereafter, the 500-seat synagogue was the centre of Jewish religious life in Topol'čany. It was considered one of the most beautiful synagogues in Czechoslovakia. In the last two decades of the nineteenth century, representatives of the Jewish community were elected for the first time to the city council, and two of its members later became deputy mayors. Around 1900, there were 1,676 Jews in Topol'čany.

The city received a further boost with the establishment of the Czechoslovak Republic in autumn 1918. Prior to that, Topol'čany had been part of Austria-Hungary. The republic recognized the Jewish minority as an ethnic group for the first time. The new democratic laws granted the Jews intellectual, religious and economic freedom.

There were great hopes for the future. Until well into the 1930s, a diverse Jewish life developed in the city. There were several synagogues, two cemeteries, a Talmud Torah school, a Jewish old people's home, a soup kitchen for the needy, a kosher butcher, a matzo bakery, the Jewish primary school, Hashomer Hatzair (Young Guard) Socialist Zionist youth organization groups and the Maccabi Association for Body Culture.[109]

'For the most part, the Jews were an acknowledged part of the population. One of my uncles, Karl Pollak, was deputy mayor. And the mayor was always one of the first to buy a Jewish calendar at the start of the Jewish year. The Jews were fully integrated in the life of the city. At least, we thought so.' Robert's sister Ruth was born in 1933. Three years later, Robert started at the Jewish primary school. Lessons there were in Slovakian, German and Hebrew.

HERBERT ADLER spent the first years of his life in Dortmund. In 1938, at the age of 9, the Sinti boy moved with his parents and siblings to Frankfurt am Main after his father, a post office worker, had gained a promotion. Sinti and Roma had lived for many centuries in Europe. They were mentioned for the first time in Hildesheim in 1407.[110]

Herbert Adler's parents were born at the beginning of the twentieth century, his father in Debrecen, Hungary, and his mother in Berlin.

'"Sinti" and "Roma" are words from the minority Romany language used in families as a second mother tongue besides the state language', says Romani Rose, chairperson of the Central Council of German Sinti and Roma.

'Sinti' refers to members of the minority living in central Europe since the Middle Ages and 'Roma' to those of south-eastern European origin. Outside German-speaking circles, Roma – or simply Rom (which means person) – is used as an umbrella term for the entire minority. Romany is related to Sanskrit, the language of the ancient Indian subcontinent, indicating that India was the original birthplace of Sinti and Roma. The widely used term 'gypsy' … [is] rejected by many Sinti and Roma as discriminatory, as it is mostly spoken in a derogatory fashion.[111]

When they moved to Frankfurt in 1938, the Adler family lived initially in a three-room apartment in Klappergasse in the Sachsenhausen district. The house was destroyed during the war and not rebuilt. When Herbert's parents, Reinhold and Margarete Adler, had further siblings, they looked for a larger apartment. They ultimately found one at Löherstrasse 21 in Sachsenhausen, on the site of which a modern building now stands. 'It was a nice five-room apartment with all the trimmings.'

Herbert went to the Frankensteiner School – at the time, for boys only. 'Our class teacher was Mr Erb. He must have been around 40. He was like a fatherly friend to us. There were around thirty boys in the class. I was never victimized by teachers or fellow pupils. I liked it there a lot.' He also felt at home with the Löhergass boys. 'I was a real Frankfurt lad.' Football was his great passion. 'We would play for hours on the Mainwiese.' He was nevertheless aware that 'something was going on with the Jews.... But what exactly? That I didn't know.'

However, he had no idea that, in August 1937, the first fifty-five Frankfurt Sinti and Roma families were interned in a camp in Dieselstrasse,[112] near the Osthafen. His parents might have known, but they never spoke to him or his siblings about it.

'One of my brothers was often hit by his gym teacher, a fanatical Nazi.' And yet, if anyone had asked Herbert whether he was afraid, he would have looked at them wide-eyed and asked what he should be afraid of. They were 'Germans, after all', had work, a nice apartment – 'Why should anything happen to us?'

# 'That's When My Childhood Ended'

Jürgen Loewenstein and Wolfgang Wermuth Right after Hitler came to power on 30 January 1933,[1] the Nazis ordered numerous restrictions on Jewish life in Germany. On 1 April 1933, the boycott of Jewish business, Jewish goods, Jewish doctors and Jewish lawyers began.[2] Uniformed Nazis stood guard in front of Jewish shops, department stores and businesses and barred people from entering, sometimes using violence. Jewish shops were daubed with slogans such as 'Jew!' or 'Shopping here can be lethal'.[3]

As co-owner of an antiques business, Wolfgang's father Siegmund Wermuth, a German soldier wounded in the First World War, was no longer able to work. He was a member of the Reichsbund Jüdischer Frontsoldaten [Reich Association of Jewish Veterans] founded shortly after the end of the First World War. In 1925, it had between 35,000 and 40,000 members in 500 local groups. Its main aim was to combat antisemitism in Germany.[4]

It was quite normal for Jewish soldiers to serve in the German army before the Nazi era. Almost 100,000 Jews had served between 1914 and 1918, some had won medals and over 20,000 had gained promotion. Among them were 3,000 officers. And 12,000 Jewish soldiers had died on the battlefields of the First World War.[5] Wolfgang's father had also been 'highly decorated'.

For Jürgen Loewenstein, everything changed radically in March 1933. He saw the parades of 'brown columns' for the first time. They marched through the streets with torches, shouting and singing. 'As a youth, I was naturally curious and opened the window.' Now he could clearly hear what they were singing: 'The Jews are everywhere, they cross the Red Sea, the waves close on them, and the world has its peace.' And then they roared: 'When Jewish blood spurts from the knife, so much the better.'[6]

He was never able to forget these verses. His grandmother, Agathe Sochaczewer (*née* Rosenthal), also heard the singing. She pulled him away from the window before the song had finished and said: 'Jürgen, look carefully at these people: they are your enemies. Never forget that.'

'That's when my childhood ended. I was not quite 8 years old.'

The Wermuth family had lots of contacts with non-Jews. Wolfgang's mother Käthe, an accomplished pianist, was invited by the neighbours to play Christmas carols on the piano. 'My mother enjoyed these festivities. It had nothing to do with her denying her own religion.' Such invitations were quite common.

Käthe Wermuth was friends with the wife of a former officer. Their daughter was the same age as Ursula Brigitte, Wolfgang's sister, who was seven years older than him. In 1935, Käthe received a letter from this woman which said more or less: 'In my position, I can no longer remain in touch with you. I beg your forgiveness, but the way of the world today also has personal consequences. Please stay away from me in future.'

Wolfgang started school in 1933 at the state primary school on Sybelstrasse. When the family moved first to Bismarckstrasse 66 and then in 1935 to Fritschestrasse 55, both in Charlottenburg, he changed to the state primary school on Witzlebenstrasse. 'There were seven Jewish children in my class out of twenty-eight pupils. Our class teacher was special. She did not favour us Jewish pupils but she felt a particular sympathy for us.' The Jewish children had religious instruction twice a week. 'We were exempt from the Christian class. And even at the state primary school there was a very good religion teacher, Miss Kaspari.' The Christian fellow pupils were curious and asked questions about the Jewish religion. 'I remember at Pesach – naturally I ate matzo, unleavened bread – and the children asked me what I was eating. I explained to them as well as I could its origins and the significance of this festival.'

There were very few Jews living in Fritschestrasse. Wolfgang made friends on the street with the neighbourhood children. 'They came to our apartment. We celebrated birthdays together. I also went to their houses. That was quite normal.'

In 1935, Jürgen was fortunate enough to go on one of the trips to Horserød, Denmark, organized by the Berlin Jewish community. 'For once I could eat as much as I wanted.'

A year later, he took part in a trip organized by the Reich Association of Jewish Veterans, again to Denmark, during the Olympic Games in Berlin (1 to 16 August 1936). 'The Nazis toned things down. They wanted to show other countries how wonderful everything was in Germany. The Jewish benches and "no Jews" signs were removed.'

The attempt by Nazi Germany to cover up the antisemitism during the Summer Games from the many visitors, athletes and journalists in Berlin was only partially successful. Antisemitic signs were still to be found, even in the vicinity of the Olympic stadiums.[7] In reality there was no interruption to the Nazi terror. Sachsenhausen concentration camp was established just outside Berlin almost at the same time as the Games, and the first fifty inmates were interned there on 12 July 1936. By the end of 1936, it already had 1,600 internees. The camp was to be a model for the large-scale expansion of the concentration camp system by the Nazi regime.[8]

Or, again, two weeks before the start of the Olympic Games, on 16 July 1936, around 600 Roma and Sinti, including many children, from the Reich capital were put in an internment camp in the Marzahn suburb of Berlin. Almost all of them were deported to Auschwitz-Birkenau in 1943.[9]

In 1938, Wolfgang's fellow pupils and neighbourhood children began to call him names ('Jude – Itzig – Lebertran [cod liver oil]'). 'I was cut off. When, in my childish innocence, I would go up to these boys, who had been in my house, they turned away. I had no reason not to like them anymore.'

Wolfgang wanted to go to the grammar school. 'There was no problem with admission.' But shortly afterwards, his parents received a letter saying that for 'race reasons' their son would no longer be accepted at the grammar school. In November 1938, Jewish children were banned from attending state schools.[10] Wolfgang was able to attend one of the twenty-four Jewish schools in Berlin,[11] at Klopstockstrasse 58 in the Hansaviertel. He later switched to the school in Joachimsthaler Strasse, the headquarters of the Jewish community after the Second World War in the divided Berlin.

A favourite meeting place after school was the Jüdisches Lehrhaus at Marburger Strasse 5 near Bahnhof Zoo. It had a library with books for young people that Wolfgang liked to go to. Apart from reading, the children played table tennis, draughts or chess. 'There was also a Jewish lunch menu. The owners were called Kugel.' On the night of the state-organized pogrom on 9–10 November 1938, during which Jewish citizens were arrested and murdered and almost all synagogues in Germany were laid waste and burned to the ground,[12] the windows of Pension Kugel were also broken, chairs thrown out onto the street and the library ransacked. At that time, the children in Fritschestrasse began to throw pieces of coal and stones at their former classmate Wolfgang Wermuth. 'There was one family – the father was some kind of civil servant – with three sons. The youngest, Dieter Neugebauer, still visited me secretly, although his parents had strictly forbidden it. His mother didn't go into a shop when my mother was in there. She waited outside until my mother left.' The concierge in the house was quite forthright. He complained about the 'Jews with their dirty feet'. Close neighbours could be heard making negative comments on the stairs. No one in the street wanted anything more to do with the Wermuths and the other Jews living there. No one wanted to know them or ever to have done so.

On 12 November 1938, Jews were banned from visiting theatres, cinemas, concerts and exhibitions.[13] This exclusion from cultural life was a severe blow for the Wermuths. 'My parents knew a lot of theatre and film people. They were friends with many of the regulars at the Romanisches Café [an artists' meeting place at Kurfürstendamm 238, now Budapester Strasse 43]. My father even played skat with the film director Ernst Lubitsch when he lived in Berlin.'

In 1938, Siegmund Wermuth had to stop working altogether, and was forced to collect rubbish. He worked occasionally for Siemens as a vacuum cleaner salesman in the outer districts, but in November 1938 this also stopped. Since 1933, the Nazis had tightened the labour market for Jews. They were now classed with 'asocials', a concept with a long tradition in political propaganda. In late 1938, German and stateless Jews had to work in special areas isolated from the other employees. This applied at first to Jews who had been forced into unemployment and then, from mid-1940, to all Jews up to a certain age.[14]

Siegmund Wermuth found it 'very decent' to be given a large radio as a retrospective Christmas bonus from Siemens:

For a long time, my father thought he was safe. He was a decorated First World War veteran. The Jews had risked their lives and spilled their blood for this country. Didn't that count for anything anymore? My father thought that they might strip the Jews of their citizenship and make them stateless, but he still didn't feel directly affected by much of what was going on. It was as if the neighbour's house was burning but my house wouldn't necessarily catch fire as a result. That's how a lot of people felt until they were up to their necks in water.

Wolfgang's parents were simply unable to believe what was happening around them. They accepted a lot, thinking that it couldn't go any further. They no longer recognized people they thought they knew. Their world collapsed around them. Literally everything slid out of control. But they still hoped that it would all pass.

In early December 1938, the Jews were banned from using certain streets and squares. The term 'Judenbann' [ban on Jews] was coined for that purpose.[15] The lives of the Wermuth and Loewenstein families were almost completely confined to their own four walls.

Of course, Jewish families – including the Loewensteins and Wermuths – in Berlin and Germany considered emigrating. But the Loewensteins didn't have enough money. Wolfgang Wermuth now had contact only with Jewish children. In his family as well, emigration became the main topic of conversation. 'Should we go? If so, where to? What about visas?' It all happened very quickly. 'Suddenly there were only sixteen children left of the original thirty or so pupils.' This made those left behind uncertain and worried. They envied the émigrés. 'At home I was consoled by being told that emigration was highly uncertain and that perhaps it would get better.' Some of the Wermuths' relatives and their families had also fled abroad.

The Sochaczewer and Loewenstein families wanted at least to get Jürgen out of Nazi Germany. He was sent to a 'hakhshara', an agricultural school, in preparation for emigration to Palestine.[16]

On 1 September 1939, Jürgen was standing on the platform at the train station in Sommerfeld (Niederlausitz) waiting for a narrow-gauge train to take him to nearby Schniebinchen. He was carrying his meagre possessions in a cardboard box tied up with string.

'Hey, kid, where are you going?' a man asked him.

'Schniebinchen.'

'Aha, you want to go to Palestine. That's where you should all go.'

Jürgen was happy to get out of Berlin. He wanted to 'start something new, to begin working and carry on learning'. And 'perhaps I'll be lucky enough to get away from Germany'.

The emigration centre was on a hill not far from the village of Schniebinchen. There were around 150 children and adolescents aged 14 and over living in three houses. Half of the day was filled with agricultural training. In the other half, they spoke about Zionism, the labour movement, kibbutzim and Palestine studies, did theatre work and played music, read German literature and had to help in the kitchen. 'Schniebinchen was isolated and we didn't get much news from outside. Everyone was waiting and hoping to make Aliyah, immigration to Palestine.'

Jürgen enjoyed the work and he learned a lot about things he had never previously heard of: 'Zionism, the labour movement, kibbutzim and equality, the history of the Jewish people and of Eretz Israel [the birthplace and refuge of the Jewish people]. But we also learned a bit about Hasidism ("The entire life of the Hasid down to the smallest detail is devoted to the service of God.")[17] and German literature.... In the evening, there were theatre and music courses.'[18] But one day Jürgen received a cruel surprise. The director informed him: 'There's no place for you here. You're not suited for community life.' For Jürgen, this decision was completely incomprehensible. But tears and shouting were of no use.

In 1933, there were 160,000 Jews living in Berlin.[19] By September 1939, forced emigration, flight and death, deportation and murder had reduced the number to just around 75,000.[20]

The Jewish school in Joachimsthaler Strasse was forced to close. Wolfgang started at the Jewish secondary school at Wilsnacker Strasse 3 in 1940. He tried very hard and was eager to learn. The big question loomed permanently in the background: when would he be able to use what he had learned? 'This question overshadowed everything.'

After Jürgen was unable to continue the agricultural training in Schniebinchen, he had a stroke of luck. At the time of his rejection, the hakhshara teacher Therese Hemmerdinger was visiting Schniebinchen from Rüdnitz and offered to accept the boy in her group.

A small group of Jewish girls and boys lived in Rüdnitz near Bernau. They were convinced that they would one day go to Eretz Israel. The work in the vegetable garden was not difficult and produced additional food. Friendships were formed and future plans hatched. We forgot what was going on in the world. The horrors of war were far away.

The first news of deportations to the East reached Rüdnitz. 'Some fellow students whose parents were on the list didn't know what to do: to go back to their families or to remain in the hakhshara. It was decided that we should all stay together.'

During this time, Wolfgang Wermuth was able to finish his schooling in Berlin at the Jewish secondary school in Wilsnacker Strasse in April 1941.

Then came the 'big bang' for him: he was recruited immediately with around 19,000 Jewish women and men from Berlin in the middle of the year for essential war production.[21] It was claimed that, without the forced labour, the economy and the conduct of the war in Nazi Germany would have collapsed at the latest by early 1942.[22]

Wolfgang was 14 years old. He was assigned to the Deutsche Waffen- und Munitionsfabriken in Berlin-Borsigwalde for an hourly wage of 27 pfennig. Work started at 6 a.m. 'I rode the S-Bahn to Friedrichstrasse, changed trains and had then to walk for 20 to 25 minutes.' They worked separately from the non-Jewish employees in 'large, locked, cage-like things'. They had to wear a blue armband with a red dot on it and were only allowed to go to the toilet in groups of ten.

Wolfgang checked bullets for cracks. 'We deliberately allowed lots of small defects to pass. We knew quite well who the ammunition was intended for. The inspection could not always be precisely traced, but we could not commit real acts of sabotage.' But it was still risky to allow defects to pass. Anyone caught doing so was likely to be deported immediately. The Jewish forced labourers had occasional contact with the non-Jewish workers. There were a few young women who secretly gave them sandwiches wrapped in newspaper. 'We had limited rations and ration cards.'

One day, Wolfgang got a splinter of metal in his eye. 'My father applied for me to be taken off the factory work.' He now worked in a small typewriter factory near the Landwehrkanal, 'where the conditions were quite decent'. Wolfgang was on the late shift from 2 to 11 p.m. 'There were more and more air raid warnings and actual air raids.'

The Jews were not allowed to eat in the factory canteen, which was reserved for 'Germans'. There was thus very little contact. Wolfgang recalls a young woman in the pay department who was always nice to him. Once she gave him a bottle of lemonade she had hidden behind a brick. He secretly returned the empty deposit bottle to her. He travelled by S-Bahn to work and his ticket was only valid for that journey. 'There would be problems if I took another route, and there were lots of controls.'

One night on the way home, Wolfgang was sitting opposite a woman. She saw the yellow star on his clothing. 'She asked me if I really had to wear the star and if I was hungry. We didn't get a lot to eat, but we weren't hungry.' The woman gave him a package to take with him. 'I'm sure she didn't have a lot herself.' In the package was a cooked meatloaf. When he told his mother about it, she said: 'You see, there are still decent people.' Things like this would give her a little hope again.

In 1940/1, one hakhshara centre after another was closed down. For Jürgen Loewenstein, this was now a common occurrence. 'We arrived at a new place, continued the work of those who were no longer there, and didn't even ask where they had gone to.' He went from Ellguth in Silesia (now Ligota Oleska, Poland), Eichow-Muhle in Spreewald, and Ahrensdorf near Luckenwalde to Paderborn.[23] From 9 January 1942, the 100-strong group lived in barracks at Grüner Weg 86.[24] They worked as forced labourers for the city. Jürgen was a road sweeper and rubbish collector.

Now and then, Jürgen and his colleagues were given food by the local inhabitants, including the owner of a bakery they passed every week: 'The baker came out of his shop and pulled out a loaf of bread from under his apron and handed it to us saying: "For God's sake don't tell my wife."' The same thing happened the following week, 'but this time it was the baker's wife who came out of the shop, produced a loaf of bread from under her apron and said: "For God's sake don't tell my husband."'

In spite of the hard physical work, the 'cultural side of life was not forgotten':

We naturally celebrated all the Jewish holidays and worked hard at learning Hebrew. We sat together in groups and listened to poems and music. Fritz Schäfer, one of our 'madrichim', gave talks, and there was lots of discussion … : 'When we get to Eretz Israel, we should realize that the Arab fellahin have more in common with us than the middle-class Jews.' Fanny Bergas, another 'madricha', gave a talk on what book we would take with us if we were alone on a desert island.

All roads to Palestine were now blocked. According to a decree of 23 October 1941, Jews were no longer allowed to emigrate.[25] Jürgen and his colleagues hoped at least to be able to stay in Germany.

In Berlin, Wolfgang's sister Ursula Brigitte was recruited as a forced labourer at Batteriefabrik Pertrix in Niederschöneweide. Here, in one of the most important industrial districts of Berlin, Jewish forced labourers had been employed since 1938. They were to be joined later by prisoners of war, and forced labourers and concentration camp inmates from other countries. In autumn 1944, a satellite camp of Sachsenhausen was installed in Schöneweide, where up to 500 women whiled away their time. Since April 1944, the manufacture of aircraft batteries, vital for the war effort, had had absolute priority at Pertrix.[26]

Ursula Brigitte Wermuth was arrested by the works security [*Werkschutz*] in July 1942, with four other women, for allegedly communicating with prisoners of war. Their 'offence': they had given them shaving brushes and toothpaste. The day after their arrest, a Wehrmacht lieutenant appeared at the door of the family's apartment. He reproached Käthe Wermuth, saying 'How could your daughter have anything to do with those gypsies?'

'You know, these people in uniform have served their country just like you', she replied. The lieutenant was taken aback at the lack of respect shown to him by a Jew. She was charged, but acquitted. In front of the courthouse, the Gestapo was waiting. 'They arrested her on the spot but later released her again.'

'After three or four days, we received an anonymous letter. It was three pages long and apparently came from a high-ranking member of the Gestapo, who had interrogated my sister. I can recall a few sentences from it. "We have questioned your daughter. I'm personally sorry, but that's how the world is today. Perhaps a new dawn will come for you one day." A few days later, the Wermuths received an official letter informing them that Ursula Brigitte was in the women's prison in Lehrter Strasse, Moabit, and that visits were only possible by special permission. But Wolfgang's mother simply went there with a package with linen and sandwiches. 'At the prison gates, a guard told my mother that she had a nerve coming to the Gestapo without permission.' By chance, Käthe saw her daughter waving from behind a barred window and was able to wave back to her. It was the last time she saw her.

After the war, Wolfgang Wermuth discovered that his sister had been deported initially to the women's concentration camp at Ravensbrück and then to Riga in Latvia, where she was shot in the forest of Rumbala in a mass execution.

The first transport of German Jews from Berlin-Grunewald train station reached Riga on 30 November 1941. The 1,000 or more Berlin Jews were all murdered in Rumbala.[27] On that Sunday, on 8 December, around 25,000 Latvian Jews from the Riga ghetto were also shot.[28]

By the end of October 1942, a further seven transports with over 6,500 Jewish children, women and men left from Berlin alone. Practically none of them survived. For example, the 959 people on the transport of 19 October, including 140 children under 10 years of age, and the 55 children under the age of 10 on the transport of 26 October, were all murdered immediately in the forest near Riga.[29]

At around this time, in Paderborn, the members of Jürgen Loewenstein's group were able to write and receive letters. They were also allowed to receive packages from friends and relatives. The letters and cards sent by Jürgen Loewenstein from Paderborn to Ernst Gross, a family friend, at Chausseestrasse 125 in Berlin, have survived. After liberation, they met up again, and Jürgen was given his letters back. On 23 December 1942, he wrote the following:

> I'm sure you know that my parents are gone. They were taken on the 3rd of this month. I've had no news since. I didn't even receive a letter, just a notification from people I don't know. Now I sit here and realize that I'm all alone, that I have no more relatives, that it's Christmas tomorrow, and Chanukah

has already passed, and there was no letter, no package with gifts, as was usually the case, and that I was alone and abandoned. But that doesn't help. Head up, don't think, just hope, hope, hope.

Here there's no change. The work is difficult (I'm now on rubbish collection) and the food is mediocre. You probably know that we don't get any meat, eggs or cake rations. But we have to make do. Sometimes we are really hungry....

Tomorrow is Christmas Eve and I wish you all the best. I hope you all keep well.... Up to now I always spent Christmas at home and, I think, at your house. But that's all finished now.

Jürgen's parents were deported to Auschwitz on the 24th transport east from Berlin on 9 December 1942.[30] The 1,060 children, women and men arrived the following day, of whom 137 men and twenty-five women were allowed to live. Jürgen's parents, Paula and Walter Loewenstein, and a further 896 children, women and men were murdered in the gas chambers.[31] Jürgen wrote to Ernst Gross in Berlin on 7 February 1943:

There are 100 of us in all.... In my room there are six boys of my age and with the same goal. They're all great guys and we get on very well together. If one gets a package or something from the city, it's shared with everyone....

One friend has his birthday on 20 February. Could you not put a small package together? A little present and a nice letter. I'm sure it would give him great pleasure.... He's completely alone, without parents. Is it too much to ask because it's not me? ... His name is Alfred Ohnhaus.

On 23 February, Jürgen wrote: 'Onny's birthday was really nice and pleasant. For a couple of hours we were able to forget everything.' The boys on Grüner Weg in Paderborn still hoped to survive the war. Many of them thought: 'We're indispensable and will hopefully remain so. Life goes on. We're young and we'll stick together.'

LYDIA HOLZNEROVÁ 'I know the Germans. They are a cultivated people. They won't behave so badly.' Lydia's father, Emil Holzner, repeated this constantly to his friend, the headmaster of the school in Hronov, a small town in eastern Bohemia, before the Germans invaded. When the invasion of the Wehrmacht in the Czech Sudetenland appeared imminent in 1938, he advised the textile wholesaler: 'Go away! Don't stay here!' But Emil Holzner, his wife Růžena, and his daughters Věra, aged 16, and Lydia, aged 9, stayed.

Lydia started school in 1936. As there were only sixty-five Jews in Hronov, there was no Jewish school.[32] 'I went to the primary school like all the children in the town.' She was the only Jewish girl in her class, but it made no difference. 'The relationship between Christians and Jews was unproblematic.'

Lydia encountered Nazis for the first time in 1937. Her family was vacationing in a spa resort, and one day young Nazi Party supporters marched through the towns with pipes and drums. 'We can do without that! We're going home', said her father. 'Why?' asked the 7-year-old. 'It was then that my parents explained to me that there could be some changes in our lives.' Emil and Růžena talked more and more about emigrating. 'I was spared these discussions. I was always sent out of the room.' Lydia recalls that her parents wanted to send Věra away. But her sister didn't want to go away. She said: 'This is my home. This is my country and this is where I'll stay.'

As the occupation of Czech Sudetenland by German troops became imminent in autumn 1938, 200,000 people left between then and summer 1939, including around 25,000 Jewish inhabitants, many of whom sought shelter and a life in the still independent Czechoslovakian provinces of Bohemia and Moravia.[33] Flight was the only way of avoiding being deported to a camp. The Holzners remained in Hronov, although the town was close to the German border.

CHANNA MARKOWICZ Channa's father always showed a marked interest in politics. The developments in Europe in the 1930s, particularly in Germany, worried him. 'It must have been 1938; he wanted us to emigrate to Russia or America.' He saw no future for himself or his family in Irshava, but his wife didn't want to leave. 'I'm not going anywhere as long as my mother lives here', she said.

DÁŠA FRIEDOVÁ Although the Fried family were the only Jews in the Czech village of Odolice, where there were also a lot of Germans as well as Czechs, Dáša Friedová and her sister Sylva had no idea of the impending dangers to their lives. 'My parents never spoke about Hitler or Nazi Germany in our presence. Perhaps they wanted to protect us.' Besides, in their children's presence, Otto and Kát'a Fried spoke French or German when they wanted to talk about serious matters. 'We didn't understand, because we children spoke only Czech.'

When, in autumn 1938, the occupation by German troops of the northern, western and southern regions of Czechoslovakia (Sudetenland),[34] including Odolice, was imminent, the Fried family fled to Prague. They had to leave almost all of their things behind. It was only then that Dáša began to sense that 'something bad is happening'.

Relatives of the Frieds wanted to leave Europe altogether. An aunt and five cousins fled to Canada. They begged the Frieds to follow them. Dáša's mother obtained a passport. 'But my father didn't want to go anywhere.' He said: 'We're Czech, we were born here and this is our land. The Germans won't be here for long. We're staying here.' In Prague, the family moved into a nice large apartment and new furniture was acquired. Dáša and Sylva went to school again. The girls played with the children of other relatives, most of whom still lived in Prague. Life returned to normal.

'My sister and I began to feel at home in our new surroundings. We no longer felt any antisemitism. And life began to be pleasant again.' Until 13 March 1939, when German troops invaded Prague. Dáša was 9 years old; her sister Sylva, 12.

Sudetenland was annexed by Nazi Germany in autumn 1938.[35] And on 15 March the following year, just one day after Slovakia declared its independence, the Wehrmacht occupied the rest of the country. The German terror began right after the arrival of the Wehrmacht, SS units and police. Jews, Roma and political opponents were persecuted, interned and murdered.[36] Dáša's father was also arrested immediately and imprisoned in Pankraz. While the family still lived in Odolice, at the time of the Czechoslovakian elections on 19 May 1935,[37] Otto Fried had offered to drive inhabitants to the polling station with the farm's vehicles. Among them were many Germans. Because Fried feared that they would vote for the pro-Nazi Sudeten German Party, which later merged with the Nazi Party, the vehicles never reached their destination: 'My father told the drivers to go somewhere else. That's why he was arrested immediately after the Germans entered Prague.' Suddenly, Dáša and Sylva became worried again. Fortunately, their father was released after a few months. 'I have never discovered what happened to him in prison.'

The girls became hopeful again. They continued to go to school and played with their relatives' children. Friends also visited them in their nice apartment. 'My mother loved to have people around her and to organize celebrations.'

JANEK MANDELBAUM In the Free City of Danzig/Gdańsk, around 35 kilometres from the Polish city of Gdynia, the Nazis won over 50 per cent of the vote in the May 1933 elections. In spite of the League of Nations mandate, Jews were increasingly discriminated against and expropriated. A modified version of the Nuremberg Race Laws entered into force there on 21 November 1938.[38] This provoked great worry and concern for Janek's parents, Majloch and Cyrla Mandelbaum. They wondered fearfully what that would mean for their future and whether they would be safe in Gdynia.

In autumn 1936, the following report on the situation of the Jews of Danzig appeared in the *Jüdische Revue* published in Mukachevo, Czechoslovakia:

> The situation of the Jews ... is determined by the fact that although a democratic constitution prevents Jews from being legally discriminated against and from becoming second-class citizens, the population is being urged through strong Nazi propaganda to boycott Jews economically.... As the dominant government party, the Nazis will do everything to pursue anti-Jewish legislation as in the German Reich.... A ban on kosher butchering was recently ordered as part of the Emergency Regulation Law. Other regulations are likely to follow.[39]

Majloch and Cyrla Mandelbaum often received visits from friends. 'They talked about politics nearly all the time. They had an idea about what was going on in the Nazi Reich.' They knew about the marginalization and repression of the Jews in Germany and wondered why Hitler and his followers hated the Jews so much. Janek's parents didn't talk about their concerns when the children were present. 'They wanted to protect us.' But Janek often listened at the living-room door – or wherever he could – and learned a lot in that way.

In the meantime, Majloch Mandelbaum made successful efforts to arrange for the family's emigration to Australia. But there was a problem: 'The regulations specified that the husband must live for six months in the country before he could fetch his family.' Janek's mother did not want to be separated for six months from her husband at times like these.

'So we didn't go. Everything would certainly have been different for the family if we had emigrated to Australia.' But no one, including Janek's mother, knew at the time what awaited the family.

The summer of 1939 had begun and Janek had just celebrated his twelfth birthday. His parents wanted him to have his barmitzvah a year later, making him a fully fledged member of the Jewish community. This celebration usually takes place on the first Shabbat after the thirteenth birthday. On this day, the barmitzvah boy has to read a portion from the Torah in Hebrew. On the following day, the barmitzvah is celebrated with family and friends.

'My father engaged a teacher to prepare me. He was meant to teach me Hebrew to study the Torah and whatever else I needed for my barmitzvah. After one or two months of lessons, the teacher disappeared and never returned. Perhaps he had fled from the impending war. The German border was just a stone's throw away.'

One day it was announced: 'Schools will not open as planned after the summer holidays.' Janek and his friends were delighted: 'Great! Longer holidays! What could be better?'

Janek's father had a premonition, suspecting that Gdynia would be one of the first military objectives of Nazi Germany. He wanted to be sure that nothing would happen to his wife and children. 'It was decided that we should go to my grandfather. My father believed that we would be safe with his father. He said he would follow us in a month.' So, one morning in August, he brought his wife Cyrla and his children Ita, Jakob and Janek to the train station. It was crowded with people: 'Many were fleeing to the interior of the country.' The Mandelbaums embarked on what was a long journey at the time, around 550 kilometres. They were to travel for more than twelve hours.

Janek's grandfather lived in Działoszyce in southern Poland, 55 kilometres from Kraków. 'It was a very Jewish town', as reflected by the population: in 1899, 4,673 of the 5,170 inhabitants were Jews;

in 1910, 6,446 out of 7,688; and in the mid-1930s, over 5,000 out of 6,700.[40] The Jewish community had a large synagogue seating 800 worshippers, a prayer house, a Talmud Torah school with 80 pupils, and a 15,000-square-metre cemetery. There was also a Jewish library with 3,000 books.[41]

Janek's grandfather was waiting for the family at the train station. He was a pious orthodox Jew in a 'black caftan with a long beard and Hasidic headwear'. He was surprised, 'if not shocked', at Janek's appearance: 'I was wearing short trousers held up by narrow braces.' He looked darkly at the boy and said to his mother: 'I don't ever again want to see my grandson leave the house without a hat.'

As they made their way back to his grandfather's house, Janek stood out: 'The town was full of Jews dressed in black. They all spoke Yiddish. There were lots of small shops with Jewish owners.' Some were also to be found on the market square near his grandfather's two-storey house. The boy felt at home in the large house, where the grandfather worked as a sign writer. To please him, Janek wore a kippa thereafter. He also went with his grandfather 'for the first time before going to the synagogue' to a mikvah – a bathhouse serving not for hygienic purposes but for cleansing ritual impurity.

Two weeks after the Mandelbaums arrived in Działoszyce, Nazi Germany invaded Poland. Seven days later, on 7 September 1939, the Wehrmacht occupied the town.

> We heard the tanks rolling from far off. The streets were empty. The Germans also came past my grandfather's house. We hid behind the curtains. He finally mustered the courage to look out on the balcony. The Germans had not only tanks but also motorcycles with sidecars and trucks full of soldiers.
>
> We heard that people from the town had been arrested. Our fear grew with every day of the occupation.

Janek hoped against hope that his father would finally arrive. But he didn't come. Instead, the family received a card one day saying that his father had been sent to Stutthof concentration camp. He had been allowed to send a message: 'I'm in Stutthof. Don't worry. I'm fine.'

Janek Mandelbaum discovered fifty years later that his father had been arrested on 14 September at the age of 36 and transported to Stutthof, 18 kilometres from Gdynia, the family's hometown.

The Nazis had already compiled lists of 'undesirable Poles' before the war. The deportation and murder of the Polish population, especially the Jews, was part of the plan to completely 'Germanize' Poland, including Gdynia and Danzig/Gdańsk. Polish leaders, including members of political parties and unions, were among the first victims. Jews who had not been shot when the Germans first invaded were arrested with non-Jews and interned in Stutthof. There, and in the thirty-nine satellite camps, the Wehrmacht interned around 110,000 people from twenty-eight countries, 63,000 to 65,000 of whom died.[42]

Mindla Czamócha, the youngest sister of Janek's father in Słomniki, lived a good 30 kilometres from Działoszyce. She had given birth to a daughter eighteen months previously, on 15 February 1938, and asked Cyrla Mandelbaum if Janek's 15-year-old sister Ita could move in to help a little after the birth. She and her husband owned a grain mill and promised 'Ita will never go hungry with us.' Janek's sister and mother agreed.

Around three months after they arrived in southern Poland, Cyrla Mandelbaum decided to move with Jakob and Janek to her older brother. He lived in a small town called Sławków, 80 kilometres from Działoszyce. Because her husband was interned in Stutthof and couldn't join them, she 'preferred to live with her own family'.

There were around 960 Jews living in Sławków. The town had been occupied by German troops at the beginning of September. A few days later, 98 men were shot by German soldiers. They were all from Sławków and the surrounding area and had attempted to escape. The synagogue was also desecrated and the German occupiers demanded a high ransom from the Jewish inhabitants. They took hostages to press their claim. And – as everywhere in occupied Europe – a Jewish council was set up in the town, which, among other things, had to recruit Jews for forced labour.[43]

When the Germans occupied Sławków, they immediately forced the people to work on the roads. In winter 1939/1940 they had to shovel snow. The snow was lying higher than me. The Jewish council was commanded every day to provide 200 or 300 people. I was not on the list because I was only 12. But I replaced people who still had some money and paid me to work for them.

Janek thought up this idea himself because his uncle was 'quite poor and had five children of his own'. They all needed to be fed 'in those difficult times', which was 'not easy'. A package, 'probably with valuable contents', that his father had managed to send shortly before his arrest also never arrived – 'And so I wanted to contribute to the living expenses.' And it worked 'quite well and I learned what hard labour means'. For a time he was assigned to an electrician as his assistant. From January 1940 to June 1942, he was conscripted for forced labour.

At the end of 1941 or the beginning of 1942, the Jews of Sławków were concentrated into a ghetto. It had no fence or wall, but they weren't allowed to leave it. There was a strict curfew from 6 p.m. to 6 a.m., and all the Jews had to remain in their homes.[44]

Janek was very worried about his mother. She tried to be strong so as to be able to look after him and his brother. 'But she was extremely worried – particularly about my father and my sister.' They weren't allowed to visit Ita. The place where she lived with her father's youngest sister was now part of the General Government[45] – the part of Poland occupied by Nazi Germany but not incorporated immediately into the Reich. The situation in Sławków, where his mother lived, was different: the town now belonged to Germany. It was impossible for her to get to the other sector. 'This situation was intolerable for my mother. She was sick with worry.' But Janek was also losing his joy and hunger for life. 'I just wanted it to be over.' He wanted to get back to his old life in Gdynia with his mother, his sister and his brother. 'With papa to meet us there.'

HEINZ SALVATOR KOUNIO In Thessaloniki, the parents of Heinz, Salvator and Helene Kounio (called Hella), were increasingly anxious at the news broadcast several times a day by the BBC. The family followed the fate of the Jews in Germany in particular, with great concern. 'My sister Erika and I realized that something worrying was going on. But we didn't know exactly what was happening.' Erika was 12 years old and Heinz 11.

Their grandmother came from Karlsbad (Karlovy Vary) in Czechoslovakia. When German troops invaded in autumn 1938, practically all of the Jews living there, as elsewhere, fled. Over 15,000 Jewish children, women and men from the border areas left their homes, as did 13,000 non-Jewish German Nazis and 155,000 to 160,000 non-Jewish Czechs.[46]

Ernst and Theresa Löwy, the grandparents of Heinz and Erika, were among them. 'My grandparents arrived in Thessaloniki as refugees. With two small suitcases. They were only able to take a few things with them. Just what they had on, plus a few clothes. They had to leave all their belongings behind. Now I began to understand that there was something terrible going on.'

The family, particularly Salvator Kounio, continued to maintain a few contacts with Germany, especially the Leitz company. 'My father imported and sold the famous Leica cameras.'

FERENC AND OTTO KLEIN Their parents in Hajdúböszörmény in Hungary also listened to the BBC every day. Sometimes their father listened to a Russian radio station broadcasting in Hungarian. 'The talk was all about war. We children often listened to the programmes as well. And we also understood very well what was going on.'

In 1938 or 1939, five of the twins' cousins had escaped to North America. 'My parents didn't want to leave.' They were convinced that what was happening to the Jews elsewhere couldn't happen to the Hungarian Jews. The twins were 6 years old; their sister Ágnes, 8. The persecution and discrimination against the Jews had already started in Hungary. In May 1938, the Hungarian government adopted the first anti-Jewish laws from Nazi Germany. The proportion of Jews in business and the professions was limited to 20 per cent. The Jews were increasingly excluded from public life in Hungary.

The anti-Jewish climate was stirred up in particular by the press, which was predominantly financed by the Germans. The 'solution of the Jewish problem', as it was cynically known, was on the agenda of various pro-Nazi parties and Christian churches. And the Hungarian army was extremely antisemitic.[47] 'My father was forced to reduce his business activities. Jews were not allowed to sell heating fuel. He was able to continue trading in building timber and roof tiles. We were still relatively comfortable.' Many Jews who had fled to Hungary from Slovakia lived in the town. It was forbidden to help them. That didn't bother Otto's mother: 'She refused to be intimidated and helped all refugee Jews with food, clothing and everything they needed.'

Otto and Ferenc could sense that their parents were becoming more and more worried as time went by. The wanted these uncertain times to end and asked themselves: 'When will the war be over?' 'When will the Germans lose the war?' It was fairly clear to them that that would be their only salvation.

'Unfortunately, the Hungarian Jews were far too trusting of the Hungarian government and other nations. But what happened was still unimaginable for most people.'

YEHUDA BACON Even before the Germans invaded Czech Sudetenland in October 1938, the 8-year-old Yehuda Bacon was already aware that there were changes taking place in Europe. He recalls that, after Austria's annexation to the Reich in March 1938,[48] Jews from there fled to Poland via his hometown of Ostrava. One of them came to his father's leather factory asking for alms. He told of the 'brutality of the German and Austrian Nazis' and wanted to 'open the eyes of the world' with his descriptions.

At the end of 1938, the Bacon family obtained the addresses from the Jewish community of people who had fled to Poland to whom packages could be sent. The wife of the rabbi to whom the Bacons sent food wrote back and said that the package was like a 'straw in the ocean to which she clutched to prevent herself from sinking'. And an acquaintance informed them from Poland: 'Our wardrobe consists of a nail on which I can hang all of my possessions.'

'That's the situation in Poland', thought the family, 'but it couldn't happen here. That was the feeling at the time.'

> The extent to which we were mentally unprepared is demonstrated by the fact that when the German troops occupied the town, we children stood at the side of the road as the tanks rolled in, trying to touch them because we had heard at home that they were made of cardboard. In addition, the jubilation – as it appeared to us – and the sea of swastikas made a deep impression, and we were keen to obtain franked envelopes from the post office with the inscription: 'The city of black diamonds [the city had large coal reserves] thanks the Führer – Day of Liberation!'[49]

51

The consequences were also felt in Ostrava: the rights of the Jewish inhabitants were gradually reduced and ultimately removed entirely.

Yehuda Bacon's family were very scared of raids. 'The houses of Jews were searched, and every pretext was used to enter and check an apartment.' When the Bacons were eating fruit once, a few drops splashed onto the floor. They were wiped up immediately 'because we Jews weren't allowed to buy fruit'. 'Aryan' friends had obtained it for them.

One day the Gestapo searched the Bacons' apartment. They found a slab of butter 'which a Polish engine driver had brought us'. He had forgotten his coat. Yehuda's mother had the presence of mind to put it around her shoulders so it wouldn't be noticed. Yehuda's father was summoned to appear, because of the butter. He went to the Jewish community to ask for support, and it intervened with the Gestapo. After a while, Isidor Bacon was able to return home. He had been interrogated by two Gestapo men. But when he was alone with one of them, he was told: 'Don't worry, nothing will happen to you.'

In early 1939, the Jewish inhabitants were registered for forced labour. In the middle of the year, two synagogues were set on fire by the Nazis.[50] Then, in October, 1,192 Jews were transported from Ostrava to Nisko in Poland, where they were supposed to build a camp. The project was abandoned in April 1940 and several hundred Jewish men were returned to Ostrava.[51] A few years later, Majdanek concentration camp was established in Lublin, 100 kilometres north of Nisko.

DAGMAR FANTLOVÁ The 8-year-old Dagmar also first learned that 'something was going on in Germany' around 1937. 'A man, probably a rabbi, turned up in Kutná Hora. He was from Germany, I don't remember which part. He had published a book. I can only recall the cover. It showed a man with a sign behind a gate on which was written: "Jude verrecke im eigenen Drecke" [May the Jews croak in their own filth].'

Dagmar heard people saying that some people were sending their children to England. This was barely discussed in her family. She and Rita were still too small. They had an aunt who wanted to emigrate with her husband, but somehow never managed to do so.

Later, there was a young man from the border region, from Cheb [Eger in German]. His parents had emigrated and he was meant to follow them later, but he didn't manage to do so. He arrived on his own in Kutná Hora. My parents invited him for lunch every Sunday. He would always say that he wouldn't go to the Theresienstadt camp and ghetto. But that's where he ended up. My father said to him in Theresienstadt: 'You see, you're here after all.' He replied: 'There's still a way out.' But he never came back.

In early 1939, the rabbi from Germany disappeared from Kutná Hora as suddenly as he had arrived. It marked the start of a new series of events. On 15 March 1939, German troops entered Kutná Hora. 'My father came to my bed early in the morning. He woke me and said: "We've lost the republic." He was crying. This was something quite out of the ordinary for me. I'd never seen my father cry before.' Dagmar got up and went to school. Nothing had changed there. 'Only the weather was bad that day.'

When she came home at lunchtime, her father spoke about a visit to a patient. 'He was driving on the left-hand side of the road. That's how it was in those days. A German column was coming in the other direction, driving on the right. They stopped him and told him he should drive on the right.' Julius Fantl came home in 'deep shock'.

One day – it must have been a holiday – the Sudeten German lodger Zotter said to Julius Fantl: 'I'd like to hang out the swastika flag.' Dagmar's father replied: 'Herr Zotter, I'm sure you know that swastikas are not allowed to be flown in Jewish houses.'

'I'd just hang it between the windows.' And that's what he did. Some time later, Zotter became the trustee of the shoe factory where he worked. This meant that all of the previous owners' rights were extinguished and transferred to the trustee.[52] Now he wanted to live in the house of the Jewish owner, which also contained the Jewish community offices. Zotter ordered the Jewish community to move to Julius Fantl's house.

One of the Jewish families in Kutná Hora had to move out of their home. 'They came to us, in the grandparents' rooms. They moved into our apartment.' On 23 October 1939, the order was given to dismiss all Jewish employees. And on 26 January 1940, Jews were forbidden from managing textile, shoe and leatherwear businesses. This and other measures, such as the obligation to register the company (7 February) and the employer's private assets (16 March), were important steps towards 'Aryanization', as it was called. What followed was the expropriation of the Jews on a grand scale.[53]

EDUARD KORNFELD When he was 6 or 7 years old, Eduard first experienced 'something like antisemitism' as he was on his way to school. Children called him a 'Saujude' ['Jewish pig']. And on the walls would be scrawled 'Zydy do Palestuny' ['Jews to Palestine'].

'At first I didn't understand what it all meant. What had the Jews or I done to deserve that? I didn't even know what Palestine was.' He thought about it a lot, and throughout his life it always hurt him deeply inside.

On 14 March 1939, the day before the German Wehrmacht invaded Bohemia and Moravia, the declaration of independence by the vassal Slovakia, the first puppet state of Nazi Germany, was announced. Prior to this, leading Slovak politicians had promised the German Reich that they would settle the 'Jewish question' on the German model. An authoritarian antisemitic one-party government, Hlinka's Slovak People's Party (named after a Slovak nationalist and anti-Jewish priest and politician), came to power. A month later, on 18 April 1939, the first antisemitic regulations were promulgated by the Slovak government. The number of Jews in the professions was drastically reduced. From then on, Jewish lawyers could only represent Jews, Jews were not allowed to have a concession for a public pharmacy, Jewish journalists could only work in Jewish newspapers, and the number of doctors with practices was limited to 4 per cent of the members of the Medical Council.[54]

It became more and more dangerous for the Kornfeld family to go out onto the street. Harassment and organized attacks on the Jews of Bratislava increased.

The Hitler Youth, the Hlinka Guard and the voluntary Schutzstaffel [paramilitary units formed by the German minority in Slovakia] beat up us Jews more and more frequently, quite brutally. For example, there was a poor Sudeten German family, whom my father had always helped. They had several children, and my father often gave them bread. Later, one of these sons joined the German SS, and one day he came and beat up my father. That was how he showed his thanks for our help. It was a terrible experience.

In 1940, there were around 18,000 Jews in Bratislava, one-fifth or one-sixth of the total number of Jews in Slovakia. There were several synagogues, eleven batei midrash (Talmud colleges), two Jewish cemeteries, a hospital, an old people's home, an orphanage, a large community hall and library, several banks, chemists, insurance companies, fifty Jewish doctors, sixty-five lawyers and thirty engineers.[55]

Between 1938 and 1942, the situation of the Jewish inhabitants of Slovakia became intolerable. 'The political climate was threatening. Our synagogues were destroyed, Torah scrolls torn and thrown onto the street. And we Jews were increasingly attacked and beaten bloody.'

The systematic anti-Jewish legislation by the Slovak state meant that only small amounts could be withdrawn from Jewish bank accounts. Or that 'we Jews were basically banned from visiting restaurants, theatres or cinemas, or from entering public swimming pools or parks'. Jews were also banned from living in certain areas and in streets named after Hitler and Hlinka. This applied to 10,931 Jewish homes in fifty-two larger towns, where 43,124 Jewish children, women and men had lived before being forced to move.

The Kornfelds were also obliged to move. 'We moved three times, I think. Once to near the Jewish school. That was still a good area. From there we moved to the Jewish ghetto', where they remained 'until the end'. Eduard's father had first had to give up his linen goods shop 'because Jews were no longer allowed to reside in that area'. In order to feed the family, he bought a bakery near the ghetto.

'One day he had to give up this business as well.' Jews were to be fully excluded from the Slovak economy. Within a short time, over 9,000 Jewish businesses – like Simon Kornfeld's – were liquidated and over 1,800 'Aryanized', in other words transferred to non-Jewish owners.[56]

Following the introduction of the Jewish Codex in autumn 1941, marriages between Jews, or 'Mischlinge', and non-Jews became a punishable offence. Extramarital sexual intercourse between them was deemed to be 'race defilement'. From 22 September 1941, the date of Rosh Hashanah, the Jewish new year – 'certainly no coincidence' – all Jews over the age of 6 had to wear a 'Jewish star'.

Finally, by 1 March 1942, 6,720 Jews were banished from Bratislava to the provinces. Those destined for 'dislokácia' were barely allowed to take anything with them. Their property was seized and sold and the proceeds used to cover the costs of the deportation.[57] The Kornfelds were able to remain in the city but lived 'in permanent and all-consuming fear'. 'We didn't know in the evening what would happen to us the following morning, and in the morning whether we would still be in the city in the evening.'

ROBERT BÜCHLER was 8 years old, his sister Ruth 6, when the satellite state Slovakia was created 'by the grace of Germany' following the declaration of independence on 14 March 1939. Now Topol'čany was also ruled by the chauvinist and antisemitic Hlinka party.

'We weren't very afraid. It was a time of deliberation. There were no major antisemitic demonstrations in our town. It was relatively quiet, albeit unsettling.'

In autumn 1939, Minister of the Interior Alexander Mach and Minister of Foreign Affairs Ferdinand Ďurčanský, two leaders of the Nazi government of Slovakia, visited Topol'čany. They addressed a large crowd from the town hall balcony. During the event, they pointed to the Jewish businesses on the market square and predicted: 'The day is not far off when all this will be in Slovak hands.'[58] This was despite the fact that the Jewish families were also Slovak citizens.

In September 1940, Robert, who attended the Jewish primary school, was not allowed to go to the state grammar school. In a decision of 13 June 1939, the Slovak government had effectively banned Jewish pupils from attending state schools.[59] The Jewish children were only allowed to attend Jewish primary schools or classes. The Jewish community of Topol'čany decided to enlarge the Jewish primary school to eight classes. But the school building was seized in 1942. Classes stopped but were later resumed, for the few remaining Jewish children spared from the Nazi actions, in the Jewish old people's home. In 1944, the school closed for good.[60]

The company where Robert's father worked was 'Aryanized' and taken over by the state. It was transformed into a monopoly called Slovpol. Josef Büchler lost his position as *Prokurist* (authorized signatory) but was allowed to remain in the company. 'My father was important for the Slovak economy.'

The family lived outside the town in a rented two-family house. The other family were Christians – the husband, head of the local council.

'We were always close to this family. My parents organized a New Year's Eve party and they were naturally invited. And at Christmas there was always a present for my sister and me under the Christmas tree.' Robert was good friends with the family's daughter, who was his age. They were together every day, went fishing and even went on holiday together. 'That might have been an exception, but it nevertheless existed as well.'

In 1940, the Büchlers were evicted from the house. 'A Slovak simply threw us out. He wanted to live there. It was as simple as that.' The Büchlers were lucky and found a 'fine apartment' in a working-class district.

GÁBOR HIRSCH Persecution of the Jews was in full flow throughout Europe. 'Our teachers', says Gábor Hirsch from Békéscsaba in south-eastern Hungary, 'made antisemitic comments. We Jewish pupils were not allowed to participate in the "levente" paramilitary training. Instead, we were given spades and hoes in preparation for the forced labour. But it was still tolerable.'

He first suspected that 'there was something threatening in the air' in March 1938. The 9-year-old heard about the entrance into Austria by German troops, the annexation to the German Reich, and the mass emigration of Austrian Jews. 'Hildegard, my non-Jewish nanny, was no longer allowed to work for Jews. She had to return to Austria.'

Two months later, at the end of May 1938, Hungary promulgated the first anti-Jewish laws on the German model.[61]

In the summer holidays, Gábor went practically every day to the lake to swim. A stream flowed through Békéscsaba and fed the pool. The family maid brought the boy his lunch in a multi-level container. 'I ate my lunch there.' He was even in the Békéscsaba swimming club, 'as long as I was allowed as a Jew'.

One summer – 'it must have been the early 1940s' – the locals had to share the pool with some members of the Hitler Youth from Germany. 'They spent their holidays in our region.' Prior to that, the Hungarian National Socialist Arrow Cross party, founded in 1937, had made a petition to the town. They demanded that Jews be banned from using the lake and steam bath. In 1941, it was rejected by the town of Békéscsaba, which claimed that there was no legal basis for the prohibition.[62]

NEVER FORGET YOUR NAME

Meanwhile, discrimination against the Hungarian Jews continued. In August 1941, the third antisemitic Jewish law entered into force, banning marriages between Jews and non-Jews. Extramarital intimate relationships between Jews and non-Jews with Hungarian nationality were penalized as 'race defilement'.[63]

'Yes, we lived with anti-Jewish laws.' But the Hirsch family were barely aware of their precarious situation. There were many Jewish refugees in Békéscsaba from Slovakia and Poland. They were invited for lunch on Shabbat by members of the Jewish community, including the Hirsch family. 'The refugees told of the violence against Jews in their countries. They related terrible stories.'

Gábor's father was optimistic. As late as 1942, he planned and built a new house on a nearby street. One corner remained incomplete. János Hirsch feared that he might not be able to keep his shop on the high street because he was a Jew. If that was the case, he wanted to turn the corner of the building into a shop, which could be done quite quickly, and to transfer his business there.

JiřÍ AND ZDENĚK STEINER 'On the day the Germans entered Prague, we were at home with my mother', says Jiří Steiner. 'German cars with yellow number plates were driving past.' They looked out onto the street, hidden behind the curtains, 'so that no one could see us'. 'Mama began to cry again and we were very afraid.' Then the lives of the Jewish inhabitants – as in all of the countries annexed by Germany – became more and more restricted and increasingly intolerable. Jiří and Zdeněk were not allowed to attend school. 'If we had gold or silver, we had to hand it in.'

The looting by the Nazis knew no limits. In the six years of occupation, the National Bank of Bohemia and Moravia alone sent nearly 43 tonnes of pure gold currency to Nazi Germany.[64]

It is estimated that there were around 55,000 Jews living in Prague in 1939.[65] A report for the period from 15 March 1939 to 1 October 1941, presented by the Central Office for Jewish Emigration set up by the Nazis in Prague, stated:

> Since the incorporation of the territory of Bohemia and Moravia into Greater Germany, the Jews have been completely excluded from public, economic

and social life.... The Jews, who have become unemployed and without means, are increasingly used for labour, particularly in construction, civil and railway engineering, regulatory work and all kinds of unskilled labour on building sites and in factories, and in agriculture and forestry.... Their bank accounts have been frozen and they are only allowed to withdraw a certain amount each month (RM 150.00 per person).[66]

Pavel Steiner's business was also liquidated. He was given a job in the Jewish community but earned nothing. The family lived from savings and what Jana Steiner, their mother, earned by selling home-made textile flowers.

One of the most incisive measures was the police regulation of 14 September 1941 stating that henceforth Jewish children, women and men had to wear a 'Jewish star'. Many other prohibitions rapidly followed: Jews were no longer allowed to enter libraries, swimming pools, cinemas, parks, certain squares and streets, sporting events, theatre and entertainment locales. They were allowed to shop only during strictly controlled hours. There was a general curfew after 8 p.m. They were only permitted to enter certain hospital departments, post offices and tram carriages. The use of boats, rental cars, sleeping and dining cars and even radios was completely forbidden. Jews were also excluded from all clubs and associations.[67]

There were notices everywhere saying 'No Jews allowed'. After August 1940, Jewish children were not allowed to attend state schools.[68] Six to eight children now met in the Steiners' home and were taught by an unemployed teacher. Some time later, they were able for a short time to attend a semi-official Jewish school.

In 1941, the family were evicted from their apartment, but were lucky enough to find other accommodation. 'The day after we moved into this apartment, Jews were forbidden from moving into new apartments.'

A year after the Germans arrived, around 5,000 Jews were deported from Prague to the ghetto in Littmannstadt (Łódź), in quick succession on five transports on 16, 21, 26 and 31 October and 3 November 1941. The third transport included 130 children and juveniles aged under 18 years, followed by a further 112 in the fourth transport. The ghetto proved to be a transit camp on the way to murder in Kulmhof extermination camp in Chełmo nad Nerem 70 kilometres away. Of the Jews deported from Prague in 1941, only 277 survived.[69]

Hagibor ['hero'] was a Jewish sports club in Prague. And, as the freedom of movement of Jewish children became more and more restricted, Jiří and Zdeněk went increasingly to the club. It was now only a small playing area next to what used to be the larger Hagibor sports ground.[70] Three times a week, the Steiner twins got up early in the morning to walk to the sports ground 4 kilometres away. Activities for children were organized there in summer until 6 p.m. Because of the curfew, they had to be home by 8 p.m. at the latest. Jiří and Zdeněk would like to have gone to Hagibor every day. This wasn't possible because there wasn't room for everyone. So many children wanted to go there. On other days, they passed the time at the New Jewish Cemetery in the Žižkov district, where Franz Kafka was buried.

The Hagibor children and juveniles stuck together: 'We spent a great time there and made lots of friendships, some of which were maintained even in Theresienstadt and Auschwitz.'

The children were supervised in Hagibor, above all, by Fredy Hirsch, a young German Jew from Aachen. Like many other Jews, he had fled to Czechoslovakia after the promulgation of the Nuremberg Laws on 15 September 1935.[71] Jiří And Zdeněk were to meet up with him again several times. During the German occupation, Hagibor was one of the few distractions. 'We weren't allowed to go to the theatre or cinema anymore.'

Later, a camp was established on the sports ground for women and men in 'mixed marriages', as they were called by the Nazis, who had refused to abandon their Jewish spouses.[72]

DÁŠA FRIEDOVÁ When Dáša and her sister Sylva, three years older than her, were no longer allowed to go to the regular school in Prague, they also met for illegal lessons in private homes.

> There were five children of my age. An unemployed woman teacher taught us all kinds of things. My sister went to a different home for lessons.
>
> The fear grew incessantly. We didn't like going outside anymore, even before Jews were prohibited from doing so. For example, I found it degrading

no longer to be allowed to walk on the pavement but only in the gutter next to it. And fewer and fewer non-Jewish friends visited us.

The Fried family had to move three times. 'Ultimately, we lived with two other families in a three-room apartment. We now had one room for four people with almost no room to play.'

Contact with non-Jewish family friends broke off almost completely. But there were still 'courageous people' who 'hid food under their coats and brought it to us', which was strictly forbidden. When Jews were ordered to wear a yellow star, from mid-September 1939, Dáša began to realize for the first time that 'we are different, although we look like everyone else'.

'People we knew' were among the 5,000 Jewish children, women and men deported in October and November 1941 to the Littmannstadt (Łódź) ghetto. 'They were only allowed to take a few personal effects and had to leave everything else behind. We didn't know at the time where they were being taken. But we quaked with fear. What was to become of us?'

While in exile, Franz Werfel, the Jewish writer born in Prague, wrote the poem 'The City of an Emigrant's Dreams':

Yes, I am right, it is the well-known street.
I've lived here thirty years without a change …
Is this the street? I'm driven by a strange
Compelling force there with the mass to meet.

A barrier looms … Before I can retreat
My arm is roughly seized: 'Please show your pass!'
My pass? Where is my pass? In a morass
Of scorn and hate I move with faltering feet.

Can the human soul endure such anxious fear?
Steel scourges that will strike me whistle near.
The last I know upon my knees I'm flung …

And while I'm spat on by an unseen crowd,
'I have done nothing wrong', I scream aloud,
'Except I spoke in your own tongue, *my* tongue.'[73]

Lʏᴅɪᴀ Hᴏʟᴢɴᴇʀᴏᴠᴀ́ fell sick a few days before the arrival of the German troops:

> I got diphtheria on 10 March 1939 and was admitted to hospital in the district capital of Náchod. Even as I child, I already knew that the Nazis were somehow dangerous. And when I woke up early on 15 March 1939, I heard people saying that the German army had entered Náchod. My mother visited me in the hospital that afternoon. I was in an isolation ward and visitors weren't allowed. We spoke through a closed window. I remember screaming and asking my mother: 'Are the Germans in Hronov?' And my mother started to cry.

She was only able to finish Year 4.

> But as my father was well known in Hronov, the headmistress of my school helped. There was an unemployed teacher in the town whom she recommended to my father. She gave him the school curriculum. The teacher came to our home and gave me lessons. My father paid him, which was illegal, of course, and risky for us and for the teacher.

Her sister Věra was able to complete her schooling at the Jewish grammar school in Brno. She could not be issued a proper school-leaving certificate, only an 'ersatz certificate'.

From June 1939, all Jewish assets were secured. German trustees were installed, especially in profitable companies like Emil Holzner's textile wholesale business. He was no longer allowed to go there.

He purchased a weaving loom and wove fabrics at home. 'Soon two other families moved in with us. There was very little room left for us. Then the trustee wanted to live in the house. We had to move out. Acquaintances in Hronov took us in. Now we had just one room for four people.' The family were still relatively fortunate. They had sufficient savings to survive for two years after the business transfer. They were even able to help relatives who had fled to Prague by giving them small or larger amounts of money. Contact with non-Jews in Hronov remained intact.

The woman who had worked as a housekeeper with the Holzners helped where she could, ran errands and brought a few items that made day-to-day living at least a little easier. Other friends hid furniture and clothing for the Holzners, because, after 1939, Jews had to declare their assets. Valuables and securities had to be surrendered.[74] A German business friend in Dvůr Králové, also in eastern Bohemia, kept Věra's trousseau. One of Lydia's uncles had married a Christian who refused to divorce. 'Whenever necessary, we called her to take care of things.'

Lydia continued to play with the neighbourhood children, even in the evening, although it was forbidden for Jews to leave the house after 8 p.m. 'It was possible because our house and the neighbouring houses had gardens in the back. We children climbed over the fence and played together after 8 p.m. The neighbours did not object, although it was risky for them.'

Lydia Holznerová never forgot one day in early 1942:

We were already forced to wear the yellow star. We only had one star. On that spring day, I put on a light coat without the star and went into town. I met my girlfriends there and we were walking around. When I got home, my father was waiting for me at the door. When I opened it, I saw he was holding a stick. He hit me with it. 'What's the matter?' I asked him. 'Look at yourself! Do I have to have people come and tell me that you're running around town without a star? You are putting your family and your friends in danger.'

Emil Holzner had had bad experiences with the Gestapo, having spent a week in prison on some unclear charge, and paying a large amount of money to be released. The experience had changed him:

When my father came back, he ordered that all of the hidden objects were to be brought back and that every last item was to be handed in. He didn't want to keep anything. Although his friends said they would keep the things, he wouldn't have it. My father never told me what the Gestapo did to him. He was completely drained when he came back.

YEHUDA BACON Yehuda particularly remembers 14 June 1940, the day German troops entered Paris.[75] As his parents were no longer allowed to work in Ostrava, they were forced to sublet some of their apartment. Mrs Florian, a tenant, was visited on that day by her son, who was in the German Wehrmacht.

He was drunk, gave us a dirty look and said: 'You'll all be eliminated soon like they're doing in the East. If I wanted to, I would just have to say the word and you'd be kicked out of your home straightaway. But I'm not like that.' Then he looked at me sympathetically and said: 'I'm sorry for you. You don't look particularly Jewish. I'm sorry on your account.'

Yehuda had initially attended a Jewish primary school in the town of his birth. He didn't go to grammar school, since the Nazi laws prohibited Jews from obtaining secondary education. To secure as wide-ranging an education as possible for the pupils, however, a few additional classes were added on to the primary school. 'Until 1941/42 the school was semi-official. Later, the classes were completely forbidden and we had "krousky", teaching circles, that were illegal and took place in private homes with six to eight pupils.'

Around the end of 1941, two 'halutzim' (Jewish pioneers for Eretz Israel, the biblical name for the land of Israel) came. They wanted originally to flee to Slovakia and said that all Jews in Prague were sitting with their suitcases packed because they could expect to be rounded up for transport at any moment. 'They asked us to flee with them. We thought that the atrocities they related were not true. Perhaps we didn't want to believe them.' Two of Yehuda's teachers, Sissi Eisinger and Jakov Wurzel, both 24 years old, came from Brno. 'And suddenly they were summoned for transport, because the people from Brno were taken away earlier.'

Yehuda can still remember their departure. 'Jakov Wurzel told us a Hasidic story, that every person has a "nitzotz", a spark, and that this spark bursts into flame once in every person. He was trying to say, I think, that everyone can show spiritual and moral greatness at some point in their life.' The pupils were so moved that they cried, 'with only a slight inkling at the time what the parable meant.

# 'The Hunt for Jews Began'

ROBERT BÜCHLER In summer 1940, the Slovak government began to compel the Jews, who had been excluded from the country's social life and economy, to carry out forced labour. In autumn 1941, the conversion of the former military barracks in Sered' and Nováky began. There, and in the existing camp at Vyhne, the Jewish population was to be isolated and concentrated. The authorities saw this as a stage on the way to the final 'solution of the Jewish question' in Slovakia.[1]

One of these camps, Nováky, was around 40 kilometres from Topol'čany, where Robert Büchler and his family lived. Many Jewish men aged between 16 and 60 were moved there from the town and forced to work.

In 1942, the rumours regarding the permanent expulsion of the Jews from Slovakia began to increase. The pro-Nazi president of Slovakia, the Catholic cleric Jozef Tiso, denied these plans. But just a few days later, on 27, 28 and 31 March, the first transports with young Jews left Topol'čany via Slovak transit camps to the East.[2] 'This came like a bolt from the blue.' The Jews were taken completely by surprise. They couldn't believe what was happening. 'The community was in shock. And before we knew it, hundreds of railway wagons had been loaded up.'

The government authorities attempted to calm things with lies, saying that the expulsions would stop. The Germans were only interested in young persons capable of working. By the beginning of April, this had already been revealed to be a subterfuge. 'The next hunt for Jews in Topol'čany began.' This time whole families were taken. 'One train after the other stood in the station, and many brothers and sisters set off on the road to no return.'

By August, the Jewish population of Topol'čany had been literally decimated. Nine of Josef Büchler's siblings had been deported with their families. Only 618 Jews of 'importance for the economy' remained. And they looked to the future with anxiety.[3]

CHANNA MARKOWICZ In March 1939, Hungary had re-annexed Carpatho-Ukraine from Czechoslovakia,[4] including Irshava, Channa Markowicz's hometown. The first anti-Jewish laws were soon to follow.

The eyes of the occupiers were drawn particularly to Jews who, despite having lived in many cases for two or three generations in the Carpathian region – the mountainous area originally belonging to Czechoslovakia, now in Ukraine – had not become citizens or could not prove their citizenship. Jews who could not prove that their ancestors had lived there permanently before 1867 were especially endangered.[5] This also applied to relatives of the Markowicz family who had immigrated from Poland.

By the end of August 1941, around 18,000 'foreign' Jews, as they were called, had been deported by the Hungarian gendarmerie via eastern Galicia to Kamenez-Podolsk [Kam'yanets' Podil's'kyi] in Ukraine. Most of them were from the part of the Carpathians annexed by Hungary from Czechoslovakia in 1939. In Kamenez-Podolsk, 14,000 to 16,000 Jews deported from Hungary were murdered on 27 and 28 August 1941, together with several thousand Jews from the surrounding area. Apart from the SS and men from Police Battalion 320, members of the Ukrainian self-defence and a Hungarian pioneer unit took part. Altogether, 23,000 Jewish children, women and men perished on those two August days in 1941.[6] 'The first of our relatives were deported in 1942. At the time we thought it couldn't get worse than it already was.' They were wrong.

EDUARD KORNFELD One day in Bratislava, came the order 'All juveniles or all girls, I can't remember which, have to register.' The family didn't know what to do. Was it going to get worse? Everyone was very afraid. There were rumours of deportation. No one knew where to. On 26 March 1942, the first transport with young Jewish women and girls from Slovakia reached Auschwitz extermination camp. *Auschwitz Chronicle* records: '999 Jewish women from Poprad in Slovakia are sent to the women's section of Auschwitz. This is the first registered transport ... The Jewish women get uniforms that belonged to the murdered Russian POWs.'[7]

The first eight Slovak transports to the East contained only young Jews – over 8,000 children and juveniles. This meant that, by the beginning of April 1942, most of the young Jews were no longer in Slovakia. From

March to October 1942, around 58,000 Slovak Jews were deported, particularly to Auschwitz, Majdanek and Treblinka.[8] Fewer than 300 were to return from the camps.[9]

Nazi Germany demanded RM 500 for each deportee for 'retraining'. In return, it promised the Slovak government that no Jews would come back and that Germany would not assert any further claims to their assets.[10]

The Kornfelds had decided in early 1942 to flee to Hungary. They didn't want to wait until it was their turn: 'In Hungary, my parents believed, it was still relatively safe for us Jews.' Eduard's 15-year-old brother Heinrich and his 11-year-old sister Mathilde were to be transported over the border by a smuggler, a farmer. The other members of the family intended to follow a few days later. On 7 May 1942, they were ready. Shortly before they were to leave, Simon and Rosa Kornfeld decided that it was better for the girl Mathilde to remain with them. 'Eduard, you should go with Heinrich.'

'So I put on one suit and another one on top of it. That's all. My father blessed us and promised that they would soon follow. No one expected that we would never see each other again. It was a farewell for ever.'

The farmer collected them from their home. 'My father paid the man. Outside the town, there was a horse-drawn cart.' This would take them to Vel'ký Meder, which had been annexed by Hungary along with the entire south of Slovakia.[11] Eduard's grandfather and one of his uncles lived there. Eduard and Heinrich were to stay there a few days and then make their way to Budapest. The farmer hurried them along. They had to cross the border before it got light.

'We followed the railway line in the direction of Vel'ký Meder. From time to time, we placed our ears to the tracks to hear whether a train was coming.' When it got light, the farmer left them. He said: 'It's too dangerous for me now. Just keep going straight on. You'll come to a village soon. Take the train from there to Vel'ký Meder.' They had arranged with their father that they would give the farmer a note as a sign when they arrived at their destination. Before the departure, their father had given them a piece of paper torn into two unequal halves and given one half to Eduard's brother Heinrich. He had kept the other half himself.

If my father was given the piece of paper intact by the farmer, he would know that we had arrived safely in Vel'ký Meder and the man would get the rest of his money.

As the farmer had not brought us to the agreed destination, my brother ripped off a small piece. I don't know if my mother and father understood the sign. Unfortunately, I never saw them again.

They reached the village between 5 and 6 a.m. An old peasant woman asked the boys: 'Are you Slovak Jews?'

'No! No! We're not from Slovakia!'

'Listen, I'm a Jew. You don't need to be afraid. I will just warn you that your Shabbat suits tell everyone right away that you're not from here. Come with me.' The woman took the boys home with her. 'First of all, we gulped down water like crazy.' They were given something to eat and then slept for a few hours. So that they wouldn't draw attention to themselves, the woman had advised them to take the train to Vel'ký Meder in the evening. 'There are so many people, including farmers from other villages. We were simply to mingle with them all.'

The train journey to Vel'ký Meder was without incident. They went to their grandfather's house. He lived there with their youngest uncle, his wife and their six children aged between 1 and 7 years. The brothers couldn't stay there because they would all have had to remain in hiding. 'We were in the country illegally. And besides we were meant to take the train to Budapest, where our parents and sister were to come.' They took the train to Budapest. Their father's uncle lived there. Eduard and Heinrich lived with him for the first few weeks. 'He was very helpful and did his best, like a replacement father.' But the family was very poor and had lots of children. Besides, 'his wife didn't want to hide us'. She was terrified that the boys would be discovered during a raid.

'We waited impatiently for our parents and sister to arrive. For weeks, even months, we heard nothing from them. We became increasingly worried as the days went by. It was unbearable.'

The brothers were living in terrible conditions. As his own family all lived in a very small apartment, their uncle had rented a room for them with a non-Jewish family. 'The room had no windows, with just a small opening onto the kitchen. It was so small that there was only space for one bed, no chairs or a table. When we switched on the light, everything was covered in red bugs. They had a very painful bite.' During the day, Eduard and Heinrich stayed out of the room. As 'illegals', they lived in constant fear of a raid. They had told the landlord that they attended 'some school or other' in Budapest. They promised repeatedly to register soon with the authorities.

They normally hid in the morning in one of the numerous synagogues in Budapest among the Talmud students there. 'No one took any notice of us.'

So they wouldn't starve, they had to think up some scheme every day. Sometimes they bought poppyseed cake, which they couldn't actually afford. There were many other things Eduard and Heinrich couldn't have bought either, even if they had had the money, because they needed ration cards: for fat, ersatz coffee, sugar, bread, meat. The same applied to restaurants.

> So I stood at the counter, took a piece from the tray and bit into it. While the saleswoman was busy with other customers, I took a second small bite. I held the cake in front of me. When the woman looked away, I quickly stuffed the entire cake in my mouth. And then I took another one, bit a piece off it, and held it as before.
>
> If possible, we repeated this several times. When the saleswoman looked away, we chewed. If she looked in our direction, we held the cake. This only worked when the shop was full.

Another strategy was to buy forged ration cards, which they sold for a profit to Slovak refugees. Eduard Kornfeld remembered all these events every day of his life as if they had just happened. Then he got a nervous disease, probably as a result of undernourishment, and kept on making involuntary movements.

One day the brothers ran into one of Eduard's former schoolmates, who was also in Budapest illegally. He told them: 'Your parents and sister were deported.' This news was 'like a slap in the face'. 'We didn't yet know anything about the gas chambers but I still had a feeling.' It was 'terrible – indescribable'.

'I'm at a loss today to explain how we managed for a whole year', he once said. 'But at some point I couldn't go on anymore. I was completely emaciated and terribly hungry.' Eduard had discovered in the meantime that refugees under the age of 15 could be legalized if they had relatives in Hungary who would stand surety for them. He knew he would have to keep quiet about the fact that he had been there for over a year, and that he would be interned initially. Without his brother – 'he was already 15' – Eduard went to the police and said: 'I arrived this evening from Slovakia. I'm a Jew.' He was arrested and sent to an internment camp. The police took his personal details and questioned him:

'When did you arrive?"

'Last night.'

'Who brought you over?'

'A farmer.'

'What did he look like?'

'I don't know. It was dark. I didn't get a good look at his face.'

'What? You went with him and don't know what he looked like?' Eduard got a 'hard smack'. 'It knocked me over. I understood straightaway. The last thing I wanted was to get hit. I imagined someone and described him.'

'You see, you knew after all! Why didn't you say so straightaway?' Eduard remained in the camp for six weeks. His uncle from Vel'ký Meder, where he and his brother had stayed at the start of their flight, stood surety for him – for accommodation, food, clothing – for everything the boy needed for his daily existence.

'So I returned to the small town of Vel'ký Meder.' Once a week, he had to report to the local gendarmerie.

HEINZ KOUNIO On 6 April 1941, the German Wehrmacht invaded Greece. The Greek army, supported by a small number of British soldiers, could not prevent the advance. Greece was divided up between the allies Bulgaria, Germany and Italy. Nazi Germany secured strategically important points for itself, including the island of Crete and the port city of Thessaloniki, which was occupied by the Wehrmacht on 9 April.[12]

Heinz Kounio recalls: 'We knew beforehand that the Germans were going to enter Thessaloniki on that day. I can remember the sunset on the evening before. The sky was red, completely red. Like blood.' The next day the Germans arrived. 'We all stayed at home. We heard a car. A small jeep – this Volkswagen – stopped in front of our house.

We observed it through a crack in the window shutter. On the vehicle was a big red swastika.' Someone got out. The doorbell rang. Then – something Heinz Kounio is still unable to understand today – his father, 'although he could speak German well', said to his wife: 'Hella, open the door.' She opened the door, where a young officer was standing. 'He was nice' and asked: 'Do you speak German?' Hella Kounio said that she did. 'Good, I would like to talk to you.'

'Please come in'; Hella Kounio led the young man onto the terrace, and he said: 'Very nice, dear lady. Please tell your husband to come with me. Don't be afraid. I'll bring him back. But he has to go with me to the shop. We need to get something from it.' Salvator Kounio came onto the terrace. 'He was now more courageous.' The officer produced an invoice and said: 'You received thirty-three Leica cameras from Germany. Where are the cameras?' They were whole sets with a camera, a normal lens, a wide-angle and a telephoto lens. His father said to the officer: 'I'm sorry but these cameras have not yet arrived. But I know where they are.'

'Where?'

'At the post office. They haven't yet been released by customs.' As the building was already closed, the director of the post office was found. He gave the cameras to the officer. The officer wrote on a piece of paper confirming the seizure of the sets. Then he brought Heinz Kounio back home unharmed. 'Those of us who had had to stay home were so relieved!' The thirty-three camera sets were sent back to Germany. The family did not receive any compensation. Every set was worth 38 gold pounds, which is what the pound sterling was unofficially called in those days. This was a bitter loss for the Kounio family. 'That was our first contact with the Germans who had entered Saloniki.'

Some time later, two rooms in the Kounios' house were requisitioned. A commissar and his orderly from the Gestapo moved in.

The Gestapo were responsible for systematically combating supposed political opponents of the Nazi regime. They were able to make arrests without legal basis. The people in their clutches were frequently maltreated, transported to concentration camps or summarily executed.[13]

As the Gestapo commissar was courteous towards the Kounios, grandfather Ernst Löwy in particular – who had had to flee from Karlsbad with his wife eighteen months previously to escape the Nazis – saw this as confirmation of his basic estimation of the Germans: a cultured people who had produced Bach, Beethoven, Goethe, Heine and Schiller could not be so evil. Of course, there were the brutal SS and some other bad Germans. But, thought Ernst Löwy, they were the exception.

In reality, however, the face of Thessaloniki had changed completely. The Germans were everywhere, giving orders and controlling everything that went on in the city. The 55,000 Jews in Thessaloniki – like their brothers and sisters in the other occupied countries – were quite literally caught in the German death trap.

Just a few days after the Nazis arrived, the Jews were banned from visiting cafés, cake shops and other public establishments. All Jews had to hand in their radios. Several Jewish newspapers were closed. Jewish houses and the Hirsch hospital were seized and were now in the hands of the German army. Finally, the members of the Jewish community council were arrested.[14] A short time afterwards, the Germans systematically looted the 500-year-old Jewish cultural and literary treasures in the city: in synagogues, private houses and public libraries, everything old and valuable was confiscated and sent to Germany.[15]

Meanwhile, Salvator Kounio was still able to go about his business, albeit at great risk. And the two children were still able to go to school. As their previous school had been requisitioned by the Germans, however, the classes were taught in a replacement building. Heinz and Erica no longer laughed. And they were not blind to their parents' constant fear.

On Shabbat, 11 July 1942, the public registration of all Jewish men between 18 and 45 years of age was ordered. On that day, between 8,000 and 9,000 Jews were to assemble on Plateia Eleftheria, 'Freedom Square'. They were forced to stand to attention in the heat for eight hours. Anyone who moved had to march on the spot until they were exhausted. At the end of the day, some 3,500 Jewish men were taken away to work as forced labourers in road and airport construction. Around 400 men died within a few months as a result of the gruelling working conditions.[16]

Following drawn-out negotiations with the German occupiers, the Jewish community managed in October 1942 to have their fellow religionists set free against payment of a large ransom. At the same time, the Germans demanded that the 500-year-old Jewish cemetery be handed over for 'military purposes'. The Jewish community refused.

In spite of this, the cemetery was still razed to the ground. No grave was spared. The gravestones were all broken up. The bones of the dead were scattered everywhere. The stones were used for road building in Thessaloniki and elsewhere. The German occupiers even built a swimming pool with them. The Jews of Thessaloniki were able to salvage only a few graves.[17] And on the expropriated cemetery site, the city of Thessaloniki built a university.[18]

The 300,000-square-metre Jewish cemetery, probably the largest in the world, was no more. The graves of around 400,000 Jewish children, women and men aged 12 years or more at the time of death were destroyed. And the graves of around 400,000 children less than 12 years old no longer existed.[19]

A few months previously, Salvator Kounio received a letter from a business associate in Germany, the owner of an optical company, who asked him to look out for his son, a soldier who had been posted to Thessaloniki. Heinz Kounio well remembers the contents of the letter, which were approximately as follows: 'Salvator, may I ask you a favour? My son is coming to Saloniki. He is very close to his family. Could you please look out for him? He might need your assistance.' As if in those days looking after a Wehrmacht soldier was the 'most natural thing in the world' for a Jewish family like the Kounios. And, indeed, a few days later, the doorbell rang. The Wehrmacht soldier Helmut Held, son of the German business associate, called on the Kounios. He was invited to lunch the following Sunday. Afterwards, he came often to the Kounios, played with Heinz and Erika and had discussions with their parents.

'The German soldier was very nice. He stayed in Saloniki for about a month. Then he was suddenly posted to Crete.' Some time later, the German police stormed the house and took their parents and the grandfather who had fled from Karlsbad. 'They were locked up by the Gestapo.' Around three weeks later, they were fortunately transferred to another prison that was not supervised by the Gestapo.

Erika and Heinz had to remain alone in their house. 'The other grandparents had already died.' A former family housekeeper, relatives and friends helped them to manage. They had also done everything possible from the outset to obtain the release of Salvator and Hella Kounio and Ernst Löwy and consulted lawyers. It took several days to achieve. They were overjoyed to be able to embrace their mother, father and grandfather again. It turned out that they had been arrested because a thank-you letter from Helmut Held opened by the German censors had contained the comment: 'Great preparations are being made here in Crete for the war in Africa.'

'The young man had basically blabbed secret war information. That's why the Gestapo interrogated our parents and grandfather.' Later, the Kounio family learned that Helmut Held had criticized Hitler while drunk. 'The young man was arrested and sentenced to death.'

'As a result of all these events, we had now completely lost our childhood innocence.'

HERBERT ADLER One day, probably in February 1941, in Frankfurt am Main:

> Two plain-clothed police officers came into my class and spoke with my teacher. Then they stood outside the door. Mr Erb said: 'Herbert, come here.' I went to him. 'Yes, sir, what's the matter?' All kinds of thoughts occurred to me. 'Have you done something wrong?' I was a typical Frankfurt lad and had got up to mischief before. But I couldn't think of anything. The teacher said to me: 'Herbert, listen, there are two criminal police officers who want you to go with them. Apparently you've done something. Go with them. You'll be back tomorrow.' He probably knew better but wanted to reassure me because he didn't know how to help me.

The boy took his satchel and left the classroom. Outside, Herbert saw that his brother Heinz was also there. They were brought home by two Gestapo men in a police car. The whole family was already there. 'They had fetched my father from work.'

Herbert, his parents and his six brothers and sisters were taken to the camp for 'gypsies' in Dieselstrasse. They were only allowed to take the most necessary belongings. Everything else, they were told, would be brought to them the next day in their new home. This was an empty promise. Their furniture, the entire contents of their apartment, were seized, including a harp and some valuable violins. His father was also a very good musician who liked to play music in his spare time. They didn't ever get anything back.

In the Dieselstrasse camp the Adler family lived in a small old wooden construction wagon. 'There was no water, light or toilets.' The furniture consisted of an old table and two chairs. At the back were two jacked-up planks for sleeping – for nine people. And for this makeshift accommodation the camp inmates even had to pay rent to the city of Frankfurt.

In May 1941, there were 160 Roma and Sinti in the Dieselstrasse camp. It was fenced in by chicken wire and two rows of barbed wire and was controlled and guarded by the police. There were roll calls every day. The inmates had to stand to attention and give the Nazi salute. Camp commandant Johannes Himmelheber used a whip to maintain discipline in the camp. At every opportunity, the police threatened to have the inmates transferred to a concentration camp and caused increasing anxiety and fear in this way. And Sinti and Roma were indeed deported to concentration camps on the basis of reports by Himmelheber.

After the war, Himmelheber continued to serve in the police. He was able to enjoy his retirement in 1952 until his death in 1971.

Herbert Adler: 'After our arrival in early 1941, we children were not allowed to leave the camp. My father and other adults were initially allowed to go to work outside.' When they first moved into the camp, he was still convinced that his father would fix it and that they would soon be able to leave again. Every day this hope dwindled, 'until I realized what they really had in store for us'.

After an armaments company purchased the site and claimed it to enlarge its operations, the camp was closed in autumn 1942.[20] The remaining Roma and Sinti, including the Adler family, were moved to the new camp in Kruppstrasse. 'The conditions there were just as bad. And in the Kruppstrasse camp, we children were forced to work, mainly loading trucks with cobblestones.' Also his little brother Rolf. He had just turned 9 years old.

'One day, when we had loaded the truck and were driving to unload it, he fell out. We shouted out loud. But the driver didn't react. My little brother was somehow dragged along. He died as a result. That was my first encounter with death.'

# Gateway to Death

WOLFGANG WERMUTH Around 66,000 Jews lived in Berlin when the first mass deportations began in October 1941.[1]

Siegmund Wermuth's only sister, Lina Steinberg, and her husband Jakob – they lived, like Wolfgang and his parents, at Fritscherstrasse 55 – were ordered to report to the collection point in Moabit, in the former synagogue at Levetzowstrasse 7–8. It was one of the largest Jewish prayer houses in Berlin and was only slightly damaged during the November pogrom in 1938. For many Berlin Jews, the synagogue was the last station on their way to ghettos, and concentration and extermination camps.[2]

The Steinbergs later sent a pre-printed postcard franked 'Litzmannstadt – General Government' to Berlin. The Wermuths now knew that their relatives were in the Łódź ghetto. The German occupiers had renamed the city Litzmannstadt. Around 164,000 Jews were confined in the hermetically sealed ghetto.[3]

On 18 October 1941, the first deportation train left Grunewald train station in Berlin for Litzmannstadt with 1,103 Jewish children, women and men.[4] Hildegard Henschel, wife of Moritz Henschel, the last president of the Jewish community in Berlin (until 10 June 1943), described the transport in a report after the war:

> On 16 October 1941, the emptying [*Ausschleusung*] of the collection point began in the morning, and the transportees were taken to Grunewald train station in pouring rain. The SS drove up in open trucks ... These trucks could only be used by children and frail persons. Everyone else had to walk in a long line through the city [around 7 kilometres].... The victims behaved admirably. Everyone knew that they must not protest. The only possible protest was suicide.[5]

The Wermuths wrote to their relatives in the ghetto but only once received confirmation that the letter had been delivered. After three months, their letters were returned with the comment: 'Undeliverable because of the danger of a typhus epidemic'. They heard nothing further from Lina and Jakob Steinberg.

'In October 1942, those of us who remained also suffered the fate of deportation.' It was the 5th, at around 5.30 a.m., when someone knocked at the Wermuths' door. 'We were already up because my father had to go to work collecting rubbish at 6 a.m.' When Siegmund Wermuth opened the door, a non-uniformed man was standing there and said: 'I'm from the Gestapo. Get dressed immediately and come with me. Your parents-in-law are already below in the vehicle.'

Wolfgang's grandparents, Willi and Mathilde Davidowitz, who had been living in Rosenheimer Strasse in Schöneberg, had been denounced by a government official by the name of Neumann:

My grandfather had two houses in Berlin. He was forced to sell them to Neumann, all done quite 'legally', of course, with sales contracts and the rest. We never saw anything of the money, which was deposited in a frozen account. My grandfather had withheld some documents from this Neumann, although he had threatened that something would happen to him if he refused to hand them over. He brought the documents to my father, who hid them in the linen drawer. Neumann got the Gestapo onto my grandfather. They appeared and put pressure on him to tell them where the documents were.

The grandparents and Siegmund Wermuth were arrested. Mother and son waited ten days for news that the three of them were in a former Jewish old people's home in Grosse Hamburger Strasse. The Gestapo had requisitioned the building in summer 1942 and set up the notorious 'Jewish camp'. This and the neighbouring Jewish boys' school formed one of the largest collection points for deportations to ghettos and concentration camps and extermination camps.[6]

On 17 October 1942, Wolfgang and Käthe Wermuth were also ordered to report to Grosse Hamburger Strasse – tantamount to their immediate arrest. They were allowed to take only minimal luggage with them and had no time to pass on things. They had to leave almost everything behind in the apartment. Before they left, 'I slashed all of the upholstered furniture and pictures with a knife.' Wolfgang wanted to leave as little as possible behind for his tormentors.

'The best thing' about the day was that he was able to see his father again. The family was taken to Theresienstadt on 30 October 1942 in a 'relatively small transport by passenger train'.[7] 'We left in the morning and arrived in the evening.'

In October 1942 alone, a large transport with 1,021 Jewish children, women and men, and three smaller transports with altogether 300, left for Theresienstadt. Only 101 people from the four transports survived.[8]

In October 1941, the Nazis decided to transform the eighteenth-century fortress of Theresienstadt into a camp for Jews from Bohemia and Moravia. Later, people from several other European countries were deported there. The impenetrable ramparts, walls and moats isolated the inmates from the outside world and prevented them from escaping. There was room for thousands of people in the various former military barracks.

By the end of June 1942, the original inhabitants had been gradually resettled. Thereafter, all of Theresienstadt was a 'coerced community', as the Theresienstadt historian H. G. Adler called it. Instead of the previous population of a few thousand, now well over 50,000 people were herded together in the former fortress at the same time. For many it was a transit station on the way to the East and the extermination camps.

Of the total of 150,000 inmates, more than 33,000 Jewish children, women and men died of exhaustion, hunger, disease and the living conditions in Theresienstadt. And around 88,000 people were deported to the extermination camps, where only around 3,500 survived. Theresienstadt was therefore, first and foremost, the wide-open gateway to death and mass murder.

The children lived initially with the adults in the barracks. Boys under 12 and girls under 16 remained with their mothers, and boys over 12 with their fathers. After Theresienstadt's civilian population had been resettled, the children and juveniles lived in separate buildings. Homes for girls, boys and trainees were established in the former school. Every room, or home, had a male or female teacher responsible for twenty to thirty children.

The camp was established by the German occupiers for two reasons. First, they wanted a central camp for the Protectorate of Bohemia and

Moravia; and second, Theresienstadt was intended for prominent Jews and other special categories.

Finally, the German occupiers wanted to maintain the fiction of the resettlement of the Jews. The Nazis therefore spoke of a 'Jewish settlement' or 'old people's ghetto', above all to deceive the rest of the world. Whenever questions were asked about prominent Jews, the answer was given that they were in the best of health in Theresienstadt. Some of the victims also thought they would be safe there during the war.[9]

On their arrival in Theresienstadt, the Wermuths were immediately separated and the large pieces of luggage seized. They were only allowed to keep their hand luggage. Everything was searched. Cigarettes, timepieces and other valuables were removed. Wolfgang was put in one of the 'juvenile homes' [*Jugendheime*], his father in a 'stretcher bearer group' [*Krankenträgergruppe*] and his mother worked in the laundry. 'Then came the great surprise. There were shops in the camp.' They were called 'sales points' [*Verschleissstellen*]. By order of the SS, the displays had to be kept full for propaganda purposes. The goods came mostly from luggage seized from the inmates or people who had died in the camp. The inmates were allowed to buy items only on a purchasing rotation,[10] at intervals of several weeks or even months. 'After about a year, my mother bought back her own dress that had been seized.'

After four weeks in the camp, Wolfgang became ill with scarlet fever. He was put in an isolation ward, but after he had recovered he suffered a further setback. In the isolation ward, he had contracted typhoid fever, which meant that he had to be isolated again. He remained in the isolation ward until April 1943. During this time, his grandparents Willi and Mathilde Davidowitz died.

In the 'juvenile home', Wolfgang was in a group with ten other boys, mostly from Berlin. Their main concern was how to survive. In 1943, an end to the war did not appear to them to be in sight. But they dreamed of a hot bath, a soft bed with fresh sheets and a table full of food where they could eat their fill for once.

Their madrich, counsellor and teacher, was Louis Lowy, born in Munich in 1920, who emigrated from Prague at the age of 15. He was very delicate. The others always had to give him some of their food, 'otherwise he would not have survived'. 'He kept us on the go.' Everyone took part in the secret lessons, a little bit of normality and an escape of a sort from reality. Lowy was later deported to Auschwitz, where he survived, emigrated to the USA, studied social work and became a professor at Boston University. He died in 1991.[11]

All boys in Theresienstadt of Wolfgang's age had to report for work in the early morning. Wolfgang did levelling work and road building and also had to dig air raid shelters and pits outside the camp. Near their workplace, a German Wehrmacht field hospital had been installed in a former gym. 'The members of the Wehrmacht who could walk often came to watch us working. Occasionally, one of them would drop a cigarette butt. For them we were prisoners. We felt like animals.'

In the field hospital, there was a corporal responsible for the clothing store. 'He was a scholar but had never joined the Nazi party and had not therefore been able to become an officer. He came from near Berlin and was well disposed towards us. I made friends with him.'

The man helped Wolfgang to smuggle a letter from Siegmund Wermuth out of the camp. It was addressed to Alice Mannheimer in Berlin. She had worked in the grandfather's watch shop and was a Christian. Her Jewish husband had already died of leukaemia in 1935.

'This woman had always stuck resolutely by her Jewish husband. She hid the belongings of those who had fled or been deported. And she also stuck firmly by us.' She sent the Wermuths packages with semolina, sugar, rice, the small amount she could save from the little she obtained with her own ration cards. Wolfgang Wermuth met her again in Berlin in 1957. She died in 1966 at the age of 87.

Wolfgang had some contact with the outside world through the corporal, who helped him and others. For example, he supplied them with boots, which they had to smear with dirt so that they wouldn't look new. When there were special announcements on the radio, he turned up the volume so that Wolfgang and the others could hear. More and more frequently, the Wehrmacht High Command would report that it had 'successfully disengaged from the enemy'. 'This meant that it had got thrashed and cleared off.'

The soldiers' food was cooked in the field hospital canteen. The Czech women who worked there secretly gave the boys tins of food. 'In that way we had enough to eat.' Wolfgang was able to give the rations he received in the camp to his parents.

During the work breaks, they often sat in a shed in which the wood fuel for the field hospital was sawn and chopped up. The man in charge was a Czech. In July 1944, he told Wolfgang of the unsuccessful attempt on Hitler's life. 'This cheered us up a bit.' The SS men became increasingly worried. The inhabitants of the 'juvenile home' feared that they would be moved somewhere else. 'Dear friends, including some from my room, repeatedly disappeared.'

'The news gradually spread that further transports were impending and that we would not be staying.'

DÁŠA FRIEDOVÁ and her family, all the Jews in Prague, all the Jews in the countries occupied by Germany, feared that 'We too will one day be deported.' The families began to 'put aside the most important things'. They knew that every person could take very little with them. 'My father couldn't or wouldn't believe it.' He would say repeatedly: 'We're a Czech family. We've never had problems, except for the argument I had in Odolice in May 1935 with the Sudeten German Party. And we're not in Odolice anymore. No one will send us away from Prague. We're staying here.'

'He either wanted to believe what he was saying so as to reassure us, or he really believed it. That's at least how I saw it as a 12-year-old girl.'

In April 1942, the Fried family received notification of transport. The discussions started up again. 'What should we pack, what can we take?'

'Take what's most important to you', said Dáša's mother to her daughter. She chose a doll. 'I had a small suitcase full of doll's clothes. I took the suitcase and the doll with me. My mother gave the silver and jewellery, all of the things we couldn't take with us, to a friend for safekeeping. She hoped and wished: "It won't last long. We'll be back soon."'

The transport collection point was at the Prague exhibition centre.[12] The Frieds had to sleep there on the floor for two or three nights. They were marched under guard to the train station. Dáša had hurt her knee and was unable to walk well. Shortly before the family set off, her father said: 'Don't show any weakness. Walk properly. So we don't have any problems.' Their train set off on 28 April 1942.[13] 'Where is the train taking us?' asked the 1,000 or so people forced to travel on it.

During the journey, Otto and Kát'a Fried attempted to console their daughters: 'The Germans won't stay here for long. Our soldiers will see to that. Look how many people are in the train. We're not alone. We don't have anything to be afraid of. We'll soon be home again.' The journey ended a few hours later in Bohušovice. The last 3 kilometres to Theresienstadt, around 65 kilometres north of Prague, had to be completed on foot.

The Frieds were happy still to be in their own country, 'where we were born'. Besides, Theresienstadt was only 70 kilometres from Lukavec, where the family had a second farm with 100 hectares of land. 'We almost felt at home.'

The women and children were separated from the men. 'We were put in a building. Young and old people together in one room. Three of us had to sleep together on a small mattress. Not at all comfortable.' Shortly after their arrival, Kat'a Friedová and her two daughters were housed in the Hamburg Barracks [Hamburger Kaserne]. Otto Fried was in another building. 'As we were only allowed in the barracks or courtyard, we had no idea where our father was.' This changed in summer 1942. 'In the evening, we were allowed outside for a time and could move around the camp. And so we saw our father again.'

DAGMAR FANTLOVÁ and her family – like all other Jews in Kutná Hora – had been ordered to register with the authorities in early 1942. 'We had to go to the neighbouring town of Kolin to do so.' They were still allowed to take the train to travel the 15 kilometres. But everyone, including the old and infirm, had to walk back. All preparations were now being made for transport.

The existence of concentration camps was known. 'But no one had a concrete idea of what they were.' They thought that they would be transported to Theresienstadt, in their own country. 'No one, I think, could have imagined how bad it would turn out to be.' At the end of May, they were notified of the transport. On 2 June, the Jews had to leave Kutná Hora.

Dagmar and Rita were each allowed to take just one book with them, because there were more important items. Most things had to be left behind. 'My mother made us wear two sets of clothes and underclothes', because what they were wearing was not weighed. But it was a very warm day.

The Fantls and their grandmother – the grandfather had already died – left Kutná Hora by train for the collection point in Kolin. After three days, they were transported on to Theresienstadt.[14] They were put in the Cavalier Barracks [Kavalierskaserne], where the armoury had been. Here they met Julius Fantl's brother and sister-in-law, who had already been deported there earlier from near Prague.

The atmosphere was very tense. The SS-Obergruppenführer and deputy Reich Protector of Bohemia and Moravia had recently been assassinated.[15] A few days later, the Czech village of Lidice, near Prague, was destroyed in retaliation: 172 or 173 men were shot by police from Halle an der Saale. Almost 200 women and around 100 children were deported, the women to Ravensbrück concentration camp, and most of the children were gassed at Kulmhof (Chełmno) extermination camp.[16]

A few days after his arrival in Theresienstadt, Julius Fantl was transferred to the Sudeten Barracks [Sudetenkaserne], and his wife Irena and the girls Rita and Dagmar to the Hamburg Barracks.

DÁŠA FRIEDOVÁ AND DAGMAR FANTLOVÁ One day Dáša Friedová and Dagmar Fantlová met in the courtyard of the former barracks. They started talking. They were both 13, very tall for their age and had the same name, although they were called Dáša and Danka, and their surnames started with the same letter. It was the start of a wonderful friendship. Dáša and Dagmar decided to stay together as long as they could. In autumn 1942, they were transferred to building L 410 for 10- to 16-year-old girls. There, they met Lydia Holznerová. In their room, or 'home', there were twenty-four girls.

'We got up early to go to work in the camp nursery, growing vegetables for the Germans. None of it was for us. Sometimes we ate grass, which was also forbidden.' In the afternoon, they went back to the 'home'. After work, there were illegal lessons. 'Our trained teachers were phenomenal, particularly Magda Weiss. Without books or paper, by talking and telling stories, we learned history, mathematics and literature.' There were girls who had no parents anymore, from the orphanage in Brno. Their parents had managed to get to Palestine and hoped that their children would be able to follow them. 'Somehow they hadn't managed. Most of these girls later died.'

One day, Dagmar's grandmother received a note ordering her to report for transport. 'A lot of old people … were sent to the East'. Dagmar never heard anything further from her grandmother.

There was strict censorship in Theresienstadt, but in order to deceive the international media, the Nazis allowed the many composers, actors, musicians, painters and writers interned there to organize the 'leisure activities' in the camp. Apart from supposedly safe standard works, Jewish artists also performed plays that were banned everywhere else in Nazi-occupied Europe. Among them was the children's opera *Brundibár*.[17] The opera was rehearsed in the cellar of their former barracks. Dagmar and Dáša also played and sang. Dagmar could read music and play the piano. Dáša learned to sing by ear. It was very important for the girls. For a few moments, they could forget the hunger, fear and suffering.

*Brundibár* was not written in Theresienstadt. The Czech Jewish composer Hans Krása wrote it in Prague in 1938. The libretto was by his friend, the Czech avant-garde artist Adolf Hoffmeister. The opera had its premiere in autumn 1942 in the Jewish orphanage in Prague. Czech Jewish artists such as Rafael and Rudolf Schächter rehearsed the opera with the orphaned children in secret, because Jews were not allowed to perform publicly.

Krása was not present at either of the two performances at the Jewish orphanage in Prague. On 10 August 1942, he was deported to Theresienstadt. The orphans followed later.[18] After the occupation of Czechoslovakia, Hoffmeister fled to France, where he was interned for seven months.[19]

The children's opera tells of a brother and sister, Pepiček and Aninka, who try to save their sick mother. The doctor prescribes milk for her. But the family are poor. In desperation, the children wonder how they can help their mother. Then they meet Brundibár, who plays a barrel organ in the market to earn money. The children also try to earn money by singing, but they are too quiet and people just laugh at them. Brundibár chases the two away. Only when a cat, a dog, a sparrow and neighbourhood children come to their aid by joining in a lullaby do passers-by stop to listen and give them money. No one listens to

Brundibár anymore. He steals the children's money from their hat. But as he tries to get away, he is caught by the children and animals together.

The opera, whose music varies from joyful burlesque to harsh dissonance, was perfect for the children in captivity in Theresienstadt. They experienced the evil represented by Brundibár every day in the camp. And the goodness, the longing, the hope of the children for a better time are evident, particularly in the finale:

For help is everywhere!
Below and in the air!
Sometimes it's all around
Sometimes it must be found
But if you ask for help, well
Listen up, we're here to say
Don't worry! Help's on the way!
And when you take a stand
Someone will lend a hand!
That's the whole point of it!
When a bully's near
Tell him you're not afraid!
You'll see him fade away!
Friends will volunteer!
And bullies disappear!

With every day, *Brundibár* became better known and more popular. It was performed over fifty times in Theresienstadt, and countless times more in back courtyards, corridors and attics. Dáša and Dagmar performed in the opera several times. 'The children sang, whistled and hummed the words and melodies all the time.' But the rehearsals and performances were interrupted repeatedly by transports to the East. The cast was forced to change time and again. The Nazis ultimately deported the last of the child musicians and singers from Theresienstadt in autumn/winter 1944. The composer Hans Krása was deported in mid-October and gassed in Auschwitz immediately on arrival.[20]

Adolf Hoffmeister survived by escaping first to France, then to Portugal and Mexico, and finally to the USA. After the war, he returned to his Czech homeland and taught at the Prague Academy of Applied

Arts. He died in 1973.[21] Practically all of the *Brundibár* actors were murdered in Auschwitz. Of the 10,000 or more children under 15 who passed through Theresienstadt, only 218 boys and girls from the 7,590 transported from there to the East survived.[22]

Dáša's father and sister were not among the survivors. 'Sylva died of encephalitis in Theresienstadt.' Her father's precise cause of death is unknown. 'My father got sick in Theresienstadt. But my mother told me that he was also beaten up. I don't know exactly what he died of.' Dáša was unable to accept the reality. 'I couldn't believe that they were both really dead, that I would never see my father and my sister again. It was like a dream from which I would wake up. Then everything would be OK again.'

YEHUDA BACON For the Bacon family from Ostrava, the train for Theresienstadt set off on 18 September 1942. It took the 13-year-old Yehuda, his father Isidor, his mother Ethel and his 19-year-old sister Hanne. Rella, Yehuda's second sister, had emigrated to Palestine in 1939.

There was terrible unease before the transport. Everyone tried to 'Aryanize' – in other words, 'to give valuables to "Aryan" friends for safekeeping'. Yehuda Bacon wrote in 1947:

> On 18 September 1942 the first transport of Jews left Ostrava. Chaos reigned in our home and probably elsewhere as well. Where should we hide our possessions? Do you think the lady will give our things back to us? Should we take some money with us? Darn it, I forgot to buy vitamins. What's wrong with me? Do you have more than 50 kg of luggage? Where are my papers? Mum, Mr Novotný has come for the fridge. Get out of my way, you're a darned nuisance, how often do I have to tell you? Go out and play! We'll carry the bag with the food with us. For heaven's sake, look how you're packing everything! They'll dig into your back as we're walking. Mum, what should I wear for the journey? This is the last time we'll take a bath in this apartment and sleep in our beds. Who knows where we'll sleep tomorrow!

Some of those destined for deportation, who saw no way out, committed suicide – a shattering experience for the children. Everything before the transport took place in an eerie atmosphere. Trucks drove up. One district after another of Ostrava was cleared out. The Jews were taken to a collection point. In his 1947 report, Yehuda described the time there:

So this is the collection point. It was like this in the summer camp, Mum. We made coffee outside in the open air and we queued with our bowls. It was great! I don't like it here. There's too much noise and people shout so loud. Why is that woman with a baby in her arms crying? Is it true that our headmaster Eberson wanted to take poison? Mum, 'All orderlies to roll call.' What's a roll call? Why is the man with the 'leader' armband shouting so much? Mrs Rawitz, have you heard that we're not even stopping in Theresienstadt? We're going to be transported on to Poland. Do you know Mr Edelstein? I've heard that he's a leader there. He might be able to get us out. I don't know him, but thousands do; how can he help? But, dad, I know his son from the Moshava, the summer camp, and Mrs Mirjam Edelstein as well. You'll see, they'll get us out. Don't be stupid. You won't be able to see him. You won't have time to speak with him. Be quiet! Damn it, can't you keep quiet here! What's up? Did someone come? Are we going now? Everyone on board. We'll take the luggage we can't carry and give it away.

The train's here, get ready! How much longer do we have to wait here? Shut up, can't you see the way the soldier's looking at us? Get a move on! Look at the way they're pointing their guns at us. Faster, faster, Jewish pig! Can't you carry? I don't feel so well. You'll have to hold on. Look, there's the train station. Mrs Procházka, can you see her? What do you say to that? Look how he's perspiring. Such a small child! Faster, faster! Finally, the train station. Stop shoving, there's plenty of room.

When a German soldier came by in the train, everyone stood up and took their hats off. Yehuda Bacon wrote in 1947:

What's going on here? What's your name. Joachim Krummholz. Slap, slap. What? Joachim Israel Krummholz. What? Don't you know your own name. Punch! Stinking Jew Israel Krummholz. Got it? Yes sir, my name is stinking Jew Israel Krummholz. It's suffocating in here, open the windows. Woe betide anyone who opens the windows, got it? Do you have any water? I can't stand it anymore.

After around twenty-four hours, they arrived in Theresienstadt, a completely new and strange world. They were met by people wearing armbands, 'semi-military caps' with yellow stripes, metal numbers on their chests, and 'GW' for 'Ghettowache' [ghetto guard]. They told the deportees to take only the bare necessities and leave everything else on the train; they would get the things later. Only a few trusted this promise, and the new arrivals took as much as they could with them.

> I was wearing all my best clothes, two and three sets. Three pairs of stockings, two shirts, sweaters, dresses, winter coat, and all kinds of pockets full of things. A travelling first aid kit in one, vitamins, sewing gear in another pocket, pencils, paper, sugar, paraffin tablets, an address book, lots of handkerchiefs, a water bottle. I think we had everything. And it was the same for everyone else.

Weighed down like this, they had to complete the journey on foot. The mood varied from despair to hope that it wouldn't be that bad after all. They would soon arrive in this 'funny town'. 'Now I know what a fortress and a barracks look like.' In the distance a barrier, a low building, in front of it an 'embankment made of wooden boxes'. As he approached, Yehuda noticed the labels on them with the name and date of birth. He suddenly realized: 'They're coffins!'

The Bacons were assigned to the attic of Magdeburg Barracks [Magdeburger Kaserne]. People came and went. They looked for their luggage. Parents and children were separated, if only for a short time. It was all very confusing. Some were waiting for transport to the East. On the very first evening, Yehuda was to say goodbye to friends whom he would never see again. His former teacher, Fanni Ziffer, was also sitting on her suitcase, ready to leave.

Suddenly, Herschl Bacon, Yehuda's uncle, appeared. He had been transported to Theresienstadt some time earlier. He attempted to reassure his relatives:

> He told us that we shouldn't be afraid, that he knew the Jewish elder and that we wouldn't be deported to Poland, that he'd sort things out for us [get us a good job], that we could live with him and then get transferred to a barracks where we'd have a bed, and that we wouldn't starve. That's how he consoled us. And we asked him thousands of questions.

The Bacons were a little less worried.

Yehuda was transferred later to the Czech juvenile home, where 10- to 16-year-old boys were housed. Unlike other children and juveniles, they didn't have to work at first. They had illegal lessons every morning, with two pupils keeping watch. After lunch, they were free until 2 p.m. and were able to see their parents during this time if they wanted. Then the lessons continued. 'In the evening we were free between 6 and 8 p.m.' They played, sang or had stories read. There were no lessons on Saturdays. A room roll call took place between 10 and 11 a.m., followed by the full home roll call. 'There were commendations for cleanliness and order, criticisms for untidiness, blocked toilets or because teachers had complained.'

Yehuda was one of the 'boys from number 5', as their room was called. They called themselves 'Dror', the Hebrew word for 'swallow'. And they had their own anthem, written by a 'chaver' or comrade:

We are thirty in a room
Everyone is different
Clever, good and honest
Bad and lazy
But we all live well together
We must hope and also
Have hope
The sun rises in the distance
It will be another bright day
We will learn and work
The past will be just a dream
Work, struggle, build up the fatherland
The past will be just a dream

From time to time, colleagues from their home went to the East with their families. 'We believed they were going to labour camps, worse than Theresienstadt but still just labour camps.'

LYDIA HOLZNEROVÁ and her family received transport notification in December 1942. Their former housekeeper helped them to take their luggage on a dogcart to the train station in Hronov.

It was already dark when they arrived in Theresienstadt. 'The entire transport was housed in the attic of some building. There were mattresses on the floor. We had to try to get out of this attic as soon as possible. We knew that those who remained there would be transported onward.'

The Holzners were the last of their relatives to be deported to Theresienstadt. 'And somehow the family managed to arrange for us to get out of the attic quickly.' They were separated immediately. Lydia was put in the 'girls' home' [Mädchenheim], where she met Dagmar Fantlová and Dáša Friedová. Her sister Věra became a carer in one of the 'children's homes' [Kinderheime] in Hamburg Barracks [Hamburger Kaserne], where her mother was also housed. The father ended up in Sudeten Barracks. Lydia also had to work during the day in the garden centre, and in the late afternoon and evening she had illegal lessons.

> We had a very musical education. Our carers, two sisters, sang in the Theresienstadt choir, along with Greta, who lived with us. In the basement of our building, there was a room with a harmonium. That's where the choir rehearsals took place. After the war, one of the singers, Karel Berman, was for many years a member of the National Theatre in Prague.
>
> He spoke to us once. We took the harmonium to our room, and he played, sang and explained the entire opera *Rusalka* by Antonin Dvořák.

'Song to the Moon' from that opera was a particular favourite, comforting Lydia in the very difficult times that were still to come after Theresienstadt. The song expresses a deep longing for love:

> Moon, high and deep in the sky
> Your light sees far,
> You travel around the wide world,
> and see into people's homes.
> Moon, stand still a while
> and tell me where is my dear.
> Tell him, silvery moon,
> that I am embracing him.
> For at least momentarily
> let him recall of dreaming of me.
> Illuminate him far away,

and tell him, tell him who is waiting for him!
If his human soul is, in fact, dreaming of me,
may the memory awaken him!
Moonlight, don't disappear, disappear!

Whenever Lydia heard the opera later on, a shiver ran down her back. She knew exactly what every note signified. 'That's how well Karel Berman explained it to us.'

There were frequent epidemics in Theresienstadt, also in the 'girls' home'. Once it was jaundice; another time, typhoid fever. 'Near the toilet was a woman who gave us disinfectant for our hands. There was an out-patients' clinic on the first floor with a doctor and a nurse. That's where we were treated.' When the typhoid fever epidemic broke out, a room was immediately made free to isolate the sick girls. Doctors were able to administer vaccinations. There were mass inspections of all those who came into contact with food. In this way, it was possible to limit the spread of the infection and those infected. 'Despite this, over 10 per cent of those with typhoid fever died.'

Looking back four decades later, Lydia Holznerová formulated it as follows: 'Theresienstadt was just about tolerable. Families were able to see one another every day. There was some healthcare and cultural life. We were allowed to write letters and receive parcels. Of course, everything was strictly regulated. But people still had some contact with the outside world.' And the Holzners were still in Bohemia. This was extremely important for them. 'When we arrived in Theresienstadt in December 1942, one of my father's sisters had already been sent to the East.' No one knew exactly what it meant to be 'sent to the East', except that it was 'worse than Theresienstadt'.

Even four decades later, Lydia was able to remember some incidents clearly – such as a transport in early January 1943. 'There was a curfew. But I looked out of the window and saw people passing by. And in September 1943 I knew some of the people.' One time, a transport arrived in Theresienstadt. 'It was Polish children. Everything was highly secret. We weren't allowed to talk to them. Some carers were sent to them, including Magda, who had been in the girls' home with us. It was said that the children were meant to have a bath, but no one wanted to. They screamed "gas", but no one knew why.'

Jiří and Zdeněk Steiner The twins were 13 when their father came home to Prague with the news: 'We have to go to Theresienstadt.' 'When we asked if we could take some toys with us, the answer was always: "no you can't"; books: "no you can't."' Only the most necessary items could be packed, and a lot was given away beforehand, including the Steiners' extensive library, to friends, acquaintances and neighbours. The transport started at the Prague exhibition centre, where around fifty people slept for two nights on the floor in one of the pavilions. Then there was the march under guard to the train station. The train arrived in Theresienstadt on 22 December 1942.

The two boys and their father were billeted in Sudeten Barracks, while their mother was in Habsburg Barracks [Habsburger Kaserne]. Jiří soon fell ill. 'I had bad diarrhoea and pneumonia.' After a few weeks, he and his brother were transferred to a 'children's home' in Hanover Barracks [Hannover Kaserne], where they also had illegal lessons. The existence of these 'homes' in Theresienstadt was due to Fredy Hirsch. Many people who knew him repeatedly point this out. As a young German Jew from Aachen, he had fled to Czechoslovakia in November 1935. In Prague, he was one of the main organizers of Hagibor, whose sports programme Jiří and Zdeněk took part in enthusiastically. Hirsch was deported to Theresienstadt on 4 December 1941.[23]

'We met our parents in the evening, although not every day. My mother often cooked something. The food was bad but tolerable. We were actually quite well off compared with what was to come. We had a theatre of sorts; there were concerts and a cabaret in the attic; and we had sports events.' But none of this could mask the fear: of illnesses such as typhoid fever, and of the transports.

Hanuš Hachenburg from Prague, who was deported to Theresienstadt in October 1942, wrote down what he and the other children were thinking. As a 14-year-old, he composed the poem *Theresienstadt*:

I was once a little child,
Three years ago.
That child who longed for other worlds.
But now I am no more a child
For I have learned to hate.

I am a grown-up person now,
I have known fear.[24]

In December 1943, Hachenburg was deported to Auschwitz, where all trace of him was lost.

# 'As If in a Coffin'

HEINZ KOUNIO Thessaloniki, 12 March 1943, around 11 a.m., military police came and ordered the Kounio family to pack their things. They were to move to the ghetto in the Baron Hirsch district near the train station, where many Jews already lived.

'Neither my parents nor my sister Erika nor I knew what horror awaited us. We gathered together what we could in the short time.' The soldiers took them first to a coffeehouse. This would be their new home. The building was locked up. Heinz noticed that the area was empty. 'I was very anxious.' He asked one of the German soldiers: 'Why is it so quiet here? Are there no people?' The soldier replied: 'You're only allowed outside for a few hours a day.'

In the coffeehouse, the family looked for a place to sleep. 'But everything was wet. The roof was leaking and the rain kept coming in. Our beds were made up of a few dirty blankets on the floor. In spite of our warm clothing, we were freezing.' The Kounio family had to share their new accommodation with a couple and their baby. 'The woman was in despair and completely bewildered at the new situation.' The baby must have sensed this: 'It wouldn't stop crying.'

Rumours had been rife in the city for some time that they would be sent to Poland. 'Some said to Lublin, others to Kraków.' The entire family was afraid of what awaited them in Poland, but no one dared to mention these fears out loud. Early next morning, they were ordered 'in an angry commanding tone' to report for registration to the synagogue, which had been adapted for that purpose.

'All possessions of any value were taken from us' in return for a receipt. The remaining cash also had to be handed over. Heinz's father was given a voucher for 600 złoty in exchange, which would be paid out in his 'new home'. This whole procedure turned out to be a complete farce. The mock seriousness was meant to keep the victims quiet. The family did not see any of the valuables or money again. They were left with just a blanket, a spoon, a fork, some warm clothing, and something to eat.

Sunday, 15 March, 2 a.m. The Germans ordered them to assemble on the central square in the ghetto. There were around 2,800 people altogether:[1] babies, children, juveniles, women and men. For two hours, nothing happened, and the tension and fear grew by the minute. 'Mothers tried to comfort their crying children. The men stared nervously into the darkness.' Then 'we heard the orders for our deportation'. Everyone had to march to the train station in rows of five.

> There were closed cattle wagons with two large doors, one of which slid to the left and the other to the right. Above there was only a small opening covered in barbed wire. We had to climb into the wagon with our luggage. It became more and more crowded. There were so many people that we couldn't sit or lie down. Not even for five minutes.

After all the names had been checked, the wagon doors were closed. Prior to this, the Germans had put two buckets in the wagon as a 'toilet' for those trapped inside, along with some bags of olives, dried figs and rusks. But no water.

The train stopped for the first time not far from the border between Greece and Serbia and stayed there for hours and hours, throughout the night and the following day, until dusk. Although the small children in particular called repeatedly for water, the wagon doors weren't opened. The small buckets for answering nature's call were not emptied either, and 'because of the crowded conditions many people didn't even make it that far'.

'It was terrible. All of the questions going through your head, and no answers. The nightmares. The incessant and penetrating crying of the young children.' It was not until Tuesday morning that the train started moving again. Shortly before, the deportees had been allowed to leave the train to stretch their legs and relieve themselves, empty the buckets and drink fresh water, surrounded by German guards.

The train rolled on northward through Belgrade and Zagreb at a maximum speed of 20 km/h. The food began to run out. 'The hunger became increasingly noticeable. Some people died.' Four days had elapsed. In a forest area close to the Austrian border, the deportees were allowed to get out of the train again. Once again, they emptied the buckets, drank water and relieved themselves. 'Here for the first time, those who had died of deprivation and hunger were taken off the train.'

The train continued via Vienna in the direction of north-eastern Europe. The deportees were no longer allowed to leave the train. 'We Jews were not allowed to pollute German soil.' Thirst became an increasing problem. The German guards took no notice even of the desperate cries of the small children. And the floor of the wagon had inevitably become one large toilet.

After the train crossed the Czech border, the people there noticed the transport. Whenever the train slowed down or stopped, Czechs attempted to pass food, water or lemonade into the wagons. But the SS wouldn't allow them to do so. Nor were the deportees allowed to leave the train.

'These spontaneous attempts to help touched me to the core.' After many rough days, the transport reached Poland. The SS informed us: 'You're going to Auschwitz.' Not to Lublin or Kraków, as some had assumed. It was the first time they had heard the name 'Auschwitz'.

JANEK MANDELBAUM Sławków, Poland,[2] one day in the second week of June 1942, 5 a.m. Banging at the door, not only at the Mandelbaums': 'Jews out! You've five minutes!' Janek's mother Cyrla, his brother Jakob, and Janek himself quickly put some clothes on. 'Everywhere we heard screaming, shouting, crying and shots. We went outside. There was total confusion. We were terrified.' The Jews from the town were ordered to assemble on the market square. From there they were driven to the local brewery outside the town and kept there. 'It was surrounded by a high stone wall.' Some hadn't even had the time to get properly dressed; some were barefoot; others in their underclothes.[3] 'On the way there, I saw two men being shot.' They had tried to escape.

The Jewish children, women and men underwent a selection: 'Children were separated from their parents. They were screaming. But it was to no avail. Fortunately, I was put on one side with my mother and my brother.' While doing forced labour in Sławków, Janek had managed to obtain a certificate as an electrician's mate. He always had it on him, thinking: 'Perhaps it will help us to stay here, because my work is needed.' He handed the paper to a German guard, saying: 'I'm an electrician's mate. My mother and brother are also good workers.'

The 'officer' said nothing, threw the certificate away, grabbed the boy by the shoulder and pushed him to one side. What Janek didn't know at the time was that he was grouped with the men fit for work, who were spared temporarily from being sent to the extermination camp. But he couldn't get his mother and brother to join him and wasn't allowed to go back to them. Janek couldn't guess which side was 'better'. All he could think of was the words his mother had whispered to him on the way to the brewery: 'We have to stay together.'

'This separation was the worst moment in my life.' Janek found himself in a group of around 100 men. Panic seized him. He searched with his eyes for his mother and brother. 'I couldn't see them anymore.' He was 15 years old. He was loaded onto a truck with the other men. They didn't know where they would be taken. Janek couldn't stop thinking about his mother and his brother. He was inconsolable and kept asking himself: 'Will I be able to find them again?' But 'I was never to see them again.'

After a few hours, the trucks reached their destination, the forced labour camp for Jews in Prady (German: Brande): 'It was already dark. We drove through an iron gate. There were some buildings. Bright floodlights shone down from watchtowers. We were beaten and driven from the trucks.'

The camp, which had been set up in October 1940, was around 20 kilometres to the west of Opole. It was on the outskirts of the village of Prady and was one of the thirteen western Upper Silesian 'Reich autobahn camps' for Jews, who worked as forced labourers on the construction of the German autobahns. Brande and the other camps were fenced in and consisted of primitive barracks. There were between 100 and 300 male inmates in each camp. A small group of Jewish women worked in the kitchens and tailor's shop.[4]

On their arrival at the camp, Janek and the other new inmates had to strip naked. Their bodies were completely shaved and 'disinfected with some chemical product' that stung terribly: 'I had difficulty holding back the tears.' Then they were given civilian clothes with the Star of David.

Gradually, the camp became a 'sick camp', as the Jewish doctor Hans-Werner Wollenberg described it in his autobiographical notes completed in 1947. Beatings and punishments were the order of the day.

Wollenberg wrote that 'those who were unable to work for more than six weeks were sent to Auschwitz'. 'Unknown destination' was the entry on the 'personnel list'. 'But we knew that it was Auschwitz.'[5]

Janek passed through the forced labour camp Gross Masselwitz (near Wrocław, now Wrocław-Maślice)[6] and Fünfteichen (Miłoszyce koło Wrocławia), a satellite camp of Gross-Rosen concentration camp,[7] to Blechhammer, from 1 August 1944 officially one of the many satellite camps of Auschwitz.[8]

DAGMAR, DÁŠA, YEHUDA, LYDIA, JIŘÍ AND ZDENĚK Between early and mid-December 1943, the Fantl, Fried, Bacon, Holzner and Steiner families in Theresienstadt were loaded onto cattle wagons. They were told that they were being sent to work in Moravia or Poland. The families discovered what *einwaggonieren* signified. 'Like being sealed alive in a coffin', said Yehuda Bacon. They were treated like cattle 'being taken to slaughter'.

Dáša Friedová remained in Theresienstadt when her dear friend Dagmar Fantlová was transported to the East. On the day of her departure, Dáša couldn't stop crying and sobbing. She thought she would never see her again. But the next day, Dáša and her mother received a transport order. While they were packing their belongings – they were allowed 20 kg – 'the pain of loss was forgotten, if only for a while'. Three days after Dagmar's departure, Dáša and her mother also left Theresienstadt. 'We didn't know where we were going to. We were told: "Theresienstadt is too full. You'll be taken to a place where a new Jewish community is being founded."'

Although Dáša had just lost her father and sister, she believed these assurances. 'In spite of everything, I was still very naïve.' Her parents had taught her to trust people. At home and in Prague, 'everyone liked us', there were no enemies. This marked the young girl: 'I still couldn't imagine that something terrible would happen to me.' The transport in the closed cattle wagons was a rude awakening for Dáša, however. 'It was packed and the air was bad. There were injured people groaning and children without their parents crying.' They had to relieve themselves in an 'overflowing bucket made of rags'. 'Terrible'.

The train stopped in Kolin, where Dáša's mother Kat'a Friedová came from. She threw some postcards she had written in Theresienstadt out of the small hole in a corner of the wagon. Dáša never discovered whether the cards were delivered.

GÉZA SCHEIN Until 19 March 1944, 700,000 to 750,000 Jews within the borders of Hungary[9] had survived, in spite of the German-style anti-Jewish legislation, discrimination and persecution.[10] This was to change overnight. Immediately after the German invasion, there was a wave of arrests among the Jewish inhabitants.[11] Countless anti-Jewish regulations and laws were rapidly adopted in early 1944: Jewish notaries, lawyers, auditors, public officials and journalists were banned from working; bank accounts were frozen; and over 365,000 hectares of land had already been expropriated by the end of 1943; telephones, motor vehicles, radios and valuables were confiscated; moving house was forbidden; restricted shopping hours were introduced; food was rationed. From 5 April 1944, Jews were obliged to wear a yellow star.[12] In this way, the Jewish population was isolated, stigmatized and branded. They were also forced into a ghetto on the island of Csepel on the Danube, today part of Budapest. 'We were living right where the ghetto was established.'

After attending primary school for four years, Géza started the Jewish secondary school in 1944. It was closed by order of the German occupiers. Géza's father, Zoltán Schein, was allowed to continue running the bakery. 'We were allowed to bake bread and other items for the Jews in the ghetto. It wasn't much, but we were still able to live from it.'

Friends of the Scheins offered to get them out of the ghetto and hide them. 'That's how well we got on with the non-Jewish inhabitants of Csepel. But my father and grandfather refused. They feared that it would cause difficulties for these people and put them at risk.' In May 1944, Hungarian gendarmes ordered the family to pack their things and go with them. 'The adults had been expecting it.' Géza, who was 11 at the time, was taken with his parents and maternal grandparents to a transit camp in a brickworks in Budakalász, around 25 kilometres away. Two weeks later, they were transported in cattle wagons, each containing 80–100 people, with the inscription 'German worker resettlement'. 'No one knew where the train was headed. The adults already guessed.' The Germans had told them that they were going East to help with the harvest.

A stopover on the way to Auschwitz was the Slovakian town of Košice (Hungarian: Kassa) around 250 kilometres away, which had been incorporated into Hungary in November 1938. The railhead there became a transhipment point [*Umschlagplatz*] for 136 transports[13] with around 380,000, mostly Hungarian, Jews on their way to the East.[14]

In Košice, the wagon doors were opened. 'We got something to eat again. Some people had died during the journey and they were removed.' The wagons were filled with new people. It took days before the people crowded in the wagons were able to see through the tiny hole that they must be in Poland. When the train reached its destination, they had to wait two more hours in the wagons. 'We could look out. We saw smoking chimneys and thought that it was some kind of factory.' But it was Auschwitz-Birkenau.

EDUARD KORNFELD After the occupation of Hungary by German troops, life for the Jewish inhabitants of Vel'ký Meder rapidly became increasingly intolerable. Eduard Kornfeld heard about the first arrests and transports. He already knew about it from Bratislava, from where he had fled with his brother Heinrich. 'I don't want to go through that again. I have to get away as fast as possible.'

The 15-year-old Eduard had met a Slovakian Jewish girl in Vel'ký Meder. She was one or two years younger than he was and, like him, had fled from Bratislava. 'I was very close and attached to her. I'd fallen in love.'

'Let's get away', he told her. He wanted to flee with her from the impending deportation to Budapest. In the hope of being able to hide in the big city, Eduard attempted to persuade the girl to come with him. But she couldn't bring herself to go.

One day in April 1944, the order came: 'All Jews to report for transport'.[15] The Jews had to march from Vel'ký Meder to the train station on the outskirts of the town. A special train was waiting at a distance from the main building. 'We weren't allowed to take much with us, only some clothes and food.' Everything else had been left behind: businesses, farms, houses, furniture, cows, poultry, goats.

The train took them to Komarno (Hungarian: Komárom) around 30 kilometres away. The Jews of Vel'ký Meder were locked up together with those Jews from the surrounding area and the remaining Jews from Komarno in the town's sixteenth-century fortress, which had been modified and enlarged between 1807 and 1877.

'There must have been around 4,000 people. There was no way of escaping anymore. The conditions in the fortress were terrible. Everything was underground. Quite far down. There was nothing to eat, no beds, nothing. We had to sleep on the bare floor.' A fire truck came just once a day to deliver water.

The Jews of Komarno and those brought there were taken away in two transports from mid-June 1944. Among them were two of Eduard's uncles and their families. 'One had six children, the other eight.' Only one of the children survived.

> We rode in the cattle wagons standing up. They were packed. The doors were locked. In Košice, where the train stopped, a few people were allowed out under guard. This was a normal train station, where there were also many civilians waiting for their trains.
>
> I saw a chance of escaping. I could have mingled with these people and disappeared. I said again to the girl whom I had fallen in love with: 'Come on, we can get lost in the crowd.' But she still didn't want to come, so I stayed as well.

GÁBOR HIRSCH Two months after the Germans entered Hungary, János Hirsch hired his son Gábor as an apprentice in his business in Békéscsaba. 'My father thought that if I'm forced to work as an apprentice electrician who already had some knowledge, I wouldn't have to do heavy labour. This idea sounds naïve to us now. But times were different and there were other laws. People knew much less than they do today. There was a war.'

As long as he lived, Gábor Hirsch could 'no longer listen to or see' discussions about this, particularly on the Internet. 'They speak as if we knew everything.' He didn't think that his parents had been really informed about the persecution of the Jews in Europe. He was convinced: 'My father János would never have deliberately exposed us to what we were to suffer later. It's unthinkable.'

In mid-May 1944, the Jews of Békéscsaba were concentrated in some 100 houses around the two synagogues. The Hirsch family's new house, which Gábor's father had built in 1942, was in the concentrated area of

Békéscsaba. The house, where the family had lived for a year, had four rooms. In May 1944, four other families had to move in, including the family of János's cousin. They were allowed to bring very little with them. 'Now there were fourteen people living in the house.' Everything had to be shared: the kitchen, the bathroom, the toilet. 'There was no privacy anymore.'

Gábor's classmate György suggested: 'You can move in with us.' The family had a farm in the country, several kilometres from any other houses or settlements. His friend's parents told Gábor: 'We can hide you until the war ends.'

'My father refused. The family should stay together. He didn't know what awaited us.' In mid-1944, the Jews from the town and surrounding area were herded together in the tobacco drying plant in Békéscsaba. There were several multi-storey buildings close to the train station. They were allowed to take '30 or 50 kilograms' with them, but limited to the bare necessities.

In mid-June 1944, Gábor was interned with his mother Ella in one of the tobacco factory buildings. He was 14 years old. At the same time, the Hungarian army had taken his father János for the forced labour service, although he was already 50, much too old for conscription into the army (18 to 46 years).[16] But the age limit had been abolished, especially for Jews. János Hirsch had already performed 'this terrible service' for some months in 1942.

Several thousand Jews were concentrated in the buildings of the tobacco drying plant in Békéscsaba. From this point on, the situation deteriorated dramatically. They suffered from hunger, overcrowding and the terrible treatment by the Hungarian gendarmes.

'During the two weeks in the tobacco buildings, thirteen people died or committed suicide. I witnessed all of that. It was terrible.'

On 24 June 1944, came the order: 'Volunteers to report for transport'. No one knew where to. 'No one reported.' Then one building with around 700 people in it was isolated, and the first transport left the ghetto in Békéscsaba for an unknown destination on 25 June.

26 June 1944: the remaining Jews from the ghetto in Békéscsaba were *einwaggoniert*. There were between eighty-five and ninety-five people in each of the cattle wagons. 'With one bucket of drinking water and one bucket to relieve ourselves'.

'People died in our wagon during the journey. How many? I don't know.' Travelling with Gábor in the transport from Békéscsaba were seven close relatives: his mother Ella (48 years), his elderly grandmother Gizella (81 years), his aunt Malvin (40 years) and her son Tibor (15 years), and his other aunt Rozsi (33 years) with her sons Jószef (7 years) and the 3-month-old baby Péter.

FERENC AND OTTO KLEIN A few days after the Germans arrived, the Klein house in Hajdúböszörmény was searched. Otto and Ferenc were out at the time. When they returned home, they saw a German car in front of their house. 'That was unusual, because there were few cars in our small town.' When the boys tried to enter, they saw their father standing at the window. 'He gave us a sign to go away.' They observed the house from a distance 'with beating hearts'. 'After about two hours, he was taken away by the Germans, handed over to the Hungarian police and locked up.' His offence: 'He was a Jew, prominent and wealthy.'

The chief of police was their neighbour and a friend of the family. He said to Lilly Klein: 'Your husband will be taken away tomorrow. Come to the police station at 9 a.m. You can take your leave of him then.' The next day, the family went to the entrance to the prison. 'My father came out. We were briefly able to take our leave of him. A car was already waiting for him. My mother was in despair. We didn't know if he would return. Anything was possible.' Shortly before, Salomon Klein had spoken for the first time about getting away. 'He didn't think the Jews were safe in Hungary anymore.' He had wanted to flee to Romania with his wife and children. 'My mother tried somehow to get my father released. But no one could or wanted to help her.'

Ferenc and Otto never saw their father again. He was taken first to the prison in Debrecen. Decades after the war, Otto Klein learned that his father died of typhus in early May 1945 at Gunskirchen camp in Austria – two or three days before it was liberated.

In early May 1944, Otto, Ferenc, Ágnes and Lilly Klein were forced to move to the ghetto in Hajdúböszörmény. They were allowed to take some food and clothes with them, but had to leave everything else behind. All Jewish families were crowded together in two streets near the synagogue. All five Kleins had to live in one room: the twins, their mother and sister and their aunt Jenny, their father's sister. The ghetto was barricaded. 'There was a temporary gate with several Hungarian policemen standing guard in front of it. They didn't bother us. I never saw them in the ghetto.' But they weren't allowed out. 'Once a week, a few Jews were let out to shop for food in the town. On their return, they were allowed to sell it to us.'

Otto and Ferenc did not take things as seriously as the adults. 'Children almost always find something to play with.' During the day, they had illegal lessons in the synagogue, particularly study of the Torah, 'instruction on how we were meant to live'.

'Our mother also tried to distract us.' She withheld bad news from the children. 'She didn't want anything to make us unhappy. But we still knew that something terrible was going on.' They had heard the adults talking: 'Jews from other Hungarian towns have been deported.' No one knew where, but everyone knew: 'We'll be next.'

Throughout his life, Otto Klein never forgot his twelfth birthday and that of his twin brother Ferenc. They had discovered that a Christian neighbour was listening to the BBC. One of the windows of the house looked out onto the ghetto. It was boarded up. But when the neighbour – 'deliberately, I presume' – opened the window inwards, noises and voices could be heard through it.

On 7 June 1944, Otto and Ferenc had their ears pressed against the boarded window. They heard the news of the previous day's successful landing in Normandy by the Allies. That gave them hope: 'Would the war soon be over?' In the last week of June, they received the order that they were to leave the ghetto the next day. No one knew where they would be going. 'My mother packed our things. We children had rucksacks. We weren't allowed to take any toys with us, only the necessities.'

Next day, they were marched to the town train station. 'The inhabitants watched but showed no reaction.' They were guarded by Hungarian police. 'They wanted to take from us the few things we possessed.'

The 1,000 or so Jews from Hajdúböszörmény were transported in cattle wagons to a brickworks in nearby Debrecen, where they joined children, women and men from neighbouring towns. They were guarded by the Hungarian gendarmerie and German SS. 'The SS gave the orders.'

They had to sleep on the bare floor. It was covered with a layer of dust several centimetres thick. 'What will happen to us?' asked Otto and his twin brother Ferenc. Some time later, they were driven by Hungarian police to Debrecen train station. German SS men took over as guards. They were once again crowded into cattle wagons. The terrible journey began. They travelled for three or four days. 'It was very crowded in the wagon. There was no possibility of lying down. We squatted on the floor and could barely sleep. There was no toilet.'

One of their cousins was also in the wagon. She was nine months pregnant. She started going into labour. 'She had labour pains and we could all hear. She probably gave birth there.' They couldn't see their cousin or make their way to her. 'The wagon was much too full.' And the indescribable heat. Their mother had managed to bring some food, but there was nothing to drink. The thirst became intolerable. They cried for water but no one cared.

There was a small window in the corner of the wagon. Otto's mother looked out and reported that they were in Slovakia. Later, she announced that they were in Poland. They didn't know where they were being taken. 'We had heard that Jews were deported to other countries.' But where? 'We weren't informed of the itinerary.'

CHANNA MARKOWICZ In mid-April 1944, the Nazis started the systematic concentration of Jews from Irshava and the entire Carpathian region. Channa Markowicz, who was almost 16, her parents and three of her four brothers were taken to a brickworks in Mukachevo, which had been transformed into a transit camp. Schmuel, the oldest brother, had already been forced to go there earlier in a Hungarian army labour battalion.[17]

'My father was optimistic. He didn't show that he was afraid. He had money, including many German coins and banknotes from the time of inflation. He took the money with him and gave it to the children in Mukachevo.'

The transports began in mid-May. By 7 June, 289,357 Jewish children, women and men from Carpatho-Ukraine, northern Transylvania and south Slovakia, which had also been annexed by Hungary, had been deported to Auschwitz-Birkenau.[18]

ROBERT BÜCHLER Towards the end of 1943, a spark of hope had been ignited among the Jews remaining in Topol'čany, Slovakia.[19] The growth of opposition meant that 'doubts arose in the new year regarding the victory of the Germans and the continued existence of the Slovak state'.

An uprising occurred in Slovakia on 29 August 1944. 'We welcomed it, but with mixed feelings. The tumultuous events were taking place far away. We in Topol'čany had nothing to do with them. The uprising only broke out officially here on 1 September. But by then troops from Nazi Germany were already advancing into Slovakian territory to put down the revolt.' After a short skirmish, SS tanks took Topol'čany on 3 September. There were approximately 1,000 Jews in the town – the remnants and those who had been freed from the camps during the uprising.

Accompanying the Waffen-SS in Topol'čany was Einsatzkommando 14, with members of the Gestapo, Security Police and Security Service. Rabbi Haberfeld was summoned to the leader of the kommando, who ordered him to calm the Jews. He also gave permission for services to be held in the Great Synagogue and promised that nothing bad would happen to the Jews. The heads of the community also spoke with him and were surprised that the commandant urged the Jews to return to their normal lives and work. Official Slovak circles followed the same pattern.

This was another subterfuge, as it turned out. Together with the Hlinka Guard, the Slovak pendant of the SS, Einsatzkommando 14 began its 'action' on 8 September. 'Within a few hours, all of the Jews had been arrested and brought to the train station – including my parents, my little sister and myself.'

In the early 1970s, Robert Büchler attempted to recall what he had thought and felt in those days:

We knew that it would be our turn sooner or later. When I saw my relatives and classmates disappear, I wanted to go as well. What bothered me was: why do we have to be the last?

We were told that the Jews were being taken to work camps. The Christians thought that it served them right: 'They'll have to work there instead of eating geese.' It doesn't matter, I thought, we can eat bread and dripping there.

I imagined that the camp would be like the gold prospector camps in Alaska described in books. I'd never been in a camp in my life. I wasn't particularly worried. I'd never been bothered that none of my deported relatives had ever written. There was a war, and they were somewhere far away. In Poland or Russia, it was said. They can't write.

My parents never spoke to me about it. But shortly before we were deported, pre-printed postcards arrived from 'Birkenau labour camp'. This caused my parents great agitation. I had never heard them talking about it before that. Until then they had never reminded us of our relatives who had been deported.

There were four packed rucksacks in the corner of my parents' bedroom. They had already been there for two years, with all the things we were allowed to take with us. When they came to collect us, my mother switched everything off. We took the rucksacks. My mother locked the apartment and gave the key to the SS man. The whole thing took five minutes.

For two years we had been waiting for this moment. We were prepared.

At first, the children found the 'trip' amusing. 'We lay on straw spread out on the floor. We made nuisances of ourselves. We laughed as we watched the adults relieving themselves in a bucket. We had a special place where we could observe everything without anyone noticing.' After the train had been travelling for around twenty-four hours, the fun began to wear off. The rain was hammering onto the roof. Everyone was tired. It was crowded in the wagon. And whenever the train stopped, everyone got up and pushed their way to the barbed-wire opening near the wagon roof. Someone climbed onto a suitcase, looked out and reported what he could see. And everyone asked: 'Have we arrived?'

# Oświęcim – Oshpitzin – Auschwitz

The train station at Oświęcim and the barracks, where Auschwitz concentration camp was to be erected eight months later, were bombarded on the first day of the invasion of Poland by Nazi Germany. A short time later, in early September 1939, the town on the Soła was occupied by the Wehrmacht.[1]

Zygmunt Kuzak, headmaster of the Salesian Monastery School, has the following recollection of 1 September:

> In the morning we heard aeroplanes. They were Polish, we thought. Bombs were dropped from them and we all realized that it was a 'friend' from the West. Panic all round ... There were fifty people in the school at the time.... The outbreak of war caused the inhabitants to flee in panic. The general fear was so infectious and dominant that in the next few days the town practically emptied.[2]

Josef Jakubowicz, 13-year-old son of a local Jewish family, remembers the arrival of the Germans as follows: 'The first German soldiers encountered ... fleeing Jews on the street, who were easy to recognize as orthodox. They shot three of them straightaway.'[3]

Jews had long formed the majority of the population in Oświęcim.[4] In 1939, there were between 7,000 and 8,000 Jews in the town, 58 to 66 per cent of the total population.[5] The Jewish inhabitants defined the town's character.[6] Jews had lived in Oshpitzin, as Oświęcim was called in Yiddish, for almost 500 years.[7] Many synagogues and prayer houses had been built in that time. The Great Synagogue was erected in the late sixteenth century. It was destroyed in a major conflagration in 1863, but it wasn't long before an even more imposing edifice was built, with room for at least 1,000 worshippers.[8] 'In the main synagogue', recalls Josef Jakubowicz, 'there was a magnificent choir: thirty trained chorists sang there. Two soloists from the Scala in Milan came once for the High Holidays.'[9]

The first Jewish cemetery was established in the second half of the sixteenth century, and the second, which still exists today, in the first half of the nineteenth. There was a mikvah; a kosher slaughterhouse; several Yeshiva schools, where future rabbis were trained; and a Jewish secondary school, as well as cultural organizations, sports clubs and foundations providing assistance to the poor and sick, among others.[10]

There were also several Jewish youth organizations offering training in preparation for Aliyah, emigration to Palestine.[11] The Zionist socialist youth organization, Hashomer Hatzair, whose young members generally supported the kibbutz movement, had a branch in Oświęcim.[12]

Jews were actively involved in the town's political life. When a town council was elected for the first time in 1867, nine of the twenty-four councillors were Jewish. In 1933, eighteen out of thirty-two were Jewish: more than half.[13] Josef Jakubowicz: 'As most of the population was Jewish, the mayor should also logically have been a Jew. But the Jewish community didn't want this, so as to avoid provoking any antisemitic feelings.... So they arranged it that the mayor was always a Catholic and his deputy a Jew.'[14] The Jewish inhabitants played a very large role in the town's economy, in commerce, handicrafts and industry. They worked in many professions, from doctors to tailors.[15]

Dampffabrik feiner Liqueure – Jakob Haberfeld, founded 1804, for example, was known beyond Poland's borders.[16] Its products were even shown on the other side of the Atlantic, at the 1939 World's Fair in New York.[17]

Jewish life in Oświęcim was vibrant until the arrival of the Germans in early September 1939. Josef Jakubowicz recalls: 'Life was bustling, colourful and enjoyable. Many scientists and intellectuals and many great scholars of orthodox Judaism lived there. Oświęcim was also known for its rich Jewish culture.'[18] The young were particularly keen on water sports, he says: 'Oświęcim had the best kayak athletes in the area. My brother, for example, won the kayak race every year. Our sports club Kadima, which means 'forward', was very well organized.... There was football, gymnastics and, of course, water sports.'[19]

In October 1939, the town was incorporated into the German Reich under the German name Auschwitz. Between 7 p.m. and 6 a.m., no one was allowed out. Anyone caught was likely to be shot.[20] All Jews over the age of 10 years had to wear a white band on their left arm with a Star of David on it. Jewish businesses and factories were closed, looted by the German troops and, a short time later, taken away from their Jewish owners. All valuables from the synagogues and Jewish households were also seized. Jews were no longer allowed to pursue their normal professions, but were enlisted for forced labour instead. One of the consequences was the complete impoverishment of the Jewish inhabitants of Oświęcim within the shortest time.[21]

During this time, Josef Jakubowicz was with friends in Sosnowiec, around 30 kilometres away. They had a bakery and gave him stale bread to take home. The 14-year-old was stopped and searched by the police on the street. 'They thought I'd stolen the bread.' A court decided: 'I was to get twenty-five strokes.' The boy was beaten terribly with a bull whip.[22]

The Great Synagogue was burned down by the German occupiers in the night of 29–30 November. The wall surrounding the Jewish cemetery was dismantled and a bunker and air raid shelter built on the site. Some of the gravestones were taken by the Nazis to the river Soła so that they could get to the water more easily to enable their horses to drink. Other gravestones were used for road construction.[23]

In April 1940, the Nazi authorities decided to install a concentration camp around 2 kilometres from the old town, initially for 10,000 inmates. From Auschwitz, the people deported there were to be transported to existing concentration camps inside the Reich.[24] The site already had stone buildings and wooden barracks that had been used previously by, among others, the Polish army.[25] The German occupiers used around 20 local Polish workers and 300 Jews from the town to clean and repair the site. In the second half of May 1940, 30 prisoners categorized as criminals, from Sachsenhausen concentration camp, were sent to Auschwitz. They received the numbers 1 to 30 and functioned in the inmate work kommandos as the long arm of the SS.[26]

A few days later, a further 39 Polish inmates from Dachau concentration camp, headed by a German kapo, arrived in Auschwitz. They were mostly young men, secondary school pupils originally from Łódź. The kommando had brought a wagon full of barbed wire to fence in the camp. Auschwitz I, the Main Camp [Stammlager], was created.[27] The first major transport arrived in Auschwitz on 14 June 1940: 728 Poles, political prisoners from the prison in Tarnów, including many young men.[28]

One of them was Kazimierz Albin, a secondary school pupil from Kraków, 17 years old. He was inmate number 118. He had been arrested by the SS while attempting to cross the border to Slovakia to join the new Polish army in Hungary or France. He was interrogated, beaten and brutally tortured. Many of the inmates were students or senior secondary school pupils. Like Kazimierz Albin, they had joined the Polish resistance against the German occupiers.[29]

They were received in Auschwitz with much shouting and blows. SS-Hauptsturmführer Fritzsch left no doubt what the real purpose of Auschwitz concentration camp was: 'Young healthy men should not survive more than three months, priests one month, Jews two weeks. The only way out of the camp is through the crematorium chimney.'[30]

Fortunately, Kazimierz Albin spoke German. This enabled him to join slave labour kommandos that offered a chance of survival – for example, in the shoemaking workshop or the SS kitchen. After over thirty months of beatings, humiliation, hunger and terror, he managed with seven other inmates in two groups to escape from Auschwitz. He made his way to Kraków and joined the underground Armia Krajowa [land army] there.[31] Very few inmates succeeded in escaping from Auschwitz.[32]

To discourage other inmates from attempting to escape, the remaining inmates from the work kommandos from which some had managed to escape were tortured or murdered. On 19 July 1943, the SS hanged twelve inmates from an inmate kommando from which three members had escaped in mid-March. Members of the families of inmates who had escaped were also rounded up by the SS and sent to Auschwitz, and put on a platform for show with the warning: 'This is what will happen to your families if you escape.'[33]

After the transport in mid-June 1940 in which Kazimierz Albin arrived, further deportations from southern Poland to Auschwitz took place in the following weeks.[34] Other large transports, with 1,666 and 1,705 inmates, respectively, arrived from Warsaw on 15 August and 22 September.[35]

Before Auschwitz became the extermination camp for European Jews, it was a concentration camp mainly for Poles.[36] The inmates were often members of the elite Polish society: lawyers; doctors; artists such as Bronisław Czech, Xawery Dunikowski or Mieczysław Kościelniak; teachers; officers; scouts; politicians; priests; academics[37] – in other words, people who were in a position to organize opposition to the German occupiers.

The living conditions for the inmates were already designed to ensure that no one deported to Auschwitz would leave it alive. The Polish historian Franciszek Piper, who, for decades as a staff member of the Auschwitz-Birkenau Memorial, has been studying the history of the concentration camp and extermination camp, summarizes the results of his research: 'The principal goal of the functioning of Auschwitz concentration camp from the beginning to the end of its existence was extermination. All other goals – such as the exploitation of inmate labour, the plundering of the property of the victims, the utilization of the corpses or medical experiments, were of secondary importance.'[38]

In 1941, the Nazis decided to enlarge Auschwitz to hold 30,000 inmates. In addition, a second camp for 100,000 people, Auschwitz II, was to be built, near the village of Brzezinka, now Birkenau, around 3 kilometres from the Main Camp. Later plans called for the enlargement of Auschwitz-Birkenau for 200,000 inmates.[39] The building of Auschwitz I meant that the inhabitants living nearby, particularly many Jews, were resettled. This violent process continued with the building of Auschwitz-Birkenau, and several villages were completely depopulated.[40]

Josef Jakubowicz was forced to help to demolish the village where his family owned a house.[41] 'Around 1,500 people' had lived previously in Brzezinka. 'The place consisted of farms and the school.' His school was there before the camp was built.

Before resettlement, it was

> normal for Jewish children to attend not only the regular school but also the Jewish school. In the mornings, we had normal lessons and in the afternoons from 3 to 7 p.m. Hebrew school, religion and Hebrew.... In Oświęcim, there was also a private Jewish secondary school. It had four classes as preparation for the Lyzeum. For the senior classes it was necessary to go to Katowice or Kraków, where it was possible to obtain the school-leaving certificate.[42]

In early April 1941, over 5,000 Jews from Oświęcim were forcibly transported to Sosnowiec, Będzin and Chrzanów, where they lived in ghettos. From there, particularly in 1943 and 1944, those who were still alive were deported to Auschwitz-Birkenau extermination camp, among other places. Very few of the former Jewish inhabitants of the town were to survive the Shoah.[43]

Josef Jakubowicz's parents, his grandfather, his three sisters, two of whom were married, their husbands and all their children were murdered. Josef was the only member of the family to survive; he was liberated from Bergen-Belsen in April 1945.[44]

Polish Catholics were also at risk of deportation. The population of the town was halved as a result of the deportations in early 1941 to around 7,600 inhabitants. Of these, around 90 per cent were Poles and 10 per cent Germans or of German origin. By October 1943, over 6,000 Reich Germans moved to Auschwitz. According to the plan of January 1943, the population was to be increased through industrialization and 'Germanization' to 70,000 or 80,000.[45]

The depopulated and seized territory covered an area of 40 square kilometres. The 'zone of interest' [*Interessengebiet*] became a restricted zone [*Sperrgebiet*].[46]

Around 10,000 Soviet youths and men designated prisoners of war were to build the Birkenau camp. From July 1941, they were deported to Auschwitz, and housed from October in a separate area of the Main Camp. Among these inmates were eighteen youths aged 16 to 18 years, a 15-year-old boy and two aged 11.

The Soviet prisoners of war were almost all murdered. On 1 March 1942, only 945 of them were still alive. By the end of January 1942, 20,500 of the inmates registered in Auschwitz had died through shooting, hunger, hanging, inhuman hard labour, diseases, beatings, freezing and 'gassing experiments' with Zyklon B in Block 11 (at the time, Block 13) and Crematorium I of the Main Camp.[47]

Auschwitz, particularly Auschwitz-Birkenau, became the main site for the extermination of European Jewry. Jewish children and their families were deported there from the first months of 1942 for the sole reason that they were Jewish. The Germans brutally denied their very right to exist. There were children already in the first transports to Auschwitz, particularly in the transports from Slovakia. Between 17 April and 17 July 1942 alone, 656 juveniles and children, including 11- and 12-year-olds, were deported to Auschwitz.[48] More than 200,000 were to follow in the next two-and-a-half years from many European countries.

The mass gassings began in early 1942 – in Auschwitz-Birkenau, initially in two converted farmhouses with gas chambers: Bunker 1 (known by the inmates as the 'red house' because of the brick walls) and Bunker 2 (called the 'white house' on account of the plastered walls).[49] At first, the Sonderkommando made up of Jewish inmates had to bury the corpses in mass graves. Later they were exhumed and incinerated on piles of wood or in pits. The fat from the corpses was collected and used to kindle the flames.

Over 100,000 corpses were exhumed between September and the end of November 1942. The ashes of the incinerated bodies were removed and emptied into the Vistula and Soła as a means of obliterating the traces of the mass extermination.[50]

Between March and June 1943, four further crematoria and gas chambers for the mass murder began operation. The ovens were built and installed by Topf und Söhne from Erfurt. Now, 4,756 bodies could be incinerated in the five crematoria within twenty-four hours. According to inmates from the Sonderkommando, the 'incineration performance' of the crematoria could be increased to around 8,000 corpses per day.[51]

In 1942, the transport of inmates for extermination stopped at a platform next to the freight station around 2 kilometres from Auschwitz-Birkenau. From May 1944, a track went right into the camp close to Crematoria II and III.[52] A selection was made there, especially by SS doctors: those who were considered fit for work – and therefore temporarily spared – were separated from the old and invalid, pregnant women and children. Around 80 per cent of the arrivals, and on many occasions entire transports, were arbitrarily deemed by the German SS to be unfit for work.[53] Under guard, they were marched or taken by truck to one of the crematoria. There they had to get undressed. Under the pretext that they were to take showers, SS men and women led them to the gas chambers disguised as shower rooms, where the Zyklon B gas was introduced, causing the occupants to suffocate to death in an agonizing process that lasted ten to twenty minutes, sometimes longer. Their bodies were incinerated by the Sonderkommando in the crematoria or pits.[54]

On the ramp, all of the new arrivals – those who were to remain in the camp and those destined for the gas chambers – had to leave their luggage behind. The Nazis stored and sorted the looted possessions in large store-rooms, including a number of barracks near the Main Camp and in thirty barracks in Auschwitz-Birkenau. The inmates called these storerooms 'Kanada' because they associated the mass of looted items with Canada as a 'land of plenty'. The SS called them 'personal effects chambers' ['Effektenkammer'] or 'personal effects stores' ['Effektenlager'].[55] This slave labour was normally carried out by several hundred inmates. When the number of transports, particularly with children, women and men from Hungary, increased in May and June 1944, this 'Kanada' kommando consisted of up to 2,000 women and men.[56]

The victims' possessions were distributed among various departments of the SS and Wehrmacht, and also among the German population. Valuables, including gold teeth removed from the victims' mouths, were transferred to the Deutsche Reichsbank.[57] The SS sold the victims' hair from eleven other concentration camps for 50 Reichspfennig per kilo – for example, to a felt factory, which converted it into yarn or hair felt stockings. By February 1943, 824 railway wagons with looted clothes and leather goods had been dispatched from Auschwitz and Majdanek.[58] Between 1 December 1944 and 15 January 1945, 99,992 items of children's clothing, 192,652 items of women's clothing and 222,269 items of men's clothing were shipped to Nazi Germany.[59]

The inmates in Auschwitz-Birkenau who were not immediately gassed were transferred from the ramp to one of the 'saunas' to be found in several sections of the camp, or the 'central sauna', or 'disinfesting and disinfection unit' ['Entwesungs- und Desinfektionsanlage'], as it was called in Nazi jargon. This was close to the mass extermination installations in Bunker II and Crematoria IV and V.[60]

In the 'saunas', the inmates were forced to get undressed. If there was not enough room – after particularly large transports, for example – they had to get undressed outside, even in freezing temperatures. Any remaining valuables and money they were carrying on their person were taken away from them. All hair, including pubic hair, was cut off, often with blunt scissors, causing painful injuries. Then the inmates were showered with cold or hot water before being given other clothing, which was often dirty, lousy, ripped or too large or too small. Finally a number was tattooed, usually on the left forearm.[61] From then on, these numbers replaced the person's name. For the 'master race', they were no longer persons. When summoned by an SS man, they had to step forward six paces, stand to attention and report – for example, as follows: 'Inmate 20034 obediently reporting' ['Häftling 20034 meldet sich gehorsam zur Stelle'].[62] The 'disinfesting and disinfection' of the reprieved inmates was carried out at great speed. They were bombarded with orders and insults in German, which they often failed to understand, resulting in beatings by the SS and kapos.[63] Sometimes, further selections were made in the 'saunas' and pregnant women who had not been detected before were sent to the gas chambers.[64]

# Children of Many Languages

From 1940 onwards, children and young people from all parts of Europe were deported to Auschwitz. This can be seen from original documents from the Nazi camp authorities; illegal copies of reports, memos and other writings; and numerous testimonies by former inmates.

BOYS FROM TARNÓW A large number of Polish secondary school pupils – most likely aged 15 and over – were already deported on the first major transport from Tarnów in mid-June 1940. The incomplete name lists do not specify precise dates of birth. The transport also included members of a youth group who had illegally distributed anti-German pamphlets and passed on news from Allied radio stations.[1]

JANEK MANDELBAUM arrived in a transport to Blechhammer via the forced labour camp Fünfteichen (Miłoszyce koło Wrocławia), a satellite camp of Gross-Rosen concentration camp.

In 1939–40, Oberschlesische Hydrierwerke AG began constructing a factory for synthetic oil in Blechhammer (Blachownia). The town was to the west of Częstochowa. Slave labourers, concentration camp inmates and prisoners of war were used to enlarge and operate the factory. The area was surrounded by a dense network of camps, including several special 'Jewish camps'. The inmates came from fifteen European countries, and around 70 per cent were Polish Jews.

On 1 April 1944, Blechhammer officially became one of the numerous satellite camps of Auschwitz. After it was taken over by the SS, they had a crematorium built in which inmates who had died as a result of the slave labour or maltreatment, or had starved or been hanged, were incinerated. Sick and elderly inmates were regularly selected and sent to Auschwitz-Birkenau, where they were almost all gassed.[2]

Janek had to wear a striped uniform in Blechhammer. 'I was not allowed to keep any personal belongings', even shoes. Instead, he was given wooden clogs. 'I could hardly walk in them, let alone run.' His feet were soon chafed sore. He had neither socks nor underwear. The hygiene conditions were disastrous: everything in the camp was dirty and stank to high heaven, particularly in the latrines, 'where we had to do our business without toilet paper'. He had no soap, toothbrush or towel, and everything was full of lice: the bunk beds, clothing, all parts of the body.

The inmates were housed in wooden barracks, usually with six dormitories, each holding thirty to forty people. They had to sleep on wooden bunk beds. The first 'soup' that Janek was served the following day was mainly hot water. And it smelled awful. 'I could hardly keep it down.' There were morning and evening roll calls every day. If the numbers were not right, the inmates had to remain standing where they were. While the missing inmates were looked for, the guards beat the others, taunted them and made them perform punishment exercises. Following the morning roll call, they had to set off for work. After marching 5 kilometres through the woods, Janek was close to collapse. Walking was a 'torture in these impossible wooden clogs'. He had to perform different types of slave labour. They had to fell trees in the woods and dig up the stumps. 'That was really backbreaking work.' But he survived.

The inmates had to work on average ten to twelve hours. With the march to work and back and the roll calls, they were busy sixteen hours a day.

After the first day of work, Janek wondered in alarm: 'How am I meant to hold out?' A further difficulty was the completely inadequate food and hygiene. 'And the constant beatings from the kapos and guards.' He made a resolution: 'I'll work as hard as I can', because he realized that 'otherwise I won't survive very long'. He had already demonstrated during the forced labour in Sławków that he was capable. There had been no complaints. In Blechhammer as well, he had to make sure that he was 'useful'.

Janek wanted to see his father and mother, sister and brother, again. He missed them terribly. He kept on thinking: 'Where are they now, how are they?' Thinking of his family gave him strength: 'More than anything, I just wanted my old life back again.'

He gradually got used to life in the camp, in spite of the great difficulties. He ate everything, tried to keep as clean as possible and worked hard. But he knew that there was always the possibility of something unexpected happening. A kapo could beat him so hard with his truncheon that he remained on the ground. Or he could get sick: diarrhoea, tuberculosis and pneumonia were rife. 'We all looked enviously at the guard dogs, because they ate much better than the slop we had.' There was no medical care worthy of the name. 'Death had many faces in the camp.'

JEWISH CHILDREN FROM SOSNOWIEC On 15 August 1942, a transport arrived in Auschwitz from Sosnowiec near Katowice, with around 2,000 Jewish children, women and men. After the selection, 75 women were tattooed with the numbers 17147 to 17221, and 27 men with the numbers 59018 to 59044. The other 1,898 people, including apparently all of the children, were gassed.[3]

FIRST TRANSPORT FROM THERESIENSTADT On 28 October 1942, the first transport arrived from Theresienstadt, with 1,866 Jewish children, women and men. It became increasingly clear that for most of the 150,000 inmates, Theresienstadt was just a transit station on the way to extermination.[4] After the selection, 215 men and 32 women with the numbers 71060 to 71274 (men) and 23275 to 23306 (women) were transferred to the camp. The other 1,619 people, including apparently all of the children, were murdered.[5]

NINETY BOYS FROM ZAMOŚĆ At the end of 1942, the German occupiers began to evict the Polish inhabitants of the Zamość region of present-day south-east Poland. Around 110,000 people, including some 30,000 children, had to give way to 'German colonists'.[6] Two transports, on 13 and 16 December 1942, brought 718 children, women and men from Zamość to Auschwitz.[7]

According to *Auschwitz Chronicle*, a further transport with Poles and Jews evicted from the Zamość region arrived on 5 February 1943. After selection, 282 men and 301 women were transferred to the camp. The other 417 people were gassed.[8]

Other boys from the three transports were killed by lethal injection on 23 February 1943. Former inmate Stanisław Głowna explained in 1946: 'In winter 1942/43 Rapportführer Palitzsch brought two boys from Birkenau, who came ... from the Zamość region. They were taken first to Block 11 [of the Main Camp] and then on the next day to Block

20, where they were both given lethal [phenol] injections by Pańszczyk [on 21 January 1943].[9] The boys were Mieczysław Rycaj and Tadeusz Rycyk.' A month later, the other 39 boys were killed by injection by Unterscharführer Scherpe.[10]

Mieczysław and Tadeusz were 8 and 9 years old. The other boys were aged between 13 and 17.[11]

KATHE LASNIK On 1 December 1942, 532 Jewish children, women and men from Norway arrived at the camp. After selection, 186 men with the numbers 79064 to 79249 were transferred to the camp. The other 346 were gassed.[12]

One of those murdered was the Jewish girl Kathe Lasnik, 15 years old. She had been arrested in Oslo five days previously. With her parents Elias and Dora Lasnik and her sister Anna, she was put on the German troop ship *Donau* in Oslo harbour. The ship brought them and the other Jewish deportees to Stettin. From there, they were taken by train to Auschwitz.[13] The transport also contained Kai Feinberg, not quite 21 years old, with his mother, father, sister, stepbrother and many relatives.[14] He survived Auschwitz. In January 1946, he reported that 'all of the women and children from our transport disappeared directly in the gas chamber around twenty minutes after our arrival in Birkenau'.[15]

The remaining men were 'quickly inspected by an SS doctor and the older and weaker men separated from the stronger ones'. The men considered unfit for work suffered the same fate as the women and children. 'Among them was my 15-year-old stepbrother.'[16]

Espen Søby reconstructed the life story of Kathe Lasnik in his book *Kathe – Deportiert aus Norwegen*. The girl's farewell letter that she was able to write to her class says: 'Thank you for everything. Now we won't see one another anymore. Tonight we were arrested.'[17]

JÜRGEN LOEWENSTEIN 'Paderborn labour camp will be closed and you will be transported to another labour camp in the East', Jürgen and his comrades were informed at the end of February 1943. 'That's OK. We'll go somewhere else and work there', thought Jürgen.

'The time has come, we're all in good spirits and everything is working out. We haven't been told much. Otherwise everything's OK. If I can …' The letter stops in mid-sentence. Words written by Jürgen on 1

March 1943, the date of the transport on a postcard, already franked and addressed to a friend of the family in Berlin. He had thrown it out of the hole in the cattle wagon without a return address. 'An order-loving German picked it up and as it was addressed and franked as it should be, he posted it in the letterbox.' It was stamped the same day at the post office in Detmold.

Two transports with at least 3,000 Jewish children, women and men left Berlin and arrived in Auschwitz on 3 March 1943. After selection, 585 men and 309 women were given numbers. The others, at least 2,106 people, were gassed.[18]

Among the deportees was the writer Gertrud Kolmar.[19] Traces of her were lost in Auschwitz. In her poem *The Great Day of Lamentation*, she wrote:

In cities, people crumpled to their knees,
Their prayers a stammering, terrified drone.
Elsewhere many a figure stood alone,
Gesturing madly, wailing among the trees.

Among those transferred to the camp was the 17-year-old Jürgen Loewenstein. He had the inmate number 104983 tattooed on his left forearm. He had been deported with ninety-eight other inmates on 1 March from the labour camp Am Grünen Weg 86 in Paderborn, where he had been forced to work for the city.[20] The transport passed through Berlin, where he was born.

The Nazis decided that the Jews who had not been deported until that time and had worked as forced labourers in Berlin armaments companies, for example, or for the city of Paderborn, should now be sent to their death. Between 1 and 12 March alone, six transports left Berlin for Auschwitz.[21] Jürgen Loewenstein describes how his group confidently stepped down from the wagon when they arrived at the camp. 'We formed a group with the madrichim, who were much older, in the middle and marched towards the end of the ramp.' When they reached a group of SS men, one of them shouted snappily: 'Paderborn work group'. 'We were loaded onto trucks, and no one was separated.'

The SS took them to the IG Farben plant in Auschwitz-Monowitz, also called Auschwitz III. At the time the largest company in Germany, with headquarters in Frankfurt am Main, it had been formed from a merger of the most important German chemical companies, such as BASF and Agfa, and was in the process of building a factory there for synthetic rubber ('Buna') and fuel for the war economy. Tens of thousands of inmates were used, of whom over 25,000 died as a result of the inhuman living and working conditions. The SS collected their wages: 4 reichsmarks per day for a skilled worker, 3 for an unskilled labourer.[22]

The first days in Auschwitz-Monowitz were the hardest for Jürgen and his comrades. 'We barely recognized one another, standing naked and shaved bare in the cold.' At the roll call at 5 a.m. on the second day, Benny Stein, one of their madrichim, was missing. 'Under his bunk was a pair of leather shoes and a note: "I was in Sachsenhausen. I won't make it. Give the shoes to the person who needs them most. I'm sorry …".' Benny Stein had walked barefoot in the night into the electrified fence.

Soon the first members of the group got sick. But they tried to stick together. 'We had the advantage that we already knew one another.' They gave the sick some of their bread rations so that they would recover their strength.

After about a month, Jürgen became feverish. He was transferred from the inmate sick bay in Monowitz to one of the blocks for the sick in the Main Camp, Auschwitz I.[23] When he began to recover, he remained in the Main Camp and was put in a kommando levelling the road nearby. The others from the Paderborn group all remained in Monowitz.

One day, Jürgen overheard a snippet of conversation between two SS men, saying that labourers were need for metalworking in a satellite camp. 'I applied and was taken.'

After around six weeks, he was transferred to the Eintrachthütte camp 50 kilometres away in Świętochłowice. This Auschwitz satellite camp had been established in May 1943. Apart from Polish and French forced labourers and Soviet prisoners of war, there were many Jews, some of whom had arrived on special trains from Auschwitz and were used to enlarge the camp, and later in the manufacture of anti-aircraft guns.[24] Jürgen helped with the assembly of flak guns. Although he worked twelve hours a day, the conditions were better than in the Main Camp. Above all, he no longer had to survive on starvation rations.

Jürgen came into contact in the camp with civilian workers. Once he spoke with a German foreman, who asked him why he was in the camp.

Jürgen replied, 'Because I'm a Jew', whereupon the man replied: 'Don't tell me that! What did you do wrong? Who did you murder? What did you steal?' Jürgen repeated: 'I'm only here because I'm a Jew, like many others.' The man said: 'I don't believe you.' 'Even people who worked with us couldn't and wouldn't face the truth. They thought that the people interned in concentration camps were professional criminals.'

HERBERT ADLER In March 1943, it was the turn of the Sinti family Adler in the 'Gypsy' camp at Kruppstrasse in Frankfurt am Main. They were also transported in cattle wagons. 'Sixty to eighty people were crammed into each wagon.' They received nothing to eat or drink for two days. 'Then we stopped somewhere. We were given bread and water. But we weren't allowed to get out. Everyone needed to relieve themselves. We did it in the wagon. There was no choice.'

The entire group was put in a section of the camp at Auschwitz-Birkenau without selection, which was unusual. The entry in *Auschwitz Chronicle* listing the day-to-day events in Auschwitz-Birkenau for 13 March is as follows: 'A transport of Gypsies arrives from Germany. 640 men and boys are given Nos. Z2200 to Z2839, and 713 women and girls get Nos. Z2480 to Z3192.'[25]

Herbert Adler, 14 years old, had the number Z2784 tattooed on his left forearm. From then on, he had to report solely with this number.

Auschwitz-Birkenau was divided into different fenced-off sections. The fence was electrified. Every camp had its own gate and watch-towers. Apart, for example, from the Women's and Men's Camps, there were at different times a Theresienstadt Family Camp [Theresienstädter Familienlager] and a 'Gypsy' Family Camp [Zigeunerfamilienlager].[26] The 'Gypsy' Family Camp and some of the other sections were divided by rows of barracks on either side with a gravel path running between. Like some of the other sections, the 'Gypsy' Family Camp consisted of thirty-two stable-like barracks, originally designed by German architects for fifty-two horses, but now housing 1,000 inmates and more.[27] This camp contained, mainly, deported Sinti and Roma families.[28] The first major 'gassing action' from this part of the camp took place on 23 March 1943: 1,700 Polish Roma children, women and men from Białystok, without numbers, were taken from Barracks 20 and 21 in the 'Gypsy' Camp and killed in the gas chambers of Auschwitz-Birkenau.[29]

The first transport with 'gypsies' from Germany arrived in Auschwitz-Birkenau on 26 February 1943.[30] By 21 July 1944, a total of 20,943 Sinti and Roma from at least sixteen countries were registered in the camp, including around 13,000 from Germany and Austria. Added to this were the 1,700 nonregistered Sinti and Roma. Thus, altogether, at least 22,643 Sinti and Roma were deported to Auschwitz-Birkenau as 'gypsies'. Around half were children and juveniles. Very few survived.[31]

Herbert Adler's father was detailed to help build a road in Birkenau. But he wasn't used to such hard work, having previously worked as a post office clerk. The constant beatings and maltreatment soon took their toll. His skull had been fractured by a rifle butt. Herbert watched his father, 'such a strong man', to whom he had looked up, as the strength was quickly drained out of him. After around six months, his father became so sick that he died as a result of the hard labour and maltreatment. 'If I'd been able to at the time, I would have beaten those responsible for his death with an iron bar. I would have beaten them to death.'

'Our mother would always tell us: "Don't do this! Don't do that! Watch out!" She was scared for us.' She didn't want anything to happen to them. Every morning Herbert watched a truck driving through the camp, taking away those who had died or been killed in the night. 'They were carried like sacks of potatoes and thrown onto the truck.'

'We lads made a ball out of rags, which we played with sometimes. Once the ball went near the electrified fence. One of the boys wanted to fetch it. Everywhere there were these watchtowers with SS men with machine guns. I watched them shoot the boy. He was 8 or 9 years old. We ran away and said to each other: "Let's not play football here anymore."'

'We could also hear the screams from the gas chambers. They weren't far away. When they closed the doors, we didn't hear it anymore. We also saw them carrying out the dead.' Once Herbert wanted to 'organize' a couple of potatoes from a wooden crate, like other children had done. He was caught, laid over a trestle and given twenty strokes with a cudgel. 'I still have the scars', he mentioned over and over again.

They were always crazy with hunger. Herbert thought: 'This is hell. I'll never get out.' One day, an SS man spotted him and asked him if he could play the guitar. Herbert said that he could. The SS man ordered him to come to the SS office in a separate building at the entrance to the 'Gypsy' Camp. He got a guitar for him, which had probably belonged previously to one of the Sinti or Roma deported to Auschwitz. 'I had to play popular songs, and the SS men sang along to them. That was their evening entertainment.' The SS man made him his odd-job-man ['Kalfaktor'] and personal slave. He had to polish his boots, iron his trousers and clean his quarters. 'In return I got something to eat, also bread and sausage, which I was able to take to my mother and brothers and sisters.'

'KALFAKTOR' The 'Kalfaktoren' were also known as 'Pipel' or 'Piepel', particularly when referring to young or very young slaves. Apart from SS men, some of the kapos appointed by the SS used these errand boys or cleaners. Wiesław Kielar, one of the first Polish inmates to be deported to Auschwitz, with the number 290, saw a good deal in his five years of internment. He worked, among other things, as a plumber and corpse carrier. He wrote later about the 'Gypsy' Camp:

> The gypsy sick bay was mostly looked after by doctors and nurses from the Main Camp and by some women from the Women's Camp. It was easy to communicate with them. It was sufficient to ask one of the children who were always running around near the wire and they would fetch the person you were looking for. The children liked to do these errands because they knew they would be rewarded. They were hungry, abandoned, incredibly dirty and ragged.[32]

There was a thin line between getting protection and more to eat and being badly maltreated. It should be noted that girls as well as boys ran the risk of being sexually abused. Halina Birenbaum from Warsaw, inmate number 48693, who was interned in Auschwitz-Birkenau and elsewhere, wrote in her book *Hope Is the Last to Die* about a block elder whom she encountered at the age of 14: 'Once she … sat me on her lap, began asking me where I came from, how old I was, what my name was. Then she announced she would make me her pipel … and she suddenly kissed me. I caught the smell of alcohol, drew back in disgust and got off her lap.'[33]

In her memoirs, Flora Neumann from Hamburg, inmate number 74559, who was deported to Auschwitz in 1943, recalled a Jewish girl from Poland called Wanda:

An SS man said that her hair shouldn't be cut. What did the girl think? Was it gratitude or fear? She began to sing.... Or was the 15-year-old being sarcastic? The SS man took her with him. What became of her? ... We never saw her again.

The SS men put many beautiful girls, half-children, into the brothel. When they were worn out, there was the gas chamber.[34]

HEINZ KOUNIO On 20 March 1943, 2,800 children, women and men arrived in Auschwitz in cattle wagons from Thessaloniki. After the selection, 417 men and 192 women were transferred to the camp and given the inmate numbers 109371 to 109787 (men) and 38721 to 38912 (women). The other 2,191 people were killed in the gas chamber.[35]

Among the boys to be transferred was Heinz Kounio. He had the number 109565 tattooed on his left forearm, his father the number 109564, his mother 38911, and his sister, a year older than he was, 38912.

'I was just 15 and had started to imagine my future life. I was still innocent. This was to change brutally.'

'Get out, get out, you pigs, you filthy dogs.' That was how Heinz Kounio, his sister Erika, his mother Hella and his father Salvator were welcomed in Auschwitz. 'It was around 11 p.m.' Everyone was afraid. As the orders were shouted in German, no one knew what was going on. 'This was the first transport of Greek Jews to Auschwitz. It contained in particular the Jews who had previously lived in the Baron Hirsch district of Thessaloniki – poor dockers, but also skilled workers, who had loaded and unloaded the ships. They didn't speak German and couldn't understand the orders. And the German SS wanted order above all!'

An SS man, 'tall, fat, with a whip', noticed the Kounio family and asked if they spoke German. Heinz's father said that he did.

Not only my wife and I but also our children speak very good German. The SS man said: 'You four are to be here every evening when transports arrive. You will be interpreters.' We started our new 'jobs' right away. 'Tell the people that they should form two groups, women here, men there. Those who can't walk should go to where the trucks are.' Everything had to be done at the double. The SS separated the elderly, the sick, babies and children. Lots of them had to climb onto the trucks. When one was full, it drove off immediately. The others were marched off. There were heart-rending scenes.

Women and men were separated, mothers from their babies and children. … And in the dry air there was a terrible stink. It smelled and tasted like burnt meat.

On the first night, Heinz was also separated from his mother and sister. Fortunately, he was able to stay with his father. The two of them, along with the others, were sorted from their transport and taken to a wooden barracks. They had to wait outside all night. They pressed up close to one another to keep warm. At dawn, they were ordered to throw the possessions they had brought with them into sacks. 'Our jewellery and gold coins in the first ones, our cigarettes and matches in the second and our ID papers in the third.' Then we were forced to undress. All of our body hair was cut or shaved off. During this time we were beaten continuously. Then we showered. 'The water was icy cold. We had to stand still. The SS monitored the scene with batons in their hands. Then the cold water was turned off and boiling hot water turned on. We were all scalded. We cried and the SS men laughed. Thoughts of revenge kept forming in my mind.' After the 'bath', we were given other clothes: 'The shirts were too small or too big, some jackets had no sleeves, and others no back.'

First of all, they were transferred to the quarantine block. They were greeted by a brutal block elder, an inmate standing in for the SS. 'He quickly showed us his "skill".' He beat the back of one of the inmates until his baton broke. There was another incident later. A man called Chalvatzis, who had come with Heinz and his family from Thessaloniki, missed the evening roll call. Completely exhausted from the long journey, he was found asleep by the block elder, who started beating him up terribly. Then Chalvatzis was taken to the crematorium.

'That was the first murder we saw in Auschwitz.' Heinz and his father asked themselves: 'How will we survive? Will we see our loved ones again?' Afterwards, they both worked as interpreters and in the tailor shop kommando making clothing for the inmates, darning socks or modifying clothes taken from transports of Jews. The families of the SS men who guarded the camp and maltreated and murdered the inmates needed clothing, uniforms and bedding.

'I often went to sleep hungry. We were required to live off a bit of bread and a thin soup. Every day I thanked God that I would see the next day.' On the other hand, Heinz was in despair, because every day he and his fellow inmates heard and saw terrible things. And whenever the roll call lasted longer than usual, Heinz was frozen. He would ask himself: 'Is there going to be another selection? Will I be chosen to stay? My father? Or are we both for the gas chamber?'

Every day new transports arrived in Auschwitz from all over Europe. On average only around 20 per cent – the young, strong and healthy people – were transferred to the camp as fit for work. Thus, the SS sent around 80 per cent – babies, children, pregnant women, the sick and elderly – to an immediate death in the gas chambers.[36] It depended on the labour requirements at the different times in the camp's existence. Frequently, a much higher percentage of people were gassed straightaway.

To create space for 'unused and fresh' people, there was never a day without new selections. The SS liked to do this especially on Shabbat, the seventh day of Creation, on which no work is allowed. It starts on Friday evening when the first three stars are visible in the sky or when it is no longer possible to distinguish between a white and a black thread. Shabbat lasts until Saturday evening.

> On these days in particular, we were extremely fearful of our fate at the roll call. The shrill voices of the SS penetrated deep. Everyone wondered whether they looked weak. We turned to our neighbours: 'What do I look like?' The weak and sick were selected for the gas chambers. A small gesture by the SS officer or doctor was sufficient: 'To the left' meant death; 'to the right' meant survival.

Every day, Heinz Kounio still shudders when he thinks about it. He is convinced: 'I survived seven selections. At the last one I was very weak and full of indescribable fear. My firm belief in God helped me to stay alive.'

Once a week the inmates were taken to a block where there were showers. They had to leave their clothes behind so they were completely naked. 'There were no towels to dry ourselves with. The Germans thought they weren't necessary for us. The air, whether warm or cold, would dry our bodies and hair.' The block was inspected once a week by an SS man. He examined every inmate 'extremely thoroughly'.

Those who weren't clean got twenty-five strokes on their back and behind with a club. The Germans didn't care whether we had the possibility at all of keeping clean.

If a flea was found in a single inmate, the entire block was disinfected. We had to undress, and our clothes were cleaned in special ovens. Then we had to shower with icy cold water. We didn't get our clothes back until the following day so we spent the entire night naked. And we didn't have anything to cover ourselves with. Many people died of pneumonia as a result.

Extreme discipline had to be kept. They were only allowed to address an SS man from a distance of at least 6 metres. Orders were not to be questioned under any circumstances. 'We had to look straight ahead during inspections. We weren't allowed to turn our heads to the left or right. We had to stand to attention completely immobile, like statues.'

Heinz rarely had a conversation with the other inmates. They had to be careful at all times and ask themselves: 'Who can I trust?' He soon realized that if he was to survive he should not have too much to do with the others. 'I had to become impervious to the suffering of other inmates, to become "inhuman" myself.'

'I have to get out alive', thought Heinz. He felt a duty: 'I want to report later what I have seen and experienced here.' So that the world would find out about the crimes of the German 'master race'.

'I had injuries all over my body from the beatings I received. I was constantly hungry, and the bunk was cold. And then there was the hard labour every day … '

Heinz made friends with a 15-year-old boy from Belgium by the name Leon Favian. 'His parents had been murdered by the Germans.' Leon was completely alone. They decided: 'If we get out of here alive, we will go to Greece together, and Leon will live near us.'

After around three months, Heinz and his father Salvator learned that his mother Hella and sister Erika were still alive. That gave them new hope and strength to get through every day. The daughter and mother worked as interpreters for the transports arriving from Greece and as clerks in the registration office. Here they had to draw up lists of inmates who had died of 'natural causes'.[37] In Auschwitz, it was not possible to distinguish between a 'natural' and a violent death. In view of the conditions in the camp, there were not many deaths that were not violent.

It was only after around four months that the boy saw his mother and sister again by chance. 'They were 100 metres away. But I recognized them immediately. I didn't wave to them. That could have had terrible consequences for me and for them. Finally, seventeen months after our arrival, I was able to speak briefly to my mother and sister for a moment when we were not being watched.' But he often looked out in vain for them. And when he saw them, there was practically never an opportunity to talk, because the SS were present. These moments enraged him.

1,196 JEWISH CHILDREN FROM BIAŁYSTOK On 7 October 1943, 1,196 children[38] and 53 carers from Theresienstadt were transported to Auschwitz-Birkenau and gassed on arrival.[39] These children had been transferred to Theresienstadt from the ghetto in Białystok on 24 August 1943. At the time, there were around 1,200 children in the group. Izio Trofimowski, the youngest child, was barely 4 years old. On the way to Theresienstadt, 20 adult supervisors and 3 women with their children were transferred to Auschwitz and gassed there. The children who arrived in Theresienstadt were kept strictly apart from the other inmates in special barracks outside camp. The SS assigned 53 doctors and other carers already in Theresienstadt to look after the children.[40]

H. G. Adler, who was deported to Theresienstadt in February 1942 and to Auschwitz in October 1944, chronicled the events in Theresienstadt and recalled the Jewish children from Białystok:

'Soon after their arrival, the children, who had already experienced all the Jewish suffering in the East in their home, Białystok, were taken in groups to the disinfection bath, where frightening scenes occurred. The children knew about the gas chambers and did not want to enter the bath chambers; they screamed desperately, 'No, no! Gas!'[41] In Białystok the children had heard that there were gas chambers disguised as showers. Inmates who had escaped from Treblinka had made this known in the ghetto in Białystok.[42]

In spite of the secrecy, the rumour spread in Theresienstadt that the children from Białystok were intended for an exchange. Their destination was Palestine or Switzerland. Evidence for this was that the children received double rations, new shoes and clothes – and the fact that the 53 doctors and carers had to confirm in writing that they would not spread any stories of atrocities.

The children improved visibly. After six weeks, their departure with their carers was announced. But instead of going abroad, their transport went on 5 October 1943 directly to the gas chambers in Auschwitz-Birkenau. It is clear that at no time had Nazi Germany intended to spare these Jewish children.[43]

DAGMAR FANTLOVÁ, LYDIA HOLZNEROVÁ, YEHUDA BACON AND DÁŠA FRIEDOVÁ At the end of 1943, Dagmar Fantlová, Lydia Holznerová and Yehuda Bacon were among the 2,504 Jews *einwaggoniert* in Theresienstadt, of whom 981 men and boys and 1,510 women and girls reached their destination, Auschwitz-Birkenau, alive on 16 December.[44]

Someone looked out and said, 'We're in Auschwitz', reported Dagmar Lieblová (*née* Fantlová). 'I'd already heard this name but didn't know what it meant. I had a terrible premonition. Then someone said: "We'll get out here and go to Birkenau." My family didn't know that Auschwitz and Birkenau were the same thing.' They had to walk from the freight station in Auschwitz to Birkenau. It was dark. They were put in large wooden barracks, in stables, in the Theresienstadt Family Camp. Their luggage had to be left behind.

'Various people from previous transports approached us. One woman wanted me to give her my pullover. I don't know whether it was a friend of my mother's but we gave her various things.' They had to go to another block for tattooing. While they were waiting in a long line, a friend came to Dagmar's mother and said: 'Have you heard that Mrs Reimanvová is a widow?' Irene Fantlová was shocked. 'It was her brother. But the woman didn't know that.' He had already been deported from Theresienstadt to Birkenau in September 1943.

Dagmar had the number 70788 tattooed on her arm. When they left the barracks, someone said to them: 'Those who have a number will remain in the camp.' They didn't know what that meant. Then they all had to go to the 'sauna'. One woman said: 'I hope you all come back.' The new arrivals had no idea what that meant either. The 'sauna' took a long time. Dagmar was thirsty: 'I drank from a tap. And then I saw the notice "No drinking – epidemic risk".' They had to get undressed and were given other clothes, more like rags. When they got back to the family camp, the woman to whom they had given their clothes returned everything to them.

The first familiar face Růžena Holznerová recognized in the family camp was her brother-in-law. She said to her daughters Lydia and Věra: 'He'll help us.'

'Suddenly, there was Uncle Max in our barracks. He brought us hot tea, which he had organized from somewhere.' So as to be able to take as much with them as possible from Theresienstadt, they had all put on two layers of clothing. Now the uncle told them to do what the Fantlová family had already been advised to do: 'Take off the pullovers, jackets, trousers, socks, cap, take off everything and give it to me.' Lydia didn't want to. 'I'll be cold.' But her mother was firm: 'Don't argue, do what your uncle says.' And so the others did so too. There followed the usual registration procedure in Birkenau. They were taken to the 'sauna', had to get undressed and hand in their clothes, were tattooed – Lydia's number was 70988 – were given clothing, which usually didn't fit and was dirty and torn. Afterwards, Lydia got her things back from Uncle Max. She had lots of spare clothing, which proved essential to survive a winter in Auschwitz-Birkenau.

After a while, Lydia and her sister were put in a barracks crowded with girls and young women. They were able to see their parents almost every day.

Yehuda Bacon observed the following scene right after his arrival in Auschwitz:

> I saw a Russian who had obtained a piece of salami from somewhere and was eating it. An SS man hit him with a truncheon and yelled: 'Spit it out, leave it!' He snatched it from him, but the man refused to let go of the piece he had already bitten in to. And I didn't understand why he wouldn't take this bit out of his mouth. He was beaten atrociously. But he swallowed the piece. Later, I understood what hunger could make a person do.

The boy spent the first night in a block with around 1,000 inmates. He met acquaintances from Theresienstadt. They told him: 'No one gets out of here, except up the chimney.' The next day, Yehuda met inmates from other parts of Birkenau for the first time, who told him terrible things about Auschwitz-Birkenau. He was tattooed with the number 168194. Initially, he and around 40 other children were put in a block which contained only old people. Many of them were starving or dying of exhaustion. 'Ten to twenty people died every day in my block.' They simply left them for two or three days so as to obtain their food rations. The block had around 500 people in it at this time. Seven children had to sleep together in a bunk. 'I remember that it was cold and that those sleeping on the outside swapped positions every two hours with those in the middle.'

Dáša Friedová arrived in the family camp four days after her friend Dagmar Lieblová. They too were taken first to the 'sauna'. They all had to get undressed and had everything taken from them. 'Suddenly we were just a pack of naked bodies.' They felt uncomfortable and were in deep shock. Dáša had the number 72726 tattooed on her left forearm.

The girl was given ragged dirty clothing that didn't fit her. She wasn't allowed to keep her shoes either. Instead, she was given wooden clogs. To keep them from slipping off, she had to hold on tight with her toes. 'This meant that I gradually got hammer toes.'

Dáša had a 'huge surprise' when she got to the family camp. 'I was reunited with Dagmar. I was amazed. It was the last thing I expected. We were both overjoyed.' And for some time they remained together with their mothers in the same barracks.

'B II B', as the Family Camp was called in SS jargon, was designed to deceive those left in Theresienstadt and the inhabitants of the annexed and occupied parts of Czechoslovakia, and also, without doubt, to fool organizations such as the International Red Cross. The aim of this section of the camp was clear: 'This is what the Red Cross delegates will be shown.' As it happened, the Red Cross never came to visit.[45]

The inmates of the Family Camp thus did not undergo selection on arrival. Families were separated by sex and housed in different barracks, but in a section where they could see one another. While Jews in extermination camps were normally forbidden from writing letters, they were actually ordered to do so by the SS at certain times. Yehuda was given a predated postcard on which he was instructed to write: 'I am well. How are you? Send us parcels.' But one group who had come from the L 417 juvenile room in Theresienstadt used the postcards to send a different message. They all started with 'Dear Moti', which in Hebrew means 'my death', and ended with the phrase, 'and that, dear Moti, is the end!'

Yehuda Bacon later discovered that the message was understood. They were instructed to put 'Birkenau labour camp near Neu-Berun' as the sender's address. The name Auschwitz was not to be mentioned, not even on the postage stamp. The cards were taken to Berlin and stamped 'Berlin-Charlottenburg'.

The card that Dagmar sent on 8 January 1944 to Fany Holická, her grandparents' former housekeeper, arrived and has been kept: 'We miss you all very much. How are aunt Janu Stryhal and Cukrs? They should write often, you too, dearest Fanynka. We long to hear from you. I'm living with mum and Ita [her sister's nickname] ... We are also [together] with father every day. We look forward to hearing from Janu and you all. Lots of kisses.'

At first, there was nothing for them to do in Birkenau. 'We had to attend roll calls for hours and were given something unidentifiable to eat. There was never enough.' Not only Dáša, but all of them, were constantly hungry. 'Sometimes we passed the time playing cat's cradle with strips of cloth tied together. I don't know where they were from or whether they belonged to someone we knew.'

The 'washroom' was in a separate block, a series of taps fitted on a long pipe. The water ran into a small channel. They had no soap, no flannel, no towel. The water was always freezing cold, even in winter. The latrines were just as bad: 'There was a row of holes on rough cast concrete. We had to sit close together like hens on a perch. Without any privacy or toilet paper. There was also a wretched smell and in winter it was unbearably cold.' Soon after her arrival in the family camp, Dagmar's mother volunteered to empty the toilet buckets in return for an extra ration of soup. 'I helped her sometimes. It was very unpleasant. But I did it.'

Lydia Holznerová complained one day to her mother: 'I'm hungry.' 'What am I meant to do? You know that I can't help you. Go and drink some water.' Towards evening, a woman came up to Lydia and said: 'Never ask your mother that again. She has enough to worry about. That's too much.' Once the 14-year-old said to her mother that she had seen a desperate man 'electrocute himself on the fence'. 'He's no hero', she replied. 'Heroism is living and surviving.'

Her mother, Růžena Holznerová, had different jobs in Birkenau that her 60-year-old husband was no longer capable of doing. 'He struggled to survive in Birkenau. He went to pieces, mentally at first and then physically. Within a very short time he became an old man.'

One name that comes up repeatedly in the descriptions by the children of Auschwitz is Fredy Hirsch. While still interned in Theresienstadt, he had been leader of the youth welfare and had looked after children. In Birkenau, he also did everything possible to improve the conditions for children. On his initiative, as Lydia Holznerová, Dagmar Lieblová and Yehuda Bacon all reported independently, small children were looked after during the day by a few women in Block 29 of the Family Camp and 8- to 16-year-olds in Block 31. As in Theresienstadt, they were divided into groups led by a madrich, a teacher, who gave them lessons, told stories and taught them songs.

Yehuda was in Block 31. The roll call ordered by the SS took place in this block. In winter or when it was raining, this was often a life-saving advantage.

Fredy Hirsch managed somehow to install a small library in Block 31, although it was forbidden to own books in Auschwitz. The selection was small. The children read the books several times: '*A Short History of the World* by H. G. Wells, *A General Introduction to Psychoanalysis* and *The Interpretation of Dreams* by Sigmund Freud, and a few children's books.' During the day Dagmar, Dáša and Lydia were also allowed to go to the children's block. Lydia's sister Věra was one of the carers.

Children, women and men died every day from the conditions in the Family Camp. All of the children, including Dáša, witnessed it. 'I saw dead people, their lifeless bodies. They were loaded onto carts and taken away.' Of the 5,007 inmates confined to the Family Camp in December 1943, only 3,256 were left alive on 11 May 1944. In just under five months, 1,751 children, women and men had died.[46]

At first, however, Dáša was 'not really sure what was going on in Birkenau'. There was 'always this whispering: What's that smell? Did you hear that someone electrocuted himself on the fence? There's something terrible going on here.' 'I became rudely aware of what was going on early March 1944. I saw men from the September transport being herded onto trucks and driven away. I saw the smoke and the flames coming out of the crematorium chimneys. And there was this terrible penetrating stench.'

Altogether, 3,791 children, women and men from the September 1943 transport from Theresienstadt were gassed in the night of 8–9 March 1944 in Crematoria II and III.[47] Until then, all of the internees, including Dagmar, had hoped that they would somehow manage to hold out. 'Some said that if you had a number, it meant you would stay and not be killed. Others reckoned we'd die anyway. There were lots of different opinions.' Everything changed suddenly after 9 March. Now everyone, including the children, realized that Birkenau was an extermination camp from which there was no escape. Girls and boys from the children's block had been gassed: 'There were now fewer children and carers', but no one spoke about it. Dáša and the other children were in shock: 'We couldn't and didn't want to speak about what we had seen and experienced. It was too terrible.'

At this time, Yehuda worked occasionally as a 'warmer' [Heizer], meaning that he prepared something to eat from the 'special rations'. Parcels, with the most valuable contents removed, addressed to inmates who had died or been murdered in the meantime, were distributed among the children. And so there was sometimes a little extra, even if it was just a soup made from a half-mouldy cake. Once, while he was cooking, the following conversation took place:

'The first serving of soup is ready!'

Looking out of the window at the crematorium: 'They've also finished the first serving there.'

Yehuda: 'We saw the smoke and knew what it meant.' Another time, Yehuda found 'some glass tubes with reichsmarks' in a loaf of bread from one of the parcels. He organized something to eat with them. He was also able to bring some to his parents. 'Sometimes I brought them soup. But my father didn't want any and would say: "You have to eat, there's no hope for us anyway."' He wouldn't even accept a couple of sugar lumps.

In mid-May 1944, further transports from Theresienstadt arrived in Birkenau with 7,503 Jewish children, women and men.[48] As soon as these people arrived at the Family Camp, they were helped by the men and women there, but also by the children. Among them was Dagmar

Fantlová: 'We helped the old people, carrying their luggage to the barracks.'

In early July 1944, the camp commandant ordered a selection in the Theresienstadt Family Camp.[49] 'I think there was an order that women from 16 to 40 and men from 16 to 50 were to be taken somewhere to work. The numbers of those to be selected were called out. My mother was over 40, my father over 50, my sister was 12 and I was just 15.' None of the Fantls were thus selected. But the block elder called out Dagmar's number. Dagmar told her that she was born in 1929. 'No, here it says 1925. You have to go.' Dagmar didn't know what that meant and went to her father, who went to the camp clerk [Lagerschreiber]. But he sent him packing: 'Everyone comes and wants to bribe me. Some want to be made younger or older so they can join some group or other.' Dagmar had to go to the selection. 'I was almost as big as I was later as an adult, still quite good-looking and not totally starved.'

SS Doctor Mengele carried out the selection. 'He assigned me to work.' Dagmar's parents were unhappy. They were afraid they would never see their daughter again. 'My mother could have volunteered, because people under 16 or over 40 were able to apply later for selection.'

Irena Fantlová was 42 at the time. She didn't report but said to Dagmar: 'You're a big girl now. You can look after yourself. But I can't leave Rita alone.' That was the last Dagmar ever heard from her parents or sister.

Dáša Friedová, Dagmar's best friend, also survived the selection. She was 15. Her mother remained in Birkenau and all trace of her was lost. Her father Otto and her sister Sylva had already died in Theresienstadt. In early July, Lydia Holznerová, 14 years old, stood in line for selection with her 22-year-old sister Věra, but wasn't picked in the first round because she was too small and young.

Věra called some young women. They took Lydia with them and went to the block where the selection was taking place. They waited there until the old and frail women went in. 'And then they pushed me in, between two old women. We had to jump over the chimney vent, which ran right through the hut. When it was my turn, I told Mengele my number and jumped. As the two old women were not able to do so, I was listed as fit for work.'

Růžena Holznerová, Lydia's mother, left Auschwitz on a large transport. 'We discovered after the war that she was gassed in another concentration camp.' Yehuda Bacon's sister Hanne was also in the group of those fit for work, but not his mother. Yehuda and Hanne persuaded her to apply again for selection. She managed to slip into the line again, unnoticed by the SS. 'And this time she came through.'

In the mid-1950s, Yehuda Bacon learned from a woman who had been deported with his sister and mother to Stutthof near Danzig that they had both contracted typhoid fever. As a result, they were not given anything to eat and died of hunger, three weeks before the camp was liberated.

Yehuda's father Isidor was 52 at the time of the selection. He remained behind until early July 1944 in the Family Camp, like women with children, the elderly and sick, and others who were not fit for work, including the young Yehuda. He was selected a short time afterwards with around ninety other children between the ages of 12 and 16 from a large group of children and taken to the Men's Camp. SS camp doctor Mengele selected 3,080 of the remaining 9,900 Theresienstadt Jews who had arrived in Birkenau[50] as fit for work. They were transported a few days later to other camps, including Stutthof, Sachsenhausen and Hamburg. The 6,700 to 7,700 children, women and men remaining in Auschwitz-Birkenau were gassed in the nights of 10–11 and 11–12 July. Among them were Lydia Holznerová's father Emil and Yehuda Bacon's father Isidor. Of the 17,517 inmates in this section of the camp, only 1,167 Jews survived.[51]

> When we were taken away from our parents and even when we knew precisely when they would go to the crematorium, none of us was able to weep. Many lost their parents, brothers and sisters, aunts, uncles, most of them their entire families. But the relationship between the remaining children and juveniles suddenly changed. We became close friends. I would have given my last rations to my friend, and he would have done the same for me.

Yehuda was put in the Men's Camp with other children and juveniles. They received special treatment there. They had more food and better clothing and they were not required to work at first. After two weeks, Yehuda was assigned to the 'cart kommando'. Instead of horses, the cart was pulled by twenty children and juveniles. They had to transport blankets, clothing and wood. They went all over the camp.

One day, they were ordered to fetch wood from the crematoria to heat the Men's Camp. It was winter and one of the inmates in the crematorium Sonderkommando told them: 'Kids, because you loaded the cart so quickly, you can warm yourselves a bit. Go into the gas chamber; there's no one there at the moment.' Some of the youths went into the gas chamber in Crematorium II. Yehuda asked the inmates from the Sonderkommando what happened in the crematoria: 'Tell me! Perhaps I'll get out of here one day and I'll write about you.' The inmates from the Sonderkommando laughed and said 'None of us will get out of here', but they nevertheless showed him the installation.

With the curiosity of children, they examined everything. Yehuda recalls: 'We went into the changing room and there were hooks there with numbers.' He asked: 'What happens in this room?' The men from the Sonderkommando explained: 'The people have to get undressed. And one of the SS men says to them: "Hurry up! Your soup will get cold. It's waiting for you."' Yehuda Bacon:

> The people were very hungry, often after a journey lasting several days. Then the SS man continues: 'Make a note of your number and tie your shoes together so that you can find your things again after the shower.' When they were undressed, they were herded into the gas chambers.
>
> Later, we went on to the room and saw a lid. 'The SS man lifts the lid', explained the inmates from the Sonderkommando and then gets the order: 'All ready! Pour in the can.' And the SS man poured in the Zyklon B gas.

Yehuda was often in Crematorium III with the cart kommando. 'We had to load and take away the ashes from the people who had been incinerated. We scattered them on the icy paths in the Women's Camp.'

CHILDREN FROM UKRAINE AND BYELORUSSIA – THE MASSACRE OF PANERIAI (Yiddish Ponar, Polish Ponary) In 1943 and 1944, children from the parts of the former Soviet Union occupied by Germany, in particular Byelorussia and Ukraine, were deported to Auschwitz.[52] German Einsatzgruppen, and the Einsatzkommandos formed from them – mobile killing units accompanied by the Wehrmacht or behind the front lines – were responsible for countless ruthless mass murders. They were energetically supported by the Wehrmacht, police regiments with German and local personnel, and local militias and willing assistants.[53]

These killing units had already been active in Austria (March 1938), Czechoslovakia (October 1938 and March 1939),[54] and in Poland after the invasion on 1 September 1939. From the very first day, Polish Jews were systematically murdered by the Einsatzgruppen, but also by Wehrmacht units.[55]

The four Einsatzgruppen operating after the invasion of the Soviet Union from 22 June 1941 consisted of around 3,000 men. In the first months alone, they and their local henchmen murdered hundreds of thousands of people on the spot, particularly Jews.[56] 'By mid-1942 the majority of the Jewish citizens of the Soviet Union who had fallen into German hands, especially those in the Baltic states, had been murdered.'[57] Moreover, outside of the actual fighting, many hundreds of thousands of non-Jewish citizens of the Soviet Union were shot as 'partisans', 'rabble rousers', 'Communists', 'saboteurs', 'gypsies', 'mentally ill', hostages, and active and passive resistance fighters, or murdered during the burning of entire villages.[58] For example, in the small Lithuanian forest village of Paneriai, twenty minutes' drive from the Lithuanian capital Vilnius, around 70,000 Jewish children, women and men were murdered in huge pits in mass executions by German SS and police units and local collaborators. Almost the entire Jewish population of Vilnius was exterminated in this way. A further 30,000 people, including Soviet prisoners of war and Polish resistance fighters, were executed in the woods of Ponar.[59]

The Polish journalist Kazimierz Sakowicz, who lived in Ponar, witnessed the crime with his own eyes. He wrote down what he saw and heard. On 5 July 1944, he was fired at by unknown Lithuanians and died ten days later as a result of his wounds.[60] In his notes of 2 September 1941, he wrote that there were '4,000 persons; … others claimed it was 4,875 – women and lots of babies…. The people were beaten before they were shot.'[61] This was just one day of many, in the forest of Ponar. Karl Jäger, responsible as head of Einsatzkommando 3 for the murder of Lithuanian Jews,[62] noted in a confidential report that, on 2 September, 817 Jewish children, 2,019 Jewish women and 864 Jewish men were killed by his unit with the aid of Lithuanian henchmen.[63]

Jäger, a member of the SS, proudly stated in his final summary ['Gesamtaufstellung'] up to 1 December 1941: 'I can state today that the aim of solving the Jew problem in Lithuania has been achieved by EK 3. There are no more Jews in Lithuania except for working Jews and their families.'[64] Under his command in Lithuania, 136,421 Jews, 1,064 'Communists', 653 'mentally ill' and 134 'others' were murdered. Among the Jewish victims were 34,464 children and 55,556 women.[65]

'The Song of Ponar' was written as a result of the atrocities committed in 1943 in the ghetto in Vilnius. The music was by the 11-year-old Alek Volkovisky, and the lyrics by the writer and poet Shmerke Kaczerginski:

1.

Quiet, quiet, let's be silent,
Dead are growing here.
They were planted by the tyrant,
See their bloom appear.
All the roads lead to Ponar now,
There are no roads back,
And our father too has vanished,
And with him our luck.

Still, my child, don't cry, my jewel,
Tears no help commands,
Our pain callous people never understand.
Seas and oceans have their order,
Prison also has its border,
But to our plight there is no light,
There is no light.

2.

Spring came to the earth,
And brought us autumn,
If the day is filled with flowers,
It must be only night that sees us.
Now autumn is growing golden on the stalks,
And it is grief that blossoms inside us.

Somewhere a mother is left orphaned,
Her child headed for Ponar.

The Vilija people in prison chains,
Also yoked in anguish.
Now ice floes race through Lithuania,
And empty into the sea.
Somewhere the gloom is breaking,
Suns are shining from the darkness.
Come quickly, horseman!
Your child is calling you!

3.
Hush, hush, spring is swelling with delight.
Around our hearts;
Until the gate falls,
Silent we must be.
Don't be joyful child,
Your smile is treachery for us now.
May the enemy see the spring,
Like a leaf in autumn.

Let the spring flow calmly,
Hush now and be hopeful.
With freedom comes your Daddy,
So sleep, my child, sleep.
Like the free frozen Vilija river,
Like the trees renewed with green.
Freedom's light is already shining,
On your countenance.[66]

LUDA (LUDMILA) BOCHAROVA Children from the former Soviet Union, in particular from Byelorussia and Ukraine, nevertheless ended up, directly or indirectly via Majdanek, in Auschwitz-Birkenau extermination camp. In 1943, for example, there were several transports from Vitebsk in Byelorussia. On 9 September, a train arrived with 1,212 people, and on 22 October another with 739.[67] There were at least 805 children and juveniles in these transports: 370 girls and 435 boys.[68] Several transports also arrived at Auschwitz-Birkenau from the Byelorussian capital Minsk, on 13 March, 18 June and 4 December.[69] Among those on the last transport were at least 60 children: 29 girls and 31 boys.[70]

Ludmila (called Luda by her family) Bocharova, not yet 3 years old, was one of these girls. Together with her 21-year-old mother Anna, she was deported to Auschwitz-Birkenau in an Einsatzkommando transport. Luda, later known in the camp as Lidia, had the number 70072 tattooed on her left forearm. Her mother, Anna Bocharova, had the number 70071.

The girl came from a family of teachers and was born on 14 December 1940 in Sambir (Sambor), near Lviv. Her sister Svetlana – Sveta for short – was two years older. Their father Alexey was serving at the Polish border as an officer in the Red Army. The family lived 1,300 kilometres away in Yenakiieve, an industrial city in eastern Ukraine with 88,500 inhabitants in 1939, where Luda was with her mother. Anna's parents-in-law also lived there. The town was occupied by the German Wehrmacht in autumn 1941.[71]

One day, an acquaintance came to her husband's father and said: 'Your daughter-in-law should get away. If the Germans find out that her husband is an officer in the Red Army, she'll be killed.' Where should she go with two small children? 'And there were Germans everywhere.'

She decided to attempt to get to Byelorussia with Luda/Lidia and Sveta. Her parents lived across the norther border of Ukraine, in a small village near Polozk (Polatsk). She hoped to survive the war there with her two daughters. But they had a journey of over 1,000 kilometres before them. And there was a war. They had to walk some of the way. Luda/Lidia was carried most of the time on her mother's back. When they finally arrived at their destination, they found abandoned and ruined houses. 'Only the oven and foundations of my parents' house remained. I stood in the ruins and cried; I had no strength anymore.'

She finally came across a neighbour of her parents. 'She didn't recognize me: my daughters and I were so thin, dirty and ragged.' Christina, the neighbour, told her that her parents and brother were alive. They had found shelter not far away in the house of Anna's uncle Sasha. 'We went to the house, but no one was there. Lunch was on the table. I sat Luda and Sveta at the table and went to look for my mother.' Anna found her by the river, washing carpets. 'Mama!' she cried, but her mother answered without turning round: 'Yurik, can't you see I have no time, go and eat, the table's laid.' Her mother thought that Anna's brother had come from the fields, where he was working with his father. Anna once again called her mother. 'Then she turned round and fainted. I shook her, and my mother came round. I told her that the children were alive.' Together they went to the house. Her daughters were sitting at the table, eating and collecting every crumb, they were so starving. 'There were no Germans anymore in the village itself.'

Partisans were fighting in the forests that covered this part of the country. Anna contacted them and helped them by watching the road and the railway line. She counted how many cars, trucks and carts went by and passed on this information to the partisans. When this became increasingly dangerous, she went with her daughters, her parents and her brother and other village inhabitants to join the partisans. They were always on the move. But then it happened. While crossing a deep river, they were caught and put in prison in Polatsk. The children were separated from them and the adults tortured by the SS. Later, all the children were assembled in the prison yard. 'The SS shot at them randomly.' Among the children were her two daughters. Sveta and other children were killed. Luda survived.

Those who remained alive were crammed into cattle wagons and transported via Minsk to Auschwitz-Birkenau, where they underwent selection. Luda-Lidia and her mother were put on the side of those who were temporarily reprieved. Anna Bocharov's parents were selected by the SS for the other side – that of immediate death.

One day, the mothers had to assemble outside with their children and stand in a line. The SS ordered: 'All children must stand in front of their mothers and the small children are to be placed on the ground.' Then came the order: 'All women three steps back!' 'Not one single mother moved.' The SS tore the children from their mothers. In this way Luda was also separated from her mother.[72] She was also looked after by other women inmates in a barracks in which there were only children. She was only able to see her mother for a couple of minutes in the evenings.

After some time, the girl was taken to an inmates' hospital block. The inmates called these blocks the 'waiting room for the gas chamber' or the 'entrance lobby to the crematorium'. They were overfull with the sick and worn out. Inmates, with or without medical training, had to work there as carers. They had next to no medicine, and their possibilities for treatment were extremely limited. The hospital blocks were barely different from the others: three-tier bunks on every floor packed with people. The paillasses on which they lay were soaked with vomit and pus. Under these conditions, even the mildest disease was life-threatening. Selections were constantly carried out and inmates subject to pseudo-medical experiments.[73]

Anna Bocharova never forgot the way Luda/Lidia screamed when the SS pushed her mother out of the hospital block. Like the other mothers, she didn't want to abandon her daughter there. But crying and imploring were to no avail. One day, however, Anna managed to obtain a slight improvement for herself and her daughter:

> At my request and with the aid of the Russian inmate doctor Olga Klimenko, I managed to get a job in this hospital block as a cleaner and could see Ludmila sometimes.
>
> Doctor Mengele came often to the building with other German doctors to select children for experiments. When the children saw the doctors, they attempted to hide, as if they were terrified of meeting Mengele. Unfortunately, my daughter was taken with others for experiments. Even after the first time, I no longer recognized her. She was so pale, almost transparent. We heard that they took blood [among other things] and replaced it with salt solution. My daughter was taken a few more times for experiments. On her return, she complained that they had given her injections. On one occasion after these painful injections my daughter had a fever and sores all over her body, which took a long time to disappear.
>
> I'm sure that pseudo-scientific experiments were conducted on my daughter. I can't say anything more because we inmates didn't know exactly what they were doing with our children. I just saw the results of these experiments.[74]

Anna Bocharova saw her daughter for the last time in mid-January 1945. She repeated to her at every opportunity: 'Never forget that your name is Bocharov, that my name is Anna and your father is Alexei.' And again and again, she implored her daughter: 'Never forget your name, never forget your name, never forget …'. 'I won't forget', Luda replied every time.

On 18 January, Anna Bocharova and other interned women were roused in the night by SS men. They had to form a line. They were informed that they were being taken to Germany. 'Some of the mothers went to the commandant and asked permission to take our children with us. We said that we would carry them. He answered: "You know where you are and who you are."' Anna was driven on various death marches to concentration camps in the West: Buchenwald, Gross-Rosen, Ravensbrück and Bergen-Belsen, where she was liberated by the British on 15 April 1945.

JACQUES, SUZANNE, DANIEL, JULES, RENÉ, NICOLE, PAUL On 6 February 1944, a transport from the camp at Drancy in France arrived in Auschwitz with 1,214 Jewish children, women and men. After selection, 166 men were given the numbers 173228 to 173393, and 49 women were tattooed with the numbers 75125 to 75173. The other 999, and thus presumably all of the children, were gassed.[75]

There were 189 children in this transport, 78 girls and 111 boys. Among them were Jacques (15), Suzanne (12), Daniel (10), Jules (7), Armand (6), René (5) and Thérèse (2), the children of Rosalie Ehrenkranz (43). Another mother deported to Auschwitz was Hélène Buchholz (40) with her four children Émile (15), Alexandre (12), Nicole (10) and Paul (5).[76]

Drancy, the central camp near Paris, was the main transit point for the transports from France to the extermination camps. Around 57,000 Jews were deported from there by train to Auschwitz-Birkenau.[77] Around 75,000 Jews in all were deported from France, including 10,000 children and juveniles under the age of 18,[78] of whom only a few hundred are estimated to have survived.[79] Around 69,000 of the deportees were destined for Auschwitz-Birkenau.[80]

According to the surviving transport lists, not all of which have been preserved, over 24,500 Jews from Belgium were deported to Auschwitz, among them over 4,600 children and juveniles up to the age of 16.[81]

GÉZA SCHEIN arrived in Auschwitz-Birkenau on 7 July 1944 with his mother Klára, his father Zoltán and his maternal grandparents.[82] The selection took place directly on the station ramp: 'The SS said that those fit for work would be put to work. They had to stand on one side. The elderly, mothers with children, the children and pregnant women were put on the other side. "They are going to a special camp."' For most, including Géza's grandparents, that meant the gas chamber.

Zoltán Schein had an inkling of what was going on. He said to his son: 'If they ask, tell them you're 15 and a baker's apprentice.' Géza was 11 but tall and strong for his age. He said that he was born on 7 February 1928, although in fact he was born on that day in 1933.[83] The SS took him at his word that he was 15.

Géza's mother was put in the Women's Camp, his father in the 'Gypsy' Camp in a wooden barracks with around 500 people. There were not even any bunks. They had to sleep on the bare, wet floor, which was sprayed with water in the evening.

Inmates who had been there longer explained: Birkenau is an extermination camp. Those who are not gassed immediately would be worked to death. The evening roll calls sometimes went on for hours as a pretext for withholding food, potato peelings boiled in water.

They had to get up at 5 a.m. 'There was another roll call and the people were counted. But the count was never right. We had to stand there for two or three hours. Then there was breakfast, if you could call it that. It consisted of a piece of bread and some kind of black liquid.'

Then they went to work at Auschwitz-Monowitz. They performed slave labour building an IG Farben factory for synthetic rubber and fuel. Within three years, around 25,000 people died in the chemical company's work camps.[84] Later Géza toiled in a coal mine in Brzeszcze, 10 kilometres away.

NINETEEN GIRLS AND TWENTY BOYS FROM MULFINGEN CHILDREN'S HOME On 12 May 1944, the children from St Josefspflege in Mulfingen, Württemberg, were transferred to the camp. Twenty boys were given the numbers Z–9873 to Z–9892 and nineteen girls the numbers Z–10629 to Z–10647.[85] The 'Z' stood for 'Zigeuner' ['gypsy'].

The Württemberg Home Decree of 7 November 1938 meant that 'gypsy' children from different homes were to be transferred to St Josefspflege in Mulfingen and concentrated there. After this date, 'gypsy or gypsy-like' children and juveniles were automatically transferred to

St Josefspflege by the Nazi authorities. Increasingly, they were children whose parents had been deported to concentration camps.[86]

On the basis of the Implementing Provisions of the Auschwitz Decree of 16 December 1942, which called for the transfer of 'gypsies' to Auschwitz-Birkenau extermination camp,[87] it was ordered that families were to be 'transferred to the camp ... together if possible'. Children housed in 'welfare homes or elsewhere' were to be 'reunited with their clan' if possible before their 'arrest'. The same procedure applied to 'gypsy children whose parents had died or were kept in concentration camps or elsewhere'.[88]

The children at St Josefspflege were not yet affected, because Eva Justin, a member of the Nazi Racial Hygiene Institute in Berlin, which, under the direction of the Tübingen neurologist Robert Ritter, examined the 'racial characteristics' of around 19,000 Sinti and Roma between 1938 and 1942,[89] required the 'gypsy children' in St Josefspflege as 'specimens' for her doctoral 'thesis'. It was published in autumn 1944 under the title 'Life Stories of Atypically Reared Gypsy Children and their Descendants'.[90]

Months before Justin's 'thesis' appeared, uniformed police from Künzelsau fetched the children in Mulfingen, on 9 May 1944.[91]

Only four of the children from St Josefspflege survived Auschwitz-Birkenau.[92]

GÁBOR HIRSCH When Gábor Hirsch arrived in Auschwitz-Birkenau from Békéscsaba on 29 June 1944 with his mother Ella and many relatives, they were immediately separated. He can recall the selection, but no longer remembers when and how he was separated from his mother. It was as if it had been expunged from his memory. It troubled him for the rest of his life.

Next, the boy was sent to the 'bath' or 'sauna' – the 'disinfesting and disinfection unit', as it was called in Nazi jargon. There, every single thing he was still wearing was taken from him and his fellow victims. He was allowed to keep only his shoes, his belt and his handkerchief.

'I had to get undressed. All the hair on my body was shorn or shaved off. A terrible procedure. No one took the slightest notice of our modesty. Then I had to shower and was disinfected, which left me terribly itchy.'

Gábor was given white underwear with 'a kind of drawstring', a shirt and striped inmate trousers, jacket and cap. 'We were hardly recognizable from earlier.'

Later they were registered. An inmate clerk wrote down their data. They were given a number that had to be stitched either onto their striped jacket or the trouser leg. 'We didn't have the number tattooed on us.'

Gábor was a 'depot inmate' ['Depot-Häftling']. Their number was not tattooed because they were 'reserves', destined to stay in the camp only for a short time. At random, they were put on a transport for another camp or were gassed in Birkenau, depending on where one or more inmates were required 'to make up the numbers'.[93]

The boy and the other new arrivals were given postcards. They were ordered to write trivial greetings to Hungary. In German. To maintain the myth of the 'resettlement of the Jews'. He wrote to a non-Jewish aunt married to his mother's brother and not deported. As it turned out after the war, his mother had the same idea. While Gábor's card was lost, his mother's card survived.

Ella Hirsch wrote in late June 1944: 'Dear sister-in-law, I'm healthy and fine. How are you? Regards and kisses.' They were ordered to put 'Waldsee' as the sender's address. Gábor Hirsch thinks he wrote 'Wald am See'.

Those who were gassed immediately after their arrival also had to write postcards. The order to write home was even given in the crematorium changing room.[94]

Most of the people from Gábor's transport who were temporarily reprieved were put in the 'Gypsy' Camp, which mostly contained Roma and Sinti families. 'Block 11 was now my "home". Apart from my 15-year-old cousin Tibor Hirsch, this block also housed several classmates from Békéscsaba, including my good friend Ferenc.'

New transports with Hungarian Jews arrived every day at the ramp in Birkenau. Gábor's block, which was already full, became more and more crowded. 'It was intolerably full.' Sometimes, there were as many as 1,200 Jewish children and juveniles in the draughty wooden barracks. There were none of the usual multi-tier bunks. The occupants couldn't even lie down to sleep on the floor because the block was so full. 'We had to sit on the floor, the first with his back against the wall, the next one between his legs, and so on, to the middle of the barracks. And it was the same from the other side. Sleep was impossible. Your whole body hurt from the unaccustomed, almost motionless sitting.'

They had to get up very early in the morning, clean the barracks and assemble outside for the roll call. Then they hung around between the latrine hut and their block. As it was very cool in the early morning, even though it was summer, they clustered together. 'We warmed one another. We stood close together, our bodies touching, sometimes twenty, thirty, as many as a hundred people.' At some point, the cluster broke apart and a new one was formed. Until the sun came and warmed them.

Finally, there was 'breakfast'. 'Hot, sweet water coloured slightly by the ersatz coffee or tea'. They were given 'dishes' to eat and drink from that the SS had mostly taken from those who had been murdered. It could be a dented pot, a large metal cup or a rusty washbowl.

Not everyone had a vessel. Several children and adolescents formed a circle and passed the cup or pot from one person to the next. Everyone was allowed 'a certain number of sips' until the vessel was empty. As the vessels were of different sizes, they were used by up to five children. Everyone watched 'with eagle eyes' to make sure that the next person didn't take more than he had.

They weren't allowed to stay in the barracks during the day. They generally sat between the blocks talking. Gábor and another boy planned how they would escape. They wanted to hide in the forest. 'It was completely irrational, but we needed this outlet.'

At lunchtime, they were given 'some kind of soup' containing dried beets, carrots or cabbage. They called it 'Dörrgemüse' ['dehydrated vegetables']. In the evening, they got 'officially a quarter of a loaf with something on it' – margarine, sometimes a little piece of sausage or artificial honey.

'Bread was the universal currency in the camp. You could "buy" lots of things with it, sometimes your own life.' Instead of the official bread ration, they often had much less: just a fifth or seventh of a loaf. The bread was often stolen – by the first block elder or other kapos who brought the food from the kitchens and hived off large quantities before handing it out. 'There was nothing we could do about it.'

After the 'evening meal', there was another roll call, 'in all weathers'. The children and juveniles had to stand in rows of ten. That made it easier for the SS men to count. 'The roll call sometimes lasted hours.' They had to stand there until the count matched the official figure. Those who were sick had to turn out as well. Those who had died in the night or during the day had to be carried to the roll call square so they could be counted.

Gábor was sent to work in the 'Gypsy' Camp. He had to keep the block clean or, if he was lucky, help to carry the food. 'The removal and disposal of the buckets full of excrement and urine was disgusting.' They stood in the barracks, often oil drums in which the occupants relieved themselves in the night. After 9 p.m., they had to stay in the barracks and were not allowed to go to the latrine hut.

The children, juveniles and adults were forbidden from leaving the 'Gypsy' Camp. 'Two or three times', Gábor was 'requisitioned' for cutting pieces of grass. They had to cut out 40 × 40 cm pieces of grass 'so as to green some other part of the camp'. The pieces of grass were cut out behind the 'Mexico' camp. This was the name given by the inmates to a section of Birkenau being built as a transit camp for Jewish women, particularly Hungarians. Gábor didn't know that his mother had been taken there after the selection.

In the 'Mexico' camp, a never completed section, the women lived under terrible conditions, 'grey from weakness and dirt', as eyewitness Seweryna Szmaglewska described it in 1946. Their clothes hung in rags from their bodies. 'Some wear only shirts, others only an apron.'[95] They didn't even have bunks. In the night, the women had to sleep on the bare earth. There was no lighting, no water, no sewer system. SS doctors held eternal roll calls and selected women for the gas chambers. 'Only an infinitesimal percentage enters the camp.'[96]

When Gábor came near 'Mexico' for the first time, he went like many others to the fence and asked one of the women inmates: 'Is there anyone there from Békéscsaba?' The woman went from barracks to barracks and looked for his mother. On this day, she was not stopped from doing so by the guards.

'And then, after some time, I saw my mother coming towards me. I was so excited. My heart beat fit to burst. We were only able to exchange a few words. What did we talk about? I've no idea.'

Shortly after their arrival, friends and acquaintances from Békéscsaba had been transported onward to various camps inside the Reich. Gábor had not been able to make friends with anyone. He was alone and in despair. 'All of the inmates in Auschwitz-Birkenau were concerned with themselves and their own plight. They were unable to care about other people's problems.'

One day, Gábor was again selected to cut out squares of grass. They were to be collected near the 'Mexico' camp, where his mother Ella was. The boy had saved a piece of bread, which he wanted to give to his mother.

'Luckily, I was able to see her again. We were only able to talk for a short time.' His mother didn't want to accept the present. 'Instead, she gave me her bread ration. She had hollowed out the bread and, as I discovered later, put some jam in it.'

Gábor was never able to remember what he talked about with his mother. 'I don't even know if she was wearing a headscarf, whether her head was shaven or whether she had stubbly hair.' He would have been happy if he could have remembered. Every day, it ate at his brain. There was much too much that he couldn't remember at all.

Gábor experienced selections many times in the camp. It often took place according to 'Goebbels's calendar', a camp jargon term named after the chief propagandist of the Nazi regime.[97] 'I don't know any more whether I heard the expression "Goebbels's calendar" in Birkenau or later on.' The fact is that the selections in the camp were often carried out on Shabbat and/or Jewish holidays. 'Or was it just a coincidence? I doubt it.'

Gábor remembered two major selections:

It was Yom Kippur, the Jewish Day of Atonement, on 27 September 1944. We children and juveniles had to assemble on a square in the camp. There was a huge number of youths.

The 'Angel of Death', Dr Mengele, and his entourage appeared. He asked for a wooden plank, hammer and nails. He fixed the plank at a height of about 150 centimetres. We all had to pass underneath. Those who didn't reach the plank, along with the emaciated and weak, were put on one side, and the stronger and taller ones on the other side. As I was one of the smaller ones, I was among those selected. We were locked in two barracks. In my block there were around six hundred children and juveniles.

A boy I knew by the name of Andreas managed to get away unnoticed. He had hidden in a block until the end of the selection and the transport of the selected children and juveniles.

The next day, Dr Epstein, the inmate doctor, came to our barracks. He picked twenty-one boys from my block including myself and saved our lives.

The doctor was probably Dr Berthold Epstein, Professor of Paediatrics at the University of Prague. After the German troops entered Prague, he went to Norway, where he was arrested and arrived in Auschwitz on 1 December 1942.[98]

'I never saw the other children and juveniles again. They were murdered in the gas chambers in Birkenau.'

A short time later, in the first half of October, Jews all over the world celebrated Simchat Torah, an expression of joy at the giving of the Law, which God handed to Moses in five books. To recall this event, there are processions and readings from the Torah, and the children are given sweets and flags. At the same time, youths were again selected for the gas chamber in Birkenau.

Gábor was in Block 13 with those selected.

'My cousin Tibor, who had been chosen as the block elder's messenger right after his arrival, heard about it. Somehow, he managed to get me moved to Block 11, where there were around 600 youths destined for the gas chamber. He said to me: "The chance of surviving is greater here, because there will probably be a second selection."' Gábor never found out whether he really knew or whether he was just trying to comfort him.

Tibor provided me with food and drink and ensured that I could wash and tidy up. He also found a clean-looking jacket for me, much too large, admittedly, but he helped me to move the buttons so that it fitted better. The idea was to improve my chances in the second selection.

There wasn't another selection, however, because some youths had tried to escape through the ventilation windows in the roof. They were caught. As a 'punishment', we were not taken away on trucks after curfew. We had to march during the day to the crematorium, with SS men and Alsatian dogs on our left and right. We were taken to the changing room, where we had to get undressed.

Quite unexpectedly, a group of SS officers came and made a second selection. We had to do some gymnastic exercises and squats. Around 50 of the 600 children and youths, including myself, were told to get dressed again. While we were doing so, the others were taken to another room. Not one of them came out again.

On the return to our part of the camp, I saw the group from Block 13. The children and youths were near the crematorium, awaiting their fate. Among them was a boy named Fredi [Alfred]. He was 16 and came from my hometown. His brother had been in the class below me at primary school.

We, the 50 still alive, were taken to the 'Gypsy' Camp. I saw my cousin Tibor there again. We embraced and cried with relief and joy. We had been certain that we would never see each other again.

On 20 October 1944, for example, around 1,000 children and youths between the ages of 12 and 18 were murdered in Crematorium III at Auschwitz-Birkenau.[99] A typical day in Auschwitz.

JOSIF (YOSHUA, JEHSUA, JECHUBA) KONVOJ was transferred, according to original documents, from Dachau to Auschwitz-Birkenau on 26 July 1944.[100]

He was born in Kaunas, Lithuania, on 1 January 1929. 'I was convinced for many decades that I was born on 1 January 1930.' The correct date was found later in documents.

Josif Konvoj can barely remember his childhood and the time in the camp.

His birthplace had a long Jewish tradition. The first Jews settled in Kaunas in the late fourteenth century, and the first synagogue was built in 1772. Twenty-five years later, there were already 1,508 Jews living in the city – around 18 per cent of the population. From 1839, Jews were allowed to vote in municipal elections. Many synagogues and a hospital were built later. The Jewish population lived above all by trading in eggs, cereal, wood, linen and cattle.

Kaunas (Yiddish: Kovno) became increasingly popular. In 1897, there were over 25,000 Jews living in the city on the Nemunas (Memel) and Neris. They played an important role in public and cultural life. There were two Jewish theatres and several Yiddish magazines and newspapers, such as *Yidishe Shtime*, as well as Jewish kindergartens, primary schools and higher education establishments.[101]

When the Soviet Union occupied Lithuania in mid-1940, there were around 37,000 Jews in Kaunas, a quarter of the total population of this small Baltic country.[102] On 22 June 1941, Nazi Germany invaded the Soviet Union. Two days later, German troops controlled Kaunas. The persecution of the Jews by the Germans and their Lithuanian henchmen began immediately. From 25 to 27 June, several synagogues were set on fire along with around 60 Jewish houses, and more than 1,500 Jews were murdered.[103]

In summer 1941, the 30,000 or so Jews who had survived the pogroms were interned in a 'small' and a 'large' ghetto in the Vilijampolė district. Neither the living space nor the basic infrastructure was anything like adequate for so many people. 'For the inhabitants this crowding was a preliminary to physical extermination.'[104]

By the end of October, more than 18,000 Jews had been shot in Forts IV, VII and IX of the fortifications surrounding the city. On 4 October, for example, 818 Jewish children, 712 Jewish women and 315 Jewish men were killed. On 29 October alone, it was 9,200 Jews, including 4,723 children.[105] By the end of 1941, six months after the arrival of German troops, almost 140,000 Jewish children, women and men had been murdered in Lithuania.[106]

In autumn 1943, the German occupying powers renamed the ghetto Kauen concentration camp. At the end of October, around 2,000 Jews were transported to Estonia, and some 700 children and elderly persons deported, probably to Auschwitz. Around 8,000 Jews remained in Kauen concentration camp, including many children such as Josif and his siblings, as well as the old and sick.[107] On 27–28 March 1944, around 1,300 Jewish children under the age of 12 were deported with older Jews over 55 – 1,000 of them – probably to Birkenau.[108] Dr Anton Peretz witnessed the events on those two days in Kauen concentration camp and wrote a report on what he had seen:

In the early morning a vehicle [drove] down the streets ... announcing on a loudspeaker: 'Anyone found on the streets will be shot.'

The women must have felt instinctively that their children were in danger. It was known that something similar had happened in another ghetto. They shouted: 'Children!'

Music was playing on the trucks to drown out the cries of the mothers and children. Then a Ukrainian and a German got out of each of the trucks. They grabbed the children and shoved them into the vehicles, sometimes with their grandmothers as well.

The child round-up lasted two days. On the first days I was lying with some children in the cellar. I had given them sedative injections. Thousands of children were caught on the first day of the round-up.

We hoped that the terror would end the following day. People didn't go to work. There was deep sadness, because children had been taken from almost every home. The people stood around on the streets. Somewhere a shot was fired and once again the trucks appeared. Everyone ran home to hide in the cellars or bunkers.

I witnessed atrocious scenes. There was a truck next to the hospital where women with children or children alone were brought, urged on by two soldiers with drawn pistols. They threw the children into the vehicle.

The mothers cried in despair. One shouted at the Germans: 'Give me my children back!'

'How many?' he asked.

'Three', the woman answered.

'You can have one.'

She approached the car. Her three children raised their heads. They of course wanted their mother. But she couldn't decide which one to take, so she left empty-handed.[109]

Around 300 of these children were shot in Fort IX near Kaunas.[110] The Konvoj family remained alive for the time being in the ghetto, and later in the concentration camp.[111] The camp was liquidated on 8 July and the houses set on fire. The remaining approximately 6,000 to 7,000 Jews were transported to camps to the west. Around 1,000 children, women and men were murdered during the liquidation of Kauen concentration camp.[112]

Josif Konvoj, his mother and one sister were transported to Dachau, probably via Stutthof near Gdańsk. In an undated transport list from Stutthof, the boy is listed as 'Jechuba Konvoj', his mother as 'Taube Konvoj' and his sister as 'Reise Konvoj'.[113] His youngest sister's actual name was 'Roza'. The birth years of Josif and Roza are not correct, although the year 1900 for the mother is right. The fact that the survivors from Kauen were transported via Stutthof to Dachau, amongst other places,[114] suggests that the names might have referred to Josif and some members of his family.

In any event, Josif was transported to Dachau on 15 July 1944. He remained there for around four weeks and was then deported to Auschwitz.[115] From there, he arrived in Buchenwald on 23 January 1945.[116]

EDUARD KORNFELD In summer 1944, Eduard Kornfeld was also deported to Auschwitz-Birkenau from the part of Slovakia annexed by Hungary. He was accompanied by two of his uncles with their families. One had six children and the other eight. The 13-year-old Slovakian Jewish girl whom he had met in Vel'ký Mader and liked so much was also on this transport.

Eduard lost sight of the girl immediately after their arrival. 'The SS were standing there with rifles, and there were also dogs.' Nothing was normal anymore. It was all so organized that he could only concentrate on himself. He had to pay close attention to what was going on. He was also very frightened.

The improbable happened: he was put on the good side in the selection. He always wondered why he wasn't sent to be gassed. 'I was one of the youngest in the wagon. Perhaps because I was relatively tall. Or because I had blond hair.' And light blue eyes …

During the regular intake procedure in the 'sauna' building, their entire bodies were shaved: 'They tore out the hair more than shaving, and pulled brutally on my penis.' Some of them were bleeding.

He was thrown a pair of trousers, a striped jacket and a cap by other inmates who had been in the camp longer. But no underwear, 'nothing'. He was only allowed to keep his own shoes.

One of them said: 'Excuse me, but the trousers are too small.' In reply, he was beaten with a whip by the SS man.

We swapped the clothes among ourselves. Naked and silent. It lasted only a few minutes. But they continued to beat us savagely.

So this was Auschwitz-Birkenau.

From then on, the 15-year-old was on the lookout all the time. He'd seen and experienced enough. 'I understood what Auschwitz was about.'

Any normal behaviour could attract draconian punishment or even mean death. He said to himself: 'I need to watch out carefully.'

Like Gábor Hirsch, Eduard was one of the depot inmates, who weren't tattooed and formed a reserve to make up the numbers for transports or the gas chamber. And also, like Gábor, he was interned in the 'Gypsy' Camp. With the growing number of transports from Hungary, the Jewish inmates also soon formed a majority in this section of the camp.

'From morning to evening it was "cap on – cap off, fall in" – beatings – squats – "dismissed" – beatings. Again and again, ten, twenty times … always on the same place. Often for hours. Day after day.'

They had to endure these roll calls twice a day in all weathers. 'Whether the sun was burning down, it was raining or bitter cold, it made no difference.' Then there were the roll call drills. These had to function perfectly first time. Otherwise, there were terrible beatings. 'I'm convinced that there can't be a military unit in the world that could form up in rows of five as quickly as we children and juveniles – 600 here, 600 there. Achieved through constant beatings.'

They only spoke to one another when no one was looking. 'Otherwise, it was forbidden.' The boy knew intuitively who was in front, next to or behind him. This was life-saving.

'Many quickly starved to death. Also in our block. I witnessed this day in, day out.'

After Eduard had been there for a few days, he spotted the huge chimney near the 'Gypsy' Camp – 'belching not only smoke but also flames'. Someone told him: 'That's the bakery.' A few days later, he met someone whom he had known from earlier. He said: 'I almost ended up in the cremmy, but was lucky.' 'What's the cremmy?' 'Crematorium, didn't you know? The people are gassed in a large room and then they're incinerated.' 'I thought it was a bakery. I was hoping to work there. I'm hungry.'

A few days later, an SS man came with the block clerk to note, among other things, who had died in the night. 'Sometimes it was ten, fifteen or twenty comrades.' The clerk said: 'We need thirty-five of you for a chocolate factory. Those who feel weak should report.'

Eduard knew that he had to fight for his life. 'Lots of kids fought to go, and I wanted to go as well.' He tried to push his way to the front. Someone held him back, pulled on his sleeve and whispered: 'Don't go!

Don't turn round! Get lost! Otherwise, you'll be for the gas!' Eduard didn't say a word, stood still as 'two others pushed their way in front of me'. He didn't turn round to see his saviour but disappeared as quickly as possible.

'It was a miracle that I was held back. The SS man and block clerk needed thirty-five to make up the numbers for the gas chamber. If they had seen that I was held back, my saviour would have been gassed right away. This was one of the many pieces of luck that rescued me from the gas chamber.'

Eduard never forgot this event. It followed him in sleepless nights and even in his dreams. 'I'm tired, I'm weak, ill, I push forward and report.' But then, every time, he survived again. 'The unknown person holds me back and says: "Don't move. They will disappear. They'll be gassed."' Once again, a fraction of a second deciding between life and death.

For Eduard, the evening couldn't come soon enough. 'If you survive until evening, it normally means you'll still be alive the following morning.' And during the day, so much could happen. Every day was like an eternity.

There were selections all the time. 'Go to your rooms!' came the order one day. Everyone had to disappear in their wooden barracks. Straightaway. Then the doors were torn open. 'Fall in!' ordered an SS man. This time it was their turn. The boy knew: 'Now it's a matter of life and death.'

They had to go outside. 'Mengele and lots of SS men with machine guns were already there.' Then came the order again: 'Fall in!' In a jiffy, they were lined up for the roll call. Ten rows, each with 110 to 120 boys formed from Eduard's block. Five rows were on one side and five on the other.

'First row step forward!' They started not on Eduard's side but on the other.

Everyone had to get undressed. We didn't have much on in the first place. We took off our jackets and dropped our trousers. Mengele inspected each row. He selected 10 boys from each group of 100.

Those selected were allowed to take their things and go back to the barracks. The others had to fall in on the camp road and were guarded by the SS. But no one knew who was destined to be gassed. But I still wanted to find out: 'Where is life, where is death?' With time I developed an animal instinct. I concluded that those who were standing on the 'road' would be gassed.

'What should I do now?' I asked myself. It was a terrible, indescribable feeling. I continued to observe the other side intently. Many people were praying. Everyone knew what it was about. To die at 15? You must be crazy! No! I want to live!

I watched those who were praying. It didn't help, but I wanted to do something. But what? I tried to concentrate to gather my last reserves of strength.

Then it was the turn of our side. First row, seven out, second row eight. Then came the next rows. I was in the last but one.

And then, Mengele went past and didn't select me. He'd already gone on to the next person. In this moment I was seized by a massive inner strength, an indescribable will to live. Suddenly Mengele turned round and made this gesture to indicate that I should step out. He selected another boy called Holzmann from my row. And from the last row he didn't take anyone.

There was another scene that he never forgot.

'That's my brother', one of them said and started to cry. And because his brother couldn't come to him, he shouted 'I want to go with him.' Although we weren't allowed to speak to the members of the 'master race', the SS man asked the boy: 'Which one is your brother?' 'That one.' 'OK, go and join him.' And they were both selected for gassing.

The 250 or so who had been selected, including Eduard, were taken together to one of the blocks. He managed to get to the barracks but had to lie down right away and passed out. 'Maybe for half an hour, maybe longer.'

The huge group who were to be gassed – 'there must have been around 3,000 children and juveniles from three blocks who were to be gassed' – were herded into the other two barracks. 'They were surrounded by the SS day and night.'

Eduard and the other boys from his block were terrified of going to the latrine hut past the barracks containing those condemned to death.

'If the numbers weren't right, they would grab one of us and send us to be gassed.'

Probably on the next evening, Eduard heard trucks coming. The doors of the barracks were torn open, the boys destined for gassing loaded onto the trucks and driven to the crematoria. 'We saw it all: non-stop crying and praying, "mama", "mother", in several languages. It was heart-rending. Many of us also started to cry. Then one said: "Stop! Just stop! Otherwise, they might have second thoughts." So we bit our hands so as not to cry.'

Later on, they found notes in the empty barracks with the names of those who had been murdered, as if to say: 'Yes, we existed. Don't forget us!' Some took the pieces of paper with them. 'I couldn't do it.'

The selections took place at shorter and shorter intervals. Eduard realized that he just had to get out of Auschwitz-Birkenau. One 'beautiful day', SS men and the block clerk stormed into their barracks: 'We need sixty men for heavy labour in the mines. If you are strong enough, you can report.'

Eduard thought: 'I'll risk it. Here in Auschwitz, I'll die anyway.' He reported along with an acquaintance from Vel'ky Meder, a boy of his age. They were examined in one of the latrines and washroom. They had to undress completely, stark naked. A thought flashed through the boy's head: 'I hope it's not the gas chamber!'

An SS man 'with a terrible face that looked like death personified' began the 'examination' by kicking each of the boys in the shins to see if they could keep their balance. Eduard stood firm and was chosen for the transport. His acquaintance was not picked. 'He fell over and was kicked out.'

CHILDREN FROM WARSAW Between 12 August and 17 September 1944, 13,720 Poles[117] – children, women and men – arrived in Auschwitz in four transports from the transit camp in Pruszków, near Warsaw. They were deported after the military uprising in Warsaw against the German occupants, from 1 August to 2 October 1944.

The uprising lasted sixty-three days, during which 16,000 Polish fighters were killed, more than 20,000 wounded and over 150,000 civilians died. They included several thousand Jews, who had been hidden by the Polish inhabitants. A further 150,000 were deported to

Germany for forced labour.[118] Finally, around 65,000 children, women and men were deported to concentration camps such as Auschwitz.[119] One of the survivors was Jadwiga Matysiak, *née* Sztanka.

I was born on 20 January 1942 in Warsaw. In September 1944 I was taken with my parents and a sister to Auschwitz-Birkenau concentration camp, where I was given the number 84876. My mother, sister and I were put in the Women's Camp. After a time, we were informed that the boys and my father had been transported to Schömberg concentration camp [a satellite camp of Natzweiler-Struthof, where – together with the sub-camp Dautmergen – 1,774 inmates died][120].

During my time in Birkenau, I was frequently separated from my mother and put in the 'Revier' [inmate 'hospital']. I was often sick, with whooping cough, measles, scarlet fever and dysentery, for example. I still have the traces on my body of phlegmon [a diffuse suppurating inflammation of the soft tissue associated with fever].

We remained in Birkenau until the end of January 1945, when we were transported to Leipzig and later to Berlin. During the time in the camp, my mother was pregnant. My youngest brother Ryszard was born … [in] Berlin[-Köpenick] on 26 March 1945. [Jadwiga Matysiak and her mother and sister were transferred[121] in January 1945 from Auschwitz-Birkenau to the Sachsenhausen satellite camp in BerlinKöpenick.][122]

We were liberated at the end of April 1945, after which we returned to Warsaw. My father and brothers were not yet there. We had no information about them. My mother was sick; she had an open wound on her leg and a festering sore on her breast. She had fever for a long time. The neighbours looked after us three children as best they could.

My brothers returned in May 1945, unfortunately without our father. He had been murdered on 24 December 1944 in Schömberg. My mother was left alone with five children.

My minor-age brothers, 17-year-old Henryk and 15-year-old Jerzy, had to look for work to feed mother and their younger siblings…. My 13-year-old sister Irena looked after us, the two youngest. My brothers and sisters attended night school at the same time.[123]

Until the German troops arrived at the end of September 1939, Warsaw was a vibrant metropolis with a thriving Jewish community, the largest in Europe at the time. The Warsaw ghetto was installed in autumn 1940.

The first deportations of Jews by Germans began in July 1942 – destination: Treblinka.[124]

The German occupiers confined the Jews of Warsaw, but also Jewish children, women and men from other parts of Poland, as well as Czechoslovakia and Germany.[125]

In March 1941, there were between 445,000 and 490,000 Jews in the cordoned-off area.[126] In January 1942, this included around 100,000 children under the age of 14.[127] This made Warsaw the largest ghetto in German-occupied Europe.[128]

The ghetto inmates were starving and fearful for their lives. By 21 July 1942, almost 100,000 Jews had died in the terrible conditions that existed in the ghetto. Around 329,000 Jews were transported from the Warsaw ghetto to Treblinka extermination camp alone from 22 July to 2 October 1942 and from January to mid-May 1943. Almost all of the Jewish babies, children, women and men deported there were murdered in the gas chambers within a few hours of their arrival.[129]

When the SS began the second wave of deportations in mid-January 1943, they were confronted by armed Jewish fighters. This uprising ended in mid-April 1943 in a Jewish popular revolt. The fighting lasted nearly a month and cost the lives of thousands of Jews. Tens of thousands were arrested and shot, or transported to labour and, above all, extermination camps.[130]

From the outset, there had been various forms of resistance in the Warsaw ghetto, which was to culminate in an armed uprising. One form of resistance is connected with the historian Emanuel Ringelblum. He was head of the underground archive Oneg Shabbat in the ghetto. From 1940, he and a group of friends and colleagues began to collect material about the fate of Polish Jews: official documents, reports, letters, surveys, diaries, wills, underground drawings and documents by Jewish resistance groups.

Parts of the underground archive were found in the ruins of the Warsaw ghetto in 1946 and 1950.[131] They included a report by the united underground organizations in the ghetto to the Polish exile government in London of 15 November 1942. Co-written by Ringelblum, it states:

> In the glow of the incomparable Polish autumn, a layer of snow glitters and shimmers. This snow is nothing but the feathers and down from Jewish

eiderdowns remaining with all of the possessions, cupboards, bags, suitcases full of clothes and linen, bowls, pots, plates and other household objects, of the 500,000 Jews evacuated to the East. Things that belong to no one anymore, tablecloths, coats, bedding, pullovers, books, cradles, documents, photographs, are piled unsorted in the apartments, courtyards, squares, covered with the eviscerated innards of the Jewish bedding, the snow from the time of the mass murder by the Germans of the Jews of Warsaw.…

Abandoned or semi-abandoned houses, streets cordoned off by barbed wire, wooden fences separating the individual blocks of houses from one another, and above all the complete absence of people, who until two months ago filled the main streets of the ghetto, hurrying about their daily business, buying and selling, working, a depopulation that we did not experience even in the centuries of the Black Death, the Plague – that's what the Jewish residential district of Warsaw looks like in September 1942.[132]

Emanuel Ringelblum, his wife Yehudit and their 12-year-old son Uri were shot, together with other Jews, in March 1944 in the ruins of the Warsaw ghetto.[133]

CHILDREN FROM WESTERBORK Between July 1942 and September 1944, Westerbork was the central transit camp for Jews deported to the East, particularly from the Netherlands.[134] The construction and maintenance of the camp was paid for with assets seized from the Jewish population.[135]

Altogether, in excess of 100,000 Jewish children, women and men were deported from the Netherlands. Over 60 trains, with more than 57,000 people, went directly to Auschwitz-Birkenau. On the transport of 19 May 1944, 245 'gypsies' were also deported, including 147 children, not one of whom survived. Less than 1 per cent of the Jews, Sinti and Roma deported from Westerbork to Auschwitz-Birkenau were alive when the camp was liberated.[136]

The Durlacher family from Baden-Baden fled to relatives in the Netherlands in 1937. Gerhard was 9 years old. In early 1942, the family was deported to Westerbork. From there they were transported first to Theresienstadt and then to Auschwitz-Birkenau.

The men between sixteen and forty-five marched naked past Mengele, their left arms in front of their chests. A few yards in front of him is a pole over which they have to jump. Recruits in a gymnasium. The signs he gives to the clerks are barely perceptible.... The *Blockälteste* [block elder] relegates the weak, the wounded, the emaciated, the limping and the bespectacled, the rejected fallen fruits, to the corner of the useless with a short jerk of his head.[137]

Gerhard Durlacher was the only member of his family to be spared. He wrote later about Auschwitz-Birkenau:

There's no language in the hell to convey what I see, hear, smell or taste. Terror and dread have cordoned off my emotions. I smell the stench of decay and oily smoke, but don't understand. I see and hear the trains, the stumbling masses of people en route to the flames, the dull blows, the naked and shorn women, their private parts exposed, three of them crouched under one grey rag, dripping with rainwater, but I don't understand. Night and day, my senses record what's happening on the other side of the barbed wire and the watchtowers, on the 'Ramp' and in the neighbouring sections of the camp, but I don't understand.[138]

ROBERT BÜCHLER Together with his mother Terezia, his father Josef and his 11-year-old sister Ruth, 15-year-old Robert Büchler was deported in autumn 1944 from Topol'čany, Slovakia, to Auschwitz-Birkenau. 'Fresh damp air' streamed into the wagon when the door was torn open.

An SS man with a helmet with a death's head on it approached and stood on the bottom step, at which those standing nearest moved back. He stood there, looked at us and yelled: 'Everyone out! Leave the luggage in the wagon!'

Everyone looked in their luggage for things that were of particular importance to them. No one got out. No one wanted to be the first.

My mother stuffed all kinds of things in her pockets: some food, soap, toothpaste. I could see a row of SS men in grey raincoats with guns and Alsatian dogs at the end of the platform. I had no idea what they were doing there. They reminded me of hunters.

Men in striped uniforms approached the train. 'Who are they?' The question nagged at me.

Two of them, youths, climbed into the wagon. Everyone looked at them. They urged us calmly to get out and to leave our things behind.

No one was in any hurry to do so. There were thousands of questions, particularly regarding the luggage.

The youths assured us that we would get the luggage later.

The first ones climbed out of the wagon.

I looked more closely at the youths. They had a number and a Star of David and their jackets had a red stripe.

My father stood motionless next to me in the middle of the wagon. He whispered to one of the youths: 'Tell me, where are we?'

It was a few moments before he answered: 'In the camp.'

'What kind of camp?' my father wanted to know. The boy appeared confused: 'Just get out and you'll be told everything outside.'

I stayed close to my father. Behind us were my mother and my sister. It took some time for the occupants to climb down. There were old people and small children among us.

At the exit there was a second youth in a striped uniform, who helped the people to climb down. When we came up to him, my father asked again: 'Where are we exactly?'

I was afraid and restless. Almost everyone had got out. My father asked the question again, this time with a tremor in his voice.

The youth looked at my father and then whispered: 'In a concentration camp.'

My father held him by the sleeve: 'What's the name of the camp?'

The youth was silent. He hesitated but then I heard him whisper in my father's ear: 'Have you never heard of Birkenau?'

The hand that was holding me began to shake. I'd never seen my father like this before.

'I'm curious, because two of my brothers have been in Birkenau for some time', he said to the youth.

'There are lots of people here in the camp. How would I recognize your brothers?' The youth went to the exit.

Now Robert remembered: shortly before they were fetched, two pre-printed postcards had arrived in Topol'čany from 'Birkenau labour camp'. They had caused great excitement in the family. His father compared the signatures of his two younger brothers with old letters from them and assured himself that they were authentic.

Robert saw his mother and sister for the last time on the ramp at Auschwitz-Birkenau. He didn't notice when they were parted. They had to stand in rows of five. Robert was very tired and wanted to ask his father something, but he was lost in thought.

SS men appeared:

I watched them and had the feeling that our fate depended on them. They conversed without taking notice of us. Then another figure appeared in a leather coat. The SS man was very tall. Then there were a couple of commands, and the row reformed as a line. The SS man stood there with his legs apart. One by one, the people went past him. With a gesture he pointed to the left or the right.

I watched it and didn't know what was going on. I was lost in thought. I had a strange sensation that I can't describe.

There weren't many left. My father stood behind me with his hands on my shoulders and said: 'If they ask how old you are, tell them you're 16. Got it?'

I didn't understand but didn't ask any more questions.

Suddenly I was in front of the SS man. He looked at me. He gestured with his finger that I should come closer.

I was rooted to the spot.

'Boy, how old are you?'

My throat was dry. I looked at him and he smiled but I was too nervous to say anything.

He repeated the question.

'I'm 16', I managed to say.

He pointed to the right.

Then it was my father's turn.

He pointed to the right again.

He came to me, placed his hands on my head and murmured a prayer.

It was mid-September 1944. Robert and Josef Büchler were put in a barracks in the former 'Gypsy' Camp. Right next to it was the Men's Camp, separated from it by an electrified fence. 'Büchler, Büchler, Büchler', shouted someone through the fence a day after their arrival. It was Jakub Büchler. Somehow, he had discovered that his elder brother had arrived on a transport – a reunion after one and a half years.

Jakub Büchler worked in the 'Effektenlager' (personal effects store), where the possessions of those murdered by the SS were stored. That enabled him to 'organize' things, despite the risk that it entailed.

Father and son were separated after two days. Robert was put in a block with around 600 children and juveniles. It was said that a scarlet fever epidemic had erupted. All children were isolated in a separate block. They were from Poland, Hungary, the Netherlands, Greece, Czechoslovakia, the Soviet Union and Germany. The block was hermetically sealed, surrounded by barbed wire.

Talking was all there was to do. The occupants told of their homes, talked about sport or their families. Some knew that their parents were no longer alive. Others hoped that they were still living. Robert imagined that he would see his sister and parents again in Topol'čany.

Food was a constant topic of conversation. They were hungry. They argued: 'My mother made it like this.' 'No, that's not the way to do it.' 'My mother's cakes were the best.' They talked about their favourite dishes, delicacies, cakes, restaurants they would like to visit when they got home again. They wanted in this way to forget their everyday existence – at least for a moment, 'but we never really managed to do so'.

One day in mid-October 1944 came the order: 'Fall in for roll call!' A selection was to be made. The children knew what awaited them. They didn't want to go out. SS men grabbed them and dragged them outside. 'The children begged and cried, screamed, kissed the SS men's boots.'

Only around 20 per cent of the children and juveniles survived the selection. Robert Büchler was one of them. They were transferred to the Men's Camp, as it was called officially. The conditions there were slightly better than in the 'Gypsy' Camp.

In the Men's Camp, the children had to work. Robert was put in the 'potato kommando'.

There were long cellars in Birkenau full of potatoes. Women had to drag them there from the trains. I was given a broom and ordered to sweep up the potatoes that had fallen out. I had almost nothing to do. But for the women it was terribly hard work. And for the first time I saw women being beaten to death by the kapos. They sank into the mud and remained there.

The next morning, Robert – 'naïve as I still was' – went to the block elder, Hans Euringer, a German, and explained that he didn't want to work in the 'potato kommando' anymore. When he was asked why, Robert replied: 'The women are beaten there.' The other inmates laughed.

Euringer, 'a decent fellow', put the boy in the 'cart kommando' led by him, where other children were also working. They had to transport things here and there in their cart and saw a lot of the camp in that way. There were two other boys from Topol'čany in this kommando. Emil Friedmann, a year younger than Robert, had also attended the Jewish primary school, and Robert had been in the same class as Jacob Schwarz. He didn't survive the Nazi regime.

In early November 1944, Robert and around twenty other children were transferred to the Main Camp, Auschwitz I, about 3 kilometres away, and, unusually, only then had the number B 14564[139] tattooed on his arm. The boys were put in Block 12, where it was 'more tolerable than in Birkenau. Everyone had his own bunk with a blanket. It was not as filthy as in Auschwitz-Birkenau, and we could wash a bit.'

The day started at 4 a.m. The boys worked in the stables, not far from Auschwitz train station. They fed the animals, cleaned them and mucked out the stalls. At around 7 p.m., they marched back to the camp. As they had enough to eat and did not have a roll call, which in winter could quickly become deadly, they were relatively better off than in Auschwitz-Birkenau. 'But here in the Main Camp, I and the other children were still exposed to the violence and threat of death every day.'

WOLFGANG WERMUTH was 15 when he was deported to Theresienstadt. At the end of September 1944, 'I was now a juvenile' – Wolfgang was ordered in Theresienstadt to prepare for transport.[140] His parents were not on the list. 'It was a great shock for them and for me.'

On arrival in Auschwitz-Birkenau in early October 1944, the inmates were subject to selection. Wolfgang landed on the 'good' side. The 'disinfection' took place a little while afterwards. 'They applied a stinging substance all over our bodies with a masonry brush. Then we were thrown underclothes sewn together from Jewish prayer shawls.'

Although he didn't realize it, Wolfgang was one of the 'transit Jews', who stayed in the camp for a short time, being put in the 'Hungarian camp' [Ungarisches Lager], the former 'Gypsy' Camp or the camp the inmates called 'Mexico' for women, which was in the process of being constructed and was never finished.

Wolfgang was put in a barracks in the former 'Gypsy' Camp with around 150 boys and men. 'We were completely isolated.'

The people from his transport who were not destined for the 'transit camp' were gassed. 'We discovered this when we arrived in the barracks. Trucks – with Red Cross insignia – fetched them. We could guess what was happening from the blazing chimneys, the ash flying through the air, and the penetrating smell of burnt flesh.' Inmates who had been at the camp longer confirmed the suspicions of the new arrivals.

Two days after Wolfgang's transport arrived, another train reached Auschwitz-Birkenau from Theresienstadt. Wolfgang discovered only in January 1980 from the Council of the Jewish Religious Communities in Prague that his parents were on that transport. Documents from Theresienstadt and research carried out at Auschwitz Memorial confirm it. Käthe and Siegmund Wermuth were most probably gassed immediately after their arrival in the camp.

'How can I get out of this hell?' Wolfgang asked himself. 'With the slop they give us to eat, we'll survive at most six or eight months, and then we're done for.' The only consolation was 'that I had friends who were in the same shemozzle'.

CHANNA MARKOWICZ and her family were deported to Auschwitz in May 1944 from Irshava in Carpathia.[141] 'It was shortly after my sixteenth birthday.' The women and men were immediately separated.

> My brothers went with my father and I with my mother. When we arrived at a sort of junction, Mengele, whose name I learned later, sent my mother to the left and me to the right. I said to her: 'Come with me!' But she didn't want to. I said again: 'Come over here, mummy.' She didn't want to because she'd been told to go to the left. A third time I called to her: 'Come over here, mummy.' Mengele heard it. He went to my mother, grabbed her round the neck with a curved walking stick and threw her on the ground.

Channa never forgot this. 'I should have gone to my mother and not called her over. That would have been the obvious thing to do. I didn't do so. At the time I didn't know where my mother and I were going.'

Channa was put in a large camp with many girls from Irshava, her home, including a cousin and her best friend with her two big sisters. 'We stayed together.'

Their heads were shaved. 'We had to get undressed and stand in a line. Those who refused were beaten with a truncheon. Then we went to the "bath" and came out with striped clothes.'

'When we were outside, I looked for my friend. I asked her sister where she was. Everyone started to laugh because she was standing next to me. I hadn't recognized her in those clothes and without her hair.'

The girls had barely stopped laughing when a young women came up to them.

She yelled at us: 'You idiots, how can you just stand there like sheep?' She was very angry. We looked at her in surprise. She continued to tell us off: 'Look over there at the crematorium. Your parents are burning there!' 'She's mad', we thought, 'how can she say such things?' We didn't believe that something like that could be true.

Channa and her friends were put in a barracks with around 1,000 girls and women. 'We slept like sardines in the bunks, head to foot to head to foot.' If one wanted to turn over, they all had to.

At the roll call, the company strength had to be counted. If someone miscounted or the numbers didn't tally, the procedure had to be repeated. This sometimes took four hours. The whole time they had to stand to attention. No one was allowed to go to the toilet. If someone relieved herself on the roll call square, 'she was beaten or killed'.

There was very little to eat. Channa couldn't stomach the soup, which was mostly just water. So all she had all day was a piece of bread and some margarine, from which she always put something aside 'for later'.

Channa was unable to comprehend a lot of what was going on around her. She was full of pain at the loss of her parents and brothers. She kept thinking in particular about her mother. She suffered from the fact that she could no longer remember what she looked like. 'I thought about this all the time.' But she couldn't conjure up her picture.

'There was a woman in our block who was very pregnant. Fortunately, our block elder was a decent Jewish woman from Czechoslovakia, who helped her. The woman gave birth. As it was forbidden to have a child, the birth and the child had to be kept secret.'

# Small Children, Mothers and Grandmothers

Adult inmates were witnesses, hundreds of thousands of times, to the suffering and death of babies and children in the camp. They experienced it on arrival, assisted at births, saw them starve to death, killed with lethal injections, shot, torn in half while still alive or thrown into the flames, or going with their mothers to be gassed.

The Nazi German state and its willing servants had complete control over the property, freedom and lives of babies, children, women and men. The protection of children, the sick and elderly, a fundamental principle even then, was turned on its head: those they could not abuse as slave labourers had no right to exist. The chance of being allowed to stay in the camp was almost non-existent.[1]

SS doctors and other ranks in Auschwitz decided in the blink of an eye between life and death. With an almost imperceptible hand gesture, Germans decided: death, death, death, death, death, death, life for now, death, death, death, death, death … 'To the right' meant temporary reprieve, 'to the left' meant death.

If a mother was carrying her child during the selection, both were gassed. It didn't matter how young, healthy or fit for work she was. If by chance the grandmother was carrying the child, she was killed with it, and the mother – if she was considered temporarily fit for work – was put in the camp.

The Jewish doctor Lucie Adelsberger, inmate number 45171, who was deported from Berlin to Auschwitz on 17 May 1943 with the 38th transport to the East, recorded her impressions of Auschwitz in Amsterdam in 1946, but her memoirs weren't published in Germany until 1956.[2]

According to SS guidelines, every Jewish child automatically condemned his mother to death. Apart from the individual chance occurrences, the camp did not keep Jewish children on. They were consigned to the fire, either living or gassed, immediately upon arrival, and they were not alone, for their mothers went with them. Every woman who had a child in tow, even if it wasn't her own but someone else's child whom she just happened to have under her care at the moment, was marked for death.[3]

Simon Gotland, inmate number 53908, was deported from France to Auschwitz in July 1942. He was forced to work mainly in the 'Kanada' kommando – among other things collecting the luggage, with other inmates, that had been brought to Auschwitz by the deported Jewish children, women and men.[4]

'The inmates were selected immediately on the ramp. Those who did not appear fit for work were sent to the gas chamber, the others to the camp. All children were gassed. If they were accompanied by their mother, the mother was also sent to the gas chamber.'[5]

Magda Szabo, inmate number A-11937,[6] was deported as a Jew from Hungary to Auschwitz in June 1942, together with her sister-in-law, who had a 2-year-old child.

'Because she was younger and weaker', Magda Szabo was carrying the child. 'And when we were standing in line, an inmate came up to me and asked if it was my child.'

She said that it wasn't. The inmate, who had evidently been in the camp longer, said to her: '"Give it … [to] the mother. Perhaps she will [get] … easier work." And I gave it to her.'

To her own mother, who was waiting for selection, she said: 'Mother, say that you're old.' Magda hoped in this way that her mother could look after the child while her sister-in-law was working.

'I was … taken [out] of the line.' She thought: 'Perhaps the children and the old women will be sent to a different camp.'

Magda never saw her mother or her sister-in-law and child again.[7]

Norbert Lopper, born in Vienna, was deported to Auschwitz in late August 1942 from Brussels, where he had escaped, together with his wife Ruth and her 16-year-old sister Sonja. He was put in the camp with the number 61983. He never saw Ruth and Sonja again.[8] One day, a 'French transport arrived' with an '18- to 20-year-old woman with a baby in her arms'.

I thought that perhaps I could do something. I tried to persuade her to hand over the child. It was better for the baby, I said. But the woman refused. [I wanted] to save her at least.... They tried to take the child away from her but she ... screamed: 'No, I won't give up my child.' ... And so she was gassed with the child.[9]

On 11 June 1944, Josef Glück arrived on the ramp in Auschwitz-Birkenau with a transport from Cluj, Romania. He was with his wife, his 2-year-old twin children, his mother, his sister and her two children aged 6 and 10 years.[10] He and his family experienced the selection as follows:

On arrival in Birkenau, we had to climb down from the wagons, leaving our luggage behind. Women and men were separated. The children went with the women. Within the women's group the young and old were separated. The children were to be given to the older women....

My wife had separated from her 2-year-old children as she was ordered to do. She gave the children to my 70-year-old mother. I never again saw my sister, who refused to separate from her children. Nor did I ever see my mother and my two children again.[11]

'A movement of the finger was sufficient', says Kitty Hart, inmate number 39934, deported to Auschwitz from Bielsko, Poland, in April 1943,[12] 'and some of the young people were sent to the camp – the old and children were sent to the left ... It was their last journey. No one came back from that place.'[13]

Rolf Weinstock from Emmendingen near Freiburg, who was tattooed in Auschwitz with the number 59000, wrote down after his liberation what he had seen in the camp in a sort of diary, which was published in 1948.[14] After their arrival in Auschwitz, the deportees had to leave the railway wagons and line up for inspection: 'A whistle blew and the bloodthirsty SS soldateska pounced immediately on the people getting out and hit them with whips. I saw eight- and nine-year-old boys crying: "Mummy, daddy!" The beasts hit them as well.... Condemned to death and perdition.'[15] 'The girls and older women also had to step out and were immediately loaded onto the trucks standing by.'

In this new chaos, suddenly, as if a guardian angel had appeared, I spotted my mother, five metres from me, in the light of a headlamp. My protector. She walked past me, arm-in-arm with other women, head held high. As she climbed into the truck she cast me a glance. She raised her arm and with a clenched fist held under her chin she called: 'Rolf, head up!'[16]

Rolf Weinstock's mother was gassed in Auschwitz in August 1942.[17] Zalman Gradowski from Łuna near Grodno in Poland (now Lunna near Hrodna in Belarus) was interned in Auschwitz on 8 December 1942. All of the members of his family were murdered on that day.[18] He was temporarily reprieved and was able to note many of his observations on paper, including the violent moment of his arrival:

And now, look my friend, what is going on here. Look who has come to welcome us. Soldiers with helmets on their heads, riding-whips in their hands, accompanied by big, vicious dogs.... Why? What are we that it is necessary to welcome us with weapons and savage dogs? We have come to work, after all, like quiet, peacefully disposed people ... Immediately after leaving the train our rucksacks were wrenched from us and even the smallest parcels were all collected together in the square. You are not allowed to take anything with you, you are not allowed to have anything on you ... The mass is divided into three groups: women with children, young and old men and from a small group of people, constituting about 10 per cent of the transport, a third rank is being formed.... The heart bleeds to see the women, exhausted by the journey, with children in arms. You would like to give them some sort of help but any attempt is met with an instantaneous reaction. You are hit on your head straightaway with something hard and blunt, so that you immediately forget your intention of going over to the other group. Women see what happens to their husbands if they try to come to their assistance. From afar they give them to understand by gestures that they should stand quietly, without moving from the spot and that they will manage by themselves somehow ... They comfort each other thinking they will soon be together and share their common lot. All sorts of thoughts keep revolving in our head. We stand helpless and defenceless. The only thing that we still feel is the pain of separation.... Lorries arrive and take women with children.... Men stand to the side and watch their nearest and dearest departing in lorries. Everyone's eyes are glued to the spot where their wives are moving on with children in their arms.[19]

There was no rule in Auschwitz without an exception. Nothing was predictable. Something that offered a reprieve one day could mean death the next. Otto Schwerdt saw mothers – in contrast to the usual practice – being forced to separate from their children on their arrival in Auschwitz, although they wanted to stay with them:

> The Nazis forced mothers who have been sent to the right-hand side to leave their small children. The women cry, scream and beg. The SS men tear the children out of their arms. I cannot describe in words how I feel when I see that. The Nazis are not human beings anymore. They rip the hearts out of the mothers' bodies. They do not show any reaction when they look into the children's frightened, pleading eyes. They hear the screams and keep pulling the children away. Tears are choking me, taking my breath away. I feel as if the world has come to an end, as if all hope and faith has died in that moment.
>
> But not the children, not the little children!
>
> Nothing, no pleading, begging, no resistance helps.[20]

Otto Schwerdt, born in Braunschweig, fled to Poland with his family as a 13-year-old in 1936. They were all deported to Auschwitz in 1943. His mother Eti, his sister Meta and his brother Sigi were gassed. Only he and his father Max survived.[21]

Seweryna Szmaglewska, a Polish author with inmate number 22090, was interned in Auschwitz from October 1942 to January 1945.[22] She witnessed 'normal' life in the camp: mothers carrying children or holding their hands were murdered. She reported in 1946: 'During this selection, a very small number of the youngest and healthiest Jewish women were sent to the camp. But women carrying children or pushing them in a pram ... were sent to the crematorium with their children. Children were detached from their parents in front of the crematorium and taken separately to the gas chambers.'[23]

Mothers with babies or small children had sometimes been allowed to take prams with them in the transports. After their murder, these prams were put first in the 'Effektenlager', also known as 'Kanada', because this country was associated, not only by Auschwitz deportees, with great prosperity. From time to time, they were sent to the German Reich and given to expectant German mothers for their babies. An entry dated 25 June 1944 in *Auschwitz Chronicle* states: 'Empty children's strollers … are taken away from the storerooms … The strollers are pushed in rows of five along the path from the crematoriums to the train station; the removal takes an hour.'[24]

The Polish actress Maria Zabrebinska-Broniewska, inmate number 44739, who was interned for two years in Auschwitz and other camps,[25] witnessed one of the pram transports. She wrote about it shortly after the war:

> At first I tried to count the number of rows, but I soon noticed that there were simply so many that it was impossible to count them fast enough.
>
> White, ivory, dark blue, light green, large and small prams filed past before my eyes, and in every one of them a short while before a healthy rosy baby had lain, its parents' future happiness….
>
> These empty prams were no doubt intended for some modern children's homes, for children of the 'chosen race'.[26]

Orli Reichert, inmate number 502, who was transported from Ravensbrück to Auschwitz on the first women's transport on 26 March 1942,[27] also witnessed one of these 'pram processions' – the title she gave to an essay describing it:

> There was once an endless line of prams moving along a road leading to the train station. They filled the entire width of the road, in rows of five. A short time before, these prams had already passed down the road in the other direction. They had come from the train station, pushed carefully and tenderly, with a cheerful being inside, little legs kicking, children's eyes looking curiously at everything, thumb stuck in mouths, smiling children's eyes communicating blissful, innocent infant dreams. The prams had come a long way and had seen lots of different countries. They were from Paris, Budapest, Brussels, Prague, Vienna and Belgrade.
>
> And now they were travelling back on the road to the train station. They were empty, and instead of being pushed tenderly by a mother, there were men in uniform behind them. They pushed the prams sullenly and

awkwardly. A strange picture. An endless line of empty prams, and the men who were pushing them had murdered the children and their mothers.[28]

Grete Salus was interned as a Jew in Theresienstadt in 1942, and in October 1944 in Auschwitz. On her arrival, she saw 'a man pushing a pram and behind him his wife hurrying on with a baby in her arms'. She spent days and nights writing her report in 1945. She would often go out onto her terrace in Prague and look out. 'There were no friends, no relatives anymore.' From her entire family, there was only one brother left, living in Palestine, as it was then. 'Writing helped me.' But the report remained in a drawer for over ten years and was not published until 1958. It describes the admission procedure in Auschwitz: 'Screams, children crying, deafening noise. Once again the order "Women and men apart!" A fat SS man snatched the luggage from people's hands. A woman behind me clung to her husband screaming, until an SS man brutally tore them apart. At the time no one knew at all how close they all were to death.'[29]

The 15-year-old Janda Weiss from Brno, Czechoslovakia, was a courier in Auschwitz-Birkenau. In that way, she witnessed many things and was also in contact with the men in the Sonderkommando. She reported in 1945:

> When the room [the gas chamber] was full, small children were thrown in through a window. [SS man] Moll grabbed infants by their little legs and smashed their skulls against the wall. Then the gas was let into the chamber. The lungs of the victims slowly burst, and after three minutes a loud clamouring could be heard. Then the chamber was opened, and those who still showed signs of life were beaten to death.... Thousands of women with shaved heads asked about their children and husbands. I lied to thousands of women, telling them that their loved ones were still alive, even though I knew very well that they were all dead.[30]

Countless infants and children died during the arduous transports, often lasting several days, to Auschwitz. Siegbert Löffler, a Jew from Berlin, witnessed this. A dental technician, he was arrested on 27 February 1943 and some days later deported to the Main Camp, Auschwitz I, and tattooed with the number 105675. He had to work there some of the time as an inmate nurse in the inmates' hospital, and also in the SS dental station squad.[31]

One day, 'eight strong inmates' were required. 'What for?' An SS man replied: 'To load furniture.'[32] They travelled by truck to the freight train station in Oświęcim, now known as Auschwitz.

> There were two or three wagons there … At the side a crowd of SS with dogs and rubber truncheons, riding whips in their hands. I thought immediately that it wasn't furniture they were loading.… [In the wagon] were ninety-four or ninety-seven, I don't remember any more, [dead] girls aged two, three, four years, dressed like Käthe Kruse dolls, as if they were going to a birthday party.
>
> I thought of my own children and lifted them slowly and tried to remove them [carefully]. An SS man hit me a couple of times on my back with a rubber truncheon … So we took them by the hair, the arms, whatever we could get hold of, and threw them out.[33]

Some of the babies or children selected on the ramp didn't get as far as the gas chamber. German SS men intervened, smashed them against walls, shot them, threw them alive into the ovens. One day, Simon Gotland, who was now in the clearing squad, had to help to unload a transport from Byelorussia:

> They had been travelling for ten or twelve days and were all dead. It took us three days … to throw out all the corpses from the transport.… One father had a girl in his arms, maybe seven years old. And the girl was still alive, but not the father … The girl was sent with the dead to the crematorium. Unterscharführer Moll, the head of the crematorium, tore the girl in two.[34]

Dov Paisikovic was taken to Auschwitz-Birkenau in May 1944 with his parents and seven siblings from Mukachevo in the Carpathian mountains, Czechoslovakia, which had been annexed by Hungary. He and one brother were the only ones to survive.[35]

The 20-year-old was put in the Sonderkommando with his father Isaak. On the first days, they were used as corpse carriers. 'One man per body', an SS man ordered: 'There was a pile of naked corpses. They were completely bloated, and we were ordered to carry them to a pit, around 6 metres wide and 30 metres long, in which corpses had already been burned.... We worked for eight days like this. Some workers threw themselves into the flames because they couldn't go on.'[36]

When Dov Paisikovic was asked by the presiding judge at the first Auschwitz trial in Frankfurt am Main how the children were taken to the gas chambers, he replied that when the gas chamber was full, the children were 'thrown over the heads'. There were also children who were killed in other ways than gassing. 'An SS man took the child from its mother and gives it a "Zuker", a sweet. And then he took the child by the hand. Before his mother's eyes he smashed it against the wall.'[37]

Nina Guseva, inmate number 65781, from Smolensk, Russia, was deported to the camp in October 1943.[38] She wrote:

> I can remember a young woman with a three-year-old child in her arms, a beautiful girl with curly blonde hair and a blue ribbon. The girl was holding a doll with plaits sticking out. The woman was taken to the camp. The SS men tried to snatch the girl from her. The mother defended her daughter with eyes wide open and crazy with despair. The hands of the perpetrator, SS man Traube, didn't even shake.[39]

The 16-year-old Gedalia Ben Zvi from Bratislava, barely more than a child himself, was transported to Auschwitz in May 1942. He was detailed to unload the arriving trains. One day a transport from Będzin, a Polish town 45 kilometres away, arrived at the camp. There was no selection. The SS wanted to murder everyone right away, including the children.[40]

> Whereas on the others [transports] people arrived with their personal belongings, these people arrived virtually without any possessions; crowded into the freight cars, about 150 people in each car. When the SS men opened the freight cars, the people actually fell out.... The corpses stank.
>
> I remember one case where a 10-year-old girl emerged from a pile of corpses – we didn't know how she survived. She started walking slowly by us, until one of the SS men "'took pity' on her and shot her.
>
> This little boy was sitting – half naked. They had evidently taken his clothes off, owing to the great heat inside the freight cars. One of the SS men was about to shoot him in the neck, and the boy turned around and still

managed to say the first words of a prayer: 'Shema Yisrael, Adonoi eloheinu, Adonoi ehad' – 'Hear, O Israel, the Lord is our God, the Lord is One.' Then the SS man threw him onto the truck.[41]

Dounia Zlata Wasserstrom, inmate number 10308, spoke several languages, including Russian and French. She arrived at the camp from France on 23 July 1942.[42] Some incidents remained etched in her memory for ever:

> In November 1944 a truck arrived with children in it.... A small boy aged four or five jumped down from the truck. He had an apple in his hand. I don't know where the children were from. [The SS men] Boger and Draser were standing in the door. I was at the window. The child stood next to the truck with the apple.
>
> Boger went up to the child, grabbed him by the feet and smashed his head against the wall. He put the apple in his pocket. Then Draser ordered me to wipe 'that stuff on the wall'. I did so. An hour later Boger called me to interpret. He was eating the apple. I saw it all with my own eyes. The child was dead. An SS man had removed the dead child.[43]

Another time, Dounia passed through a hut in which corpses were lying, all naked.

> Something was stirring among the dead; it was a young girl who was not naked. I pulled her out to the camp road and asked her: 'Who are you?' She answered that she was a Greek Jew from Saloniki.... 'Why are you here?' 'I can't live with the living any more. I want to be with the dead.' I gave her a piece of bread. In the evening she was dead.[44]

Zdzisław Soleski, inmate number 96244, from Kraków, watched as 'SS men smashed the heads of children who were crying out of fear of the crematorium against a tree'. And 'when the corpses from the wagons were taken away on trucks, there were people still alive among the dead bodies'. 'When they were tipped into the pit with the burning corpses, we heard a terrible scream every time for a few seconds.'[45]

The children and their parents who had been convicted by the Gestapo police court in Katowice were also murdered immediately. The court met from early 1943 at intervals of several weeks in Block 11 of the Main Camp, Auschwitz I. Interrogations and investigations were also carried out there. The convicted defendants were Poles who, for example, had resisted the German occupation of their country. Thousands of children, women and men were shot without prior registration immediately on arrival at the camp, on the 'black wall' or 'death wall' in the yard of Block 11.[46]

The former inmate Bolesław Zbozień, inmate number 22557, witnessed an incident of this nature, standing on a table and looking through a gap in the bricked-up window in the yard of Block 11. A woman with her infant in her arms, two children aged around 4 and 7 years, and a man were led to the execution site:

> Until the end of my days, the scene that took place before our eyes will remain etched in my memory. The woman and the man did not resist when Palitzsch [SS Rapportführer][47] placed them in front of the 'death wall'. Everything took place in silence. The man took his child's hand in his own left hand. The second child stood between them, and they also held hands. The mother held the youngest child tightly to her breast. Palitzsch first shot the infant in the back of its head, shattering its skull … and causing a good deal of blood. The infant flapped like a fish but the mother held it even tighter to her. Palitzsch now aimed at the child standing between them. The man and woman … stood motionless like stone monuments. Palitzsch wrestled with the oldest child, who didn't want to be shot. He threw it on the ground, lay it on its back and shot it in the back of the head. Then he shot the woman and, last of all, the man. It was terrible.[48]

Another witness of the executions on the 'black wall' was Francizek Gulba, inmate number 10245, who was interned in Auschwitz in February 1941. He was put in Block 11 as a punishment and could see what was going on in the yard. He and his comrades would climb onto the three-tier bunks, which gave 'an excellent view from above'.[49]

> One evening, several persons were brought to Block 11 … There were children, women and men in the group…. Their hands were tied behind their backs with wire…. Finally a woman and child were brought in – we assumed it was a mother and her daughter. The mother … held the daughter's hand.

Both were dressed only in a blouse. Palitzsch shot the mother first. When she fell to the ground, the child flung itself onto the body and cried in despair: 'Mummy, mummy!' Palitzsch aimed at the girl but missed her, because the child continued to embrace her mother's body. Then the block elder came and held the girl so that Palitzsch could take better aim. A moment later the child was dead.[50]

The Polish inmate Władysław Girsa, inmate number 12601, one day had to do some masonry work close to one of the crematoria in Auschwitz-Birkenau. He was around 30 metres from the killing site and could look through the half-open door of the crematorium: 'I saw a little girl (around 8 years old) run up to an SS officer crying. She kneeled in front of him and stretched out her hand. From her behaviour I assumed that she was asking for help. In response to her pleading the SS man kicked her so hard that she fell down and didn't get up again.'[51]

Jan Szpalerski from Warsaw, inmate number 119468, who was deported to Auschwitz-Birkenau on 29 April 1943, was forced to work as a slave labourer in the carpentry kommando. In this way, he was able to see lots of sections of the huge camp with his own eyes.[52] One day in summer 1944, he had to erect a hut with other inmates near Crematorium IV. While he was putting on the roof, he saw inmates from the Sonderkommando transporting people on narrow carts from the crematorium gas chamber to the nearby burning pits:

It was at a time when the Auschwitz crematoria … no longer had the capacity to cope because of the intensity of the extermination of the Jews, making it necessary to burn thousands of corpses in the open air in pits dug specially for that purpose.

Then three trucks arrived: dumpers loaded with children who were still alive, which turned in the direction of the pits. The vehicles reversed to the edge of the pits, lifted the bed and dumped the children directly into the flames…. Some of the older children jumped out in horror and turned around blindly to flee. Unfortunately, they didn't know that there was no way out. The SS men began effortlessly to shoot them and toss them back into the pits dead or alive. This incident convinced me that there was a hell on earth.[53]

Krystyna Żywulska (*née* Sonia Landau), member of a Jewish family from Łódź, wrote about another day 'when the ovens couldn't handle so many corpses'. She was arrested in Warsaw in June 1943 and sentenced to death, but after two months in prison was deported to Auschwitz.[54]

> We could distinguish only women and the children.... They hugged their children closely. Small children were carried by their mothers, older children clung to their mothers' skirts, and still older children looked around with suspicion.... About an hour later, the chimney of the fourth crematorium, which was just behind our dormitory, began to gush flames. Simultaneously, smoke began to rise from the hole that had been dug near the crematorium.... The wind moved the cloud in our direction. The smoke covered the sun and the bright light of the day turned into frightful darkness. The smoke carried the smell of burning goose, only much stronger.[55]

Kalman Bar On from Ilok – part of former Yugoslavia, now Croatia – who, with his twin sister Yehudit, fell into the hands of SS doctor Mengele,[56] saw wheelchair occupants and babies being thrown alive into the flames: 'There was a small copse next to the crematorium with a large burning pit. Wheelchair occupants and babies were thrown into the pit and burned alive. For ten weeks I heard the screams of the burned victims, from July to September (1944).'[57]

Because of a shortage of gas in mid-1944, Camp Commandant Rudolf Höß ordered that less gas should be introduced into the gas chambers.[58] After liberation, Hermann Langbein, inmate number 60355, from Vienna, who, as a clerk to the SS camp doctor,[59] saw and heard a lot, wrote several books on Auschwitz. In *Die Stärkeren*, he described the gas shortage in 1944:

> Many were just numbed but not dead and were thus transported live on the carts to the crematorium ovens and incinerated there. Höß gave another order to save gas. Piles of wood were collected outside the crematoria. The children of Hungarian Jews were thrown into the flames. The children were chosen because they were lighter. Strong men were picked from every transport, who were ordered to throw the children – including their own children – into the flames. Then the men were gassed.[60]

Seweryna Szmaglewska also heard that:

> because great economies are being made in the use of gas, small children are being burned alive. Therefore, they are at once separated from their elders and led inside separately. One day a small boy, perhaps five years old, escaped from the SS escort as they reached the entrance to the crematory and ran with all the power of his two little feet back along the railing. But where could he run, where could he hide?[61]

All infants and children who got as far as one of the crematoria – in other words, who were not killed beforehand by the SS and/or thrown alive into the fire pits outside – were murdered in the gas chambers. There were slave labourers who witnessed or saw what happened in front of the crematorium, in the entrance to the gas chambers, and in the gas chambers themselves.

Otto Wolken, inmate number 128828, a doctor from Vienna, arrived at the camp on 9 July 1943. He worked as an inmate doctor in Auschwitz-Birkenau.[62] In mid-April 1944, as so often before, he was once again witness to 'a tragedy':

> From the Lublin camp (Majdanek), 299 girls and two infants came to the camp. We, the medical orderlies, were ordered to examine them. They were all healthy young persons. We were told they would only be with us for a while and would then be sent to the Women's Camp. Late in the evening they were fetched by the 'Hundekommando' [SS guards with dogs trained to attack humans].… For hours we heard the desperate cries from the crematorium of these girls, who knew what was to become of them. We also heard the shouting and shooting by the guards. We couldn't see anything but could only guess the tragedy that was taking place. We knew that they were destined for the gas chambers when we saw the Hundekommando.[63]

'Krystyna Żywulska saw lots of transports arrive. They went "straight on to the little white house". This was a converted former farmhouse with a gas chamber disguised as a shower. "A little blond girl picked a flower. Our chief [from the SS] became furious. How could she destroy flowers! How could she spoil the grass! She had the whole road to walk on. A cultured civilized German could not stand the sight of such destruction.

He ran up to the child, who could not have been more than four years old, and kicked her. The child tumbled and fell on the grass. She didn't cry; she only clutched the flower stem – the flower was gone. She stared at the SS man with wide-eyed surprise. Her mother lifted the child and went with the others. The child turned her head and continued to look at our chief over her mother's shoulder. "The eyes of that child condemned the whole German nation", Tanja said hatefully, walking next to me.'[64]

Ota Kraus and Erich Kulka came from Prague and Vsetín in Czechoslovakia. They had been in Auschwitz-Birkenau since autumn 1942 and were in a group of artisans who carried out repairs throughout the camp. Both of them saw a lot.[65]

> The child was impatient at having to wait so long. She kept on asking her mother how long it would be before they started. With tears in her eyes, the mother tried to comfort her: 'Be good, it won't be long now, we'll soon be going to Granny and Grandpa. We've just got to have a bath, then we'll put on some nice clothes, and off we go …'
>
> But the child would not quieten down; it seemed to sense that something unusual was going on. Fearing that the child's whining might provoke the SS men on guard to violence – for they did not draw the line at beating children – the mother said to her: 'Do a little dance for us, then, and we'll soon be off to see Granny.' In a trice the girl was happily dancing. Several women and children formed a circle while the little girl performed a charming quadrille in their midst in this antechamber of death. Even the SS seemed to be taken with the unusual sight. But the dance was never finished …
>
> [SS man] Kramer suddenly burst into the room, and shouting, 'This isn't a theatre!', gave the order to move the people into the gas chamber.[66]

Rudolf Höß, Commandant of Auschwitz, wrote in his autobiography:

> The smaller children usually cried because of the strangeness of being undressed in this fashion, but when their mothers or members of the Special Detachment comforted them, they became calm and entered the gas chambers, playing or joking with one another and carrying their toys. I noticed that women who either guessed or knew what awaited them nevertheless found the courage to joke with the children to encourage them,

despite the mortal terror visible in their own eyes. One woman approached me as she walked past and, pointing to her four children who were manfully helping the smallest ones over the rough ground, whispered: 'How can you bring yourself to kill such beautiful, darling children? Have you no heart at all?'[67]

On the basis of the findings in the Warsaw Höß trial (March 1947) and the Kraków trial of forty SS men and women (November/December 1947),[68] Jan Sehn, Director of the Institute of Forensic Expertise in Kraków and member of the Main Commission for Nazi Crimes in Poland, presented an early and detailed study of the events in Auschwitz. It contains a precise description of the extermination of children, women and men on an industrial scale:

The people from these transports were driven immediately from the loading ramp to the area where the gas chambers were located. Those who were not capable of walking were driven there on trucks. Thousands and thousands of people moved from the loading ramp in unending lines towards the crematoria....

In the middle of the road running parallel to the train platform a constant stream of trucks transported the old and sick and children to the gas chambers. SS men with machine guns ready to fire lay in the ditches by the side of the road.

One of the SS men made a speech to the group of people assembled on a small square in front of the gas chamber, assuring them that because there were dirty and lousy people in their midst and that no one was allowed in the camp in that condition they were to be taken to the bathing and disinfection room.

Even prisoners from the special detachment (Sonderkommando) did not tell the victims the truth in the undressing room. They told them only of the alleged bathing and de-lousing, reminding them to fold their clothes neatly and remember where they had put them so they might find them again quickly after the disinfection.

During this time, the gas chamber was warmed with the aid of portable baskets filled with burning coke ...

After the Jews had undressed, they entered the gas chambers. Here there were shower heads and water pipes, so that the room looked like a shower.

Usually the women and children entered first and then the men, who were always a smaller group. With beatings and harassment by dogs ... around 3,000 victims were crowded into one gas chamber. Then the doors were quickly closed and the waiting disinfectors immediately dropped Zyklon into the gas chambers through specially designed vaporizers to ensure a rapid and maximum effect. This device caused gas to form straightaway ...

According to stokers employed in the crematorium, as soon as the gas chamber was closed the victims crowded towards the door, pressed against the peephole, damaging the electrical wiring and ventilation systems.

Half an hour after the gas had been introduced, the doors were opened and the ventilation switched on. The corpses were pulled out immediately and taken by lift to the ovens above.

The corpses were generally in a seated position. They had a pink skin colour with occasional dark pink and green spots. Some had foam on their lips, others had bled from the nose. Many corpses had their eyes open, and very many had become entangled in their death struggle.

The majority of the bodies were near the door. Fewer victims were near the places where the Zyklon was introduced. From the position of their bodies, it was clear that the people there had tried to escape and get nearer the door.[69]

Marina Wolff, interned from 1942 in Auschwitz-Birkenau, reported to the German-Israeli author Inge Deutschkron about a transport with 'around 150 children', which arrived one day in the camp. The children were holding hands:

One was carrying the youngest with difficulty, accompanied by female SS guards marching briskly.... They stopped in the field opposite the crematorium.

A woman guard instructed the children in a loud voice: 'Get undressed nicely and fold your clothes neatly so that you can find your things again afterwards. And then we'll go to the shower.'

The children began to undress. Then a five-year-old girl suddenly threw a large red ball. The others ran after it, caught it, threw it in the air and played for a while in the warm September sunshine.

They were small children, the oldest perhaps ten. At the edge of the field a very small child – two years old, at least too small to play with the others

Dáša and her sister Sylva Friedová, three years older than her. 'I have only good memories of the first nine years of my childhood. It was a nice, happy time.'
© Alwin Meyer Archive

Heinz with his father Salvator, mother Hella and sister Erika Kounio in Thessaloniki. 'We were an open-minded family interested in culture. Books, theatre and concert visits were part of our lives.'
© Heinz Salvator Kounio

Dagmar Fantlová and her sister Rita. 'My father was a doctor, and my mother a housewife. I had a younger sister called Rita. We lived peacefully in Kutná Hora until 1939.'
© Rita McLeod

Moshe Špíra from Mukachevo in the Carpathian region was deported to Auschwitz at the age of 13. He survived but was never able to talk about his childhood or Auschwitz.

© Alwin Meyer Archive

Gábor Hirsch in the small Hungarian town Békéscsaba. 'My father owned an electrical supply and radio shop. In its heyday, he employed between ten and fifteen trainees.'

© Alwin Meyer Archive

Jürgen Loewenstein lived at Grenadierstrasse 4a (now Almstadtstrasse 49) in the centre of Berlin. 'People at the time said that the Jews were to blame for everything and that all Jews were rich. This was in blatant contradiction to the social situation in which my family and others lived.'
© Alwin Meyer Archive

Wolfgang with his parents Käthe and Siegmund Wermuth and his sister Ursula Brigitte. 'I was a real Berlin lad. My family were always aware of their Jewish identity and never denied it.'
© William Wermuth

Janek Mandelbaum, born in Gdynia (Poland), a few years after liberation. 'I lived there for the first twelve years of my life with my father Majloch, my mother Cyrla, my sister Ita and my brother Jakob. Until then we had a good and interesting life.'
© Jack Mandelbaum

The twins Jiří and Zdeněk Steiner from Prague, aged 3 or 4. 'Our family had lived for several generations in the city. We were liberal Jews. We celebrated all the holidays and went to the synagogue on Saturday mornings.'
© Alwin Meyer Archive

When Eduard was 2, his family moved to Bratislava, where his father, Simon Kornfeld, opened a flourishing linen goods shop. 'We were strictly religious. We went to the synagogue not only on the holidays but also on Shabbat. Anything else would have been unthinkable.'
© Ruth Kornfeld

Channa Loewenstein (*née* Markowicz) with her daughters Noomi and Noga.
'There are no pictures of me as a child. They all got lost when we were deported
from Irshava (Carpathia) to Auschwitz.'
© Alwin Meyer Archive

Yehuda Bacon's parents: 'Jews were commonplace in Ostrava.'
© Yehuda Bacon

Yehuda with his sisters Hanna (l.) and Rella. 'Relations between Jews and non-Jews were relatively good. I didn't personally experience any antisemitism at first.'
© Yehuda Bacon

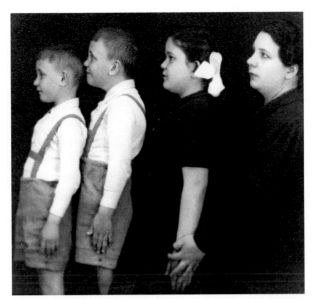

The twins Ferenc and Otto Klein with their sister Ágnes and their mother Lilly. Their father, Salomon Klein, was a hardworking businessman. 'My parents loved each other and us children very much.'
© Alwin Meyer Archive

Old postcard showing the synagogue in Hajdúböszörmény (Hungary).
© Alwin Meyer Archive

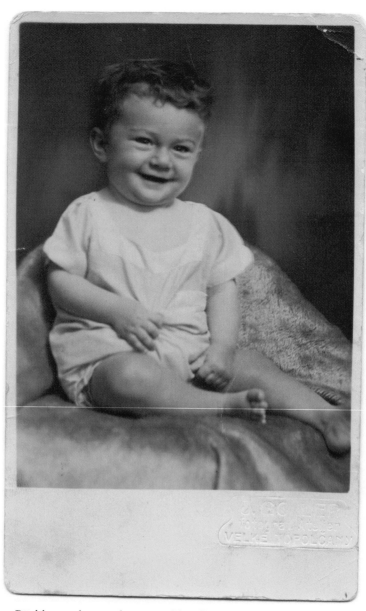

Robert Büchler aged around 1 year in Topol'čany, western Slovakia. 'My father's ancestors had lived for around 200 years in the city … Of my grandparents' thirteen children, five were tailors like my grandfather. Everything they sold was hand-made.'
© Alwin Meyer Archive

Lydia and Věra Holznerová in Hronov, Czechoslovakia. Their father, Emil Holzner, said repeatedly: 'I know the Germans. They are a cultivated people. They won't behave so badly.' But he was wrong.
© Alwin Meyer Archive

Anna Polshchikova gave birth to her son Viktor on 15 October 1944 in
Auschwitz-Birkenau. She was able to breastfeed him, something only a few
mothers in the camp were capable of. They both survived, also something that
very few managed.
© Archive of the Auschwitz-Birkenau Memorial and Museum

Lidia Rydzikowska was born Luda Bocharova in Ukraine. She was deported at the age of 4 to Auschwitz and separated from her mother Anna, who told her: 'Never forget your name, never forget it …'
© Archive of the Auschwitz-Birkenau Memorial and Museum

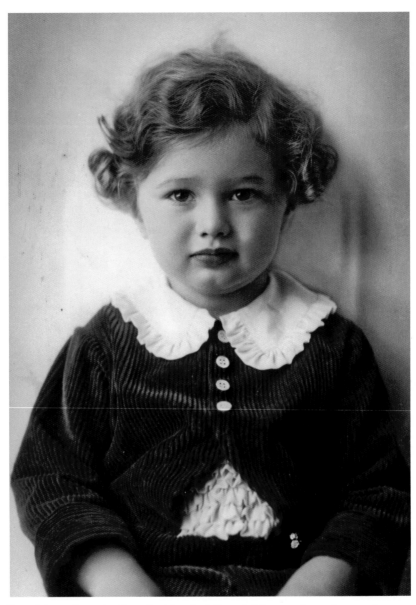

Géza Schein from the Danube island of Csepel (Hungary), aged around 2 years. His father Zoltán was a baker. 'We were allowed to bake bread and other items for the Jews in the ghetto. It wasn't much, but we were still able to live from it.' © Zoltan Kozma

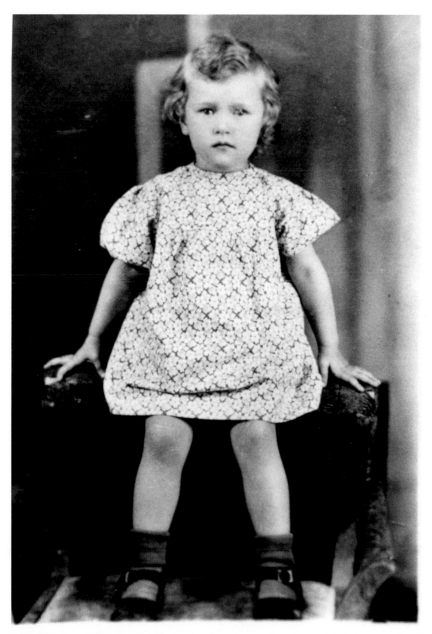

Called Barbara Wesołowska for over seventy years, her name at birth on 27 April 1944 in Auschwitz-Birkenau was probably Katya Kulik. Because her arm was too small, her inmate number was tattooed on her thigh.
© Barbara Wesołowska

At the age of 6, Vera and Olga Grossmann were abused by SS Doctor Mengele for his experiments. The photos were taken around 1950 in London.
© Vera Kriegel

On the lower photo, Olga is in the bottom row (2nd from l.) and Vera in the second row (2nd from r.).
© Vera Kriegel

He was called 'Kola' in Auschwitz. When he was liberated from the camp, he didn't know how old he was nor where he came from. The photo was taken around eighteen months after his liberation. He used it many years later to search for his family.

© Alwin Meyer Archive

Éva/Ewa was deported to Auschwitz on 20 May 1944 in a transport of Hungarian Jews. After liberation, the little girl was adopted by Karolina and Jósef Krcz from Poland. She was unable to find any of the members of her family again.
© Ewa Krcz-Siezka

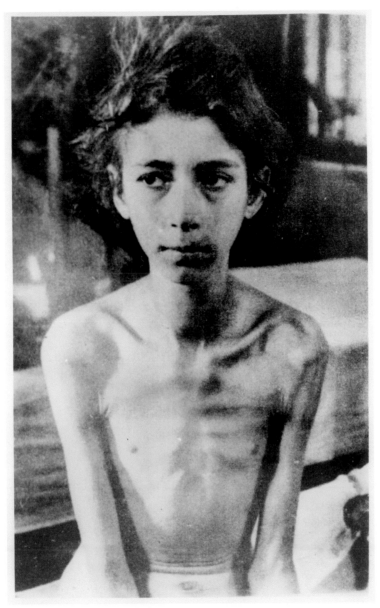

Judith Rosenbaum was deported from Hungary to Auschwitz with her twin sister Ruth in early June 1944. Both were liberated. Ruth's feet, which were frostbitten from having to stand for twelve hours in winter as a punishment, had to be amputated. She died on 23 March 1945.
© Archive of Auschwitz-Birkenau Memorial and Museum

The suitcases of Pavel Kohn and Peter Perl were found after the liberation of Auschwitz. At least 232,000 babies, children and juveniles under the age of 18 were deported to Auschwitz, including 216,000 Jews and 11,000 Sinti and Roma.

© Alwin Meyer

The ramp at Auschwitz-Birkenau extermination camp.
© The United States Holocaust Memorial Museum

Babies and children were almost always killed immediately. If a mother was carrying a child during the selection, both were gassed.
© The United States Holocaust Memorial Museum

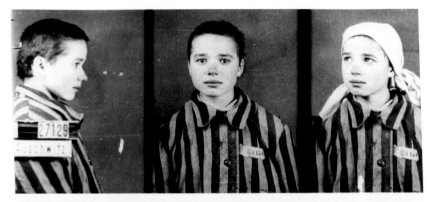

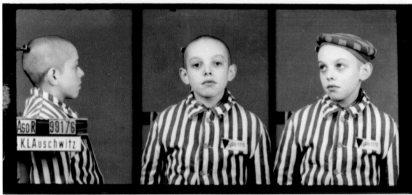

Krystyna Trześniewska died in Auschwitz on 18 May 1943 aged 14.
Anatol Wanukiewsicz arrived on 1 February 1943 aged 13. He survived.
Jaroslav Lisin arrived at the camp on 2 October 1942 aged 13.
© Archive of Auschwitz-Birkenau Memorial and Museum

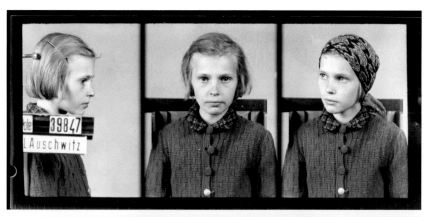

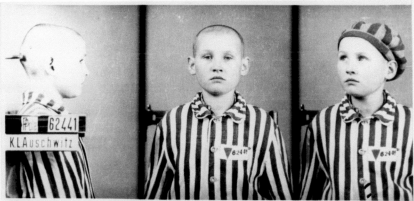

Maria Matlak was deported to Auschwitz on 2 April 1943 aged 15. She survived.
Leonard Grosicki arrived in Auschwitz on 1 September 1942. He survived.
Unknown, arrived in the camp on 8 August 1942.
© Archive of Auschwitz-Birkenau Memorial and Museum

Jews were normally forbidden from writing, but occasionally they were even forced by the SS to do so, particularly in the Theresienstadt Family Camp. They had to write that they were well. In that way, the Nazis attempted to maintain the myth of the 'resettlement of the Jews'. Dagmar Lieblová wrote to Fany Holická, her grandparents' former housekeeper. She signed the postcard, which has survived, with her pet name 'Danka'.
© Rita McLeod

Géza Schein, aged 12 years. Jean Markiel, a fellow inmate, secretly drew this pencil portrait in Auschwitz-Birkenau in 1944 and gave it to the boy.
Drawing: Jean Markiel. © Archive of Auschwitz-Birkenau Memorial and Museum

"Muselman"

After liberation, Yehuda Bacon occupied all his free time with painting. He drew and painted women with children, the fear of the inmates, or the half-starved people known as 'Muselmänner' and usually close to death.
Picture: Yehuda Bacon. © Archive of the Auschwitz-Birkenau Memorial and Museum

As a child, Yehuda Bacon experienced the limits of humanity and beyond. He managed to create a meaningful existence above all through his art. 'My pictures saved me.'
Picture: Yehuda Bacon. © Alwin Meyer Archive

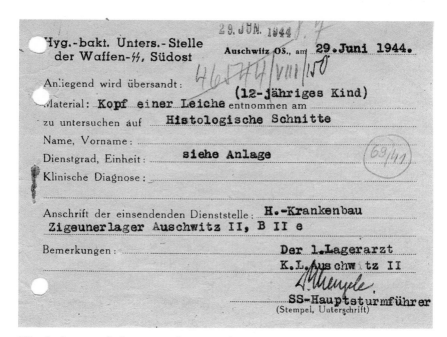

Hyg.-bakt. Unters.-Stelle
der Waffen-SS, Südost

29. JUN. 1944

Auschwitz OS., am **29.Juni 1944.**

Anliegend wird übersandt:

**(12-jähriges Kind)**

Material: **Kopf einer Leiche** entnommen am ............

zu untersuchen auf **Histologische Schnitte**

Name, Vorname: ............

Dienstgrad, Einheit: ............ **siehe Anlage**

Klinische Diagnose: ............

Anschrift der einsendenden Dienststelle: **H.-Krankenbau**
**Zigeunerlager Auschwitz II, B II e**

Bemerkungen: ............ **Der 1.Lagerarzt**
**K.L.Auschwitz II**

**SS-Hauptsturmführer**
(Stempel, Unterschrift)

'Head of a corpse': document from Auschwitz Đ signed by SS Doctor Mengele.
© Archive of Auschwitz-Birkenau Memorial and Museum

Cot in one of the surviving barracks in Auschwitz-Birkenau, in which babies, children and juveniles had to live.
© Alwin Meyer

– was sitting. Like a kindergarten teacher the [SS guard] Irma Grese clapped her hands:

'That's enough playing, Leave the ball where it is. Now let's hurry up and go to the shower.'

The children obeyed and ran down the steps to the crematorium

The little girl also crawled awkwardly after them as well as she could on her knees. Irma Grese saw her and gave her dog to an SS guard and picked up the girl. The gas chamber steps were too high for her little legs....

We saw Irma Grese one more time, when she came out of the crematorium, fetched the dog and went back quietly with it to the camp. After twenty minutes, the ventilators started up and the process was over. In front of the crematorium were the pants, the ribboned dresses – and the red ball.[70]

It was probably on the Jewish New Year in 1944 that Josef Glück saw SS doctor Mengele and three SS 'leaders' come into his section of the camp. They were driving a large group of Jewish boys from Hungary 'who were all healthy'. 'These children knew, sensed, what was happening. They all ran off.' The SS men grabbed them and drove them into barracks number 11. 'After two days, trucks arrived.... They were sent to be gassed.' Among them was his nephew, Andreas Rapaport. On the wall in Block 11 he had written in Hungarian in blood: 'Rapaport, André, élt tizenhat évet' [André Rapaport lived sixteen years].

Josef Glück saw the boy as the SS led him off. He called out: '"Uncle, I know I'm going to die. Tell my mother that I thought of her until the last moment." But I couldn't tell her because she was already dead.'[71]

'One day after opening the gas chambers, the men of the Sonderkommando', says Krystyna Zywulska,

heard the quiet whimper of a living baby. Although they had already witnessed the worst scenes you could imagine, this time they were numb with terror. It turned out that the child was still alive because during the gassing it continuously sucked its mother's breast, resulting in gas not having access to the lungs.... Moll [SS man in charge of the gas chambers], who was on duty, was called. Enraged, he threw the child into a burning furnace alive.[72]

Seweryna Szmaglewska wrote in her eyewitness account *Dymy nad Birkenau* [*Smoke over Birkenau*] in 1946: 'A young Jewess from Łódź ...

stands ... bleeding among the women, her eyes staring benumbed at the pillar of smoke.' In the face of the inconceivable things she witnessed in Auschwitz-Birkenau, there is one sentence that recurs repeatedly: 'The Germans are human beings. And we, the Jews, are human too.'[73]

For the Polish actress Maria Zarębińska-Broniewska, what she saw and suffered in Auschwitz haunted her for the rest of her life. She died just two years after liberation, on 5 July 1947. The 'Auschwitz experiences', said a friend, 'attached themselves undetected to her organism, and dwelled for a long time', until they 'cruelly extinguished' her 'broken will to live'.[74]

Before that, she wrote down her experiences. The children remained engraved on her heart:

> I saw hundreds of children getting out of the trains and going to their death. Now, as I write down what I saw, I am still surprised that as a mother who loves not only her own child but all children in the world, I didn't go mad. For days, I would be haunted by a face or a figure of a child from the train who was doomed to die. How often did I see them playing behind the barbed wire – a little girl in a green coat, a boy playing with a ball, or a baby in pink rompers in the arms of its happy mother.[75]

The mothers and children enjoying a temporary reprieve in the Theresienstadt Family Camp were generally gassed six months later in a number of actions without selection. As the Nazis required slave labourers to clear the ruins after the air raids in Germany, a selection was carried out in the Family Camp at the end of June 1944. Mothers with children were also allowed to 'apply'. The 21-year-old Ruth Bondy from Prague, inmate number 72430, who was deported to the Auschwitz-Birkenau Family Camp in December 1943, was asked by some women before the selection what they should do.

> At first I avoided giving them a direct answer. 'How should I know. I don't have a child of my own.' But when that didn't seem to satisfy them, I said: 'I think if I had a small child, I would stay with him.' They nodded – they had long made up their mind and they just wanted my confirmation. For years the heavy burden of responsibility has stayed with me. The mothers were

young and could have survived and founded new families. It was only after my own daughter was born that I was reassured. I would never have left her alone at that moment when she was more in need of my embrace than ever.

Only 'three of around six hundred mothers with children' decided in June 1944 to apply for 'selection'. The others all stayed with their sons and daughters. Until the end.[76]

# 'DI 600 Inglekh' and Other Manuscripts Found in Auschwitz

> People who worked in the camp looked death in the eye every day, they were beaten, they had other tragedies. But we saw the most terrible things of all. We did the dirty work of the Holocaust.[1]

These are the words of Ya'akov Gabai, inmate number 182569, one of the few surviving witnesses of the Jewish Sonderkommando in Auschwitz-Birkenau. Together with his brother Dario, inmate number 182568, he was brought to Auschwitz on 11 April 1944 in a transport from Athens. The two worked as slave labourers in the crematoria in Birkenau as 'corpse pushers' [*Leichenschieber*] and 'corpse draggers' [*Leichenschlepper*].[2]

Filip Müller, inmate number 29236, from Sered' near Bratislava, was deported to Auschwitz on 13 April 1943 at the age of 20, with a transport of Slovakian Jews. He was soon assigned to work in Crematorium I in the Main Camp, later in the crematoria in Auschwitz-Birkenau. For almost three years, he was forced by the Germans to dispose of the bodies of the murdered victims.[3]

As a young man, he had to watch as tens of thousands of people lost their lives – including many babies, infants and children. When the members of the Sonderkommando had to clear the dead out of the gas chambers, there were sometimes children whose hearts were still beating. These children were then shot by the SS.[4]

SS-Hauptscharführer Moll, in charge of the gas chambers at Auschwitz-Birkenau, snatched children away from their mothers as they were on their way to the crematorium. He took them behind Crematorium IV where there were two large pits in which the corpses were burned.

'And he threw ... the [living] children into the boiling [corpse] fat.' Afterwards, Moll said he could now 'eat his fill' because 'I have done my duty.'[5]

Simon Gotland, born in Warsaw and deported in July 1942 from Frankfurt to Auschwitz, worked for several weeks as a helpless slave labourer in the Sonderkommando.[6] He had to dig the large pits in Auschwitz-Birkenau mentioned by Filip Müller, into which the gassed victims were thrown. 'And although we piled on 2 to 3 metres of sand, the blood still seeped through.'[7]

In the first half of 1942, Auschwitz-Birkenau became the centre of the mass extermination of the Jews by the Germans. As a consequence, the gassing and burning of the children, women and men was transferred from the Main Camp, Auschwitz I, to Birkenau.[8]

The 'most terrible of all', the work in the crematoria with the gas chambers and the bonfires and burning pits, was carried out by members of the Sonderkommando under orders from the SS. They were Jews, kept strictly segregated from other inmates in Auschwitz-Birkenau.[9]

The SS forced the members of the Sonderkommando, under the threat of death, to cut off the hair from the dead women, tear out the gold teeth and search the corpses for hidden valuables. The SS forced them to drag the murdered victims to the crematorium ovens and to push them into the ovens. There were also burning pits outdoors in which the men from the Sonderkommando were permanently confronted by their own death, piling the corpses or throwing them into the already burning pits. They had to smash the bones of the gassed victims who had not completely burned – while suffering constant physical and psychological violence from the SS – remove the ashes and tip them into the Soła and Vistula.[10]

'We're the only ones', says Ya'akov Gabai, 'who saw the tragedy of the Jews with our own eyes.'[11] As witnesses of the mass extermination and 'holders of the secret', all men in the Sonderkommando were regularly murdered and replaced by other inmates.[12] Thus, of over 2,100 Jewish inmates in the Sonderkommando, only around 110 survived.[13]

One form of resistance by the Sonderkommando inmates was to make notes on what they saw and experienced in the camp and to bury them – as testimony for later – in the area of the crematoria in Auschwitz-Birkenau. Eight containers with hidden manuscripts have been found to date in Auschwitz-Birkenau. They include testimonies by Zalman

Gradowski, Leib Langfus and Zalman Lewental. Five manuscripts are in Yiddish, and one each in French and Greek.[14]

The testimonies suggest that there are still very many more manuscripts buried in the earth in Auschwitz-Birkenau. They have not been found today and in some cases might have been destroyed as a result of climate influences.

Henry Porebsky, a surviving inmate of the 'electrician kommando' whose work took him all over the camp, reported after liberation that there were manuscripts buried between the changing room and the gas chamber in Crematorium III: 'The containers were not placed directly under the walls of the building because it was feared that the crematoria … might be demolished … Nor could they be buried near trees, as these might be felled and uprooted.… As far as I recall, at least thirty-six containers of various sizes and volumes were buried in this way.'[15]

Zalman Gradowski wrote in his discovered manuscript: 'Dear finder, search every inch of the earth. Under it there are dozens of documents buried, by me and by others, which shed light on everything that happened here.'[16]

All of the records found to date are by inmates forced to work in the Sonderkommando. Under mortal danger, they wrote down what they had seen with their own eyes. Other inmates supported them. For example, an inmate from the 'Kanada' kommando provided Gradowski with writing paper.[17]

Two manuscripts written in Yiddish by Zalman Gradowski have been found in Auschwitz-Birkenau. The first was discovered by Szlama (Shlomo) Dragon on 5 March 1945 near the ruins of Crematorium II. It was in a German aluminium water bottle. Dragon himself had the inmate number 80359 indelibly tattooed on his left forearm, and was a member of the Sonderkommando like Gradowski.[18]

The first manuscript by Gradowski to be found consisted of a notebook and two-page letter dated 6 September 1944. The letter was completely legible, but the first lines of each page of the notebook had become smudged on account of moisture and could not be deciphered.[19]

The second manuscript by Gradowski was made publicly known by Chaim Wolnerman, who had been an inmate in Auschwitz-Birkenau.

After he returned to his hometown of Oświęcim in March 1945, he searched for several months in the nearby former Auschwitz camp for traces of relatives, friends and acquaintances. He went from block to block. As he put it, his disappointment was immense. Unfortunately, he found nothing he was looking for.

What he found, to his surprise, was a list with names of people who had been deported to Auschwitz. He came across a pile of artificial limbs, a mountain of shoes, a large number of stockings, children's toys and paper bags containing women's hair. He also found glass jars with embryos in SS doctor Mengele's former hospital block. Wolnerman gave both the list of names and the jars with embryos to the Main Commission for Nazi Crimes in Poland.

On his tours of the camp, he often met people looking for 'treasures' in the former extermination camp. And he himself found gold teeth in the ashes of the burned victims.

One day, a young man came to Wolnerman and offered him a manuscript in Yiddish, which he had found in a rusty tin can near one of the former crematoria. Wolnerman skimmed a few pages of the manuscript and realized immediately that it was an important document, and bought it from the young man.

In early 1947, Wolnerman and his wife Jetta, who had been liberated from another camp, emigrated to Israel. He continued to concern himself on and off with the manuscript but was not able to publish it until 1978, in Yiddish and at his own expense.[20]

This second manuscript by Gradowski found in Auschwitz-Birkenau had the title: 'In harz fun gehinem' [In the heart of hell].[21]

After marrying his wife Sonia, Gradowski lived in the Polish town of Łuna near Grodno (today, Lunna, near Hrodna in Belarus). The town had been occupied in mid-1939 by the Soviet Union. Around two-thirds of the population, including the Gradowskis, were Jewish. On 28 June 1941, German troops occupied the town. The Jewish inhabitants were persecuted and forced to work, and in October 1941 concentrated in a segregated ghetto.[22]

In the night of 2 November 1942, the ghetto was closed and around 1,500 Jewish children, women and men interned in Kielbasin transit camp in cold and damp underground barracks without any sanitary installations. Many died of typhoid fever as a result.[23] The systematic deportation of the Jews from Kielbasin began at the end of November. Zalman Gradowski was interned in Auschwitz on 8 December 1942. All of the members of his family were murdered on that day:[24] 'My wife Sonia, my mother Sara, my sister Estera-Rachel, my sister Liba, [my] father-in-law Rafael, [my] brother-in-law Wolf'.[25]

In the second text, Gradowski describes the fates of several individuals, including many children. In this manuscript, he relates, in particular, the events of Purim night on 8 March 1944, when the 3,791 people, including a large number of children, who arrived from Theresienstadt in September 1943 were gassed.[26]

'IN HARZ FUN GEHINEM': The families were already separated, torn apart, deported there: the lonely wife cried in one hut, the husband in another, and the larger children in the third crypt, sitting there and crying, calling for their mothers and fathers ...

Strong young boys and girls thought only of their parents. Who knew what was happening to them there. And young men, full of courage and strength, sat there stunned by grief, thinking of the young wives and children from whom they had only just been parted....

Soon we would bear witness. With our own eyes we would have to watch our own destruction, as five thousand Jews, five thousand vibrant, thriving souls, women and children, young and old, would pass under the truncheons of civilized brutes. At the authorities' disposal would be rifles, grenades and automatics, as well as their constant four-footed companions, their vicious dogs; these would chase and savagely attack the Jews, who, distracted and confused, would run blindly into the arms of death....

Hopeless, baffled, crushed, they began to run to the trucks, dodging the snapping of the dogs and the blows of the enraged beasts. And more than one fleeing woman fell with her child, so that the accursed earth already drank warm blood from young Jewish skulls....

From the rows of naked people, many broke from the line and fell wildly, weeping and crying; naked children recognized their mothers and kissed, embraced, rejoiced that they had been reunited here. And a child felt lucky to have a mother, a mother's heart, accompanying him to the grave....

There a mother sat naked on the bench, holding her daughter, a girl not yet fifteen years, on her lap. She pressed her head to her breast and kissed all her limbs. And streaming hot tears fell on the young flower. Thus the mother mourned for her child, whom she would soon lead to death with her own hand....

Mothers passed with small children in their arms; others were led by the hands of their little ones. They kissed their children – a mother's heart cannot be bound – kissed them all along the way....

Suddenly the naked procession came to an abrupt halt. A pretty girl of nine, whose long, intricately plaited braids hung in golden strips down her childish shoulders, had approached followed by her mother, who now stopped and boldly addressed the officers [SS men]: 'Murderers, thieves, shameless criminals!'[27]

The first manuscript by Leib Langfus was found in April 1945 by Gustaw Borowczyk from Oświęcim in a broken fruit jar near the ruins of Crematorium III in Auschwitz-Birkenau. The finder took the manuscript home. As it was written in Yiddish, he was unable to read it. Large sections were also damaged by moisture. It took until November 1970 for the manuscript to be given to the Auschwitz Memorial by the finder's younger brother Wojciech Borowczyk.[28]

Leib Langfus was a rabbinical judge from Maków Mazowiecki,[29] around 80 kilometres north of Warsaw. On 5 September 1939, German troops entered the town. Around half of the inhabitants were Jews. They were immediately taken for forced labour, had to cut off their 'payot' (sidelocks), and their synagogue was deconsecrated. In February 1940, 500 'invalids' and older people from the town were murdered, and in August a further 20 Jews and Poles were shot in front of the synagogue.

In autumn 1941, the Jewish inhabitants were concentrated in a segregated ghetto. Through flight and 'transfer', around 5,500 Jewish children, women and men had to carve out an existence in the crowded ghetto. Some were housed in cow stalls and stables. Hunger and cold, coupled with infectious diseases, caused the mortality rate to rise. In July 1942, 36 Jews were shot or hanged.

Finally, in mid-November 1942, the Jews from Maków Mazowiecki were transferred to the ghetto transit camp in Mława and then deported to Auschwitz, a month later. Among the 5,000 Jews was Leib Langfus, who was to be recruited for slave labour in the Sonderkommando at Auschwitz-Birkenau.[30]

'SHEMA YISRAEL': 'We arrived on the following evening at the involuntary destination', wrote Leib Langfus in the manuscript discovered in 1945. 'The train stopped at Auschwitz.' Soon afterwards, he saw 'a square teeming with SS men'.

The closely spaced high posts illuminated the square so brightly that they dazzled and confused the people.

The people were driven first in great haste from the station. The rucksacks and parcels had to be left behind. Everything the people brought out of the wagons had to be thrown onto a pile.

Those who had died during the journey were dragged out of the wagons by a group of Jewish workers.

Women were called out, but particularly the men and children. Completely numbed and surprised, the men hurriedly kissed their wives and children, embraced them and took their leave. A terrible wailing was to be heard.

The gendarmes began to drive the crowd forward; they endeavoured to hurry the people up as much as possible. As a result many people didn't manage to say goodbye forever to their nearest and dearest....

The men looked anxiously towards the lines of women and children. They moved; they watched them climb obediently into the trucks that took them directly to their death, as it later transpired. In answer to our questions about where they were going, we were told that they were going to special barracks where they would live and that we could meet and talk to them every [Sunday]....

People were pressed together [as much as possible]. It is difficult even to imagine that there was space for so many people in such a small [room]. Those who didn't want to go in were shot for [resisting] or torn to pieces by dogs....

Then all the doors were hermetically sealed and gas dropped down from a small hole in the ceiling. The people locked inside could no longer do anything. So they wailed with bitter pitiful voices. Some wailed in despair, others sobbed frantically, and a terrible crying was heard. Some recited 'Vidui' [confession], others 'Shema Yisrael' ['Hear O Israel' – the Jewish profession of faith].

Because of the masses of people, they fell on one another as they died until there was a pile of five or six up to a metre high. Mothers froze on the ground sitting with their children in their arms, and the men died embracing their wives. Some of the people formed a shapeless mass.

Others stood bent over; the lower part of their body was standing, the upper part from the stomach upwards was lying. Some had turned blue because of the gas, others looked quite fresh, as if they were sleeping.

There was not space for all of them in the bunker [as the two farmhouses converted into gas chambers were called]; some were kept in a wooden barracks until 11 a.m. the following day. In the morning they heard the despairing voices of those being gassed and realized immediately what awaited them.[31]

A fruit jar with a metal lid was found near the ruins of Crematorium III in Auschwitz-Birkenau on 17 October 1962, containing a notebook and loose sheets wrapped in wax paper. Half of the text written almost completely in Yiddish (one sheet is written in Polish) could still be deciphered, but the rest had become damp over the years and was illegible.

The entire manuscript was initially attributed to Salmen (also spelt Zalman) Lewental from Ciechanów near Warsaw. The notes, 'Die 600 inglekh' ['The 600 Boys'] and 'Die 3,000 nakete' ['The 3,000 Naked Women'], were thought to have been written by him because they were hidden in the notes with his name on them.[32] Professor Ber (Bernard) Mark, long-standing director of the Jewish Historical Institute in Warsaw, discovered, however, that the actual author of these notes was again the rabbinical judge from Maków Maszowiecki, Leib Langfus.[33]

Every day, every hour, all inmates in the Sonderkommando saw babies and children, alone or with their mothers, grandmothers and adult carers, being driven into the gas chambers at Auschwitz-Birkenau. Leib Langfus recorded the scenes for posterity:

'DI 600 INGLEKH': At noon, 600 Jewish boys of twelve to eighteen years old were brought in, dressed in long striped camp clothing, threadbare and torn. They wore shoes or wooden clogs on their feet. The children were so beautiful, well formed and seemed to shine in their rags.

This was during the second half of October 1944.[34]

They were led by twenty-two armed SS men. As they came into the courtyard, the Kommandoführer ordered them to undress there.

When the children saw the clouds of thick smoke, they realized at once that they were being taken to their death. They began to run in all directions within the courtyard, mad with fear, pulling out their hair and not knowing how to save themselves. Many of them began crying in terror, and they all started to moan.

The Kommandoführer and his assistants beat the children savagely in order to force them to undress. He beat them until his club broke, whereupon it was replaced with another, and the man continued to beat the helpless children on the head. The strong men won.

The children undressed automatically, frightened to death. Naked and barefoot, they clung to each other to protect each other from the blows. And yet they still did not go in....

The soft and pure voices of the children became increasingly bitter and heavy. The loud crying began to echo into the distance.

We stood completely frozen and as if paralysed by these miserable cries.

With satisfied smiles, with no trace of mercy, and with victorious pride, the SS rushed the children into the bunker with cruel blows. The Unterscharführer stood on the stairs and if one of them went to his death too slowly, he was beaten savagely with the rubber truncheon.

Nevertheless, a few confused children were still running backwards and forwards looking for a way out.

The SS men chased them, rushing and whipping them, until they had taken control of the situation and finally shoved them inside.

They were unimaginably happy. Weren't any of them ever fathers of children?[35]

'DI 3,000 NAKETE': The order came. 'Juden, antreten!' ['Leave the ranks.'] Then the blocks were filled with Jewish girls. During the selection, nobody paid attention whether they looked well or not, whether they were sick or well. They were lined outside the block and later they were led to Block No. 25;[36] there they were ordered to strip naked; allegedly, they were to be examined as to their health. When they had stripped, all were driven to three blocks; 1,000 people in a block ... and there they were shut for three days and three nights, without getting a drop of water or a crumb of bread, even.... One of us, looking at the immensity of unhappiness of those defenceless, tormented souls, could not master his feelings and wept. One young girl then cried, 'Look what I have yet lived to see before my death: a look of compassion and tears shed because of our dreadful fate. Here, in the murderers' camp, where they torture and beat and where they torment, where one sees murders and falling victims; here, where men have lost consciousness of the greatest disasters; here, where a brother or sister falls down in front of you, and you cannot even vouchsafe them a farewell sigh – a man is still found who took to heart our terrible situation and who expressed his sympathy with tears. Ah, this is a wonderful thing. The tears and sighs of a living [man] will accompany us to our death, there is still somebody who will weep for us.' ... An emaciated young girl lay apart and was moaning softly, 'I am ... dy ... ing, I ... am ... dy ... ing'; a film was covering her eyes which turned this way and that ..., begging to live ... A mother was sitting with her daughter, they both spoke in Polish. She sat helplessly, spoke so softly that she could hardly be heard. She was clasping the head of her daughter with her hands and hugging her tightly. 'In an hour, we both shall die. What a tragedy. My dearest, my last hope will die with you.... A shiver passed through the body of the young girl, she cried out desperately, 'Mamma!' And she spoke no more, those were her last words.[37]

# Births in Auschwitz

Pregnant women in Auschwitz found themselves in a particularly hopeless situation. When the Women's Camp was being built (from March to August 1942 in the Main Camp, then transferred to Auschwitz-Birkenau),[1] they were automatically killed by phenoline injection into the heart, gassed or beaten to death, regardless of whether they were Jewish or not.[2] Pregnant Jewish women from other concentration camps were also transferred to Auschwitz exclusively for gassing.[3] Mothers who gave birth in secret in Auschwitz often heard only the first cries of their new-born babies.

> Pregnant women in the concentration camp had the symbol 'SB' (Sonderbehandlung – special treatment) marked on their file cards, which meant gassing. Until 1943, the basic principle applied that women who arrived pregnant at the camp or became pregnant while there were not allowed to live. If they nevertheless gave birth, the child and its mother were killed by phenoline injection.[4]

This was one of the core statements by Professor Jan Olbrycht, inmate number 46688, expert witness at the Kraków Auschwitz trial (24 November to 22 December 1947), based on Nazi documents found in the former extermination camp.

The inmate doctor Lucie Adelsberger, who was deported from Berlin to Auschwitz on 17 May 1943, wrote in her report, recorded in Amsterdam in 1945–6: 'As soon as the newborn saw the light of day, the inconceivable happened: The Jewish child was forfeited to death, and with him, his mother. Within a week both were sent to the gas chamber.'[5]

The pregnant women whose condition had been overlooked at the initial selection on the ramp and who had been transferred to the camp were likely to undergo an immediate secondary selection carried out during the disinfesting and disinfection in the 'saunas', where they had to undress completely. Women who were discovered to be pregnant were gassed immediately.[6]

The doctor Sima Vaisman, born in Bessarabia (now mostly Moldova) and deported in January 1944 from Drancy in France to Auschwitz-Birkenau, was able to observe how the SS proceeded. In her testimony, which she wrote down eight days after returning to Paris, she stated:

> The [SS] doctor comes to examine the naked living goods he has sought out for the camp! Thin, sick and above all pregnant women could have slipped past him unnoticed, so he carefully examines those who look pregnant, courteously, with quasi-paternal concern. He tells them that it is in their own interest to admit to him whether they are expecting a child and whether they are tired ... He wants to give them light work and additional food. Touched by such kindness, the women admit without thinking. They are placed on one side and are given a coat to throw over their shoulders. They put a child with them who has slipped into the sauna unnoticed ... And they are taken to the crematorium.[7]

Alter Feinsilber (later he called himself Stanisław Jankowski) was arrested in France at the end of March 1942 and deported to Auschwitz. After five months, he had the number 27675 tattooed on his chest and was assigned in November 1942 to the 'crematorium kommando' in the Main Camp. 'We lowly workers were used generally for all activities connected with the burning and transportation of the bodies, feeding the crematorium ovens and removing the ashes.' In July 1943, he had to perform slave labour in the Sonderkommando in Auschwitz-Birkenau. He made the following statement in June 1945 about the initial selection of pregnant women: 'I noted that pregnant women arriving at the camp were shot immediately. If the pregnancy wasn't detected, the woman could give birth secretly but had to sacrifice the new-born child, otherwise they would both have been killed.'[8]

Simon Gotland was deported from France in 1942. He was forced to work mainly in the 'Kanada' kommando, where he sorted the belongings of the deportees – at least 80 per cent of whom were killed immediately upon arrival – for shipment to the German Reich. With other inmates, he was responsible, among other things, for collecting the deportees' luggage. One day, he opened a wagon from one of the numerous transports and discovered that the occupants were mostly hospital patients. 'In this wagon there was also a woman screaming loudly. She was pregnant and the child was half-out. She was giving birth. I entered the wagon and pulled the child out of the woman.'

Gotland ran to another wagon where he had seen food. He brought some to the woman and her new-born baby. This was noticed by SS-Rottenführer Baretzki, who was on ramp duty at this time. He approached and saw the woman and the baby: 'He hit me and the woman. The child fell on the floor and he kicked it. The baby was spun a few metres away. Baretzki yelled: "Bring that piece of shit here!" When I brought the child, it was already dead. After I had unloaded the others from the wagon, I looked for the woman. She was also dead.'[9]

It was 'terrible to witness', said Julian Niewiarowski, inmate number 5596, 'when an SS man smashed a newly born child against a wall or a tree'. It was 'more than refined physical death': 'The mothers fainted, tore out their hair or killed themselves.'[10]

Women were sometimes able to conceal their pregnancy for a long time and gave birth secretly in the camp. This took place often in Auschwitz-Birkenau in the walled flue running through the centre of the barracks from the brick oven, but also in the bunks or on the ground. The newly born babies had scant chance of survival. SS doctors, medical orderlies and their assistants took the children away from their mothers and killed them.[11]

On 29 September 1946, the local newspaper *Die Union* in Dresden published an article on Auschwitz-Birkenau entitled 'Geburt im KZ' ['Birth in a Concentration Camp']. The by-line was signed 'O. R.'. It stated:

> Birkenau, the concentration camp where dirt, vermin and epidemics vie with one another. The stables where we live are dark and full of mud. Live? It's night. Anyone walking in the camp at this time will hear the desperate wailing and moaning of women, stacked ten- or twelve-high in the bunks

– stacked in the true sense of the word, because there is no room for them to lie next to one another. Watch out where you walk, where you place your feet, so as not to trip over one of the corpses that lie in masses on the ground around the barracks. Don't disturb them; let them sleep. Their struggle is over.

Come with me to the hospital – antechamber to the crematorium, as the inmates called it – and I will show you a picture that you will never forget. Hold on to the door, so that the wind doesn't tear it out of your hands. And don't be surprised. Nothing should surprise you here. There is a woman lying on the ground. She has her jaw tightly clenched. She is seeking with her hands to support herself in the mud, which they call a floor here. Next to her is a nurse holding pieces of newspaper and lighting them one after another. Why is she doing this? Does she want to set fire to the barracks? No, it's to provide light. Because a child is being born, and we don't have any other light than this.

You must observe everything closely, and you will see that the woman is lying in the dirt on the ground without a blanket or a sheet, that there is no basin of water next to her, because we only have water when it rains. Don't forget to take a look at the young doctor who is kneeling next to the woman and helping her. Have you ever seen so much despair in a young face? She is not wearing a white coat; she doesn't have sterile rubber gloves on her hands, but her head is shaved bare and her face is pale and desperate – not only tonight. 'I can't see any more babies', she told me yesterday. Do you know why?

And now, watch closely, the child is arriving. The woman on the ground digs her hands even deeper into the dirt; she screams and screams. The doctor kneels next to her, works quickly and skilfully with her young, thin hands. One more scream, a last effort, and the child is there. The mother sinks back exhausted and closes her eyes.... She cries. Look around and don't forget. Everyone standing around is crying. Sweet, tiny child. You won't be taken to a basin with warm water. You won't be wrapped in soft, white swaddling. You will be rubbed down with pulp and wrapped in rags.... We love you, tiny thing. You are passed from arm to arm, and we kiss your tiny feet that have just emerged from their warm enclosure into hardship and misery, and what you can feel warm on your face is not the sun. It is the tears, hot, bitter tears, which we shed for you and in anger at humanity that allows such a thing to happen.[12]

One night, shortly after she had fallen asleep, Margita Schwalbowá was awakened by a scream. A woman, a nurse, had gone into labour. She was lying on the third tier of a wooden bunk. The darkness was interrupted for a moment by the lighting of a newspaper.

> A colleague assisted with the birth. Our nurse no longer screamed, no longer cried, only her eyes were large and deep like our darkness. She is not alone in the bed; her bedfellow does not even move, she is so tired. She lies dozing next to the woman giving birth. The child is born in deep and insane darkness. 'Give me something, I have to cut the umbilical cord.' Someone rips off a piece of shoelace.... Two days later the young mother and her son were gassed.[13]

Margita Schwalbowá, inmate number 2675, a Slovakian doctor, arrived in Auschwitz on 28 March 1942. She was enlisted first in the women's hospital in the Main Camp in Block 25 at Auschwitz-Birkenau, which was a transit station to the gas chamber.[14]

Judith Sternberg, a nurse from Wrocław deported to Auschwitz in February 1943 and forced to work in the hospital, wrote about Block 25 in a report entitled 'In der Hölle von Auschwitz':

> One day an SS man named Tauber[15] visited our block in order to make selections for the gas chamber. He couldn't have been more than twenty-five years old. When he entered our block we all had to stand at attention. 'Well, then, let's start right away', Tauber said.... One after another, the patients had to march past him, and whoever was unable to stand was deposited naked on the stone floor. Again and again he kicked the patients with his hobnail boots, in the belly or the back, until the blood ran. Of about nine hundred and fifty women, eight hundred were written down for the gas chamber. The block was almost emptied. The women prayed to God; they screamed for help; they prostrated themselves before the SS men, begging for their lives. Beatings were their answer.[16]

Julian Kiwała, inmate number 9143, was block elder for around three months at the end of 1942 in the 'hospital' in the Birkenau Women's Camp. In the evening, he had to return to the Men's Camp, where he slept.[17] After liberation, he recalled a transport arriving in Auschwitz at the end of 1942 from Majdanek:

> Among the women in the transport were three mothers with babies a few weeks old and three pregnant women almost at term. They were housed in Block 24, where they gave birth to three children the following day.... For several days we hid the newborns from the SS men ... These children were the favourites of the entire block. At first we [secretly] organized food for the young mothers – milk and white bread – from the kitchens in the Men's Camp.

One day, after about two weeks, the mothers and babies were transferred by the SS to Block 25, the 'death block'. When Julian Kiwała heard about this on his return to the Men's Camp, he hurried immediately to the 'mortuary', which was also in this block. He discovered that 'the six women and six babies were no longer alive. All of the corpses had the mark of an injection on the chest in the region of the heart.'[18]

In the first half of 1943, the registered non-Jewish pregnant women interned in the camp were allowed to give birth, but their babies still had 'no right' to remain alive.[19] 'Until May 1943, all children born in Auschwitz were brutally murdered by drowning in a barrel or bucket. This procedure was carried out by Nurse Klara and Nurse Pfani.' After each birth, the mothers heard a loud gurgle and sometimes lengthy splashing from the room. A short while afterwards, the mother could see the body of her child, gnawed by rats, thrown outside, wrote the midwife Stanisława Leszczyńska, who was interned for two years in the Women's Camp in Birkenau and assisted many women giving birth.[20]

Irmgard Konrad (*née* Adam) from Wrocław, who was deported to Auschwitz in early 1943, saw how close life and death were to each other in the Women's Camp.[21] A few days after her referral to the hospital, she was the helpless witness to the drowning of a baby: a mother had had a child. 'This Klara had induced the birth' and came with a small baby. Irmgard had not seen a new-born baby before.

> And she [Klara] took the baby, placed it on a table, fetched a bucket and drowned the child. And I stood there. Of course I yelled at her. But I can

still hear what she said: 'Why should I be gassed for this Jew brat? New-born Jewish children are not allowed to live and have to be registered as dead.' That's how they drowned new-born babies in Auschwitz in a bucket. Later, when I got out of Auschwitz, it took me a long time to get over it. [I was still not over it] when I became a mother myself.[22]

From around mid-1943, the SS allowed new-born babies of non-Jewish mothers to remain alive. Some of them were entered in the camp register and had a number tattooed like adult inmates. As their left forearm was still too small, the number was tattooed on the thigh or buttocks.[23] Babies of non-Jewish Germans or of women 'deemed to be German' were not tattooed in Auschwitz, nor were the babies of women arrested during the Warsaw military uprising from 1 August to 2 October 1944 and deported to Auschwitz, or those born in Auschwitz who were considered 'racially valuable'. These babies were to be examined in 'new settlement facilities', as they were called, for their suitability for 'Germanization'.[24]

This form of child abduction, known as 'Germanization', even took place in Auschwitz. In November 1943 alone, 542 children from Auschwitz were taken in a single transport to the German camp at Lebrechtsdorf (Potulice, Poland). There were 301 girls and 241 boys up to the age of 13. Most of them were from the Vitebsk region of Byelorussia.[25] Blond and blue-eyed children in particular were taken from their mothers. Some of them still live in Germany, possibly unaware of how their lives were determined by force. In Poland alone, Nazi Germany abducted as many as 200,000 children for 'Germanization'.[26] The precise numbers are not known.

The non-Jewish pregnant women after mid-1943 who were allowed to live had, nevertheless, to work until shortly before the birth. The Polish writer Seweryna Szmaglewska, inmate number 22090, who was interned in Auschwitz from November 1942 to January 1943, testified at the Nuremberg Tribunal in 1946:

I noticed then a woman in the last month of pregnancy. It was obvious from her appearance. This woman, together with the others, had to walk 10 kilometres to the place of work and there she toiled the whole day, shovel in hands, digging trenches. She was already ill and she asked the German supervisor, a civilian, for permission to rest. He refused, laughed at her, and together with another SS man, started beating her. He scrutinized her work very closely. Such was the situation of all the women who were pregnant. And only during the very last minutes were they permitted to stay away from work.[27]

In spite of the greatest efforts and care by adult inmates, non-Jewish babies also had practically no chance of survival in the camp. The French journalist Marie-Claude Vaillant-Couturier, arrested as a resistance fighter and transported to Auschwitz on 27 January 1943, stated at the Nuremberg International Military Tribunal on 28 January 1946: 'Yes, in principle, non-Jewish women were allowed to have their babies, and the babies were not taken away from them; but conditions in the camp being so terrible, the babies rarely lived for more than four or five weeks.'[28]

The conditions in the barracks were unimaginable. Even in winter, they were almost never heated. The cold penetrated everything. Icicles hung from the ceiling. The stench, infectious diseases and vermin were the order of the day. Stanisława Leszczyńska:

> The rats getting fat on the corpses were as big as cats. They were not afraid of people and when they were chased away with sticks, they often just tucked their heads in, clawed the bunks tightly and went onto the attack; the rats were particularly attracted to the repellent body odour of the very sick women, who were unable to wash and who had no fresh clothing.[29]

In spite of their attention, the mothers, emaciated by hunger, cold and disease, could not prevent their babies being bitten or gnawed by rats. The exhausted women, who had not been able to wash or obtain fresh clothing after the birth, were also attacked day and night by the rats. Their fingers, ankles, noses and ears were bitten off.[30]

Children were born in several sections of the camp, separated by electrified fences, including the Theresienstadt Family Camp, which existed from September 1943 to May 1944. There were numerous transports bringing Jewish children, women and men from the Theresienstadt ghetto to Auschwitz-Birkenau. Like the new-born babies, they were initially allowed to live. Many died in the inhuman conditions and the rest were gassed at intervals of around six months in several 'actions'. Of the 17,517 inmates in this section of the camp, only 1,167 Jews survived.[31]

In contrast to the situation in the Theresienstadt Family Camp, the babies born in the 'Gypsy' Camp, which was also later liquidated, were all registered by name and tattooed with a number. The main register of the 'Gypsy' Camp, which has survived until the present day, lists 378 births there. The first babies entered in the main register were Anna Malik and Peter Wachler, who on 11 March 1943 were given the numbers Z1936 and Z2086. The last babies listed in the 'Gypsy' Camp were Renate Ernst, number Z10803, born on 13 June 1944, and Oskar Weindlich, number Z10077, born on 20 June 1944.[32]

There were scarcely any supplies there either for the mothers or for their babies. There were not even nappies. After liberation, Elisabeth Guttenberger (inmate number Z-3991), deported from Munich to Auschwitz with several members of her family in March 1944, described the situation in the 'Gypsy' Camp:

The children died first. Day and night they cried for bread; soon they were all starving. The children born in Auschwitz did not survive long either. The only thing that the SS were bothered about with these new-born babies was to ensure that they were properly tattooed. Most died within a few days – at the most two weeks after their birth. There was no care, no milk, no warm water, not to mention powder or nappies.[33]

Hermann Langbein from Vienna also saw the 'Gypsy' Camp with his own eyes and described the mothers and their new-born babies:

The sick women and children were lying in the neighbouring barracks.... There were six babies – they can only have been a couple of days old – on a straw bag. What did they look like! Spindly limbs and bloated stomachs. On the bunks next to them were the mothers, emaciated, with burning eyes.... A wooden shelter had been built on the back wall [of the barracks], the mortuary. I'd already seen a lot of corpses in the concentration camp. But I was still shocked. A pile of corpses, a good 2 metres high. Practically all children, babies, youths, with rats scurrying over them.[34]

The 'Gypsy' Camp existed from February 1943 to August 1944. At least 22,643 Sinti and Roma were deported to Auschwitz-Birkenau as 'gypsies'. Around half were children and juveniles under 18, including almost

9,500 boys and girls younger than 15. Only a few survived.[35] Altogether, around 21,000 Sinti and Roma were murdered in Auschwitz.[36]

Some children were born in the inmate hospital camp installed in November 1944 in the former 'Gypsy' Camp[37] and above all from autumn 1942 in the barracks and hospital block in the Women's Camp in Auschwitz-Birkenau.[38] On the initiative of the inmate midwife Stanisława Leszczyńska, there was a 'delivery room' in the Women's Camp in Barracks 16 (numbering from 1943), in which children were born in three-tier bunks behind a curtain. The room moved several times: from December 1943 until well into early 1944 it was in Barracks 17, then later in Block 10, renumbered as Barracks 24 in 1944.[39]

As so often with Auschwitz, words cannot adequately express the situation. The term 'delivery room' is completely misleading, because there was no 'room' meeting even the most rudimentary European or North American standards for pregnant women and new-born babies in Auschwitz-Birkenau. All 'accommodation' in Birkenau was extremely primitive, draughty, covered in blood and faeces, with no protection against the heat of the summer or the temperatures as low as minus 25°C in winter. 'Delivery room' suggests some kind of normality, but this was completely absent in Auschwitz-Birkenau.

There were also pregnant Jewish women in the transit camps.[40] These sections were created in June 1944 because of the vast number of transports with Hungarian Jews. Around 438,000 people were transported from Hungary. In view of the large number of Jewish children, women and men arriving in Auschwitz-Birkenau at the time, they could not all be selected and gassed on the spot and were transferred to the camp. In summer 1944, there were on average 30,000 to 50,000 Jewish babies, children, youths, women and men in the transit camps. For practically all of them, it was merely a 'waiting room for the gas chamber'.[41]

Births took place not only in the Women's Camp, Theresienstadt and 'Gypsy' Family Camps or the transit camp, but everywhere occupied by women: outdoors at the morning and evening roll calls,[42] while performing slave labour outside the camp, secretly in a ditch somewhere, under a tree or behind a building. If they were discovered by the SS, it would mean instant death for mother and child.

There were also pregnant women on the death marches that set off from Auschwitz, especially after August 1944. Those who couldn't continue or attempted to escape because they were about to give birth or were weak or sick were likely to be shot. Alina Cielemięcka-Naciążek saw this on the freezing cold and icy roads in January 1945. She was four months pregnant. After liberation, she spoke of her experiences on the death march:

> Suddenly we heard the screams of an inmate women who had gone into labour.... As she couldn't go on, she climbed down into a ditch by the road. The other women were horrified. They couldn't help her and had no way of making the SS men stop. They weren't allowed to stop either. The pregnant woman's mother wanted to stay with her daughter but was pushed away by the SS. After a while they heard shots. This was a terrible experience, especially for us pregnant women.[43]

Months before, in the Women's Camp at Auschwitz-Birkenau: an 'expectant mother', reported Stanisława Leszczyńska from the Women's Camp, 'saved her bread ration for a long time so as to be able to organize a bedsheet'. She 'ripped it into rags to make nappies and clothing' for the child.[44] It was only thanks to the women in the 'Effektenlager', who sorted the possessions of the interned and murdered, that the babies were provided with the bare necessities. These women risked their lives to obtain cloth for nappies and clothes to wear. Washing nappies was extremely difficult because water was in short supply. As it was forbidden to hang washing visibly, the mothers dried the home-made nappies on their backs and legs.[45]

There was no additional food for the babies. They did not normally receive a drop of milk, just the usual rations: 'coffee', 'soup', bread and margarine. Stanisława Leszczyńska: 'The mothers' breasts, shrivelled from hunger, merely irritated the mouths of the new-born babies, produced a reflex movement and made them even hungrier.' The babies died gradually of starvation. 'Their skin was as thin as parchment, through which tendons, blood vessels and bones were visible.'[46]

Jewish babies continued to be killed at birth, even after the killing of non-Jewish babies had been suspended in mid-1943. They were drowned, given lethal injections, gassed or beaten to death. Mothers had their breasts bound so that they couldn't feed their babies, or else the SS wouldn't allow the umbilical cord to be cut and tied after the birth. The baby was thrown into a bucket with the placenta. Two inmate midwives risked their lives to disobey this prohibition and carry a baby to a bunk. For these and other cases, there was another method. Because the Jewish mothers were not allowed to breastfeed their babies, even if they were capable of doing so, the babies usually died quite quickly. The Jewish babies who survived were killed with phenoline injections.[47]

One of the Jewish women who gave birth in Auschwitz testified: 'He [Mengele] bound my breasts so that I couldn't feed the baby. But he wanted to see how long it could survive without food.'[48]

Mengele also ordered Ruth Elias (alias Ruth Iliav), who had been deported to Auschwitz in December 1943 from Ostrava, Czechoslovakia, to bind her breasts. She was nearly 21. 'The labour pains start. An inmate midwife lays me on the ground and helps me to give birth.' It was a girl.

My child cries, the first sound it makes, and my heart weeps. Mengele ordered me not to feed the baby. He orders me to bind my breasts. I'm not allowed to breast-feed my child. She cries with hunger, she wants to eat. I chew up a piece of bread and stick it in my child's mouth. Mengele comes every day and after eight days he orders: 'Be ready tomorrow with your child. I'll come and fetch you.'

Ruth Elias cries and wails.

I know that tomorrow we will die. A stranger sits at my bed and talks to me. Talks and talks and talks. She calms me: 'Don't despair, I'll help you.' After the lights were turned off at 9 p.m., she returned with a syringe in her hand. 'Give me the child, it's a strong dose of morphine. It will kill the child.' 'I can't murder my own child!' 'You must. I'm a doctor and have to save lives. The child is not viable, half-starved; it has nutritional oedema. I have to save you. You're young.' After resisting for two hours I was so worn down that I did the deed. Yes, I'm a child murderer. Dr Mengele! Child murderer! I was hysterical. The SS doctor came back and asked: 'Where is your child?' Ruth Elias answered: 'Died last night.' 'Died? Show me the body.' But to find a small, starving child's body killed by a morphine injection among thousands of corpses is too much even for the all-powerful Dr Mengele. He says merely: 'You're lucky. You can travel to work on the next transport.'[49]

Anni Sussmann from Vienna and Lilli Segal from Berlin met in early August 1944 on their arrival in Auschwitz-Birkenau. They both came from Jewish families and had fled from the Nazis to France, where they were arrested by the Gestapo.[50] 'We were very concerned about Anni. When she arrived at Auschwitz, she was five months pregnant', writes Lilli Segal. 'She knew that pregnant women were either selected for extermination or … that medical experiments were carried out on them.' So as not to attract attention, Anni had always stood at the back during roll calls. One morning at the end of September, she went into premature labour.

> The first problem was to find a bed in a dark corner with a little bit of straw that wasn't too dirty. No one had a cloth or a piece of paper to wipe the bed at least a little bit. The child lay in a puddle on the boards. Anni gave birth to a boy. Mengele took the child away immediately. He only had one treatment for babies: a phenoline injection in the heart.[51]

Abortions by serial injection or surgical interventions, without regard for the month of pregnancy, were conducted by order of the SS at different times in the hospital block, the Women's Camp, the inmates' hospital and the transit camp.[52] This is confirmed by the inmate doctor Janina Kościuskowa in her 1962 report 'Kinderschicksale im KZ-Lager Auschwitz': 'A transport arrived once with one hundred pregnant women; they were put in the Revier [inmate hospital], where a perforation [puncture of the uterine wall with a pointed instrument] was performed regardless of the stage of the pregnancy. Many paid with their lives.'[53]

Auschwitz-Birkenau was like a jungle in which it was easy to get lost. No one could predict how one and the same matter would be treated the following day by the SS. Something that was in order today might well mean death the next day. Nothing was foreseeable. The main purpose was still extermination. Pregnant Jewish women sent to the Women's Camp, and thus able to survive temporarily by performing slave labour, could only stay alive if they had a miscarriage, the pregnancy was interrupted or the baby born in the camp was poisoned or otherwise killed. Otherwise, the Jewish child and its mother were destined for one of the gas chambers.[54]

Gisella Perl, a doctor from Sighetu Marmaţiei, Romania, was deported to Auschwitz with her family in 1944. Her husband, her only son and her parents all lost their lives.[55] She was chosen by Mengele to establish a department for pregnant women and to report pregnancies to him. She did so only once: 'The woman was taken immediately to Mengele's laboratory. Mengele stepped on her abdomen to cause a miscarriage. Mother and child were dissected and then burned.'[56]

In order to save at least the mothers' lives, Perl had the bitter duty to perform abortions:[57] 'It was up to me to save the life of the mothers, if there was no other way, then by destroying the life of their unborn children.' She performed abortions on condemned women – without being able to assure the necessary hygiene conditions, 'kneeling down in the mud, dirt and human excrement … always in a hurry, always with my five fingers, in the dark, under terrible conditions. No one will ever know what it meant to me to destroy these babies…. It was again and again my own child I killed to save the life of a woman', at least temporarily.[58]

The Jewish doctor Lucie Adelsberger wrote in her Auschwitz report in Amsterdam in 1945–6: 'Medical ethics prescribe that if, during labour, the mother and the child are in danger, priority must be given to saving the life of the mother. We prisoner physicians quietly acted in accordance with this regulation. The child had to die so that the life of the mother might be saved.'[59] As the poison available in the camp was not sufficient for that purpose, one mother had no alternative but to strangle her baby. 'She was … a good mother who loved her children more than anything else. But she had hidden three small children back home and wanted to live for them.'[60]

In her memoir *I Survived Auschwitz*, written directly after the war, Krystyna Żywulska recalled babies delivered one day to her block.

> Their mothers were already working. There were several of them. One of them had been born somewhere behind a hut. It belonged to a Jewish woman. No one fed the Jewish baby. Mothers did not have food. Why feed the child? It

was not registered anywhere and if it were the mother would also be punished by death. Thus, no one took care of the child. It cried, whimpered, grew weak and swollen and finally died.

In her 'survival report' in 1946, Krystyna Żywulska recalled 'a Jewish woman' who one day

gave birth to a child on the stove in plain view of the whole hut. In the hospital, where each moment brought death to someone, a new-born baby wailed. 'I won't let it die, I won't strangle it', the mother decided. 'It's my first baby. It must bring me luck. Help me. I'm sure some miracle will save the baby.' She spoke with such determination. She entreated everyone with such fervour that they decided to help her. The strangest thing was that the mother could feed the child.

And, in case of a surprise visit by the Germans, the child was hidden under straw pallets.

It survived for about a month. Then the order came that 'all Jewish women must be signed out regardless of their condition. The mother had to be notified, but no one could muster courage to do that. Dr Fruma, a quiet and gentle woman, somehow procured a sleeping drug and injected it into the child. The mother, senseless with pain, was dragged out of the hut.'[61]

'To you, my dearest', wrote another woman who gave birth to a child in Auschwitz, 'I – a mere skeleton covered in skin – gave all my last strength'. 'In amazement at the miracle of life', like her fellow inmates, she had no choice later but to end her son's life:

When, soon afterwards, I was injecting morphine into your body, secretly given to me as an act of utmost mercy, to protect you against a cruel death, I could hardly perceive anything. They bound my head in wet rags and I simply pressed you to me to ease the long, endlessly long, struggle.… All the same, the pain never abated.[62]

Sometimes, women who had secretly given birth were able to hide the new-born girl or boy for a while with the aid of other women. But, even for these babies, death was inevitable sooner or later. Zofia Stępień-Bator (inmate number 37255) described such a situation after liberation. She was deported from Radom, Poland, to Auschwitz on 1 March 1943. She was used to heavy physical labour from external kommandos, first in agriculture and later laying railway tracks. She became ill with pneumonia and typhoid fever[63] and was transferred to the inmates' hospital. When she recovered, she noted her surroundings: she noticed a woman with an infant.

> The child was carefully hidden. After the evening roll call, when there was little risk of encountering SS men, fellow inmates came to this woman. They helped her to change the baby.... The women said that the camp doctor knew about the baby. He had allowed the woman to get used to the child – but then one day he ordered the child to be brought to him, and he gave it a [fatal] phenoline injection.[64]

Erich Kulka from Czechoslovakia was interned on 4 November 1942 in Auschwitz-Birkenau with his wife Elly and his 11-year-old son Otto. He and his son later managed, in the night of 23–24 January 1945, to escape from one of the death transports. His wife was taken to Stutthof, where she died of typhus on 19 January 1945.[65]

In Auschwitz-Birkenau, he was one of a group of craftsmen carrying out repairs all over the camp. He therefore saw a lot in the different parts of the camp.

> One woman gave birth to a child [in the Theresienstadt Family Camp]. The child was three months old when the camp was liquidated. She gave it a sleeping potion and hid it at the bottom of her bag. She managed to bring it to the Women's Camp. The supervisor discovered the child but didn't say anything and allowed the woman to keep it. The Rapportführer (SS man Buntrock) was also moved, admired the woman's courage and also allowed her to keep the baby. The next day, however, (SS-Oberscharführer) Boger came with [a] list. There was a child missing in the camp. He then ordered the woman and child back to the Family Camp. They were both gassed.[66]

Olga Lengyel, born in Cluj, Romania, was transported to Auschwitz in mid-1944 with her husband Miklós, her children Arvad and Thomas, both not yet 12 years old, and her parents. She was the only one to survive. As an inmate doctor, she could not accept that mothers and their new-born babies were sent to the gas chamber. She said to herself: 'We must at least save the mothers.' Lengyel gave a detailed account in her book, published in French in 1946 as *Souvenirs de l'au-delà*, and a year later in English as *Five Chimneys*: 'The fate of the baby always had to be the same', she wrote: 'After taking every precaution, we pinched and closed the little tyke's nostrils and when it opened its mouth to breathe, we gave it a dose of a lethal product.... Without our intervention they would have endured worse suffering, for they would have been thrown into the crematory ovens while still alive.'

These acts placed a terrible burden on her mind. 'I try in vain to make my conscience acquit me.' Elsewhere she writes: 'And so, the Germans succeeded in making murderers of even us.... The only meagre consolation is that by these murders we saved the mothers.... I still see the infants issuing from their mothers. I can feel their warm little bodies as I held them.'[67]

Until about the beginning of November 1944, all Jewish children born in the camp were killed by the SS and never registered officially.[68] 'Before November 1944, however, eight new-born babies with Jewish mothers were registered for some unknown reason as inmates and given inmate numbers',[69] wrote the Polish historian Helena Kubica, who, as a long-standing researcher at the Auschwitz Memorial, was able to study the documents and testimonies there. There were also instances of non-Jewish women who had just lost their babies taking the babies of Jewish women in their place. In this way, they were able to save a few of them.[70]

ANNA AND VIKTOR POLSHCHIKOV Anna Polshchikova had been deported from the Soviet Union (Crimea, Ukraine) to Vienna and was a forced labourer there for two years before being deported from Vienna to Auschwitz in February 1944.[71] She had the inmate number 75560 tattooed on her arm. In her memoirs, she described the birth of her son, the fear for his life, the tragedy and hopeless situation of Jewish women and their children, and breastfeeding other mothers' babies.

Very few women were able to breastfeed their new-born babies. They had no milk and were also too weak, often closer to death than to life.

Anna Polshchikova was one of the few women who could still breastfeed her child. She also acted as a wet nurse for other new-born babies. That way, the young woman saved these babies from dying.[72]

To make room for her in the hospital block at Auschwitz-Birkenau, another woman had to get up.

> The poor woman could barely stand, even with the help of other inmates, and she died the next day. There were around one thousand patients in the block and a pile of corpses in the washroom. Among them were some small children. A healthy baby boy came into the world in the middle of the night on 15 October 1944. The Polish women looked lovingly at him and said: 'What a beautiful boy!'
>
> On the day my son was born I saw a beautiful Jewish woman from Czechoslovakia in the bed opposite me. She was crying: 'Why are you crying?' With tears in her eyes the poor woman replied: 'Last night I gave birth to a little girl after my husband and I had longed for one. But we are not allowed to have children. I'm a Jew and my daughter was killed today.' ... I didn't know how to comfort the poor woman. The much longed-for little girl of another Jewish woman didn't want to die. The little girl started to gasp for air, groaning and emitting a death rattle. These sounds were heart-rending. I had goose flesh over my whole body. All round there were insults and cries of indignation. Why was the Jew forcing the child to suffer, and why couldn't she strangle it once and for all like everyone else and put it out of its misery.

As if it was a normal everyday event for a woman to strangle her own child. 'Someone came and took the shivering Jewish mother away, crazy with despair', unable to suffocate her child. 'My God, what torture it was for a mother!'

A Jewish woman from Romania sat to Anna's left. She had had a son, strong and healthy like his mother.

> Jewish woman were not allowed to breastfeed. Their children usually had to be killed within three days. If a Jewish mother failed to suffocate the child, she was sent to the crematorium on the fourth day with the child. All Jewish women knew about this. 'To hell with the Germans!' I cried and squeezed some milk onto the spoon. Carefully I dripped the contents of the spoon into

his mouth, and he almost choked. But then he sucked with his gums on the filthy, mushy spoon. I couldn't pull it out of his mouth.

Voices yelled at me from all sides: 'What's the matter with you? Do you want to go with him to the crematorium?'

A fat healthy woman in a white coat suddenly appeared from nowhere and asked in Russian: 'Where's the Jewish baby that refuses to die?' The killing took place before my eyes and before the eyes of the completely stunned mother. The woman with the injection turned out to be a doctor from the neighbouring block. She lifted the dead baby from her knee, took its tiny hands and threw it on the pile of bodies in the washroom.[73]

Anna Polshchikova fed seven babies in Auschwitz-Birkenau. She and her son were liberated from there and returned to Yalta on the Crimean peninsula.[74]

The incomplete documentation makes it impossible to know how many pregnant women were deported to Auschwitz or how many children were born there. Numerous eyewitness accounts indicate that many children were born in Auschwitz, however, including a large number of Jewish boys and girls, in spite of the basic SS principle that all pregnant Jewish women were to be murdered immediately on arrival. At least 378 Roma and Sinti children were born in Auschwitz as well, along with a large number of Byelorussian, Polish, Russian and Ukrainian children, and children of other nationalities. On 27 January 1945, around sixty children born in Auschwitz were liberated, several of whom died shortly afterwards as a result of their internment.[75] Survivors apart from Viktor Polshchikov included Katja Kulik (after adoption, Barbara Wesołowska), Krzysztof J. (pseudonym) and Angela Orosz-Richt.

BARBARA WESOŁOWSKA has been her name for over seventy years. Research since the 1960s by the former Auschwitz inmate Tadeusz Szymański, the journalist Edmund Polak and the historian Helena Kubica suggests that her name at birth on 27 April 1944 in Auschwitz-Birkenau was Katya Kulik.[76] The camp number was tattooed on her thigh. Her mother is thought to have been Fyedora Ustinovna Kulik. Her parents lived in a small village near Vitebsk, Byelorussia. Her father, Nikolai Ivanovich Kulik, helped the partisans. 'And when the Germans came, they shot him in August 1943.'[77] All of the inhabitants of the village were to die. At the mass execution, her mother was shot in the leg. 'She and another women remained motionless between the corpses. All the others were dead.'

Fyedora and the other woman waited several hours before climbing out of the pile of bodies. They wanted to escape to the neighbouring village but were arrested and interned in Auschwitz on 9 September. Fyedora Kulik had the number 61985 tattooed on her. *Auschwitz Chronicle* states: 'Nos. 61417–62169 are given to 753 female prisoners sent from Mobile Strike Commando [Einsatzkommando] 9 in Vitebsk in White Russia. [They] are suspected of collaborating with or helping partisans active in White Russia.'[78]

'My mother was pregnant.' Fyedora Kulik gave birth to twins, Katya and Viktor, in the camp. Both the boy and the mother died in Auschwitz. Katya was moved in autumn/winter 1944 to Lebrechtsdorf (Potulice) near Bydgoszcz. The midwife Stanisława Leszczyńska reported: 'The heart-rending sobs of the mothers accompanied the departing baby transports' from Auschwitz.[79]

Lebrechtsdorf had a detention centre and a central 'transformation facility' for children, where they were examined to determine their suitability for 'Germanization'. On 11 November 1943, 148 children under 2 years of age, and 3,180 under 14, were interned there. There were 1,585 girls and 1,595 boys.[80] At around the time Katya Kulik was moved to Lebrechtsdorf, there were 122 infants and babies under the age of 2.[81]

Katya was not even a year old when she was liberated from Lebrechtsdorf on 21 January 1945. She was admitted to hospital in Będzin near Katowice. Władysława Wesołowska learned from a neighbour that a train with the children liberated from Lebrechtsdorf had arrived in her town in early March 1945. There were children without parents available for adoption by foster families. 'I went to the hospital straightaway', said Władysława. She was given a girl, whom the doctors reckoned was 7 or 8 months old. She was called 'Basia', short for Barbara, the name given to her by the other children liberated with her. Władysława Wesołowska: 'She had the number 73528 tattooed on her left thigh. I recall that other children also had tattoos.'[82]

Władysława Wesołowska took the little girl home with her: 'After we adopted Basia, we put an advertisement in the newspaper looking for her parents.' But no one replied. 'I [still] don't know who Barbara's parents are', she said in July 1961, 'and the tattooed number indicates that she was born in the camp'. Children who arrived with Basia told her in March 1945 that they had been interned together in Auschwitz. They recalled one of the barracks where she was born:

> Two female inmates visited the barracks repeatedly. The older one was called 'grandma' [Oma] and the younger one referred to Basia as 'little daughter'. One day they came, kissed Basia and said tearfully: 'We won't see each other again.' Later, another woman came, whose baby had died in the camp. She breastfed Basia. The children didn't know what happened to the other woman who had breastfed Basia before.[83]

Decades later, Barbara Wesołowska recalled the meeting with her adoptive mother: 'Władysława Wesołowska took me home with her [in March 1945] from the hospital in Będzin. She adopted me. She was my Polish mother, my "mama". I had a new name and family, because at the time I didn't know my biological family or my name.' After leaving school, she trained as a hairdresser and worked for many decades in that profession. She has a daughter, Lidia, and is now retired and lives in Będzin near Katowice, Poland.

KRZYSZTOF J. (pseudonym) was born in Auschwitz-Birkenau in late December 1944. He had the inmate number 188784 engraved on his left thigh, recalled his mother. The bigger he grew, the more illegible the number became. He grew up in Kraków, and by the age of 13 had been in hospital eighteen times because of the time in the camp. In 1979, he moved to Germany where he met and fell in love with a German woman. They couldn't get married. 'That would have killed my mother. The thought was intolerable for her, after everything she, her family and I had suffered under the Germans.' He had two children. 'That's all I have to say. I don't want my name mentioned or a photo because of the way others might react.'

ANGELA OROSZ-RICHT 'My Jewish mother didn't want me to share the terrible experiences she had had in the camp. She wanted to protect me from the consequences of Auschwitz and barely talked of it.' Her mother Vera told her of the day of her birth in Auschwitz-Birkenau shortly before Christmas 1944: 'I don't know the exact day of your birth. I just know that it was three days before the SS celebrated Christmas. If that was 24 December, then you must have been born on the 21st. if it was the 25th, then you were born on the 22nd. I can't remember.'

Vera didn't tell her daughter much else. 'This changed with an interview that my daughter Kathleen taped for a school project when she was sixteen on the roots of her family. We were deported from Hungary to Auschwitz-Birkenau on 25 May 1944 – my mother Vera Bein (*née* Otvos) with me inside her and my father Dr Avraham (Tibor) Bein, who was a lawyer.'

Angela's parents met in Sárospatak, a small town in north-eastern Hungary. They married in Budapest in March 1943 in the presence of friends and relatives. The young couple lived in Sárospatak. 'My mother was an educated, well-brought-up woman.' She spoke fluent French, Hungarian, Slovakian and German. 'After finishing school she wanted to go to university but was not allowed to do so because of the antisemitic Hungarian laws.' Instead, she became the governess of a boy who had lost his mother.

Jews had lived in the small town since the first half of the eighteenth century. According to the 1941 census, Sárospatak had 1,036 Jews out of a total population of 13,213.[84] This changed on 19 March 1944 when German troops invaded Hungary. Until then, 700,000 to 750,000 Jews had lived in Hungary in spite of the German-style anti-Jewish legislation, discrimination and persecution. The German occupation was accompanied by a wave of arrests of Hungarian Jews. Countless anti-Jewish regulations and laws were hurriedly adopted in early 1944. Jewish notaries, lawyers, auditors, civil servants and journalists were banned from working. Bank accounts were frozen and over 600,000 acres of land were expropriated. Telephones, motorcycles, radios and valuables were confiscated. Jews were not allowed to move house, and had limited shopping hours and food rations. On 5 April 1944, they were forced to wear a yellow star.[85] In this way, the Jewish population was isolated, stigmatized and branded.

On the morning after the Pesach (Passover) festival on 16 April 1944, there was a loud hammering at the door of Vera and Avraham Bein's apartment. Hungarian gendarmes took them away in a cattle truck. Just after Pesach, there was not even any bread in the house for them to take with them. They were concentrated in a ghetto in the neighbouring town of Satoraljaujhely. These were their last days as a family.

A few weeks later, Angela's parents were once again loaded onto a cattle wagon. After an arduous journey of around three days, they arrived in Auschwitz on 25 May.

> On the ramp at Birkenau my parents were confronted by SS doctor Mengele, who designated almost everyone to be killed straightaway. My mother told Mengele that she was pregnant. She hoped for sympathy. She had already been separated from my father. He didn't survive. Mengele said to my mother: 'You stupid fool.' He pointed to the right-hand side. He considered her fit for work and allowed her to stay alive for the time being.

Angela's mother was assigned to a kommando working outside the camp confines performing heavy physical labour building roads or in the fields.

'She subsequently became a human guinea pig. When she was around seven months pregnant, she was subjected by Professor Carl Clauberg and his team to sterilization experiments.' From 1942 to the end of 1944, Clauberg performed this extremely cruel mass sterilization in Auschwitz, above all on Jewish women. Many hundreds of women had irritant fluids injected into their womb, 'as a direct application of the Nazi race theory and policy in which Jewish women were not allowed to live'. Other Jewish women whom Clauberg designated as being 'unusable' were worked to death or gassed.[86]

'The substance injected into my mother was extremely painful. The procedure was repeated several times. And there was still the foetus inside her. That was me. And somehow I survived.' Angela Orosz-Richt is convinced that her mother became infertile as a result of the experiments.

In spite of the constant threat of death in Auschwitz-Birkenau, Vera Bein and her unborn daughter survived. When she started going into labour, she went to the block elder, an inmate from Czechoslovakia. 'Her father was a doctor so she knew a little bit about it.' She managed to organize hot water, a sheet and some scissors. 'She told my mother to lie on the top bunk. She climbed up there as well and helped with the birth. That's how I came into the world.' After the birth on 21 or 22 December 1944, Angela was so weak that she couldn't even cry. She was so undernourished that she weighed only 1 kg. Three hours after giving birth, her mother had to attend roll call. 'It is impossible to imagine the strength and courage required to do that.' It was freezing cold and she was dressed in rags. She stood there for a long time and prayed that her new-born baby would still be alive when she returned. Vera Bein shivered and thought: 'I have a child. I have to stay alive!'

Angela and Vera Bein were liberated from Auschwitz-Birkenau on 27 January 1945. On that day a boy named György was also born. His mother, Erzsébet Faludi, also from Hungary, couldn't breastfeed her son. Angela's mother helped. She was 'marked by the constant hunger, but she had enough milk left over to feed the other woman's baby. This was one of many miracles that occurred in this insanity. So my mother nursed both children.' That was the start of a long friendship between the two mothers and their children.

Mother and child were not able to return to Hungary until November 1945. In the ruins of post-war Europe, they took a roundabout route as far as Sluzk in Byelorussia. 'Although it was almost a year since my birth, I still weighed only 3 kg. I was very sick and could hardly move.' The doctors consulted by her mother feared that she would never be completely healthy. But her mother didn't give up. In the end, she found a doctor who looked after her for many years, 'until my bones were strong enough for me to walk'.

Angela Orosz-Richt lived until 1973 in Hungary, before emigrating to Canada, first to Toronto and later to Montreal. She was a social worker and bookkeeper. She has two children, Kathleen and David, and grand-children Asher Yehuda, Faigie, Yechiel, Dassy Vera, Bethseva, Chana Vera and Nuchem. Her mother Vera died in 1992 of spine and lung cancer at the age of 71. 'The nightmares returned. SS doctor Mengele was standing at the door of her hospital room. Even morphine didn't help.' Her mother died on 28 January. 'She didn't want to die on 27 January, because that was the date she had been liberated from Auschwitz forty-seven years earlier.'

A few years ago, Angela Orosz-Richt asked her daughter Kathleen: 'Has the Holocaust influenced your life in any way?' Kathleen replied:

My whole life has been centred on the Holocaust. When I was just four, I had to start fending for myself because I needed to be prepared just in case another Holocaust occurred. And you always said to me and my brother: 'Your generation would never survive a Holocaust, because you're spoiled.' As a young woman I expressed my fear before the birth of my own child. You 'exploded' and said: 'You have a wonderful life, why are you so anxious? Look at nana and the circumstances in which she gave birth to me in Auschwitz!'

Angela travelled to Auschwitz, 'where I was born', with her daughter Kathleen at the end of 2015 to celebrate the seventieth anniversary of its liberation. Her lawyer accompanied her and said that a trial was about to start in Germany against a former SS man. He asked her to testify. She replied: 'I will never go to Germany and do not wish to meet any Germans – ever.' The trial of the SS man Oskar Gröning began on 21 April 2015. He was charged at Luneberg District Court with being an accessory to the murder of 300,000 people. 'When I read the media reports of the trial', says Angela, 'I changed my mind. I travelled to Germany and testified on 2 June 2015: I was born in Auschwitz. I weighed 1 kg. I have a duty to tell my mother's story.' She also wanted to be the voice of the children in Auschwitz and countless other camps who had not survived. 'I want to point my finger at the perpetrators.' Forgive these mass murderers? 'That's out of the question for me. I have no right to do so.'[87] She recalls those in her own family who were murdered – her father Tibor Bein, who failed to survive the inhuman conditions in the camp, or her uncle Matisyahu Otvos, her mother's brother, who was shot as a forced labourer in Hungary.

Angela returned to her birthplace for the seventy-fifth anniversary of the liberation and intends to go back as long as she is able. 'I want to be where my mother was when I was born.' She continues to hold on to the thought that her mother was doomed in the extermination camp. 'And yet she remained unbroken and believed that she and I would survive.' This optimism touches her deeply today.

More than before, Angela Orosz-Richt is convinced that 'the Holocaust could happen again'. Why is that? 'Because the world has not learned the lessons of the Shoah.' Some had learned, but too many had not. That's why, she said, we've seen 'more genocides' since 1945: 'People were murdered by the thousands, hundreds of thousands! In Rwanda. In Srebrenica. In Syria. In so many places. And antisemitism, the oldest form of racial hatred, thousands of years old, is still alive.' She says there are still people who are convinced that 'all Jews are rich', 'that Jews are too influential'. That Jews control Hollywood, the media or Wall Street. The Internet, Angela points out, is full of this rubbish. It spreads 'like wildfire', remaining largely unchecked.[88]

# 'Twins! Where Are the Twins?'

The twins Jiří and Zdeněk Steiner from Prague were taken by SS doctor Mengele when they were 14. Ferenc and Otto Klein from the Hungarian town of Hajdúböszörmény were 11, and Olga and Vera Grossmann from Turiany in eastern Slovakia were just 6 years old when they were preyed upon for Mengele's experiments.

In Auschwitz-Birkenau, SS-Hauptsturmführer Mengele was particularly interested in twins. When they arrived on the ramp, he requisitioned them for his pseudo-medical experiments. Most were aged between 1 and 16 years.

Mengele had long been interested in 'race research'. In his first doctoral work in 1935, he claimed, on the basis of 123 lower jaws examined by him in the Munich State Anthropological Collection, that the race of a subject could be determined from their skeleton. 'His study, which was graded summa cum laude, would be regarded today as madness rather than science',[1] says medical historian Udo Benzenhöfer.

Mengele arrived at Auschwitz at the end of May 1943. He was head camp doctor in the 'Gypsy' Camp, later in the men's hospital, and doctor in the SS field hospital. He also served in other hospital blocks, including the one in the Women's Camp. He effectively had power over all of the children, women and men in the different sections of Auschwitz-Birkenau and those on the transports that arrived almost every day.[2]

'For many inmates, Mengele embodied the selections process.'[3] It is true that he sent masses of children, women and men to the gas chambers, supervised executions, accepted the fact that inmates died as a result of his experiments, and killed subjects when they were no longer of use to him.[4]

But it is also true that all SS doctors in Auschwitz selected, supervised gassings and sought out twins for Mengele's experiments. Pharmacists, medical orderlies and dentists also made selections. They all served the extermination of inmates.[5]

Mengele felt omnipotent in Auschwitz, tried out all kinds of things in his human experiments, studied noma (cancrum oris), tested procedures for sterilizing men and women, conducted bone marrow transplants, did experiments to change eye colour, and carried out research on twins.[6]

With a doctorate in philosophy and medicine, he was interested in both Jewish and Sinti and Roma twins. They were selected, measured, X-rayed, infected with viruses, their eyes cauterized, and finally killed and their bodies dissected.

The nurse Elżbieta Piekut-Warszawska, who was arrested in Kielce and deported in late May 1943 to Auschwitz-Birkenau, arrived in the twins' block in the Women's Camp in July 1944. In her memoirs, she writes:

After the selections on the ramp, around 350 pairs of twins aged from one to sixteen years were housed in this block. Some were of the same sex, others of different sexes. The parents of these children were gassed. The twins were Jewish children from France, the Netherlands, Belgium, Hungary and Germany. They still looked healthy and pretty, but were scared and tearful....

After just a few weeks the children showed the first symptoms of avita-minosis [which can cause scurvy], throat and eye infections, oedema of the extremities, and pneumonia. The greatest danger was the rats, which were as big as cats and roamed day and night. They were even capable of killing children while they slept at night....

After three weeks, we were told that a commission would be coming to our block. At lunchtime one day in August, Dr Mengele appeared in our block with two German Unterführer and the camp elder Stena. After the inspection ... he ordered the children to be brought in groups sorted by number (they all had a number tattooed on their arm) and age to the surgery in the Men's Camp, where they were to be 'examined'. They underwent anthropometric, radiological and morphological examinations in preparation, as a Polish doctor informed me, for later experimental operations.

For the anthropometric examinations the children had to undress, after which measurements were taken for two to five hours with precision instru-ments (protractors, compasses, slide rules). During the examinations the pairs of twins were compared to see whether their measurements were identical. Copious notes were taken. For the children it was a terrible experience.... The subsequent morphological examinations were particularly dramatic. Blood was taken first from the finger and then from the vein, sometimes twice or three times.... They screamed, struggled and refused to be touched. They were terrified of needles. The staff ultimately had to use force. ... Between July and October the number of children still alive dropped to around 300.

The children also had liquids dropped into their eyes. I couldn't see what was happening because the children were taken to another room. One of the twins had drops in both eyes and the other in one eye only. I was instructed to observe the reactions and not to interfere in the event of changes, redness or swelling. For the victims the process was extremely painful: their eyelids swelled, and their eyes stung and watered profusely.[7]

At the end of October 1944, the children from this block were transferred to another section of the camp. The surviving twins and new additions were moved around continuously and often put, together or separately, in different sections of Auschwitz-Birkenau.[8]

'The conditions here', continues Piekut-Warszawska

were worse, because we were in a block for adults with multi-tier bunks and no stove. The children were further examined. Diseases attacked the worn-out organisms even more. Swellings in the mouth, scurvy, enlarged eyes and diarrhoea occurred. Children died. The victims were kept behind after the examination. I have never discovered what happened to them.[9]

Forty years after the liberation of Auschwitz, a Mengele tribunal was organized in February 1985 at the Yad Vashem Memorial in Jerusalem. There were 29 women and men who testified. Many of them had been children in Auschwitz and often the only members of their families to have survived. Vera Alexander from Slovakia, inmate number 5236, arrived in the camp on 19 April 1942 and was block elder[10] in the 'Gypsy' Family Camp. She testified in Jerusalem:

There was a set of twins, Guido and Nina, barely four years old. Mengele took them and brought them back perversely mutilated. Their backs had been sewn together like Siamese twins. Mengele had also joined their veins. The wounds were full of pus, and they screamed day and night. Somehow their mother – her name was Stella, I recall – obtained morphine so as to put an end to her children's suffering.[11]

The inmate doctors rounded up in Auschwitz from all over Europe knew very well what happened to the twins 'kept behind', as they were forced by Mengele to assist in his 'experiments'. They were faced by an extremely difficult dilemma: to save lives or to remain alive themselves, to remain human or to make a 'pact with evil'.[12]

Two months after Dr Miklós Nyiszli, inmate number A 8450, arrived on the selection ramp with his wife Margareta and daughter Zsuzsana on 29 May 1944[13] from Viseu de Sus, 'split off' from Romania to Hungary in 1940, he was forced to work for Mengele. At the end of July 1945, he gave recorded testimony for the first time, in which he spoke, among other things, about 'fourteen gypsy twins' guarded by the SS in the 'work room' next to the 'dissection room':

> Then they brought in the first twin, a fourteen-year-old girl. Dr Mengele ordered me to undress the girl and place her on the dissecting table. Then he administered an intravenous injection of Evipan [a narcotic] in her right arm. After the child had gone to sleep, he felt for the left ventricle and injected 10 cc of chloroform. The child twitched briefly and was dead, whereupon Dr Mengele had her taken to the mortuary.
>
> That night, all fourteen twins were killed in this way. Dr Mengele asked us how many corpses we could dissect in a day. He reckoned we could do seven or eight. We answered that if he wanted precise scientific work from us, we could manage four on average. He agreed with this number.[14]

In a memoir published in Hungary after the war in 1946, Nyiszli stated that 'by order of the fanatical SS doctor Mengele, who thought he was a genius', he had opened up hundreds of bodies. 'I cut the flesh from the bodies of healthy girls for Dr Mengele's bacterial cultures. I bathed the corpses of cripples and dwarves in calcium chloride solution and boiled them in tubs so that the properly prepared skeletons could be sent to museums in the Third Reich to provide proof to future generations of the need to exterminate "inferior races".'[15]

After killing his 'scientific material', the mass murderer Mengele sent blood samples, eyes, heads and other preserved body parts to the Kaiser Wilhelm Institute of Anthropology in Berlin-Dahlem.[16] The package was stamped 'Urgent, vital war material', says Nyiszli. 'I sent countless packages of this type to Berlin-Dahlem during my time in the crematorium, to which detailed responses with scientific opinions or instructions were received. I created a separate dossier for this correspondence. The Institute almost always expressed its deep gratitude to Dr Mengele for the rare material he sent it.'[17] Miklós Nyiszli saw and heard a lot in Auschwitz-Birkenau. He said of Mengele's 'research aims': 'To advance one step in the search to unlock the secret of multiplying the race of superior beings destined to rule was [for Mengele] a "noble goal".'[18]

In her testimony at the first Frankfurt Auschwitz trial, from 20 December 1963 to 20 August 1965, Ella Lingens, inmate doctor from Vienna, who arrived in Auschwitz in February 1943, recalled Dr Mengele:

> He was the first person to rid the Women's Camp of lice. He sent a whole block to be gassed, then disinfected the block, brought a bathtub and had the inmates of the next block washed in it. In the meantime, this block was disinfected. And so it went on. After this action, the A camp was free of lice. He had started, however, by gassing around 750 women from the first block.[19]

JIŘÍ AND ZDENĚK STEINER were loaded in a cattle wagon with their parents in Theresienstadt[20] on 6 September 1943: 'Sixty to eighty people with luggage herded together in one wagon.' When they arrived two days later in Auschwitz,[21] nothing happened at first. The doors remained closed. Suddenly a small package flew through the small opening in their cattle truck. 'We were surprised', says Jiří Steiner, 'and when we opened it we found in it a piece of salami. It was from one of the German soldiers who had accompanied the transport.'

Then the SS dragged them brutally out of the wagon. They were divided into two groups: women, girls and infants on one side, men and adolescent boys on the other. Luggage had to be left behind. They had to fall in and were marched a good 3 kilometres in rows of five in a long column, beaten with sticks by the SS to drive them along. On the way, they saw people behind barbed wire fences in striped uniforms without hair.

The first night they had to sleep on the damp ground as there were no bunks. In the middle of the night, they were woken with much yelling and beating with sticks. A total of 5,006 Jewish girls, boys, women and men were registered and tattooed.[22] Pavel Steiner, their father, had the number 147741, Zdeněk the number 147742 and Jiří 147743. Their mother Jana's number is not known.

In the morning they were sent to the 'bath'. The men were shorn. They were given inmate clothing – Jiří an old pair of military trousers that were much too big for him, a torn shirt and a much too large coat. They were only allowed to keep their shoes. They were put in the Theresienstadt Family Camp in Auschwitz-Birkenau.

For the 5,006 people who had been promised 'work in Moravia', everything they now saw and heard was incomprehensible, mad and absurd. And the inmates interned in the other camp sections in Birkenau wondered why the sick, old and children were being kept alive and why children, women and men were in the same section of the camp, something that was not at all customary in Auschwitz. They were initially interned in the Theresienstadt Family Camp.

At first, the smaller children and girls were allowed to stay with their mothers and the older boys with their fathers. This enabled Jana Steiner to see her husband and two sons, who were in the same block.

Later, Jiří and Zdeněk were taken to the children's block during the day. At first, there was only one, but a second block was established after the arrival of a further transport from Theresienstadt. The walls were painted white and had scenes from Walt Disney's *Snow White and the Seven Dwarves* on them. They had been painted at the request of Fredy Hirsch, who had looked after the children in Theresienstadt, by a friend, the artist Dinah Gottliebova, who was also interned in Birkenau. She painted characters from the film, which she had seen in Brno before the war, on the walls of the barracks for the children in the Theresienstadt Family Camp.

Chairs and tables were later brought into the children's block. The food was better there than in the rest of the camp. 'The three- to five-year-olds were right next to the door. On one side were the girls, on the other side the boys, arranged by age, with a teacher for each. We, the oldest, were fourteen and right at the back.' There were proper lessons for the children. 'Our teacher was amazing. He taught us literature, mathematics, Czech, history, English and geography, all without pencils or paper.' If an SS man appeared, someone immediately started, for example, to recite a fairy tale in German. The younger ones in particular wanted to know what it was like outside the camp.

FERENC AND OTTO KLEIN The transport of the twin brothers Ferenc and Otto Klein, who were deported with their sister Ágnes and their mother Lilly, ended in May 1944 on the ramp of Auschwitz-Birkenau. 'We were able to look out. We saw the barbed wire.' One person said: 'That's a camp.' The doors opened. Orders were hurled at them. 'Out! Everybody out! Leave everything! Quick, quick, quick!' It was chaos. 'Some people were beaten terribly. It was brutal.'

An inmate who had been ordered to do this work approached them and, pointing to Ferenc and Otto, asked their mother: 'Are the two children twins?' 'Yes, they're my twins', she answered. 'Then wait here.' He went to Mengele – 'I learned the name later' – to inform him. A short time later, the inmate returned and said: 'Good, I need them both.' The twins were immediately taken to one side.

Ferenc and Otto observed the selection, saw families being torn apart. Their mother, aunt and sister had to stand in a line. A short glance by the SS doctor, who decided everything: 'Our mother and aunt went to the left, on the path to death', although they didn't know it at the time. 'Our sister went to the right, the path of the living' – which offered a temporary reprieve.

They were no longer able to speak to their mother, aunt and sister. 'It went so fast.' And they weren't in a normal state of mind: they were intimidated and frightened. The twin brothers underwent the painful registration process, with disinfection, beatings and tattooing.

The *Auschwitz Chronicle* entry for 27 May 1944 states: 'Two Jewish twin brothers who receive Nos. A-5331–A-5332 and six female Jews who receive Nos. A-6028–A-6033, are admitted to the camp after the selection from an RSHA transport from Hungary. Boys and healthy individuals are probably admitted as "depot prisoners". The remaining people are killed in the gas chambers.'[23]

The twin brothers were Ferenc and Otto Klein.[24] They were both put in the men's inmates' hospital. 'After everything was "finished", two SS men took us there.' The hospital had long been referred to by the inmates as the 'waiting room for the gas chamber' or 'entrance lobby to the crematorium'.

The boys were taken to the washroom, where they were forced to shower and received other clothing. Zvi Ernö Spiegel was their kapo in the hospital. Kapos were inmates who were forced to assist the SS. 'He was an extremely nice and decent man.'

They met Zvi Ernö Spiegel in the washroom. 'He was a twin and a Jew from Hungary like us.' He asked: 'Do you have anything in your pockets that you want to keep?' They had snapshots that their sister Ágnes had taken of family members and friends. As she didn't know where to leave the photos, she had given them to her brothers. They had them in their pockets together with a miniature Torah. They gave everything to Spiegel. After they had showered and received other clothing, he returned everything to them.

'We were put in Block 15. It contained around 110 twins, but also inmates with skin diseases, small people and triplets. We had to carry the small people when we went to the wash block. Otherwise they would have had difficulties for not being able to keep up.'

Most of the twins were from Hungary. 'There were also some Czechs and Germans. Among them was a very nice young German boy. He was about seventeen and his name was Feingold. He was very religious and was always praying. His sister survived and moved after liberation to Basel, Switzerland.'

At the start of the deportations from Hungary, practically only twins were left alive, registered and transferred to the camp. On 17 May 1944, nineteen twin brothers and single twins arrived; on 18 May, twenty twin sisters; on 19 May, seven twin brothers and single twins; and on 20 May, fifty-eight twin sisters and single twins, twenty-four twin brothers and single twins.[25]

OLGA AND VERA GROSSMANN 'Twins! Where are the twins? Twins out!' It was these yells that greeted the 6-year-old twin sisters Olga and Vera Grossman on their arrival at Auschwitz-Birkenau extermination camp.

Their parents, Isack and Šarolta (Shari) Grossmann, were with them. They came from a small eastern Slovakian village called Turiany (after 1948, Turany), where their father had been a successful building contractor. The family owned a large house, woods and land.

The family started to have problems in 1941. Warned through rumours and announcements in official speeches of anti-Jewish measures, the

Grossmanns left their home one day – the year is unknown – to escape from the Hlinka Guard, the Slovakian equivalent of the SS. 'My father often paid for the hiding places with money', says Vera Kriegal (*née* Grossmann). 'I have a very clear memory of hiding under sacks full of dry corn in an attic. The Guard were looking for Jews in hiding. The people whose attic we were hiding in told us that we had to be quiet and shouldn't move or cough. Because if the Guard found us they would be killed.'

Olga and Vera were filled with a 'terrible feeling', as their mother also later recalled, that never left them for their entire lives, because, as Vera Kriegel put it: 'If I did something wrong it could mean the death of my parents and sister.'

One day the family were again in hiding in a house.

In the middle of the night there was loud shouting. Men from the Guard were at the door and yelled: 'Come out or we'll shoot!' I remember a young man pulling me out of bed. I started screaming: 'I want to stay in bed! Let me stay here. I'm not going anywhere.' I started struggling and kicking. But it didn't help.

Olga and Vera were 6 years old when they were arrested. Together with their parents, they were put in a camp in Sered', around 60 kilometres east of Bratislava, where Jews were interned as forced labourers. It was also a collecting point for deportations to Auschwitz.[26]

In late October / early November 1944, the family was transported to Auschwitz-Birkenau.[27] There was straw on the floor of the wagon. Somewhere there was a bucket for doing the necessary. It was very stuffy. There were only small openings and the wagon was packed. People cried for something to eat and drink. There were mothers with babies sucking at the breast. My sister Olga and I were so thirsty; we also wanted to drink, but there was nothing. That was really bad.

When the wagon door opened in Auschwitz-Birkenau, the dead fell out first. 'And then the people who were still alive fell on the dead. Outside were the Nazis with dogs, whips and guns. They beat us and shouted: "Hurry! Hurry up, damned Jews. Hurry up! Hurry up!" They wouldn't leave us alone.'

The twin sisters had no idea where they were. 'Our father was pushed into a line where there were only men. We never saw him again. Everything happened so quickly that we had no time to think.' That was probably 4 November 1944, the arrival date next to the names Olga and Vera on a list drawn up after liberation.[28]

As the family had spoken German as well as Slovakian in Turiany, they could understand everything that was being shouted and said. But Šarolta Grossmann was still unsure what to do when there was a call for twins. 'In the end, my mother decided to tell the truth', says Vera Kriegel (*née* Grossmann). 'A Nazi approached and took us to the man called Mengele', as she later discovered.

> Mengele scrutinized us. My mother had fair skin, blue eyes and dark hair. Olga was taller than me, also had fair skin but brown eyes. My skin was a little darker and I had brown eyes and resembled a 'gypsy'. I took after my father. Mengele didn't believe at first that we were twins, because we didn't look identical. He said to our mother: 'You're not a Jew. You're an Aryan.' But my mother answered: 'I'm a Jew and those are my twins.'

Then he measured her face. With his fingers he measured the distance from her forehead and her ears to her nose. He repeated: 'You're Aryan.' Our mother replied: 'I'm a Jew.' 'Good, then come with me.'

Šarolta Grossmann had to leave her children with a group of women, who then marched away from the ramp.

> We saw a pit with flames in it. There was screaming and crying. Children were taken from their mothers, who struggled to keep them, but they were brutally torn away. We could see men in uniform grabbing the children and throwing them alive into the flames. The babies were thrown into the air and torn apart like chickens. The Nazis laughed and had fun.

Olga had the number A26945, Vera A26946 and their mother A26944 tattooed on them.

For the sisters it was hell: 'The Nazis were diabolical. They brainwashed us: "You're worthless. And if you're worthless, then you deserve to die. You're no good for anything." They wanted to have complete control over us. People found that impossible to bear. Some simply wanted to get it over with.'

Vera Kriegel has a clear memory of the terrible things she saw in Auschwitz, day in, day out. Even if she wanted to, she can't get them out of her mind. 'Once there was a mother with four children and they said to her: "You can keep one child. Which one do you want?" What is a mother supposed to do? She didn't want to pick out one child. She threw herself onto the electrified fence and killed herself. That was her answer.'

Olga and Vera were supposed to be separated from their mother, but Vera wouldn't allow it.

> I clung tightly to my mother. A Nazi tried to tear me away, but couldn't manage. I screamed and kicked. It took three of them to pull me away. My mother told me later that everyone who saw the fight I put up had tears in their eyes. Olga and I were brought to a barracks. Our mother came soon afterwards. We were so happy.

One day they were locked in 'a kind of wooden cage'. 'My mother, Olga and I and two other girls. I don't know what happened to them. The cage was so small that we could hardly move or lie down.'

The 4-year-old twin sisters Hanna (Channah) and Sarah (Susan) Seiler, who were taken to Auschwitz-Birkenau from Berlin, were also put in a cage like this.

> Hanna and I were shut in a wooden cage of about 1.5 square metres in area. They gave us some terrible-tasting soup and bread. We were completely isolated in this cage at one end of the barracks....
>
> The experiments on our bodies started very soon afterwards. We were taken to a spotless white laboratory and placed on a table. We were given an injection in the spine and then returned to the cage. This procedure was repeated every few days for a certain time. The pain from the injection lasted until the next one.
>
> Soon after the first injection, my sister started getting convulsions. I didn't know what it was. She was sitting in the corner of the cage and suddenly went stiff. Then her face, arms and legs started to convulse as if she had no control over them. Dr Mengele's assistants were in front of the cage observing

us. Sometimes Mengele himself was also there. I don't know whether I had the same, but I suppose so. ... One day – it must have been in December 1944 – Hanna was bought back to the cage and started having the convulsions as usual. This time they didn't stop but lasted all night. When she stopped, her entire body was motionless. Even though I was so young, I knew that something terrible had happened. I screamed.... Then Dr Mengele came and lifted her out of the cage. I knew she was dead. We were 4 years old.[29]

Olga and Vera Grossmann remained in this or another wooden cage with their mother and two other girls for around two weeks. They precise duration is unknown.

Olga Solomon (*née* Grossmann) relates that the two twins were then taken to a laboratory 'for experiments to be performed on us'. 'All I know is that this went on for hours and hours, days and days. We had to get undressed and our fingerprints were taken. Every day Mengele came to the barracks for blood tests – with a smile on his face! I'll never forget that smile.' He was 'terribly nice' to them.

Vera Kriegel (*née* Grossmann): 'They gave us injections in the spine. We didn't know what was in the injections. It was the first experiment Mengele conducted on us.

Then Olga and I were separated from our mother. The injections made us dreadfully sick. We were dizzy, vomited and felt terribly weak.'

Another experiment was conducted elsewhere. They also fetched their mother for it. It was not in a barracks. 'We were brought one after another to a room', says Vera. There they had drops put in their eyes, which were very painful.

'In the room was a wall full of human eyes of different colours staring at us. It was a collection of butterflies. I was shocked and left the room trembling.'

Mengele wanted to change the eye colour by injecting methylene blue so that they would meet 'Aryan requirements'. He was looking for a way of turning the brown eyes of blond children into blue ones.[30]

Vyera Pavlovna, inmate number 74107 from the village of Hlyn'ske near Poltava in Ukraine, also spoke about this change of eye colour. She was interned in Auschwitz with a large group of young girls and women at the beginning of January 1944 and gave birth to a child there in May of that year. With her in the barracks were two other mothers who had just given birth.

In February 1945, Pavlovna testified:

> German doctors conducted experiments on the new-born babies to change their eye colour. They took the child and dripped a fluid into its eyes. Then they observed the reaction and added more drops.... There was a Polish woman – I don't know her name – whose child was subjected to these experiments, which flushed out the baby's eyes.... They put several drops in the eyes of an eighteen-month-old Russian girl, whose name I don't know. Her eyes became red, and she died after three days.[31]

Mengele once had Vera brought to a room. He asked her all kinds of questions.

> There was a long-haired blond woman in the room, whom I didn't know. I had to stand naked in front of Mengele. He turned me around with his whip and showed me to this woman. It didn't hurt but it was worse than being beaten.
>
> I don't know what he was trying to do. He just said to me: 'You're a good little girl. Here's a present for you.' He gave me a piece of bread, sugar lumps and chocolates. I took them to my sister and mother and shared it with them.
>
> We didn't see our mother very often. She was always asking: 'Where are they? Where have my daughters been taken?' She always knew where we were.
>
> One day they took us to what I suppose was the 'Gypsy' Camp. There were around a hundred children in our barracks, maybe more. We weren't allowed out. They gave us injections again. We had sores all over our bodies and very high fever. Lots of blood was taken.
>
> One night during the curfew there was a commotion in the barracks. It was dark but I saw that children were being taken away. I fell back to sleep.
>
> When I woke in the morning, I wanted to turn round in my bunk. As it was very narrow and we could only turn over together, I had to wake the girl who was between Olga and me. But she couldn't be roused. She was dead. I don't know what had happened. But I saw that the barracks was empty. There were only six or seven of us left.
>
> Her twin sister Olga could never forget the Women's Camp where they were kept for a time. There was a block with lots of children, including babies.

It was full of wailing, crying and moaning. A fear crept up on me. There were also pregnant women there lying on bunks. I saw something terrible there. I saw a baby taken from its mother's lap and thrown live into the burning stove. I've never ever got over that. This image is etched in me forever.

OTTO AND FERENC KLEIN were 12 when they fell into the clutches of SS doctor Mengele. 'We had no idea what was going on around us.' They were examined repeatedly from head to foot. Mengele's assistants took blood, injected them with 'some substances or other', cut samples of hair, printed their fingers and toes, dropped 'some liquid' in their eyes. Afterwards, they could barely see for a while. They always felt 'quite terrible' afterwards.

'Mengele examined us in person three or four times. Zvi Ernö Spiegel, who knew several languages, was our interpreter. He spoke kindly to us. He examined me and Ferenc from top to bottom. He checked our fingers, noses, skin, teeth, hair.... All of his observations were noted. And everything was photographed.'

When Otto and Ferenc were with Mengele for the first time, they had to undress completely. The photos in their pockets fell out. Mengele wanted to look at them. He put three photos to one side, 'one of our father, one of our mother, and one of my brother and me with our Jewish teacher, who had a beard'. He looked carefully at the picture of the teacher and asked the twins: 'What did you learn from the Christians?' Otto was surprised at his brother, who answered like a shot: 'We learned everything from Jews. We've learned nothing from Christians.'

Mengele didn't pull a face or react in any way. He didn't punish Ferenc and Otto. Nothing.

The children talked to one another about what they had gone through and discussed what the examinations might be for. 'No one knew for sure.' But they all knew that 'Mengele needs us for his experiments.' If they had a dispute with someone, they would threaten to tell Dr Mengele. On the other hand, it was also clear that they were completely dependent on Mengele.

After just a couple of days in Birkenau, Otto and Ferenc realized what was going on in the camp. The other twins had told them what the selections meant. They heard about the gas chambers and saw Crematorium III with their own eyes, which was right next to their section of the camp, separated only by barbed wire. The boys saw people going in 'but never coming out again'. They saw smoke and flames belching out of the chimneys, smelled a certain odour, which they could taste on their tongue.

My brother and I knew that we would probably never see our mother and aunt again. We were unable to express our feelings at the time. Under normal circumstances we would have reacted strongly. But we were also in a terrible and hopeless situation. Like all twins we asked ourselves every day and every night: 'How will we survive?' We knew that we would need a huge amount of luck.

Otto and Ferenc didn't feel 12 years old anymore. 'Anyone in this situation grows up immediately.' The twins were constantly reminded of something their mother had told them a short while before: 'People who are killed just because they are Jews go straight to heaven.'

Harassment and maltreatment of inmates by the SS were daily occurrences in Birkenau. This included 'exercises' such as leapfrog, rolling or duck-walking. The inmates had to perform these sadistic exercises until they were exhausted.

The SS were able to relax by playing real sport. There were many renowned athletes, national and international champions and Olympic Games participants in Auschwitz-Birkenau. Football matches were organized near Crematorium III for a time.[32]

Otto and Ferenc were witnesses: 'The matches took place on Sundays. We boys had to chalk the field. The SS watched, but I think there were also matches against inmate teams. I know for certain that two Hungarian twins from our barracks played. They were twenty years old and outstanding footballers.'

The football field was only a few metres from the ramp. One Saturday, a transport arrived while the boys were marking the field. 'It must have been 22 July 1944.' From the small opening in the cattle wagon, someone called out: 'Do you speak Hungarian?' The 12-year-old Otto replied: 'Yes.' From the wagon, the voice said: 'The dog's dead.'

They didn't understand at the time what was meant. 'Later we heard that an attempt had been made two days before on the life of the dog,

Hitler.' The new arrival could not have known that the attempt had been unsuccessful.

JIŘÍ AND ZDENĚK STEINER One morning in March 1944 came the order to fall in at the lower section of the camp. The inmates marched off to the quarantine camp taking all of their belongings with them. They went quietly to the quarantine camp, convinced that nothing could happen to them and that they were merely going to a new family camp. The SS man and Erster Schutzhaftlagerführer Schwarzhuber had stated that they were due to be transported to a camp in Upper Silesia. At the same time, a rumour circulated that they were all in fact to be gassed. 'We didn't believe it, however, because we thought it couldn't happen.'

They waited the entire day. Nothing happened that day, 7 March 1944, nor on the next morning. In the early afternoon came the order: 'Stand by in the barracks. Rapportführer Buntrock is coming!' When he arrived, he read out the names of some doctors. 'And then we heard our number. We were terribly afraid, because my father's number wasn't read out, and our mother was not in the barracks. Buntrock assured our father that he would see us again in the evening.'

Jiří and Zdeněk were taken with other twins from this barracks to the main gate of the quarantine camp. 'There were already people there from other blocks, pairs of twins, doctors and nurses' – altogether around seventy people.

They were taken to the 'hospital' in the Theresienstadt Family Camp. 'We went to sleep. Perhaps they had given us something, I don't know anymore.'

When Jiří and Zdeněk woke up the next morning, they were told that the transport had departed. 'Everyone knew what had happened but we weren't told anything.'

The brothers learned that trucks had driven off in the direction of the crematorium. 'And flames came out of the crematorium chimney.' At first, Jiří and Zdeněk didn't want to believe that their parents had been murdered. 'We even made plans about seeing them again.'

Their teacher and protector Fredy Hirsch had committed suicide on 8 March.[33] He didn't want to be a passive witness to the impending extermination.

Jiří and Zdeněk Steiner were 14 years old when they met Mengele, a 'tall, slim man'. 'He had a high forehead and appeared very arrogant. But his facial expression could change in the fraction of a second to a smarmy smile.'

Mengele had them brought to the 'Gypsy' Camp. With feigned concern, he asked the Steiner twins if there was anything they wanted. 'My brother and I answered simultaneously: "We would like to be with our parents." He assured us that we would soon see our parents. He didn't say where.'

They were examined for the first time by inmate doctors. The length of their fingers, nails and noses was measured, in fact 'just about everything that can be weighed and measured'. The hair and skin colour were noted, and finger and toe prints made. Then they were returned to the hospital in the Theresienstadt Family Camp. 'And camp life went on as before.'

At this time, Mengele had requisitioned around 150 sets of twins aged between 3 and 16 years. The boys were in the hospital, the girls in the Women's Camp. 'We twins lived in a barracks with small people.'

The measurements by the inmate doctors continued:

They took X-rays, photographed us from all sides, tested our eyesight, hearing, nervous system and heart. They took blood samples (around fourteen times in eighteen months), which were sent to a laboratory somewhere. It was said that various substances were tried out on us, but I have no proof of this. But throughout our time in the camp, we were in very bad health.

Jiří maintains that the examinations went on endlessly on account of the Jewish inmate doctors. 'Many examination results were lost and had to be obtained again. We were never finished so Mengele couldn't order our extermination.'

They were spared from the selections that took place in July 1944 in the Theresienstadt Family Camp. 'I saw women and men, completely naked, standing and waiting in long lines in front of the barracks.' Fellow inmates later confirmed that Mengele had determined who should live and who should die.

Right after this selection, twins, doctors and nurses were transferred to the hospital camp near the crematoria. Mengele still needed them. The inmates there received only rudimentary treatment from the inmate doctors. 'Blood was taken in the new camp. This was not good for our weakened bodies.'

Jiří and Zdeněk had to clean the block. They met an inmate from the Sonderkommando, which worked at the ovens in the crematorium for those who had died in the gas chambers. 'He told us how our parents died.'

Again and again, for more than fifty days, Hungarian transports, which had begun in May 1944, arrived at the ramp in Auschwitz-Birkenau. Jiří and Zdeněk could see Mengele 'how he carried out the selections, how he picked those destined to die'. Jiří also saw with his own eyes 'the liquidation of the "Gypsy Family Camp"':

> I was lying in the 'hospital' at the top of a multi-tier bunk. I could see through a hole in the wall. The 'gypsy' women were wailing terribly. Their section of the camp was right next to the Men's Camp. They were not crying but giving out an indescribable high-pitched sound. I will never forget it. One truck after another left from the 'Gypsy' Camp.

On that day and the following night, 2 and 3 August 1944, the Nazis gassed between 4,200 and 4,300 Sinti and Roma. The corpses were burned in a pit.[34]

Mengele continued his experiments with the twins. 'He was very concerned about us. No doubt we were the guarantee for his "scientific" and SS career.'

But one day Mengele was not there. 'One of our tormenters, the camp doctor Thilo, organized a selection. My brother and I were selected for the crematorium. This information left us more or less unmoved. We had become completely indifferent. We just said to ourselves that there was nothing to be done. We would be reunited with our parents in heaven, with God.'

Otto and Ferenc Klein were also selected for the gas chamber. But Mengele returned that night and 'rescued his twins'. How long would his protection last? How long would the experiments go on? They had heard that some people had disappeared without a trace and others had become very sick as a result of the experiments.

All of the twins were afraid of the chimneys. They believed nothing and no one. They looked through the barbed wire fence to see what was going on in other parts of the camp. They saw adults walking into the electrified fence. One sign of the twins' fear was the 'gas chamber game'. Jiří Steiner: 'We threw stones into a hole in the ground and shouted "gas, gas, gas!" They were the people who went to the crematorium. We even discussed how to build the ovens.'

In winter 1944–5, the Steiner twins were detailed to carry water. They had to walk about a kilometre with buckets of water. 'This work was terrible because I often got completely soaked until I realized that I only had to half-fill the buckets. Afterwards it got a lot easier.'

Occasionally they could hear firing in the far distance. The children had an idea: 'We pressed our ears to the ground and could now hear the fighting at the front quite clearly. We kept on pressing our ears to the ground. We heard the roar of artillery. We heard the front approaching. We couldn't get enough of it. Our hopes for survival grew and grew.'

Jiří and Zdeněk and the other children and juveniles in that section of the camp once again dreamed of being liberated. 'We talked of soft-boiled eggs, fresh rolls with butter, clean shirts, leather shoes and school.'

# 'To Be Free at Last!'

On 23 July 1944, the Red Army and units of the Polish Armia Krajowa liberated Majdanek extermination camp located in a suburb of Lublin in the east of Poland. On 3 November 1943 alone, 18,000 Jews were murdered there by the SS in a single day during the 'Aktion Erntefest' ['Harvest Festival Action'].

Starting in early 1944, the surviving inmates from Majdanek were deported to camps to the west. A large number of mostly Byelorussian children were transported in early April to Dzierzążnia, a satellite camp of the Litzmannstadt (Łódź) juvenile detention camp.

Before Majdanek was liberated, the SS had attempted to obliterate the most obvious traces of their crimes. They were not entirely successful: members of the SS camp staff were arrested, documentation of the crimes found[1] and intact mass extermination facilities secured.

For that reason, the SS wanted to eradicate all traces of their crimes in Auschwitz. In the second half of 1944, files, documents – including inmate files – and transport lists were destroyed. The pits in which the corpses had been burned or the human ashes from the crematorium ovens had been tipped had to be cleaned, covered over, flattened and greened by the inmates.

The crematoria were dismantled and later dynamited. Incineration ovens, dismantled wooden barracks and the possessions of the Jews murdered in the gas chambers were removed, for the most part to Germany. Between December 1944 and mid-January 1945 alone, over 1 million articles of clothing were prepared for transport. And on 23 January, the thirty barracks comprising the 'Effektenlager', the store where the possessions of the murdered inmates were kept, were set on fire by the SS.

More than 80,000 children, women and men were transferred from mid-August 1944 to mid-January 1945 to concentration camps farther to the west. Many were subsequently required to work as slave labourers in armaments companies in Germany and Austria.

The camp gradually emptied out. The SS concentrated the remaining inmates in a few sections. Twins, the sick and 'unproductive elements' had to remain in Birkenau and continued to live in fear of their lives. The ultimate intention was to murder all of the children, women and men remaining in Auschwitz. The fact that most of them survived is due above all to the rapid advance of the Red Army. Later, however, after the withdrawal of the SS, about 600 more inmates were found shot in Auschwitz I and Auschwitz-Birkenau.

Work began in the last quarter of 1944 on dismantling and then dynamiting the crematoria. Prior to this, the technical gas chamber installations and ovens had been removed to within the Reich, along with a large amount of building material and the possessions belonging to the murdered inmates.[2]

The twin brothers Otto and Ferenc Klein had to help. 'We loaded sacks full of clothes and other possessions onto a handcart, which we had to pull to the ramp and load onto wagons.'

One day an SS man called Otto and Ferenc over to him. 'Here, take these canisters to the crematorium.' They did so. At Crematorium III, SS men were waiting for the boys and opened the three containers, which were 'full of explosive'. Holes were made in the brick walls. 'The SS stuffed the dynamite into them.' Before the SS blew up the crematorium, the boys were warned: 'Get under cover! Lie down!' Then the building was blown up. 'The crematorium collapsed.'

Early December 1944. Gábor Hirsch was suffering increasingly from the effects of camp life. He was becoming weaker and weaker every day. His body was covered in festering wounds. He had ulcers in his mouth. 'I couldn't eat anymore.'

Around his fifteenth birthday on 9 December, he was transferred to the 'hospital'. This barracks was barely any different from the others: three-tier wooden bunks were filled with sick inmates. The straw on which they had to lie was saturated with excrement and pus.

Inmates – with or without medical training – had to work in these blocks. They tried to assist the sick but had practically no bandages or medicine.

'It was here, in the "hospital", that I was finally tattooed. I had the number B–14781.'[3] It was one of the last inmate numbers assigned in Auschwitz.

In the second half of January, the SS drove a further 58,000 people from the Main Camp, Auschwitz-Birkenau and the forty or more satellite camps westward to the interior of Austria and Germany. Some 8,000 to 9,000 inmates, mostly sick or incapable of walking or being transported, were left behind.[4] Gábor was one of them.

In mid-January 1945, the noise of the artillery was now clearly audible. Everyone in the camp knew that the front was approaching.

Many SS men disappeared. 'For us, the guards that were still there were practically invisible.' Their hope of surviving grew, but Otto and Ferenc Klein still lived in fear of being killed after all.

On 18 January, Otto and Ferenc Klein, Jiří and Zdeněk Steiner and Gábor Hirsch were presented with the choice of embarking on a 50-kilometre march, walking the 3 kilometres to Auschwitz train station or stating that they were incapable of walking.

Gábor Hirsch was so weak that he would not have survived a march. He reported sick and was transferred to the men's hospital. He was extremely afraid of being shot. 'With the Germans, you never knew.'

Otto and Ferenc Klein opted for the short walk to Auschwitz train station or to stay in the camp.

Jiří and Zdeněk were not sure what to do. They had only one wish: 'To be free at last!'

They contemplated what they should do. 'We knew that the long march would mean certain death. But we didn't want to stay in the camp either.' They had heard that the SS were going to blow it up.

'Put us down for the three kilometres', they decided. Zdeněk whispered softly: 'Perhaps we can run off.'

In the afternoon, around 150 sick inmates left the men's hospital and set off on the 50-kilometre march.[5] The very sick remained behind, along with twins and a small group of inmate doctors and nurses.

On 20 January, Jiří and Zdeněk saw SS men putting luggage in their car. 'They came into the camp to find tailors from among the inmates who could make or repair civilian clothing for them. And they also needed carpenters to build sleds for them.'

The SS had evidently abandoned the watchtowers. They did not appear to be there anymore.

'We went on an "excursion" and got as far as "Kanada"' – as the inmates called the barracks where the SS stored and sorted the possessions they had taken. 'We found ourselves in the midst of a gigantic treasure trove. Clothing, linen, suitcases, sewing machines, spectacles, medical instruments …'.

They got scared and took only the most important things – a jacket, a pair of trousers, a blanket. They said to themselves: 'Perhaps we can come back.'

On the morning of 22 January, a Security Service unit stormed into the men's hospital where Jiří and Zdeněk were. The inmates referred to these so-called camp infirmaries as antechambers to hell, to the gas chambers. 'All Russians fall in!' they ordered. They were taken behind Block 14 and had to line up in a ditch full of water. 'Practically all of them were shot' – along with a lot of other inmates who had been looking for food in other parts of Birkenau, or for ways of escaping.[6]

In this situation, Šarolta Grossmann attempted to escape one night with the twins Olga and Vera. A man and his two boys joined them. 'We didn't know where we should go. We only knew that we had to get away.'

They spent the night in some 'unfinished building'. But when they looked out into the snowy landscape the following morning, they decided to return to their section of the camp. They would not have survived in the snow and cold without food and drink.

'All Jews fall in', came the order on 25 January 1945. In the afternoon, a Security Service unit had arrived with the intention of taking around 350 Jewish children, women and men from the camp, including Otto and Ferenc Klein, Jiří and Zdeněk Steiner and Šarolta Grossmann, but not her twin daughters Olga and Vera, who were separated from her.[7]

The twin sisters were in a barracks with other children. Vera could see her mother from the entrance. She wondered how she could get to her. She went back into the barracks and said to Olga: 'I'm going to run, and then you can follow me.'

The SS allowed them to join the group. 'We couldn't believe it, but perhaps they thought they could kill us sometime on the way.'

Their mother was quite far back in the column. But the people asked: 'Who do these children belong to?' And the twins were passed from one row to another. 'Until we finally fell into our mother's arms.'

Their guards asked them who couldn't walk. According to Jiří Steiner, five people reported. 'They were shot', as were others who couldn't keep up during the march. People dropped dead in the snow. 'It was terrible. We didn't know what would happen to us.'

'The shooting wouldn't stop', recalls Olga Solomon (*née* Grossmann). 'We hid under our mother's jacket.'

'Suddenly Germans arrived on motorcycles', says Otto Klein. 'They shouted something. We couldn't understand. Then the guards disappeared with the other Germans. We never saw them again.'

'And then for a moment, a short moment', says Olga, 'there was a strange silence.'

Those left behind were still afraid. They couldn't believe what had happened. They said to themselves: 'Perhaps the Nazis have only gone off for a short time and will be coming back again soon.' But then they began to realize what this unexpected piece of luck meant. They shouted for joy.

Some ran across the fields into a wood. Jiří Steiner: 'We didn't know where to go. It was terribly cold.'

Some suggested going to the Main Camp, where they could best hide.

They were at a bridge on the road from Birkenau to Auschwitz. Vera Kriegel (*née* Grossmann): 'We thought that the bridge might be dynamited. Some men went down to check. It took a while. We were freezing and hungry.'

But there was no explosive under the bridge, and they were able to cross. 'We arrived at the Main Camp, Auschwitz I. And the inmates left there asked where we had come from. They said we had been very lucky.'

There was coffee and soup with rice. The people were so starving that everyone wanted to get to the food. 'But there was a man who said: "Wait! Here is a woman with two children. They should eat first."' A year later, this man, Jan Simsović, a Pole, inmate in the Main Camp, married Šarolta Grossmann. 'So we lost one father in Birkenau and found another in Auschwitz.'

A day and two nights passed. In the Main Camp, an inmate council was formed. It decided that no one should show themselves at the window or go out. They wanted to give the impression that the camp was empty.

The chatter of machine guns woke them on 27 January. 'The firing was continuous – until midday', reported Jiří Steiner. Then they heard silence. 'I associate this expression, "to hear silence", with that time. There was really an unusual silence' – for two hours. 'We sat there without saying anything. Someone prayed.'

In the early afternoon, Jiří had a 'strange feeling'. He went to the entrance. He wanted to open it just 'a little bit'. 'Outside, in the middle of the snow-covered main road through camp, was a young man wearing a white coat with a cap with a red star.' Jiří shouted: 'The Russians are here!'

Everyone ran out, also from the other barracks. 'Everyone took something with them: a piece of bread, the most precious things we had. We gave it to him. Then some of us put him on our shoulders and carried him around.'

A few minutes later, other Red Army soldiers arrived. 'They sent everyone back to the barracks.' They said: 'This is the front. Do you want to get shot?'

Otto and Ferenc Klein remained in the barracks where they were hiding. They didn't yet trust themselves. 'Then a Russian soldier came to our barracks. He could see that we children were scared. He tried to comfort us. "I'm a Russian soldier, not a German. Don't be afraid."

Now we knew that it was over. We were free. We had survived. What happiness, what a great day. We had a future again.'

In view of his very poor health, Gábor Hirsch had remained in Auschwitz-Birkenau. He had hidden under the straw on a bunk in one of the barracks. 'I was so weak that I could barely walk.'

After a few hours, he moved. Then he heard, from all over the barracks, 'Pst, pst, pst.' He realized that he was not the only one to have 'this great idea'.

Several hours passed. Now the occupants began to show themselves. Gábor lay down with two adults in the block elder's abandoned room. His condition quickly deteriorated. The two adults didn't want to take responsibility for Gábor. They took him to a hospital barracks.

'I was so weak that I couldn't walk. If I had to go somewhere, I held on to the barrack wall, but mostly I crawled on all fours. I also had terrible diarrhoea.'

On account of his poor health, he has no memory of his liberation. 'I couldn't even get to the next bunk without dirtying myself again.' But he was free.

Shortly after the liberation, Russian cameramen filmed the situation in Birkenau. Gábor Hirsch thinks he recognizes himself in one of the pictures:[8] 'The boy with the blanket supported by a medical orderly could be me, but I'm not sure.'

A few days later, Gábor was taken in a cart pulled by mules to the former Main Camp, where both the Red Army and the Polish Red Cross had set up field hospitals. Russian doctors examined the boy. They found a purulent, very painful mouth ulcer, extreme malnutrition and tuberculosis.[9] He consisted merely of skin and bones. 'I was 15 years old and weighed 27 kg.' He was bedridden for weeks. He slowly recovered and put on weight. 'The Russians really fed me up.'

Jiří and Zdeněk Steiner were examined by the Red Army medical commission. They were both also 15 years old. Jiří weighed 28 kg and was 1.30 m tall. He wasn't to grow much taller later on, either. He can be seen in a film taken by the Red Army front cameramen a few weeks after liberation. He is standing in a group of adults at the fence. 'I'm the boy with the bandaged hand.' His hand was broken.

On 24 February 1945, all of the former inmates still in Auschwitz gathered together. They pledged 'to do everything possible in their future lives to prevent fascism from recurring'. For Jiří Steiner, this oath has always been of great importance.

According to the decades of research at the Auschwitz Memorial, at least 232,000 children and adolescents under the age of 18 were deported to Auschwitz, including 216,300 Jews and 11,000 Sinti and Roma; 3,120 were non-Jewish Poles, 1,140 were Byelorussians, Russians and Ukrainians, as well as from other nations. On 27 January 1945, only about 750 children and adolescents under the age of 18 were liberated from Auschwitz. Of them, 521 were 14 and under and there were around 60 new-born babies.[10]

One Soviet forensic commission immediately examined a representative group of children. Its report states: 'There were 180 children among the inmates liberated in Auschwitz – 52 under the age of eight and 128 aged between eight and fifteen. All of the children had arrived in the camp in the second half of 1944 ... The medical examination revealed that 72 children had pulmonary and lymph node tuberculosis, 49 were suffering from malnutrition and complete exhaustion, and 31 from frostbite.'[11]

# Transports, Death Marches and Other Camps

The rapid advance of the Red Army forced the SS, particularly after autumn 1944, to gradually close down Auschwitz-Birkenau. Transport after transport, death march after death march was set in motion. Inmates from Auschwitz and satellite camps were moved to concentration camps farther to the west.

Weak and sick children, women and men were mostly left behind in Auschwitz or killed shortly before the camp was liberated. The SS drove tens of thousands of inmates back and forth on long marches or crammed them into railway wagons and sent them, sometimes for weeks, on random journeys. Those who were too weak or sick to continue were shot immediately. Many died of cold, starvation or thirst.[1]

DAGMAR FANTLOVÁ AND DÁŠA FRIEDOVÁ were transported in summer 1944 from Auschwitz-Birkenau to the west of Nazi Germany. They were taken in cattle wagons to Hamburg not by the SS but by the Wehrmacht. The train arrived at its destination on 6 July 1944, a date that Dagmar Lieblová (*née* Fantlová) has never forgotten.

In Hamburg, the girls and women were put in one of the warehouses in the port. 'It was a huge room. We slept in double bunks. In another part of the room there was also a dining area with tables and benches as well as washing facilities and a toilet.' They were even given a bowl, a spoon, linen and a blanket. The living conditions bore no resemblance to those in Birkenau. In the room with them were women from Hungary who had come to Hamburg via Auschwitz. Russian prisoners of war were housed on another floor.

For breakfast they had ersatz coffee, 'but then we had a proper midday meal: potatoes and salted herrings'. This was something they had never seen in Auschwitz-Birkenau. 'We were astonished.' But they only got this food on the first day. Afterwards, there was just a thin soup and bread.

The women and girls also had to work on Saturdays, clearing rubble from bombed houses. Sunday was a free day. Dáša and Dagmar didn't know how they would stand this hard labour for even a week.

There were air raids almost every night. They were woken from their sleep and had to go to the warehouse basement on Dessauer Strasse, which still exists today. From there, they travelled by launch to work, 'to Moorburg, Wilhelmsburg and other districts in Hamburg and the surrounding area. We worked in different factories.'

Two months after their arrival, Dáša and Dagmar were transferred to the Neugraben women's camp, a satellite camp of Neuengamme. They had to dig ditches for water pipes in the forest, collect bricks from the harbour in Harburg and, in winter, clear the snow.

Near the forest where Dáša and Dagmar were working was a house inhabited by a woman and her son, who was still a child, but he didn't dare to approach them. They were guarded by customs officers who were 'very lax'.

> Once the boy's mother requested to the guard that we bring the heather we had been gathering to her garden. We did this. The woman invited us into her house. This was quite unusual. We had ersatz coffee and a piece of bread and cheese. It was the first time in years that we had been in a normal house, sitting in a 'proper' kitchen with a family, if only for a short time.

The son's name was Wolfgang and he was 12 years old. His friend Jürgen must have been two years younger. At the end of December 1944, the boys brought the girls a large bag 'full of potatoes, carrots, cabbage and a few other things'. 'It was a Christmas present from the boys, which brought us immense pleasure. That's something else I've never forgotten.'

The next station for Dáša and Dagmar was the Neuengamme satellite camp Hamburg-Tiefstack near the Billweder Bucht in the present-day Billbrook district. They were required there to collect and stack bricks from bombed houses. It was one of the last camps to be built, in early February 1945. It is not known how many of the 500 or so Jewish girls and women from Czechoslovakia[2] died of malnutrition, the brutality of the guards, the consequences of the long internment or in air raids.

When the two girls returned one evening from work, they discovered that the camp had been bombed. Some women were dead and others lay wounded in the hospital.

The survivors arrived in early April 1945 at Bergen-Belsen. They had been taken by train to Celle and had to walk the last 25 kilometres to the camp. 'It was a terribly long way. You didn't look back. You tried to stay alive.'

LYDIA HOLZNEROVÁ AND HER SISTER VĚRA arrived together with 'around 250 Czech Jewish women', probably in July 1944, at Christianstadt, a satellite camp of Gross-Rosen. Further transports arrived with a large number of Jewish women from Germany, the Netherlands, Austria, Hungary, territories occupied by Hungary, and Łódź ghetto. Many had passed through Auschwitz-Birkenau on death marches and in cattle wagons on their way to Christianstadt, including several pregnant women who had remained undetected in Auschwitz and whose babies had been stillborn or died at birth. There were also several girls[3] younger and older than the 14-year-old Lydia.

They all lived in barracks in the forest and had to work in a munitions factory. Most women were employed filling bombs, grenades and explosive charges. In doing so, they came into contact with strong and toxic chemicals that caused anxiety, unconsciousness or convulsions.[4]

Lydia had to fell trees and chop wood in the forest 'to make wood gas to power the vehicles'. Her sister worked on an excavator, where a Czech man offered to help them. He took letters from Lydia and Věra for posting.

This enabled us to communicate again from Christianstadt with our hometown of Hronov. The man was even allowed to have parcels for us sent to his address. First of all we were sent clothing from home, organized by our old housekeeper. My aunt, a Christian, was also there and helped us. I was sent a pair of spectacles and something to eat. And we got shoes from the shoemaker in Hronov. We had traced our feet on a piece of paper and sent it home.

Lydia and Věra had to leave Christianstadt in early February 1945. 'It was an "evacuation", a death march.'

They slept on the way in barns and stables. After four or five days, some people, including Lydia and Věra, decided to escape. 'We hid deep in the straw and didn't come out.' They stayed there for a day and a night.

'There were originally five girls and young women. I was the youngest. My sister was there too. We met a stream of Germans fleeing from Poland or from the Red Army. We made a mistake. We should have run with the stream.' But they were drawn in the opposite direction. They found themselves in Upper Lusatia, not far from Bautzen. Bohemia was a stone's throw away.

After half a day, they ran into members of the Hitler Youth. 'They asked us straightaway to roll up our sleeves. They saw the tattooed numbers and knew who they were dealing with.'

The youths took them to the nearest police station. There they were told that they would be shot.

> We were given a pick and shovel. We really believed that we were going to have to dig our own grave. But we were taken to a factory. There was a German there who looked after us. We were able to wash and were given something to eat. The man wanted to keep us as workers. He negotiated with someone but we were not allowed to stay.

The next day, a transport arrived in Bautzen, with Polish, Hungarian and around ten Czech women. With them, Lydia and Věra were forced to march in the direction of Dresden. The date was 14 February 1945, the day Dresden was fire-bombed by the British.

The women had to march back in the other direction. After two days, they met Czechs who had fled from Dresden. 'They suggested that we also flee. But we were afraid. We were guarded by soldiers.'

They arrived in Aussig (Ústi nad Labem). 'We were now in Bohemia. We hoped to get to Theresienstadt, where we thought there would be relatives or acquaintances. It was a stone's throw away.' But they had to march in the direction of Marienbad (Mariánske Lázně).

On the way, they were meant to spend the night in Pürles (Brložec). 'My sister came suddenly and said: "Do you remember what this name means in our family? We often spoke about Pürles."' Lydia didn't know.

'This is where our grandfather was born.' There wasn't a barn in the village big enough for all of the women. The Polish, Hungarian and Czech women and girls slept in different farms.

'We arrived at a house. It wasn't very big. At the gate was the farmer. My sister went up to him and asked: "Excuse me, but did you know the Holzners?"' The man was flabbergasted. Věra whispered: 'This is either the end or something else is about to happen.' They turned again to the man: '"This girl and I are Holzners." He asked us to prove it.' They showed him photos of their parents that had been sent to them in Christianstadt. The girls and women went into the farmer's barn, but at midnight there was a knock on the door: 'The Holzners have to come out.'

'We didn't know what would happen. Věra said: "Stay here. I'll go out."

After a while she came back. "It's OK."'

They were taken to the farmer's kitchen. He pointed to a woman sitting at the table. 'She's a friend of your family.' He had fetched her from Karlovy Vary (Karlsbad) around 40 kilometres away.

The woman said: 'We knew nothing about your internment. We talked about how we could help you. I went to the guards. I tried to buy your freedom. But it wasn't allowed. But we can help you as long as you are here.'

The sisters were able to wash and got plenty to eat for the onward route, also for the other women. 'And on the journey we were constantly being brought food.'

Shortly before they had to leave Bohemia, an old man came to them. He brought a loaf of bread. 'I used to play cards with your grandfather. Here's something for the route.'

Prior to this, Lydia and Věra had had another 'remarkable encounter' in Theusing (Toužim).

In the town, a young SS man was pushing women in our column. My sister shouted at him: 'Why are you pushing them?' We were bold because we knew the Nazi rule was coming to an end. 'Are you from Theusing?' Věra asked the SS man. 'Do you know Rudolf Holzner? He's my cousin and he was also on a transport like this.' As he left the SS man said 'I went to school with him.'

Shortly afterwards, he returned with butter and ham. 'We didn't accept it because we didn't want to take anything from someone who hit and tormented our comrades. It was beneath our dignity.'

Their column eventually headed for Flossenbürg concentration camp in the Upper Palatinate about 100 kilometres away. After three days, they continued on a goods train to Bergen-Belsen. By now, it was early April 1945.

CHANNA MARKOWICZ probably travelled in autumn 1944 in a cattle wagon to Hamburg, where Dagmar Fantlová and Dáša Friedová had gone some months before. She was housed 'somewhere' in the harbour area, where it was 'much better' than in Birkenau. There were flushing toilets and showers. They slept in double beds. Everyone had his own place to sleep. Above the bed was a shelf with a pewter plate 'for personal use'. In the mornings, they were served a hot 'thick soup'. Everything was 'unusual'.

All over the city, the girls and women who were still captive had to clear the rubble after the air raids, usually in destroyed factories, for example in Eidelstedt and Wedel.

They travelled to Wedel by boat. They were given white work coats and large blue handkerchiefs to wear on their heads. 'Without the striped uniforms, we looked more human again.'

They were guarded by an older Wehrmacht soldier. He put the younger ones in a separate group. 'Although he didn't have much', he often gave them some of his bread. When they were working close to a beet field, they were allowed to pick beets. And when it rained, Channa and her comrades were allowed to shelter. They didn't have to work very hard, only when an SS man came to check on them.

Channa experienced many air raids. But, as inmates, they were never allowed in the air raid shelters. Once they were on a factory site when there was an air raid warning. Channa was sitting under a tree but then suddenly thought: 'No, I mustn't stay here.' She got up and went to another group of trees, and at that moment a bomb landed where she had been.

Another time, they were in the middle of Hamburg. 'There was a huge air raid shelter there.' When the sirens howled, they were not allowed to go there. The air raid shelter suffered a direct hit. They were unharmed.

In the city, they rode to work under guard by tram. As the tram was travelling past a bombed-out house, a wall collapsed. There were lots of dead and injured. Channa suffered injuries to her head and spine. Others performed first aid straightaway. She was later operated on by inmate doctors.

'Somehow I kept on having good luck.'

WOLFGANG WERMUTH was put on a transport westward from Auschwitz-Birkenau at the end of September 1944.[5] 'It can't get any worse', he and his fellow inmates thought. 'We just wanted to get out of Auschwitz.'

Because of troop movements and destroyed track, the cattle wagons went back and forth 'like on a chess board'. Wolfgang was interned in the next few months in Dachau concentration camp, in 'Aussenkommando Landsberg',[6] in Landshut satellite camp and in one of the Kaufering satellite camps.

Between mid-1944 and April 1945, Jews from all over Europe, particularly survivors of the ghettos in Łódź, Kaunas and Siauliai, Lithuania, were transferred to the eleven camps belonging to the 'Kaufering-Kommando'. These camps probably didn't all exist simultaneously. The inmates were required to build gigantic underground bunkers for aircraft production with concrete ceilings 5 metres thick to protect them from Allied air raids. The structures were not all completed.[7]

Wolfgang was probably sent first to Kaufering IV (near Hurlach). They had to build huts in the ground, digging pits with a tent-like awning over them. For camouflage purposes, they were covered with earth and grass. 'Inside there were only bunks.' There were no blankets, despite the sub-zero temperatures. 'The conditions were terrible. People were dying like flies.'

In January 1945, the inmates were taken in open wagons to Landshut, another Dachau satellite camp. It existed from around September 1944 to April 1945 and was occupied by some 500, mostly Jewish, inmates. Many of Wolfgang's comrades died in just a few months.[8]

They had to transport boulders and debris in tipper wagons from one place to another. 'It was just to keep us busy and served no purpose. It was just as brutal as in Kaufering.'

In Landshut, there was an SS-Unterscharführer called Henschel. 'To judge by his dialect he was from East Prussia.' He was particularly vicious. He hit the inmates with a thick electric cable and a belt buckle. 'I was beaten several times with the cable. He brutally maltreated my friends Walter Bär from Cologne and Hugo Kozen from Berlin.' Both died as a result.

Years later, in May 1968, Wolfgang Wermuth submitted an affidavit to the senior public prosecutor at the court of appeal in Berlin-Charlottenburg: 'This man is responsible for the death of my two closest inmate friends.... I suppose that this murderer Henschel is spending his retirement like a good citizen and father somewhere in West Germany. An investigation should be carried out.'[9]

The public prosecutor Kouril launched an investigation on 10 May 1968 'on suspicion of murder', and passed it on to the public prosecutor's office at the Landgericht (district court) in Landshut.[10]

Charges were never brought against the SS man, since – according to the Central Office of the State Justice Administrations for the Investigation of National Socialist Crimes in Ludwigsburg – he could 'no longer be identified'.

Ultimately, Wolfgang and other inmates were once again transported in open wagons to the main camp at Dachau near Munich. 'We were all in terrible condition.'

Wolfgang managed to survive somehow until Dachau was liberated on 29 April 1945.[11] 'I can still remember: I was completely apathetic. Suddenly the barracks door flew open, Americans entered and shook their heads as they beheld the people crawling and lying there. There were war reporters there as well. They photographed me.'

HERBERT ADLER was transported sometime from Auschwitz-Birkenau to the west. 'I can't remember the exact date or month.' He and other children and youths were sent first to Sachsenhausen, then to Buchenwald and finally to the Men's Camp at Ravensbrück.

Sachsenhausen concentration camp, around 40 kilometres from Berlin on the outskirts of Oranienburg, existed along with around eighty-five satellite camps from mid-1936. The Gestapo used it, among other things, to try out new ways of killing. Other concentration camps such as Buchenwald, Ravensbrück and also Auschwitz were planned from there. And it was an SS officer training camp for the rapidly growing number of German concentration camps throughout Europe.

Around 200,000 people from many countries were interned in the main Sachsenhausen camp and satellite camps, including some 20,000 women, but also children and juveniles. It is estimated that 35,000 to 40,000 people died there through medical experiments, hunger, diseases, maltreatment, slave labour or mass executions. Thousands of Soviet prisoners of war were shot in September and October 1941 alone.[12]

Among the peope transferred to Sachsenhausen in 1944 were around 200 Sinti and Roma,[13] including Herbert Adler[14] and other youths from Auschwitz.

When they arrived in Sachsenhausen, they asked each other: 'Which block were you in at Auschwitz-Birkenau?' One answered: 'I was in Block 31.' Another said: 'I was in Block 27.' Herbert Adler asked them: 'Do you know what happened to my mother and sisters?' No one could, or wanted to, answer.

At some point Herbert was transferred to a satellite camp of Buchenwald. Among the first inmates there were Sinti and Roma. Hundreds had been deported to Buchenwald in June 1938. Only around 100 were still alive in early 1939.[15]

Herbert was sent to work in an underground kommando in one of the many satellite camps.[16] 'Rocks were broken with a drill. The SS guarded and watched us constantly. When there was blasting, we had to take cover behind rocks. The SS men then went out. After the blasting we had to load the rocks onto carts. We got almost nothing to eat.'

When the SS liquidated the 'Gypsy' Family Camp in Auschwitz-Birkenau in 1944 and killed many of its occupants, Sinti and Roma were transferred on several transports to Buchenwald, among other camps. One such transport left on 2 August 1944, when 1,408 Sinti and Roma were taken from Birkenau to Buchenwald on a freight train. The transport arrived a day later. Among the new arrivals were 105 children between the ages of 9 and 14, and 393 youths and young adults aged 15 to 24.[17]

After their departure, a camp curfew was ordered in Auschwitz-Birkenau, and a block curfew in the 'Gypsy' Camp.[18] The entrances to the huts where the remaining Sinti and Roma lived were boarded up. Eight trucks entered the 'Gypsy' Camp under the cover of darkness. The doors were opened and the Sinti and Roma driven out.[19]

Lucie Adelsberger, a Jewish doctor from Berlin, witnessed the clearance: 'We hear the curt orders of the SS, the screams of the children. I recognize a few of the voices: the older ones resist audibly, cry out for help, shriek, Traitors! Bastards! Murderers! A few minutes of this, then the trucks drive off and the screams fade away in the night.'[20]

Rudolf Weisskopf (after the war, Vitek), a Czech dermatologist deported to Auschwitz-Birkenau, who was forced to work in the 'hospital block' in that part of the camp, also witnessed the last hours of the inmates in the 'Gypsy' Camp.

'The deathly silence in the otherwise so noisy camp was quite unusual. In the morning, after a night spent in dull inactivity, we were greeted by the silence of death. The camp was deserted with no sign of life. The air stank and the sky was covered with clouds of black smoke.'[21]

That morning, 3 August 1944, the 'Gypsy' Camp was almost completely empty. Between 4,200 and 4,300 Sinti and Roma infants, children, women and men had been gassed the previous night.[22]

But not all of them were dead. Two small girls had hidden under blankets and were still alive. They had been overlooked during the clearance. There was also a young Roma woman, who had hidden in the sewage system. A few days later, the two girls and the young woman were shot.[23]

Of those who had been transferred to Buchenwald in early August, 200 Sinti and Roma were returned to Auschwitz – directly to the gas chambers in Birkenau. Among them were also many children.[24]

Herbert Adler was finally transferred from Buchenwald to Ravensbrück with other boys who had come with him from Auschwitz. In the village of Ravensbrück, around 90 kilometres north-east of Berlin, the largest central women's concentration camp on German territory was installed from 1939. Women from Poland, Germany and the Soviet Union in particular were deported to Ravensbrück, but there were also inmates from Austria, Belgium, Czechoslovakia, France, Hungary, Luxembourg, the Netherlands and Scandinavia.

In the second half of 1944, Slovak and Hungarian Jewish women and 12,000 Polish and Jewish women and children from Warsaw were interned in Ravensbrück. 'Up to 3,000 women and children lay on straw, without blankets' in a tent specially erected for them. The first 440 Roma women were already deported to Ravensbrück from Burgenland, Austria, in June 1939.[25]

Altogether, around 132,000 women and children and 1,000 girls were registered there.[26]

Apart from the Women's Camp, there was also a small Men's Camp in Ravensbrück. Between April 1941 and the end of April 1945, around 20,000 inmates were detained there.[27] One of them was the Sinti boy Herbert Adler.

> We were housed not far from the women. One day I saw my sister Wanda, two years older than me, through the fence for the first time in a long time. She had also arrived on a transport from Auschwitz. I couldn't talk to her. We could only signal to each other from a distance. But neither of us understood what the other was trying to say.

Tens of thousands of children, women and men from over forty nations interned in Ravensbrück did not survive to see the camp liberated.[28] They were murdered, died of hunger, disease or medical experiments, maltreatment, on the death marches or through slave labour. Between early January and the end of April 1945 alone, it is estimated that at least 5,000 to 6,000 women and men were murdered in the gas chambers at Ravensbrück.[29]

As Allied troops approached the camp, the SS ordered its evacuation. In the second half of April 1945, over 20,000 inmates marched off in columns.[30] In one of these columns – 'we drove in trucks' – was Herbert Adler with around thirty-five other children and youths.

'Suddenly we heard shots. We were in a wood. And then the Russians were there and captured the SS men. That must have been somewhere near Parchim. It was the beginning of May.'

GÉZA SCHEIN Mid-September 1944: selection in Auschwitz satellite camp Jawiczowice (Jawischowitz). Géza Schein was told by a kapo that the SS had decided that the sick and weak should remain behind. Those fit for work were to be sent to the Reich.

The next station: the former 'Gypsy' Camp in Auschwitz-Birkenau. 'I went back to the block where my father was. And then Dr Mengele came for an examination. An older Polish kapo said that the children had already been medically examined. Mengele departed again.'

Some days later: Géza Schein and his father were loaded onto freight cars. 'I was happy to have my father with me. There were only a few adults, mainly children, who had been declared fit for work.'

20 September 1944: Géza and Zoltán Schein were transferred to Mauthausen concentration camp in Austria.[31] The accommodation and food were a little more tolerable for the boys than in Auschwitz-Birkenau. He had to perform 'inhumanly hard' labour in the stone quarries for up to sixty hours a week and was 'maltreated by the SS as well'.

Fear was his constant companion. Death lurked everywhere. After surviving a workday and the night, 'the fear started up again'. He would ask himself constantly: 'Will I survive until this evening and tomorrow morning?' Because: 'Death lurked in every nook and cranny', even 'where I didn't expect it'.

13 December: Géza was transferred with 190 children and youths to Gusen, a satellite camp around 5 kilometres away.[32] Of the more than 60,000 inmates transferred there since May 1940, only an estimated 25,000 survived.[33]

Zoltán Schein was one of the inmates shot in Gusen: 'My father joined the resistance group in the camp. I helped him. I carried secret messages to his comrades. The group was discovered and ten inmates were shot during the roll call, including my father. Now I was completely alone.'

The boy worked in aircraft production in Gusen. The aircraft manufacturer Messerschmidt had transferred some of its production there. In May 1944, around 35 per cent of the entire production at the Messerschmidt factory in Regensburg was now carried out by slave labourers in Gusen and Flossenbürg.[34]

At the end of January 1945, Géza returned to Mauthausen. It was bitterly cold. They lived in tents. There were no bunks. The inmates had to sleep on the floor, head to foot, foot to head, 'like sardines'.

At the end of March, they were forced to walk to Gunskirchen, 60 kilometres away. The inmates were guarded by older Wehrmacht soldiers. They were 'around sixty'. Only at the end of the column was there an SS unit. 'They had the task of shooting anyone who couldn't keep up.'

After a while, Géza couldn't stand it anymore. 'If you don't give me something to eat, I won't continue', he said to one of the soldiers. The man gave him something to eat.

When they passed through Linz, inmates, including Géza, stormed a bakery. 'But the shop assistants chased us out and even called the SS.' For fear of being shot, they ran off in haste.

Géza and his comrades had more pleasant experiences as well: 'People offered us food from the side of the road.' The soldiers encouraged them: 'Take it, it's for you.'

They often met other groups of inmates during the march. During a short rest at the side of the road, a transport of around fifty women passed them. 'Is there anyone from Hungary, from Csepel?' called Géza.

'My child, my dear, you're alive?!' cried a woman – his mother, whom he hadn't seen or heard anything of since the selection on the ramp of Auschwitz-Birkenau in July 1944. A happy reunion – Géza said nothing about his father's death.

Mother and son were able to meet and talk every day at the Gunskirchen satellite camp. Klára Schein told Géza what she had been through: various kommandos in Birkenau, including slave labour in a nursery growing vegetables for the SS guards. Transport to Frankfurt am Main in August 1944 to clear rubble after air raids. Transfer some months later to Ravensbrück and work on the land. In March 1945, evacuation march to Gunskirchen.

'We didn't work here. We had to collect the corpses every day. People were dying of exhaustion. Around 80 per cent of the inmates were so weak that they could barely move.'

3 May: 'Towards midday, the SS became very restless. They packed everything they could, got into trucks and drove off. We heard machine gun fire.'

On 5 May, the US army arrived. 'We were free!'

Together with the soldiers, some of the former inmates set off in pursuit of the SS men in jeeps. 'Some were shot, others taken prisoner.' The SS storehouse was opened. 'Particularly the people who were most emaciated devoured large quantities of food.' It was too much for their starved organisms. Without realizing it, some of the recently liberated inmates quite literally ate themselves to death.

The US troops recognized this fatal consequence and started to regulate the serving of food. 'The people were angry with the Americans. They reckoned they weren't getting enough to eat, although it was the best course.' Only in this way could many of them be saved.

Janek Mandelbaum had been 'pushed to and fro' since June 1942, wherever his labour could be exploited again. He was in seven camps: Brande (Prądy), Fünfteichen (Miłoszycekoło Wrocławia), the Auschwitz satellite camp Blechhammer (Blachownia), Gross-Rosen (Rogoźnica), Dyhernfurth II (Brzeg Dolny), Bad Warmbrunn (Cieplice Zdrój) and Dörnhau (Kolce).[35]

'Every camp was different. But they were all crowded. The food was miserable. It was dirty everywhere. And there were lice. Morning and evening roll calls in all weathers, often lasting hours. Everywhere the same terrible SS rules.' Janek suffered from extreme cold, oppressive heat or stuffy cold and damp weather. He felt constantly harassed. And there was this permanent, terrible hunger. He would often imagine the perfect meal: chicken soup with home-made noodles, roast duck with lots of side dishes, prepared by his mother Cyrla. He tried not to think so often about his family: 'I missed them so much!' It caused him unspeakable pain to see them in his mind's eye. But not to think about them was impossible. He wanted finally to have his old happy life back.

One of the worst camps was the main camp at Gross-Rosen, 65 kilometres to the west of Wrocław. Around 120,000 people were deported there, and it was one of the largest labour camps. The inmates had to quarry granite. More than 40,000 people were worked to death or murdered there.[36] When Janek arrived in Gross-Rosen with other inmates, there was no room for them. 'We had to sleep in the barracks on the bare concrete floor, side by side.' There was no room to lie on their back or front. 'When one person turned over, everyone had to do so.' Here, he was number 16013. It had to be sewn on his clothing so that he could be recognized at all times as an inmate. He no longer had a name but had to say: 'Inmate 16013 reporting.'

Danger lurked everywhere, and he had to be on his guard, because one wrong move meant certain death. The work in the quarry, carrying blocks of granite on the steep site was 'indescribably difficult'. He was not the only one to suffer from the brutal conditions. Some could no longer endure it and took their lives: 'They jumped down one of the mine shafts.' At some point, Janek no longer saw death just as a threat. 'I learned in the camps that death could also be a kind of release, liberation from pain and suffering.' Nevertheless, he wanted to stay alive at all costs. 'To do this you needed above all a large amount of good fortune.'

One night he woke up with severe stomach pains. He had diarrhoea and just managed to get outside the barracks. His stool was full of blood. He managed to get back to his bunk. The next morning, he couldn't get up. A 'not so bad' kapo helped him to the hospital barracks, something he had not seen from the inside in any of the other camps. An inmate doctor gave him a 'coal-like substance' for the diarrhoea. He had to stay there and was given a bunk. In subsequent days, he had to take more of the bitter-tasting medicine. He also witnessed dead inmates being carried out. He said to himself: 'I have to get out of here as soon as possible.' Although he was very weak, he succeeded somehow. The kapo made sure that in the next few days he was only given light work. That way, he managed to survive.

Already at Blechhammer, an older fellow inmate called Aaron had given him useful tips for survival. And in autumn 1943, he had the good fortune to meet Moniek (Moses), who became 'like a second brother' to him. Moniek was from Wolbrom near Kraków. Immediately after the arrival of German troops in September 1939, the Jews were persecuted, locked up and forced to work. At that time, there were around 5,000 Jews in Wolbrom. Added to this were some 3,000 Jewish children, women and men in early 1940 who had been driven out of Kraków. In July 1941, 120 youths were deported to Pustków forced labour camp near Rzeszów. During the Nazi regime, 4,500 Jews from Wolbrom were murdered. Of these, 800 were shot on the spot and piled into three mass graves that they had had to dig themselves beforehand.[37]

Moniek was two years older than Janek. He had been separated in 1940 from his parents, two sisters and two brothers and had been interned ever since in camps. His motto was: 'Work as little as possible and don't draw attention to yourself. That way you'll survive.' Even in the camp, his new friend made him laugh through his 'funny ways'. 'He would clown around whenever he could.' Janek thought a lot and wondered: 'How can God allow such atrocities?' Moniek, however, refused to give it a thought. 'Just think of the moment. Believe in the future.'

It was now winter 1944. 'It was bitter cold.' Janek and Moniek were driven with other inmates to bombed-out houses, where they were forced to clear the rubble. 'They had been damaged in Allied air raids. Our hope for an end to the war grew with every aeroplane we heard.'

April 1945 came. Janek and Moniek were transferred from the Gross-Rosen satellite camp Warmbrunn (Cieplice Zdrój) to Dörnhau (Kolce). They had to walk. In mid-April around 200 inmates arrived, of whom over 85 died before 8 May. An unknown number failed to survive the march to Dörnhau.[38]

Dörnhau had been installed in a former factory building at the end of November 1943. Up to 2,000 inmates were interned there simultaneously. They were employed in twelve-hour shifts on road building, tree felling or tunnelling mines in the Owl Mountains. From October 1944, the camp assumed the function of a central 'hospital' camp. Many people died through deliberate neglect. Seriously ill inmates were also taken from Dörnhau to Auschwitz.[39] In Dörnhau, there was hardly anything to eat. 'They gave us no more than a bowl of soup per day, lightly flavoured water.'

One evening, the SS bolted the gates of the factory building. 'That had never happened before.' When Janek woke the following morning, he learned that two inmates were attempting to break down the gate. He and other fellow sufferers helped. The gate finally fell off its hinges. They cautiously went outside. 'The guards had disappeared.' The Red Army arrived soon afterwards. That was 9 May.

'It's over. The war is over. We're free. Finally free.' Janek and Moniek and all of the liberated inmates capable of doing so jumped for joy. Many embraced and danced around 'like crazy'. 'We were in an area that had been abandoned by the German civilian population, who had fled from the Russians. Moniek and I, along with other former inmates, investigated the area.' They found abandoned houses and entered. 'It was heaven to be in a real house again.' They found clothes, food – everything they needed. They stayed for a few days wherever they felt like it. For the first time for ages, they slept again in 'real feather beds'. Once they had eaten all the food in one house, they occupied another. They had only to look after themselves. 'What a wonderful feeling.' Janek was no longer inmate number 16013.

EDUARD KORNFELD After a journey in a cattle car from Auschwitz that lasted several days, Eduard Kornfeld ended up on 29 September 1944 at Dachau.[40] Then they continued to some of the over 150 satellite camps of the main camp, which had been established on 22 March 1933.[41]

He was first sent probably to Kaufering IV near Hurlach, then to Kaufering IX, thought to have been near Obermeitingen.[42] After once again passing through Dachau, he was then transferred to Riederloh II, also known as the Steinholz camp, near the village of Mauerstetten, around 3 kilometres from Kaufbeuren. The people deported there were enlisted to build a new percussion cap factory, to lay tracks and to work in the forests. The slave labour was performed for Dynamit AG, Berliner Baugesellschaft and the Hebel company.

The camp was only established in autumn 1944, but after just a short time the conditions there were already atrocious as a result of the inadequate food and clothing, the miserable hygiene conditions, the maltreatment, hard labour and the penetrating cold of the autumn and winter months.[43]

The camp was deep in the forest. There were only a few blocks. No one could find us there. It was desolate. I once said: 'Even if the Messiah came, he wouldn't find us.' I had a terrible time in this camp. For me it was worse than Auschwitz. It was the most brutal camp, without gas chambers but an extermination camp nevertheless.

Eduard lived in Block I, where he was reunited with the 'nice, tall lad' he had known in Auschwitz. 'I saw a youth, tall and emaciated. He had straw in his hand. He looked more like a living corpse, just skin and bones.' Eduard looked more closely at his face and thought: 'I know that face.' He spoke to him: 'Don't I know you?' The youth replied quietly in Hungarian: 'You've come to a good place.' 'What block are you in?' The youth was in Block II. Eduard promised: 'I'll visit you.' Then the youth took some of the straw lying on the floor to sleep on and left. He could barely walk. Eduard went later to Block II. He had no idea what to expect. 'I went in. People, dead or lying delirious with fever on the straw. They had no food, no water – nothing. They were the rejects left to die. Hell, I thought, is a piece of cake by comparison. I heard: "Mama, water, water".'

He took some kind of container, fetched water from outside and gave one of them a drink. The others were crying: 'Water, water!' There must have been a hundred of them. But he didn't find his friend.

Suddenly I realized that everyone had assembled outside for roll call. I knew that my life was in danger. As I ran I heard the camp elder reporting to the

271

SS camp commandant that one was missing. Still running, I shouted: 'Here I am!' I could have been beaten by the camp elder or shot by an SS man, but they left me alone. 'Leave him, we'll give him something for Christmas!'

Eduard's name was noted. He didn't visit the death block again. It made him even more afraid. 'The people were dying there like flies, every day ten, twenty, thirty loaded onto the sleds', pulled away and unloaded far from the camp.

Eduard and the other inmates had to dig ditches for water pipes outside the camp. It was winter, with deep snow, bitter cold and the ground frozen solid. The work was 'inhumanly hard'. The SS drove them on: 'Faster, work!' they ordered all day, beating the inmates brutally at the same time. 'I witnessed the following scene. There was a young man, a pharmacist from Hungary. An SS man hit him and shouted: "Work harder!" The young man asked: "What right do you have to hit me?" The SS man repeated the man's question several times, hitting him on the head at the same time until he was dead.' That's how many died, 'frozen, beaten or shot'. They had to bring the dead 'home' to the concentration camp in the evening. So that the count would be right. Eduard and his comrades soon had no strength anymore.

Shortly before Christmas 1944, Eduard received his 'Christmas present'. There were seven of them who were punished in this way. In Block I there was a narrow table. 'Undress!' they were ordered. Several SS men were present. 'Sentenced to twenty-five strokes' was the punishment. They had to bend naked over the table. With a 'kind of hard rubber truncheon' an SS man hit the first inmate 'with all his might'.

The inmate screamed like an animal. I was sure they would murder him. After around five strokes we didn't hear a peep anymore. Apart from the noise of the beating it was as silent as the grave. Until the last stroke. The inmate had to stand up and take his things. At the same moment he started laughing and couldn't stop. Like a 'madman'. It was not the laughter of a human being. And this procedure was repeated again and again. I was the fifth. The SS man hit me. The pain was excruciating. We had no flesh anymore, practically just bones. I was … convinced that my backside would be shredded to ribbons. After the fifth or sixth stroke I couldn't feel anything anymore. Nothing. But I was the only one to carry on screaming. I thought: 'If he notices that it doesn't hurt, he'll hit me even harder.' When he was finished with me, I also had a laughing fit. I couldn't control it. I don't know what it was. I have no explanation for it.

Eduard could no longer sit. 'The pain was too intense.' Decades later, he still couldn't lie on his back.

Two days later was Christmas. It turned out that the beating was only part of the 'Christmas present'. In the morning, Eduard and his comrades were made to go in the dying block. They had to fetch the dead from the block and load them onto a sled. Those who normally did this work had the day off. Eduard was unable to enter the block. 'I kept thinking of the nice tall youth who had become an emaciated skeleton and whom I had seen right at the beginning in the dying block. Terrible. That was enough for me.' He remained outside and helped to load the bodies. Others went in. They had to see 'who was not moving, who was cold'. They had to pick out the dead from the living.

When the sled was full, Eduard pushed it from behind, while others pulled it from the front or pushed it from the sides. Suddenly the camp commandant stood behind Eduard, grabbed him by the collar – it wasn't difficult, he weighed next to nothing – and threw him onto the pile of corpses. Eduard wanted to crawl off. 'No, stay there, you'll soon be joining them', said the SS man to him. 'I was already an old hand so I played dead and remained lying on the corpses. I knew that if I moved I'd be a gonner. He would have stayed and watched as I was buried alive.' The SS man lost interest in the youth and went away 'to hit others'. Eduard quickly crawled down and mingled with the others who were pulling from the front. 'That way he wouldn't recognize me again. All of us wretches looked the same. Like fifty eggs that are also difficult to tell apart.'

Outside the camp, a large pit had been dug. The corpses were meant to 'disappear' in it. Eduard wanted to unload the dead bodies slowly and carefully. The camp commandant was soon at his side again and snarled without recognizing him: 'What? Not like that!' The member of the 'master race' ordered the corpses to be laid at the edge of the pit. 'Then he pushed them in with his boot.' Down below, other inmates had to cover everything with earth. 'That was my Christmas present.' From then on, Eduard always pulled the sled from the front. He no longer drew attention to himself. That way he survived.

One day, someone called Eduard a 'Muselmann'. In the camp jargon, this term was used to describe someone who was so starved and deprived that he was barely alive. 'Muselmänner' were tormented particularly by the SS and kapos. They usually survived only a short time. 'This designation was terrible for me. I would never have called someone a "Muselmann" because I knew it was a death sentence. That was the end, doomed to die.'

He had long felt sick and very weak and had often had nothing but mouldy bread to eat, but he didn't realize how bad he looked. 'Without a mirror I had no possibility of seeing myself. There was still a spark at Auschwitz. But now in this concentration camp hardly at all.'

In the four months of its existence, around 1,300 mostly male Hungarian and Polish Jews passed through Riederloh II. On 8 January 1945, when it was evacuated, it is estimated that there were only 200–300 sick and emaciated inmates there.[44] A memorial stone was erected in the late 1940s at the mass grave in Mauerstetten-Steinholz to recall the suffering and death of Jewish youths and men in Riederloh II. The inscription reads: 'Fraternal grave of 472 Jewish inmate victims of the Nazi labour camp in Riederloh near Kaufbeuren.' In 1951, the Mauerstetten municipal authority decided to reassign the concentration camp site as a residential zone. The latest version of the *Chronik der Gemeinde Mauerstetten* states: 'After the district of Kaufbeuren acquired the site in 1952, the municipal council adopted a decision in 1953 to develop the former Steinholz camp [i.e., the Dachau satellite camp Riederloh II] as a residential zone.' In subsequent years, the site of the former camp was to become 'a pleasant home' for around 500 new inhabitants.[45]

Back to 1945: Eduard continued to move around. He was transferred from Riederloh II to Dachau, probably on 8 January, and from there at the end of the month to Augsburg-Pfersee, and then in April again to the 'Kaufering-Kommando'.[46] Towards the end of the war, there were still around 10,000 inmates in the camps there. Ernst Kaltenbrunner, head of the Reich Security Main Office, originally ordered their liquidation. To that end, in an operation code-named 'Cloud AI', the Nazi Luftwaffe was to bomb the Kaufering camp complex, among other sites. The operation was not carried out, however. Instead, the inmates in most of the Kaufering camps were evacuated on foot and by train in the second half of April, towards Dachau.[47]

'We set off on foot. If someone could no longer walk, he was shot without ado on the spot.' Eduard pulled himself together. He had a strong will. He wanted to stay alive. But he was at least a 'half-Muselmann' and felt very weak. Added to this was the fact that he didn't have any proper shoes anymore, but just a piece of wood covered with a piece of cloth held in place by wire. 'And the cloth was worn.' This is all he had to walk in, demanding a good deal of ingenuity from his weakened body. After they had been walking for two or three hours, a huge bus appeared. It came to collect the tired and weak. 'But no one wanted to board.' They suspected a trick and thought: 'We'll be taken somewhere in the forest and shot.'

Eduard nevertheless considered going. He knew that he wouldn't be able to hold out for long. He said to his comrades who were with him: 'I'm going.' They replied: 'Are you mad? We'll help you.' 'No, I can't go on. Look at my broken wooden shoes. The wire is chafing my feet. I already have lots of sores. Every step hurts.' 'No, don't do it. You'll be shot. We'll help you.' Eduard gave up. 'They were decent fellows although they had trouble walking as well.' He didn't board the bus. It drove off almost empty.

Towards midday, they were allowed a break. Then, when they started up again, every step 'was even worse than the last'. Eduard had no strength left. At any moment he could have collapsed. And then they would shoot him on the spot. It would be better to go a little way with the bus. He said to the others: 'If the bus comes back, I'll get on board. I don't care, I can't go on anyway and they'll shoot me. So I might just as well get on the bus.' The bus came back. Eduard got in. He was sure that they would shoot him. No one stopped him anymore.

The bus filled up. No one said a word. The bus set off. 'Everyone ate their last piece of bread or whatever else they had, convinced that it would be their last meal, their last moment.'

They drove to a forest region. Every time they came into a new part of the forest, the youth said to himself: 'This is it. Now they'll mow us down.' And when the bus slowed down on a bend, he felt a 'fearful tension' that went right through him: 'This is it. Now we're going to get out. Now ...'

Even after the war, Eduard Kornfeld was haunted by thoughts of this bus ride. 'I dreamed of it. I had a precise recollection of the journey. Every single detail is indelibly printed in my mind.' In 1989, he saw a picture of a similar bus in *Der Spiegel* magazine. It was one of the buses used in the Nazi era to take 'euthanasia' victims, above all the sick and 'handicapped', to the killing institutes in Grafeneck near Reutlingen, Brandenburg, Bernburg an der Saale, Sonnenstein in Pirna, Hadamar near Limburg and Hartheim near Linz. The children, women and men to be murdered had to get undressed and were than gassed, mostly with carbon monoxide. Tens of thousands of victims were exterminated in this way.[48]

'At first I was shocked to see the picture of the bus. But it was something of a relief as well. Now I had proof that this bus that had been haunting me actually existed.' In April 1945 the bus did actually take them to Dachau, something Eduard could not have imagined in his wildest dreams.

One day news spread among the inmates: 'The Russians are here.' They believed that they would be liberated. But the SS were still there and started shooting at them. It went on for one or two more days before Eduard saw the SS leaving in trucks.

> I felt uneasy. No one knew what was going on, and I was still afraid. I simply remained somewhere in the camp and watched in silence. And then I heard the clanking of a tank. Americans, not Russians, appeared from all sides. I was free! It was incredible. An indescribable feeling. The joy. I was so happy. But I was still weak, very weak.

When units of the US army liberated Dachau on 29 April 1945, Eduard was just skin and bones. He weighed a mere 27 kg. They were free but the dying went on. Two-thirds of the 32,000 or so inmates liberated from the main camp were sick and completely debilitated. A typhoid fever epidemic was spreading through the former camp. In May alone, a further 2,221 ex-inmates were to die.[49] Many people were unable to tolerate the much richer food. Eduard recalls that an American officer apologized right after the liberation that he couldn't give them any of their rations and that supplies would soon be arriving.

Eduard was examined by a US army doctor. It was the first time he had heard English. The 'devastating' diagnosis was left and right tuberculosis. 'I was put in the army field hospital. Like me, lots of people had terrible diarrhoea. Many died. After busy nights there would be completely different people lying next to me in the morning.' Eduard didn't want to die and said to himself: 'I want to live; I have to live.' The worst thing was that 'all around me I saw people dying every day'. He wondered: 'Why should I be the one to survive?' But he wanted to live. 'After Auschwitz, after everything, why should I die now?' He had no strength in his bones. He couldn't get up unaided. And when he stood up, he couldn't put one foot in front of the other.

His condition improved after a few weeks. The desire grew in him to return to Bratislava. At the end of May, the longed-for day of departure arrived. He travelled back to the Slovakian capital by road and rail.

CHANNA MARKOWICZ, DAGMAR FANTLOVÁ, DÁŠA FRIEDOVÁ AND LYDIA HOLZNEROVÁ ended up with their evacuation transports in Bergen-Belsen. They all hoped to experience their redemption, their personal liberation, there.

From June 1940, prisoners of war were interned by the Wehrmacht in Bergen-Belsen and its satellite camps Fallingbostel, Oerbke and Wietzendorf. Around 40,000 Soviet prisoners of war alone lost their lives there. In April 1943, the SS took over part of Bergen-Belsen, and it became a concentration camp for Jews, some of whom were to be exchanged for captured Germans abroad. From August 1944, thousands of women from Auschwitz-Birkenau arrived there. From December of that year, the camp was the destination of many transports from concentration camps near the front.[50]

When Channa, Dagmar, Dáša and Lydia arrived in Bergen-Belsen at the end of March / beginning of April 1945, the camp was hopelessly overcrowded. Hunger, epidemics and a very high mortality rate were characteristics of the everyday life of interned children, women and men. Dáša was immediately struck by the

numerous head-high piles of corpses. It was teeming with people. We had to sleep sitting on the bare floor. There was almost nothing to eat. On the last few days we didn't get anything at all. The people died even more quickly.

We witnessed it all. A human tragedy of the worst kind was being played out before our eyes.

For Dagmar as well, the conditions in Bergen-Belsen were unimaginable. 'It was only possible to last there for a few days. There was no water and hardly anything to eat. The hygiene conditions were atrocious. The barracks were overcrowded. We sat close together and there was no room to lie down. And then the lice. And outside the piles of corpses.'

'How did we survive?' wondered Channa afterwards. 'Everywhere there were half-dead people lying around. They were all infested with lice. The dead were constantly being carried away. They were stacked in the forest like wood: a row of five and then another row laid perpendicularly over it.'

'We survived', says Lydia, 'because we were only there for a short time.' On 15 April, the British liberated the camp. 'We couldn't have put up with it for much longer.'

There were 55,000 children, women and men in the camp. Around 10,000 corpses lay around unburied.[51] Between February and mid-April 1945 alone, around 34,000 people died. In spite of the aid provided immediately by the British, a further 13,000 people died by the end of June 1945 as a result of their internment.[52] Others succumbed to the unaccustomed rich food, which their starved organisms were unable to digest.

Soon after the liberation, Channa heard that survivors were breaking open the camp food stores. She took some tins but a struggle broke out for the food. Channa dropped the tins. 'Luckily', as it turned out, 'because many people got diarrhoea after eating and died.'

On the day of liberation, British soldiers threw tins over the barbed wire. Dáša saw someone running around with a white flag saying: '"Don't take it, don't eat it." We didn't understand but were cautious and just ate some rusks and drank powder milk dissolved in water.'

Channa, Dáša, Dagmar and Lydia couldn't believe that they were finally free, but they were no longer capable of visible emotions. They were too weak. Dagmar: 'But inside we were immensely happy to have survived.'

The survivors were gradually transferred to the barracks of the former Bergen-Hohne military training area and to hospitals in the surrounding area.[53] Many buildings were transformed into emergency hospitals.

'I can't remember whether I was really happy.' Dáša felt a little safer in the new surroundings. 'The people were friendly, the rooms clean.' She slowly got used to eating properly. Every day, her confidence and belief in a personal future grew.

Her friend Dagmar and Channa both had typhus. Channa was put in one of the emergency hospitals established by the British. Her eyes were swollen and red. And she was still suffering from the effects of the tram accident in Hamburg. 'When I think what I looked like …'.

Dagmar was put in a hospital in April, where she spent her sixteenth birthday. While Dáša was taken to Prague by truck with other former inmates in late May / early April, it was several years before Dagmar could lead an independent life.

Dáša felt 'completely alone' and 'a little lost'. For the previous three years, except for a few days, she had always been close to her friend and had slept next to her. 'We thought and felt like twins.'

Because of their health, Dagmar, Lydia and her sister Věra were not able to return home until the summer. Dagmar was on the first train from Bergen-Belsen to Czechoslovakia.

Channa was taken to Sweden with other young women to recover and get back on their feet. Some of the women were put in hospitals, others in a sanatorium in Malmö. The initial period was occupied almost exclusively with Channa's medical treatment.

For Yehuda Bacon, Robert Büchler and Heinz Kounio and his father Salvator as well, the Red Army unfortunately didn't reach Auschwitz soon enough. Nine days before liberation, on 18 January 1945, they were marched off by the SS on one of the many death marches that left Auschwitz at the time and whose unknown destination many were not to reach.

The northern winter was raging. At night, the temperature dropped to below minus 20 degrees. In the distance, they could hear the artillery. Even 'our German guards had to admit', says Heinz Kounio, 'that "the Russians" would soon be there.'

Many people in our group had no shoes. Their feet soon had frostbite. The first victim was a German Jew. He couldn't walk anymore and lay down in the snow. He begged an SS man to shoot him to put an end to his suffering. The man was glad to shoot him – and would have done so anyway, because no one was to be left alive.

The road was covered with dead bodies, probably the victims of an earlier death march. On the very first day we also 'lost' around one in four of our group.

The death march routes were lined with mass graves. Near Rybnik, just 60 kilometres from Auschwitz, around 290 frozen Auschwitz inmates were found.[54]

Heinz thought constantly of his mother and sister. 'I wonder where they are. Will I ever see them again?'

His thoughts were confused. On the one hand, he longed to be dead. He was desperate and at his wits' end. On the other hand, he didn't want to give up and end that way. 'That's not the reason my mother brought me into the world.' Every minute, he wrestled with himself and attempted to screen out the bad thoughts.

ROBERT BÜCHLER was in another of the many inmate columns that left Auschwitz-Birkenau at intervals on this day. He was utterly desperate. In the confusion in Auschwitz, he had lost contact with his group. He didn't know anyone he was with. He felt completely alone. They were marching fast. 'Anyone who failed to keep up got a bullet.'

On the way, they met a group of women. Robert spotted Elsa Rosenthal from his hometown of Topol'čany. She had been deported in March 1942. The young woman was pulling a handcart. She took out a loaf of bread and gave half to the boy. It was the only thing Robert had to eat in the next four or five days.

After two days and nights, the group arrived at Loslau (Wodzisław Śląski) in Upper Silesia. Railway transports with thousands of people were being organized. Heinz Kounio and his father were put in an open wagon used previously to transport coal.

Robert was also put in an open coal wagon almost half-full of snow, directly behind the locomotive. The driver sometimes gave the boy hot water from the boiler to drink. The people, packed together, got nothing to eat. In their despair, they ate bits of coal they found in the wagon.

On 23 January, the train arrived at Buchenwald after a journey lasting several days. Of the thousands that had boarded in Loslau, most had died. 'In my wagon fewer than ten were still alive.' They were completely exhausted, overtired and weak from hunger and cold.

HEINZ KOUNIO AND HIS FATHER SALVATOR arrived in the open coal wagon at Mauthausen in Austria. There had been about 100 people in their wagon. 'Around twenty of them were so sick that they had to lie down.' The others stood. 'We were exposed to the elements without protection.' It was bitterly cold. And the faster the train travelled, the more intolerable their physical and mental state became.

The wind bit into their faces. They had nothing to eat or drink, and had to eat snow. Their morale was at its lowest ebb. None of the twenty sick inmates lived. 'Every dead person meant more space for the living.' But everyone else got sick during the journey.

After Heinz and his father had climbed down from the wagon, they had to walk another thirty minutes to the camp. 'It was almost impossible.' They were weak and completely exhausted, which only earned them insults and beatings from the SS guards.

They arrived at the camp on 25 January 1945[55] and had to spend the entire night outside in sub-zero temperatures. Then they were searched for hidden valuables, as in Auschwitz, and their body hair was once again shorn. They showered first in cold and then in boiling hot water causing considerable scalding. All the time, the new arrivals were beaten with truncheons.

Around 800 to 900 inmates were interned in barracks originally designed for 100 people. Most of them slept on the floor, as there was nowhere near enough bunks for everyone.

Heinz nevertheless fell asleep through exhaustion, but woke up frequently. Someone's foot was in his face, a head on his stomach, and sometimes there were two or three inmates on his feet.

Four days after their arrival in Mauthausen, they were gathered for a further transport. Heinz thanked heavens to be able to leave this 'godforsaken place'. The hope that they would survive was revived. The train set off eastward to the town of Melk, around 85 kilometres away, site of one of the many Mauthausen satellite camps scattered all over Austria.

People from all over Europe were deported to Melk. The inmates were enlisted to build tunnels in nearby Roggendorf. Under the code name 'Quartz', underground production facilities for the armaments industry were to be built. They offered protection from air raids. The SS were paid by the construction companies – including Holzmann AG, Siemens and Wayss & Freytag – for the inmates' forced labour.

Because of the high groundwater level, the inmates were usually up to their ankles in water. They were often showered by falling sandstone. Pushing the loaded carts was regarded as a punishment. This slave labour was carried out mostly by Jews.[56]

Salvator and Heinz Kounio were enlisted to dig the tunnels into the mountain. They worked round the clock. Heinz was initially on the first of three shifts starting very early in the morning and ending in the afternoon. Then it was his father's turn and he didn't return to the camp until after midnight.

> The camp was completely run down. We weren't able to change our clothes even once. Even those who had been there from the beginning of the camp had never had anything else to wear. They were completely ragged, filthy and infested with lice.
>
> A large number of inmates were sick. They had swollen arms and faces, open wounds, dislocated knees … And there was next to no medicine in Melk.

Heinz found a slim pocket diary in the camp and organized a pencil. He felt that 'freedom could not be long in coming'. He didn't want to forget anything, and now he could write it down. From then on, from 30 January 1945, he wrote his first testimony to what he saw and experienced in the diary, which only had room for a few lines per day.

Under the heading 'Characters in the Melk camp' he described the SS medical orderly Gottlieb Muzikant.

> He had a nasty character, and his face reflected the darkness of his soul. Committing a crime was for him the simplest thing in the world.

In the hospital he had only one aim: to finish off those whom the others hadn't managed to kill. Regardless of how sick they were, without Muzikant's permission no one could be admitted. His recurrent excuse was that there were no beds available.

He only changed a bandage once, when it was absolutely necessary. And when the bandage was changed, the air was full of the stench of rotting flesh. If Muzikant heard a complaint he threw both the patient and the doctor [himself an inmate] out onto the street. I often wondered: 'Did Muzikant and the others never have a family? No one to care for them? Did they ever consider what would happen when the circumstances changed and the war was over?'[57]

Selections were carried out regularly in the hospital. More than 1,400 inmates were selected and sent back to Mauthausen. Many of them died there.[58]

ROBERT BÜCHLER By contrast, Robert Büchler was extremely surprised at the way they were received in Buchenwald after days of travel in the open coal wagon.[59] The admission was relatively calm and without beatings. The old inmates gave them a friendly welcome. The new arrivals remained suspicious. 'Some of us well remembered the tricks of the SS and their assistants.' They were worried about what was awaiting them. Robert had an encounter right at the start that was to leave a lasting impression.

We were standing in line in front of the inmate registry. When it was my turn to go in, I was confronted by an inmate who must have been sixty years old. As usual he asked for my personal data. When he asked where I was from, I said 'Czechoslovakia'. The man lifted his eyes from the form and looked at me in surprise. He spoke to me in Czech and said it was the first time an inmate had given his homeland as an answer, a country that didn't exist at that time.

The man was spending his sixth year in the concentration camp. He appreciated my honest answer. When the form was completed, he asked me for my inmate's cap. He filled it with food. This was the first time I'd eaten after starving for days.

Buchenwald concentration camp was established in July 1937. It was on Ettersberg hill near Weimar, just 10 kilometres from the city centre, from a city that in the 1920s had still been an open and lively cultural venue, where the modernist architect Walter Gropius founded the Bauhaus in 1919.

The 265,000 children, women and men interned in Buchenwald and its satellite camps until April 1945 came from all over Europe. The camp was 40 hectares in area and had more than 135 satellite camps.

For Jews, there was a segregated area for the people arrested during the anti-Jewish November pogroms (November 1938 to February 1939). From April to December 1938, 13,687 Jews were sent there. There was also a special fenced zone for Poles and Viennese Jews – a tent camp (September 1939 to February 1940). The 'Little Camp' was a separate camp within the overall camp. People were interned there to ease the overcrowding and to ensure that the camp as a whole continued to function. They were housed mainly in windowless Wehrmacht stables. Originally designed for around 50 horses, they accommodated almost 2,000 people.

Slave labour and pseudo-medical experiments, shootings, deadly injections or hangings were the dominant features of the camp. The victims were 'plundered' as in Auschwitz, and their gold teeth extracted.

Around 56,000 children, women and men died in Buchenwald, including some 8,000 Soviet prisoners of war and 11,000 Jewish children, women and men.

At the time Robert Büchler was in the camp in early 1945, Jews were the largest inmate group – 36,000 out of a total of 112,000 inmates.[60]

Robert was put first in the empty Block 57 in the 'Little Camp'. The block elder, a German political inmate, and others, mainly Russian prisoners of war, still in their uniforms, welcomed the new arrivals. The first thing he said to them was: 'Comrades, you're not in Auschwitz anymore. There are no gas chambers here. Don't be afraid!'

These words made a deep impression on Robert. 'They gave us the courage to continue struggling for our lives. The block elder demanded mutual aid and solidarity so that we could arrive at the day of liberation together.'

Dr Jonas Silber from Metz reported in 1945 on the children in Buchenwald: 'The number of child inmates in Buchenwald concentration camp is estimated at about 900. The age group between fourteen and eighteen makes up about 85 per cent of the total number of children.'[61]

Between mid-January and mid-February, one transport after another arrived in Buchenwald.[62] Block 57 was soon full. At the roll call, the block elder announced that all children and youths were to be put in a separate block.

'We suspected a trick. We had enough experience. Everyone thought it was a trick to kill us. The block elder and his assistants attempted to calm us.'

They were offered the alternative of children's block or transport. Robert trusted the block elder. After some hesitation, he opted for the children's block. He was disappointed that only a few youths made the same choice.

'There were twelve boys in the first group to go to the children's block, aged between eleven and sixteen years.' All had arrived two days previously in one of the transports from the East. Robert knew some of them from Auschwitz.

'Block 66,[63] where we were taken, was at the perimeter next to the fence. Normally it had room for around 200 inmates. But at that time the camp was so full that more and more people were crowded in there.'

The 'first man' in the children's block was Gustav Schiller, a Polish Jew. He must have been 35 and was the block elder's deputy. He was an 'impressive personality' with a strong sense of justice.

As he determined what went on in the block, he ensured that the sick and weak were not neglected. He was always there when food was served to ensure that the meagre rations were fairly distributed. Schiller had good self-control and mastered the greatest difficulties. He used all of his energy to improve the terrible conditions in the block for everyone.

After a month, there were more than 500 children and youths in the block. There were not enough bunks. The food was completely inadequate. 'We were tormented by an unimaginable hunger. Additional rations were given to the inmates who went to work. And they were sometimes able to organize something. The non-Jewish inmates occasionally received food parcels, and also packages from the International Red Cross.'

'We could scarcely believe that we could also share the miracle we'd heard so much about.' They were hugely surprised when it was announced one day that Red Cross parcels were to be distributed in the tent camp. Six boys were each given a 12 kg parcel with food and warm clothing.

'Our joy was even greater when we learned that the non-Jewish inmates in the "Big Camp" had donated some of the parcels to us. We regarded this deed as a great demonstration of solidarity. And this gesture was also good for morale and strengthened our will to live. Every day demanded our full physical and mental strength.'

The 'miracle' was repeated twice more.

The conditions in the children's block continued to deteriorate. The overcrowding became worse. 'It was unbearable.' And most children and youths were completely emaciated and very weak. It is astonishing that Robert did not get sick, 'because there was a typhoid fever epidemic in the camp, which killed many people'.

It was now early April 1945. The children and youths in Block 66 could sense that the front was drawing nearer. They spotted Allied fighter planes every day.

One morning, an order was announced over the loudspeaker: 'All Jews to fall in immediately for roll call.' Chaos and panic broke out. The block elder and his deputy in the 'Little Camp' were taken completely by surprise. They told the children and youths to stay in the block and to resist any attempt to make them leave, 'by force if necessary'.

A large group of camp guards, an inmate policing group formed by the SS, appeared and ordered everyone outside. No one moved. They were not to be intimidated. The group departed again.

On 10 April, with the US army only a few kilometres from the camp,[64] the feared order came again: 'All Jews to fall in for roll call!' This time, armed SS men came into the 'Little Camp'. They used brute force to drive the children and youths out of the huts. Those who wanted to save themselves would have to run away outside. Only a few managed to hide somewhere.

After thirty minutes, it was all over. The SS men escorted them to the roll call area in the 'Big Camp'. Thousands streamed there, including non-Jewish inmates. The area was surrounded by SS men with machine guns. Escape was impossible. They were split up into groups of 100. Under SS guard, they were forced to leave the camp.

'We were lucky to have to wait because we were among the last.' Because, suddenly, low-flying US aeroplanes shot over the camp. Panic broke out.

At first I didn't realize what was happening. I ran instinctively with the other inmates. Behind me I heard shots. The SS were firing at the fleeing people. I ran like crazy. After a few minutes I stopped and tried to figure out where I was. I was somewhere among the barracks in the 'Big Camp'. I decided to go to my Czech friends who were housed in a separate block. The door was locked. I had to knock for a while until they opened it for me. They were right to hesitate: no one wanted to risk being caught helping escapees.

After a while, SS men stormed into the block and drove the inmates to the roll call area. They were also ordered to leave the camp in groups of 100.

Robert Büchler found himself with a group of older inmates. He didn't know anyone. They had to leave the camp at a trot, accompanied by SS men. 'Those who stayed behind were immediately shot.'

They reached Weimar train station in the night, where they were herded into cattle wagons. 'Some fainted, remained lying on the floor and others trod on them. The crowding was terrible.' In the early hours of the morning the train set off, but it was soon stopped. The locomotive suffered a direct hit from an American air raid. The people got out of the wagons but were rounded up again by the SS and forced to continue on foot.

It was 11 April 1945. On this day, Buchenwald concentration camp was liberated by the US army.

'We knew that the front was very close and tried to slow down the pace.' But the SS drove them eastward at a trot. 'On this sad day many old comrades who had survived the torments for years and were so near to being liberated were killed because they couldn't keep up.'

It was evening and the SS wanted to take a break. Some of the SS men disappeared into an isolated tavern in the forest. Robert lay dog-tired on the road. At first, he failed to notice what was going on around him. His comrades had gone off into the forest.

I acted by instinct, without looking around. I ran for all I was worth until I was in the middle of a group of people. Sometimes someone would fall down in front of me. I stumbled over the body in the dark, fell, got up, carried on running. I have no idea how long we ran. When we stopped, I collapsed.

His comrades told him later that those who had run away were shot down by the SS. They had trouble getting him up again. 'I was in a very critical condition. Everyone tried to help me. They looked after me with great concern.'

The group of around fifty men and youths was in the Thuringian Forest. In the morning, they decided to leave the forest. The road took them to the village of Eisenberg. Unarmed German soldiers were waiting in the market square for the Americans to arrive.

They went to the police station and asked for something to eat. A policeman accompanied them to the next village and instructed the mayor to feed them. They were taken to a barn. A sack of potatoes was boiled in a large copper. They were able to wash at a fountain. After eating, they collapsed in the straw and slept.

The next morning, US army tanks were standing on the main street in the village. The men went up to them and explained that they were liberated inmates from Buchenwald. A couple of telephone calls were made. Two trucks arrived and took the group to the glassworks around 25 kilometres away in Jena, where they were examined and disinfected by US medical orderlies. They were given new clothing and housed in a former Hitler Youth holiday camp on the banks of the Saale.

Robert Büchler drove a few times to Buchenwald with a former inmate and Jewish doctor from Czechoslovakia, who had somehow managed to requisition a car from the US army. The doctor took care, in particular, of the approximately 500 children and juveniles from Block 66 who had witnessed the liberation. Of the 200 who had been taken off the evening before, very few were still alive.

In early May, Robert was asked by a doctor if he would be willing to talk to a group of apprentices at the Zeiss works. He agreed to do so. He spoke to around a hundred of them in the works canteen about his time in the concentration camps. 'But I had the feeling that they didn't really believe me.'

YEHUDA BACON's death march took him, after several days, to the Auschwitz satellite camp Blechhammer, about 90 kilometres away. Here, they were loaded into freight cars. 'Fortunately I was in a closed wagon.'

The train was bombed en route. The first wagon was hit and many people were killed. They had very little to eat and there was no water at all.

The route took them through Ostrava, Yehuda's old hometown. The doors were opened there. He was given bread and something to drink by 'some Czech aid organization'.

After several days of travel, the conditions in the wagon became worse and worse. The occupants relieved themselves in torn-off bits of blanket taken from Birkenau, which were then thrown out of the opening. When there were no blankets left, 'we did everything on the floor in a corner of the wagon'. 'The smell was terrible.'

The meandering journey took two weeks before arriving in Mauthausen. The camp was established near Linz in August 1938, five months after the annexation of Austria to the German Reich. There were granite quarries there, where the inmates were to be worked to death as cheap labour. From 1943, the inmates were forced increasingly to perform slave labour in the armaments industry.

The inmates called the camp 'Mordhausen' ['Mord' means 'death' in German]. It was one of the most brutal camps in the system. People were beaten to death, shot and hanged; they starved, froze and were killed by lethal injection or gas. Over 200,000 people were deported to Mauthausen and its satellite camps. Around half of them died.[65]

The adults who arrived in Mauthausen with Yehuda were enlisted to repair track damaged in air raids. 'Many died doing so.'

The boys remained in the camp. They had to clean the barracks floors and haul rocks for 'some unknown purpose'.

In the second half of April 1945, they set off again in the direction of Wels. 'The march from Auschwitz-Birkenau to Blechhammer was nothing compared with this death march.' Many failed to reach camp at Gunskirchen, around 60 kilometres away, dying as a result of the deprivations or being shot by the guards.

This camp had been established at the end of December 1944. It was in the forest and consisted until April 1945 of makeshift barracks. It was even more crowded than Mauthausen. In the last days before it was liberated, there was nothing to eat. Around 150 people died every day as a result.[66]

When the US army liberated Gunskirchen on 5 May, a few days after Yehuda's arrival, he was completely emaciated, weighing just 34 kg.

He was so weak that he was taken immediately to the hospital in Steyr. 'I had typhus and felt wretched.' I stayed there until 11 June. On that day, he set off home to Czechoslovakia.

HEINZ KOUNIO In mid-April 1945, Heinz Kounio and his father Salvator were evacuated from Mauthausen to Ebensee satellite camp. 'We were all emaciated and very, very weak.' Many died on the march to Melk train station or in the cattle wagons that were to take them to Ebensee. Others were killed during the transport by the SS.

When they arrived at Ebensee train station, they were formed up in ranks after leaving the wagons. 'A high-ranking SS man hurried towards us. I had a funny feeling that something terrible was going to happen.'

During the train journey, some inmates had been shot trying to escape, but others had managed to flee. A selection took place at the train station. Over twenty inmates were selected at random.

Among them was Salvator Kounio. Heinz wasn't selected. He wondered anxiously: 'What should I do? Should I join my father?' They had survived together for so long. 'And now?' He joined his father. 'Whatever was to happen, I wanted to be with him.' He wished to share his father's fate.

The selected inmates had to throw away everything they had with them. They were told unmistakably that they would be going before a firing squad, as retribution for the inmates who had escaped.

The firing squad arrived. Some of us begged the SS men to spare us. 'We didn't run away. We're innocent.' But the SS didn't listen. They beat the people who were begging.

We had to march to the place where we were to be shot. I lost any sense of reality. They were going to shoot us. But I couldn't and didn't want to believe it. All of the inmates were crying and shouting.

But my father didn't cry. He tried to comfort the others saying out loud: 'What's happening to us is unjust, but it will put an end to our suffering.'

I was so proud of my father!

Another higher-ranking SS man from the camp approached. He asked the SS men guarding us how many new arrivals there were. He was given a number that included those who had been selected. And then something incredible happened. Because we had been included and the count had to be right, we were also taken to the camp.[67]

Ebensee had 18,500 inmates at this time, the highest number it was to reach. As a result, the number of guards was also increased to over 600 men. Most were members of the Wehrmacht, which meant that not only the SS were responsible for the conditions in the camp.

Ebensee was established in November 1943 by the Nazi leadership for a huge underground bomb-proof armaments project. The tunnels built there by the camp inmates were intended for the Peenemünde rocket research centre. Having been transferred to Usedom, it was bombed by the British Royal Air Force in mid-August 1943.

Because of the rapid advance of the Allied forces, the Nazis were unable to implement the transfer of the rocket research centre to Ebensee. Instead, the tunnels were used from early February 1945 to make fuel and engine parts for trucks and tanks.

Although the end of the war was near, the construction of the underground tunnels continued. As in Melk, the inmates in Ebensee were also leased out by the SS to the companies building the tunnels. The forced labourers were guarded by supervisors and employees of these companies.

The inmates had to work day and night in eleven-hour shifts. Some details worked in three eight-hour shifts. The inmates had to toil for seventy-seven hours a week and were in a constant state of extreme exhaustion as a result.

Ebensee was overcrowded. The food rations were so small that the inmates were constantly hungry. Ebensee became a starvation camp. Many of the inmates looked like skeletons.[68]

The work was often followed by roll calls lasting hours, with insults and beatings. One day, it was Heinz's turn. He was accused of moving too slowly and was punished by twenty-five hard strokes with a whip on his back and posterior.

It took hours for the pain to diminish sufficiently for him to lie down. So as not to freeze, he covered himself as well as he could with an old piece of paper. The guards spotted him, and he received seven additional strokes of the whip.

'Afterwards I couldn't feel anything anymore.' This lasted about a week, but then the pain was all the worse as a result of the countless deep wounds. 'I couldn't sit down at all.' The 'indescribable' hunger was also unbearable. 'All we got for breakfast was "tea", dirty, warmed-up water.' Drinking it caused him to vomit.

> After the hard and energy-sapping slave labour in the morning, there were two litres of water for lunch. It was called 'soup' but contained nothing but a few dirty potato peelings.
>
> Then we went back to work. In the evening we were exhausted. All we got to eat was a small piece of 'bread' made from potato peel ground into 'flour'.
>
> Many of us tried to get hold of the bones thrown to the SS dogs. We licked them to at least have the sensation of meat in our mouths. We also broke them into small pieces and then ate them.
>
> During the work we lifted pieces of tar. We licked them like chewing gum. Everyone tried it out at least once.
>
> The pain of hunger woke us in the night. It was unbearable.
>
> We were desperate. The pain and hunger were worse than in any of the previous camps. I was sure that my father and I would die sooner or later of the torment and constant hunger. I longed to die so that this interminable martyrdom would come to an end.
>
> What kept me alive was the presence of my father and the constant thoughts of my mother and sister. I had to stay alive in case they were also alive so that we could share a future together.[69]

At the end of April, the longed-for news made the rounds among the inmates: 'The Americans are close by!' Heinz Kounio's hope that he and his father would survive the camp was given 'new sustenance'. Every day the air raid sirens wailed.

People continued to die in the camp, 'even faster than before'. More and more inmates were starving to death. There were corpses everywhere. By now, the SS didn't care whether they were taken to the crematorium.

'There were isolated instances of cannibalism. The German guards were indifferent to that as well.' On the other hand, the inmates continued to perform slave labour.

One morning, when Heinz Kounio was returning from work, he was greeted by a devastating piece of news: Leon Favian, 'my only friend', had died of hunger in the night. Heinz had made friends in Auschwitz with the 15-year-old from Belgium. Since then, they had always been together. 'His parents had been murdered by the Germans.' Leon was completely alone. They decided that if they came out alive, they would go together to Greece, and Leon would live near him.

They had survived Auschwitz and Melk. Soon they would have been free together.

Heinz took Leon's death very hard. He was shocked, embittered, inconsolable. 'I just kept bursting into tears.' He would never again hear his voice, never again feel his presence. 'He was like a brother to me! Since then I have kept his memory alive in my heart.'

But a day later, finally: 'Freedom! My joy was indescribable. We ran outside. We cried like babies. Finally the Americans were there!'[70] They liberated Ebensee concentration camp at 10.45 a.m. on 6 May.

Around 27,000 men and boys had been deported to Ebensee from all over Europe. More than 7,000 died in the camp from the hard labour, malnutrition and epidemics, or were killed by benzene injections to the heart. Other inmates selected by the SS doctors as unfit for work were returned to the main Mauthausen camp, which was tantamount to a death sentence.

The US army found between 1,000 and 1,200 dead scattered around the Ebensee site. They were buried in a mass grave.[71]

And the dying continued: 'On the first day of our arrival, we found 450 among the sick inmates who had already been dead for a while', wrote the director of the United Nations Relief and Rehabilitation Administration (UNRRA). 'Through comprehensive measures such as cleaning the camp, improving nutrition and enlarging the hospital, the conditions in the camp improved and inmate fatalities decreased within eight days from 450 to 18 per day.'[72]

JÜRGEN LOEWENSTEIN As the front came nearer, the inmates in the Auschwitz satellite camp Eintrachhütte in Świętochłowice were evacuated westward. Jürgen was taken to Mauthausen in a cattle wagon at the end of January 1945. There were so many inmates herded into the wagon that they had to stand for the whole journey. Many died during the transport, which arrived in Mauthausen on 25 January 1945.[73]

The camp was also overcrowded. They were asked: 'What are you? What can you do?' Jürgen hesitated barely a moment before replying:

'Skilled worker. Fitter.' After four weeks, he finally received the reply: 'OK, come with me!'

Jürgen was transported with a small group to the Saurerwerke satellite camp in Vienna.[74] The factory specialized in manufacture under licence for the Swiss truck and bus company Adolph Saurer. During the war, tank engines and tractors were made there. Apart from 5,000 forced labourers, 12,000 concentration camp inmates were to be enlisted for it.[75]

'Survival in Auschwitz, Mauthausen, everywhere, was a matter of pure luck. Many people from our transport were sprayed on arrival in Mauthausen with ice cold water. It was winter and they had no possibility of drying themselves.'

A good four weeks later they had to leave Vienna for Mauthausen – with a stopover in the satellite camp of Steyr-Daimler-Puch AG in the Münichholz district of Steyr.[76] During the Nazi era, the factory in Steyr became a major part of the armaments industry with 50,000 employees, around half of whom were forced labourers. It is not known precisely how many inmates from Mauthausen were enlisted to build plants or for the manufacture of aeroplane engines.[77]

They were given only one loaf of bread for the 165-kilometre journey. They marched first to Steyr, and then later to Gusen satellite camp 40 kilometres away.

During the march, they lived from water, sorrel and grass. The population didn't help them. 'In our striped uniforms we looked like prisoners, despite the fact that we were just skin and bones. No one wanted anything to do with such criminals.'

They slept in the open or in barns. All of them were infested with lice. At each stopping place or overnight halt, the first thing they did was to undress and 'crack' lice. The inmates were guarded by members of the Wehrmacht. At the end of the column were SS men. 'Anyone left behind was shot.'

They didn't have proper shoes, just wooden clogs. Walking was a permanent torment. One of Jürgen's comrades repeated constantly: 'Come on, stick it out! We have to stick it out. Just keep going.'

It took weeks until they arrived in Gusen, 5 kilometres from Mauthausen. 'Practically no one survived the death march.'

A short while later, on 5 May 1945, Jürgen and the others who were still alive were liberated by the US army.

# Dying? What's That?

KOLA (MIKOŁAJ) When the last inmate transport left Auschwitz in mid-January 1945, a much smaller number of SS men remained behind to guard children, the sick and those unfit for transport. The Polish civilian population living in the vicinity heard about this. Some of them found the courage to enter the camp. Through them, the news spread that there were children there without food or supervision.

The news also reached Emilia and Adam Klimczyk,[1] who lived 13 kilometres from the camp in Jawiczowice near Brzeszcze. As they were childless, they decided to take in one of the children from Auschwitz. They made inquiries and discovered that the SS men in the camp shot intruders, along with inmates who attempted to escape.

On 24 January, three days before the camp was liberated by the Red Army, the Klimczyks set off for Auschwitz-Birkenau. 'We passed through a clearing in the forest with wood stacked up to burn the corpses', said Emilia Klimczyk. 'We entered the actual camp through a hole in the fence.'

At that moment, an SS motorcycle patrol arrived. Adam Klimczyk hid behind a pile of wood while his wife took refuge in an empty barracks. The SS men stopped, looked around and then left when they heard aeroplanes approaching.

'All over the camp there were bodies of murdered inmates, diverse objects, burning pits', reported Adam Klimczyk later. 'And everywhere was the smell of the smouldering bonfires.'

In a nearby barracks, there were women. They were watching and called out to Emilia when the SS men had left: 'I entered the barracks where there were lots of women and a group of children – boys, 7, 8, 12 years old.' But she wanted a child who would not remember the terrible things and to whom she could say: 'You are my child.'

She would have preferred a little girl to take home with her. And in one of the other barracks there were 'very pretty Jewish girls'. But they were already 14 years old or more. In addition, she feared that they would not be able to feed an older girl properly, 'as we had very little to eat ourselves'.

In another barracks, there were three small children along with the older ones. But they clung to each other and were inseparable. 'And I couldn't and didn't want to take in three children because of the shortage of food.'

Emilia spoke in this barracks to Polish women inmates who were looking after the children. They pointed to a boy. As the Klimczyks were afraid that the SS patrol would return, and persuaded by the women, Emilia decided to take this boy with her.

The women told her that the boy's name was 'Kola' (short for Mikołaj). No one could say where he was from, how old he was, or what his surname was.

Another boy, perhaps 6 years old, approached Emilia and begged her to take him. But one of the others assured her that he would survive until the camp was liberated.

'And so I took Kola. He ran to me, held out his little hands and said in Polish: "I want my mother." How could I not take him? Fate had led me to him.'

Emilia wrapped the child, who was perhaps 2 years old, in a cloth and took him from the camp with her husband.

Stanisława Jankowska, camp number 20203, was one of the inmate women who was looking after the children in Auschwitz-Birkenau at the time. She kept a diary from 21 to 28 January 1945 in an exercise book she had managed to find somewhere and which is now in the Auschwitz Memorial. 'Chronicle of the Last Days of Auschwitz' was the title she gave to it. Kola's rescue was described as follows: '24 January – The Klimczyks from Brzeszcze reported about an orphan.' On another page, the names and address are noted: 'Adam and Emilia Klimczak, née Krzak – Rudolf Krzak, 1 boy Mikołaj.'[2]

'Rudolf Krzak' was Emilia's father. In Polish documents, the name of the father is written after a woman's maiden name. The different spelling – Klimczak rather than Klimczyk – is no doubt due to the difficult conditions in Auschwitz-Birkenau at the time.

GÉZA SCHEIN Seven months earlier, Emilia Klimczyk had noticed a child by the name of Géza in the coalmine in Brzeszcze. The boy had been deported from Hungary to Auschwitz in mid-1944 at the age of 11 with his parents and maternal grandparents.

On the ramp in Auschwitz, his father Zoltán realized what was happening. He said to his son: 'If they ask, tell them you're 15 and an apprentice baker.' The SS believed him.

Géza's mother Klára was sent to the Women's Camp, while he and his father were put in the 'Gypsy' Family Camp. Both had to perform slave labour in the construction of a factory in Auschwitz-Monowitz for synthetic rubber ('Buna') and benzene for the Frankfurt-based company IG-Farbenindustrie AG.

Géza and six other boys had to drag bricks and mortar and unload carts. 'And we had to collect the bodies lying around everywhere.' The dead had to be counted, otherwise the SS would have suspected an attempted escape and would have made life even harder for the other inmates.

Dr Bárdos, a doctor from Géza's hometown Csepel, was one of the first dead bodies that the boy saw.

'There was a rumour that the children were to be taken to the gas chambers. The Roma from my father's village gathered the children, including me, and hid them. I owe my life to this Roma.' After around a month, 'I slipped into a group that was to be sent to the mines.'

At first, the inmates had to march every morning and evening to and from the mine in Brzeszcze, 13 kilometres from Birkenau. After a time, barracks were installed in Jawiczowice, which was close to Brzeszcze, where the 150 boys, all Jewish children from Hungary, were forced to live in very difficult conditions.

Géza worked on the surface sorting the coal by size and quality and shovelling it onto huge piles. It was hard work and he often collapsed with exhaustion. 'The adults helped me because they were afraid that as a child I would not be able to keep up and would be punished by the SS for it.'

There were also Polish civilians working underground in the mine. Some women prepared food for their husbands in a shared kitchen at the mine. Among them was Emilia Klimczyk, who some months later with her husband was to risk her life to rescue little Kola from Auschwitz-Birkenau.

The children were filthy from the work in the mine. But there was little water for washing and no soap or towels. Scabs formed on their skin, developing into open wounds that wouldn't heal.

'In the mine group there was a boy whose precocious seriousness and sadness caught my attention', said Emilia Klimczyk later. 'I decided to look out specially for him. I also continued to give food to the others, but for him I brought additional delicacies from home.'

The boy was Géza Schein: 'I felt an attraction to this woman. She brought me bread, potatoes, fruit and medicine.'

It was autumn 1944. Géza suspected that he would not be able to stay much longer in the mine. He wanted to thank the Polish woman – he didn't know her name at the time – and make a gift for her.

'Once he managed to come to the kitchen', said Emilia. 'He gave me to understand with his eyes that he wanted to tell me something. In a corner of the room, where the SS men couldn't see us, he flung his arms round my neck with tears in his eyes and said in broken Polish: "I love you, mummy."'

Géza gave her a small drawing (10.5 × 14.8 cm) with a portrait of himself. A fellow inmate (Jean Markiel) had drawn it secretly in Auschwitz-Birkenau and given it to Géza. From then on, the boy had carried the drawing against his body under his clothes.

ÉVA A few days after Auschwitz was liberated, a boy by the name Stanisław (Krcz)[3] set off for the former Auschwitz-Birkenau camp. Like the Klimczyk family, he had heard that children were still there.

When the Germans occupied Poland, his parents, Karolina and Józef Krcz, lived with their children Stanisław and Genia, opposite Auschwitz train station.[4] The building in which they lived belonged officially to the concentration camp site. This meant that, particularly in 1943 and 1944, they inevitably witnessed the arrival of mass transports. They were woken in the night by shouting and often heard shots. If someone escaped from the camp, their house was searched. Karolina Krcz: 'We lived in permanent fear of being resettled or interned in the camp.'

Stanisław Krcz, who already attended school, once secretly observed an SS man taking out his rage on an inmate. After brutally beating him, he ordered the inmate to flee. When the inmate left his workplace, the SS man fired at him. 'He missed. The SS man, surrounded by kapos, brutally murdered the inmate. He placed a bar on the neck of the inmate, who was lying on the floor, and then stood on the bar.... I was horrified by the calm way in which he committed this crime.'

During the occupation, the Krcz family was 'resettled' in another district. Stanisław's sister Genia became very sick. There were barely any doctors and no medicaments, and there were also extreme food shortages. Genia died, the family believes, of pneumonia. Stanisław: 'It's difficult to describe how devastated my mother was after the loss of her daughter. There was nothing I could do to comfort her.'

'I thought', said Stanisław, years later, 'that a child might help my mother with her depression, a girl to replace my dead sister Genia.' That was why he went to the former Auschwitz-Birkenau camp.

He found a barracks with around sixty small children. He met a woman and told her directly what he was looking for. She pointed to a little girl called Éva, saying that she had arrived at the camp with her parents and a younger brother in a transport from Hungary. On their arrival, her mother had refused to be separated from her, whereupon an SS man had beaten her to death with a rifle butt. All of the members of Éva's family were dead. Fellow inmates had looked after her and protected her from selection.

Stanisław took the girl with him and immediately called her by the Polish name 'Ewa'. Éva/Ewa[5] never forgot that moment: 'I can even remember the route I took with Stanisław. He carried me across the tracks. And there was a heavy snowstorm.'

Amazed at the boy, adult inmates gave him a roll with seven drawings, portraits of Sinti and Roma, as it turned out years later, by Dinah Gottliebova, who had been interned in Auschwitz-Birkenau in September 1943 at the age of 20. By order of SS doctor Mengele, the young woman from Brno had drawn pictures of Sinti and Roma for his pseudo-medical 'race research'.[6]

'Here's a child for you to make you stop despairing about Genia.' These are the words Stanisław used when he handed over the girl to his mother. The family lived in Oświęcim. And from the very first day, Ewa – like every small Auschwitz child, she spoke a mishmash of Yiddish, German, Polish, Russian, Czech and Hungarian – called Karolina Krcz 'mama' and Stanisław 'tatinek', the Czech for 'dad'.

Ewa wore a blue satin dress, a striped coat and red leather boots. If she had not been so filthy, you might have thought she was going on outing with her parents. But she looked completely neglected.

Karolina feared that it would be impossible to keep the 2-year-old Ewa alive. She was undernourished, had an over-large head and a bloated stomach. Her forehead was covered in scabs and her entire body with small ulcers, and her hair was full of lice. Her eyes were bloodshot and festering. The inmate number A5116 could be seen clearly on her left forearm.

Ewa required intensive care and effort before the colour returned to her face. In the difficult supply situation immediately after the war, Karolina had to scour the surrounding villages to obtain milk, butter and eggs.

While Ewa's physical condition gradually improved, the psychological consequences of camp life proved more difficult to overcome. For a long time, she would wake up in the morning crying. For years afterwards, she was terrified of dogs and ran away whenever she saw one. And she was extremely nervous.

She was incapable of playing. 'With other children she was strangely serious; she never enjoyed herself and was very withdrawn', said her new brother Stanisław, who tried repeatedly to arouse her interest. When he gave her a toy, she didn't know what to do with it and would just stare at it or throw it away.

But Ewa developed a feeling of security. 'My mother was everything to me. I was treated like her own child, perhaps even better.'

LIDIA The Rydzikowski family also decided a few days after liberation to take home a child. Previously, Ryszard Rydzikowski had sought his wife Bronisława's brother Julian Chyciech in the former concentration camp. 'The Nazis had interned him there.'[7]

Ryszard was unable to find out anything. He was horrified by what he saw in Auschwitz-Birkenau. 'Above all, I have never been able to forget the wretched state of the children I saw there.'

He asked a woman, 'a Jew, she had a star on her inmate's clothing', who had remained behind to look after the children, if he could take one of the children home with him. 'They don't have any parents. All of them can be taken', the woman replied.

Ryszard went home. At first, he was unable to talk. Later in the day, he related everything to his wife, Bronisława Rydzikowska. 'I already had two children who had been killed in the war.' So they decided to adopt one of the children.

Next day, they went to Auschwitz-Birkenau. Bronisława: 'There were lots of corpses in the camp. Those who were still alive looked like skeletons. We went into the barracks where the children were. Two older girls came up to me and begged: "Take us with you!"' Bronisława preferred a child who needed special care.

'Suddenly I felt someone stroking my legs. I looked down and in front of me was a tiny little girl. "Take me, auntie", she said.'

One of the women looking after the children said that the child's mother had been shot a couple of days earlier by an SS man. She pointed to a dead woman in inmate's clothing in a ditch.

The Rydzikowskis took Lidia, as the child was called, home with them.[8] 'When I look at Lidia sometimes and remember what she looked like then, my eyes fill up with tears', said Bronisława years later.

Lidia's head had been shaved bare. She was starving and her lips had a large deep cut on them. It took more than two years for this wound to heal. Her thin legs were frostbitten up to the knees.

When she undressed the child, the Rydzikowskis noticed bite marks on her backside. Lidia said that she had been bitten by a dog in the camp. The inmate number 70072 was tattooed on her arm. Lidia looked about 4 years old.

The Rydzikowskis put her in the bathtub right away. 'She looked like a skeleton. Her body was covered with ulcers, which were crawling with lice.'

The first time the girl ate something, she was stricken by painful stomach cramps. Foam came out of her mouth.

A doctor was called. 'For a long time she was terrified of doctors. Then she began to scream. He had to take off his white coat. Only then was he allowed into the room.' The doctor ordered a strict diet, but the child could still not keep anything down for a long time afterwards. 'It went right through her.'

Lidia's pathology was very complicated. She had severe haematorrhoea, pneumonia and meningitis. At first it was feared that she wouldn't survive. She was in treatment for a long time. Lidia felt: 'My Polish parents spared neither effort nor money to save me.'

At first, Lidia cried every afternoon. She was afraid of everyone and hid in a corner of the apartment. When her adoptive parents approached, she screamed even louder.

'She would stop crying', said Bronisława, 'if we gave her a bundle of old clothes and ordered her back to the camp. Then she would jump into bed, pull the blanket over her head and fall asleep.'

Lidia was surprised when other children cried. For a long time, she would repeat: 'No one cried in the camp.'

The child spoke more Russian than Polish, also mixed with some Czech and Yiddish. She often sang two Polish children's songs, 'Ta Dorotka' and 'Jedzie pociąg z daleka' ['Our Train Comes from Far Away'], and she also knew some Polish and Jewish prayer melodies. But she could no longer remember who had taught her them.

When Lidia played with other children, she would occasionally order them to kneel down and put their hands up. Then she would run among them and shout: 'Mengele's coming. Be quiet, or else you'll be put in the Revier [inmate hospital block] and in the oven.'

And if someone fell down while playing, she would pull him or her up and say: 'You're for the oven.' Or she would stand them in a line and give them each a piece of wood that looked like a thermometer and say: 'You're done for.'

Not only her playmates but also adults would look at Lidia sometimes in amazement. They wondered what she must have seen, heard and been through. Why did she remember the name Mengele? The Rydzikowskis had never heard of it and only later did they learn about the SS doctor's crimes.

KOLA was 3 years old when the Klimczyk family risked their lives to rescue him shortly before the camp was liberated. He was one of the youngest inmates in Auschwitz.

It took a considerable time to delouse Kola and clean him up. His feet were badly frostbitten. He looked like a skeleton, his little body was almost transparent and his stomach bloated from undernourishment. He had been bitten by dogs, was covered with ulcers with a layer of scabs on his head, his eyes were gummed together with pus and they ran continuously for a long time.

On his second day at home with the Klimczyks in Jawiczowice, Kola began to look closely at his adoptive mother. He said: 'You're not my mother. You're auntie.'

Like the adult inmates in Auschwitz, the boy had a number tattooed on his left forearm. Emilia Klimczyk: 'It was terrible, because lots of Germans were returning at this time. They passed the house and some even entered. I had to make sure that Kola was always wearing a long-sleeved shirt or pullover and didn't roll up the sleeves.' Even though the camp was about to be liberated, there would have been terrible conse-quences for the Klimczyk family if the number had been discovered.

Whenever Kola saw Germans passing or entering the house, he would scream: 'We have to run away, otherwise they'll shoot us!'

Kola was often sick, very thin and barely grew. He contracted tuber-culosis and had to go to hospital. He needed endless medical treatment. His adoptive parents feared that he would not survive. Adam Klimczyk took him often to the sea or the mountains, which helped Kola to recover. But the family were constantly worried and unsettled by him.

In the first years, Kola's behaviour was strongly influenced by his camp experience. Clearly remembering that his feet had been frostbitten, he would stand unsteadily so as not to put too much weight on them. If his hands were cold, he would clasp them together in a special way like the inmates in the camp so as to warm them again.

He was fanatical about cleanliness and order. Kola didn't like it when someone touched his things or moved them somewhere else. And he would often stand lost in thought.

Everything was new for the boy. The only food he knew was 'kartoshki', potatoes. He had a habit of smelling everything before he ate it.

He spoke a mixture of Russian, Polish and German. When he played with other children, he gave them orders in German. He referred to food in Russian and feelings in Russian and Polish. And words of endearment and belittlement were always in Russian.

He was very nervous and suffered frequently from cramps. He couldn't stand to see uniforms: 'Mum, we have to run, there are Germans here', he would say on such occasions. And nocturnal disturbances or knocks at the door caused indescribable anxiety.

Whenever the Klimczyks had visitors, they had to sit on the sofa, put their hands on their knees and remain motionless. Kola would go up and down and scrutinize the visitors like a guard.

When Emilia Klimczyk visited her mother, they talked with Russian soldiers who were billeted with them. Unnoticed, Kola grabbed a pistol lying on the table, pointed it at the soldiers, shouted in German: 'Hände hoch' ['Hands up'] and pulled the trigger. Everyone held their breath – only the soldier knew that the gun was not loaded.

The Klimczyks couldn't understand why Kola was so terrified of rats and tractors. They asked German prisoners of war who were working in a nearby coalmine and had apparently been guards in Auschwitz-Birkenau. One of them said that the child must have seen corpses being piled up with a tractor so that they didn't have to be touched. And there were lots of rats in the barracks.

One day, Kola saw a foreman in a miner's uniform in the mine in Jawiczowice. 'Buy me a gun and a sword', he asked his adoptive mother. Asked what he intended to do with them, he explained: 'I want to kill this man in uniform and cut him up.' When Emilia pointed out that killing was wrong, the child looked at her in astonishment verging on disbelief.

Although he got enough to eat, he would always hide away bits of food when he thought no one was looking. In the camp, the tiniest thing had immense value.

Even as a child, it seemed to Kola that lying was vital to survival. 'The child often lied, believing that he had to', recalled Emilia. 'We tried to break the habit and told him that if he did something bad we wouldn't punish him if he owned up to it.'

Kola didn't change. Ultimately, the Klimczyks lost patience. 'Get dressed, we're going on a journey', said Emilia angrily. 'Where are we going?' asked the astonished boy several times, but didn't get a reply until he was dressed. 'You lie and don't love us, so we're going to give you away.'

'That did the trick', said Emilia:

> Kola pulled himself together and promised not to lie any more. He owned up to his pranks: once, he and some other boys trampled the wheat in a field. When the owner came all of them ran away except for Kola. I had to pay for the damage but Kola wasn't punished. The child realized that he had done something wrong.

One of the beliefs that Kola retained from Auschwitz-Birkenau was that people didn't die, but were killed. The Klimczyk family realized this fairly soon. They were distraught. When a relative died, the Klimczyks took him to the wake. They uncovered the body and told him to look closely at it. He searched for traces of blood, bruises and bullet wounds. But he found nothing. Emilia said to him: 'He died.'

'What does "die" mean?' asked Kola. 'Who beat him to death?'

His adoptive mother tried to convince him again. 'He wasn't killed. He died.'

But Kola asked again: 'Died? What do you mean?' He couldn't understand it. For years afterwards, whenever a relative or neighbour died, he would ask 'Who killed him?'

Another time, there was no meat in the shops. Kola said to Emilia: 'Kill me, then you'll have some meat.' She explained patiently that people didn't kill. He replied: 'But I've seen blood flowing and people being killed.' It had been a common sight in Auschwitz-Birkenau.

Kola believed that the way adults who had not been in the camp as inmates thought and reacted was due to a lack of experience. They were like children who had no idea what life was really about.

BEN SHEMEN Immediately after the war, representatives of the Youth Aliyah ('aliyah' means 'ascent' to the Promised Land, Israel) in Europe set out to search for surviving Jewish children and adolescents. They were to be taken to homes and villages such as Ben Shemen, a children's village between Tel Aviv and Jerusalem, founded by Siegfried Lehmann, a paediatrician from Berlin.

He began his Jewish pedagogical and social work in Berlin early on. In 1920 he went to Lithuania and set off for Palestine, as it was at the time, with fifteen boys and girls from the children's home in Kaunas. With this small group, he founded the Ben Shemen Youth Village in 1927.[9]

The Youth Aliyah was officially founded as the Aid Committee for Jewish Youths in Berlin on 30 January 1933, the day Hitler came to power, by the teacher, social worker and poet Recha Freier. The aim was to rescue Jewish children and juveniles from the Nazi regime and to help build a Jewish state. By the end of November 1938, more than 3,000 children and juveniles had arrived in Palestine from the countries ruled by the Nazis, some of whom found a new and safe home in Ben Shemen or in kibbutzim.[10]

The brutal antisemitism in Nazi Germany shook Freier to the core, as she wrote in her poem *Earthquake*:

The city garden
The gold shimmering gate
Closed??
A big white cardboard sign
A frame of black paper
'Admission prohibited for dogs and Jews!'[11]

After Germany started the war, collection points for Jewish children and juveniles were set up in many countries. A race against time began as the German troops advanced. '13,000 children from Germany, Austria and Czechoslovakia', wrote Freier, were brought to safety in Belgium, Britain, the Netherlands and Scandinavia, where they were put in homes or with private families.[12]

Among those rescued were Lutz Kann and his sister, who both arrived in Palestine:

In 1939 my sister and I came to Israel. My sister was just fourteen and arrived on a Kindertransport from the Netherlands. It was very bitter for our parents. There were parents who couldn't separate from their children, and then it was too late and they were transported to Riga or Auschwitz. But how were they to know? No one could imagine it, the mass murder![13]

During the war years from 1940 to 1945, at least 11,500 Jewish girls and boys from the countries occupied by Nazi Germany managed to escape to Palestine, sometimes by very roundabout routes.[14] Among them was a group of around 1,000 Jewish children and juveniles from Poland. Their story of survival as the 'Tehran children' became known. After the invasion of Poland by German troops on 1 September 1939, hundreds of thousands of Polish Jews, but also over a million Christians, fled to the Soviet Union. There were mass arrests, persecutions and deportations to Siberia, as a result of which many children lost their parents.

After the Germans invaded the Soviet Union on 22 June 1941, at least 116,000 Polish refugees set off in early 1942 on the long and arduous journey to Iran. Among them were around 1,000 Jewish children and juveniles. From the Central Asian Soviet republics, they travelled by train via Krasnovodsk (now Türkmenbaşy) and then by ship to Bandar Pahlavi (now Bandar Anzali) on the Caspian Sea. Others came via Bukhara

(Buxoro), Kazan and Ashgabat (on the Iranian border) to Bandar Pahlavi. All of the children had scratches, skin infections and diarrhoea, and some were seriously ill with malaria, tuberculosis or typhoid fever. Many were completely emaciated because of the enduring hunger.

The Jewish Agency for Palestine established an orphanage in Tehran for the Jewish children who arrived in Iran between April and August 1942, where they were treated and mostly recovered from their serious diseases. In early January 1943, over 700 children with adult accompaniment travelled by truck to Bandar Shahpur on the Persian Gulf and from there by freighter to Karachi, Pakistan, and through the Red Sea to Suez, Egypt. They finally travelled by train through the Sinai desert and arrived in northern Palestine in mid-February. A second group with over 100 children travelled overland through Iraq and arrived in the Promised Land at the end of August 1943. Altogether, around 870 'Tehran children' found a new home in Palestine, often in kibbutzim.[15]

In 1946, the first children rescued from Auschwitz and other camps arrived in Ben Shemen. Practically all of them had lost their parents.[16] Aryeh Simon, long-time director of the children's village, recalled:

> The children who arrived in our care carried the traces of their suffering on their bodies and in their hearts. We did what we could with our limited means to help them to find their way to a happier normal life. We were shocked to discover that some of them identified with the Nazi ideology. They had not been brainwashed. What their brief lives to date had taught them can be summed up in a single sentence: 'You are either on top or underneath, kicking or being kicked, hangman or victim.' The conclusion, so it appeared to them, was obvious.[17]

Richard Levinsohn, who worked for fifty years as an educator and gardener in Ben Shemen, spoke of his experiences:

> I particularly recall one boy whose story I didn't know at first because he wasn't in my group. I was looking for participants for a performance of the story of the Little Muck by Wilhelm Hauff. I chose the pupils without regard for their past. But it turned out that most of the children who volunteered had a difficult and sad past.

I discovered that Mosche Hurwitz, the boy who was to play the king, was always very aggressive and had been in Auschwitz. He had worked there on the crematorium ovens and had had to push his parents on a wheelbarrow after they had been gassed. It was important for him to play a main role and to be integrated in the team.

Benjamin Hildesheimer was another Auschwitz survivor. Although he had been through a lot, his suffering was not immediately apparent. He played the leading role in the 16 mm film *Adamah* (The Earth) made by us in 1947. In this role we sought to express what we had seen in all the children from the camps who were unable to assimilate.

There were children who didn't want to do anything. They said that they had already worked enough for Hitler. Others didn't believe that there was enough to eat for everyone and that no one had to steal. Then there were children who always hid bread in their bags because they couldn't break the habit of saving food.

Children like Benjamin had lost their faith in people. They were attached to animals, dogs, horses …

We distributed the children from the camps in existing groups. We didn't leave them to themselves. They came together with 'normal' children. This community life contributed greatly to their reintegration.

It took a while to restore their faith in humanity. Although the terrible memories remained, within a few years practically all of them had become used to a normal life.[18]

# Alive Again!

Find someone in the family! Not to be alone! How else were the liberated children and juveniles to find their way in a world out there, which they no longer recognized, or were completely unfamiliar with?

Many of the children from Auschwitz who knew something about their families made their way back home – even when they suspected that mothers and fathers, sisters and brothers, were no longer alive. Perhaps an uncle, an aunt or a friend had survived. Find someone! Not to be alone!

Almost no one was able to return immediately. They were so marked, debilitated, sick from the camp that they had to be taken care of in emergency field hospitals or clinics until they had recovered somewhat. Some of them remained for a short while, others for many years.

They all believed in a free world that would welcome them with open arms. But for many this remained a dream. The Jewish children and juveniles, in particular, who returned to their homes found that nothing was as it had been before. Many were met with hostility: 'What are you doing here? Why didn't you stay where you were? We don't want you here.' They were not welcome.

And those Jewish girls and boys who returned to their looted apartments and houses soon began to wonder how they could continue living in the village, town or street from which they and their families had been deported. This house, this street, the school would always remind them of the people who had died. Practically none of the neighbours, practically none of the supposed friends of the family, had helped them in any way.

HAVING TO REMEMBER Especially the small children who had spent a long time in the concentration or extermination camp were unable after their release to relate to everyday items. They didn't know them. Tables served as seats; chairs were projectiles; eating utensils as tools. They didn't know how to wash. Games were alien. Some couldn't even walk properly, but marched in step as they had done after the roll calls. And there were those who couldn't even remember their parents.

The children were noticeably irritable, and their moods fluctuated greatly. For a long time, they were suspicious of their new surroundings. They were in constant fear of having things snatched away from them: clothing, food, toys. They defended them as if their life depended on it. When someone left, for many of the younger ones – like Kola Klimczyk – it was as if they had died, an experience they had suffered on a daily basis in the camp.[1]

It was difficult or even impossible for them to acquire a taste for life. They couldn't help but remember the camp. When they undressed, they automatically searched their clothing for lice. They broke into panic at the sight of a uniform. If they didn't look closely or if they found it impossible to look in the direction of the uniform, they naturally assumed it was an SS man. When they went through a gate, they were reminded of the gates separating the various sections of the Auschwitz-Birkenau camp. The sound of an unknown language reminded them of the camp: perhaps they wouldn't understand the order and would be killed because they couldn't carry it out. When their hair was cut, they were reminded of how they had been shaved bald in the camp. They were unable to use metal eating utensils or to stand in long lines. A visit to the doctor caused panic in those children and juveniles who had been abused in the camp for medical experiments. A train journey immediately reminded them of the deportation. And there was the permanent fear of the freedom that they had to deal with afresh every day.

They would hide food as a strategy for survival. They defended things as if their life depended on it, because in the camp even the smallest items had inestimable value. Every small crust of bread meant that they could survive for one or two days. Only those who had a secret supply could be sure of staying alive. Even spoiled food was not to be thrown away. They would be incredulous if adults suggested that they do so: 'You've no idea!'

At first, the children and juveniles avoided any kind of work. They had to conserve their strength. In the camp, they had learned that they would only survive if they remained in good health. And besides, they would tell themselves that they had worked enough for the Germans. It was difficult for them to keep to the normal conventions. In the camp, everyone had used familiar forms to talk to one another. Outside, it was often different. It appeared to them that for the others money and superficial forms of politeness were more important than compassion and sincerity. Wasn't it enough just to have food, a roof over one's head and a school to go to?

Basically, many of the children and juveniles had lost their trust in people. In the outside world, it was no longer as easy to recognize duplicity. They discovered repeatedly that there were bad people 'outside' as well. They were often disappointed.

And there was the reluctance to really talk about the atrocities they had experienced. Those who had not been in the camps already found them peculiar and would only find them more so. The children only felt understood by former camp inmates. They therefore sought contact with children, young people, and also older people, who understood them without them having to explain. Auschwitz came alive especially at night, as they were forced to remember how hunger had gnawed at their innards; the cold that penetrated through to the bone; the stench of burning flesh; the selections by the SS that had taken away their mothers and fathers, brothers and sisters, grandparents, uncles and aunts, friends; and the fear that their own number would be called out. At these moments, the ever-present threat of death in Auschwitz became all too real.

FEELING OF ABANDONMENT The idea of being taken in by people as substitute parents was difficult to assimilate at first. Who were these people who were holding their hands, welcoming them with open arms and giving them a goodnight kiss?

A total of 732 children and juveniles who had survived concentration and extermination camps, slave labour and death marches were sent to Great Britain in 1945 to convalesce. Most of them were boys and young men, but there were also 80 girls and young women. They travelled under the patronage of the Central British Fund (now World Jewish Relief). The fund was a Jewish aid organization that had already energetically supported refugees during the Nazi rule. The children and juveniles were put in transit homes all over the British Isles, including Windermere in the Lake District and Durley near Southampton.[2]

An unnamed carer reported on her observations:

Much worse than the physical condition is the mental state. It fluctuates between noisy, exaggerated joy, depression and apathy, and many of them have bad nightmares. In their sleep they see themselves and their comrades being mistreated, persecuted and threatened with shooting. But there is also another recurrent dream: 'I dreamt that I got a letter.' The feeling of abandonment weighs more heavily on them than what they experienced in the camps.... They survived the torture and deprivations but now they find themselves in a kind of vacuum and don't know what to do with themselves. They seek a point of reference in this large, alien and incomprehensible world.[3]

They were often the only survivors in their families. They had been humiliated, uprooted, in a state of emotional chaos, as illustrated by the recollection of an evening discussion for older girls in one of the English homes:

Everyone complained about trivial matters; they were all agitated, and then they finally burst out: 'Why are we still here? It would be much better if we were dead.' 'We laugh a lot and are high-spirited, but that's just a façade. We want to deceive ourselves so as to forget how unhappy we are.'

'We're now much sadder than we were in the concentration camp. There we lived from one day to the next. Where can we get a piece of bread? Will they beat us again? Will we be in the next group to be gassed? That's as far ahead as we thought.' They all spoke at the same time. 'Now we're in England and they tell us that we should start a new life, but we can't shake off the old life. Not a day, not an hour passes without our remembering what they did to our parents and brothers and sisters. Only now do we realize what we've lost and how rootless we are. A new life? Why and for whom?' 'People have sympathy for us, but they don't need us. Whether we live or die, we won't leave behind a hole. We don't belong to you and should be long dead, like our families.'[4]

But with patience, sensitive psychological and social care and a welcoming home in beautiful natural surroundings, many of the uprooted children gradually learned that they no longer had to fight for food or human warmth. Mick (Abraham) Zwirek from Płock, Poland, who had survived two ghetto internments and four concentration camps, summed up the new feeling: 'When I woke up in the morning and looked around, I thought I was in heaven. There were white sheets on the bed and white bread to eat.'[5] Harry (Chaim) Olmer from Sosnowiec, Poland, also survived arduous slave labour and several concentration camps. He said: 'The return to humanity began' in Windermere.[6]

In April 1945, a group of small children arrived from Auschwitz in a children's home near Kraków. Years later, one of the carers still clearly recalled a girl from that time. Her behaviour was so remarkable that she never forgot it.

At first, the staff of the children's home thought that the 5-year-old girl was dumb: 'She would look on intelligently but never said a word.' After about three weeks, she began to speak, had fits of rage, flailed around unexpectedly when she played, hit the other children. Then she would become quiet and withdrawn again.

The girl had been brought to the home in rags. For a month she didn't want to exchange them for other clothes. 'If you bring me a new dress you will put me in the ovens.'

Finally, they managed to persuade the girl that there were no ovens in the children's home. Only then would she put on the new clothes.

'For a very long time', says the carer, 'the child was tormented by nightmares and screamed out loud in her sleep. Without waking up, she would speak scrambled words in German and shook all over.'[7]

BEING UNABLE TO TELL ANYONE In many countries, doctors, nurses, families and organizations selflessly tended the children and juveniles. In spite of this care, the children were also confronted by an atmosphere of indifference, rejection, suspicion, criticism and coldness. One of the openly spoken and deeply hurtful reproaches was to ask how they could have allowed themselves to be herded like sheep into the concentration camps instead of dying a hero's death in the resistance.

Quite a few children who had seen themselves deprived of their families, their homes and their roots asked themselves: 'What have I survived for? Who could have guessed that the world outside could sometimes be so repellent?'

Liberated children and juveniles who returned to the Soviet Union were eyed with misgivings and met by an atmosphere of mistrust. People wondered whether they had not in fact been members of the SS or other Nazi criminal organizations. They stood under a cloud of suspicion and were sometimes treated as traitors who had worked for the Germans. Some were not allowed to return to their families. Others were cut off after their return, forbidden from going to school and university or from working. Some former concentration camp inmates were even deported to Siberia and put in camps there.[8] To avoid this, they had to keep quiet for years about the fact that they had been forced labourers in Germany or concentration camp inmates.

Nadezhda Tkacheva, who is thought to have been deported from the region of Saratov via Vitebsk to Auschwitz in 1943 at the age of 6, recalls: after the war, 'we were regarded with suspicion by our fellow citizens, as if we had gone to the camp of our own accord'. She had her camp number surgically removed. Then 'I was sick for a long time', she reports. 'My mother had attempted to treat the wound with vinegar. We did everything possible to get rid of the scars on our skin.' She did not wish to be recognized and branded forever as an Auschwitz survivor. Nadezhda kept quiet for many decades about her past.[9]

The Russian documentary film *Painting Death* by Julia Gerra recounts the story of Krystyna and Ludowika, born in Warsaw in 1929 and 1930 and brought up by their mother, since the father had died.[10]

On 1 August 1944, the first day of the Polish military uprising in Warsaw, they were visiting an aunt and playing in the garden. Suddenly there were shots. Their aunt was killed and their cousin was shot before their eyes.

Another aunt, who was also there at the time, shouted to them: 'Hide!' They ran to a cemetery where they knew of an old crypt where they could stay out of sight. They remained there for two or three days.

Their hunger finally overcame their fear and they managed to get to the house where they lived with their mother. The fighting in Warsaw was still going on all around them. On several occasions they brought bandages and water to the wounded Polish fighters.

After the uprising had been put down, Krystyna and Ludowika were arrested along with their mother and force-marched to Pruszków, 15 kilometres away. Here the girls were separated from their mother and transported in a cattle wagon to Auschwitz-Birkenau. 'We children had our temperature taken along with blood samples on several occasions. Some of the children failed to return.'

After about three months, Krystyna and Ludowika were moved to Neuengamme near Hamburg.[11] They were very weak and were put in the sick bay, where they were treated with medication. The Polish women inmates took special care of them, encouraging them to get up and feeding them a spoonful at a time. This gave them the will to live, and they didn't want to die anymore.

Krystyna and Ludowika were probably in one of the Neuengamme satellite camps. They were liberated in April or May 1945.

On return to Warsaw, they looked in vain for their mother but met a man, presumably a member of the Red Army, who wanted to bring them to a place where they would receive medical treatment and could go to school. He took them to the train station and put them on a train. But the train didn't stop in Poland and only did so when it reached Babruysk around 600 kilometres away in Byelorussia.

In the town, which was also in ruins, they were advised not to tell anyone they had been in a concentration camp. Only later did they realize that anyone who had been in a German concentration camp was likely to have problems and would not be able to find work or study.

Krystyna changed her name to Kzenia and Ludowika to Lidia. For the ten years they were together, Kzenia didn't even tell her first husband that she had been in a concentration camp. Even between themselves, the sisters avoided the subject. It was their secret.

This did not change for them until the 1970s, when a film came out based on the true story of a Russian mother who had been separated in Auschwitz from her little boy. They were reunited decades later after the boy had been brought up by a woman in Poland.

Jewish survivors were also prevented from emigrating to what was then Palestine. One of them was Eduard Kornfeld's older brother.

One day, Eduard received a letter from Cyprus. He was surprised and excited and wondered who could possibly have written to him from there. The letter was from his brother Heinrich, with whom he had fled to Hungary and hidden in Budapest, where he had had to leave him at the end of 1943.

'I was indescribably happy to discover that he was still alive. He had located me with the help of Jewish organizations.'

After the invasion by Germany on 19 March 1944, Heinrich had managed to get to one of the safe houses in Budapest of the Swiss diplomat Carl Lutz, who had immediately recognized the perilous plight of the Hungarian Jews. After tough negotiations with the German authorities and the Hungarian government, he was given permission to issue around 5,000 letters of safe passage for emigration to Palestine.

He interpreted the agreement to mean that one letter could be issued for each family. Besides, the names were entered in joint passes – sometimes 1,000 people in one pass. In this way, they were protected by the Swiss legation. And the holders of these letters of safe passage were housed temporarily in seventy-six safe houses that the vice-consul had managed to acquire. In this way, Carl Lutz and his assistants rescued over 60,000 people – around half of the surviving Hungarian Jews.[12]

Eduard's brother boarded the ship that was to take him to Palestine. 'But the British captured the ship and detained it in Cyprus.'

More than 70,000 would-be immigrants attempted, in the three years between the end of the war and the founding of the State of Israel, to reach Palestine on a total of 140 ships. Before they reached the coast, however, most of the ships were captured. The passengers were taken prisoner and in some cases, as with Heinrich Kornfeld, transported to Cyprus.[13]

This was a bitter disappointment, particularly for those who had been freed from German concentration camps by the British army.

EMOTIONAL SURVIVAL The liberated children and juveniles were often more familiar with impending death than they were with living. They would restlessly and desperately ask themselves searching questions: Who am I? Is my mother still alive? Where is my brother? Was my father gassed? The inmate number, tattooed on the forearm, thigh or buttocks, was the only thing that small children had to tell that they had been in Auschwitz.

They had to learn to see life from a different perspective from how it had been in the camp. They had to learn to come to terms with the emotions of survival. They had to rediscover their youth so that they could grow older like other people.

Many married early, often to people who had also survived the Shoah. Who else could they share their life with? They were connected by the experience of having survived the atrocities. For a long time in some cases, everyone else remained alien.

CHANNA MARKOWICZ AND ISRAEL (JÜRGEN, ROLF) LOEWENSTEIN
Channa was transported from Auschwitz-Birkenau via Hamburg to the Bergen-Belsen concentration camp, from where she was liberated on 15 April 1945, suffering from typhoid fever. She was put in a hospital set up there by the British.[14] It soon became the largest hospital in Europe. Medical students were fetched from the British Isles to help look after the many patients and to assist the British Red Cross, Jewish teams and a group of Quakers.

Many were so debilitated and sick that they were beyond rescue: 9,000 former inmates died by the end of April, followed by another 4,000 children, women and men in May.[15]

Channa survived. She travelled via Lübeck to Sweden on the ship *Ingrid*.[16] Some passengers had to spend a further time in hospital, others were put in a sanatorium in Malmö. At first, their lives revolved exclusively around getting well again.

They had enough to eat, but always felt it was not enough. 'It was only later that we realized that in our state of health it was not good to eat too much.'

The people looked after them with dedication and devotion. 'We looked like animals. But they came nevertheless and gave us sweets and other things.'

After Channa's health had improved, she was taken in by a family. She went to school. Her class consisted solely of former inmates. She was taught in English, Swedish and Hebrew. 'The standard was not very high.' But it was sufficient to complete the 'Folkskola'.

With the help of the Red Cross, Channa had discovered that her older brothers Schmuel and Jakov were alive. She wanted to go to them as quickly as possible. 'My brothers didn't want me to come. They didn't say why.' It was only when visiting her brothers many years later in 1964 that she discovered the reason.

At the end of the Second World War, Irshava was part of the Soviet Union.

My brothers had returned home in 1945. They lived with my uncle, who had the largest garage in the area. He had not been deported and had to repair cars and aeroplanes. He had a lot of influence. He managed to prevent a train full of Jews from departing by bribing the gendarmerie.

After the war, Schmuel and Jakov worked in his garage. They didn't want me to come because the situation at home was not good. Many returnees from the camps had been sent straight to Siberia.

After completing their schooling, Channa and her comrades were hired by a chocolate factory. The company gave them accommodation. It was a 'miniature paradise'. They lived comfortably, had enough to eat and were able to buy things. All of Channa's friends were given bags of chocolates.

But they all knew that they didn't want to remain in Sweden. Their goal was Palestine. Although Channa had been sent immigration papers for the USA by her uncle, when she began to hear more about Israel, her mind was made up: 'I don't want to go anywhere but Israel to live in a kibbutz. I want to help build the country.'

As the British controlled Palestine, Channa entered the country as a tourist on a Swedish passport. The date was 29 April 1948, her twentieth birthday.

She decided to go to Dorot kibbutz in the south. At the time, the kibbutz lived from farming. Channa worked at first in the kitchens and later as a carer in the kindergarten. There was a radio in the kibbutz and there was one programme that Channa never missed: the search announcements with the names, dates and places of birth of those who were missing. The programme was broadcast every day for several hours. Channa hoped to hear something of her family. She wrote letters until her fingers bled. Later, the newspapers published long lists with the names of the missing. 'But I didn't find anyone.'

Channa Markowicz met her future husband, Jürgen Loewenstein, in the kibbutz. He was from Berlin and had been deported to Auschwitz at the age of 17.

Jürgen was in desperate physical condition when he was liberated from the camp. 'My lungs were ruined.' He spent a year in a hospital, the TB clinic at Baumgartnerhöhe in Vienna.[17]

When he was discharged from the sanatorium after nine months, he asked himself: 'What do I do now? I want to go to Palestine.' Even as a youth, he had wanted to go there. 'My life goal was to live as a Jew in my own country. But who needed a sickly individual like myself bearing the marks of the camp?'

Back to Germany? After everything that he had experienced, that was never an option. Besides, 'no one in my family was still alive'. Jürgen decided: 'I'll look for something positive.' In Vienna, he found work in a centre for Jewish displaced persons, Jewish refugees housed in a school at Alserbachstrasse 23. Jürgen's name at this address was printed in the New York newspaper *Aufbau* on 1 March 1946 under the heading 'Jews in Vienna – 1st list of returnees from concentration camps'.[18]

At the time Jews from Poland, Hungary and Romania were beginning to flee to Vienna. They had returned initially to their homelands, but they had no family or friends there anymore. And they also often received a cold welcome from the non-Jewish population. They wanted to go to Eretz Israel.

I was working in the secretariat, compiling lists of those who wanted to emigrate. They travelled illegally to France or Italy. There were also those who wanted to join family members in the United States of America. But that was quite difficult. They needed an affidavit from relatives living there that they would support the new immigrants.

Anyone could travel to Palestine, however young or old, healthy or sick. The journey was illegal and many ships were captured by the British, who sent the passengers to Cyprus, where they were interned. This didn't change until the founding of the State of Israel in 1948.

Jürgen also wanted to go to Palestine/Israel. His aim was to live and work in a kibbutz. He would have liked to go in 1946 but he was not healthy enough. He didn't know whether he would tolerate the climate, and he didn't want to be a burden in the kibbutz. Added to that was the fact that he was doing a good and meaningful job in Vienna.

In 1947, he travelled to a Zionist seminar in Italy, where he met young women and men from Hungary, with whom he was to found the kibbutz Yad Hana some years later. It was with them at another seminar near

Rome that he experienced the founding of the State of Israel on 14 May 1948.

Jürgen Loewenstein travelled by ship to Israel in 1949.

Jürgen Loewenstein met Channa Markowicz shortly after his arrival and they got married soon afterwards. Together they followed the appeal by friends to establish the kibbutz Yad Hana. Most of the founder members came from Hungary and Austria. They had all gone through the terrible experience of deportation and concentration camps, and practically all of them had seen their families murdered by Germans.

> We talked about the past so as to get to know one another better. But mostly we talked about our hopes for the future. We wanted to live together and build up something, one for all and all for one. We saw the kibbutz as an opportunity for a socialist future where everything is shared and no one has private income. We wanted to build a completely new land and to live as a people in our own state where we felt safe so that what had happened to us and our families would never again occur.

In Israel, Jürgen didn't want to be called by his German names anymore. 'The Germans gave me the additional name "Israel" so that everyone would know immediately that I was a Jew, different, not wanted.' When he arrived in Israel, he left Jürgen Rolf behind in Germany. He felt that 'Israel' was more appropriate – the name of his new homeland, Medinat Yisrael, as the land is called in Hebrew.

Their kibbutz was named after Hannah Senesh (Szenes), a Hungarian Jew, resistance fighter and poet. She went to Palestine in 1939, studied initially in an agricultural college and then joined a kibbutz. In 1943, she volunteered for the British army and joined a Jewish brigade tasked with helping endangered Jewish communities. In 1944, she was parachuted into Yugoslavia with the aim of reaching Budapest. She crossed the border in early June, as trainload after trainload of Hungarian Jews were transported to Auschwitz and other death camps. She was arrested immediately, tortured and shot on 7 November. She was 25 years old.[19]

She wrote poems, even during her dangerous mission and while in prison. In *We Gathered Flowers* written in 1944, she expressed her hopes:

We gathered flowers in the fields and mountains,
We breathed fresh winds of spring,
We were drenched with the warmth of the sun's rays
In our Homeland, in our beloved home.

We go out to our brothers in exile,
To the suffering of winter, to frost in the night.
Our heart will bring tidings of springtime,
Our lips will sing the song of light.[20]

Yad Hana kibbutz was founded in 1950 under very difficult conditions. There was little to eat 'because there was not much in the entire country'. If they had a few olives and half a boiled egg for breakfast, that was already a feast. As there was no sugar, they sweetened their tea with jam. They could only dream of chicken, and apples were far too expensive.

When Channa bought a pair of shoes for £2 10s with the money she had earned in Sweden, everyone just shook their heads. How could she spend so much money?

Channa worked in the fields planting vegetables, with which the kibbutz earned revenue. 'When we arrived in the country, we lived in tin huts. Wooden huts were already something special.'

For many years, they had only a horse and no tractor. The kibbutz had just a few cows, which were milked by hand. The members worked in all weathers without a break, for eight hours a day. They had to wash their clothes by hand. Food was prepared on spirit burners.

In 1953, Channa began to work as a carer in the children's homes. She already had two daughters, Noomi, born in 1949, and Noga, born in 1952. 'I have always loved children.' She worked for over thirty years and was blessed with a third daughter, Naawa, in 1959.

One thing was of prime importance to the kibbutz founder generation: 'We wanted to be on good terms with our Arab neighbours.' Israel Loewenstein: 'We wanted to do better than the Germans. We worked together in the fields. We shared the water supply with the neighbouring Arab village. Their children played with the Jewish children in the kibbutz swimming pool. So that the feeling of hate would be overcome for ever.'

Israel Loewenstein returned to Auschwitz for the first time in 1965. As a delegate of the International Auschwitz Committee, he took part in the twentieth anniversary commemoration of the liberation. Thousands of former inmates from all over the world attended the event. It was a moving experience for Israel Loewenstein, not least as he met up again with people who had been in the camp with him.

When he went to the block where he had been interned, it was full of people, and there was no room for him to contemplate his own history.

In the 1960s, the kibbutz received a first request for a visit by a group of German vicars. 'A general meeting of the kibbutz was convened. We had a long discussion. In the end, we decided to make contact again with the Germans for the purpose of meeting and understanding one another.

The German group came and we spoke initially in English. We didn't sit in a circle but back to back. But it was a start.'

Channa Loewenstein learned how to make pots and to model sculptures. She made clay portraits of the people around her but also in memory of the 6 million who had been killed at the hands of other human beings. One of her works was called *My Parents* in commemoration of Awraham and Zseni Markowicz, who had been gassed in Auschwitz.

For many years, she gave courses in sculpture. 'Anyone can make something out of clay, whether they are one year old or 120.'

She always lived and worked in the kibbutz and didn't want to move to the city. Over the years, the original idealism was accompanied by a large degree of scepticism. 'Today people come to the kibbutzim because the life there is more comfortable than in the city. Everything has more of a material emphasis than those who founded and built up the kibbutz wanted. I always knew that the kibbutz was not an oasis but also influenced by people from outside.'

She believed as long as she lived that the time in the kibbutz was 'the most beautiful in our life'. Nowhere else could she have met 'such a community of people'.

For Channa and Israel Loewenstein, a dream came true in spite of all the economic and other problems that were a permanent feature of the kibbutz. Until Channa's death on 27 December 2014, they enjoyed living in a nice house. 'Today we have stone houses with all conveniences.

Everyone has a radio and television. You can even go to university', she said proudly.

On the other hand, Channa was sorry that, because of economic constraints, for some years her kibbutz had no longer existed 'in its original communal form. We have become a "normal" village.' The houses are now owned privately, some of the land leased, and there are no joint festivities anymore, no healthcare within the kibbutz. 'Everyone has to look after himself.' The *chadar ochel* or dining hall as a central meeting place no longer existed. This was something that Channa had difficulty coming to terms with.

The Loewensteins travelled several times to Berlin, for the first time in 1980. They went to East Berlin, because Israel wanted to show Channa 'his' Berlin, or at least what was left of the old Scheunenviertel. On this day, the positive memories prevailed. 'People always try to push aside bad memories.'

They visited Paderborn, where Israel had been a forced labourer in 1942–3, for the first time in summer 1989. Only ten of the hundred or so members of the Paderborn group survived the Nazi era.

The visits to Paderborn were important experiences for Channa and Israel: 'We didn't speak there just about the past; it was important for us to meet the people who live in Paderborn today to discuss and clarify current and past problems of life and particularly the relationship between Germans and Jews. I think I made new friends there.'

Surviving documents enabled Israel Loewenstein, who died in February 2018, to trace the fate of his parents. They confirm that Paula and Walter Loewenstein were taken from their apartment on 3 December 1942 and deported on 9 December to Auschwitz on the twenty-fourth transport to the East. A day later, the arrival of 1,060 people was registered. The entry for 10 December in *Auschwitz Chronicle* states: 'After the selection, 137 men and 25 women are admitted to the camp and receive Nos. 81263–81399 and 26621–26645. The remaining 898 people are killed in the gas chambers.'[21]

Israel's parents were probably among those murdered. 'At any event, I never again heard anything from them.'

In the records on Theresienstadt in the kibbutz Givat Haim, Israel found his grandmother's name, Agathe Sochaczewer (*née* Rosenthal), deported on 7 August 1942 from Berlin to Theresienstadt. Only one person from this transport survived until liberation. Israel's grandmother died in Theresienstadt on 6 December 1942.

On 16 April 2002, three 'Stolpersteine' (stumbling blocks) were unveiled for Israel's parents and grandmother at Almstadtstrasse 49, their last place of residence before deportation. 'Stolpersteine' is the name given by the artist Gunter Demnig to the concrete cubes on which 10 × 10 cm brass plates are fixed with brief details of the victims of the Nazi dictatorship engraved on them. Over 75,000 'Stolpersteine' have been installed in around 1,200 cities and municipalities in Germany and in twenty-five other countries since 1995. The blocks recall murdered Jews, Sinti, Roma, Social Democrats, Communists, homosexuals and euthanasia victims.

'It means a lot to me that my parents and my grandmother are recalled here. These "Stolpersteine" are very personal for me. They are a discreet mark of the special respect that is due to them.'

DÁŠA FRIEDOVÁ (DASHA LEWIN) was taken with other former inmates at the end of May / beginning of June 1945 by truck from Bergen-Belsen to Prague. Aid committees on the streets of Prague greeted the returnees. They wrote down their names, displayed long lists, informed the people who had arrived and who was looking for family members.

Dáša found one of her mother's brothers again. Jan Schlappl was married to a non-Jew and had survived in a labour camp in Bohemia.

His wife Marie asked Dáša on her arrival: 'What would you like to eat?' She replied: 'Potatoes and knackwurst.' She had dreamed of this in the camp. Her aunt had thought that after all the years of deprivation she would want something special and repeated in disbelief: 'Potatoes and knackwurst?' 'Yes', Dáša replied. And that's what she was served.

She remained only for a short time with her uncle's family because there was not much room there. 'My uncle, his wife, her sister and the two children lived together in a two-room apartment.' For a while afterwards she lived with a family by the name of Kott. Irma Kottová had been with Dáša and her friend Dagmar in the camp. 'They had a nice apartment in Prague-Vinohrady.' Dáša had the maid's room.

In Prague, she found a friend of her parents. He was a professor and took her to the village of Bernartice near Milevsko, where his parents had a house. Dáša had private tuition with him. After six weeks, she finally had her school-leaving certificate. She then applied successfully to a commercial college in Prague. Her fellow students helped her to cope. 'They knew that I was alone. The girls were always inviting me to their homes.'

Dáša often spent the night with Vilma Vávrova, who became a close friend. 'Her mother was pleased at our friendship. Whenever I visited Vilma, she washed my clothes.'

By this time, Dáša had rented a small room. Vilma's mother visited frequently, cleaned, washed her clothes and looked after her belongings. 'I couldn't manage with normal daily affairs. I had never learned to wash clothes, to sew or to cook. Because I had been in the camp, every meal was a good one. For example, I bought precooked goulash and ate it for three days in a row. "Heavenly", I thought.'

One day she visited an old friend of her father. 'I was completely taken aback when he produced the money that my father had given him to look after before our deportation.' With this money she was able to pay her way while at school.

Through the Red Cross, Dáša discovered an uncle who had fled from the Nazis to Canada. He and an aunt who had also fled to Canada regularly sent her parcels. She was supported as well by UNRRA, the United Nations refugee organization.

After graduating from commercial college, Dáša was given back some of her family's possessions: the 100-hectare farm not far from Terezín (Theresienstadt). Dáša moved to the farm in Lukavec. 'I felt at home there. It's a wonderful place to live.' Someone who knew about farming helped her. He managed the farm and she took charge of the paying salaries and purchasing. They were able to grow vegetables and strawberries.

The Communist Party came to power in Czechoslovakia in 1948. 'I was forced to give up my property and work.'

Dáša was allowed initially to continue living in her family's house. She was ordered to report for work in a factory in Neštěmice near Ústí nad Labem. 'I had to fill small bags with baking powder.' She travelled by train to work at 4 a.m. and returned home at 5 p.m. 'That was really tough.'

Dáša had many different jobs in subsequent years. She worked in a sugar factory, then she did the payroll for another company, was employed in a mine office, then in a planning institute, and finally in a language school in Prague.

'Wherever I was, people would look at me askance and say to my face: "What are you doing here with your bourgeois background?" They were not interested in what I'd gone through in the camp or that I'd lost my family. Or they said: "You have relatives in North America. You can't be trusted. You could divulge company secrets."'

In the planning institute Dáša made friends with Lily Špirová. 'She invited me to her home every Friday. As I only had a washbasin in my room, I always took a bath when I visited.' She often spent the whole weekend with this Jewish family.

In 1960, Dáša met and fell in love with a 'gentleman from California' at this family's house. His name was Maury Lewin. He was from Los Angeles and was visiting his father, who lived in Prague. They married on 25 April 1962 in Prague after waiting two years for permission from the Czech authorities to marry and emigrate to the USA.

The young married couple left Prague in June 1962. All of their friends came to the train station to see them off, including Dáša's best friend Dagmar, who had been living in Prague since the 1950s after years in the sanatorium.

Dáša feared that she would never see Dagmar, whom she had met in Theresienstadt, or her other friends ever again. 'I thought that the Communist government of Czechoslovakia would not let me back in.' They said goodbye with tears in their eyes. 'My life is falling apart', thought Dáša as she waved through the carriage window at the friends she was leaving behind.

With her marriage and move to the USA, she changed her name from Dáša Friedová to Dasha Lewin.

Soon after her arrival in Los Angeles, she found work with the cosmetics manufacturer Neutrogena. The company had around forty employees and was growing rapidly. Dasha Lewin enjoyed her work and she studied at the University of California at the same time. Every time the company grew, her position there improved, and she rose to become vice-president.

In summer 1966, she returned to Prague for the first time since her move. It was surprisingly easy to obtain permission. Afterwards, she and her husband frequently visited Dagmar and her husband Petr and stayed with them in Prague. They had extended breakfasts together and talked at length in the night.

In 1992, Dasha and Maury bought a house in Prague. The Velvet Revolution in 1989 had also opened up new possibilities for them in Czechoslovakia. After their retirement, they spent many summers together in Prague.

Dasha and her husband travelled extensively and were often in Germany, including Berlin. Whenever she met Germans who were a bit older than she was, she couldn't help wondering if any of them had been responsible for sending people to their death.

In 2002, Dasha and her husband visited Auschwitz-Birkenau for the first time. 'As soon as I entered the barracks in Birkenau, I remembered what I had been through there. I could see it all in my mind's eye. And when we saw the hair and the spectacles in the exhibition, I remembered that I had also lost my glasses in Birkenau. I felt sick to my soul.'

Everywhere in Birkenau the earth was mixed with the ashes of those who had been murdered. Dasha filled a small plastic bag. 'I took the earth to our family grave in Prague.' To the Jewish cemetery, where Maury Lewin found his final resting place in 2006. 'One day I would like to be buried here next to my husband', said Dasha at the time. She died a year later and was buried next to him.

Dasha never regretted going to California. She and her husband had a nice house and friends and were integrated in the Jewish community. They felt safe and had a good life until Maury's death.

In Los Angeles, Dasha was one of the founders of Facing History and Ourselves. She spoke on many occasions to school classes. 'We tried to highlight the mistakes, tragedies, humiliation and degradations of the past and present': education as an answer to antisemitism and racism. She was aware of the limitations. 'In spite of Auschwitz, people are still marginalized, taunted, beaten, raped and murdered.' She was convinced: 'Many people have learned nothing.'

Dasha saw her personal experience with the opera *Brundibár* in California as a hopeful sign. It was very popular with schools and children. She would introduce the opera, describing how it had been performed in Theresienstadt and speaking of the life there. 'We touch a nerve in the children. Especially the children acting and singing in the opera, but also those in the audience. That hit home more than any talk.'

After a performance in Seattle, a boy came up to her, took her hand, kissed her arm at the place where her number was tattooed and said: 'I never want to live the way you had to.' Dasha felt the tears well up in her eyes.

She didn't want sympathy: 'No child should ever have to put up with what I experienced. I will do what I can to help.' She would think repeatedly of the finale of *Brundibár*, the most successful children's opera in the world today:

> You must build on friendship,
> walk the path together,
> trust in your strength,
> stand firm with each other.

DAGMAR FANTLOVÁ wrote to Františka Holická in mid-April 1945, immediately after her liberation from Bergen-Belsen. After the Fantl family had been deported, Františka had to move out of the apartment in her hometown of Kutná Hora. Dagmar received a reply from Professor František Malý, where the grandparents' former housekeeper had been renting a room since the end of 1942. He said that Dagmar could live in his house until her parents returned.

After Dagmar was finally able to get back on her feet following several months in hospital, she took the first train possible from Bergen-Belsen to Czechoslovakia in the summer of 1945.[22]

František Malý met Dagmar in Prague and drove in a borrowed car to Kutná Hora. 'I had a bath straightaway and something to eat. Everyone was afraid that I would eat too much. But it was already three months since the liberation. I had got used to eating again. I was constantly hungry and never full. This feeling of never having enough was to last for the next two months.'

Dagmar was still in very poor health. In early August, she was taken to a sanatorium in eastern Bohemia. 'Only, as I later discovered, because a doctor's daughter should have a place to die. I must have been seriously ill.'

She spent two and a half years in the sanatorium. Her parents and sister had not returned. František Malý was her guardian.

Dagmar was able to return to Kutná Hora in February 1948.[23] She had to take care of herself, rest a lot and gradually accustom herself to a 'normal' life. She started playing piano again and wanted to improve her English and go to school. 'I had only had five years of schooling and wanted at least to complete the Quarta [year 7].'

She did this at the age of 20, and two years later even managed the Abitur [school leaving certificate and university entry qualification]. She started a five-year course of German and Czech studies at the University of Prague. Almost every weekend she travelled to her grandparents' former housekeeper, whom she called 'Aunt Fany'. During the semester breaks, she had to work to earn money. The small annuity she received, later a scholarship, was not enough to live on.

She got married in October 1955 and was called Lieblová thereafter. The family of her husband, Petr Liebl, had also been in the camp. 'My husband came from České Budějovice (Budweis), which was bilingual at the time. He grew up speaking both Czech and German. But after the camp, his family didn't want to speak German anymore.'

Dagmar's first daughter was born in February 1956. 'I named her Rita, after my sister.' She completed her studies in autumn of that year and took on a position as a teacher in a secondary school while her husband completed his mathematics degree.

In May 1959, Dagmar Lieblová gave birth to a second daughter, Zuzana. A year later, she was offered a position in a Prague language school. Her husband had the opportunity at the time to work for twelve months in a computing centre in the Soviet Union. 'We travelled there with the children, who were four and a half and one and a half at the time.'

Returning to Prague in 1961, they moved into a housing association apartment they had bought and remained there until 1965, before moving to Ghana for three years. Dagmar taught German and occasionally Russian at the Institute of Languages, while her husband was a mathematics lecturer at the university.

The family returned to Prague in July 1968. In the night of 20–21 August, Soviet ground and airborne troops invaded Czechoslovakia with the assistance of units from East Germany, Poland, Hungary and

Bulgaria: a violent end to the Prague Spring, the attempt at 'socialism with a human face'. Academic friends of the family returned to Africa, and in some cases from there to the West.

Dagmar was heavily pregnant, and in September her son Martin was born. She couldn't and didn't want to leave her homeland. 'I love Prague. This is my home. I would never be able to stay away too long', she said many times.

She taught for over twenty years at the Institute of Translation Studies of Charles University. After her retirement in 1991, she worked as a freelance translator, translating a book about Jugendstil and several guides to Prague into Czech, and articles in the series *Theresienstädter Studien und Dokumente* into German.

Until her death in 2018, she was passionate about her honorary chairmanship of the Terezín Initiative founded in 1991. Former Jewish inmates in Theresienstadt and other Nazi concentration camps had a great need after the downfall of Communism to have an independent association of their own, she related.

'We recall the victims of the Nazi regime through eyewitness accounts in schools, cultural events and the publication of newsletters. It is important for us that no one forgets these crimes. We also provide assistance with health problems and attempt to improve the quality of life of particularly needy survivors.'

In the last decade of her life, Dagmar Lieblová accompanied numerous Czech, German and international youth groups and school classes to the former camps in Theresienstadt and Bergen-Belsen. She has attempted to provide explanations to the young people, spoke about her own experiences, answered questions, had discussions with the young people and recalled 'those who didn't make it'.

Dagmar's husband, now also deceased, worked from 1991 as a tourist guide in Prague, 'which he enjoyed immensely'. Her daughters have long completed their studies. Rita is a psychologist, married a Canadian in 1987 and now lives in Canada. 'She is happy and contented.' Zuzana is a doctor and has three sons called Mikoláš, Daniel and Vavřinec. Martin studied mathematics for a time and worked afterwards in an international media group. He is the father of three children called Helena, Klara and Vojtěch.

Every year, Dagmar's friend Dasha came to Prague from Los Angeles to visit with her husband Maury Lewin, until the summer of 2006, when Maury died unexpectedly at the age of 75. 'And Dasha died just a year later.' Dagmar Lieblová, her husband Petr and their children visited Dasha and Maury several times in California. When Dagmar visited for the first time on her own in 1986, they went on an excursion with a tourist agency. 'The courier would say: "Your sister's already here." We didn't say anything – she thought Dasha and I were sisters.'

EDUARD KORNFELD was liberated from Dachau at the end of January 1945. After spending several weeks in a US army field hospital, he was fit enough to return to Bratislava.

The liberation of Czechoslovakia had begun in eastern Slovakia in September 1944. In mid-March 1945, the first Moravian village was liberated by the Red Army. Eduard's hometown of Bratislava was liberated at the end of April.[24]

'The Czech people welcomed us very warmly. They gave us all kinds of food. We were invited to people's homes to recover. Lots of people brought cakes to the train platforms because they had heard that we were returning from the camps. They even wanted to give us money. It was incredible.'

When Eduard arrived in the part of Czechoslovakia controlled by the Red Army, he was questioned in the train by Russian soldiers because he was wearing SS riding breeches and had an SS cap with him, together with heavy boots from the Americans. He had been given these things in Dachau. 'There was no other clothing there.' The SS rank insignia and death's head had been removed, however. In Dachau he had been given a provisional ID card, which he now had to produce. The Russian soldiers were surprised at his clothing but, realizing that he had been in the camp, they left him alone.

Eduard received so many gifts – bread, cakes, drinks – that he left a lot behind when he changed trains. It was impossible to carry everything with him. Later, in Slovakia, the situation was completely different. 'No one cared a jot about us.' There was not even enough to eat there.

When he arrived in Bratislava, the first thing was to find somewhere to live. He asked everywhere. Some houses had been set aside for 'uprooted' returnees like himself. But they were bare and didn't even have beds. Eduard then went to one of the apartments that had been owned by his parents. 'But strangers were living there.'

Someone told him that there was a clinic where he could report. It was in a house where a rabbi had lived previously. He stayed there. One of his cousins discovered him there a few days later. She, her seven brothers and sisters, her parents and another uncle, his wife and their six children had been deported with him in June 1944 from Komárno to Auschwitz. She was the only one to have survived.

12 July 1945: Eduard was in relatively poor health and was still suffering from tuberculosis. Together with around 300 other survivors, he was sent on this day to a state sanatorium in the High Tatra mountains. His cousin was also in the group and took loving care of him. 'She was like my dearest sister.'

There were around 200 Jewish and 350 non-Jewish patients in the sanatorium. They got on quite well together. 'I felt most comfortable, however, with the Jewish boys and girls.' The Jewish children and juveniles had quickly found each other, as if connected by a thread. They formed groups of around 30 people and talked about everything together.

At first Eduard thought: 'They all come from non-religious Jewish families.' None of them was a practising Jew. They ate everything that was served to them – not least as there was no kosher food just after the war. They were mostly given pork, ham and even bacon. 'It's good for you', they were told.

Although the Jewish children and juveniles assumed that the others were from non-religious households, it turned out that they had all been brought up religiously. This might well have been the reason why they all felt most comfortable in each other's company.

On the other hand, 'they were not interested in religion anymore'. They were put off by it. After Auschwitz, Dachau and Bergen-Belsen, they had been unable to retain a belief in God. Eduard also 'struggled and thought a lot' after being liberated. He firmly believed at the time: 'That's not possible, there can't be a God.' He thought of the hundreds of innocent lives he had seen taken, in Auschwitz, Dachau and Bergen-Belsen. He decided that he wanted nothing more to do with religion.

The care, the medical treatment, the discussions, the regular meals, had their effect. Many returned slowly to the world. Eduard no longer thought of the atrocities 'every second of the day'.

They were sometimes a bit high-spirited. 'Sometimes we would simply run away from the sanatorium.' They would travel to Bratislava for a couple of days. The 330-kilometre journey took six to seven hours. They would sleep somewhere in the train station. 'We weren't allowed out, in fact. It was strictly forbidden. But we were young. They couldn't kick us out. Where would we go? We didn't have homes anymore.'

On one of these visits to Bratislava, they ventured into an area where lots of Jewish families had lived before the Nazis. That was in 1946. The children and juveniles from the sanatorium were all camp survivors, and they were all without parents. They ran through the streets 'in pure delight' and chatted excitedly. It was Friday evening. Then, through a window, they saw the lit Shabbat candles.

> We cleared off at once to another street. The sight of it! We hadn't talked about it. No one said anything. But the pain was too great, the memory of home and the lost world. It was like being stabbed with a knife. We felt as if we were running away from a machine gun.
>
> For many years, every Jewish holiday was a time of suffering for me. I didn't want to think about it but I couldn't help recalling my wonderful childhood, the holidays and festivals. The pain was indescribably intense.

Eduard's cousin had by now been sent by a Jewish organization to a sanatorium in Switzerland, after her condition had failed to improve in the High Tatra. 'We were told that Davos, which was world-famous, was the right place to recover. And my cousin was insistent: she wanted me to come to Switzerland as well.' Eduard's condition had improved in the meantime, but then he had a relapse. 'It went on like that for a while.'

One time, when he thought he was on the road to recovery, he went to Bratislava. He wanted to go regularly to the doctor and to start a new life. He had managed to recover the apartments that had belonged to his parents and was able to live well from the rent. But his health deteriorated again. He had neglected the treatment. The temptations of the newly found freedom were simply too great.

At the same time, the 'atmosphere under the Communists became increasingly unbearable'. Expropriations, enforced conformity of the media, arrests of democratic politicians and dissidents were commonplace. The 'restructuring' of the country on the Soviet model was well under way. And to cap it all, Eduard was enlisted into the army, despite his health. He protested, said that he had been in Auschwitz and produced his disabled pass. To no avail. The authorities told him: 'You look well enough for office work.'

He called his cousin in Switzerland and told her everything. She said immediately: 'Don't stay there. Come to Davos. Right now!'

That was easier said than done. Eduard needed a passport to leave. 'Except for prominent politicians, no one was allowed to leave the country at the time. The legal possibilities for leaving were strictly controlled by the Communists.'

Eduard thought of a way out. He looked up a very good friend with whom he had shared a room in the sanatorium in the High Tatra. Right after the war, he had obtained a leading position in the Zionist socialist youth organization Hashomer Hatzair, which prepared juveniles for Aliyah, immigration to Palestine/Israel and life in a kibbutz. In 1950, organizations such as Hashomer Hatzair were banned as foreign organizations.

This friend was now working in a ministry in Bratislava. He spoke to his supervisor about Eduard and managed to obtain a passport valid for a limited duration. It said 'via Austria, Italy and so on to Palestine'. But Eduard still wanted to go to Switzerland.

He left the country by train on 28 August 1949, 'three days before the passport expired'. He had only been allowed to take the bare necessities with him: a couple of shirts, trousers, underwear, shoes. He was also given 100 Austrian schillings from the Slovakian Tatra Bank. 'I kept the closest eye on this money. It was all I had.'

The first stops on the way to Switzerland were Vienna and Steyr. Altogether, he remained three months in Austria.[25] He was put in one of the camps set up after the war to temporarily house displaced persons (DPs) from Germany, Italy and Austria. In these camps and elsewhere at the end of 1946, there were an estimated 250,000 Jewish children, women and men who had survived the forced labour, concentration and extermination camps and the death marches.[26]

With the aid of the American Jewish Joint Distribution Committee, which had been supporting persecuted Jews throughout the world since 1914, Eduard was able to continue the medical treatment for his lungs. 'One side on Monday, the other on Thursday.' He was in continuous contact with his cousin in the sanatorium in Davos. 'She did everything to enable me to get to Switzerland as quickly as possible.' She was helped by an uncle and aunt of Eduard, and their children, who had lived in Yugoslavia and escaped from the Nazis via Italy to Zurich. One of their sons had been murdered in Zagreb.

Eduard finally obtained a visa. To fetch it, he had to go to the Swiss consulate in Salzburg, which was a further worry. 'I didn't have a valid passport anymore. I needed one without fail for the Swiss authorities.'

Eduard found help from a former school colleague, whom he had met in the DP camp. 'He knew all the tricks' and put an extension in the passport. 'What he wrote was full of mistakes, neither proper Slovak nor proper Czech.' Fortunately, no one noticed, and Eduard got his immigration papers. It was the end of November 1949, and after his relatives had sent him a ticket, he was finally able to travel to Switzerland.

Eduard was admitted immediately to the Etania Jewish sanatorium in Davos, where he once again met his cousin, who had ultimately made it possible for him to come to Switzerland. He was suitably grateful to her.

A few days after his arrival, one of the 'nice lads', with whom he was sharing a room, said to him: 'Come, I'd like you to meet a nice kid.' They entered his room. 'He was in plaster from head to toe. I was shocked to see him. He had pulmonary and spinal tuberculosis.'

That is how Eduard Kornfeld and Otto Klein met. 'He was a really nice lad' and it was the start of a wonderful friendship.

Like Eduard and Otto, many of the patients in the Etania sanatorium were concentration camp survivors. They spoke constantly about it, as they had done in the sanatorium in the High Tatra and were to do for decades afterwards, whenever they met. 'That was our salvation; otherwise we would have gone mad.'

In 1951 came the long awaited day: at the age of 22, Eduard was finally able to leave the sanatorium. He was offered a trainee position in Zurich as a gemstone setter, but he needed a residence permit to start there. The Swiss refugee aid organization made an application for him to the Swiss immigration authorities. They replied saying that he had to leave Switzerland within three months. After a number of personal interviews, however, he managed to have his residence permit extended again and again.

In Zurich, he lived with an 'elderly Jewish gentleman', whom he had met a few months previously in the sanatorium. He was a widower and lived alone in a four-room apartment. Eduard could have lived with him rent-free but he didn't want to. 'I didn't want to feel like a beggar.' They agreed on a rent of 100 francs a month, although as an apprentice he only received 250 francs.

The apprenticeship was without problems, but once a year Eduard had to report to the immigration authorities in Zurich. 'I was only given a residence permit for twelve months at a time.' After completing his apprenticeship, he obtained employment in the long established and well-known Meister company on Bahnhofstrasse, which had been making, selling and repairing clocks, watches, jewellery and silver since 1881.

After a couple of years, he decided that he wanted to become independent. He had acquired sufficient experience and wanted to be his own boss and to work in his own way. Now he needed approval not only from the immigration authorities but also from the department of employment. 'I said that because of my frail health I wanted to set up a workshop at home.'

He was given the necessary approval and he set up a small workshop in the apartment of the old Jewish gentleman, where he now worked on contract for several Zurich jewellers. His work was highly appreciated. Without asking the immigration authorities and department of employment, he rented a small workshop on Bleicheweg so as to be close to his customers. It was just round the corner from Bahnhofstrasse, where the jewellers had their businesses. This made it much easier for Eduard to work and it paid off. His business grew and he was soon supplying jewellers wholesale.

'I often had to struggle in order to succeed. Without a strong will and perseverance I would never have reached my aim of not having to count every cent. I wasn't given any handouts.'

He finally obtained a permanent residence permit and, two years later in 1965, Eduard acquired Swiss citizenship and the red passport with a white cross that went with it.

Eight years earlier, he had met Ruth Meissner during a holiday in the Swiss mountains. They married three years later. He found it difficult to talk to her about his life. At first, they knew only that he had been in

Auschwitz and that she had fled from the Nazis with her family, first to Prague and then to Italy and finally to Switzerland.

'I didn't want to burden our newly found happiness with the sad story of my family and all the terrible things I had experienced.'

It was years before they were able to speak about what had happened to them during the Nazi era. Sometimes they would hear things incidentally, particularly when they were with other survivors. 'All night, until they were ready to collapse', they would talk about their families and about Auschwitz.

Eduard and Ruth Kornfeld had three children, two sons and a daughter. The oldest, Alexander, was born in 1963, Rita in 1964 and Richard in 1967.

FERENC AND OTTO KLEIN Their protector in Auschwitz, Zvi Ernö Spiegel, who had been their block kapo and repeatedly warned the twins about the dangers in the camp, was liberated with Ferenc and Otto at the end of January 1945. He was 28 years old, and spoke all of the Slavic languages as well as Hungarian, Yiddish and German. He was afraid to stay in Auschwitz, fearing that the Germans would return, and wanted to leave immediately. 'The thirty-six children and juveniles, all twins, said that we would go with him.' He agreed and helped them. 'Without him we wouldn't have made it.'

A day after liberation, they set off on foot. Ferenc and Otto wanted to go to Budapest and from there to Bucharest, and then directly to Palestine. 'Our home had been taken from us.' After all they had been through, they didn't want to stay in Europe. 'We knew that our mother was no longer alive and hoped to find our father and sister somewhere.'

In icy cold weather – 'it was 20 degrees Celsius below zero' – they started out on an odyssey lasting several weeks. They had to walk at first but later found a military truck that took them in the direction of Kraków. The truck had an accident and one of the twins was killed. Another child was later run over by a truck.

They arrived in Kraków a few days later. 'We were stuck there for ten days. The Russian soldiers didn't allow us to cross the Vistula.' Zvi Ernö Spiegel ultimately found a 'Polish office' that issued them 'a kind of pass for the Vistula bridge'. The journey continued, on foot at first and then in Russian military trucks.

They spent one night in a wooden hut where straw was stored. 'It was freezing. We set fire to the straw and the hut burnt down in no time.' They fled in fear of what the villagers would say.

'They're Jews', people hurled at them in another village. 'We were not wanted. They threw stones at us.' A Russian soldier intervened and took them to a nearby nunnery. The nuns allowed them to sleep in the chapel. 'It was locked. As there were no toilets in the church, we had to do our business where we were. We were all sick from the camp and had diarrhoea.' Once again, the survivors feared the consequences, so they broke the windows and fled.

Their meandering journey – 'we didn't even have a map' – took them to the Polish–Russian border. A Russian officer who spoke Yiddish asked them: 'Who are you? Where are you going? Do you want to enter the Soviet Union? You can do so, but you won't get out again. I advise you to go back to Poland as fast as possible.'

He helped them – 'he was fabulous' – and attached a railway wagon to a Russian military train heading for Slovakia. In two days, they covered more distance than they had in the previous six weeks.

More and more twins left on the way and changed trains, travelling to Prague, for example. Ferenc and Otto and others left the train at the Polish–Slovak border. They wanted to get to Budapest.

In Miskolc, where their mother's family had lived, they had to change trains. At the station, by chance, they ran into a Jew whom they vaguely knew and asked him about their family. He told them 'some of your mother's brothers, an aunt, a male and a female cousin are alive'.

They went to a house where relatives lived. Otto rang the doorbell. A cousin opened the door and asked: 'What do you want?' The twins answered: 'Don't you recognize us?' When they told her, 'she almost fainted'.

She summoned her father, who saw immediately that something was wrong with Otto. He felt his forehead and said: 'You have a temperature. You can't go on. You're staying here.' Otto had a high fever.

Their relatives told them that two of their mother's brothers had hidden from the Nazis and avoided deportation in that way. Their aunt had gone to Budapest. 'She survived there with forged papers.' The third uncle had been saved by the Swiss consul Carl Lutz.

Word spread among the liberated Jews of Miskolc that Otto and

Ferenc had been interned in Auschwitz. They all wanted to know if the stories about the gas chambers were true. 'They'd heard about them but couldn't believe it.' The twins told them what they had seen with their own eyes. 'Now they believed the terrible truth.'

The 13-year-old twins stayed in Miskolc. They both had tuberculosis. 'Fortunately, my brother was not as sick as I was. I had tuberculosis not only of the lungs but also of the spine.' Otto was put in a hospital run by the American Jewish Joint Distribution Committee, the most important pan-European aid organization for liberated Jews.[27] He was later transferred to a sanatorium in Budapest.

'For months my whole body was in plaster and I could barely move. But I wasn't in the hospital the whole time. My brother and I lived with our uncle. He looked after us and gave us a new life. I wasn't allowed to go to school because of my illness and had private lessons.'

In August 1945, the twins saw their sister again. 'She had heard that we were in Miskolc.' They only discovered that she was alive two days before she arrived. 'What an occasion it was when we were able to hold her in our arms again.' She lived with her brothers at her uncle's house.

They went to their hometown Hajdúböszörmény together. 'Everything from our house had disappeared.' Otto was not able to retrieve even a single keepsake. After 1948, under the Communists, their land and houses were declared abandoned property and taken over by the state. Their house was demolished, and apartments were built on the site. Nothing that their family had owned was ever restituted to them.

Otto and Ferenc remained for three years in Miskolc with their sister Ágnes. They tried to emigrate for the first time in 1946. Four of their mother's brothers lived in the USA, having emigrated there early in the twentieth century.

'We went to the US consulate in Budapest but were told we needed a valid Hungarian passport in order to apply for a visa.' After they had obtained passports, there were 'repeated problems with the issuance of a US visa.'

Their passports were valid until the end of 1948. 'We have to get out now, otherwise we'll never get out', they thought, after the Social Democrats had been forced to unite with the Communists and bourgeois parties were banned.[28] An uncle who lived in Paris obtained a French visa for them. The twins and their sister travelled with the uncle and aunt with whom they had lived in Miskolc. They had a transit visa for Switzerland. Otto was still very ill. He got out at the border station in Sargans. An uncle living in Zurich had arranged for him to go to a sanatorium in Davos.

It was with a heavy heart that he left his twin brother. They had been together for all of their lives, apart from the four months Otto had spent in a Budapest hospital. He had managed then because it had only been for a limited time. They had not even been apart in Auschwitz. 'And now?' When would he see Ferenc again? He was 'quite anxious'.

Otto's relatives travelled on to Paris, where they waited a year for a US visa. At the end of 1949, they emigrated to the USA with the aid of an uncle who lived in El Paso, Texas. It was he who paid for Otto's time in the sanatorium.

Otto Klein met Eduard Kornfeld, who also had tuberculosis, at the Etania Jewish sanatorium in Davos. They became close friends. Many of the patients in the sanatorium were often the sole survivors of former large Jewish families. Day and night, for years, they talked about persecution, camps, murder. Otto Klein: 'These discussions enabled me to carry on living in spite of Auschwitz. For me they were the best therapy.'

In Davos, Otto was put in plaster again. 'For a year and a half.' His only wish at first was to leave the sanatorium in good health. It took him five years.

Finally, in 1953, at the age of 21, he was discharged. He hoped to be able to meet up again soon with his brother and sister in the USA, but he didn't have a visa. In the meantime, he attended a private business school in Basel, where he learned German. He graduated two years later.

But now he had incredible problems with the immigration authorities. A relative stood surety for him and promised to finance him, 'So that I wouldn't be a burden to the Swiss.' But it didn't help. Otto had to leave Basel canton.

In 1955, he went to Geneva. In Basel, he had had a residence permit only for three months at a time. He went to see the immigration authorities in Geneva. 'What do you want to do here?' 'Study French?' The official looked at him questioningly. 'Do you think you can learn the language in three months? I'll give you a year.'

After that, Otto had no great difficulties anymore. His residence permit was extended every year. He was later given a permit to settle, renewable every three years. He became a Swiss citizen in 1968, 'which was quite an achievement'.

His sister Ágnes married Tibor Schaechner in New York in April 1956 and had three daughters, Lillian, Audrey and Susie. Tibor was from Budapest. After the German troops occupied Hungary on 19 March 1944, the 16-year-old had to toil in a labour battalion building tank barriers. One day he missed the transport and took public transport to the building site. Before they reached the city limits, the bus driver told him that the work battalions would be broken up and that he and the other boys were to be deported. Tibor jumped out of the bus and survived in this way. 'Of 179 boys in his work battalion, not one returned.'[29]

Ágnes studied in El Paso and San Antonio and obtained bachelor's and master's degrees. Otto Klein: 'My sister then devoted herself to social work in El Paso.' She needed dialysis for many years, and died in Texas in 1998.

Ágnes Schaechner (*née* Klein) refused to talk about her experiences in Auschwitz-Birkenau and the other camps. Shortly before she died, she nevertheless told Otto Klein something: 'not much, just that she had been in the Women's Camp in Birkenau. In October 1944, at the age of 14, she was taken somewhere in north Germany and performed slave labour in several camps, including in a secret underground factory making aircraft parts.'

Otto's sister was liberated on 9 April 1945, by members of the 9th US Army, from Salzwedel,[30] a satellite camp of Neuengamme, established in July–August 1944, a good 100 kilometres north of Magdeburg. Women worked at the Polte-Werk on twelve-hour shifts making infantry and flak ammunition. Most of the 1,520 girls and women, including Ágnes, were from Hungary, but there were also some from Poland, Greece, Czechoslovakia and Germany. Women from other camps arrived in March–April, and around 3,000 were liberated a short while afterwards. Ágnes Klein was 15 years old.[31]

In a video interview with the managers of the Holocaust Museum in El Paso, Ágnes Schaechner explained why she never spoke of her experiences in Auschwitz and the camps: 'I was thinking why not, and

I believe I wanted to be as "normal" as I could be. I didn't want to be "different". I wanted to be just a normal, regular person.'[32] She didn't want to talk about Auschwitz-Birkenau or for it to be an important part of her life. She just wanted her daughters, her husband, her relatives, friends and life in El Paso to be the centre of her life – and not Auschwitz-Birkenau and the other camps.

After his arrival in the USA, Ferenc Klein had purchased a small truck in Brooklyn, New York, and made local deliveries. He performed his military service in the US army in Japan. Then he went to El Paso and had a successful office-supply wholesale business.

He never married. He died of kidney failure in 1986, at the age of 54. Otto never really recovered from this: 'It was an indescribable shock for me. I was touched to the core. In spite of the distance, I always had an emotional tie to my brother. We saw each other at least once a year in Israel, the US or Switzerland.'

Otto married in 1976 but later separated. 'Although she wasn't Jewish', he was able to talk to her about his past. She had read a lot about the Nazi era. For a long time after their separation, she would call and tell him about an article or book he should read.

Otto travelled several times to Hungary after 1968. On his visits, he recognized lots of places from earlier and rediscovered other things. 'But I didn't know anyone. No one!' Not in Miskolc, where he had lived for several years, nor in Hajdúböszörmény, where he was born and spent the first eleven years of his life.

In 1969, only 16 Jews were left in Hajdúböszörmény of a pre-war population of 1,000.[33] The synagogue Otto went to as a child still stands. 'But the last time I was there it had become a furniture warehouse.'

For around fifteen years, Otto visited schools to talk about his life. He gave interviews for newspapers and appeared on the television. He had very good experiences with schoolchildren and juveniles. 'Now people ask us about Auschwitz', he said once. 'Quite unlike the first decades after the war: non-Jews were not interested.' At least that was 'my experience'.

Otto returned to Birkenau and Auschwitz for the first time in 1986. He made his way alone through the huge site of the former camp. He went to where Block 15 had been, the blown-up crematorium, the former Women's Camp, where his sister had been interned. 'It all came back to me immediately. I remembered so many things, as if they had happened yesterday.'

GÁBOR HIRSCH After Russian doctors had fed him up for weeks in the field hospital set up in Oświęcim, Gábor was taken by the Red Army to Katowice at the end of March 1945. This marked the start of an odyssey lasting over five months. He passed through numerous villages, towns and rural districts in Poland, Ukraine, Byelorussia, Romania and Hungary. Everywhere the earth was soaked with the blood of countless people brutally murdered by the Germans.

One of the places he stopped after Katowice, for example, was Czernowitz (now Chernivtsi, Ukraine), the historical capital of Bukovina. It belonged to the Ottoman Empire in the sixteenth century, the Habsburgs from 1775, Romania from 1918, the Soviet Union from 1947, and Ukraine from 1991.

Jews were first mentioned in the city's history in 1408. In 1930, there were 45,592 Jews living there, 41 per cent of the population. It was a literary centre, with Jewish writers such as Paul Celan and Rose Ausländer living there. This ended overnight when Nazi Germany invaded the Soviet Union. Einsatzgruppe D murdered 1,500 leading citizens, and on 1 August a further 682 Jews were shot. The remaining Jews were put in a ghetto and deported.[34] Today, there are only around 1,000 Jews living in Chernivtsi, 0.5 per cent of the population.

Rose Ausländer, who survived the forced labour and persecution in Czernowitz, wrote many years later of the former multilingual city of culture: 'In this atmosphere, anyone who was intellectually alert was almost obliged to confront philosophical, political, literary or artistic questions or to be active themselves in these areas. A sunken city, a sunken world.'[35]

Gábor Hirsch was in Czernowitz at the time of Germany's unconditional surrender on the eastern front. 'That was 9 May 1945, a day after the western front. We celebrated both occasions.'

Finally, on 6 or 7 September 1945, he returned to Hungary, after another endless meandering journey. 'I never knew where the train was heading and what would come next.'

Seven months had passed since he had been liberated. He had travelled over 3,500 kilometres, a huge detour through south-eastern Europe. 'The direct route through Slovakia would have been just 550 kilometres.' The train stopped in his hometown Békéscsaba. Gábor needed to go on to Budapest, where former camp inmates could obtain identity papers. At the train station he met people, who fetched his uncle: Imre Hirsch, one of his father's brothers, who had also survived Auschwitz and had already returned to Békéscsaba.

'My uncle hurried to the train station. He brought me a jug of milk, which I drank with great enjoyment.'

Imre Hirsch had been arrested immediately after the Germans invaded Budapest and put in a camp. 'His wife had just had a baby.' Two months later, he was deported on the first Hungarian transport to Auschwitz and from there to Gross-Rosen. 'He never forgave himself and throughout his entire life he reproached himself: "In the darkest moment I abandoned my family." Even though he could have done nothing about it.'

In early September 1945, Imre Hirsch said to his nephew Gábor at the train station in Békéscsaba: 'Your father also survived.' The boy discovered that his father had already opened the store again. At the time he was on business in Budapest. They sent him a telegram. 'My father was waiting for me at the train station. As I had had bad experiences on the way back to Hungary, I distrusted all adults, even my own father. I refused to accept an extra roll from him in the restaurant. "Why?" he asked. "I don't trust anyone anymore", I replied.'

Next day Gábor obtained his identity papers. His father provided him with the essentials, bought him a shirt, trousers, a jacket and a pair of shoes. Then they went back to Békéscsaba.

Gábor's father had returned from forced labour in October 1944. His house and business in Békéscsaba were returned to him. 'Both of the houses had been looted.' There were strangers living in his house. 'They had to leave.'

Gábor had a private tutor to help him to catch up with his schooling. 'It took two or three months, and then I passed the exams for Years 4 and 5.' He returned to his old secondary school and his former class. But he no longer felt comfortable there and couldn't get used to living in Békéscsaba. 'There was a feeling of antisemitism.' Gábor wanted to get away.

He completed Year 7 in a Jewish secondary school in Budapest. But he didn't get on there either. 'Partly because the subjects were different, partly out of laziness, and partly because of the temptations of the big city.' He failed four subjects.

The family held counsel. It was decided that Gábor should go to a technical college in Szeged, around 90 kilometres from Békéscsaba. 'And that's what happened.' His grades improved. 'The advantage was that I was able to do the Matura [university entrance qualification], but in other subjects.' In 1951, he passed the technical Abitur.

In the meantime, the political situation in Hungary had changed radically. In 1948, the Social Democratic Party was forced to merge with the Communists to become the Hungarian Working People's Party. After a 'cleansing action' in 1949 and subsequent years, the Communists were in sole charge of the country's fate.[36] His father was now considered a capitalist and exploiter. In 1951 he was obliged to give up his business, and decided, 'like the majority of Hungarian Jews at the time', to move to Budapest. 'Jews could live more anonymously there.'

After 1951, the Gábors – his father, his stepmother Rozsi Schwartz, whom his father had married in 1947 – lived together in the Hungarian capital.

Gábor was now 22 and wanted to study at the university, but he wasn't accepted. He never knew why. 'Was it because of my grades?' But he knew students who had got in with much lower grades. He felt he had been treated unfairly.

He found a job in a measuring instrument factory. Fortunately, he met up a short while afterwards with a fellow student from the technical college, who told him about a recently established university that trained teachers for technical colleges. Gábor applied and was accepted. He completed his studies in 1954 with a qualification as an electrical engineering teacher. But he wanted to continue studying and become a professor of engineering. He passed the entrance examination.

He worked during the day in a radio factory, and studied after work at the University of Technology in Budapest.

After Stalin's death in 1953, reformers in the Communist states exerted increasing pressure on the Stalinist leadership. There was a popular uprising and in October 1956 hundreds of thousands of people demonstrated in Budapest for free elections, a multi-party system, freedom of the press and national independence.

Soviet tanks rolled into Budapest and bloodily put down the uprising. Thousands of people died in the fighting. More than 200,000 Hungarians fled to Austria or Yugoslavia.[37] Gábor was one of those who fled. 'I no longer wished to live in Hungary under these conditions.'

At the end of 1956 at the age of almost 28, Gábor reached Nickelsdorf in Austria. He had walked the whole way. His feet were festering and he had stomach ulcers. 'Leftovers from Auschwitz' made themselves felt again. He was taken to hospital in Vienna, where he discovered that, unlike other countries, Switzerland was taking in sick refugees so as to relieve Austria. He accepted the offer. In the first week of December 1956, he continued his journey to Switzerland, where he was put in Military Hospital 25 in Lenk im Simmental, around 70 kilometres from Bern. Six weeks later, he went to Zurich. He wanted to continue the studies he had been forced to interrupt in Hungary and was accepted by the Swiss Federal Institute of Technology (ETH). He received a bursary of 270 francs a month from the Hungarian Student Commission and sublet a room in Zurich.

He was able to continue with the fifth semester of electrical engineering studies. 'I graduated in 1958.' He was taken on immediately afterwards as a research assistant at the ETH.

In 1962, he had the opportunity of working as an exchange assistant at Imperial College in London. He had hoped to be able to learn to speak proper English, 'but I was only allowed to stay for six months. Otherwise I would have forfeited the rights I had acquired in Switzerland as a foreigner.'

In 1964, he found a position in the private economy as a development engineer for the Swiss subsidiary of a US company that manufactured copiers, typewriters and calculators.

He wanted finally to become a Swiss citizen. He felt at home in Switzerland, had a good job and had a network of contacts. To his great surprise, he was informed by the Swiss authorities in Zurich: 'You have to live for at least six years without interruption in Zurich itself.' He had been abroad for six months and had therefore to start from scratch. He finally completed the residence qualification in 1972.

He retired in 1995 and was now able to devote more time to the former camp inmates living in Switzerland. He organized meetings, and the Contact Centre for Survivors of the Holocaust was established in April 1997. Apart from communication and awareness-raising, it also served as an information centre for survivors seeking compensation and assistance.

After retiring, Gábor started to fill in the still existing gaps in his biography. For decades, his recollections of the most terrible time in his life had been 'chaotic and fragmented'. 'For a long time, I had no possibility of talking with people who had suffered a similar fate. Many people in my surroundings had a quite different past. I grew up in a largely non-Jewish environment.'

After 1995, he travelled frequently to Hungary, wrote hundreds of letters and collected many photos and documents, posted articles and queries on the Internet, put advertisements in newspapers. He looked constantly for the people who were with him in Auschwitz-Birkenau. People from all over the world contacted him. There were several get-togethers in Hungary. 'We talk about our conflicting memories and try to put them in order.'

Gábor died in August 2020. He never forgave himself for not having talked with his father about the forced labour; with his uncle, who was deported on one of the first transports to Auschwitz; or with his cousin, who was interned with him for a long time in the 'Gypsy' Camp.

For many decades, he didn't know what had happened to his mother. 'In the first years after liberation, in Hungary, I had the feeling that she would turn up again one day.' He said to himself at the time: 'Then I'll move in with her.'

Later, he discovered from his cousin Böske, who had been interned in one of the transit camps in Auschwitz-Birkenau with Gábor's mother: 'A selection took place on 25 September 1944. Your mother and mine left the camp on that rainy day carrying their shoes.'

In 1994, he sent an inquiry to the Arolsen International Archives. He was informed in September 1998 that his mother had been transported from Auschwitz-Birkenau to Stutthof near Danzig (Gdańsk). She was registered there as Ella Hirsch on 27 September 1944. Gábor obtained the transport lists from the archive of the Stutthof Memorial. It showed that 4,501 women, including 1,849 Hungarians, were deported to Stutthof on that transport.[38]

In 1999, he traced the route taken by his mother and the other women from his hometown to Stutthof. He wanted to know how many women from his home had been deported there. He discovered at the Memorial there: 'There were seventeen women from Békéscsaba. My mother died there on 18 December 1944.'

There has not been a Jewish community in Békéscsaba for a long time now. The two Jewish cemeteries were still visited by friends and relatives. In 2003 and 2004, a synagogue was even erected at the Neolog Cemetery, where a commemoration took place in June 2004, recalling the sixtieth anniversary of the deportations from Békéscsaba. Gábor was there, as he was every time afterwards.

Today, the two once magnificent synagogues in Békéscsaba are now, respectively, a furniture store and a store and warehouse for refrigeration equipment. That hurt him terribly.

GÉZA SCHEIN and his mother Klára were liberated from Gunskirchen. They were both suffering badly from typhus and were taken to the nearby town of Wels to obtain medical treatment in a hospital set up in the Alpenjäger barracks. 'Not only the sick but also former inmates of Gunskirchen were recovering there.'

Géza is included with his name and his date and place of birth in a list of 30 June 1945 drawn up by the International Red Cross in Geneva.[39] It was at this time that he left the hospital with his mother.

They had to wait a further two months, however, before they could find space in a train to take them home. Five or six carriages with former inmates were attached to a train with Hungarian gendarmes and soldiers from the Arrow Cross party, which had collaborated closely with the Nazis but now insisted that it had always been 'respectable'.

The train took two weeks to travel the 280 kilometres to the border. 'As we passed through the Hungarian towns, we saw lots of ruins.'

A week later, the train had completed a further 170 kilometres and arrived at Kelenföld train station in Budapest. After one and a half years, Géza and Klára were finally in Csepel, which they found to have changed profoundly. Here too there were ruins, empty shop windows, people clearly marked by the war. Many familiar faces were gone. Very few Jews had survived.

The walls of the Schein family's former apartment were still standing. The windows were gone, as was the furniture. 'The neighbours told us who had taken it.'

The 12-year-old Géza was enrolled straightaway in school, with German as a compulsory subject. 'After all I'd been through, I didn't want to learn German and was expelled from the school as a result.'

Decades later, he saw things differently.

Of course it was stupid of me, but as a child I didn't think that way. Of course, I knew Germans who had been in the camp. But the memory was still quite fresh and I didn't want to see any Germans. But I can't hold a grudge like that against a whole nation all my life. I've learned that in the meantime.

Géza didn't want a German-sounding surname either. It was changed to Kozma.

Like his ancestors, he became a baker and worked for over forty years in the bread factory in his native town of Csepel.

JiŘí AND ZdenĚk SteiNer were taken by truck in early March 1945 by members of 'our army' from Auschwitz to Slovakia, to the village of Spišská Nová Ves. There was one woman whom Jiří was never to forget: 'She asked us what we would like best. We said that we would love a boiled egg.' The woman went off and scoured the entire village for eggs.

In Spišská Nová Ves, Jiří and Zdeněk were looked after for about a month by a Jewish family. They had difficulties adapting to a 'normal' life.

At the beginning of April, they were taken to the military children's home in Lučivná in the High Tatra. 'We were fifteen years old and had a lot of trouble adapting there as well. We would cry a lot and get upset over the slightest thing.'

In early August, the entire home was transferred to Prague. The twins learned that an uncle of theirs lived there. He was sick, but he and his wife took them in. They stayed there for a year. Here they continued their secondary schooling for a while.

'Two children were too much for my aunt, who didn't have any children herself. She was irritable, and so were we.'

The twins struck out on their own. They separated for the first time in 1946. Jiří went to Litvínov and started as a trainee in the chemical industry. Zdeněk began training in a textile company in Aš at the border with Germany.

Nine days before their eighteenth birthday, tragedy struck: Zdeněk died in a road accident on 11 May 1947. 'We survived the camps ... If we hadn't separated, who knows? ... It broke my heart. First my parents gassed in Birkenau and then my brother dying in an accident.' Jiří suffered deep depression for years after.

He finished his training 'but with great difficulty. I was terribly clumsy. So many jars I held in my hand in the laboratory got broken.'

It was not until his son Petr was born in 1957 that 'new hope began to germinate in me after the death of my parents and my brother'. He felt more confident of his abilities and 'about life in general'. 'My son was my pride and joy.'

Jiří returned to Auschwitz for the first time in March 1966. He chose that month deliberately because many members of his family had been driven into the gas chambers on that day twenty-two years previously. 'There were my parents, and many uncles, aunts and cousins.' Of the family of eighteen, only three survived. Before he died in October 2002, Jiří returned to Auschwitz several times because he realized 'how much of that time' was still in him. He went to the lake in Auschwitz-Birkenau, which is filled in with the ashes of countless people murdered in the camp. Whenever Jiří went there, he felt as if he was standing at his parents' grave. It mattered little to him that their ashes might have been somewhere completely different. This was the grave of those who had been murdered and thus of his parents as well – the place he could mourn them.

Jiří had various jobs – for example, in a culture house as the editor of a juvenile magazine. He published articles about the Nazi occupation of his country, about Auschwitz and his personal experience there. For more than twenty years, he was public relations officer for the Czech State Insurance, wrote the newsletter for members as well as articles about accident prevention and developed children's games to teach them road safety.

After his retirement in 1991, Jiří was press spokesman for the Association of Resistance Fighters and Political Prisoners, which offered support for former inmates and their families. In the last years of his life, however, he became seriously ill with Parkinson's disease and was hardly able to work anymore.

He married for a second time in 1973. His wife Eva meant everything to him. He was also a proud grandfather.

The children of his son from the first marriage are called Petr and Helena. He hoped to tell them his family history 'when they are grown up and can understand it'. This was something of great importance to him and his 'last great task'. His wife Eva confirmed many times that he did indeed manage to pass on some of this history to his grandchildren.

LYDIA HOLZNEROVÁ AND HER SISTER VĚRA were able to return to their hometown of Hronov in Czechoslovakia in July 1945, three months after their liberation in Bergen-Belsen. As they were later to discover, they were practically the only survivors among their many relatives.

The old housekeeper and her husband lived on the ground floor of the Holzners' house. An aunt came to Hronov with her two children and it was agreed that they would live with the sisters for mutual support. Lydia Holznerová was 15 years old at the time. She weighed 36 kg and her head had been shorn on account of the lice she had had in Bergen-Belsen. 'I was ashamed to come home.'

The two sisters were examined in the hospital at Náchod. 'The doctor was very good. The treatment he proposed helped us, and we slowly regained our strength.'

Lydia and Věra were taken care of. They were given clothes, food coupons and furniture for two rooms. 'We didn't need anything else because we knew that our aunt was moving in with all her household goods.'

Lydia and Věra were able to live in a family again.

> The aunt didn't replace our mother, but she knew all about it and I didn't have to explain anything to her. That made the return to a new life easier for me. Our old housekeeper also told us about the people in the village: those we could speak to, those whom I didn't need to know anything about, and those we should spit in the face of.

A few months after the end of the war, they received a large package with Věra's trousseau, which her father had left with a German friend in

Dvůr Králové. He made sure it was returned, even though he himself had moved to Germany in 1945.

Lydia soon met up again with Dita Polachová, with whom she had shared a double bed in Theresienstadt. They had told each other everything about themselves at the time, and when the housekeeper opened the door, Dita said: 'You must be Mariechen.' As they toured the house, Dita knew exactly how it had been: 'That must have been your nursery, and that was the living room.'

Věra's school leaving certificate was now recognized. She had completed it at the Jewish secondary school in Brno before being deported by the Germans, but had only been issued a replacement certificate. Věra soon left for Prague to study, just like her older cousin. Lydia's cousin completed her schooling in Náchod, but Lydia herself had lost contact with her former classmates.

In Hronov a one-year refresher course was offered for children who had suffered under the German occupation. 'In my class was also my best friend, whom I had known since I was four.' This helped Lydia a lot. She passed the course and then attended commercial college, where she graduated in 1950. In September of that year, she moved with her aunt to Prague, where her cousin was now also studying. Lydia worked for decades in the office of a scientific technical society.

When she retired in 1990, she joined the recently created Theresienstadt Initiative, an association of former Theresienstadt inmates, and was its honorary secretary.

Throughout her life, Lydia remained in touch with the women she had come across in the various camps. They met regularly, and one day she encountered Dagmar Fantlová (Lieblová) again.

She felt closest to her sister Věra, who ran a children's library in Prague for many years until her retirement. Until Lydia's death, they lived together in an apartment in the Vinohrady district of Prague. Their shared past had made them inseparable.

OLGA AND VERA GROSSMANN Four months[40] after their liberation, the twin sisters and their mother Šarolta Grossmann had recovered sufficiently to leave Oświęcim and return to Slovakia, 'no easy task in a Europe that had been devastated by war'. They reached their hometown of Turiany in May 1945. The reception was anything but welcoming.

Strangers lived in their house and they refused to move out. The Grossmanns even received threats. They didn't want to remain in Turiany and left for Stropkov and from there went to Košice.[41] It was there that Šarolta Grossmann married Jan Simšović in 1946.

Jews had lived in Stropkov since the late seventeenth century. There was a synagogue, a yeshiva, a Talmud college and many businesses, workshops and companies owned by Jews. In April and May 1942, almost all Jewish children, women and men in the city were deported to the East, including Auschwitz. Only 162 Jews from Stropkov survived.[42]

Olga and Vera were sent by their mother to a convalescent home in the Tatra. They were still both very weak, undernourished and consumptive. They remained in the mountains for six months.

'The situation in the country was highly unstable. Attempts were made to bring the surviving children somewhere else so that they wouldn't suffer anymore.'

The twins were sent in April 1948 to Britain, and from there to a kind of sanatorium in Ireland.[43] It was in a castle in Delvin, about one hour's drive from Dublin. There were around 100 girls, most from Czechoslovakia, sent there to convalesce and regain their strength. Most stayed for a year.

Olga and Vera had to learn again how to play, something they had not had an opportunity to do for a long time. They didn't like some of the games, however, because they reminded them of Auschwitz: 'Hide and seek would make us feel very anxious. Having to hide was terrifying for us.'

Many children stuffed themselves with food on account of their experiences in the camp, because they were not sure when they would next get something to eat. Other children wailed when they saw a policeman.

During this time, many of the girls' parents emigrated to the United States, Canada or Israel. Practically all of them left with their parents. The remaining twenty girls, including Olga and Vera, were sent to England. 'We remained there for another four years.'

The twins lived in Stamford Hill in north London and attended Avigdor Secondary School, a Jewish school that offered the 11-year-old girls their first experience of regular schooling.

They were taken in by the Posens, a very religious family with seven children of their own and four foster children. They came from Frankfurt am Main and had a large house. 'Now we had a new home, and the Posens took loving care of us', says Olga, 'but we missed our mother a lot.' They were nevertheless happy to be able to start afresh. 'We were free, studied hard, played sport and had lots of friends.'

When thirteen of these remaining twenty girls were collected by their parents, those left, including Olga and Vera, wondered why their parents didn't come for them. They all missed their families terribly. Rabbi Solomon Schonfeld, the headmaster, told them: 'The situation in Israel is still unstable. You have to be patient. Your mother would like to have you with her in Israel but she also wants to be sure that you get a good education.'

As they hadn't seen their mother for so long, however, the twins were not content to wait. 'One day we even ran away', recalls Olga. 'But after a few hours we came to our senses and went back.'

In the end, they decided to write to their mother. 'First we went to Oxford Street and bought an English–Slovakian dictionary', says Olga. 'We wanted to write to our mother in Slovakian in our own way with our own words. It took us three days to translate the letter but we managed in the end.'

Rabbi Schonfeld gave the twin sisters, 'Miss Olga and Miss Vera Grossmann, born on 22 April 1938', a personal reference:

> have been known to me for about five years. She comes from a strictly orthodox home in Czechoslovakia and has been brought up here in London in the same strict orthodoxy, both at school and at home. They are determined to make the Torah the guiding principle of their life. I am confident that Olga and Vera now joining their parents in Israel will always keep up the teachings of orthodox Judaism.[44]

Olga and Vera's mother had emigrated to Israel in 1949 with her husband and the two daughters she had had in the meantime. In autumn 1952, she became very ill. 'She thought she was dying. Our mother wanted to see us at all costs.' So the twins, now 14 years old, arrived in Israel.

'We docked in Haifa on 6 January 1943. English was the only language we spoke properly. But the main thing was to be with our mother again.

Her children were practically all that she had. From our stepfather we had four more sisters. So there were six of us altogether.'

Jan Simšović treated Olga and Vera like his own children. No one in his family had survived the Nazi era. The Simšović family had bought an old house in Haifa. It had two rooms. They couldn't afford anything else. The eight of them lived in these crowded conditions, which proved very difficult. 'We both had to find work. We wanted to continue school and later go to university but we had no money. So we all found work so as to support the family.'

The twins married young, Olga at the age of 17 and Vera at 18.

Vera's husband Shmuel Kriegel was from Poland. His family had been able to escape from the Nazis to the Soviet Union, and his father and brother fought in the Red Army. As a 12-year-old, Shmuel had to work so as to support his mother and sister.

When he married Vera, Shmuel had no possessions. After the marriage, he took a relatively well-paid job laying a pipeline in the Negev desert. His wife, now Vera Kriegel, continued to live in Haifa, and he was only able to see her every two weeks. They had no choice, because they also had his parents to support. And Olga helped her parents.

Vera Kriegel became pregnant and in 1957 gave birth to Isack, named after her father.

The constant separation from her husband became a problem. Shmuel tried to persuade her to come to the Negev, as he had much better earning opportunities there. But Vera didn't want to leave Haifa and abandon her family, her twin sister and her mother. It was not until 1962 that she moved with Isack and Frit, her 8-month-old daughter, to Dimona, a city founded in the desert in 1955 in the northern Negev. Finally, she was able to lead a normal family life.

Olga remained in Haifa. Her married name was now Solomon. Her husband, who held a high position in the Israeli military, died in 1994. 'That was a tragedy for me. I was so happy with him. All those years he treated me and protected me like a child.'

Vera Kriegel returned to Auschwitz for the first time at the end of 1985. On the occasion of the fortieth anniversary of the liberation of the camp, twenty Jews from Israel and the USA recalled their suffering and their murdered family members. There were also eight twins in the group who as children had been subject to experiments by the SS doctor Mengele.

Vera didn't want to go to Auschwitz at first. 'I already knew it and had had enough.' But she changed her mind. When the group arrived at the Memorial, they were greeted by reporters and television teams. 'It took all of my strength not to show how wretched I felt.' The group travelled on to Majdanek, where Vera broke down. 'The past caught up with me. I started to wail.' She has no memory of what happened afterwards.

Olga Solomon could never summon the strength to go. 'I couldn't and can't go back to the place of my worst suffering, which still gives me nightmares and sleepless nights.'

Vera and Olga don't want sympathy. 'That would simply embarrass us.' Of the perpetrators, they say today: 'Shouldn't we pity these people for allowing themselves to descend to become such barbarians?'

HERBERT ADLER was most probably liberated by the Red Army in the second half of April 1945 on a death march in a forest area 100 kilometres from Ravensbrück concentration camp.

> One of the Russian soldiers immediately took us children and juveniles away. We stayed together and were brought to a large bank that had been hit by a bomb. The inside was still intact, however. We were given beds, mattresses and something to eat. They did everything humanly possible for us.
>
> The Russians then wrote down our names with the help of the German Red Cross and asked: 'Where are you from? And you?' They said: 'I'm from Cologne, I'm from Würzburg, I'm from Hamburg, I'm from Bremen …'.

The children were given new clothes and a *laissez-passer*. Two members of the Red Cross got on the train with them and accompanied them to their destinations.

With Herbert was a boy called Jakob (Benjamin) Müller, also from Frankfurt am Main. They had been together in all the camps, from Auschwitz-Birkenau to Ravensbrück and had become friends.

When they arrived in Frankfurt, they were asked where they lived. Herbert replied: 'Löherstrasse 21'. 'That's in Sachsenhausen. I know it well.' They drove there. But the house where the family once lived was in ruins. Herbert said: 'I have an uncle who wasn't locked up because he had a "German wife". His name is Valentin Adler and he lives in Fahrgasse.' But that house had also been destroyed. 'And then Jakob

Müller said: "You can stay with us."' He knew that his mother and sisters had returned home. 'I stayed with the family for about two weeks.'

In the meantime, the Red Cross had found Herbert's uncle in Wächtersbach, a good 50 kilometres from Frankfurt.

When they took their leave of each other, both of the boys cried. 'We'd been together for so long.' They had formed a strong bond on account of their difficult experiences. They promised: 'We'll meet up again.' But it turned out differently.

The uncle lived with his family in Wächtersbach. 'When I arrived, I was so exhausted from everything that I couldn't speak.' Herbert had to lie down. The next day, he told the family about his father's death. His mother, his four sisters, the three other brothers had all remained in Auschwitz and had probably been gassed on the spot.

'That was a shock for my uncle and his family. They couldn't understand it.' Finally, the uncle asked Herbert: 'And the others?'

'Yes, Wanda and Heinz also got out of Auschwitz. I saw Wanda from a distance in Ravensbrück. But I don't know where they are.'

A few months later, his brother Heinz arrived in Wächtersbach, followed a short time later by his sister Wanda. They all lived in temporary accommodation with the uncle and his family. Their apartment was much too small in the long term for the seven of them. Herbert's uncle went to the mayor, who helped them find a larger house with a small garden. 'I was able to recover there a bit.' Herbert gradually got back his strength.

Although his family had its roots in Germany, he had decided in the camps that if he survived he would not come back to Germany. 'I could never have a hundred per cent confidence again.' But over the decades, he gradually revised his opinion.

Herbert wanted to train as an automobile mechanic but couldn't find an employer who would take him. He got a job in a forestry company, helping to clear trees. Then he worked for a while in a construction company. Finally, in the mid-1950s, he was hired by the Neckermann mail order company. Outside of work, he was a musician and often appeared in combos at US bases. 'They loved it.'

He met his wife, a bookkeeper, at a sports club in Wächtersbach. He played football and his wife Lieselotte was a handballer. 'One day there was a celebration with the local clubs. I saw her there for the first time and we got to know each other.' They got married, and in February 1949 their daughter Elvira was born. Around 1955, they moved to Frankfurt. 'My daughter is married and has two children.'

He always found it difficult to make friends with people who hadn't been in the camps. When people heard that he'd been there, in Auschwitz, and had seen 'all that suffering, they automatically withdrew'.

'When I first got back, it was very difficult for me.' He told his wife everything. But for years she worried about him. Every night he would cry out and talk in his sleep, saying things like: 'Why are you hitting me? What did I do?' It went on like that for years.

He didn't like it if anyone tried to tell him what to do and what not. 'That's how it was then. In the concentration camp I had to do everything I was told. But now I'm free', he would say repeatedly. 'I'll decide what I can do and what not.'

His wife advised him to see a therapist. He was in therapy for around two years. And with time, the subject of Auschwitz gradually faded into the background. But he was helped most years later by being able to talk about Auschwitz and the other camps at events, in schools or church communities.

His meeting with Andreas von Schoeler, the mayor of Frankfurt at the time, made a deep impression and gave him courage to talk about the past. 'That must have been 1992 at the Brunnenfest in Sachsenhausen.' Herbert was playing there with his combo. After the performance, the mayor asked him about the number tattooed on his arm. They got into deep conversation. The mayor invited Herbert to speak at a large public event. At the event, he was pleased to note the interest that people took in his life story.

'It was never easy to speak about it, but at the same time it was an outlet.' Decades after the war, he would still wonder to himself: 'What did you go through? Is it humanly possible that people would do that to one another?'

He became an honorary member of the board of the Central Council of German Sinti and Roma. In that function, he worked above all at seeking compensation for the former forced labourers and supported the erection of a memorial to the Sinti and Roma murdered by the Nazis. But he was not to live to see it completed in the German capital Berlin.

As long as his health permitted, he travelled every year in early August to Auschwitz-Birkenau to the international day of remembrance of the Sinti and Roma, recalling the night of 2–3 August 1944, when the 4,200 to 4,300 Sinti and Roma remaining in Birkenau were gassed.

And when I'm at the Auschwitz Memorial, I stand for half an hour alone in front of Block 21, where I was forced to live with my father, my mother and my brothers and sisters. But the barracks are no longer there, just black stones with numbers on them. And the others I come to Auschwitz with leave me alone. They know I'm standing there for my father, my mother and my brothers and sisters. And at the end I say to myself: 'For me you're not dead. You live in my heart.'

In Birkenau, the 'Gypsy' Camp was not far from the ramp where the people arrived from everywhere. We could see the selection by the SS. And how many were sent to the gas chambers.

That was difficult to stomach.

His sister Wanda would say to him repeatedly: 'I don't know how you can stand all that, how you can do all that.' And he always replied: 'If I don't do it, who will?'

Wanda Michaelis (*née* Adler) once described how it was for her: 'I felt for a long time as if I was being followed. I was scared of everyone and didn't trust anyone. It's impossible to describe in words how terrible it was.'

Until his death in October 2004, Herbert talked tirelessly about Auschwitz. He sought to stay calm and objective, but inside he was still seething.

WOLFGANG (WILLIAM) WERMUTH weighed 39 kg when he was liberated from Dachau at the end of April 1945. He was sent immediately to the Outer Camp Hospital set up by the US army.[45] He was discharged several months later.

Together with other former inmates, he organized an old Wehrmacht truck to take them back to Berlin. There were forty of them, and they didn't get far. The truck broke down in Regensburg and they were unable to find another means of transport. They were accommodated initially in a refugee camp.[46] Many of them remained in the city, where a Jewish community soon formed again. Some of Wolfgang's comrades 'remained there all their lives'.

In 1946, Wolfgang ran into somone in Regensburg completely unexpectedly. 'Hey, Bubi', called out a 'ragged ex-soldier' on the street. 'Bubi' had been Wolfgang's nickname in Berlin. It was Dieter Neugebauer, recently released from US captivity. They had been neighbours in Berlin. In 1938, he had still played secretly with Wolfgang. 'We were naturally delighted to meet up again.' Wolfgang took him for a night to the refugee home, gave him 10 marks and something to eat the next morning, and then Dieter left. 'Unfortunately, I never again heard from him. Something must have happened to him, otherwise I'm sure he would have got in touch.'

Wolfgang's father had said repeatedly in Theresienstadt: '"If you get out alive, write to Rose Koppe in Providence, Rhode Island. She'll help you." She had married my father's cousin.' He had memorized her address. So he wrote to her through the US army post office. 'Two weeks later came the reply with a huge package.' The relatives wanted Wolfgang to come to them in the USA.

He was 20 years old when he boarded the *Marine Marlin* in Bremen on 21 February 1947 and emigrated to the USA.[47] He arrived in Providence on 2 March. 'I felt too old to go back to school.' He started working in a print shop but then decided to train as a watchmaker.

Wolfgang soon changed his name to William, which was easier to pronounce. He remained for seven years in Providence before taking a position in the watch and jewellery department of a renowned department store in Hartford, Connecticut. The owner's family came originally from Baden-Württemberg. 'They were Jews who had come to America in 1847 and started their lives there afresh.' Out of solidarity, the owner Beater Auerbach hired lots of immigrants.

William Wermuth returned to Berlin for the first time in 1957. 'I tried to straighten out my grandparents' inheritance situation.' He met people he had known as a child and retraced his footsteps from those days. He discovered an archive in Passauer Strasse. 'I found documents referring to our seized apartment at Fritschestrasse 55. It had been sold cheaply after our arrest and deportation. The proceeds, 533 reichmarks, went to some Nazi women's group.'

He didn't want to return for good to Berlin. 'That was out of the question.'

Back in Hartford, a year later he met Gisela Herford. Her family had emigrated to the United States in 1927. They were married on 28 August 1960 by a rabbi from Bad Nauheim, who had been released from Buchenwald in 1938 and just managed to escape to the USA.

Gisela's mother never felt really at home in the USA and she yearned increasingly to return to Europe. But she wanted to stay with her daughter. The Herfords had relatives in Switzerland. William wanted to try it out there with his wife and mother-in-law. They wanted to settle in Zurich, but unexpectedly the immigration authorities refused to issue residence permits.

They gradually got used to the idea of returning to Germany after all. They looked at a map for the cities closest to Switzerland so as not to be too far from their relatives. They decided on Konstanz. But William wanted to know more about what to expect there. 'I had to find out what it was like.' He had newspapers sent and wrote to the local chamber of industry and commerce. It sent him information about the job market, rent prices and the city's history. 'It looked very nice.'

He would probably not have returned to Germany on his own. It was a 'psychological feat of strength'. He said to himself: 'I'll give it a go.' His friends in Hartford merely shook their heads. They said: 'We can't understand why you would all do such a thing, especially you, a survivor.'

In 1970 the three of them moved to Konstanz. The mother-in-law felt visibly at home there. William quickly found a position in the watch and jewellery department of a department store. 'I had to work hard to come to terms with my past and my thoughts. Only then is it possible to feel the pulse of a nation.'

He never hid the fact that he was Jewish. He stayed at home on Jewish holidays. 'There were never any problems.'

He took early retirement after fourteen years. He and his wife were involved in the life of the Jewish community. 'For years the community didn't flourish, but at least we had a community. The members were all old, but that changed with the arrival of Jewish immigrant families from Russia. Now there is even a new generation in the community.'

He and his wife were only able to speak about the camps with a few non-Jews. They avoided intensive discussions about politics, religion or Auschwitz. 'There was no point. In the USA it was different.' They were disappointed that conversation in Germany was often superficial. 'Many people feel concerned only when their own material life is affected, when the talk is of salaries and working hours.'

The Wermuths settled well enough in Konstanz. They often thought about leaving Germany again, particularly 'when we heard about anti-Jewish incidents, Nazi goings-on and xenophobic attacks'. But at such times, William said to himself and to his wife: 'If people like me left, the "final victory" [*Endsieg*] would be almost complete.'

ROBERT BÜCHLER was offered numerous possibilities for convalescence after his liberation in April 1945. One group was to be sent to Sweden. Dr Winter, a US army doctor, suggested that he go to a sanatorium in France. But Robert wanted to see his parents. He was sure that at least his father was living. In early July, Robert travelled by bus from Jena to Prague.

In Prague, he slept in the residence and centre for doctors. Every day, he went to the Jewish community offices. He ate in a soup kitchen. It was here that he met a man from Topol'čany, who told him: 'Your father is at home.' Robert was not to be held back. He had to return to his hometown. But in those days, this was easier said than done. Not all the trains were running, because the track was missing and bridges had been blown up. It took him some time before he managed to get to Topol'čany.

At the train station, Robert met someone he had known from earlier. Robert asked him: 'Are there still Jews here?' The man replied that there were but he didn't know where. But he said that the 'Jewish soup kitchen' had been set up again. There was also a provisional prayer house there. The small synagogue had been repurposed as a warehouse by the Nazis, and the large synagogue had been completely destroyed.

'We don't know whether your father is here. But there are some Büchlers in the town', Robert learned from former camp inmates. His father's sister was still alive. She had fled into the forest with her family shortly before the last deportation from Topol'čany. And there, 'as fantastic as it may sound', she had lived in a hole in the ground.

> The first thing I asked my aunt was: 'Where is my father?'
>
> My aunt looked at me strangely and said: 'Your father? Where should he be? Isn't he with you?'

'No.'

'And where were you?'

'We were deported to Auschwitz.'

My father's sister was beside herself. She broke down in tears. She didn't know what to do. Finally, she said: 'Your father isn't here.'

That was a terrible moment for me. I couldn't control myself. I burst into tears. I was sick. My disappointment was unbounded. I was lost. I didn't know what to do.

Only this one sister and two of my father's brothers, who had been lucky enough to survive the concentration camp, were still alive. 'The man in Prague must have thought that one of the two brothers was my father.'

Robert was taken in by an uncle, who lived in straitened circumstances with his wife and two children in temporary accommodation. He had a place to sleep, hang his clothes and eat. But he didn't find what he was looking for. 'I needed a point of reference, someone whom I could talk with about my future. And that was missing there.' A more likely candidate was the Zionist socialist youth organization Hashomer Hatzair [The Young Guard], which he had joined.

He wanted to attend commercial college in Bratislava.[48] An uncle arranged it for him and offered to put him up. But there was practically no space, and the college sent him a list of all the things he had to buy. It was too expensive. He couldn't and didn't want to ask his uncle. 'Who will pay for it?' Robert asked himself. 'What am I to do now?'

The friends from Hashomer Hatzair said to him: 'What's the problem? You're independent and can do what you want. Join us in the youth home. You belong there.' Right after the war, Hashomer Hatzair had founded homes for orphaned children and juveniles returning all over the country from the camps.

To his uncle's bafflement, Robert moved in with the friends from the youth organization, who sought to help as many of their members as possible to get to Palestine, later Israel, to live in kibbutzim. Robert saw this as a meaningful future perspective. With the others, he prepared intensively for life on a kibbutz. It was to be called Lahavot Haviva in memory of the Slovakian parachutist Haviva Reik, who emigrated to Palestine in 1939, later joined the Haganah paramilitary organization and was dropped behind German lines to organize Jewish resistance in Slovakia. She was captured by the SS and executed in November 1944.[49]

In 1949, Robert emigrated to Israel. He worked with his friends for some months in an existing kibbutz to gain practical experience and learn as much as possible. Together with around 100 women and men, practically all of whom had been deported to concentration camps during the Nazi era, Robert Büchler founded Lahavot Haviva in October 1949.

> It didn't bother us much at the time. But unconsciously the fact that we had been in the camps was very important. We sought to form a community, because this offers more security. That's why we wanted to live in a kibbutz. We wanted to create something. But the living and working conditions were difficult. Only a few from my group remained in the kibbutz. Many of them were concentration camp survivors.

Years later, the thought occurred to him: 'The group should have been more mixed, then perhaps not so many would have left.'

In the kibbutz, Robert married Esther Herz, whom he already knew from Czechoslovakia. She had been deported to Auschwitz as a 12-year-old. She had twelve siblings, but only one brother and one sister survived the Nazis.

Robert never heard anything more about his parents and sister. He wrote to everyone, including the German Red Cross. In vain. He merely received two postcards from a woman whom he had met by chance in Israel. Josef Büchler had sent them in 1942 to her family. 'That's all I have of my father.'

Robert and Esther had two daughters and a son. Ruth, born in 1954, was named after his sister, and Anat, five years younger, after her mother. Joséf was born in 1967. Ruth and her husband Saadi have three sons, Omer, Star and Ilaj. Anat has a daughter called Shiba and a son called Tor. Joséf and his wife Inbal are the proud parents of two sons, Royi and Tal.

Robert worked initially on a building site in the kibbutz and then in the fields. He took courses in joinery and worked as a joiner for twenty years. Until his death in August 2009, he still did repairs on the side one or two days a week.

After the kibbutz had got beyond its difficult early days and started to be profitable, Robert was finally able to fulfil a dearly held wish. The kibbutz put up the funds to enable him to study and graduate in history at the University of Tel Aviv. Some years later, he took courses in Jewish studies and modern Jewish history at the Hebrew University in Jerusalem.

After completing his studies, Robert worked most of the year in the Moreshet Archives at the nearby Givat Haviva Institute, a large documentation, research and teaching centre run by the left-wing kibbutz movement in Israel.[50] He was director of the research institute and archive, and was involved in researching and documenting the Shoah and the history of the Hashomer Hatzair youth organization.

'Every year thousands of Jewish and Arab students from all over Israel take part in our courses on the Shoah and Nazi era. We also take youth groups to the memorials such as Auschwitz-Birkenau and places in Europe that used to have Jewish communities. Here the students can learn themselves about some of our roots and Jewish heritage.'

Robert tried several times to visit his former homeland. In vain. He couldn't get a visa. 'We're still persona non grata in Czechoslovakia', he wrote in November 1988. Finally, in June 1990, he and his wife were able to return to Prague, 'not without mixed feelings', and to their birthplaces in Slovakia. 'The political upheavals at the time made it possible. After forty-one years it was high time. And much to our surprise, most of the people we met were friendly and open.'

Afterwards, Robert returned several times to his old homeland and investigated the former Jewish life in Topol'čany. It can be traced back to the fourteenth century. The new Jewish cemetery, which had opened in the previous century, was the only surviving and clearly visible sign of Jewish life there.

Like practically all other Jewish infrastructure, the old cemetery opened at the end of the eighteenth century was destroyed during the Nazi era. A road had been built through it. A few of the gravestones were transferred to the new cemetery, but it was the oldest ones that were broken up. In the absence of written documentation, they would have been a valuable source of information about the community's history.

After the war, the remains of the old cemetery were transferred. The city administration used the space for housing. Today, there is no trace of this first cemetery. And finally, the small synagogue, which had been used during the war as a warehouse, had to give way in the 1960s to housing.

Thanks to the attention of the few remaining Jews in the town and to donations from all over the world, the new cemetery remained intact. Today, the cemetery is in immaculate condition, in stark contrast to the former Jewish community of Topol'čany, which has completely disappeared.

Robert Büchler was co-founder of the International Buchenwald Committee. He organized several meetings in Israel of the inmates of Block 66 and spoke many times at conferences and events at the present-day Buchenwald Memorial. In 1976, his book about the history and fate of the Jewish community in Topol'čany was published, followed in 2003 by the highly acclaimed *Encyclopaedia of Jewish Communities in Slovakia*, which he edited.

For many years, he was also active in the Public Committee of Auschwitz Survivors and the Peace Now movement. For him the most important thing was that there should be no more war and hatred. 'And that's why I live in this kibbutz, in a community without much money or possessions. They aren't worth anything. All that really counts is peace.'

YEHUDA BACON was liberated from Gunskirchen in early May 1945 and was sent to the hospital in Steyr in early June to help him to recover.[51] Then he set off immediately for Czechoslovakia. 'I thought that I might find my mother and my sister again.'

He was admitted to a convalescent home in Štiřín Castle, 30 kilometres south of Prague, established by the Christian Czech humanist Přemsyl Pitter. Here and in other confiscated castles, Jewish children from the ghettos and concentration camps, but also German orphan children, found a temporary refuge.[52] The Jewish children came not only from Czechoslovakia, like Yehuda Bacon, but also from Carpathian Ruthenia, Austria, Poland and Romania.

In Štiřín, I and the others had the opportunity for the first time in a long time to lead a safe and quiet life. Here we experienced the human kindness and sympathy that we had been deprived of for so long. Above all, we were shown the love that we had had to do without for so many years. It was particularly difficult for us children to readjust. I was in bad shape, both physically and mentally. It took a while for me to get back on an even keel. A team of doctors, educators and nurses helped and took intensive care of us. And not to forget that it was in Štiřín that I had my first art lessons.

One of the teachers of the children coming from the camps was Hans G. Adler, himself an Auschwitz survivor, who later devoted himself to research into the persecution of the Jews by the Nazi state, and was to become one of the chroniclers of the Theresienstadt ghetto. In 1985, he recalled how he met Yehuda Bacon shortly before his sixteenth birthday in July 1945: 'I was assigned to a group of Czech-speaking adolescents, mostly boys, practically all of whom had spent some years in Theresienstadt, Auschwitz and Mauthausen and had met in Theresienstadt in 1942/43. Yehuda struck me particularly: an expressive, youthful, almost childlike face with the features of an old man and a disoriented gaze.'[53]

Yehuda was marked by his years in the camp. He was distrustful of everyone. He felt as if he was 80 years old. Adults who had not been in the camps were like 'children with no experience of life'.

After his return to 'normal life', his development went in two directions. On the one hand, he wanted to learn and devoured knowledge with an insatiable appetite. He wanted to make up for his lost childhood because he realized 'how much I had missed through my time in the camps'. On the other hand, he was happy to escape into the intact child's world that he had known for just a few years in order to blot out the terrible experiences for a moment: 'I was suspicious of everyone. And I refused any physical work. We had learned in the concentration camps to save our strength and not to waste it. That made us weak. We had to conserve enough energy for the moments when it was really needed. That was the only way to survive.'

Adler recalls the time after liberation:

Yehuda was withdrawn at first but we soon got very close. I was particularly moved by his insatiable thirst for knowledge on all subjects, particularly philosophy, theology and religion. Our discussions were marked by a primal urge to communicate in a most intimate fashion not only the diverse aspects of a terrible time of persecution but also a stream of subtle reflections about a vast array of experiences, formed within a deep but damaged mind.[54]

367

Everyday experiences inevitably reminded Yehuda of what he had gone through in the camp. Immediately after the war, he witnessed a burial with a large coffin and music. He couldn't help laughing and thinking: 'Are the people crazy to make such a performance about a body?' Or when he was at a play or concert, he couldn't help thinking how long it would take to gas the audience. He tried to imagine how much clothing, how many gold teeth and sacks of hair would remain.

He recalls that the death of one of his teachers was the first time he was able to cry again – thirteen years after his liberation.

Yehuda spent practically all of his spare time painting. His talent had already been spotted when he was a child. In Theresienstadt and Auschwitz, he had also made illegal sketches of everyday camp life, which had been lost. Now he recreated them all again from memory. His subjects were the extermination machinery, the crematoria, the barbed wire enclosures, the watchtowers, the SS men, the suffering of the inmates. He drew the half-starved figures who were known in the camps as 'Muselmänner', mothers with their children, and lots of self-portraits whose expression was repeated in the faces of his fellow sufferers.

In autumn 1945, Adler showed some of Yehuda's work to the painter and academy professor Willy Nowak. 'Nowak agreed immediately to take him on as a private pupil.' Nowak wrote to Max Brod, a writer and dramaturge living in Tel Aviv, about Yehuda. Brod and Hugo Bergmann, who taught philosophy at the Hebrew University, offered their support to the young artist, and he was awarded a scholarship to study at the Bezalel Academy of Art in Jerusalem.

David Gat, formerly David Weinbach, was one of the youths living with Yehuda at Štiřín Castle. He had been deported to Auschwitz in 1944 at the age of 16 with his mother, sister and three brothers. Decades later, he recalled the moment when the children and juveniles expressed the wish to emigrate to Palestine.

This came as a shock to Přemsyl Pitter. He asked them: 'What's wrong with here? What don't you like about Czechoslovakia? Why do you want to leave?' They discussed with him for two hours. 'But then he realized that our minds were made up and he concluded: you're free and can do what you think is right. But he still often brought the subject up again.'[55]

Přemsyl Pitter remained an influential figure for youths like David

Gat and Yehuda Bacon. 'I have never forgotten how he tried to make us understand that it was what was inside a person that was the most important. Not fashionable clothes or superficial words. These values remained deeply embedded in me. They have helped to form my life.'

Yehuda remained in the Štiřín convalescent home for about nine months. When he left for Palestine in 1946, he didn't have to pay any tuition fees. 'Nothing else was settled.'

He received plenty of assistance. His sister, who had come to Palestine in 1939 and lived in a kibbutz, arranged somewhere for him to sleep. He received clothing from the Youth Aliyah. He was able to eat lunch in a children's home 'on a little stool' thanks to the intervention of a distant relative. 'I was a starving artist.'

But he was happy to be able to study art. Auschwitz remained the main subject of his work. Because he wanted to testify, he signed his pictures not with his name but with the number tattooed on his left forearm in Auschwitz: 168194.

Not everyone understood the residual problems from his time in the camp. 'That was very hard for me', he recalls. 'But they simply had no time or means to build the land of Israel and defend the territory given to us Jews, and at the same time to attend to the people from the German concentration camps who came from Europe to Israel. It was not until many years later that attention was paid to the survivors.'[56]

Years after liberation, his thoughts were still mostly in the concentration camp. 'I was only interested in looking inwards, but the result had a symbolic effect on others, and my creativity was transformed into art, I hope, because the statement it made was strong and direct enough to signify something to others.'

In his work, Yehuda took stock of himself. As a child, he had felt confronted – every day, every hour, sometimes every moment – by the relentless threat of extermination. He grieved and attempted to interpret in his pictures what he had seen and experienced. As a child, he had been forced to look far beyond the limits of humanity. With the greatest determination, he searched to give a meaning to what the soul of a Jewish child, his soul, had been exposed to.

Yehuda completed his studies at the Bezalel Academy of Art in 1955, after which he continued studying in London, Paris and Florence. Shortly after his return to Israel, he was appointed as a lecturer at the

Bezalel Academy, where he remained as professor of graphic art and drawing until 1994. Since then, he has been a freelance painter.

He travelled often to London and New York on study trips. His works have been exhibited throughout the world: in Antwerp, Copenhagen, Vienna, Oslo, Stockholm, Helsinki, Princeton, London, Berlin, Hamm and Dortmund, to mention but a few. His pictures have been purchased by many collectors, galleries and museums around the globe.

Yehuda had a daughter from his first marriage, called Hanna after the sister who perished in Stutthof.

In 1970 he married Leah, a long-standing lecturer in literature at the Hebrew University in Jerusalem. They have two sons, Benjamin Israel – 'he was named after our fathers' – and Hannan Brachiahu. 'Hannan was the suggestion of my wife's mother, who had a relative with a similar name in her family.'

In 1961, Yehuda Bacon testified as a witness in the Eichmann trial in Jerusalem, an event which helped to increase acknowledgement and understanding for the concentration camp survivors in Israel.[57] Eichmann was responsible for the deportation and extermination of the Jews as part of the 'Final Solution'.[58]

More than 100 witnesses testified. Yehuda relates: 'The Eichmann trial transformed the Shoah from a painful trauma to the central element in Israel's national conscience.'

Eichmann was sentenced to death, but Yehuda was one of the seventeen signatories of a letter opposing his execution. They called on Prime Minister Ben Gurion to commute the death penalty to life imprisonment. But the death sentence was confirmed and Eichmann was hanged in late May 1962. It was the only death sentence ever to be carried out in Israel.[59]

Yehuda was also a witness in the Auschwitz trial in Frankfurt am Main from December 1963 to August 1965. More than 210 concentration camp survivors testified.[60] The defendants were former SS members and one former kapo.[61] They were charged 'alone or with others with cruelly or maliciously killing people … out of bloodlust or for other base reasons' in the area of Auschwitz concentration camp or 'of knowingly assisting, through actions or advice, in the commission of crimes'.[62]

For Yehuda, there was something surreal about the Auschwitz trial. The perpetrators were sitting in the dock, without uniform and without power. Even nineteen years after the war, he well remembered the former SS men. He was 'shocked at the lack of feeling and remorse' of his torturers. He nevertheless considered it his moral duty to record the full truth. 'I recounted everything, all of the atrocities. I described how SS man Baretzki beat inmates to death. But I also felt obliged to relate how he secretly brought bread for us children.'

Yehuda also had the opportunity to speak a little about his family. On 30 October 1964, the counsel for the secondary charge, Henry Ormond, asked him: 'Who else was with you when you came to Auschwitz?' Yehuda replied: 'My parents and my sister. But I also had an aunt with two children, and lots of cousins.' Ormond: 'And how many survived?' Yehuda: 'Just me.'[63]

There is no doubt that the Auschwitz trial marked a turning point in the history of the Federal Republic of Germany. For the first time, the German public were provided with an unambiguously authentic and detailed picture, communicated by a German court, of the Nazi persecution of the Jews. There was a strong and lasting reaction. The newspapers, not only in Germany, provided daily detailed reports on the trial.[64] The coverage by Bernd Naumann in the *Frankfurter Allgemeine Zeitung* is regarded as exemplary.[65] The younger generation in particular, who had not personally experienced the Nazi dictatorship, were motivated in this way to face up to their country's recent past.[66]

The liberating feeling for Auschwitz survivors like Yehuda from being able to testify was, often enough, compromised by the humiliating cross-examination by the defence counsel and the scandals that accompanied the trial. For example, there is film of police officers saluting not yet arrested former SS officers during the trial recesses.[67]

Yehuda's testimony in the trial was one of the reasons for coming to Frankfurt. But he also wanted to know how Germany and the Germans were reacting to the trial. 'It was as if suddenly another world – the 1960s – and the world of our yesterdays came together for a few days in one room. There were school classes who came to listen. Perhaps it left an impression.' He wondered at the time: 'What would happen if everyone in the gallery were to go home and say at the dinner table: "I was there today and it was very interesting." And what then?' In October 1964, Yehuda asked himself: 'What will happen to us, the survivors? Where are we on this chessboard?'

The sentences were pronounced in August 1965. Six of the twenty defendants were sentenced to life imprisonment. Others were given prison sentences ranging from 3 years and 3 months to 14 years. One defendant was sentenced to 10 years' juvenile detention. Three of the defendants were acquitted.[68]

After years of feeling like an outcast, Yehuda found his way back to a normal life – through his painting, the love of his wife, his two sons and his daughter from his first marriage, and the friendship of Hans G. Adler and Martin Buber. One day, he realized: 'I've said what I want to say about Auschwitz. I wanted to create something else and not become a "professional concentration camp survivor". I didn't want to be identified exclusively in this way anymore.'

This evolution can be clearly seen in Yehuda Bacon's work. His early pictures are in dark and gloomy black and grey tones, the figures have stiff bodies, blank expressions, eyeless sockets. It took a long time for life to return to these bodies.

The new realization began to find expression in Yehuda's pictures and the human relations depicted in them. He creates a world of interwoven memories and fantasies in the form of double or multiple faces symbolizing good and evil. With great sensitivity, he portrays the relationship between mothers and children or between young couples.

Yehuda reached for his paint palette and gradually his pictures became saturated with colour. In his recent pictures, mostly coloured abstracts, the weight of the past can be seen only in faded tones. Today, Yehuda's pictures are not directly to do with Auschwitz. He now signs them with his name and not his camp number.

'Many of my pictures contain references to the camp experience, but hidden and discreet.' But if you look closely, you can still see them.

Yehuda's way back to a fulfilling existence is due above all to his art. 'My pictures saved me.'

JANEK MANDELBAUM and his friend Moniek were liberated in May 1945 from a satellite camp of Gross-Rosen in Dörnhau (Kolce). They didn't want to live in one of the zones controlled by the Russians in Europe.

So they set off for Frankfurt am Main in western Germany. 'We'd heard that the Americans had most to eat.'

At that time, getting to Frankfurt was no easy task. The city was around 700 kilometres away from where they were. They had to manage somehow to make their way there. They walked some of the distance, but also took trains and sometimes got a ride in an army truck.

> It was a terrible journey. There were very few trains at the time. Lots of rolling stock and track had been destroyed. The train would travel for a while, and then we would have to get out and walk for several kilometres. Then there was another train, and then we were picked up by an army truck. Finding something to eat was an even greater problem. But we managed, and after a few weeks we finally arrived in Frankfurt.

There were around 184,000 Jews in post-war Germany, including tens of thousands of children and juveniles, like Janek, under 18 years of age. Around 50,000 of the survivors came from extermination and concentration camps.[69]

For a long time after the liberation of Europe, many of the children and juveniles who had survived the Shoah had nowhere to go. They were looked after above all by Jewish organizations, which brought the survivors to the western occupation zones and offered them a temporary home in refugee camps or other facilities in the land of the perpetrators.[70]

Their aim was to make it possible for as many Jews living in Europe as possible to emigrate to Palestine. After the contempt and mass murder that the Jews had been subjected to since 1933 through Nazi Germany, they had no future in that country. For many people, this was self-evident. They wanted to create a Jewish state in Palestine so as to ensure their future safety.

Janek and Moniek found temporary refuge in the displaced persons camp in the Zeilsheim district of Frankfurt. Between 1945 and 1948, it held an average of 3,000 Jewish children, women and men. There was a kindergarten, synagogue, schools, a library, and a social and cultural life.[71]

'We were examined by a doctor in Zeilsheim. I weighed 36 kg. Six years earlier, when we fled from Gdynia, I was only twelve and weighed 50 kg.'

Long lists were posted every day in the camp with the names of people looking for their families. Janek and Moniek studied the lists every day. Janek would have dearly loved to find the names of his father, mother, sister and brother. 'That would have meant that they were still alive.' But he didn't even find a name he recognized.

One day, however, he spotted the name of his cousin Arek Mandelbaum. He found where he was and was informed by Arek: 'Sigmund Mandelbaum is living in a refugee camp in Landsberg am Lech near Munich.' Sigmund was his favourite uncle, his father's youngest brother. He once again began to hope that his parents and siblings were still alive.

Janek set off for Munich to see his uncle. Once again, the journey was full of difficulties: 'Very little was moving at the time, and there were many obstacles to overcome.' The reunification with his uncle was a moving experience. 'It was an intense encounter. He had been in Auschwitz, Buchenwald and Stutthof and had suffered enormously. But I recognized him immediately.'

His uncle announced the terrible news:

'Your father is dead. He died in Stutthof in October 1944.' My uncle arrived in Stutthof a day later from Buchenwald. I don't know how my father died.

When I learned that he hadn't been liberated, that he had spent five years in a concentration camp, suffering every day, every hour – it's very difficult for me to speak about it – that he did not live to be liberated, I would have 'preferred' that he had died on the first day in Stutthof. Then he would have been spared a lot of suffering.

And although I knew my uncle was telling the truth, I refused to believe it. My father dead? It was simply unacceptable, impossible. He was such a strong-willed person.

Janek wanted to go to Poland to look for his mother, sister and brother. He managed to get to his hometown of Gdynia in overcrowded trains and on foot. There were ruins everywhere – the port, the docks. He didn't find anyone he recognized. Strangers were living in the family's apartment. 'They were unfriendly and tried to get rid of me.' All of the family's possessions had disappeared. He returned to Gdynia many times. 'I didn't get anything back.'

Of the 4,500 Jews who had lived in Gdynia at the end of 1938, only 33 returned after the war. A further 10 settled in Sopot and 8 in Gdańsk. In subsequent years, practically all of them left the Trójmiasto [tri-city] region of Gdynia, Sopot and Gdańsk.[72]

Things were no different in Działoszyce, where his grandfather lived and where Janek, his mother and brother and sister had fled in August 1939. 'There were strangers living in the house there as well.' The inhabitants told him: 'Your grandfather and his wife were shot by the Germans.' They had been driven with 1,200 to 2,000 other Jews to open pits near the Jewish cemetery and murdered.[73]

In Słomniki, where Janek's sister Ita had found refuge with her mother's youngest sister, the neighbours told him: 'My sister was collected at the end of 1942 with my aunt's baby [Josef Czarnocha, born on 23 July 1941], whom she was looking after.' On 7 September 1942, a few days before her eighteenth birthday, Ita was transported to Bełżec and murdered there.[74]

Bełżec extermination camp in the Lublin district was established by Germans to murder Jews. In 1942 at least 435,000 children, women and men, particularly Jews from Poland, were gassed.[75] Many of the Jews in Poland were liquidated on the spot, however, as confirmed by the doctor, historian and collector Zygmunt Klukowski and his *Diary from the Years of Occupation 1939–44*. He witnessed the expulsion of the Jews of his hometown Szczebrzeszyn (60 kilometres from Bełżec) on 21 October 1942. On the first day, around 1,000 were taken away, and 400 to 500 were murdered in Szczebrzeszyn itself. Klukowski noted: 'You cannot even imagine the barbarism of the Germans.'[76]

Janek, his mother and his brother had lived with an uncle in early 1940 in Sławków. Through subsequent research, he discovered: 'My mother Cyrla, my brother Jakob and my uncle and his family were taken from Bukowno train station, seven kilometres away, to Auschwitz in cattle wagons' on 11 June 1942.[77] This is the last news he had of them.

There was nothing to keep him in Europe anymore. He wanted to get away 'as quickly as possible'. On 15 June 1946, he boarded the *Marine Perch* with his uncle Sigmund and his cousins Arek and Robert Mandelbaum. They arrived in New York ten days later. The new immigrants were welcomed by members of the Joint Distribution Committee, a Jewish aid organization. They were taken to a hotel and asked: 'Where do you want to go?' They had a choice of several cities.

'I didn't want to stay in New York. It was too big for me. They suggested Kansas City. I asked: "Why there?" They said: "Jews from Germany went there in 1938. It must be a nice place." I asked: "Why?" "We never heard from them again", was the surprising answer. "They must be getting on well there."' That was enough for Janek, who soon changed his name to Jack, because it was simpler for the Americans. He was given a ticket and 5 dollars, and off he went to Kansas City.

Many of the others who had chosen that city started working in factories, earning 50 dollars a week. But Jack wanted to do something else. He got a job with a clothing wholesaler, sweeping the floors and transporting packaging material. He earned 22 dollars a week but had to pay 18 for his room. It was difficult for him at first.

Nine years later, he was still with the same company but had worked his way up, was much better paid and spoke good English. He saved every cent possible and in 1952 became a US citizen. 'My boss died in 1957. I bought the company with the money I had saved and a loan.' Jack Mandelbaum developed the company into a flourishing import business. 'I managed to do so only because for a time I suppressed the memory of the atrocities during the Nazi era. Otherwise, I wouldn't have made it.'

On 26 September 1948, he married his wife Shirley and they became the proud parents of four children, Sharon, Barry, John and Mark.

Apart from Sigmund, the only one of Jack's many uncles and aunts to survive was 'the clever, beautiful Hinda'. In 1950, he arranged for her to come to Kansas City. 'She was never able to talk about Auschwitz.' Jack didn't push her. She died in 1965. 'With her a lot of my family's history disappeared forever.'

Moniek, whom he had befriended in one of the camps, emigrated to the USA in 1950 and found work in the construction industry. He and his wife Erica had two sons. Jack and Moniek remained good friends. The only difference: 'Moniek never returned to Europe. The Nazis destroyed his family, he would say. We didn't do anything to them, he would repeat in our conversations. "I will never set foot in that part of the world again."'

As the years passed, Jack felt an increasing urge: 'I had to go back to Gdynia and the other places in Poland that played a major role in my family's life.' This was the only way to shed light at least on some of the family's history. Documents, family photos, mementos – practically everything had been irretrievably destroyed during the Nazi rule. He managed at least to obtain a photo of his father Majloch from relatives in 1968. He was given a photo of Tauba Goldwasser, his mother's older sister, by a cousin from Israel. 'That was a happy day for me', as she bore a strong resemblance to Cyrla Mandelbaum. 'Nothing remained of my sister Ita and my brother Jakob – only my memories of the years of our happy childhood together.'

HEINZ KOUNIO AND HIS FATHER SALVATOR were liberated in May 1945 from Ebensee, a satellite camp of Mauthausen. He is quite certain: 'If the Americans had come just two days later, I would most probably been among the dead.' A photo shows him in the first days after liberation: every single rib can be seen. Heinz Kounio was quite literally just skin and bones.

'My father took the photo.' The Americans had given him a simple camera. Afterwards, Salvator took photos of everything he considered important – particularly the people who had survived. He also took photos in other Mauthausen satellite camps, everywhere he interpreted for the Americans.

Two days after liberation, the first of two US field hospitals was established. Many former inmates were sick and had to be tended.[78] 'Although I must have looked like a corpse, my brain was still working.'

The former inmates improved every day thanks to the treatment they received. 'We were deliberately given very little to eat, mostly fluids' – whatever their weakened systems could stand. 'I felt like an old man. The German Nazis had stolen my childhood and youth. Nothing and no one could bring it back.'

Heinz and Salvator Kounio arrived back in Thessaloniki in July – 'as quickly as we could.'

His mother and sister Erika had been transferred from Auschwitz to other camps. In spring 1945, they were in Malchow,[79] a satellite camp of Ravensbrück. In early May, they set out on a foot march in the direction of Schwerin. The roads were chaotic. It was clear to them that the Nazi regime was collapsing.

They met other columns of inmates on their way. Erika would ask men who had been in Auschwitz: 'Did you know the Kounios?' They were told several times: 'No, they are no longer alive.'

Hella and Erika Kounio were ultimately able to hide in the woods with three other Greek women. They remained undiscovered and were liberated by the Red Army on 5 May.

There were no vehicles available. They set off on foot and reached the American zone. There were no trains to Greece, but they got as far as Belgrade by truck, where they found a place to stay in a private house. Hella wrote to a cousin in Switzerland, who informed her: 'Salvator and Heinz are alive. Go back to Thessaloniki as soon as you can.'

It took a while but finally, in September, they managed to get a train to take them home. 'We arrived in the evening.... And there they were in front of us. How thin they looked! But how warmly they embraced us!'[80]

They recovered both their home and their business premises. Both were empty. Christian friends had stored the Kounios' furniture and household objects before the family was deported to Auschwitz. 'We managed to recover a lot', says Heinz.

Father and son soon began to start up the photo shop again. 'We set about the work with a passion. We wanted to look forward and get ahead.'

Heinz married in 1953. He and his wife have four children: two sons – Salvator and Solon – and two daughters – Hella and Regina. The two sons took over the photo shop in 1985.

Heinz's father died in 1960 and Heinz continued to run the business, which exists to this day in the centre of Thessaloniki. In 1985, he said to himself: 'I've worked enough now. I want to devote my life to coming to terms with the Shoah.'

His first book was published in 1982. Originally available only in Greek, a revised version was published later in the USA under the title *A Liter of Soup and Sixty Grams of Bread: The Diary of Prisoner Number 109565*.

Since 1992, he has been trying to put names to the Jewish children, women and men from Thessaloniki and all over Greece who were deported to Auschwitz and murdered there. He was helped initially by the few documents from the Jewish community in Thessaloniki that had survived the war. But these were far from sufficient. Heinz began to send out letters to respondents all over the world, initially to the many Jewish communities. In this way, he was able to identify the few survivors of Auschwitz, who were now in Israel, South America and even in Japan.

Heinz has managed to collect the names of 37,000 people on three continents. He has identified 25,000 children, women and men from the Jewish community of Thessaloniki who were deported by the German Nazis, often to the Auschwitz-Birkenau death camp. Their memory is preserved on a large commemorative panel in the city's Jewish museum. Bella Alaluf is a typical example. She was born in 1923 in Thessaloniki and, like Heinz, was deported in the first transport to Auschwitz on 15 March 1943. She survived the original selection and on 30 July 1943 was deported to Natzweiler-Struthof concentration camp, around 50 kilometres south-west of Strasbourg. She was gassed there in August 1943 along with the other 86 Jews transferred from Auschwitz, 46 of them from Thessaloniki. The journalist Hans-Joachim Lang wrote about their lives in his book *Die Namen der Nummern*.[81]

In 1987, with his mother and wife, he visited Karlovy Vary (Karlsbad), where Hella Kounio, *née* Löwy, grew up. They went to the well-preserved Jewish cemetery, where her brother Heinz Erich Löwy is buried. Hella Kounio wrote to former Auschwitz inmate Tadeusz Szymański, a long-standing member of staff of the Auschwitz-Birkenau Memorial:

'Our cemetery and the old synagogue there are still standing. I wanted to visit my brother. He died at the age of nine during an appendix operation. His grave and the graves of all other family members are there. The last remaining Jews will also be able to be buried there. None of the graves were damaged. This was our old hometown.'[82]

They drove on to Bochov, fifteen minutes away. This is where Hella Kounio was born and where her grandfather had lived. He owned a small house and store on the market square, selling trousers, cloth, coats, curtains and the like to the local farmers.

She wrote in 1987:

To the left is a small village, Buchau, now Bochov. We drive straight to the market square. The old one is still there. The inhabitants are Czech; the Germans have gone. And there is my grandparents' house. It has been freshly painted. The farmers do it themselves. In the upper storey are flowerboxes with flowers. Underneath is my grandfather's former little shop. It's still a shop today. The market square is well tended. The Steiningers had a shop here. There was an auxiliary synagogue where Jewish services were held. That used to be there as well.[83]

379

Heinz's mother also wrote about the joint visit to the Auschwitz-Birkenau Memorial:

> The (former) camp makes us feel as if we are all still there. Everything has been left as it was. Everything is alive. There are throngs of people in civilian clothing. They all want to keep the memory alive: 'Never again Auschwitz'.... If you go through the (former) camp with your heart and mind open, you relive the experience as an Auschwitz inmate. Morning and evening roll call. Everyone had to be accounted for. If someone died or was beaten to death at work, the corpse was placed next to the living and the report stated: 'four hundred living and two dead'.... Everyone who survived must tell their grandchildren and great-grandchildren and never forget.[84]

JOSIF (JOSCHUA, JEHSUA) KONVOJ was lying in hospital in the Lithuanian capital Vilnius in mid-2004. For Jews, the city had been a spiritual capital for centuries, so much so that it was known as the 'Jerusalem of the East'. One day, a doctor brought Josif the latest issue of the *Jerusalem of Lithuania* newspaper. As he was browsing through it, he spotted a death notice: 'On 21 February this year Mojsche Konvoj (Konvojas) died in Canada. He was born on 13 October 1929 in Kaunas and was interned in the ghetto there from 1941 to 1943 and then deported to Dachau. He was liberated in May 1945.'[85]

After liberation, Josif had never heard of anyone with the same surname as him. He wondered: 'Do I have relatives in Canada? How can that be?' A friend of his worked in the Jewish community in Vilnius. He advised him to contact the editor of the newspaper. The newspaper gave him the email address of a travel guide from the USA, who frequently visited Lithuania with Jewish groups, many of whom had lived there before the Nazis came. The guide gave him the email address of the deceased's family. He sent condolences to them 'because they had the same name as him'. They replied asking him to tell them about his life. After his liberation, Josif had very little recollection of the time before. Surviving documents indicate that Josif arrived in Dachau on 15 July 1944 at the age of 15. He remained there for four weeks before being transported to Auschwitz. From there, he arrived on 23 January 1945 in Buchenwald, where he was liberated in April.[86]

He was able to relate about himself and his family:

I know that we lived in Kaunas near a river. There was a bridge. And I addressed my father as 'Alter'. I think that's how everyone referred to their fathers in Yiddish. I can recall that medical experiments were carried out on me in Auschwitz. I don't know exactly what and how. That and the terrible time in the ghetto and the other camps have made me lose my memory. I'm convinced of that.

The family in Canada wrote and asked him to send photos of his childhood. He didn't have one single photo of himself or his family from Kaunas. Then they asked him to tell them his number from the camp and to send a blood sample. He did so. The first blood sample got lost, and the second was analysed in Jerusalem and New York. The result was clear: 'I had a brother called Zalman/Selman (Jerry) Konvoj in Canada and a sister, Selda/Zina (Konvoj) Boruchovitz in Israel.' His sister had even lived in Kaunas until 1971. She had married in 1949 and since then had a different surname. 'That's why I didn't find her.'

He met his brother and sister several times and stayed with them in Canada and Israel. They were able to fill in some of the blanks in his memory. In mid-1941, the three of them had been interned with the rest of the family in the ghetto in Kaunas – with his father David, a tailor, his mother Taube (*née* Singer) and his second 6-year-old sister Roza and a 3-year-old brother called Yehuda. Like the other children, the 12-year-old Josif had had to work in the ghetto as a messenger and plumber's mate. He also had to help with burials.[87] In 1944, they were all transferred to various camps. His parents, sister Roza and brother Yehuda were murdered. 'It was a powerful and confusing moment when I met my brother and sister for the first time. It can't be put into words.'

When his brother Zalman visited him in Lithuania, they travelled together to Kaunas, their birthplace. 'He showed me where we had lived. There was the river and the bridge. I remembered them – but not much else.' But from then he knew. 'The visit to Kaunas was so overwhelming that we were both weak and could hardly put one foot in front of the other.' When he travelled to Kaunas later, he could only stay for a short while. He felt, as long as he lived, that it was better for him not to go to Kaunas at all. That's how much it affected him emotionally.

Josif remembered that he was liberated by the US army in April 1945 while on an evacuation march from Buchenwald. 'I was so weak that

I couldn't walk. My comrades from Czechoslovakia carried me.' An American told him to come with him, but his comrades wouldn't allow it. As he had almost no recollection of the past, they urged him to come with them. So he ended up in Czechoslovakia, where he had a new home for years with Jan and Žofia Pokornych in Oslavany near Brno.[88] The couple had no children.

'I was admitted straightaway to hospital. When I had recovered, I attended a Czech school. I had learned a bit of Czech from my comrades in the camp.'

He then worked from 16 September 1946 to 9 November 1948 in the Oslavany electricity company.[89] 'I trained there as an electrical engineer.'

His Czech mother urged him: 'You have to go to Kaunas and look for your mother and father and your relatives.' The Soviet embassy in Prague was contacted, and he travelled to Kaunas with a member of the embassy. But he was unable to find out anything about his family.

He had neither a Lithuanian nor a Czech passport or ID. They said: 'You're a citizen of the Soviet Union and should have returned home after liberation.' Because he had failed to do so, he was a 'bad person'.

> I was arrested and imprisoned for two or three days. A Soviet officer took me to Vilnius. They threatened to send me to Kazakhstan or Siberia. Fortunately it never happened. I was allowed to stay in Vilnius. That was in 1949.
>
> It remained complicated. I couldn't get a job because I had been abroad. I had to rewrite my CV. The answer was always: 'You were abroad and cannot therefore be given the job.'

One day he was given a piece of advice by a high-up official: 'If you want a job, you shouldn't mention the camp and the time abroad.' He followed the advice and was hired. He had to dismantle old electricity meters in Vilnius and replace them with new ones. He did this for twenty years. Afterwards, he worked in a company making micromotors, and was ultimately organization manager in a welding factory. He retired in 1998.

He married his wife Elena in 1950. Their son Vechislav was born two years later, and a daughter Galina in 1962.

Josif enjoyed his many visits to his 'Czech parents'. 'After the years in the camp, they looked after and treated me like their own son. My feelings for them could not be stronger.'

When his 'Czech father' died in 1981, he naturally attended the funeral in Oslavany. When his 'mother' died in 1989, he was unable to attend because he was in hospital himself – in fact, Josif Konvoi suffered heavily from a variety of illnesses throughout his life. He died in Vilnius, Lithuania, on 28 January 2018.

# Who Am I?

As they grew older, the children from Auschwitz who did not know their names or where they came from began increasingly to wonder about their origins. They asked: 'Who am I?' When searching for parents, the inmate number was often a help, because boys and girls were tattooed immediately after their fathers and mothers. The women and girls had Women's Camp numbers, and the men and boys numbers from the Men's Camp.

KOLA KLIMCZYK, who was rescued from Auschwitz-Birkenau by Emilia and Adam Klimczyk shortly before the camp was liberated, attended primary school in Jawiczowice, Poland. His fellow pupils had no idea that he had been in Auschwitz. They asked: 'Why do you have a number and not us?' Kola also wondered why none of his relatives had a number. 'Why do I have one and not my parents?'

The Klimczyks did not want to hide from the boy that he wasn't their biological child, but they didn't want to talk about Auschwitz at first. They wanted to protect him and to offer the security of a home.

For a long time, Kola was not interested in lessons. His mother brought him to school. As soon as she left, he would escape through the back door. Or he would disrupt the class and distract the teacher by not remaining in his seat. 'What's the matter with her? I wanted to ask someone a question, so I went to where he was sitting. I wasn't bothering anyone.'

Things changed later. The boy had no trouble learning his lessons and he enjoyed music and playing with paints.

If any of his classmates touched him, he reacted aggressively.

By the time he was 10, it was impossible to avoid the subject of Auschwitz anymore. The Klimczyks tried to answer his questions carefully and to tell him what they knew about him and Auschwitz.

When he was 14, he started middle school in Oświęcim. At this time, he began to wonder: 'Who am I? A Jew, a Pole, a Russian? I must be a

Jew or a Slav, like most of the people in Auschwitz.' He became increasingly uneasy. 'Everybody wants to know who they are and where they come from.'

The first time he said he was going swimming. But when he returned, he admitted: 'I was at the Memorial.' He often visited the former camp 13 kilometres away, went into the barracks, examined every nook and cranny in the huge Birkenau complex. According to his adoptive mother, 'Kola hoped to find the solution to the puzzle that was his life.' He was looking for a clue, a scrap of paper, that would tell him something about his family. But in vain.

On one of his visits, Kola met Tadeusz Szymański, a former inmate of Auschwitz, Gross-Rosen and Buchenwald. He worked at the Auschwitz-Birkenau Memorial, paying special attention to the children who had been interned there.

After the camp was liberated, a Red Army film crew had shot film in Auschwitz in late February to early March 1945. One sequence shows a group of children behind barbed wire. They are holding dolls in their hands. Then there are close-ups, and one of the children shows the inmate number tattooed on its arm.

Szymański wanted to know where these children were and what had become of them. He wrote hundreds of letters, contacted people all over the world and found Auschwitz children in Australia, France, Israel, Italy, Poland, Czechoslovakia, Hungary and the USA.

In Poland alone, he contacted around twenty-five of the liberated children from Auschwitz. He organized meetings and helped the children to deal with everyday problems. Their shared past bonded them together.[1]

He was helped by a group of women, former inmates of Auschwitz who now lived close to the former camp. Many were friends and supported one another.

With the aid of the International Red Cross and other aid organizations, Szymański and the women wanted to help the children to find their parents. In isolated cases, they were also initially successful, which gave hope to the others, including Kola.

When Russian, Ukrainian and Byelorussian families heard that there were other children from Auschwitz still living close by, a lively correspondence developed between them and the Polish women.[2]

Hanka (Hanna) Paszko read a letter in the 27 November 1960 issue of the *Nowiny Gliwickie*, a daily newspaper published in Gliwice, from Zinaida Bulakhova, who lived in Vitebsk, Byelorussia. She was writing in an attempt to find her two daughters, Gala and Raia. Their Auschwitz inmate numbers, 77252 and 77253, had also been published.

The first number was very close to the one tattooed on Hanka's arm, as far as she could decipher it. She thought: 'Perhaps this woman from Vitebsk is my mother.'

Hanka had been liberated from Auschwitz at the end of January 1945. She had lived initially with an elderly woman in Kraków and was then in a children's home, and then in a convalescent sanatorium with a ward for pulmonary diseases. She was ultimately adopted by a 'dear woman' from Zabrze near Katowice. From then on, she was called Hanka Paszko.[3]

Szymański relates that there were numerous incidents in the Harbutowice children's home near Kraków, where Hanka lived from May 1945 with six small children who had been liberated from Auschwitz.

> The children all slept in one large room. A boy called Tolek [short for Anatol] was so sick that he was to be put in a separate room so as not to infect the other children. But they protested and said: 'No selection! He has to stay here!' In the end a compromise was found: one of the girls was allowed to sleep in the same room as Tolek so as to watch out for him.

The children recognized almost none of the food they ate. One day, they were served the beetroot soup borscht. When they saw it, they had no idea that such a soup existed. 'They shouted: "What are you giving us? Blood? We can't eat that!"'[4]

Hanka remembered that her name was Luda (short for Ludmila). In the children's home, the other children would sing the Polish song 'Ludu mój ludu' ('People my people') and look strangely at her. From then on, she decided that she wanted to be called Hanka.

She also remembered the name of one of her brothers, Olek or Alek. And she had a good recollection of how the number had been tattooed on her arm. She had attempted to pull away and had been held down. 'It hurt a lot.'

And then, in late 1960, she had to deal with the question of whether Zinaida Bulakhova was really the mother of Hanka/Luda. Letters were exchanged. Finally, with the aid of infrared radiation, it was possible to determine that her number was 77263.[5]

In 1961, Nina Gusieva, who had been deported to Auschwitz in 1943 from Smolensk, published a report on her deportation, the Women's Camp and the children there. It contains clues to Hanka/Luda's real parents. Nina recalled a girl called Luda Betsludova, whom she described as a shy, withdrawn child. And although she was hungry, she never asked for anything.

Once she heard the child crying in the night. She was evidently so hungry that she was forced to ask for a piece of bread. But Nina had nothing to give her. She spoke to her in an attempt to soothe her. The 3-year-old girl liked being talked to and said that she loved Nina 'up to the sky and even higher'.[6]

The number on Hanka/Luda's arm confirmed that Zinaida Bulakhova was not her mother. But she remained in contact with the women from Vitebsk and the surrounding area, where many mothers were still looking for the children they had been forced to abandon in Auschwitz and other camps.

Valentyna Ivanova Betsludova, who lived in Orsha, some 80 kilometres from Vitebsk, also heard about the contact with Hanka Paszko. She wrote: 'Hanka, you might be my daughter. Do you remember your brother Alik?'

When Hanka read these lines, she felt certain she had found her mother, even though she had only a vague memory of a brother called Olek or Alek.

Things moved quickly. Letters were exchanged and Hanka sent Valentyna the earliest photograph she could find. Valentyna immediately recognized her long-lost daughter Luda.

Hanka learned about her and the story of her family. She was born in 1940. Both her parents were teachers in a small Byelorussian village. As the family had supported the partisans, they were arrested in July 1943. Her father was shot. Valentyna, who was pregnant at the time, was transported with Hanka/Luda and two older brothers to Majdanek.

Hanka/Luda probably arrived in Auschwitz on 15 April 1944, her mother two days later in Ravensbrück.[7] *Auschwitz Chronicle* states:

'Prisoners from the Lublin concentration camp (Majdanek) are transferred; 988 women and 38 children were received.'[8]

After the liberation, Valentyna looked for her daughter and sons. Alik was found, but there was no trace of Hanka/Luda. Valentyna lived for years in hope and doubt, wondering: 'Can my daughter still be alive? She was so small.'

After she heard of Hanka/Luda's existence, she wanted to visit her daughter straightaway. She wanted Luda to live with her.

In mid-May 1962, they finally met up. Hanka travelled to Orsha in Byelorussia. As the train pulled into the station, she saw an excited group of people waiting for her. And there was her mother. 'She embraced me, trembling with joy and excitement, unable to say a word.' Her brother Alik and his wife, together with her other brother Edik, born in the camp, whom she had never seen, were also there.

They travelled to the small village where her mother and Edik lived. Valentyna no longer worked as a teacher but managed the *kolkhoz* library.

They exchanged few words at first. Relatives, friends, neighbours and acquaintances all came to visit. They embraced and kissed Hanka and were happy that the lost daughter had been refound. Some of them could speak a little Polish and asked her about her life. Hanka said she had finished school and was working. She later studied law and worked as a legal adviser in a textile factory.

'They were happy to note that I'd been well brought up in Poland. But they also said: "You're different."' Her mother watched her all the time. She couldn't take her eyes off her, wherever she was standing, sitting or working. 'She looked at me as if she were trying to read my whole life in my face.'

Hanka had the feeling that her mother had an important question to ask. 'Will you stay here?' she finally said once when they were alone. 'I can't say at the moment. Perhaps later.'

Later she said to her mother: 'I'm going back to Poland.' Valentyna had to understand, even if it was hard to accept, that they would never be able to make up for the time apart. Luda had been raised and cared for by another woman, who had become her mother. She had become 'a different person', who felt at home in Poland. The prospect was almost unbearable for Valentyna.

After about a week with her biological mother, Hanka visited the women from Vitebsk with whom she had been in contact while looking for her family. She had information and photos of other children from Auschwitz living in Poland who didn't know who their biological parents were. They had been waiting impatiently for Hanka, curious to hear her news.[9]

KOLA (MIKOŁAJ) KLIMCZYK Hanka Paszko told the women of Vitebsk, who had also been looking in vain since the liberation for their missing children, about Kola Klimczyk. On the very first day, she met Marusya Lanilovna Kozlova, who was looking for her son named Nikolai (Kolya for short) Andreyevich Kozlov.[10]

The Polish first name Mikołaj is similar to the Byelorussian Nikolai. The Polish short form for Mikołaj, Kola, could be the reason that, in the confusion of Auschwitz-Birkenau, Kolya for Nikolai became Kola for Mikołaj. Moreover, because of the diversity of languages in the camp, small children in particular spoke a mixture of several languages.

Hanka Paszko wrote a letter to Kola while she was still in Byelorussia:

I arrived in the Soviet Union on 13 May 1962 to visit my mother.... It was very moving. I met practically my entire family. But there are still emotional moments like this to come for me. Now I'm in Vitebsk ...

I met Marusya Lanilovna Kotslova, who is looking for her son Kola. And this is where the story starts. I can't say anything for certain, but there's a strong resemblance between you, Kola, and Mrs Kozlova. You have the same eyes and nose. I showed her a photo of you.... She thinks you look like her Kola.

In the letter, Hanka quotes Kola's putative biological mother: '[I want] to let him live where he is, but we would like to see him very much'.

'There is, however, the problem with the number', continued Hanka in the letter. 'It is unclear.'[11] For a long time, Kola's number had been read as 185852.[12] It was so blurred, however, that it could never be determined for certain.

His putative mother's number was 77362. Like Luda Betsludova (Hanka Paszko's mother), Marusya Kozlova had been transferred to Auschwitz-Birkenau from Majdanek on 15 April 1944. The girls and women from this transport were most probably given the numbers 77235 to 78222.[13]

'Kola, I don't know whether you are interested in this', wrote Hanka from Vitebsk regarding a meeting between Kola and his putative biological mother. But she emphasized the importance of sending photos from his childhood.

Galina Kozlova and her mother Marusya obtained Kola's address from Hanka. His putative sister wrote to him straightaway:

> Please excuse me for having decided to write to you. But I'm doing so because I'm looking for my brother Nikolai Kozlov ... When we saw the photo that Luda showed us, Mum and I recognized you, but not immediately, because you're grown up now. We looked at your face and decided that you looked like my father who is unfortunately no longer alive.
>
> Mum has already forgotten your number. She says it could be 183962 or else 183982 or 189962 [Marusya had already given the number 183962 earlier to the Soviet Red Cross[14]]....
>
> Kolya, we know that you have found a good home and that you have been adopted by good people. That's fine, but you can imagine how much I would like to see my brother and Mum her son. This situation is hard for us. It's difficult for us to know that you live somewhere but without knowing how you are....
>
> Kolya, please don't think that we want you to come and live forever in the Soviet Union. No, stay where you are.... After having raised you for so many years, your adoptive parents can't give you back to us. But we must see you.... My heart tells me that you are my brother.[15]

The reply came promptly, not from Kola but from his Polish adoptive parents Emilia and Adam Klimczyk. They enclosed photos in the letter to Hanka Paszko for the Kozlov family. Marusya and her daughter Galina (Gala) wrote by return of post:

> We received the letter from Luda (Hanka) and were excited and delighted to see the photos. We can't describe how grateful we are to you for writing this letter and sending us the photo of Kola. As soon as I saw the photo of Kola in a white shirt and open jacket with the happy child's smile on his face, my heart was filled with inexpressible happiness and joy....

The last time I saw Kola was in January 1945.... I can remember exactly what he looked like. We thank you and your wife many, many times for this happiness and the joyful experience on the day when we see our beloved son again.

All of our family and relatives are grateful that you have raised him to be what he is now ...

I saw Kolya on 19 January.... On that day I was only allowed in for an hour. Kolya couldn't stop crying. I persuaded him not to cry. On that day I brought him something [to eat] that I had saved up all week. He already understood everything and knew that I could be punished for it.... That was the last day I spent with him, and I can't stop thinking about it. Afterwards we were marched on towards Germany – to Neustadt [a Ravensbrück satellite camp], where we were liberated.

Immediately after my return, I started to look for my children.... In 1946 I found my elder daughter, Gala, in a children's home in Kyiv.

When I returned home in 1945, there was nothing there. I had to start out from scratch. I learned that my husband had died in the war. I remarried in 1947 ...

We are looking forward very much to meeting you, Kola's adoptive parents.... We thank you for the invitation. I we hope that we can always live happily as friends. And that we can always be like a large family.[16]

The Klimczyks encouraged Kola: 'Go to your mother!' His adoptive father, now retired as a miner, gave him money. Emilia packed his suitcase.

Kola's years of longing, hope and wishes appeared now to be over. As a 20-year-old, he travelled for the first time to Vitebsk in autumn 1962 to his putative biological mother, Marusya Kozlova. She told him all the details of the family's history that she had not already written in the letters. He was born in November 1941 and was thin and frail for his age. The family was arrested by Germans in May 1943. They shot his father straightaway and his mother, together with his sister and himself, were sent first to Majdanek and then to Auschwitz-Birkenau.

Kola's sister was then transported to the children's and juvenile camp in Litzmannstadt (Łódź). His mother was put on an evacuation transport to Germany, was liberated there and returned to her home. She began immediately to search for her children.

Her daughter was able to say approximately where she came from. She set off for Lviv, where the Soviet authorities had established a centre after the war to identify the parents or relatives of these children. In this way, the mother and daughter were reunited.

Marusya Kozlova continued to search for her son. She had seen the film shot a few weeks after the liberation of Auschwitz showing a group of children. For years she searched in vain, but she never gave up hope and was convinced that her son Kolya was alive.

For Kola Klimczyk, it was important for his presumed biological mother to see his tattooed number. 'And she knew that I had two distinctive moles on my back and the sole of my foot.' This convinced him that she was his mother and that, after seventeen years, they had found each other again.

When Kola travelled for the first time to Vitebsk, his Polish adoptive mother told everyone she was sure her adoptive son would return. But secretly, and unbeknown to anyone, she complained bitterly to Tadeusz Szymański: 'She reproached me heavily. She was clearly jealous of the other, biological mother. She complained to me for having encouraged her to look for his family. She feared that Kola would like his biological mother more and that she would lose him.'

Kola soon found himself confronted by this dilemma: Who is my real mother? The biological mother, who had to abandon him in Auschwitz when he was 3, or the Polish mother, who rescued him?

For Kola, now 21 years old, the answer was clear. He returned to Poland, to the country that had become his home, whose language he spoke, and where he had spent most of his life, where his adoptive parents had helped him to get on with his life.

This was a bitter disappointment for my mother Marusya Kozlova. She cried when I left for Poland. She had lost me now for a second time. But I couldn't remember her and couldn't establish any real emotional ties with her. I had practically no connection with the person who had given birth to me. She was nothing like the mother I had imagined. She was a stranger. By contrast, I couldn't imagine a stronger emotional bond than the one I had with my Polish mother.

Moreover, Kola admitted, decades later, that he wasn't sure that Marusya Kozlova really was his mother. A maternity test was never carried out to resolve this unanswered question. Kola Klimcyzk died in November 2001.

Because Kola had no emotional attachment to his putative biological mother and was not even certain whether they were related, he remained distant from her after the first visit to Vitebsk and often waited a considerable time before answering letters from her or her daughter Gala.

After Kola's return to Poland, for example, Marusya wrote to him: 'Hello, the son I gave birth to. We are all well. We wish you all the best for your life and good luck at university. Study hard and stay healthy.

Kola, the son I gave birth to. Please answer this letter. Why don't you write? Are you angry about something? Have I done something wrong? I don't feel as if I have.'[17]

A short time later, Kola received a letter from his presumed sister Gala: 'Dear Mikołaj, I'm sorry to bother you and to write so directly. But as you don't want to write back to us, I feel obliged to remind you that it is your duty to reply. Your family is waiting to hear from you. And please let us know if you need anything ... We were so sad after you left.... Kola, please write back.'[18]

Kola had written in the meantime. Gala replied on 18 December 1962: 'Dear Kola, no we weren't at all angry with you for not writing for so long.... Tell us something about yourself. How is your family? Your [step]sister has got married. We were at the wedding but we were sad that you weren't there. If you have a [recent] photo, please send it to us. Your sister Gala.'[19]

In a second undated letter in which she describes a second wedding, she writes:

Thank you very much for your letter. It's true that we were very angry with you for writing so little. But only until your letter arrived. We thought you didn't have time for us.... The wedding was very nice. It's a shame that you weren't there. My son Sasha listens to Polish radio all the time. He thinks it's Uncle Kola speaking ... Live where you want, ... but give a sign of life from time to time. It's your duty.[20]

Kola was unable to fulfil the expectations of his Byelorussian family, and would not have been able to do so even if he had been certain that Marusya Kozlova was his biological mother. He wrote around once a month – at least at the outset. He travelled several times to Vitebsk and stayed for a long time there. The Kozlovs also visited him in Kraków.

'In every letter, at every meeting, there was the subtext', as Kola intimated on several occasions: 'My Byelorussian "mother" always hoped, without saying it, that I would live with her in Vitebsk or at least spend more time with her than I could or wanted to. From her point of view that was quite understandable, because as far as she was concerned I was her son.'

She had finally found her son, but he continued to live over 1,000 kilometres away, spoke another language, had other habits and was completely different. In spite of all his doubts, Kola remained in regular contact with the Kozlov family in Vitebsk as long as he lived. He felt he owed it to them. But he could never give 'Mama Kozlova', as he called her, the lost time after Auschwitz.

Marusya suffered from the situation. In Auschwitz-Birkenau, she had had to abandon Kolya under indescribable circumstances. Now that she had found him again, she just wanted to hold on tight to him, to have him around all the time. Now it was possible, but she was still not able to fulfil her dearly held wish. It was very difficult for her to accept and put up with this situation.

Kola studied in Kraków and became an architect. He visited his Polish parents as often as he could and kept his room in the house there.

He was generally suspicious of others. 'I don't trust everyone who is friendly towards me', he said once. He kept his distance at first, and it was only after a long time that he formed friendships.

In the last years of his life, Kola worked as an architect in Kraków. He designed housing estates, school, offices and kindergartens. He lived in the Nowa Huta district with his wife Ewa and their daughter Dorota, born in 1982. He and his family prospered. And Kola was able to pursue his hobbies, painting and music. As in his schooldays, he enjoyed 'playing with colours'.

GÉZA KOZMA (SCHEIN) Emilia Klimczyk was delighted when Kola returned home from Vitebsk in autumn 1962. She was now sure that he would stay with her. And she was now at liberty to fulfil a long-held wish. She wanted to find out what had become of the Jewish boy from

Hungary to whom she had given food in the coal mine in Brzeszcze in 1944 and who had then given her a portrait done by a fellow inmate.

It was to take a good ten years for this wish to be fulfilled.

In early 1973, an exhibition, 'Message to the Living', took place in the Hungarian National Gallery, with pictures, photos and documents from the Auschwitz Memorial. Among the exhibits was a 10.5 × 14.8 cm piece of cardboard with a pencil drawing, *J. Markiel: Portrait of a Hungarian Boy*, with the question 'Who knew him?'

A newspaper published the drawing and the question. 'A woman from Brzeszcze (Poland), who worked in the camp kitchen is asking for information about this boy.' The article was about Emilia Klimczyk and how the boy had given her his portrait. 'Although we are convinced that the boy was murdered in the gas chambers, we are publishing the drawing at the woman's request. Please notify us if you knew him.'[21]

Géza Kozma himself notified the newspaper the next day. The day before, he had returned from work in the afternoon, eaten something, then, as always, rested on the couch in the living room. He picked up the newspaper on the table and leafed through it.

Suddenly he shouted out loud. He jumped up, showed his wife the picture and said: 'That's my portrait! And it says that someone is looking for me.'

The newspaper contacted the National Gallery, which in turn got in touch with Tadeusz Szymański from the Auschwitz Memorial, who had been given the portrait by Emilia Klimczyk with a request for assistance – as he had done previously with her adopted son Kola.

'Now I have a second son', said Emilia, when Szymański brought her the news from Géza Kozma. Géza was no less delighted to discover that this woman was alive and even looking for him. 'I have never forgotten this Polish mother.'

Afterwards, and until his untimely death in January 1991, Géza, who was a baker like his ancestors, travelled at least once a year to Poland to visit his 'Polish mother' and 'Polish father'. Until he died, he referred to Emilia as 'mama'. In many conversations, he always emphasized: 'She helped me a lot and I regard her as a mother. I will never forget her.'

Géza had a very close relationship with Kola. 'It was nice to see how the relationship between the adopted Byelorussian child and the Jewish boy from Hungary developed. They regarded each other as brothers, as the sons of Emilia and Adam Klimczyk', said Szymański.

Whenever Géza came to Poland, Kola met him at the train station in Kraków and they travelled together to the Klimczyks in Javiszowice. Kola also occasionally visited Géza's family in Budapest, either alone or with his wife. They went on excursions and holidays together.

The two communicated as they had in the camp, through gestures and drawings and a few words of German, Russian, Polish and Hungarian – difficult for outsiders to understand, but they managed to communicate everything they wanted to say.

Whenever Géza came to Poland, he visited the Auschwitz-Birkenau Memorial and walked through the Women's Camp, past the 'Gypsy' Camp, the remains of the crematoria, where his grandparents had been gassed and cremated, to Block 18 in the former Main Camp, where an exhibition recalled the Jews from Hungary who had been deported to Auschwitz. At this time, there was still a black wall with countless names of those who had been murdered, including his grandfather Sándor Ungár.

'After the time she spent in the various camps, my mother never regained her health. She spent many months in hospital. She waited constantly for my father to return. I didn't tell her that he had been shot in Gusen. That gave her hope that he would one day return, and courage and strength to continue living.'

Géza's mother Klára died in 1959 at the age of 49 as a result of her internment. She lived long enough to see her son marry Ilona Horváth in 1953 and to enjoy her grandchildren Zoltán and Klára, named after Géza's paternal grandparents.

Zoltán later became a master mason, carpenter and roofer, and for many years was also the chauffeur to a minister in the Hungarian government in Budapest. He has two daughters, Susanne and Katharine. His sister Klára worked for many years as a shoemaker.

In 1961, the family moved to a new apartment in the Pesterzsébet district of Budapest, where Géza and Ilona lived until 4 January 1991. On that day Géza died at the age of 59 in a Budapest hospital, following an operation. His wife and children described it as 'the tragedy of their lives'.

Géza remained embittered throughout his life at the fact that he was refused membership of the Hungarian League of Antifascists and

Resistance Fighters. 'I was rejected. They wrote that I was much too young to have been a resistance fighter.'

Lidia Rydzikowska A few days after their liberation from Auschwitz, Bronisława and Ryszard Rydzikowski took in a little girl by the name of Lidia, as she was called in the camp. Straightaway, Lidia told her adoptive parents about the camp and her life before. During the first days with the Rydzikowskis, she said that she had come to Auschwitz 'with my mummy in a red wagon'. And one day, as she was crossing the railway bridge in Oświęcim with her father, she pointed to a red cattle wagon in a passing train and said that it was like the wagon she had travelled in.

Lidia often recalled the moment when Germans fetched her. 'My grandmother and I cried a lot, but mummy said that I shouldn't cry because the Germans were watching.'

She came from Minsk. Her mother's name was Anna and her father was Lenard. He went to the front, she said. She vaguely recalled her brother Mikhail. He had often pushed her around in a wheelbarrow and tipped her into the sand. But she could no longer remember whether he had been with her in the camp.

One day, when Ryszard Rydzikowski suggested buying a sledge, Lidia said to him: 'Wait, daddy, when Mikhail comes he'll buy me one.'

Sometimes the child was asked what her surname was. The adults thought she was saying 'Batjar', which in the Polish spoken particularly in the Lviv region means something like 'scoundrel'. (The city had been called Lwów until September 1939, when Soviet troops invaded. It had been a Polish city until then and most of its inhabitants were Jews and Poles.) They would smile when she told them, thinking that she was joking.

As she grew older, Lidia learned to express herself better. She used other variants, but mostly she said that her name was Lidia Baciarówna. Her recollections of the first years of her life became more and more detailed:

I remember the wooden barracks. It seemed very large at the time. That's where I saw my mother. She had long black braids. I'm almost sure she was my mother. She was beautiful. I always thought she was the most beautiful.

When the SS men took the women away, my mother broke out of the ranks and ran to me. The SS man shouted and shot her. I never saw her again.

A boy came up to me, took my hand and said: 'Come with me.'

When we assembled for the roll call, an SS woman came into the barracks with a large black dog. We were afraid of the dog and quickly moved away.

Once I fell from the second tier of a bunk bed. I began to cry out loud and then a woman comforted me and gave me something to eat.

In the camp, people always frightened us by saying that Mengele would come. I didn't know what or who he was.

I remember the dead, who were covered with grey blankets, and also the rats. They were so dangerous that whenever we saw one we would scream and hide under the bunks.... Before the Rydzikowski family took me in, I was in some kind of hospital. Almost all of the others there were adult men. I was shown to everyone, and then I returned to the barracks, where the children were. I cannot say why I was there or what kind of hospital it was.

I remember my mother now approaching me and asking if I wanted to go with her. I said 'take me, auntie, I'll be a good girl.'

I was in the barracks at the time, eating half-cooked peas from a large red bowl.


Looking back, Lidia says: 'I don't know whether I saw all those things myself or whether someone else described them so realistically that I felt as if I had witnessed them. I think I probably saw it all myself. But I didn't realize the enormity of the tragedy taking place before my eyes.'

Lidia was officially adopted by the Rydzikowkis in June 1947. A month earlier she had been baptized as Ludmila-Lidia (Luda/Ljuda for short). Her age was determined by the local doctor and her date of birth given as 2 January 1940. There was no place of birth on the birth certificate. Lidia was given her Polish parents' surname.

Lidia attended primary school in Oświęcim from 1947 to 1954. She also went to music school for a while. 'At some point, my ambition was to be an operetta singer.' She tried on several occasions to write poems. 'They were published in school magazines.' Years later, she still had the urge 'to write or create something'.

While at school, she tended to avoid her fellow pupils. Ryszard Rydzikowski: 'She preferred to be alone.' She would often run barefoot in the fields and regularly lost her shoes. She was particularly fascinated by geese. She went to where they were feeding and chased them away.

After finishing her basic schooling, Lidia went to the chemical technical college in Oświęcim, graduating in 1958. She wanted to go to university, but the family couldn't afford it. Bronisława: 'Soon after the war, I had to go to work because my husband couldn't manage alone to pay for our daughter's upkeep and schooling. Lidia wanted to carry on studying and we wanted her to as well, but I became sick with anaemia and we had to abandon the idea.'

In 1958, Lidia began working in the laboratory of the chemical works in Oświęcim, where her father also worked. 'But my adoptive mother was afraid I would have to do shift work and wouldn't manage. She found me a position in the installation planning office at the chemical works.'

In the late 1950s, Lidia began to wonder increasingly: 'Who am I? Where do I come from? I can't get it out of my mind.'

In late summer 1958, she heard a missing persons announcement on the radio, which touched her. She wrote to the Polish Red Cross:

I am looking for my father. It could be that there was a missing persons announcement on the radio by the International Red Cross in Switzerland for Lidia Baciarówna. That could be me. During the occupation I was deported as a child to Auschwitz, where my mother died. I would like to find my father or someone from my family.

A month later, she received a reply from the Polish Red Cross: 'We have no information about your father at the moment.'

Lidia continued searching, 'although it appeared impossible that I would find my father'. She wrote to many offices but always received negative answers.

The 18-year-old refused to give up. She was helped by the former Auschwitz inmate Tadeuz Szymański and a work colleague, Henryk Porębski, who had also been in the camp. She obtained the address of the German Red Cross and wrote to Germany for the first time in summer 1959. The letters went back and forth. Lidia sent photos taken some years after the liberation and pictures of what she looked like now. She provided every tiny detail of her life that she could remember and gave her camp number, 70072. And then, on 20 January 1962, came an unexpected but dearly hoped-for reply from the German Red Cross in Hamburg:

It gives us pleasure to inform you that your mother did not die, as you think, but lives in the USSR. Anna Bocharova submitted a missing persons announcement through the Soviet Red Cross. The details provided were: Lyudmila Bocharova, born 1940, father's first name Alexei, mother's first name Anna, place of birth Novi Szambor, Dragobychskaya Oblast. Your identity was confirmed by the number 70072, which you indicated and which was given by the Soviet Red Cross for the girl being sought.[22]

Her biological mother had the number 70071. And as the numbers were tattooed first on the mother and then on the daughter, it was clear that this must be her mother.

The Rydzikowskis could hardly believe it. The letter from the Red Cross was passed from one person to another.

On 14 February 1962, the first sign of life from Lidia's family came from Ukraine in the form of a telegram: 'We are happy that you are alive. Who collected you from the camp? Where did you grow up? How are the Rydzikowskis? Do you remember your mother? We look forward to a visit. Mama, papa and sisters.'[23]

When Lidia received these first lines from Ukraine, she initially reproached her biological mother: 'You've waited until now to look for me. If I had been a mother, I would have done much more to find my daughter.' But Lidia didn't yet know all the efforts her mother had made since the end of the war to find her.

One day, before the telegram arrived, the postman told Lidia that there was a telephone call for her. The Rydzikowskis didn't have a phone, so she was meant to go at 10 a.m. the following day to the post office in Oświęcim. Lidia's refound mother in Ukraine had booked a telephone call.

Anna Bocharova, her husband Alexei and a friend of the family who spoke some Polish waited on tenterhooks at the post office in Yenakiieve in the south-east of Ukraine for the call to Oświęcim.

When the connection was finally made, Anna shouted in excitement: 'Lyuda, my daughter, can you hear me?' Lidia, who spoke a little Russian, replied: 'Mama, I can hear you!' She couldn't remember a single word of the call.

Immediately after receiving the letter from the German Red Cross, Lidia had written to Ukraine:

Dear mother, papa and sisters,

You can't imagine how happy I was when I received the news that my mother was alive. I can hardly believe it. It's like a dream.

I have often thought about you. I've been to the [former] camp and lit candles, because I thought you were no longer alive and that I would never see you again. I thought that my real name, my origins, my date of birth and my family would remain an unsolved puzzle forever.

I remember some moments in the camp, but I have only a blurred memory of how we were separated and what you look like....

How did you get back to the USSR? Were you still in Auschwitz when the camp was liberated? How old are you? How many sisters do I have? Are they older or younger than me? I don't remember them. I'd be interested to know when exactly I was born. How old is father?

Was he really at the front? And why do I claim to have a brother Mikhail?

Please write and tell me what you do, where you work. I would so much like to see you....

I'm sending a couple of photos and await your letter and pictures with impatience. Kisses to you and my sisters from your daughter Lyuda.[24]

Shortly afterwards, Lidia received a letter from her mother:

Greetings, our dearest daughter Lyudochka!

Yesterday we received the joyous news that they had found you, and in the letter were two photos of you.

My dear little one, the memory I have kept of you all my life is exactly the one on the photos of you when you were younger. You are a little taller and more robust but your face is the same as it was when we were separated.

My dearest little child, you were four years and one month old at the time. You, my little child, don't remember perhaps or have forgotten, but I, my little one, have never forgotten you by day or by night. We have survived all of the fateful blows in Auschwitz and you have been with me constantly these last seventeen years.

After liberation, I started immediately to look for you. I wrote everywhere but all in vain, but I was determined to keep looking for you all the days of my life. And then the longed-for day arrived, and now I am very happy, my little daughter, to discover that you are alive....

I beg you, my dearest little daughter, to write to me everything about your life, how you are living and with whom. If you have foster parents, please express to them my enormous gratitude for caring for and protecting you. Tell them that for your biological mother they are the most precious people in the whole world....

Lyudochka, little child, we have received your photos as a grown-up. You look exactly like your father, with the dimple on your chin and nose. Only your eyes are like mine.

Lyudochka, little child, we will get a photo of the family taken and send it to you.

My little child, I would like to carry on writing forever, but I'm so happy that I can't write any more. Goodbye for now and kisses.[25]

A few days later, the sisters Svetlana, Rimma and Olga, and even an uncle, wrote. In March 1962, Lidia received an invitation to the Soviet Union for three months. The invitation also extended to her adoptive parents and her husband – Lidia had married in December 1961.

In autumn, she finally left. Lidia's mother was at the train station in Moscow to meet her. They embraced and cried. Anna Bocharova had always thought of her daughter as a child. In front of her was an adult woman.

Thousands of women and men who had lost their children in the war prepared a huge reception for Lidia. She was welcomed like a cosmonaut who had just returned to Earth. Newspapers, the radio and television reported on it, since it was the first time in ages that one of the children of Auschwitz had been reunited with her parents. It nourished the hope of others that perhaps their own children would be found.

From Moscow, they set off on the 1,000-kilometre journey to Yenakiieve, where the Bocharovs lived. The mother and daughter visited numerous factories to relate their lives.

Despite all of the to-do, they finally found time to talk. Lidia learned about her forgotten childhood and got an idea of those aspects that had remained in the dark. Her father had been a teacher and she was born on 14 December 1940, almost a year later than the doctors in Oświęcim had determined.

Anna Bocharova had seen her daughter in Auschwitz for the last time in mid-January 1945. She told Lyuda many times: 'Never forget that

your name is Bocharov, that my name is Anna and your father is Alexei.'
Lyuda replied: 'I won't forget, mama.'

Anna was evacuated to Bergen-Belsen as the Red Army approached.
She was liberated there by the British on 15 April 1945.

She returned home to Ukraine and began to work in an orphanage. 'I
thought I might find a trace there.' She visited many children's homes. 'I
saw thousands of children who had no parents anymore.' An Auschwitz
survivor told her that he had seen a child who looked like her daughter
and that a Ukrainian woman had taken her.

When Anna gave birth to two daughters in 1947, relatives said: 'Give
them the names of your two dead daughters. The war took Svetlana and
Lyudmila and in this way you will keep alive their memory.'

'No', she replied, 'I think that Lyuda is alive. Svetlana was shot, so
one of them can be named Svetlana, but I don't agree to Lyudmila. She's
alive.' And on 14 December 1947, the Bocharov family celebrated Lyuda's
(Lidia's) birthday, as they had done the years before and would do for all
the years thereafter.

The Bocharovs never abandoned hope and wrote letters everywhere.
The replies were all negative – until January 1962.

On her first visit to Ukraine, Lidia was accompanied by her husband
and her Polish parents. During the stay, the two mothers became more
and more jealous of one another. Anna wanted her refound daughter to
stay in Yenakiieve, but Bronisława wanted her Lidia to return with her
to Poland.

The jealousy was evident in many everyday scenes. Ryszard
Rydzikowski, Lidia's Polish father, clearly recalls one particular occasion
at the Bocharovs: 'Lidia was taking a bath. She called her biological
mother to wash her back. My wife protested. She wanted to do it, as she
had done all those years. They argued until they finally agreed that both
of them should do it.'

Lidia ultimately returned to Poland with her adoptive parents. 'I now
have two mothers and two fathers', she said on her next visit to Moscow
and Ukraine. It was not to be her last visit. She went to see her biological
mother many times. And the Bocharovs also visited her in Poland.

Lidia's story touched many women and men, especially in Russia,
Ukraine and Poland. She received many moving letters from people,
including a soldier who had been one of the liberators of Auschwitz. He

recalled a small, black-haired girl with whom he had played. Could it have been Lidia?

Ewa Krcz Karolin and Jósef Krcz from Oświęcim took little Ewa from Auschwitz-Birkenau at the end of January / beginning of February 1945. On 21 August 1949, the day Ewa started school, the Oświęcim local court approved her adoption by her Polish foster parents. Her assumed date of birth was marked as 15 November 1942.

'All of the relatives, acquaintances and neighbours knew from the outset that I was a child from the camp.' It was the same at school. 'The children noticed that I had a number, but it was of no importance. They knew about it.'

Ewa did well at school. She discovered music. The family bought a piano. She completed seven years at the music school in Oświęcim and graduated from high school in 1960.

While she was at school, there was a group of students who wanted to visit the Auschwitz-Birkenau Memorial. 'One of them was me. The former extermination camp left a strong impression', said Ewa once. 'But it didn't awaken any memories. I can only vaguely remember some kind of shower – and my fear of dogs.'

The subject grew in importance for Ewa. 'Who was I and where did I come from?' With the aid of Tadeusz Szymański, she began to investigate. It was established that she had arrived in Auschwitz-Birkenau on 20 May 1944 in a transport of Hungarian Jews. The Memorial chronology, based on original documents from the Nazi camp authorities and statements by former inmates, has the following entry:

> 34 male Jews (twin brothers and any boys born as a twin), given Nos. A-2507–A-2540, and 58 female Jews (twin sisters and any girls born as a twin), given Nos. A-5079–A-5136, arrive in an RSHA transport from Hungary and are admitted to the camp. Some of the young and healthy individuals are probably admitted as 'depot prisoners'. The remaining people are killed in the gas chambers.[26]

Ewa had the number A 5116.

In 1962, she and Szymański contacted former inmates in Hungary, the Association of Partisans and newspaper offices. In autumn 1962, the journalist László Rózza published an article entitled 'Who is Ewa Krcz?' in the newspaper *Népszabadság*. Many Hungarian publications took this information and printed photos of Ewa. Hundreds of readers wrote in. Many said, 'I'm certain that's my child',[27] in the hope of finding their long-lost daughters.

Some merely recalled that 'a sweet, almond-eyed, black-haired girl was deported from the neighbouring apartment'. One woman wrote that her Ewa had pierced ears and that perhaps that could be verified.

One person objected:

> What's the point of reopening old wounds, because there is no single family that hasn't lost members. I think it a great sin on your part to raise false hopes in these people, who believe that this former inmate A 5116, Ewa Krcz ... is their child. What is it but an illusion to think that after eighteen years this adult woman will bear any resemblance to their four- or five-year-old girl?

The newspaper responded: 'What we are doing in the name of humanity is not to raise false hopes but to arouse a sense of humanitarian solidarity. We don't think it is an illusion for Ewa to want to find her parents and relatives again.'[28]

Ewa Krcz received a telegram: 'Little Ewa, father, brother found.' Over fifty possible relatives sent messages, all convinced that Ewa was their daughter.

The Hungarian Red Cross contacted her. 'Please look carefully at these two photos, an old lady and a young married couple, the child's parents, say that you are Jutka (Judit) Stolcz. Others also believe that Jutka Stolcz and Ewa Krcz are the same person. Think carefully! Can you recall the faces of the young couple? Or that you were once photographed with a fluffy toy dog?'[29]

More and more people took an interest in Ewa's story. The girls in a class at Kossuth Zsusza secondary school in Budapest invited Ewa to visit them and offered to pay the travel costs. The media continued to report. 'Twenty-year-olds, help! If the parents are alive, shouldn't we find them?' was the headline in one Hungarian newspaper.

On 7 July 1963, Ewa Krcz travelled with Tadeusz Szymański to Budapest. She remembers the discussion with her Polish brother Stanisław, who had collected her shortly after the camp was liberated and spoken to a woman who said that her parents were no longer living. 'I didn't think so much about the parents for that reason. But I thought it possible that there might be someone from the family. The fact that so many people claimed to be my parents caused problems.'

The girls at Kossuth school prepared a great welcome. They showed Ewa Budapest, went on excursions, swimming, dancing, and made friends.

The encounters with the people who thought she was their lost child were quite different. Without exception, they tried to persuade Ewa to recognize them as her real family. They all assured her: 'You are our child.'

Every family wanted to make a great celebration. Every apartment, every house was decorated, the tables festively laid. She was shown photos that were supposed to prove that she looked like the people on them – countless pictures of a smiling little girl crawling on all fours, who a few months later was to be deported to Auschwitz.

'I remember the first visit. The husband knew I was coming. He was a tailor by the name of Goldfinder. He had made everything ready. We rang the doorbell. He opened the door. He was holding a huge bunch of roses. When he saw me, he fainted.'

When he came to, he said again and again: 'I knew the child was alive. I've always known it.' His wife tried to calm him. 'Don't get so fixated. We're not even sure that she's our daughter. What will you do if she isn't?'

Ewa was confused. Tears flowed. She said to Tadeusz: 'What a welcome! What an experience! Maybe I'm related to them. He must be my father!' But Tadeusz placated her. 'Wait! We've still got a lot of visits.'

Another time, they visited an old woman. Old photos were shown, letters from long-dead aunts and uncles.

'Look at the high forehead, the bushy eyebrows, the arch of the upper lip. It's clear, isn't it?' And with trembling fingers, she traced the contours of the little girl's oval face, hopefully seeking similarities between the faded photographs and the woman from Kraków sitting in front of her.

In Nagykanizsa, 200 kilometres southwest of Budapest, Ewa was joyfully welcomed. Gyuli Schlesinger also believed that he had found his daughter again. With tears in his eyes, he told Ewa 'that his wife, [her] mother, was no longer alive'. He assured the press and radio reporters who were present that he didn't want any sensationalism but merely hoped that Ewa was his own child.

'Evi!' Ewa was greeted in this way in one village. The Weinert family thought they had got a second daughter. The meeting of Evika and Ewa left a marked impression on Tadeusz:

> When we were sitting in the room, a typical Hungarian village room, Ewa sat next to Evika. They embraced. They looked at one another, saying almost nothing. And when one of them spoke, the other barely understood what was being said because of the language barrier. But they managed to communicate what they wanted to say. It was the language of love. And sometimes no words are needed to express love.

Ewa quickly realized that it would be very difficult to find her family. 'During the first visits, Ewa was uneasy', Tadeusz recalled. 'But it wasn't despair or anger that people were trying to fool her. She wanted to find someone. Sometimes the supposed parents were so pushy that she had to tell them.'

Ewa became more and more reserved, but not always. Tadeusz: 'It seemed to me that if she liked someone, she supported this family. She wanted to help them.'

Her companion asked them all: 'When was your child deported?' Sometimes they would reply: 'In August 1944. But what business is that of yours? She's our daughter.' But Ewa was deported to Auschwitz-Birkenau on 20 May 1944.

There were some cases where everything fitted. It was possible that these people were Ewa's parents. In the end, twelve of the fifty-four families remained.

Ewa and Tadeusz returned to Oświęcim on 23 July 1963. Professor Ökrös[30] from the Forensic Institute in Budapest compared Ewa's blood group and fingerprints with those of the possible parents. There were no matches; much to everyone's disappointment, none of them could be Ewa's parents.

In subsequent years, however, she maintained contact with some of them. One was the journalist and painter Peter Imre from Budapest. Until his death in 1976, he took care of 'his daughter', sending her money, for example, so she could go to university, attending her wedding in 1965.

From 1966, Ewa Krcz-Sieczka, as she was now called, worked as a dentist in a town in western Poland. She was passionate about her work. She has three daughters, Agata, Anne and Renate, born in 1968, 1969 and 1974. The two elder ones studied medicine, much to Ewa's pleasure. She tried indirectly to convey to her children the hope that they would do something to help humanity – as a direct consequence of her own life.

She didn't want to bother her daughters too much with the subject of Auschwitz. If her daughters asked her, for example, why she had a number tattooed on her arm, she explained to them. She always resisted requests for interviews from journalists, historians or film makers, who wanted to ask her children what it was like to have a mother who had been a child in Auschwitz.

Ewa never really gave up her hope of finding her biological parents. The hope was rekindled above all when the Hungarian director László Nádasy completed a film entitled *Éva A 5116* in the 1960s. It was shown in many countries – but without the hoped-for outcome.

She has never forgotten the discussions, meetings and people she met in Hungary. Looking back, she said once: 'There was a tragedy in every home. Their child Ewa had been deported. And then someone came to visit – and it wasn't their child. All of my encounters in Hungary were more difficult for me than the most difficult exams I had to sit.'

For years, she remained in touch with a man who had emigrated from Hungary to Sweden and believed that he was her father. As the years went by, however, she began to ask whether there was any point.

She received several inquiries from families. For example, the son of a Jewish family living in California wrote: 'I'm writing to you because my father corresponded with Ewa Krcz to find out whether she was his daughter. We would be happy to invite Ewa to Israel to do blood tests and whatever else is necessary to find out whether she is part of our family.'

Ewa was unable to comply with such requests. The experiences and the long search for her parents had been too exhausting and painful.

# '… The Other Train Is Always There'

None of the surviving children of Auschwitz could forget the ultimately indescribable terrible experiences they had to go through in the death camp. The pain is always there. The mother who was murdered, the father, the sister, the brother, the grandparents, the friends, aunts and uncles. And as they grow older and no longer have to look after their own families, the memories of Auschwitz often return even more powerfully. They remain alive throughout their lifetimes and beyond, with them and their descendants. The consequences of Auschwitz are suffering without end – today, tomorrow, the day after tomorrow and far beyond.

In the late 1950s, for example, doctors from Kraków began to study the effects of the war and concentration camp internment on former inmates. Polish psychiatrists and also fifty children of the camps, including boys and girls who had been in Auschwitz, investigated this subject over a long period. Eighteen of the children had been born in the camps.

Dr Wanda Półtawska was one of the psychiatrists to study these children. She had been arrested herself at the age of 19 for being active in the Polish resistance movement and interned on 23 September 1941 in Ravensbrück women's concentration camp. Terrible medical experiments were performed there on her and on other girls and women: incisions were made in their legs and the wounds infected with bacilli, and then the legs were put in plaster. Many died during the experiments or years later.

She had been at the University Psychiatric Clinic in Kraków since 1952. She and her colleagues discovered that the youths and adults – as they were now – whom they examined suffered from nervousness, headaches, sleep disorders, anxiety and apathy.[1] In 1966, for example, she reported on a 27-year-old woman who had probably been deported to Auschwitz as a 4-year-old in mid-1942:

On several occasions she returned to the subject of the family.... Her earliest memory is the image of her mother; she claims to recall her face and that she had a child in her arms, then a large fire, her mother's screams and tears. She also remembers a large number of children, perhaps a hundred....

Asked what she would like to change in her life, she just sighed and said like a small child: 'That mummy and daddy were here, but that's not possible. I'm completely despondent, my fate remained in Auschwitz. How often do I consider taking my life, but alone I can hardly help myself. If only I had someone close, someone who could help me.' ...

On the day of the examination, she began suddenly to scream in the night ..., repeating the word 'mummy, mummy' and crying in her sleep. In the morning she had no recollection of what had happened in the night.

She suddenly started talking about the Germans, saying she was still afraid of them and accusing them: 'I damn them and have a terrible fear, I'm continuously afraid of them. If it hadn't been for the Germans, I would have a different life....'

She feels very isolated and abandoned. It is terribly painful for her that she has no parents, and she particularly misses her mother. She feels forgotten, abandoned and unloved....

She repulses anyone who tries to approach her. She fears people, although she is much in need of their friendly assistance. But she is convinced that people only want to exploit her in the way her previous experience has demonstrated. She has a pronounced inferiority complex and quickly abandons plans for fear of failure. She feels that she can never succeed.[2]

A young woman, now 23 years old, was born in Auschwitz-Birkenau in 1943. Her mother also survived.

After the birth of the child, ... who was allowed to live, in Birkenau in 1943, she [her mother] kept the child for six weeks but could not breastfeed it and fed it with herbal tea. The child was not bathed once in these six weeks....

She is very attached to her mother and does nothing without her. The mother accompanied her to the examination. She had married the previous year and was now expecting a child. She was looking forward to it but was afraid that the child might be nervous. She spoke enthusiastically about her husband.

She often thinks about Auschwitz and says: 'Because of this internment [and her health] she cannot be a musician.' ... She speaks casually about her 'failed life'.... She continues: 'I'm still afraid of the Germans.' ...

She has a fairly precise insight into her mental state, which helps her resolve conflicts and take an objective view of reality. The tests reveal anxiety and suppressed aggression, which the subject is unaware of and which manifest themselves in an excessive anxiety and restless concern for her loved ones.[3]

The doctors in Kraków reported on a 36-year-old woman who was deported at the age of 10 and spent three years in various camps:

'I'd like to forget but it isn't possible. I would like at least for these memories to fade, but they lose nothing of their power and cannot be erased.'

She talks of her time in the camp: 'I was panic-stricken with fear, it was one long horror that for some unknown reason I survived. Now I'm not afraid of anything specific but there are moments ... during the day when I cannot suppress the irrational fear that wells up in me. My body drips with perspiration and I tell myself: don't be stupid, the war is long over. But that doesn't help; it's incurable.' ...

Asked if she has children, she answers typically: 'I'd love to have children but I am terribly afraid that a child could go through what I did and so I can't bring myself to have one, although I know it's silly.' ...

She fears and hates the Germans. She was surprised herself when on a journey through German territory she found that German children provoked the greatest hatred in her. She couldn't control this feeling and cut short her stay....

She regards her life as 'messed up and there's nothing to be done because the shadow of the past follows me'....

She is not very active, lives without purpose or ambition and is completely without energy. There is a feeling of emptiness and a ruined life in everything she does. She returns unwillingly to her camp experiences, but during the examination it turns out that these are the only problems that she addresses, as if her life had stopped at the moment of liberation.[4]

For these children of Auschwitz, Germans and the German language are for ever associated with fear. Four children expressed themselves like this, for example:

'My attitude to the Germans is decidedly hostile and I don't believe in German–Polish friendship.'

'When I suddenly hear German spoken on the radio or while I'm on a trip, I drop everything.'

'I associate every word of German with the yelling in the camp and with the kapos. I refused to go on a business trip to Germany. They're all the same there.'

'The word Germans is enough to provoke fear in me. People can't understand it.'[5]

ANGER, FEAR, HOPE … For the women and men who survived Auschwitz as children and juveniles, the relationship to Germany and the Germans remains difficult. In the first years after liberation, they were all furious and enraged by what the Germans had done to them and their families. They feared and hated the Germans in equal measure.

Yehuda Bacon wanted no further contact of any kind with Germans. While still in Auschwitz-Birkenau, he and other children and juveniles asked themselves: 'What will become of us if we survive? The Germans, all Germans, were for us like the SS, the murderers.' They wanted revenge. The children made a pact: 'After the war, we'll build a high wall and leave the Germans to starve behind it.'

When Yehuda returned in 1945 as a 15-year-old to his Czech hometown of Ostrava, he saw a group of German prisoners of war being ordered to shovel snow. He recalled: 'During the occupation my father had had to do exactly the same thing.' And he had had to watch this deep humiliation. 'My first reaction was to kill one of the Germans with a stone.' But he did nothing. At that moment, he realized: 'Why should I hit him? I don't know the man. I don't know if he committed any crimes.'

For many years, Otto Klein, one of the many 'Mengele twins' from Hungary, had a 'strong hatred and thoughts of revenge'. In 1955, he entered German territory for the first time again. When he met middle-aged or older men, he immediately wondered: 'Were you a Nazi?' He said once: 'I never wanted to blame the entire German people, only those who committed the crimes or allowed them to be committed.'

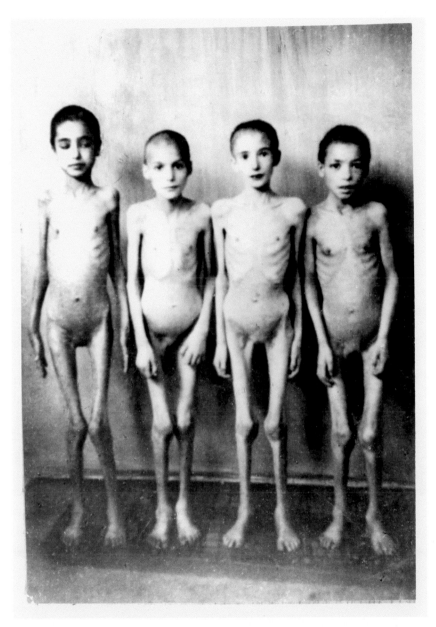

SS Doctor Mengele 'claimed' twins on the ramp in Birkenau for his experiments in the extermination camp. They were selected, measured, X-rayed, infected with viruses, their eyes cauterized, and finally killed and their bodies dissected. © Archive of Auschwitz-Birkenau Memorial and Museum

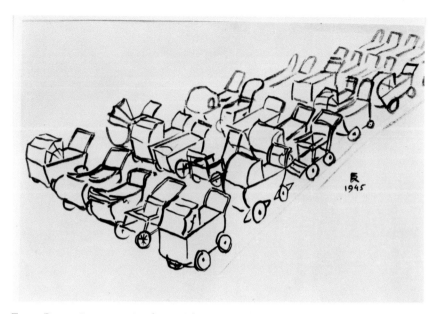

Franz Reisz: *Prams in Auschwitz*. The watercolour was painted in Paris in 1945.
© Archive of Auschwitz-Birkenau Memorial and Museum

Mother and child, murdered in Auschwitz.
© Archive of Auschwitz-Birkenau Memorial and Museum

Angela Orosz-Richt (*née* Bein) was born in Auschwitz-Birkenau around 21 December 1944. That she survived as a Jewish girl is quite exceptional, since all Jewish babies in Auschwitz-Birkenau were normally killed with their mothers. She lives today in Montreal.
© Angela Orosz-Richt

These children were liberated in Auschwitz on 27 January 1945. The photos were taken soon after the children were rescued.
© Alwin Meyer Archive

Auschwitz-Birkenau, late January 1945. Only 750 children and juveniles aged under 18 were liberated from the camp, including 521 aged 14 or younger, and around 60 new-born babies, several of whom died a short time afterwards. © Archive of Auschwitz-Birkenau Memorial and Museum

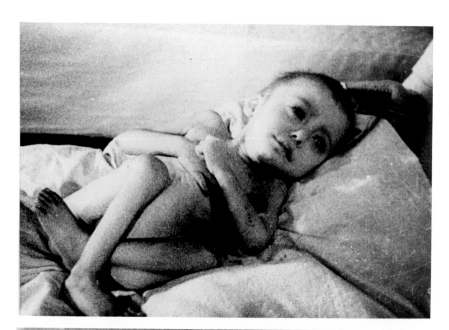

All children liberated in Auschwitz were extremely weak and suffered from tuberculosis, pleurisy, eczema and severe frostbite and other diseases, as was the case with Alice Ziemlich and Gertruda Mangel (bottom photo). The two girls, aged 14 and 12, had extremely frostbitten feet, possibly after having been forced to stand twelve hours in winter as a punishment.
© Archive of Auschwitz-Birkenau Memorial and Museum

Jiří Steiner a few weeks after liberation in the former camp: 'I'm the boy with the bandaged hand.' His hand was broken. In May 1945, there were still over 450 children in field hospitals established in the former camp. Most were Jewish boys and girls.

© Archive of Auschwitz-Birkenau Memorial and Museum

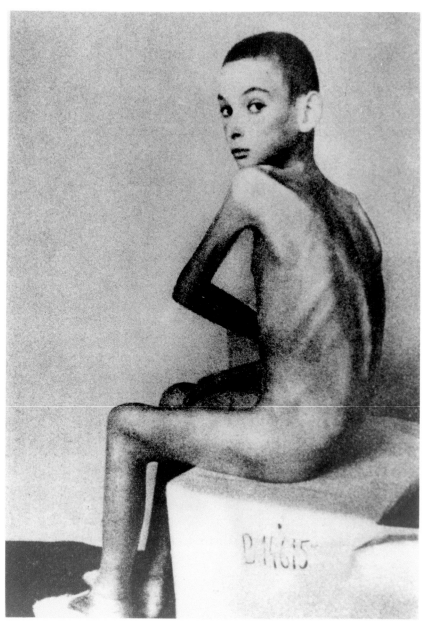

István (Stephen) Bleyer shortly after liberation in Auschwitz. The 14-year-old had frostbitten feet with two open sores. 'I couldn't walk and was very weak.' In 1951, he moved from Hungary via Italy to Canada, became an architect and President of the Montreal Holocaust Memorial Centre (since 2016: Montreal Holocaust Museum). He died in March 1997.
© Archive of Auschwitz-Birkenau Memorial and Museum

Gábor Hirsch believed that he was in this photo taken after the liberation. 'I think the youth with the blanket being helped by the medical orderly must be me. But I'm not absolutely certain.'
Top photo © Alwin Meyer
Bottom photo © Archive of Auschwitz-Birkenau Memorial and Museum

Very many Hungarian families who had lost a daughter called Éva were convinced that Ewa, who lives today in Poland, was their daughter: 'Definitely!' They all prepared great celebrations. They crowded round her and didn't want to let her go.
© Tadeusz Szymański

Channa and Israel Loewenstein with their daughters Noomi, Noga and Naawa. Neither of them ever regretted the decision to help establish a kibbutz. They constantly repeated: 'For us Israel is a new country built by those of us who survived the Holocaust.'
© Alwin Meyer Archive

Seventeen years after being liberated, Kola Klimczyk found his presumed biological mother in Vitebsk (Belarus).
© Tadeusz Szymański

Thirty-seven years after Auschwitz: Kola Klimczyk with his daughter Dorota.
© Alwin Meyer Archive

Lidia with her Polish adoptive mother Bronisława Rydzikowska. Seventeen years after the end of the Second World War, she found her biological mother, Anna Bocharova, in Ukraine.
© Archive of Auschwitz-Birkenau Memorial and Museum

Barbara Wesołowska, aged 17. She was probably born Katya Kulik in Auschwitz-Birkenau. The inmate number is tattooed on her left thigh.
© Barbara Wesołowska

Herbert Adler and his sister Wanda in Frankfurt am Main. 'My mother, three of my four sisters, three of my father's brothers: all died in Auschwitz.' He played football all his life (last row, 2nd from r.).
© Alwin Meyer Archive

Otto Klein 'always had this one dream': 'My brother and I are locked up. We are helpless. Will we survive?'
© Alwin Meyer

Dagmar Lieblová (*née* Fantlová) with her husband Petr on their wedding day in Prague. Her grandchildren were her pride and joy. She can be seen in the photo playing with Daniel (r.) and Vavřinec, the sons of her daughter Zuzana.
© Rita McLeod

Robert Büchler with photos of his parents Terezia and Josef (above) and his sister Ruth, four years younger than him. 'On the ramp at Birkenau I saw my mother and my sister for the last time. My father also died.'
© Alwin Meyer

Tauba Goldwasser, his mother's older sister, bore a strong resemblance to his mother. 'I only have a photo of my father.'
© Jack Mandelbaum

Majloch Mandelbaum, Janek's father. 'He did not survive the Stutthof concentration camp. When I learned in 1945 that he had not been liberated, that he had spent five years in a concentration camp and suffered every day, every hour – it is very difficult for me to talk about this.'
© Jack Mandelbaum

Jack (Janek) Mandelbaum with his children Sharon, John, Barry and Mark
in Kansas City. 'My father Majloch, my mother Cyrla, my sister Ita and my
brother Jakob were all murdered.'
© Jack Mandelbaum

Eduard and Ruth Kornfeld's family.
© Ruth Kornfeld

Eduard Kornfeld with photos of his murdered siblings: 'My sister Mathilda was murdered aged 12, my brother Jozef aged 9, Alexander was 8 and Rachel 6. My father, Simon Kornfeld, was 43, my mother Rosa 37.'
© Alwin Meyer

The twin sisters Vera Kriegal and Olga Solomon with their mother Šarolta Grossmann in Israel.
© Vera Kriegel

Vera with her children Isack and Frit at the Auschwitz Memorial.
© Vera Kriegel

Maury and Dasha Lewin in Los Angeles. 'For many decades', says Dasha, 'I couldn't admit to myself that my sister Sylva and my mother were dead. I wasn't so sure about my father.' For many decades, she continued to look for her family. 'This hope gave me some inner peace.' But no one came back.

Heinz Salvator Kounio in Thessaloniki. 'Of the 56,000 Jews who lived here, only 1,950 survived.'
© Alwin Meyer

Gravestone at the new Jewish cemetery. 'The old one was completely destroyed.'
© Alwin Meyer

Yehuda Bacon taught and passed on his skill and knowledge for many years at the Bezalel Academy of Arts and Design in Jerusalem, where he was a professor of graphic art and drawing. Since then, he has worked as a painter. His paintings have been exhibited in many countries.
© Alwin Meyer

Yehuda Bacon: self-portrait aged 15.
© Yehuda Bacon

Halina Birenbaum (*née* Grynsztein) was interned in the Warsaw ghetto at the age of 13, and then deported via Majdanek to Auschwitz. Her father, mother and younger brother were murdered. Only Halina and her older brother Marek survived.

© Halina Birenbaum

'I didn't want my children to be like the children of German mothers. I was always afraid of that. There was no sign of it, but I wanted to prevent it through their upbringing.'
© Alwin Meyer

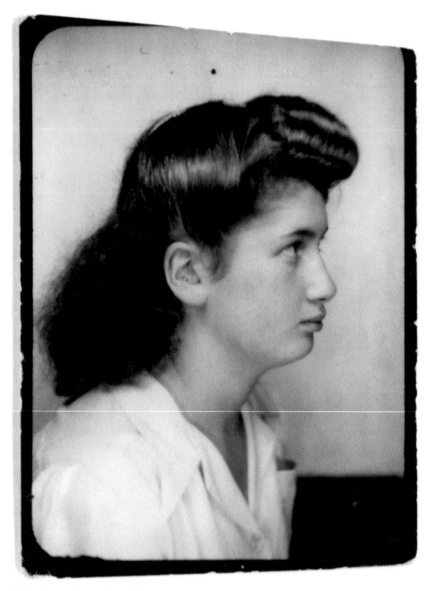

Halina Birenbaum (*née*) Grynsztein) two years after her liberation.
© Halina Birenbaum

Géza Kozma: 'After the war and everything my family and I had suffered, I didn't want the German-sounding name "Schein" anymore. So I changed it.'
© Alwin Meyer

Emilia Klimczyk helped Géza to survive when he was 12.
© Alwin Meyer Archive

Josif Konvoj from Vilnius: 'I can recall that medical experiments were carried out on me in Auschwitz. I don't know exactly what and how. That and the terrible time in the ghetto and the other camps have made me lose my memory. I'm convinced of that.'
© Alwin Meyer

After 1957, Gábor Hirsch travelled many times to Germany. It would have been impossible for him directly after being liberated. 'I also had to struggle with ideas of hatred and revenge.' He made a resolution never to buy German goods.

This gradually changed while he was still in Hungary. His interest in radio technology played a role. 'The scientific literature in German was quite good.' He began to read the magazine *Radio Mentor – Europäische Monatsschrift für Radio, Phono, Television, Electro* published in Berlin. His uncle took out a subscription for him from the 1950s onwards.

Gábor 'never had particular problems with young Germans, much less with the present generation. Some reserve towards the older generation remained after everything that I and my family had suffered under the Germans.'

After being liberated, Eduard Kornfeld also had an 'indescribable hatred for all Germans'. He wanted to revenge himself on 'the murderous nation'. He thought to himself: 'I'd like to fly, obtain an aeroplane with an atomic bomb and drop it on Germany. I wanted to kill as many German children, women and men as possible.'

For years, he asked himself how he could avenge his parents and brothers and sisters, murdered by the Germans.

> In the 1950s, when he was an apprentice gem setter in Zurich, he saw a way of taking revenge: There was a box with poison powder, including a toxic substance we used to clean the jewellery. The key to this box was in a jar I had access to. I could have got my hands on the poison. Then I could have poured it into the water supply somewhere in Germany to kill as many Germans as possible. I felt this mad urge for many, many years. Every day I had to struggle with myself.

– But he didn't do it.

In 1966, he was supposed to go to Germany on business. He thought about it and wrestled with himself for a long time. 'Should I go or not?' In the end, he went. It was terrible. He felt 'surrounded by murderers'. He couldn't trust anyone.

'In the hotel my name, Kornfeld, gave away the fact that I was Jewish.' He always locked the door but couldn't help thinking: 'Perhaps they'll poison my food or drink.'

Decades after liberation, he still regarded every German a few years older than him as a murderer. He thought about every young German he saw or met: 'His father is a murderer or is related to one.' Throughout his life – he died in September 2020 – he wondered: 'Was his grandfather involved with the killing?' He no longer hated younger Germans. 'They are not responsible for the crimes committed by their forefathers.' But he avoided contact with Germans 'as far as possible', nor did he feel comfortable in Germany.

Thomas Buergenthal, who was deported to Auschwitz as a 10-year-old, felt the same.[6] After being liberated, he lived for a time with his mother in Göttingen. 'At the beginning I would sit on the balcony. On Saturday or Sunday in particular, people would go for a walk, fathers and grand-fathers with the children. And my father was not among them. I thought that if I had a machine gun, I would shoot them all.' This changed when he played with children and met people who were friendly.[7]

Dagmar Lieblová relates an incident in a station café in Erfurt. She was sitting there late one evening with a friend, 'also Jewish'. The police came around midnight. Dagmar was deep in conversation and had forgotten where she was. Suddenly she heard the command: 'Your papers please!'

'I was taken completely by surprise.' She began to tremble. She was no longer accustomed to hearing German spoken that way. Looking back, she says: 'There must be something in people, in me, deep down, that emerges when I'm reminded of the past.'

One might ask why Dagmar studied German of all things, and later lectured in the subject.

> Of course, I didn't speak German immediately after the war. I couldn't speak it so well at the time. But I enjoyed my studies from the outset. We had very good lecturers and professors. I liked my course. It was also interesting to see what was happening in Germany. And, of course, I can't keep every-thing apart. German was also spoken in Auschwitz-Birkenau, Hamburg and Bergen-Belsen. But it's not the fault of the language.

Israel (Jürgen) Loewenstein returned to German soil for the first time in 1965. He travelled to East Germany to attend the twentieth anniversary of the liberation of Sachsenhausen. Then he went to East Berlin, through the streets of the former Scheunenviertel to the last house his family had lived in. He found the grave of his grandfather, who had died in late 1939, in the Jewish cemetery in Weissensee.

When he met older people, he couldn't help asking himself: 'Who is that? What did he do in the war?'

He wanted to visit Lotte Büchner, whom he had met at an agriculture and forestry congress in Romania. When he knocked at the door of her apartment on Chausseestrasse, a young man opened the door.

'Good evening. I'm Jürgen.'

'Who?'

'I'm Jürgen from Israel.'

'What? You're Jürgen?'

'Yes, what's the matter?'

'I imagined you quite differently.'

'How?'

'With sidelocks, a caftan and a large hat.'

'Why?'

'I never understood what my mother-in-law meant when she said she knew a Jew.'

'Have you never seen a Jew?'

'No, never. Where would I see one? You must understand that that was drummed into me in the Hitler Youth.'

On another occasion, Israel (Jürgen) Loewenstein heard: 'You work in the fields?' The man looked at Jürgen's hand and continued: 'You work in the kibbutz? Jews work?'

He has never understood how such notions about the Jews could continue to exist. 'People still have the most absurd ideas.'

The last time he went to the Auschwitz-Birkenau Memorial was in summer 2004. He accompanied a group of pupils from the Albrecht-Haushofer-Oberschule in Berlin-Heiligensee. Prior to the visit, he had shown them what was left of the Berlin he had known: the Scheunenviertel, the Jewish school in Grosse Hamburger Strasse, and the grave of the philosopher Moses Mendelssohn.

'They were most impressed by the "Stolpersteine" (stumbling blocks) of the small children murdered by the Nazis. Some of them started to cry.'

And, at the Auschwitz-Birkenau Memorial, they saw with their own eyes for the first time what they had hitherto known only from books, reports or films: the Main Camp or Auschwitz I with the entrance gate and the macabre slogan 'Arbeit macht frei' ['Work sets you free']; the black wall where the inmates were shot at close quarters; the standing cell, a 90 × 90 cm hole where up to three inmates had to stand all night, maybe for smoking a cigarette, before working twelve hours the next day; the wooden barracks in Auschwitz-Birkenau where 1,000 or even more inmates were crammed together; the ruins of the huge crematoria at the end of the camp in which people were gassed; the lake in Birkenau filled with the ashes of the cremated children, women and men.

Israel remained with the group all of the time they were exploring the camp. He answered questions, gave explanations, talked about his own experiences and those of his wife Channa in Auschwitz, and even consoled the young pupils.

'Meetings like this with young people helped me after the war to re-establish a balance in my life. It gave me the strength and confidence to resume the life that had been interrupted by the Nazis. And it restored some of my faith in humanity.'

MANY WERE NOT RECOGNIZED AS PERSECUTEES The attitude to Germany and the Germans has been repeatedly tested, particularly when it comes to assuming medical and hospital expenses. The claims were often rejected, even though the treatment was essential for diseases resulting from the camp internment.

For example, Mirjam M. was deported to Auschwitz as a 12-year-old. She doesn't like to talk about it and, if so, uses another name.

In the mid-1980s, Mirjam received medical attention in Israel, having been diagnosed with a severe psychiatric disorder resulting, according to the psychiatrist, from her 'persecution during the Second World War'.

Her doctor in Jerusalem prescribed psychiatric treatment four times a week for two years. He was paid $20 per session. Mirjam applied to the Amt für Wiedergutmachung [Reparation Office] in Saarburg, Rhineland-Palatinate, for payment of the costs.

The authorities passed on the matter for appraisal by a neurologist and psychiatrist in a small town near Koblenz. In his confidential neurological appraisal, he offered a completely different diagnosis from the one by his Israeli colleague:

[Her written] statement reads like the delusions of a psychotic sadist.... The psychiatric findings are those of an immature person with an extremely avoidant personality disorder, defective concentration and memory of the recent past, anxiety and tension. She fails at everything and is depressive....

Experiences normally fade with time. It cannot be denied that the subject's personality as such is the result of this marked experience.... M. is a teacher at an institute and a woman with a naturally highly sensitive character who has greater difficulty processing her persecution than a normally reacting young person....

Her current condition is not connected with the persecution but is due to her character.[8]

The claim that the experiences of the camp fade with time was refuted worldwide early on by many doctors and therapists. Professor Leo Eitinger, a reputed Czech-Norwegian psychiatrist and former Auschwitz inmate, has repeatedly pointed out that mental consequences became more likely as the former concentration camp victims grew older: 'Examinations revealing unconscious material clearly show that the wounds are deep and the scars often merely superficial.... The strength to deny or combat old memories dwindles during serious illnesses or when our vitality is weakened as a result of other events, such as ageing.'[9]

In any case, the Amt für Wiedergutmachung refused several times to pay the costs of Mirjam's treatment, in spite of written and telephone protests by German friends. She had to pay the costs of her persecution-induced disease herself.

In general, for decades, German doctors and authorities were quite strict in the matter of recognition of concentration camp internment trauma and reparation. Medical costs and pensions were paid by postwar Germany only if the victims could credibly demonstrate that there was a clear connection between the experience of internment and the present-day suffering, which was practically impossible to do.[10]

It was not uncommon for the post-war examiners to be former Nazis, some of whom were highly incriminated. Christian Pross, a Berlin doctor and internationally acclaimed specialist in the treatment of extremely traumatized subjects, wrote a pioneering study on this subject. He stated that many of the appraising doctors continued to identify with the aggressor and 'suppressed their own fear, shame and feelings of guilt' caused by the confrontation with the suffering of the victims by denying and trivializing this suffering.[11]

For decades, with few exceptions, German doctors failed to address the specific diseases of the survivors and ignored foreign studies on the subject. Pross:

> Numerous … studies have pointed to the fundamental differences between prisoner-of-war and concentration camps, which consist not only in the fact that there were no crematoria in the former but also that the aim of extermination, genocide and total marginalization of the inmates was absent. Many German experts did not recognize the concentration camp survivors' suffering as persecution trauma, as the returnees from Russia had also been exposed to the same deprivations but had not demonstrated such suffering.[12]

Not even one in two applications was recognized under the Federal Compensation Act (Bundesentschädigungsgesetz), adopted on 29 June 1956 retroactively to 1 October 1953. The law provided for a measly DM 150 as compensation for each month of internment – DM 5 per day in Auschwitz.[13]

The Polish Association of Former Child Inmates pointed out in late 1990 that 'over one thousand child inmates' living at that time in Poland had received 'no compensation from Germany for the injustice'. These children were all under 16 when they were interned.[14]

According to a calculation in 1989, around 90 per cent of the money was received by survivors who at the time of the persecution could demonstrate that they were German or had a geographical connection to Germany within the Reich borders in 1937. In other words, only 10 per cent of the total amount was paid to foreign victims – although they accounted for 90 per cent of the survivors.[15]

Several of the surviving children of Auschwitz whose stories are related in this book had to wait over forty years before receiving compensation for their forced camp internment. Prior to this, the Federal Compensation Act, which was sprinkled with extremely complicated provisions, had to be revised several times. Many survivors had already died and received nothing.

For around thirty-five years, Mirjam M. has been receiving a small pension from the Federal Republic of Germany for her concentration camp internment. Another child of Auschwitz has only obtained anything since the end of August 2011, over sixty years after being liberated.[16] 'But even if I were to obtain a lot', he pointed out, 'no one could make good the experience.' For both, recognition of their suffering and that of their families is what counts. This is the real meaning of 'reparation'.

EVERYDAY EXPERIENCE OF THE PAST The children and juveniles who survived Auschwitz and other camps still have to live today with the constant memory of the past. The experience is relived in sleepless nights, in nightmares, in everyday scenes, in the reactions of people. Keys with room numbers on a board in a hotel become the eyes in the photographs on the wall of SS doctor Mengele's laboratory. Everyday smells become the stench that recalls Auschwitz.

Vera Kriegel (*née* Grossmann) has travelled many times to Europe and North America, confronting school classes, church communities and politicians with her past. She often has flashbacks like the one that occurred during a visit to one European city.

I was hit so powerfully by a smell that it remained in me. In my mind, in my entire body. I just couldn't get rid of it. I went to my hotel room. I went to bed. I was beside myself. I was in a terrible state. All because of a smell. I pulled the bedclothes over my head. But I just couldn't get rid of this smell. I took a shower. But the smell wouldn't go away. It was in my head.

The next day she went to look for it. Finally, someone told her that the snack kiosks in this city use pig fat for frying. Vera believes that the smell recalled the stench of burnt human flesh coming out of the crematorium chimneys in Auschwitz-Birkenau.

Her twin sister Olga Solomon is also haunted by her experiences: 'I never said anything to my family but they noticed that there were seats at our dining table where I couldn't sit. Opposite our apartment was a lamppost that looked like a watchtower and reminded me of Auschwitz.

When the lamppost with its grey lamp was replaced one day, I cried for joy.'

Otto Klein rarely dreamed about Auschwitz-Birkenau, but he occasionally had a recurring dream: 'My brother and I are locked up. We are helpless. Will we survive?'

Eduard Kornfeld had terrible nightmares. 'I often dream that I'm in Auschwitz-Birkenau, in a room in the crematorium. And I know that I'm about to be gassed. We are pushed inside. I think: "Where can I hide?" But there's no way out. The SS push us into the gas chamber. I wake up covered in perspiration.'

Auschwitz was ever-present for Eduard. He sometimes heard or read people saying: 'Enough with the Holocaust and Auschwitz.' He would like to have told these people: 'What would you say if it was your mother who had been put in the gas chamber?'

He was at a loss to understand people who said he should finally forgive and forget. These people understood nothing of his situation. It was easy for them to talk – they didn't go through it themselves.

He often pointed out: 'There was not just one concentration camp. There were more than a thousand. And the Germans murdered with a ruthlessness that would be unimaginable today. But I saw it with my own eyes. How can I forget, much less forgive, these bestial crimes? I have no right to do so.'

Channa Loewenstein was deported to Auschwitz-Birkenau from the Carpathia region (now Ukraine) in summer 1944, with her parents and three of her four brothers. The women and men were immediately separated.

> My brothers went with my father and I with my mother. When we arrived at a sort of junction, Mengele, whose name I learned later, sent my mother to the left and me to the right. I said to her: 'Come with me!' But she didn't want to. I said again: 'Come over here, mummy.' She didn't want to, because she had been told to go to the left.... Mengele heard it. He went to my mother, grabbed her round the neck with a curved walking stick and threw her on the ground. My mother was on the wrong side.

Especially as she got older, Channa thought about her mother with increasing intensity. Again and again, she relived the moment when she lost her mother on the ramp at Auschwitz-Birkenau. She couldn't understand, couldn't forgive herself and was inconsolable that she hadn't gone over to her mother. 'I should have gone to my mother and not called her over. That would have been the obvious thing to do. I didn't do so.'

Channa cried a lot. As she got older, this recollection, the constant memory of this one moment, became a heavy and unbearable burden.

WHY DID I SURVIVE? Practically all of the children of Auschwitz are tormented by the question of why they survived and not their parents, brothers and sisters, relatives and friends. Jürgen Loewenstein is convinced: 'Surviving Auschwitz was a "matter of pure luck".'[17]

Eduard Kornfeld recalled those who, 'in spite of the conversations and the solidarity among the surviving children and juveniles', could not continue to live with this burden, with the memory of the murdered family members, the memory of Auschwitz and the other camps.

> It is extremely tragic, but many committed suicide, including friends from the sanatorium where I spent many years. One of my room mates lived later in a suburb of Zurich. He took his life there, in another sanatorium.
>
> In Davos there was a girl of my age, a very nice girl. She had already been discharged from the sanatorium and had rented a small apartment in the town. She was funny, quick-witted and always in a good mood. But one day she hanged herself.
>
> There was another young woman with whom I was friendly in Davos. She was three or four years older than me. Suddenly she stopped speaking. No one was able to approach her anymore. She stopped eating and drinking. She was force-fed for a time. But it didn't help. In the end she died.
>
> The list goes on.[18]

Eduard never considered suicide. He hadn't survived Auschwitz, Kaufering, Riederloh II, Augsburg-Pfersee and Dachau to kill himself after liberation. 'My will to survive was stronger than the death wish.' He wanted to get healthy, to build a new life and found a family.

Vera Kriegel suffered for years from severe depression. Her children, Isack and Frit, would ask why she felt so miserable. The answer every time: 'I have a headache.'

She and her twin sister Olga Solomon cannot forget what Auschwitz and Mengele did to them as children: 'He gave us orders and could do with us whatever he wanted. He experimented with us, took blood and gave us injections whenever he felt like it.' If they had not done what he wanted, they were afraid that he would have hit them or worse. 'And the constant questions …'.

She cannot stand people who attempt to give her advice and tell her what she should do and not do. They are too reminiscent of her helpless situation in Mengele's laboratory.

'I'm difficult to live with', she admits. 'Criticism for me is like a personal affront.' Every day is a struggle for survival. 'I have to show myself and others that Mengele didn't win.'

Everyone knew her as Vera, who wanted to live, who laughed and was fun. 'But that has always been just my outer self. Inside I'm completely different.' She puts up a façade. It's as if there are two Veras. 'One Vera goes out and enjoys life. The other Vera wants to die.'

Stella Müller-Madej from Kraków, who was deported to the 'hell of Auschwitz' at the age of 14, reports similar feelings.[19] 'I'm two people: one is civilized and sociable, the other just wants to be left alone and have nothing to do with people.'[20]

Olga Solomon spent half of her life in hospital. For a while she had difficulty living in the 'normal' world after Auschwitz. When she became pregnant for the first time, she experienced everything again. 'I don't know what Mengele injected into Vera and me when we were six. And then having to wait nine months for the birth. And always this fear: who knows what will come out? "Please God, let me have a healthy child." Luckily both the first and second child were healthy.'

Ludmila M. was 3 when she was liberated from Auschwitz. At the age of 42, she had to apply for an early pension: 'I am in permanent psychiatric treatment. It's very difficult for me to live with Auschwitz. My daughter has also suffered for many years. No one can really help us. We would like to be free of this history. It's not possible. We will never be free of Auschwitz. In recent years it has even got worse.'

BELIEF IN GOD Others lost their belief in God in Auschwitz. 'Where was He?' asked Channa Loewenstein. She found it difficult to live without believing in God. She said repeatedly: 'The only thing I believe in since Auschwitz is fate.'

Jiří Steiner was religious, 'but in summer 1944, when my parents were gassed', he decided to 'cut off from it'. 'It was in Auschwitz-Birkenau.' He had seen the smoke coming out of the crematoria and asked himself: 'Can a god permit that?' And the answer was 'no'.

Heinz Kounio is of a different opinion. 'I survived seven selections. At the last one, I was very weak. Full of indescribable fear. I am convinced that my firm belief in God helped me to stay alive.'

For Eduard Kornfeld, the question of God arose again with the birth of his children. Although he still wondered how God can exist against the background of Auschwitz, he wanted to give his children the same religious upbringing that he had. He didn't want to pass on his doubts to them. 'I also owed it to my grandparents.'

On the other hand, he didn't want his children to seek the meaning of life with a guru or in a sect. And he didn't want them to become Christians. 'Practically everyone who shipped us Jews to the camps was a Christian.' He hoped his children would find support in the religion of his forefathers.

He celebrated Shabbat in the family and lit the candles on Friday evening. 'Then I feel the blessed warmth that I felt as a child. It was so peaceful and nice.'

Yehuda Bacon recalls Martin Buber,[21] the Jewish philosopher, theologist and Bible translator, who died in 1965. He learned from him that Hasidim (the pious) speak of two types of suffering. The suffering that comes from God teaches us something. The suffering that comes from evil pulls us down. While we are suffering, we cannot recognize this, however. 'The most important thing we can learn from this is to better understand the suffering of our fellow human beings.'

Otto Klein went to the synagogue on the High Holidays and to say 'yahrzeit' for his parents and siblings. He lit a candle and said Kaddish for the salvation of the dead: 'May there be abundant peace from heaven, and life, for us and for all Israel.'

The belief in God gave him strength. 'Even in Auschwitz, my brother and I always hoped that God would free us.' Some people who went through all that would say: 'He doesn't exist. Where was He? He turned his back on us.' Otto Klein didn't dare to doubt God. 'That would have been the end.'

'Deep down in my heart I always remained a Jew. No one and nothing could beat that out of me. Not even Auschwitz.'

How to protect your own children? Most of the children of Auschwitz whose stories are told in this book avoided speaking to their own children, particularly when they were little, about their time in the camp. They wanted to protect them.

Channa and Israel (Jürgen) Loewenstein:

> We wanted to give our children a better start in life than we had. Nothing should stand in their way. That's why we didn't talk in detail about our time in Auschwitz. It has often been said: 'Are those who went through that really normal? Is it possible to be normal?' We didn't want our children to walk around all the time with the feeling that they were the children of parents who had been 'mentally damaged' in Auschwitz and for them to wonder 'am I normal?'

Géza Kozma only told his children about Auschwitz after a newspaper article about him appeared: 'They are not like the experiences you talk about when you come back from a trip.'

Vera Kriegel only spoke in general terms to her children about Auschwitz and never wanted to go into detail. Years later, she wondered: 'Perhaps it was a mistake, but I didn't know how to relate these things to my children.'

'Of course my children know', said Dagmar Lieblová, 'that I was in a concentration camp. It's part of my life.' But their interest was not the same. The eldest daughter listened. 'The second daughter wanted to know more about the family history. But it was all connected: there was only one cousin left. And only half of my husband's family remained after the war. My mother-in-law's relatives had all gone.'

Richard, Eduard Kornfeld's youngest son, began to ask questions when he was just 8. 'He wanted to know everything about Auschwitz.' His father gradually told him his story, but only when he was asked. In this way, the older children Alexander and Rita also heard about it.

Gábor Hirsch always meant to travel to Auschwitz to find out about his mother. But for a long time, it was not possible. While he was at university, he didn't have the time and had to think of his future. 'And before I obtained Swiss nationality it was too risky.' After his marriage and the birth of his sons, he had to look after the family. 'We wanted to live!' Later, after his naturalization and his children had grown up, he no longer had the courage.

He had only told his sons fragments. 'Whenever they asked' – about their grandparents and his life in Hungary and the terrible time in Auschwitz.

The 'change of heart' came between his son Mathias's high school graduation and the start of university. Mathias decided to take part in a study trip by juveniles from the Schweizerischer Israelitischer Gemeindebund to Poland. They were investigating the roots of Hasidism and also wanted to visit the scenes of the Shoah, including the Auschwitz Memorial.

Gábor said to his son: 'If you go, I'm coming too. That way it will be easier for me and perhaps for you as well.' It was the best way for him to recall the past and to speak about it with his son. On their way to the Auschwitz Memorial, Mathias heard for the first time the chronology of his father's past.

Two years later, Gábor visited Auschwitz with his youngest son Michael, who also heard his father's full story for the first time.

This time, he ventured into the former 'Gypsy' Camp, where he had spent the most terrible time in his life. 'I had to summon up an enormous amount of willpower.'

In the Memorial archive, he found documents about himself and some of his family. He met historians who were investigating the children liberated from Auschwitz. He learned about a twin by the name of Otto Klein, who had been liberated from the camp in 1945 at the age of 12 and lived in Geneva.

After his first two visits to Auschwitz with his sons, Gábor changed. His wife Margit, who died in August 2017, remembered: 'My husband opened up and spoke a lot more about his past.' The visits to the Memorial really 'opened the floodgates'.

The children and grandchildren of the survivors often know much more than their parents and grandparents suspect – from the unsaid, from hints and comments. The children of Auschwitz inevitably passed on their experiences to their children and grandchildren, even if they did their utmost to protect them. It is part of the family history that could not and cannot be hidden. The children and grandchildren could sense how their parents and grandparents suffered.

For Noomi and Noga, the first-born daughters of Channa and Israel Loewenstein, it was 'quite normal' that they had no grandparents. 'We all came from the concentration camps to the kibbutz', sometimes as the only survivors of large families. As the elderly had been the first to be murdered in the camps, none of the children in the kibbutz had grandparents. This changed when new members came to the kibbutz who had not been in the camps. Now some of the children in Yad Hanna had grandparents. The Loewenstein's third daughter Naawa once asked her mother, even before she started school: 'Where are my grandparents?' Her mother replied: 'You don't have any. They're dead.'

Naawa wasn't happy with this answer and kept asking every day about her grandparents. One day, she returned 'in triumph' from the kindergarten and said to her mother: 'Why do you keep telling me I don't have any grandparents? I have grandparents, but they're no longer living.'

When Noga, the middle daughter, was in secondary school, there was discussion of an exchange with a school in Siegen. 'My daughter and another boy from Yad Hanna were against an exchange with Germany', recalled Israel, 'although they knew that we were in favour of these contacts.' The exchange did not take place until Noga and Dror Feiler – the boy next door, today a renowned Swedish-Israeli musician and composer – had left school.

THE FOLLOWING GENERATIONS of the survivors are highly affected by the story of persecution of their parents and grandparents, as Yehuda Bacon and his wife Leah discovered.

Yehuda Bacon decided not to hide from his sons that he had been in a concentration camp.

> My wife and I decided to tell them everything as soon as they asked. When they were small, of course, we didn't say anything. Then came a period when they showed a great interest in everything. They wanted to know how it was.

I told them in what I thought was a suitable manner. They also read books on the subject, which they took themselves from the bookshelves.

The children, Benjamin and Hannan, were sick for many years. For no apparent reason, one of the boys stopped talking for a year. One of the first things he asked when he started speaking again was: 'How were the people burnt?'

Yehuda Bacon: 'Although we had always avoided it, our son must have heard something when he was young, when friends visited and we spoke about Auschwitz.'

Yaakov Gilad is a well-known Israeli musician. His mother is Halina Birenbaum (*née* Grynsztein). She was interned initially at the age of 13 in the Warsaw ghetto, and then deported to Auschwitz via Majdanek. Her father was deported to Treblinka, her mother to Majdanek, and her brother Chielek also to Auschwitz-Birkenau. Only Halina and her elder brother Marek, who managed to hide in Warsaw during the German occupation, survived. Halina was liberated in early May 1945 in Neustadt-Glewe, a satellite camp of Ravensbrück; Marek in the Polish capital on 17 January. Halina has lived since 1947 in Israel and has two sons.[22]

Yaakov Gilad and Halina Birenbaum were interviewed by the Israeli director Orna Ben-Dor Niv for her biographical film *Because of That War*. She asked about the impact of the Shoah on the survivors' children.

Yaakov Gilad:

I wanted to be like everyone else, but I couldn't be. Why did I feel different? First, I have a very small family. I realized early on that everyone else had aunts and uncles, and there were only the four of us. And we only became four when I was five years old. Until then we were only three. Also, my mother had a tattoo and the children were always asking me what it was....

I remember the simplest things, such as children's games. She took a towel, knotted it and said: 'That's how we made dolls in the ghetto.' Everything reminded her of her childhood in the ghetto. Her childhood memories are connected with the ghetto. My childhood memories were always connected with her memories.[23]

His mother Halina Birnbaum:

When he was two, I thought he was already old enough, a child who could walk unassisted, sit and stand and to whom I could already tell everything. I was eager to tell him about my family, those who had died in the Shoah and were no longer there. I wanted to share this with him as soon as possible. He should learn about my mother and my brother. Although he was still so small, I wanted to fill his world with my experiences 'there'.

I told him nothing about the atrocities, but still. As soon as he was able to take it in, he asked about the number. I told him that bad people had done that during the war. He continued to ask and I continued to tell him. I didn't realize that it would be so terrifying.[24]

Yaakov Gilad: 'If I got bad grades or broke something, she [my mother] would say: "Did I survive Auschwitz for that?" Even as a small child I heard this. Through my actions I had to provide the justification for her being alive.'[25]

Halina Birnbaum: 'I didn't want my children to be like the children of German mothers. I was always afraid of that. There was no sign of it, but I wanted to prevent it through their upbringing. My two sons were not always in agreement with me. And they didn't always understand my being different.'[26]

Jiří Steiner once took his son to Auschwitz and wanted to tell and show him everything, to 'pass on my recollections'. 'Petr couldn't stand this confrontation with my and our history.' His son has never returned to the Auschwitz Memorial.

The eldest granddaughter of grandparents who were both interned when they were young in Auschwitz describes a visit to a restaurant in Brussels.

'There were my parents and my two adult siblings.' The restaurant they had chosen appeared friendly and they looked forward to a couple of pleasant hours together as a family. There was a man and a woman speaking French sitting at one of the four windows. There was a small gallery with several tables. The family sat down there.

The waiter came. They ordered. It took half an hour but then the dishes were served.

The door to the restaurant opened. A couple with two small children entered. They looked around and then climbed up the short staircase to the gallery and sat down.

'We heard the sound of their voices. We were shocked: they were speaking German. They were Germans. We hadn't expected that and weren't prepared for it. We felt uncomfortable, although we had often had brief contact with Germans. But we were not prepared for it in these surroundings.'

The family discussed what they should do. They took their plates and sat in the farthest corner of the gallery.

That didn't work. 'They weren't loud and looked friendly but we couldn't and didn't want to hear this language. It made not only my parents but also us children uneasy. We knew our grandparents' story. These Germans reminded us of Auschwitz. A terrible feeling rose up in us. We struggled to control it but in vain.'

They quickly left the restaurant. Days later, although they were no longer in Brussels, they still hadn't got over the experience. For families born after the war, the past had intruded involuntarily into the present.[27]

Contact with Germans has also remained complicated for Jack (Janek) Mandelbaum's son Mark. 'It was always difficult for me. It's difficult for me today – because I know these "things", the past in all its detail. I know about the terrible things Germans did to my family and relatives.'

'Fortunately', says Jack Mandelbaum, 'I didn't talk about my past to my children until they were seventeen or eighteen. I married a "real American girl". That's probably why we didn't speak about it in front of our children before then.'

And yet, even when they were young, Jack and Shirley Mandelbaum's children found the situation difficult. They knew: 'My parents, their grandparents, were no longer alive, likewise my sister and my brother, their aunt and uncle.'

His son Mark adds: 'We knew that we had no grandparents except for our maternal grandmother. From about the age of four I went to the memorial service recalling those who failed to return from the war. That wasn't easy for me.'

Jack continues: 'In families where both parents survived, children were told, sometimes while they were still young, about Auschwitz, other concentration camps and the suffering of their own families. They probably knew too much too early. They couldn't live with this knowledge. Some of these children went on to commit suicide.'

IS MY MOTHER PERHAPS STILL ALIVE? Many children of Auschwitz still ask today whether their families were really gassed – or whether they are still alive somewhere. They continued to search for a long time, and some still do so today – if only in their dreams – for their parents.

Dasha Lewin (*née* Friedová) could never really believe that her mother Kát'a and her sister Sylva were gone forever. Several times, she came across articles in the newspapers reporting the sudden reappearance of people thought dead.

> My sister and my mother had to be still living. Because of his age, I wasn't so sure about my father. I was never able to admit that Sylva was dead – although I knew she had died in the camp. It was the same with my mother. I didn't care what other people said. Not even the crematoria in Birkenau, which I had seen operating with my own eyes, could convince me.

For many, like Dasha, it was the hope that someone was alive that kept them going. 'It's like a dream', she said sometimes, 'which I'll wake up from. Then everything will be all right.' But no one came back.

Her husband, Maury Špíra Lewin, was also interned in Auschwitz as a child. Until his death, he could not talk about it. 'Over the years', says Dasha, 'he did tell me a few things.' He spent the first thirteen years of his life as Moshe Špíra in Mukachevo (Ukrainian Mukacheve, Hungarian Munkács) in the Carpathian mountains. He was deported to Auschwitz in 1944 and liberated somewhere in Germany in 1945. He was sick and had to spend two years in hospital.

Research carried out at the time indicated that none of his family had returned to Mukachevo. Maury arrived at a Jewish children's home in New York in 1947 as a 'homeless child of the Shoah'. Some months later, he took up the offer of a Jewish organization and went to California. In Los Angeles, he met the Lewin family. Their only son had died in a car accident. The mother, Elise Lewin, suffered greatly from the loss of her son. Many people encouraged her: 'If you help another child, you might feel better.' Maury moved in with Howard and Elise Lewin, who adopted him a year later.

Years later, it was discovered that his biological father was still alive. He had somehow landed in Prague on his way back from Russia and had remarried. Maury's mother and his siblings, except for one sister, Sara Lipa, had all died during the Shoah. Sara went to Israel. Maury visited her there for the first time in 1953, later several times with his wife Dasha.

Maury carried a piece of paper wrapped in cellophane with him at all times. Written on it in block letters were the names of various concentration camps in the following order: 'Auschwitz, Bełżec, Bergen-Belsen, Birkenau, Buchenwald, Chełmno, Dachau, Emsland, Gross Rosen.' He also noted the name 'Bullenhuser Damm'. At house number 92–94 in the night of 20–21 April 1945, SS men had murdered twenty Jewish children aged between 5 and 12 years – ten girls and ten boys, including two sets of siblings. Before they were murdered, they had suffered the torture of medical experiments as inmates of Neuengamme concentration camp. The children had live tuberculosis bacilli injected under their skin and introduced by a rubber tube through the air pipe into their lungs. They came from France, Italy, Yugoslavia, the Netherlands and Poland.[28]

He had also written 'Forest of Below – Wald von Below' on the piece of paper he always carried with him. Here, near Wittstock, the SS had herded together more than 16,000 inmates. They were forced to live in an enclosure in a forest without accommodation or food. They sought protection from the weather in holes or self-made shelters. They ate herbs, bark and roots. The cemetery in Grabow contains 132 graves of inmates who died in the forest camp or a field hospital.[29]

It is not known why Maury carried the piece of paper with him everywhere, or whether he was liberated from Auschwitz or another camp or in the Forest of Below. Dasha Lewin did not know either.

Dasha and Maury Lewin are buried in the New Jewish Cemetery in Prague. Their graves can be visited there by taking the underground line A to Želivského. The entrance to the cemetery is directly opposite the exit to the station.

Eduard Kornfeld and his older brother Heinrich, who had lived in Israel since the late 1940s, met as often as possible in Switzerland and Israel. The brothers had difficulty talking about their terrible past. 'Almost nothing about our parents, our siblings. My brother and I were both embarrassed to cry in front of one another and to hurt each other with our memories.' On a few occasions, Eduard had the firm intention of talking about it but never managed to do so. The brothers could not get past this one point. They were not able to deal with it together – it was too painful.

The brothers never again heard anything about their parents and siblings. One surviving transport list confirms that the mother and father, the two sisters and two brothers were deported on 4 June 1942 from the forced labour and transit camp at Patronka near Bratislava.[30] The destination is not mentioned. According to the Yad Vashem memorial in Jerusalem, around 2,000 Jews were deported to the East between June and September 1942 from the Patronka camp. The men capable of working were transported to the east of Poland and from there to Majdanek. The children and women were taken to the Bełżec and Sobibor death camps.[31]

Yehuda Bacon would like to forget Auschwitz and the other camps but is incapable of doing so. He mentions the international remembrance days in many countries. They are important for him, but in particular for people who were not in the camps, 'for the future's sake', so that horrendous crimes like Auschwitz are never repeated. He would be happy to live without this memory of Birkenau and the other camps, the recollection of a time in which playing and childhood were abruptly taken away from one day to the next, in which his parents, one of his two sisters and practically all of his relations were killed.

'Our family now all have fulfilled and good lives', said Margit Hirsch, the wife of Gábor Hirsch. Both sons, Mathias and Michael, have been to university, have good jobs and a settled existence. But Margit makes no secret of the fact that 'there are times when my husband is completely absent, lost in thought and dealing with his time in Auschwitz'. During that time, he is unapproachable.

After his retirement, Gábor spent practically all of his time conducting research and attempting to bring order to his confused and fragmented memories of the most terrible time in his life. He also looked for people who had been with him in Auschwitz-Birkenau. Little by little, he attempted to piece together the story. Margit believed that her husband had found a way to come to terms with 'the Auschwitz thing'. He had been lucky. As Gábor himself said, 'I don't know how I could have lived with myself if I had been one of the perpetrators. I'm happy that I was a victim and not a perpetrator.'

WELL OVER 20,000 JEWISH COMMUNITIES were destroyed by Germans between 1933 and 1945.[32] 'I'm the last Jew in the village', says Adolph Smajovich-Goldenberg. He lived in Bilky (Bilke) in the Carpathian mountains. The village is now in the extreme south-west of Ukraine. Bilky is one of the many places in Europe which no longer has any Jewish life. 'If the Germans hadn't come it would probably look quite different here. I can still remember my childhood. There were around one thousand Jews living here. We had a synagogue, a rabbi, Jewish schools, and lots of the shops on the main street belonged to Jews. After the liberation, only about sixty Jews returned, including my two brothers.'

His father, Samuel Goldenberg, made windows, doors and cartwheels. 'He was a good, hardworking man. My father died before we left.' In May 1944, Adolph was deported to Auschwitz at the age of 16 with his mother and his two sisters, Mirjam and Helen. His brothers Moshe and Wilhelm had been enlisted previously into the Hungarian army as forced labourers. In reality, it was slave labour, which only around 20 per cent of the Jewish men survived.[33]

'My sister Mirjam, who was twelve, and my mother Frida were gassed straightaway in Auschwitz.'[34] The Jewish cemetery in Bilky has survived and is tended, thanks above all to donations from survivors and their families living all over the world.

There used to be a large Jewish community as well in Mukachevo, some 45 kilometres away. In 1941, there were 13,488 Jewish children, women and men there, over 40 per cent of the town's population. In May 1944, the Jews of Mukachevo were deported to Auschwitz. Only around 2,000 survived.[35]

Today there are 250 Jews – if that – in Mukachevo. The rabbi is Chaim Shlomo Hoffman, born in 1938 in Debrecen, Hungary, around two and a half hours away by car. He barely knew his father.

I was deported to Bergen-Belsen with my mother and my three sisters in 1944. I was the youngest in the family. I was almost seven when we were liberated. My father didn't return from Buchenwald. At first we were in Hungary. I cried every night and couldn't sleep, reliving everything I had seen and experienced. It has never gone away completely. It's like a computer – stored in the memory.

The flourishing Jewish life in Thessaloniki that existed for centuries has also disappeared since the Shoah. Heinz Kounio: 'Of 56,000 Jews who lived here, only 1,950 survived.'[36] For many centuries, well over 50 per cent of the inhabitants of Thessaloniki were Jewish. The language they had brought with them from Spain remained the lingua franca in the city for over 400 years. When Heinz Salvator Kounio and his father returned to Thessaloniki in July 1945, many things had changed completely. 'The familiar sounds, the Judaeo-Spanish, the smells, the Jewish flair all still exist but they are not the same.' The survivors returning from Auschwitz and the other camps found the districts and streets in which Jewish children, women and men had lived, studied, laughed, worked, prayed and loved completely empty. The people living in the houses today might not even know who had lived there before and what happened to them.

Almost none of Heinz's contemporaries returned from Auschwitz. In 1945, many families had but one surviving member, who had lost father and mother, sisters and brothers, grandfathers and grandmothers, aunts and uncles – alone in the world and left to their own devices.

'We were happy that we, my parents, my sister and I, survived and that we are so close and can help one another.' On the other hand, the Kounio family is filled with sadness and anger that twenty-two close relatives died. They were murdered by Germans because they were Jews. The mere thought of this is unbearable, both for those who suffered in Auschwitz and elsewhere and for the new generations of Jews – and will always be so.

INCURABLE WOUNDS In spite of everything, many of the children of Auschwitz began a new life after Auschwitz, studied, learned professions, went to school, had children, celebrated and lived. What an amazing achievement – that for many children of Auschwitz and their families a future was possible despite their memories.

'Yes, it's true', says Jack (Janek) Mandelbaum.

We founded families, sought a new life, married, had children. We went to work and built new homes. All that kept the terrible memories at bay. But now that we are older, we can no longer keep the memories in check. We have to live with them every day. It doesn't help to say 'it was so long ago' and just carry on. That doesn't work. The pain is there, every day, every hour. I get up in the morning, wash and shave, look in the mirror and say to myself 'I will get through the day.' Others who weren't in the camps can't understand this.

Otto Klein was very concerned about antisemitism, above all in Europe. 'Today again more and more synagogues and cemeteries are being damaged, Jews spat at on the street, beaten up and killed.' He no longer wanted to read the newspaper or watch the news on television. Every day, he heard or read about antisemitism in Europe. This was not only difficult for him. Otto wondered: 'What will the future be like for the Jews if something effective isn't done soon?' He was afraid again.

Throughout his life, he had both Jewish and non-Jewish friends. 'But I felt most comfortable among Jews', he always said. 'The shared roots and ideas are a strong and reassuring link.' He was fed up of having to defend Israel, 'this small piece of land', to non-Jewish friends and acquaintances. He believed that 'very few people understand the situation' in Israel and mostly 'know nothing'.

Even seventy-five years after being liberated, Eduard Kornfeld mistrusted people. 'Still!' He recalled something Anne Frank wrote in her diary: 'I still believe, in spite of everything, that people are truly good at heart.' Eduard, by contrast, said 'I believe in the evil in people.' His experiences in Auschwitz, in Riederloh II and the other camps, and even after the war, allowed no other conclusion. He remained mistrustful. There were people he could trust, but it took a very long time. He had unconditional trust in his wife and his children and would have done anything for them.

He was most at home and free in Israel. Here, 'among my people', he felt 'I'm like everyone else. No one would dream of persecuting me.' In Israel he immediately found a connection to people and could communicate very well because there were no barriers. If he had not contracted tuberculosis in the camp and had been better able to put up with the heat, he would have moved to Israel long ago. On the other hand, he was grateful that Switzerland had taken him in decades previously and allowed him to found a family and an existence there. Switzerland became a real home for him.

In the last decades, Jack Mandelbaum has often visited his old hometown Gdynia. That way he can be close to his murdered family, in the place where he spent the happiest days of his childhood with his mother Cyrla, his father Majloch, his sister Ita and his brother Jakob. His son Mark relates:

> Many people cannot understand why my father has spent the summer months in Poland for so many years. I don't think anyone has the right to question his decision, but many do so anyway. If others don't want to go to Europe, it's their decision, and that's fine. When I see my father in the place he grew up, I can sense how happy he is.

During this time, he is where he wants to be.

Since 1945, Jack Mandelbaum has sought tirelessly for a photo of his mother Cyrla. He has been unable to find one anywhere in the world. He has asked and sought repeatedly in Israel, in Poland, in the USA. Decades ago, he placed an advertisement on the Internet. He promised a reward of 10,000 dollars to anyone who could give him a photo of his mother. But no one has responded. 'I would love to have a photo of my mother. That would give me indescribable pleasure. It would be the happiest day of my life.'

If the children of Auschwitz still alive today had one wish, it would be to see their mothers, fathers, sisters and brothers again. They would so much like to touch their faces, speak to them, have their favourite meal cooked by their mother, enjoy their hair being stroked, or feel a kiss on the cheek. These elderly people would so much like to embrace their mothers, fathers, sisters and brothers again, to dine together, and to visit their children and grandchildren with them.

'The horror of Auschwitz will be with me for the rest of my life', says Angela Orosz-Richt, who was born in Auschwitz-Birkenau. 'I'm afraid for my children, my grandchildren, my great-grandchildren. Aggressive antisemitism is once again rearing its head in Germany, in Europe, and other parts of the world. Quite openly. This is intolerable for me, my family, for all Jews in the world.' That's why she doesn't stop talking to people about Auschwitz: in youth clubs, schools and the Musée de l'Holocauste in Montreal. 'I have to speak up for those who can no longer do so. I have to relate the story of my mother and the murdered Jews.' So that Auschwitz is never repeated in any form.

Yehuda Bacon and others are asked by friends all over the world: 'Why do you of all people visit Germany?' He answers: 'I didn't want the Nazis to turn me into one of them.' He doesn't want to be someone full of hate. He has crossed Germany several times by train. But he also says something that applies to many survivors and their descendants: 'I can enjoy the countryside, but the other train is always there – the train to Auschwitz.'

# Note on the Interviews

The statements by the children and juveniles who survived Auschwitz, Auschwitz-Birkenau and other concentration camps and extermination camps are based for the most part on lengthy interviews with them and their families and friends recorded on tape and film from the 1970s onwards. The dates were as follows:

Herbert Adler – mid-March 2004 in Frankfurt am Main

Yehuda Bacon – summer 1976 in Jerusalem / 16 October 1984 in Jerusalem (interviewed by Jörn Böhme) / 10–16 March 1988 in Jerusalem / 14 October 1994 in Jerusalem / 9 July 2008 in Jerusalem

Halina Birenbaum – 13 June 1989 in Berlin-Lichtenrade / mid-January 2005 in Oświęcim

Robert (Joschua) Büchler – 8 October 1984 in Jerusalem (interviewed by Jörn Böhme) / 8–15 March 1988 in Givat Haviva / 12 October 1994 in Givat Haviva / 11 July 2008 in Lahavot Haviva

Gábor Hirsch – 5 June 2004 in Esslingen

Schlomo Hoffman – 8 July 2005 in Mukačevo / 28–30 July 2006 in Mukačevo

Lydia Holznerová – 29–30 March 1988 in Prague

Krzysztof J. – 11 March 2007 in Oldenburg / 5 December 2013 in Berlin

Věra Jilková-Holznerová – summer 2004 in Prague

David Jozefowicz – 26–27 September 1988 in Bad Dürrheim

Otto Klein – 1–2 June 2004 in Geneva

Adam and Emilia Klimczyk – 16–17 September 1990 in Jawiczowice and Oświęcim / 3 August 1994 in Jawiczowice

Dorota and Ewa Klimczyk – 27 September 2010 in Kraków

Kola (Mikołaj) Klimczyk – July 1972 in Jawiczowice / 15 November 1984 in Kraków / mid-May 1985 in Berlin / 16–17 September 1990 in Jawiczowice and Oświęcim / 1 August 1994 in Kraków (with his wife Ewa) / 2–3 August 1994 in Oświęcim

Eduard Kornfeld – 6–7 June 2004 in Zurich

Heinz Salvator Kounio – 21 July 2008 in Thessaloniki

Josif Konvoj – 9 August 2012 in Vilnius

Géza Kozma – 24–26 April 1984 in Jawiczowice and Oświęcim / 11 November 1988 in Budapest

Zoltan Kozma – 13 August 2005 in Budapest

Ewa Krcz-Siezka – 16 November 1984 in Lubin

Vera Kriegel – 9 March 1988 in Dimona / 10–12 October 1994 in Yad Hanna

Erich Kulka – 13–16 March 1988 in Jerusalem

Richard Levinsohn – 14 March 1988 in Ben Shemen

Dasha Lewin – summer 2004 in Prague / 17–20 October 2006 in Los Angeles

Dagmar Lieblová – 29–30 March 1988 in Prague / 13 September 1990 in Prague / 8–9 August 1994 in Kutná Hora and Prague / summer 2004 in Prague / 16–18 September 2017 in Cloppenburg

Channa (Hanna) Loewenstein – 15–16 March 1988 in Yad Hanna / 10 October 1994 in Yad Hanna / 14–15 July 2008 in Yad Hanna

Israel Loewenstein – 8 October 1984 in Yad Hanna (interviewed by Jörn Böhme) / 12–15 March 1988 in Yad Hanna / 10 October 1994 in Yad Hanna / 8 and 13 July 2008 in Yad Hanna / 10–11 July 2010 in Yad Hanna

Mirjam M. (pseudonym) – 12 August 1986 in Frankfurt am Main / 14 October 1994 in Tel Aviv / July 2006 in Tel Aviv

Jack (Janek Manela) Mandelbaum – 5 August 2012 in Sopot / 10–12 September in Berlin / 17–18 September in Cloppenburg / 10–13 July 2019 in Naples, FL

Mark Mandelbaum – 5 August 2012 in Sopot

Angela Orosz-Richt – 26–27 June 2019 in Montreal / 27 January 2020 in Berlin

Bronisława and Ryszard Rydzikowska – 16 September 1990 in Czaniec / 6 August 1994 in Czaniec

Lidia Rydzikowska-Maksymowicz – July 1972 in Oświęcim / mid-November 1984 in Czaniec / 17 September 1990 in Oświęcim / 4–5 August 1994 in Czaniec and Oświęcim

Aryeh Simon – 15–16 March 1988 in Givat Haviva

Adolph Smajovich-Goldenberg – 9 August 2005 in Bilky / 29 July 2006 in Bilky

Olga Solomon – 10–12 October 1994 in Yad Hanna

Jiří Steiner – 30 March 1988 in Prague / 13–14 September 1990 in Prague / 10–11 August 1994 in Prague

Tadeusz Szymański – July 1972 in Oświęcim / 15–16 May 1979 in Berlin (with Jürgen Pieplow) / 30 January 1983 in Oświęcim / 17 November 1984 in Oświęcim / 1–2 December 1989 in Cloppenburg / 30 November 1991 in Berlin / 24–25 March 1992 in Oświęcim / 17–18 December 1992 in Oświęcim / 1–2 April 1993 in Oświęcim / 27 October 1993 in Oświęcim / 19–21 January 1994 in Oświęcim

William Wermuth – 12–13 July 1988 in Konstanz

Barbara Wesołowska – 25–26 March 1992 in Będzin

# Notes

Apart from the interviews above, there were numerous other unrecorded interviews with the children of Auschwitz and their families. All interviewees also made records, letters, documents and photos available. The interviews and personal documents and correspondence (letters, emails and telephone calls) are not generally mentioned specifically in the notes. The following sources were also used.

(All translations are by Nick Somers, unless otherwise marked.)

## Preface

1   See, in particular, Raul Hilberg, *The Destruction of the European Jews* (Chicago 1961), and Götz Aly, '*Endlösung*' – *Völkerverschiebung und Mord an den europäischen Juden* (Frankfurt am Main 2017).

2   Franciszek Piper, 'Mass Murder', in Wacław Długoborski and Franciszek Piper, eds., *Auschwitz 1940–1945: Central Issues in the History of the Camp*, vols. I–V, trans. from Polish by William Brand (Oświęcim 2000), vol. III, pp. 11–52, 205–31; Auschwitz-Birkenau Memorial and Museum (Teresa Świebocka, Jadwiga Pinderska-Lech and Jarko Mensfelt), *Auschwitz-Birkenau: The Past and the Present* (Oświęcim 2016), pp. 6–12.

3   Auschwitz-Birkenau Memorial and Museum, *Auschwitz-Birkenau*.

4   Piper, 'Mass Murder'; moreover, from the first day of occupation onwards, Jews were ruthlessly murdered in the countries invaded by Nazi Germany, by German 'Einsatzgruppen' and 'Einsatzkommandos' (mobile killing units), but also by Wehrmacht units. According to the United States Holocaust Museum, 1.3 million Jews were shot by Wehrmacht and SS units or killed in gas trucks on the territory of the former Soviet Union alone: United States Holocaust Museum, Documenting Numbers of Victims of the Holocaust and Nazi Persecution | The Holocaust Encyclopedia (ushmm.org).

5   Auschwitz-Birkenau Memorial and Museum, *Auschwitz-Birkenau*, p. 12 (prepared by Piper).

6   Helena Kubica, *Geraubte Kindheit – In Auschwitz befreite Kinder* [Stolen Childhood: Children Liberated in Auschwitz] (Oświęcim, October 2021), pp. 7, 59. Altogether, 400,000 babies, children and women were registered in

441

Auschwitz, including over 23,500 children and juveniles, almost all of whom were murdered.

7   Ibid., pp. 17, 33, 64.

8   Helena Kubica, *Pregnant Women and Children in Auschwitz* (Oświęcim 2010), p. 13; see also George M. Weisz and Konrad Kwiet, 'Managing Pregnancy in Nazi Concentration Camps: The Role of Two Jewish Doctors', in *Rambam Maimonides Medical Journal* (Israel), 9.3 (July 2018).

9   Alwin Meyer, *Mama, ich höre dich – Mütter, Kinder und Geburten in Auschwitz* (Göttingen 2021), pp. 104–62.

## Life Before

1   For further details of Heinz Salvator Kounio and his family, see also Heinz Salvator Kounio, *Ezisa to thanato: To imerologio tou arithmou 109565* (Thessaloniki 1982), and Kounio, *A Liter of Soup and Sixty Grams of Bread: The Diary of Prisoner Number 109565* (New York 2003).

2   Hugo Gold, ed., *Die Juden und Judengemeinden Böhmens in Vergangenheit und Gegenwart* (Brno and Prague 1934), p. 255; see also I. Ziegler, *Dokumente zur Geschichte der Juden in Karlsbad (1791–1869)* (Karlsbad 1913), pp. 7–141.

3   Gustav Treixler, 'Geschichte der Juden in Lichtenstadt, Neudek und St. Joachimstal', in Gold, ed., *Die Juden und Judengemeinden Böhmens*, p. 378.

4   Gold, ed., *Die Juden und Judengemeinden Böhmens*, pp. 258–9.

5   Albertos Nar, 'Die Juden von Thessaloniki', in Niki Eideneier and Hans Eideneier, eds., *Thessaloniki – Bilder einer Stadt* (Cologne 1992), pp. 73–7; see also M. Atlas, 'Was sah ich nach 500 Jahren von der Goldenen Zeit des Judentums in Spanien', in *Zeitschrift für die Geschichte der Juden*, 3–4 (Tel Aviv 1965), pp. 175–82.

6   Georg Bossong, *Die Sepharden – Geschichte und Kultur der spanischen Juden* (Munich 2008), pp. 45–58, 92–4; Aron Rodrigue, 'Der Balkan vom 15. bis 20. Jahrhundert', in Elka-Vera Kotowski, Julius Schoeps and Hiltrud Wallenborn, eds., *Handbuch zur Geschichte der Juden in Europa, Sonderausgabe* (unmodified reprint in one volume of the 1st edition 2001) (Darmstadt 2012), pp. 296–9; Nar, 'Die Juden von Thessaloniki', p. 78; Ioannis K. Kassiotis, 'Thessaloniki unter osmanischer Herrschaft', in Eideneier and Eideneier, eds., *Thessaloniki*, p. 46.

7   Quoted from *Die Welt*, 28, 10 July 1903.

8   Joseph Nehama, 'Zuflucht Saloniki: Die Sepharden im osmanischen Exil – Eine Auswahl (1492–1556)', in Nehama, *Histoire des Israélites de Salonique* (Bochum 2005), pp. 90–9, 124–56; Manuel Gogos, 'Saloniki – Mutter Israels', in Niki Eideneier, ed., *Die Sonnenblumen der Juden – Die Juden in*

*der neugriechischen Literatur* (Cologne 2006), pp. 18–28; Esther Benbassa and Aron Rodrigue, *Die Geschichte der sephardischen Juden – Von Toledo bis Saloniki*, trans. Lilli Herschhorn (Bochum 2005), pp. 96–101, 107–10 – original title: *Histoire des Juifs séphardes: De Tolède à Salonique.*

9 Charalambos K. Papastathis, 'Bildungswesen und geistiges Leben in Thessaloniki zur Zeit der Osmanischen Herrschaft', in Eideneier and Eideneier, eds., *Thessaloniki*, pp. 126–7.

10 Nar, 'Die Juden von Thessaloniki', p. 78.

11 S. Bénédict, 'Das Schulwerk der Alliance in Saloniki', in *Ost und West*, 1 (January 1907), pp. 64–6.

12 Benbassa and Rodrigue, *Die Geschichte der sephardischen Juden*, pp. 144–52.

13 Iakov Benmayor, 'Thessaloniki Ir Va' Em Be' Israel', in *Cultural Forum of the Jewish Community of Thessaloniki*, vol. I, *Thessaloniki*, 2nd edition (Thessaloniki 2005), p. 33; Gogos, 'Saloniki', p. 21.

14 Christos Safiris, 'Die verwüstete "Mutter Israels" – Ruhmes- und Leidenstätten des Judentums in Thessaloniki', in Eideneier, ed., *Die Sonnenblumen*, p. 11; see also Mor. J. Cohen, 'Brief aus Saloniki', in *Die Welt*, 24, 16 June 1899.

15 Elkan Nathan Adler, *Jews in Many Lands* (London 1905), p. 141.

16 Adler, *Von Ghetto zu Ghetto – Reisen und Beobachtungen, Nachdruck, Nachwort und Erläuterung von Joachim Schlör* (Teetz 2001), p. 214, back cover.

17 Adler, *Jews in Many Lands*, pp. 141–2.

18 Esriel Carlebach, *Exotische Juden – Berichte und Studien* (Berlin 1932), p. 19.

19 Nar, 'Die Juden von Thessaloniki', pp. 78–83; Benbassa and Rodrigue, *Die Geschichte der sephardischen Juden*, pp. 71–93; Rodrigue, 'Der Balkan', pp. 300–1; Nehama, 'Zuflucht Saloniki', pp. 56–63, 109–15.

20 Gogos, 'Saloniki', p. 22.

21 Papastathis, 'Bildungswesen', p. 127; see also *Die Welt*, 4, 23 January 1903.

22 Bossong, *Die Sepharden*, p. 105.

23 Rena Molho, 'The Judeo-Spanisch – A Mediterranean Language in Daily Use in 20th Century Salonica', in *Cultural Forum*, p. 14; see also *Die Welt*, 8, 24 June 1899.

24 Georg Herlitz and Bruno Kirschner (founders), *Jüdisches Lexikon – Ein enzyklopädisches Handbuch des jüdischen Wissens in vier Bänden* (Berlin 1927–31), vol. IV/2, p. 1148; Benbassa and Rodrigue, *Die Geschichte der sephardischen Juden*, p. 62; see also M. Kayserling, *Sephardim: Romanische Poesien der Juden in Spanien – Ein Beitrag zur Literatur und Geschichte der Spanisch-Portugiesischen Juden* (Leipzig 1859), pp. 140–4.

25 Samuel Usque, quoted from Nehama, 'Zuflucht Saloniki', p. 98.

26 Nar, 'Die Juden von Thessaloniki', pp. 78–81; see also 'Die Juden von Saloniki

– Eine Reiseerinnerung', in *Im Deutschen Reich* (published by the Central-Verein deutscher Staatsbürger jüdischen Glaubens), 1 (January 1917), pp. 12–17.

27 Benbassa and Rodrigue, *Die Geschichte der sephardischen Juden*, pp. 102–7.

28 Gogos, 'Saloniki', p. 23.

29 Nar, 'Die Juden von Thessaloniki', p. 81.

30 Katrin Boeckh, *Von den Balkankriegen zum Ersten Weltkrieg – Kleinstaatenpolitik und ethnische Selbstbestimmung auf dem Balkan* (Munich 1996), pp. 212–19; Fränkel, 'Von den heutigen Juden Salonikis', in *Ost und West*, 3 (March 1913), pp. 254–76; 'Griechenland – Neue griechisch–jüdische Konflikte in Saloniki', in *Die Welt*, 28, 10 July 1914.

31 Jannis D. Stefanidis, 'Geschichte Thessalonikis von 1912–1940', in Eideneier and Eideneier, eds., *Thessaloniki*, pp. 57–8; Bossong, *Die Sepharden*, p. 109; 'Das Schicksal Salonikis', in *Die Welt*, 19, 19 May 1914.

32 Benmayor, 'Thessaloniki', p. 37.

33 Boeckh, *Von den Balkankriegen*, pp. 270–2; George Horton, 'Saloniki', in *Supplement to Commerce Reports*, Annual Series No. 7B, Washington DC, 2 October 1918.

34 Stefanidis, 'Geschichte Thessalonikis', p. 61; Hagen Fleischer, 'Griechenland', in Wolfgang Benz, ed., *Dimension des Völkermords – Die Zahl der jüdischen Opfer des Nationalsozialismus* (Munich 1991), pp. 244–5.

35 Nehama, 'Zuflucht Saloniki', p. 25.

36 Nar, 'Die Juden von Thessaloniki', p. 83.

37 Herlitz and Kirschner, *Jüdisches Lexikon*, pp. 62–3; Benmayor, 'Thessaloniki', p. 37.

38 Bénédict, 'Das Schulwerk der Alliance in Saloniki', p. 64; Bossong, *Die Sepharden*, p. 93; Cohen, 'Brief aus Saloniki'; Andreas Karkavitsas, 'Thessaloniki', in Eideneier, ed., *Die Sonnenblumen*, p. 55; Carlebach, *Exotische Juden*, pp. 26–7.

39 Adler, *Jews in Many Lands*, p. 142.

40 Elke Sturm-Trigonakis, 'Jüdisches Leben in Thessaloniki – Ein Gespräch mit Andreas Sefiha', in *Tranvia – Revue der Iberischen Halbinsel*, 55 (June 1999), pp. 5–7; M. Ehrenpreis, 'Saloniki, das Zentrum der Sephardim', in *Menorah*, 11 (November 1926), p. 626.

41 'In medieval Hebrew, the Iberian peninsula was called Sefarad. Before and after the expulsion of the Jews from Spain in 1492, the Jewish communities on the Iberian peninsula and the communities with Iberian origins were known as "Sephardic". As a result of an extension of the meaning but also because of cultural contacts in the past and certain common features of the

rite, practically all non-Ashkenaz [central, northern and eastern European Jews], particularly North African and Middle Eastern Jews are called "Sephardic"': Benbassa and Rodrigue, *Die Geschichte der sephardischen Juden*, pp. 8–9. The definition in the *Neues Lexikon des Judentums* states: 'Hebrew name for the Jews in Spain and Portugal before their expulsion in 1492, later settling in south-eastern Europe, North Africa and Asia, but also in Holland, England, north-western Germany and America': Julius H. Schoeps, ed., *Neues Lexikon des Judentums*, new revised edition (Gütersloh 2000), p. 758; see also Herlitz and Kirschner, *Jüdisches Lexikon*, vol. IV/2, pp. 330–6, and vol. III, pp. 464–6.

42  Carlebach, *Exotische Juden*, pp. 8–9; see also Ehrenpreis, 'Saloniki, das Zentrum der Sephardim', pp. 623–9.

43  Bossong, *Die Sepharden*, pp. 88–92, 98–107; Herlitz and Kirschner, *Jüdisches Lexikon*, vol. III, pp. 464–6.

44  Adler, *Jews in Many Lands*, p. 142.

45  Rodrigue, 'Der Balkan', pp. 311–13.

46  For further details of the life of Heinz Salvator Kounio and his family, see also the book by his sister Erika Myriam Kounio-Amariglo, *From Thessaloniki to Auschwitz and Back: Memories of a Survivor from Thessaloniki*, trans. Theresa Sundt (London 2000).

47  See also C. Z. Klötzel, 'Saloniki', in *Neue Jüdische Monatshefte*, 10 (25 February 1917), p. 282.

48  *Jüdische Stimme* (Vienna), 20 November 1934.

49  See, for example, Max Wurmbrand and Cecil Roth, *Das Volk der Juden – 4000 Jahre Kampf ums Überleben* (Frechen 1999), e.g., pp. 330–1, 404–16.

50  Yad Vashem, ed., *Black Book of Localities Whose Jewish Population Was Exterminated by the Nazis* (Jerusalem 1965), pp. VI, 1–440.

51  Shmuel Spector, Editor-in-chief, *The Encyclopedia of Jewish Life Before and During the Holocaust*, 3 vols. (New York 2001), vol. II, p. 848.

52  A. H. Teller, 'Geschichte der Juden in Bilin und Umgebung', in Gold, *Die Juden und Judengemeinden Böhmens*, pp. 34–7.

53  Arno Pařik, *Die Prager Synagogen* (Prague 1986), pp. 54, 60–1.

54  Jürgen Franzke, ed., *Orient Express – König der Züge* (Nuremberg 1998), pp. 104–5.

55  For further details of the life of Gábor Hirsch and his family, see Gábor Hirsch, *Als 14-jähriger durch Auschwitz-Birkenau – Aus dem ungarischen Békéscsaba sieben Monate Konzentrationslager überlebt und über Kattowitz, Czernowitz, Sluzk zurück 1933–1945* (Konstanz 2011).

56  Randolph L. Braham, *The Politics of Genocide – The Holocaust in Hungary*,

condensed edition (Detroit 2000), p. 146; Spector, ed., *Jewish Life*, vol. I, p. 99; Hirsch, *Als 14-jähriger durch Auschwitz-Birkenau*, p. 20.

57 Gábor Hirsch, undated manuscript about the fate of his family and his birth-place Békéscsaba.

58 The Central Database of Shoah Victims' Names at Yad Vashem, page of testimony for Jakob Silberstein, submitted by his niece Lenke Singer on 21 June 1999.

59 Zdeněk Jelínek, 'Tragédie kutnohorských židů', undated manuscript, translated from Czech to German by Petr Liebl.

60 Gottlieb Bondy and Franz Dworský, *Geschichte der Juden in Böhmen, Mähren und Schlesien*, vol. I (Prague 1906), pp. 237–8.

61 Rabbi Abraham Stein, *Die Geschichte der Juden in Böhmen* (Brno 1904), p. 40.

62 Jelínek, 'Tragédie kutnohorských židů'.

63 Klaus-Dieter Alicke, *Lexikon der Jüdischen Gemeinden im deutschen Sprachraum*, 3 vols. (Gütersloh 2008), vol. II, pp. 261–3.

64 Stein, *Die Geschichte der Juden in Böhmen*, p. 39.

65 Alicke, *Jüdische Gemeinden*, vol. II, p. 262.

66 'Synagoga Kolín', www.cestyapamatky.cz/kolinsko/kolin/synagoga.

67 Jelínek, 'Tragédie kutnohorských židů'.

68 Eike Geisel, *Im Scheunenviertel – Bilder, Texte und Dokumente*, 2nd edition (Berlin 1981), pp. 10–32; Horst Helas, *Die Grenadierstraße im Berliner Scheunenviertel – Ein Ghetto mit offenen Toren* (Berlin 2010), pp. 11–36.

69 See, for example, Susanne Willems, *Der entsiedelte Jude, Albert Speers Wohnungsmarktpolitik für den Berliner Hauptstadtbau* (Berlin 2002).

70 Linke Poot (Alfred Döblin), 'Östlich um den Alexanderplatz', first published in *Berliner Tageblatt*, 29 September 1923, quoted from Geisel, *Im Scheunenviertel*, pp. 120–3.

71 Alicke, *Jüdische Gemeinden*, vol. II, pp. 576–8.

72 Alfred Etzold, *Ein Berliner Kulturdenkmal von Weltgeltung – Der Jüdische Friedhof Berlin-Weißensee, mit einem Beitrag von Jürgen Rennert* (Berlin 2006), pp. 13–45.

73 Alicke, *Jüdische Gemeinden*, vol. I, pp. 73–6; Spector, ed., *Jewish Life*, vol. I, p. 33.

74 Spector, ed., *Jewish Life*, vol. I, p. 127.

75 Claudia-Ann Flumenbaum, 'Von den Anfängen bis 1789', in Andreas Nachama, Julius Schoeps and Hermann Simon, eds., *Juden in Berlin*, 2nd revised edition (Berlin 2002), p. 9.

76 Michael Brenner, 'Die Weimarer Jahre', in Nachama et al., eds., *Juden in Berlin*, pp. 137–80; Elke-Vera Kotowski, ed., *Juden in Berlin – Biographien* (Berlin 2005), pp. 65, 68–9, 173, 227, 243, 285–6.

77 Avraham Barkai, Paul Mendes Flohr and Steven M. Lowenstein, *German-Jewish History in Modern Times*, vol. IV, *Renewal and Destruction 1918–1945* (New York 1998), pp. 37–40.

78 Ibid., pp. 40–3.

79 Jarosław Drozd, *Lost in the Whirlwind of War – The Jewish Community in Gdynia/Poland* (Gdynia 2008), pp. 145–9.

80 Ibid., pp. 56–65; Museum of the History of Polish Jews, 'History of the Jewish Community in Gdynia', https://sztetl.org.pl/en/towns/g/35-gdynia/99-history/137291-history-of-community, and 'Demography', https://sztetl.org.pl/en/towns/g/35-gdynia/100-demography/20726-demography.

81 Hille J. Kieval, 'Die Juden in Böhmen, Mähren und der Slowakei', in Natalia Berger, ed., *Wo sich Kulturen begegnen – Die Geschichte der tschechoslowakischen Juden* (Prague 1992), pp. 23–8.

82 Milada Vilímková, *Prager Judenstadt* (Prague 1990), pp. 85–7.

83 Ibid., pp. 143–83; Jindřich Lion, *Jüdisches Prag /Jewish Prague*, trans. Nick Somers (Vienna 2005), pp. 77–81.

84 Stein, *Die Geschichte der Juden in Böhmen*, pp. 157–8.

85 Vilímková, *Prager Judenstadt*, pp. 9–79.

86 Jindřich Lion and Jan Lukas, *Das Prager Ghetto* (Prague 1959), pp. 54–60; Lion, *Jewish Prague*, pp. 128–33.

87 Spector, ed., *Jewish Life*, vol. II, pp. 1020–1.

88 Israel Gutman, ed., *Encyclopaedia of the Holocaust*, 4 vols. (New York 1995), vol. III, p. 1185.

89 Yeshayahu A. Jelinek, *The Carpathian Diaspora – The Jews of Subcarpathian Rus' and Mukachevo* (New York 2007), pp. 31–341.

90 Ibid., p. 14.

91 Livia Rothkirchen, 'Das tschechoslowakische Judentum: Entwicklung und Niedergang (1918–1939)', in Berger, ed., *Wo sich Kulturen*, p. 108.

92 Jelinek, *The Carpathian Diaspora*, Map 3, p. xx.

93 Interview with Adolf Smajovich-Goldenberg, Bilky, Ukraine, 9 August 2005.

94 Spector, ed., *Jewish Life*, vol. I, p. 550.

95 Yehoshua Weiss, 'Nagymegyer (now Veľký Meder)', manuscript, 2000.

96 Spector, ed., *Jewish Life*, vol. III, p. 1384; Guy Miron, Editor-in-chief, *The Yad Vashem Encyclopedia of the Ghettos during the Holocaust*, 2 vols. (Jerusalem 2009), vol. II, pp. 514–15.

97 Weiss, 'Nagymegyer'.

98 David Groß, 'Verlauf der Geschichte der Juden', in Hugo Gold, ed., *Die Juden und Judengemeinden Bratislava in Vergangenheit und Gegenwart* (Brno 1932), pp. 3–10.

99  Spector, ed., *Jewish Life*, vol. I, pp. 182–4; Alicke, *Jüdische Gemeinden*, vol. III, pp. 3380–5; Aron Grünhut, *Katastrophenzeit des slowakischen Judentums – Aufstieg und Niedergang der Juden in Pressburg* (Tel Aviv 1972), pp. 182–201.

100  Herlitz and Kirschner, *Jüdisches Lexikon*, vol. IV/2, pp. 478–9; Grünhut, *Pressburg*, p. 160.

101  Tatjana Tönsmeyer, 'Vom Desinteresse zur Hilfsbereitschaft – Solidarität und Hilfe für verfolgte Juden in der Slowakei', in Wolfgang Benz and Juliane Wetzel, eds., *Solidarität und Hilfe für Juden während der NS-Zeit*, Regionalstudien 4 (Berlin 2004), p. 20.

102  Spector, ed., *Jewish Life*, vol. I, p. 481.

103  Miron, ed., *Ghettos*, vol. I, p. 158.

104  Ibid., pp. 485–6; Spector, ed., *Jewish Life*, vol. II, pp. 831–2.

105  Hugo Gold with Ferdinand Kraus, 'Geschichte der Juden in Mährisch-Ostrau', in Hugo Gold, ed., *Die Juden und Judengemeinden Mährens in Vergangenheit und Gegenwart* (Brno 1929), pp. 372–8; Annegret Nippa and Peter Herbstreuth, *Eine kleine Geschichte der Synagoge aus dreizehn Städten* (Hamburg 1999), pp. 260–73; Alicke, *Jüdische Gemeinden*, vol. II, pp. 2637–40.

106  Gold with Kraus, 'Mährisch-Ostrau', p. 373.

107  Quoted from ibid., p. 374.

108  Ibid., p. 377.

109  Robert Yehoshua Büchler, *Quellen zur Geschichte der Jüdischen Gemeinde zu Topoltschany und ihre Schicksale* (Jerusalem 1976), pp. 95–152; Spector, ed., *Jewish Life*, vol. III, p. 1314.

110  Romani Rose, ed., *'Den Rauch hatten wir täglich vor Augen' – Der Nationalsozialistische Völkermord an den Sinti und Roma* (Heidelberg 1999), pp. 13–14.

111  Romani Rose, ed., *Der Nationalsozialistische Völkermord an den Sinti und Roma*, exhibition catalogue, permanent exhibition, Auschwitz State Museum (Heidelberg 2003), p. 13.

112  Peter Sandner, *Frankfurt, Auschwitz – Die nationalsozialistische Verfolgung der Sinti und Roma in Frankfurt am Main* (Frankfurt am Main 1998), pp. 78–84, 123.

'That's When My Childhood Ended'

1  Leni Yahil, *The Holocaust: The Fate of European Jewry*, trans. Ina Friedman and Haya Galai (Oxford 1990), pp. 53–4; Reinhard Sturm, 'Zerstörung der Demokratie 1930–1933', in Bundeszentrale für politische Bildung, ed., *Weimarer Republik*, new revised edition (Bonn, November 2011), pp. 54–73; Martin Gilbert, *The Holocaust: The Jewish Tragedy* (London 1986), pp. 30–1.

2 Helmut Eschwege, ed., *Kennzeichen J – Bilder, Dokumente, Berichte zur Verfolgung und Vernichtung der deutschen Juden 1933–1945* (Frankfurt am Main 1979), pp. 36–7; Gutman, *Holocaust*, vol. I, pp. 234–7.

3 Wolf Gruner, *The Persecution of the Jews in Berlin 1933–1945: A Chronology of Measures by the Authorities in the German Capital*, trans. William Templer (Berlin 2009), pp. 59–60.

4 Barkai et al., 'The Organized Jewish Community', in Barkai et al., *German-Jewish History*, vol. IV, pp. 95–6.

5 Michael Berger, '"... liebt nächst Gott das Vaterland" – Jüdische Soldaten und ihre Rabbiner im Ersten Weltkrieg', in *Der Schild* (published by the Bund Jüdischer Soldaten), 1, 1 November 2007; S. Neufeld (Ramat Chen), 'Die Frühvollendeten', in Hugo Gold, ed., *Zeitschrift für die Geschichte der Juden*, 2/3 (1970), pp. 87–8; see also Peter C. Appelbaum, *Loyalty Betrayed: Jewish Chaplains in the German Army During the First World War* (London 2014).

6 'Die Juden ziehen dahin, daher, sie ziehen durchs Rote Meer, die Wellen schlagen zu, die Welt hat Ruh'; 'Wenn das Judenblut vom Messer spritzt, geht's noch mal so gut.'

7 Reinhard Rürup, ed., *1936 – Die Olympischen Spiele und der Nationalsozialismus*, 2nd edition (Berlin 1999), pp. 131–41.

8 Hermann Kaienburg, 'Sachsenhausen – Stammlager', in Wolfgang Benz and Barbara Distel, eds., *Der Ort des Terrors – Geschichte der nationalsozialistischen Konzentrationslager*, 9 vols. (Munich 2005–9), vol. III, pp. 18–21, 28.

9 Rose, '... *täglich vor Augen'*, pp. 65–8; see also Johannes Heesch and Ulrike Braun, *Orte erinnern – Spuren des NS-Terrors in Berlin*, 2nd revised edition (Berlin 2006), pp. 89–95.

10 Gruner, *Persecution*, p. 117.

11 Spector, ed., *Jewish Life*, vol. I, p. 128.

12 Gruner, *Persecution*, pp. 116–17.

13 Joseph Walk, ed., *Das Sonderrecht für die Juden im NS-Staat – Eine Sammlung der gesetzlichen Maßnahmen und Richtlinien – Inhalt und Bedeutung* (Heidelberg and Karlsruhe 1981), p. 255.

14 Wolf Gruner, *Jewish Forced Labor under the Nazis: Economic Needs and Racial Aims, 1938–1944* (Cambridge 2006).

15 Gruner, *Persecution*, p. 118.

16 Israel (Jürgen) Loewenstein, 'Ich habe ein Zuhause gefunden', in Evangelischer Arbeitskreis Kirche und Israel in Hessen und Nassau, ed., *'Wer hätte das geglaubt!' – Erinnerungen an die Hachschara und die Konzentrationslager* (Heppenheim 1998), pp. 28–32.

17 Leo Trepp, *Die Juden – Volk, Geschichte, Religion* (Wiesbaden 2006), pp. 304–5.

18 Loewenstein, 'Zuhause', p. 28.

19 Barkai et al., 'Population Decline and Economic Stagnation', in Barkai et al., *German-Jewish History*, vol. IV, p. 33.

20 Gutman, *Holocaust*, vol. I, p. 200.

21 Gruner, *Forced Labor*, p. 212.

22 Arbeitskreis Berliner Regionalmuseen, ed., *Zwangsarbeit in Berlin 1938–1945* (Berlin 2003), p. 17.

23 See Förderverein für eine Internationale Begegnungsstätte Hachschara-Landwerk Ahrensdorf e.V., ed., *Herbert Fiedler, 'Träume und Hoffnungen'*, nos. 1 and 2, 'Ein Kibbuz in Ahrensdorf' and 'Unser Landwerk Ahrensdorf, Luckenwalde', undated.

24 Arbeitskreis Berliner Regionalmuseen, ed., *Zwangsarbeit*, p. 17.

25 Gruner, *Persecution*, p. 147.

26 Gabriele Layer-Jung and Cord Pagenstecher, 'Berlin-Schöneweide', in Benz and Distel, eds., *Der Ort des Terrors*, vol. III, pp. 12–123.

27 Alfred Gottwaldt and Diana Schulle, *Die 'Judendeportationen' aus dem Deutschen Reich 1941–45* (Wiesbaden 2005), p. 121.

28 Data from the Jewish Community of Latvia on its website, https://jews.lv/en/jewish-cemeteries-and-memorial-sites/rumbula-memorial. Other studies put the number at around 27,000 Latvian Jews from the Riga ghetto murdered on 30 November and 8/9 December 1941 in the forest in Rumbala; see *Newsletter of the Fritz Bauer Institut zur Geschichte und Wirkung des Holocaust*, 26 (Autumn 2004).

29 Gottwaldt and Schulle, *'Judendeportationen'*, pp. 132, 134, 255, 257, 258, 259.

30 Ibid., p. 399.

31 Danuta Czech, *Auschwitz Chronicle 1939–1945* (New York 1997), p. 283.

32 Spector, ed., *Jewish Life*, vol. I, p. 532.

33 Eva Schmidt-Hartmann, 'Tschechoslowakei', in Benz, ed., *Dimension des Völkermords*, p. 356.

34 Detlef Brandes and Václav Kural, 'Der Weg in die Katastrophe 1938–1947', in Brandes and Kural, eds., *Der Weg in die Katastrophe – Deutsch-tschechoslowakische Beziehungen 1938–1947* (Essen 1994), pp. 11–25. 'The term "Sudetenland" was an umbrella term for the Germans in Bohemia, Moravia and Silesia. It was similar to designations such as Carpathian Germans or Alpine Germans. It was used initially in the early twentieth century .... The term "Sudeten" ... did not catch on immediately and did not gain in significance until after 1918, when – according to Josef Pfitzner – the integration of the Bohemian and

Moravian Germans in the newly established ČSR marked "a new historical era of the Sudeten Germans" that "shook up their existence". The name was used increasingly in political dialogue and became an ideological term. This gifted and cultured professor of history at the German University in Prague was instrumental with his works in the 1930s, particularly the book *Sudetendeutsche Einheitsbewegung* in 1937, in bringing about this ideological shift. It is the association of these terms with the Nazi ideology that has given these words a negative connotation in the general Czech consciousness': Zdeněk Beneš and Václav Kural, eds., *Geschichte verstehen – Die Entwicklung der deutsch-tschechischen Beziehungen in den böhmischen Ländern 1848–1948* (Prague 2002), pp. 98–9.

35  Beneš and Kural, eds., *Geschichte verstehen*, pp. 138–49.

36  Václav Kural, 'Zum tschechisch-deutschen Verhältnis in der tschechischen Politik 1938–1945', and Eva Hahn, 'Verdrängung und Verharmlosung: Das Ende der jüdischen Bevölkerungsgruppe in den böhmischen Ländern nach ausgewählten tschechischen und sudetendeutschen Publikationen', in Brande and Kural, eds., *Der Weg*, pp. 93–118, 135–60; Václav Kural, 'Heydrichs Terror – ein auslösender Faktor zur Radikalisierung der Transferpläne', in Beneš and Kural, eds., *Geschichte verstehen*, pp. 180–5.

37  Alena Mípiková and Dieter Segert, 'Republik unter Druck', in *Tschechien, Informationen zur politischen Bildung 276*, published by the Federal Office of Political Education.

38  Gutman, *Holocaust*, vol. I, p. 346.

39  Richard Bergern, 'Die Juden von Danzig', in *Jüdische Revue* (Mukachevo/Czechoslovakia), (October 1936).

40  Museum of the History of Polish Jews, 'History of the Jewish Community in Działoszyce', www.sztetl.org.pl/de/article/dzialoszyce/5,geschichte; Spector, ed., *Jewish Life*, vol. I, p. 350.

41  Museum of the History of Polish Jews, 'History of the Jewish Community in Działoszyce'; Spector, ed., *Jewish Life*, vol. I, p. 350.

42  Danuta Drywa, 'Stutthof – Stammlager', in Benz and Distel, eds., *Der Ort des Terrors*, vol. VI, pp. 477–529.

43  'Sławków', *Encyclopedia of Jewish Communities in Poland*, vol. VII, www.jewishgen.org/yizkor/Pinkas_poland/pol7_00356.html; Miron, ed., *Ghettos*, vol. II, pp. 723–4.

44  'Sławków'; Miron, ed., *Ghettos*, vol. II, pp. 723–4.

45  Gutman, *Holocaust*, vol. II, pp. 549–50.

46  Jaroslav Macek, 'Geschichte der Grenzgebiete 1938–1945', in Brandes and Kural,eds., *Der Weg in die Katastrophe*, pp. 57–75.

47 Christian Gerlach and Götz Aly, *Das letzte Kapitel – Der Mord an den ungarischen Juden 1944–45* (Frankfurt am Main 2004), pp. 19–90.

48 Gutman, *Holocaust*, vol. I, p. 127.

49 Envelope stamped 14 March 1939, original owned by the author.

50 Spector, ed., *Jewish Life*, vol. II, pp. 949–50.

51 Nippa and Herbstreuth, *Eine kleine Geschichte der Synagoge*, pp. 278–82; see also Gutman, *Holocaust*, vol. III, pp. 1062–5.

52 Jaroslava Milotová, 'Zur Geschichte der Verordnung Konstantin von Neuraths über das jüdische Vermögen', in *Theresienstädter Studien und Dokumente 2002* (Prague 2002), pp. 75–115.

53 Wolf Gruner, 'Protektorat Böhmen und Mähren', in Wolf Gruner and Jörg Osterloh, eds., *Das 'Großdeutsche Reich' und die Juden – Nationalsozialistische Verfolgung in den 'angegliederten' Gebieten* (Frankfurt am Main and New York 2010), p. 159.

54 Ladislav Lipscher, *Die Juden im Slowakischen Staat* (Munich and Vienna 1980), pp. 31–6.

55 Spector, ed., *Jewish Life*, vol. I, p. 184; Grünhut, *Pressburg*, pp. 159–201.

56 Lipscher, *Die Juden*, pp. 63–77.

57 Ibid., pp. 80–4; Miloslav Szabó, 'Slowakische Rassegesetze (1939–1941)', in Wolfgang Benz, ed., *Handbuch des Antisemitismus – Judenfeindschaft in Geschichte und Gegenwart*, vol. IV (Berlin and Boston 2011), p. 388.

58 Quoted from Büchler, *Topoltschany*, pp. 126–9.

59 Lipscher, *Die Juden*, p. 64.

60 Büchler, *Topoltschany*, pp. 126–9.

61 Gerlach and Aly, *Das letzte Kapitel*, pp. 48–50.

62 Hirsch, *Als 14-jähriger durch Auschwitz-Birkenau*, p. 26, and the document translated into German, from the Arrow Cross party on 7 August 1941, on the CD provided with the book.

63 Gerlach and Aly, *Das letzte Kapitel*, pp. 48–50.

64 Drahomír Jančík, 'Germanisierung und Ausbeutung der tschechischen Wirtschaft und des jüdischen Vermögens zur Zeit der Okkupation', in Beneš and Kural, eds., *Geschichte verstehen*, pp. 126–7.

65 Schoeps, ed., *Lexikon des Judentums*, p. 670.

66 'Bericht der Zentralstelle für jüdische Auswanderung in Prag über die Entwicklung und die Lage der Juden im Protektorat Böhmen und Mähren vom 15. März 1939 bis zum 1. Oktober 1941', in *Theresienstädter Studien und Dokumente 1996* (Prague 1996), pp. 265–6.

67 Ibid.

68 Lucie Ondrichová, *Fredy Hirsch – Von Aachen über Düsseldorf und Frankfurt*

*am Main durch Theresienstadt nach Auschwitz-Birkenau* (Konstanz 2000), p. 29.

69  Jaroslava Miltova, 'Der Okkupationsapparat und die Vorbereitung der Transporte nach Łódź', in *Theresienstädter Studien und Dokumente 1998* (Prague 1998), pp. 40–69; Gottwaldt and Schulle, *'Judendeportationen'*, pp. 66–9, 73, 78, 81, 83.

70  See also Martina Schweibergová, 'Hagibor: ein Ort mit lehrreicher Geschichte': https://deutsch.radio.cz/hagibor-ein-ort-mit-lehrreicher-geschichte-8562028.

71  Ondrichová, *Fredy Hirsch*, pp. 9–35.

72  Schweibergová, 'Hagibor'.

73  Franz Werfel, *Poems*, trans. Edith Abercrombie Snow (New Jersey 1945), p. 113.

74  Jančík, 'Germanisierung und Ausbeutung', pp. 124–37.

75  Bernhard Brunner, *Der Frankreich-Komplex – Die nationalsozialistischen Verbrechen in Frankreich und die Justiz in der Bundesrepublik Deutschland* (Frankfurt am Main 2007), pp. 31–44.

## 'The Hunt for Jews Began'

1  Lipscher, *Die Juden*, pp. 90–3.

2  For the developments in Topol'čany and Slovakia, see also Büchler, *Topoltschany*, pp. 93–173.

3  Ibid., pp. 159, 161–6.

4  Albert S. Kotowski, '"Ukrainisches Piemont?" – Die Karpatenukraine am Vorabend des Zweiten Weltkrieges', in *Jahrbücher für Geschichte Osteuropas*, 49 (2001), p. 94; Gerlach and Aly, *Das letzte Kapitel*, pp. 482–3.

5  Gerlach and Aly, *Das letzte Kapitel*, p. 74.

6  Ibid., pp. 74–5.

7  Czech, *Auschwitz Chronicle*, p. 148.

8  Lipscher, *Die Juden*, p. 119.

9  Schmidt-Hartmann, 'Tschechoslowakei', p. 373.

10  Lipscher, *Die Juden*, p. 119.

11  Gerlach and Aly, *Das letzte Kapitel*, pp. 482–3; Gutman, *Holocaust*, vol. IV, pp. 1365–6.

12  Gutman, *Holocaust*, vol. II, pp. 610–12; vol. IV, p. 1325; Fleischer, 'Griechenland', pp. 245–6.

13  Gutman, *Holocaust*, vol. II, pp. 612–16.

14  Nar, 'Die Juden von Thessaloniki', pp. 83–4.

15  Benbassa and Rodrigue, *Die Geschichte der sephardischen Juden*, p. 235; Gutman, *Holocaust*, vol. IV, p. 1325.

16  Fleischer, 'Griechenland', pp. 250–1; Bossong, *Die Sepharden*, p. 110.

17 Stella Salem, 'The Old Jewish Cemetery of Thessaloniki', in *Cultural Forum*, pp. 58–9. Other publications also described the situation: see, for example, Benbassa and Rodrigue, *Die Geschichte der sephardischen Juden*, p. 236: '[War administration councillor Max Merten] demanded a ransom from the Jews of Saloniki of 3,500 million drachmae, subsequently reduced to 2,500 million. The Jewish community also agreed to hand over the centuries-old Jewish cemetery to the municipal authorities, which they had wished to take possession of in all the years between the wars. The cemetery was rapidly demolished.' Gutman, *Holocaust*, vol. IV, p. 1326: '[The Jewish community] ransomed its young men... Part of the money was raised in Salonika and Athens; the rest came from the transfer of the five-hundred-year-old graveyard to the municipality, which systematically destroyed it.' Bossong, *Die Sepharden*, p. 110: 'In December 1942 the Nazi thugs razed the Jewish cemetery in the heart of the city ... to the ground.' Fleischer, 'Griechenland', pp. 250–1: '[Several weeks of] negotiations between the military authorities ... and the Jewish community [ended] with an agreement ..., by which the last of their hard-pressed brothers were bought free. After drawn-out negotiations ... the ransom in billions ... was agreed ... In addition, the historical Jewish cemetery ... was transferred to the Greek municipal authorities.' Rene Mohlo and Vilma Hastaoglou-Martinidis, *Jüdische Orte in Thessaloniki* (Athens and Braunschweig 2011), pp. 23–4: '[Merten] offered [the release of the Jewish forced labourers] from the labour camps against payment of 3.5 billion drachmae. The community did its best to raise the demanded sum but was unable to do so in its entirety. Using this as a pretext, Merten on 6 December 1942 followed the advice of the collaborating governor of Macedonia, Vasilis Simonidis, and ordered the municipal authorities to destroy the old Jewish cemetery.'

18 Eberhard Randholz, 'Das griechische Jerusalem – Tagung über die Geschichte der Juden von Thessaloniki', Deutschlandfunk, 19 October 2004.

19 'Jewish Cemetery', in *Cultural Forum*, pp. 50, 55–8. Other publications state that the Jewish cemetery in Thessaloniki had '300,000 graves' (Bossong, *Die Sepharden*, p. 110), 'over 300,000 graves' (Molho and Hastaoglou-Martinidis, *Jüdische Orte in Thessaloniki*, p. 24), or '500,000 graves' razed to the ground (radio broadcast by Simone Böcker and Chrissi Wilkens, 'Stadt der vielen Erinnerungen', Deutschlandfunk, 25 September 2010).

20 Sandner, *Frankfurt – Auschwitz*, pp. 129–35, 146–56, 269–74.

## Gateway to Death

1 *Wegweiser durch das jüdische Berlin* (Berlin 1987), p. 367.

2 Heesch and Braun, *Orte erinnern*, pp. 152–7.

3   A. Eisenbach (Centralna Żydowska Komija Historyczna Łódź), *Getto Łódźkie, Warszawai* (Łódź and Kraków 1946); Bella Guttermann and Avner Shalev, *Zeugnisse des Holocaust – Gedenken in Yad Vashem* (Jerusalem 2008), p. 88.

4   Gottwald and Schulle, '*Judendeportationen*', pp. 70–1.

5   Hildegard Henschel, 'Aus der Arbeit der Jüdischen Gemeinde Berlin während der Jahre 1941–1943 – Gemeindearbeit und Evakuierung von Berlin 16. Oktober 1941–16. Juni 1943', in *Zeitschrift für die Geschichte der Juden*, 1/2 (Tel Aviv 1972), pp. 33–7.

6   Heesch and Braun, *Orte erinnern*, pp. 67–73.

7   See also 'Transportliste' from the 'Gestapo Bereich I Berlin' to Theresienstadt, ITS (International Tracing Service) Arolsen 1.2.1.1/11192842, 1.2.1.1/11192843 and 1.2.1.1/11192844.

8   Gottwald and Schulle, '*Judendeportationen*', pp. 67–73.

9   H. G. Adler, *Theresienstadt 1941–1945: The Face of a Coerced Community*, trans. Belinda Cooper (New York 2017), see also Wolfgang Benz, 'Theresienstadt', in Benz and Distel, eds., *Der Ort des Terrors*, vol. IX; Guttermann and Shalev, *Zeugnisse*, p. 479; Hilberg, *Destruction*, vol. II, pp. 437–8.

10   Adler, *Theresienstadt*, p. 398.

11   Heinz Kersting, *Louis Lowy – Bridge-Builder across the Atlantic and Important Teacher of German Social Workers*, Institut für Beratung und Supervision, Aachen, 22 September 2002.

12   See also Adler, *Theresienstadt*, pp. 59–60.

13   See also '"Karteikarte" aus Theresienstadt mit dem Namen von Dagmar Friedová', ITS Arolsen 1.1.42.2/4984405.

14   Ibid. See also '"Karteikarte" aus Theresienstadt mit dem Namen von Dagmar Fantlová', ITS Arolsen 1.1.42.2/4976030.

15   Gutman, *Holocaust*, vol. I, p. 230.

16   Stefan Klemp, '*Rücksichtslos ausgemerzt*' *– Die Ordnungspolizei und das Massaker von Lidice* (Münster 2012), pp. 11–23.

17   Patricia Tosnerova, 'Die Postverbindung zwischen dem Protektorat und dem Ghetto Theresienstadt', in *Theresienstädter Studien und Dokumente 2001* (Prague 2001), pp. 106ff.; Adler, *Theresienstadt*, pp. 522–5; Wolfgang Benz, *Theresienstadt – Eine Geschichte von Täuschung und Vernichtung* (Munich 2013), pp. 115–16; Milan Kuna, *Musik an der Grenze des Lebens*, 2nd edition (Frankfurt am Main 1998), pp. 168–9, 205–14.

18   Kuna, *Musik an der Grenze*, pp. 168–9, 205–14; Joachim Lange, 'Mit Grandezza und leichter Hand', in *die tageszeitung*, 21 October 2014.

19   Adolf Hoffmeister, biography, www.batz-hausen.de/dhoff.htm.

20   See also Kuna, *Musik an der Grenze*, pp. 210–14; Lange, 'Mit Grandezza'.

21  Hoffmeister, biography.

22  Miroslav Kárný and Margita Kárná, 'Kinder in Theresienstadt', in *Dachauer Hefte 9* (Dachau 1993), pp. 14–31.

23  Ondrichová, *Fredy Hirsch*, pp. 52–4, 57–65.

24  Hanuš Hachenburg, *Theresienstadt*: https://rabbijohnrosove.wordpress.com/2015/04/15/terezin-a-poem-by-hanus-hachenburg-zl.

### 'As If in a Coffin'

1  Czech, *Auschwitz Chronicle*, p. 445.

2  List of names of the Sławków action on 11 June 1942 with the names of the inmates and Jews designated for deportation, including Cyrla, Janek and Moniek (Jakob) Mandelbaum, issued by the Council of Elders of the Jewish community in Bendsburg (Będzin) on 13 June 1942. For the date of arrest and deportation, see also 'Sławków'.

3  See 'Sławków'.

4  Hermann F. Weiss, 'From Reichsautobahnlager to Schmelt Camp: Brande, a Forgotten Holocaust Site in Western Upper Silesia 1940–1943', in *Yad Vashem Studies*, 39.2 (2011), pp. 81–120.

5  Hans-Werner Wollenberg, 'Meine KZ-Erinnerungen', manuscript, completed in Berlin on 7 May 1947, pp. 46–96.

6  See Martin Weinmann, ed., *Das nationalsozialistische Lagersystem* (Frankfurt am Main 1990), p. 646.

7  Barbara Sawicka, 'Fünfteichen (Miłoszyce koło Wrocławia)', in Benz and Distel, eds., *Der Ort des Terrors*, vol. VI, pp. 295–301.

8  Franciszek Piper, 'Das Nebenlager Blechhammer', in *Hefte von Auschwitz 10* (Oświęcim 1967), pp. 19–39.

9  Gerlach and Aly, *Das letzte Kapitel*, p. 7; Hilberg, *Destruction*, vol. II, p. 844.

10  Gerlach and Aly, *Das letzte Kapitel*, pp. 37–90.

11  Varga, 'Ungarn', in Benz, ed., *Dimension des Völkermords*, p. 341.

12  Gerlach and Aly, *Das letzte Kapitel*, pp. 132–48.

13  Ibid., p. 275.

14  Michael Okory, *Kaschau war eine europäische Stadt – Ein Reise- und Lesebuch zur jüdischen Kultur und Geschichte* (Wuppertal 2005), p. 15.

15  The 'inmate sheet [Häftlingsbogen]' from Dachau states: 'Arrested on 15 April 1944 in Nagymegyer', ITS Arolsen 1.1.6.2/10146355.

16  Gerlach and Aly, *Das letzte Kapitel*, p. 162.

17  See Jelinek, *The Carpathian Diaspora*, pp. 271–4, 288–310.

18  Gerlach and Aly, *Das letzte Kapitel*, p. 275; for the transports from Carpatho-Ukraine, see also Jelinek, *The Carpathian Diaspora*, pp. 308–10.

19 For the 'incidents' in Topol'čany between the end of 1943 and mid-September 1944, see Büchler, *Topoltschany*, pp. 166–70.

## Oświęcim – Oshpitzin – Auschwitz

1 Josef Jakubowicz, *Auschwitz ist auch eine Stadt: Durch acht Lager in die Freiheit – ein Überlebender des Holocaust erzählt*, 2nd edition (Nuremberg 2005), pp. 41–2; Augustyna Mościńska, 'Jan Knycz, Zeitzeugenberichte', in Internationale Jugendbegegnungsstätte in Oświęcim, ed., *Oświęcim am ersten Tag des Krieges* (Oświęcim 1999), pp. 43, 48–50.

2 Zygmunt Kuzak, quoted from 'Jan Ptaszkowski, Zeitzeugenberichte – Einwohner der Stadt Oświęcim erzählen über den September 1939', in Oświęcim, ed., *Oświęcim am ersten Tag des Krieges*, p. 7.

3 Jakubowicz, *Auschwitz*, p. 43.

4 Robert Jan van Pelt and Debórah Dwork, *Auschwitz: 1270 to the Present* (New York 1996), p. 33.

5 Lucyna Filip, *Juden in Oświęcim 1918–1941* (Oświęcim 2005), pp. 46–7; Jakubowicz, *Auschwitz*, p. 16.

6 Yosef Landau, 'Oshpitzin – Family and Community Life', in Yitzchak Kasnett, *The World That Was: Poland*, second printing (Cleveland Heights, OH 1999), pp. 56–68; Jakubowicz, *Auschwitz*, pp. 20–36.

7 C. Wolnerman, A. Burstin and M. S. Geshuri, eds., *Oświęcim: Memorial Book*, hectograph (Jerusalem 1977), pp. 141–5; van Pelt and Dwork, *Auschwitz: 1270 to the Present*, pp. 33–6.

8 Wolnerman et al., eds., *Oswiecim; Auschwitz Memorial Book* (Jerusalem 1977), pp. 107–12; Filip, *Juden in Oświęcim*, pp. 54–65.

9 Josef Jakubowicz, 'Jüdische Bürger in Auschwitz – Erinnerungen', in *Dachauer Hefte 17* (Dachau 2001), p. 145.

10 Wolnerman et al., *Memorial Book*, pp. 107–12; Filip, *Juden in Oświęcim*, pp. 65–80, 88–91, 131–7.

11 Filip, *Juden in Oświęcim*, pp. 102–6.

12 Heinrich Ehlers, Talma Segel and Arie Talmi, eds., *Haschomer Hazair – Ein Nest verwundeter Kinderseelen* (Vienna 2006), pp. 12–16.

13 Filip, *Juden in Oświęcim*, pp. 25, 115.

14 Jakubowicz, 'Jüdische Bürger in Auschwitz', p. 147.

15 Jakubowicz, *Auschwitz*, pp. 23–5.

16 Wolnerman et al., *Memorial Book*, pp. 155–60; Filip, *Juden in Oświęcim*, pp. 40–1, 154–61.

17 Henryk M. Broder, 'Unser Haus in Oświęcim', in *Der Spiegel*, 10 August 1998.

18 Jakubowicz, *Auschwitz*, p. 22.

19 Jakubowicz, 'Jüdische Bürger in Auschwitz', pp. 149–50.

20 Filip, *Juden in Oświęcim*, pp. 168–9.

21 Ibid., pp. 172–94; Jakubowicz, *Auschwitz*, pp. 41–8.

22 Jakubowicz, 'Jüdische Bürger in Auschwitz', pp. 149–50.

23 Filip, *Juden in Oświęcim*, pp. 59, 69; Jakubowicz, 'Jüdische Bürger in Auschwitz', p. 148.

24 Danuta Czech, 'Entstehungsgeschichte des KL Auschwitz, Aufbau- und Ausbauperiode', in *Auschwitz – Nationalsozialistisches Vernichtungslager* (Oświęcim 1997), pp. 30–2.

25 Franciszek Piper, 'The Origins of the Camp', in Długoborski and Piper, eds., *Auschwitz 1940–1945*, vol. 1, p. 53; Sybille Steinbacher, *Auschwitz – Geschichte und Nachgeschichte*, 2nd revised edition (Munich 2007), pp. 13–15.

26 Czech, 'Entstehungsgeschichte', p. 33.

27 Ibid., pp. 30–44.

28 Czech, *Auschwitz Chronicle*, p. 13.

29 Kazimierz Albin, *Steckbrieflich gesucht* (Oświęcim 2008), pp. 12–61.

30 Quoted from ibid., p. 62.

31 Ibid., pp. 171–212, 225–327.

32 See, e.g., Tomasz Sobański, *Fluchtwege aus Auschwitz* (Warsaw 1989); *Escape from Auschwitz* (Westport, CT 1986), pp. 51–111, by Erich Kulka, who escaped with his 12-year-old son Otto during the evacuation.

33 Tadeusz Iwaszko, 'Häftlingsfluchten aus dem Konzentrationslager Auschwitz', in *Hefte von Auschwitz 7* (Oświęcim 1964), pp. 25–57.

34 Czech, *Auschwitz Chronicle*, pp. 14, 15, 19.

35 Ibid., pp. 26, 29.

36 Yisrael Gutman, 'Auschwitz – An Overview', in Yisrael Gutman and Michael Berenbaum, eds., *Anatomy of the Auschwitz Death Camp* (Bloomington and Indianapolis 1998), pp. 10–16.

37 Piper, 'Origins', pp. 48–9; Christoph Heubner, Alwin Meyer and Jürgen Pieplow, *Lebenszeichen – Gesehen in Auschwitz* (Bornheim and Merten 1979), pp. 109–51; Państwowe Museum Auschwitz-Birkenau and Stiftung Neue Synagoge Berlin and Musemspädagogischer Dienst Berlin, eds., *Sztuka w Auschwitz 1940–1945 – Kunst in Auschwitz 1940–1945* (Bramsche 2005), pp. 351–89.

38 Franciszek Piper, 'Functional Goals and Tasks of the Camp', in Długoborski and Piper, eds., *Auschwitz 1940–1945*, vol. I, p. 139.

39 Czech, 'Entstehungsgeschichte', pp. 39, 48.

40 Irena Strzelecka and Pitor Setkiewicz, 'The Construction, Expansion and Development of the Camp and its Branches', in Długoborski and Piper,

eds., *Auschwitz 1940–1945*, vol. I, pp. 70–4; Annabel Wahba, '"Mir gehört Auschwitz" – Die bedrückende Last einer Erbschaft: Die Israelin Zypora Frank hat ein Grundstück in Polen geerbt', in *Süddeutsche Zeitung*, 14 August 1998.

41 Jakubowicz, *Auschwitz*, p. 47.

42 Jakubowicz, 'Jüdische Bürger in Auschwitz', pp. 141–2.

43 Filip, *Juden in Oświęcim*, pp. 180–202; see also Jakubowicz, 'Jüdische Bürger in Auschwitz', pp. 148–55.

44 Jakubowicz, *Auschwitz*, pp. 103, 100–11.

45 Steinbacher, *Auschwitz*, pp. 53–4, 57, 59.

46 Strzelecka and Setkiewicz, 'Construction', pp. 70–4, 83.

47 Jerzy Adam Brandhuber, 'Die sowjetischen Kriegsgefangenen in Auschwitz', in *Hefte von Auschwitz* (Oświęcim 1961), pp. 15–62; Czech, 'Entstehungsgeschichte', pp. 39–48; Piper, 'Mass Murder', pp. 95, 116–33.

48 Helena Kubica, 'Children and Adolescents in Auschwitz', in Długoborski and Piper, eds., *Auschwitz 1940–1945*, vol. II, p. 217.

49 Piper, 'Mass Murder', pp. 135–43.

50 Ibid.

51 Ibid., pp. 144–68; see also Annegret Schüle, *J. A. Topf & Söhne – Ein Erfurter Familienunternehmen und der Holocaust* (Erfurt 2014), pp. 63–74.

52 Tadeusz Iwaszko, 'Deportation ins KL Auschwitz', in *Nationalsozialistisches Vernichtungslager*, p. 86.

53 Tadeusz Iwaszko, 'Reasons for Confinement in the Camp and Categories of Prisoners', in Długoborski and Piper, eds., *Auschwitz 1940–1945*, vol. II, pp. 21–2.

54 Ibid., pp. 165–76.

55 Heubner et al., eds., *Lebenszeichen*, pp. 16–19; Andrzej Strzelecki, 'The Plundering of the Possessions of the Jewish Victims of Mass Murder', in Długoborski and Piper, eds., *Auschwitz 1940–1945*, vol. II, pp. 149–55.

56 Strzelecki, 'Plundering, pp. 150–1.

57 Ibid., pp. 155–9; Andrzej Strzelecki, 'Ultilization', in Długoborski and Piper, eds., *Auschwitz 1940–1945*, vol. II, pp. 399–406.

58 Andrzej Strzelecki, 'Die Plünderung des Besitzes im KL Auschwitz ermordeten Juden', in *Nationalsozialistisches Vernichtungslager*, pp. 259–70; Strzelecki, 'Utilization', pp. 407–12.

59 Jan Sehn, *Konzentrationslager Auschwitz-Birkenau* (Warsaw 1987), pp. 148–9.

60 Andrzej Strzelecki, 'Geschichte, Rolle und Betrieb der großen Entwesungs- und Desinfektionsanlage im Konzentrationslager Auschwitz-Birkenau', in Teresa Świebocka, ed., *Architektur des Verbrechens – Die Gebäude der 'Zentralen Sauna' im KZ Auschwitz-Birkenau* (Oświęcim 2001), pp. 11–26, 33.

61 Ibid., pp. 33–42; Iwaszko, 'Reasons for Confinement', pp. 20–1.

62 Tadeusz Szymański, 'Bericht seiner Verhaftung', in Heubner et al., eds., *Lebenszeichen*, pp. 45–6.

63 Iwaszko, 'Reasons for Confinement', p. 22.

64 Strzelecki, 'Große Entwesungs- und Desinfektionsanlage', pp. 37–8.

## Children of Many Languages

1 Irena Strzelecka, 'Die ersten Polen im KL Auschwitz', in *Hefte von Auschwitz 18* (Oświęcim 1990), pp. 21–36, 68–110.

2 Piper, 'Blechhammer', pp. 19–39; see also Ernst Koenig, 'Auschwitz III – Blechhammer', in *Dachauer Hefte 15* (Dachau 1999), pp. 134–52.

3 Czech, *Auschwitz Chronicle*, p. 217.

4 Ibid., p. 328; Wolfgang Benz, 'Theresienstadt: Ein vergessener Ort deutscher Geschichte?', in *Theresienstädter Studien und Dokumente 1996* (Prague 1996), p. 12.

5 Czech, *Auschwitz Chronicle*, p. 260.

6 Roman Hrabar, Zofia Tokarz and Jacek E. Wilczur, *Kriegsschicksale polnischer Kinder* (Warsaw 1981), pp. 50–3; Helena Kubica, *The Extermination at KL Auschwitz of Poles Evicted from Zamość Region in the Years 1942–1943* (Oświęcim 2006), p. 24.

7 Czech, *Auschwitz Chronicle*, pp. 284–7; Kubica, *Zamość*, pp. 26–39, 43–78, 136–51, 238–41.

8 Czech, *Auschwitz Chronicle*, p. 323.

9 Ibid., p. 310.

10 Quoted from Roman Hrabar, Zofia Tokarz and Jacek W. Wilczur, *Kriegschicksale polnischer Kinder* (Warsaw 1981), pp. 64–5; see also Czech, *Auschwitz Chronicle*, p. 336.

11 Czech, *Auschwitz Chronicle*, pp. 310, 336.

12 Ibid., p. 276. Later research showed that the Jews from Norway were not deported to Auschwitz from the port of Bergen but were concentrated in Berg camp, around 100 kilometres south-west of Oslo. They were then deported from the port of the Norwegian capital via Stettin to Auschwitz. See Kai Feinberg, 'Ich erkläre an Eides statt (Eidesstattliche Erklärung im Nürnberger Prozess)', in Gerhard Schoenberner, ed., *Wir haben es gesehen – Augenzeugenberichte über die Judenverfolgung im Dritten Reich* (Munich 1964), p. 266; Hermann Sachnowitz (written by Arnold Jacoby), *Auschwitz – Ein norwegischer Jude überlebte* (Frankfurt am Main, Vienna and Zurich 1981), pp. 12–32; Werner Renz, 'Holocaust-Forschung', in *Newsletter des Fritz Bauer Instituts*, 21 (autumn 2001), p. 55.

13 Espen Søbye, *Kathe – Deportiert aus Norwegen* (Berlin and Hamburg 2008), pp. 103–32.

14 Feinberg, 'An Eides statt', p. 266.

15 Feinberg, quoted from Søbye, *Kathe*, pp. 133, 184.

16 Feinberg, 'An Eides statt', p. 267.

17 Kathe Lasnik, farewell letter, quoted from Søbye, *Kathe*, p. 14.

18 'Häftlingspersonalbogen' des Vernichtungslagers Auschwitz with the name Jürgen, Rolf Loewenstein, 3 March 1943, no. 104983, ITS Arolsen 1.1.2.1/499816; Czech, *Auschwitz Chronicle*, p. 343.

19 Gottwaldt and Schulle, 'Judendeportationen', p. 410.

20 Margit Naarmann, 'Ein Auge gen Zion … : Das jüdische Umschulungs- und Einsatzlager am Grünen Weg in Paderborn 1939–1943', *Paderborner Beiträge zur Geschichte* 10 (2000), p. 61.

21 Gottwaldt and Schulle, 'Judendeportationen', pp. 408–18; Naarmann, 'Ein Auge gen Zion', pp. 51–61; Felix Moeller, 'Der Protest der Rosenstraßen – Eine Woche im Berlin des Jahres 1943', in Thilo Wydra, *Rosenstraße* (Berlin 2003), pp. 25–57.

22 Strzelecka and Setikiewicz, 'Construction', pp. 108–18; Steinbacher, *Auschwitz*, pp. 37–49; Czech, 'Entstehungsgeschichte', pp. 40–2.

23 'Transfer to Auschwitz (Main Camp) from Buna inmate sick bay', 29 March 1943, with the name Jürgen Löwenstein, ITS Arolsen 1.1.2.1/529970.

24 Franciszek Pipe, 'Das Nebenlager "Eintrachthütte"', in *Hefte von Auschwitz 17* (Oświęcim 1985), pp. 91–155; Andrea Rudorff, 'Eintrachthütte', in Benz and Distel, eds., *Der Ort des Terrors*, vol. V (Munich 2007), pp. 211–14.

25 Czech, *Auschwitz Chronicle*, p. 352.

26 Strzelecka and Setikiewicz, 'Construction', pp. 80–113.

27 Jürgen Pieplow, *Majdanek, Stutthof, Gross-Rosen: Arbeitsmappe Polen* (Berlin 1992), 'Pferdestall'; Rose, 'Völkermord Roma im "Zigeunerlager" des KL Auschwitz 1.3.1943–2.8.1944', in Wacław Długoborski, ed., *Sinti und Roma in Auschwitz-Birkenau 1933–44* (Oświęcim 1988), p. 301.

28 Vlastimila Kladivová, 'Sinti und Roma im "Zigeunerlager"', in Długoborski, ed., *Sinti und Roma*, p. 301.

29 Czech, *Auschwitz Chronicle*, pp. 358–9.

30 Ibid., p. 338.

31 Michael Zimmermann, 'Die Deportation der Sinti und Roma nach Auschwitz-Birkenau', in Verband der Roma in Polen, ed., *Das Schicksal der Sinti und Roma im KL Auschwitz-Birkenau* (Oświęcim 1994), pp. 45–83; Kladivová, 'Sinti und Roma', p. 301; Kubica, 'Children and Adolescents', p. 288.

32 Wiesław Kielar, *Anus Mundi*, 10th edition (Frankfurt am Main 2004), p. 252.

33 Halina Birenbaum, *Hope Is the Last to Die: A Coming of Age under Nazi Terror*, trans. David Welsh (London 1996), p. 101.

34 Flora Neumann, *Erinnern, um zu leben, vor Auschwitz – in Auschwitz – nach Auschwitz*, 3rd revised and enlarged edition (Hamburg 2006), p. 50; see also Hermann Langbein, *People in Auschwitz*, trans. Henry Friedlander (Chapel Hill, NC 2004), pp. 406–12.

35 Czech, *Auschwitz Chronicle*, p. 356.

36 Piper, 'Mass Murder', pp. 205–31.

37 Helene Kounio, statement, Auschwitz Memorial, Oświęcim, 19 April 1962; Erika Amargilio (Heinz Kounio's sister), 'Bericht', in Lore Shelley, ed., *Schreiberinnen des Todes – Lebenserinnerungen internierter Frauen, die in der Verwaltung des Vernichtungslagers Auschwitz arbeiten mussten* (Bielefeld 1992), pp. 64–73.

38 Bronka Klibanski, 'Kinder aus dem Ghetto Bialystok in Theresienstadt', in *Theresienstädter Studien und Dokumente 1995* (Prague 1995), pp. 94–105.

39 Czech, *Auschwitz Chronicle*, p. 501.

40 Adler, *Theresienstadt*, p. 128; Klibanski, 'Białystok', pp. 93–4, 102.

41 Adler, *Theresienstadt*, p. 127.

42 Ondrichová, *Fredy Hirsch*, p. 66; Klibanski, 'Białystok', p. 94.

43 Klibanski, 'Białystok', pp. 94–105.

44 Czech, *Auschwitz Chronicle*, p. 548; Miroslav Kárný, 'Theresienstädter Familienlager in Birkenau', in *Hefte von Auschwitz 20* (Oświęcim 1997), p. 223.

45 Kárný, 'Theresienstädter Familienlager', pp. 224–37.

46 Ibid., p. 174.

47 Czech, *Auschwitz Chronicle*, p. 595.

48 Ibid., pp. 627–8.

49 Ibid., p. 656.

50 Kárný, 'Theresienstädter Familienlager', pp. 224–37.

51 Czech, *Auschwitz Chronicle*, pp. 662–3; Kárný, 'Theresienstädter Familienlager', pp. 217–23.

52 Czech, *Auschwitz Chronicle*, pp. 351, 421, 485–539; Kubica, 'Children and Adolescents', pp. 265–8; Projektgruppe Belarus, ed., *'Dann kam die deutsche Macht' – Weißrussische Kinderhäftlinge in deutschen Konzentrationslagern 1941–1945* (Cologne 1999), pp. 12–23, 62–81.

53 Hilberg, *Destruction*, vol. I, pp. 271–390.

54 Gutman, *Holocaust*, vol. II, pp. 433–9.

55 Frank Golczewski, 'Polen', in Benz, ed., *Dimension des Völkermords*, pp. 419–26.

56 Gert Robel, 'Sowjetunion', in Benz, ed., *Dimension des Völkermords*, pp. 510–22, 560.

57 United States Holocaust Museum, Documenting Numbers of Victims. In the territory of the then Soviet Union alone, 1.3 million Jews were shot on the spot or killed in gas vans.

58 Wolfram Wette, 'Sowjetische Erinnerungen an den deutschen Vernichtungskrieg', in Paul Kohl, ed., *Ich wundere mich, dass ich noch lebe: Sowjetische Augenzeugen berichten* (Gütersloh 1990), pp. 295–8.

59 Rachel Margolis and Jim Tobias, *Die geheimen Notizen des K. Sakowicz – Dokumentezur Judenvernichtung in Ponary 1941–1943* (Frankfurt am Main 2005), pp. 7–46; Vilna Gaon State Jewish Museum, ed., *Catalogue of the Holocaust Exhibition* (Vilnius 2011), pp. 81–5.

60 Margolis and Tobias, *Geheimen Notizen*, pp. 12–14; Vilna Gaon State Jewish Museum, ed., *Lithuanian Holocaust Atlas* (Vilnius 2011), pp. 292–6.

61 Kazimierz Sakowicz, 'Aufzeichnungen', quoted from Margolis and Tobias, *Geheimen Notizen*, p. 59.

62 Ernst Klee, *Das Personenlexikon zum Dritten Reich – Wer war was vor und nach 1945* (Frankfurt am Main 2003), p. 280.

63 Margolis and Tobias, *Geheimen Notizen*, p. 15.

64 Quoted from Klee, *Personenlexikon*, p. 280.

65 Gutman, *Holocaust*, vol. II, p. 733.

66 Alek Volkovisky and Shermke Kaczerginski, 'The Song of Ponar', www. yadvashem.org/yv/en/exhibitions/music/shtiler-shtiler.asp.

67 Czech, *Auschwitz Chronicle*, pp. 485, 511.

68 Kubica, 'Children and Adolescents', p. 216.

69 Czech, *Auschwitz Chronicle*, pp. 351, 421, 539.

70 Kubica, 'Children and Adolescents', pp. 216–17.

71 'Demography of Ukrainian Towns', pop-stat.mashke.org/ukraine-cities.htm.

72 For details of Ludmila Bocharova and her family, see also N. Krylova, 'Person number 70071', in *Ogoniok*, 7 May 1983.

73 Irena Strzelecka, 'The Hospitals at Auschwitz Concentration Camp', in Długoborski and Piper, eds., *Auschwitz 1940–1945*, vol. II, pp. 291–346.

74 Anna Vasilyevna Bocharova, statement, Yenakiieve, 13 February 1969, Yenakiieve city archive.

75 Czech, *Auschwitz Chronicle*, p. 581.

76 Serge Klarsfeld, *French Children of the Holocaust: A Memorial* (New York and London 1996), p. 411.

77 Franciszek Piper, *Die Zahl der Opfer von Auschwitz* (Oświęcim 1993), pp. 187–8.

78 Hilberg, *Destruction*, vol. II, p. 657.

79 Klarsfeld, *French Children*, p. 8.

80 Juliane Wetzel, 'Frankreich', in Benz, ed., *Dimension des Völkermords*, p. 127.

81 Piper, *Die Zahl der Opfer*, p. 197; Serge Klarsfeld and Maxime Steinfeld, eds., *Die Endlösung der Judenfrage in Belgien* (Paris 1980), p. 88.

82 'Häftlingskarte' with arrival date 7 July 1944, inmate number 103820 [Géza Schein], ITS Arolsen 1.1.26.6/2528868.

83 See 'Häftlings-Personal-Karte', Geza Schein, KL Mauthausen, ITS Arolsen 1.1.26.3/1743693.

84 Steinbacher, *Auschwitz*, p. 42.

85 Czech, *Auschwitz Chronicle*, p. 624.

86 Johannes Meister, 'Schicksale der "Zigeunerkinder" aus der St. Josefspflege in Mulfingen', reprint from *Württembergisch Franken Jahrbuch 1984*, pp. 198–206.

87 Anita Geigges and Bernhard W. Wette, *Zigeuner heute – Verfolgung und Diskriminierung in der BRD* (Bornheim-Merten 1979), pp. 327–8.

88 Quoted from Meister, 'Zigeunerkinder', p. 207.

89 Tilman Zülch, 'Sinti und Roma in Deutschland – Geschichte einer verfolgten Minderheit', in *aus politik und zeitgeschichte*, 30 October 1982.

90 Meister, 'Zigeunerkinder', p. 207.

91 Christoph Knödler and Hans-Joachim Treumann, 'Die Zigeunerkinder in Mulfingen', project by Year 12, Deutschordengymnasium, Bad Mergentheim, as part of the Deutsche Geschichte school competition, 1980–1, pp. 59–66.

92 Meister, 'Zigeunerkinder', p. 228.

93 Brigitte Mihok, 'Die ungarischen Juden', in Benz and Distel, eds., *Der Ort des Terrors*, vol. V, p. 149; Strzelecka and Setkiewicz, 'Construction', vol. I, pp. 98–100.

94 Kárný, 'Theresienstädter Familienlager', p. 162.

95 Seweryna Szmaglewska, *Smoke over Birkenau*, trans. Jadwiga Rynas (New York 1947), p. 295; Strzelecka and Setkiewicz, 'Bau, Ausbau und Entwicklung', pp. 115–17.

96 Szmaglewska, *Smoke over Birkenau*, p. 296.

97 See, e.g., Aron Bejlin, 'Zeugenaussage beim Auschwitz-Prozess', in *Der Auschwitz-Prozeß – Tonbandmitschnitte, Protokolle, Dokumente,* published by the Fritz Bauer Institute and the State Museum Auschwitz-Birkenau, Digital Library 101 (Berlin 2004), pp. 16325–7.

98 Ernst Klee, *Auschwitz, Täter, Gehilfen, Opfer und was aus ihnen wurde – Ein Personenlexikon* (Frankfurt am Main 2013), p. 109; Langbein, *People in Auschwitz*, pp. 338, 426; Ulrich Völklein, *Joseph Mengele – Der Arzt von Auschwitz* (Göttingen 1999), p. 135.

99 Czech, *Auschwitz Chronicle*, p. 736.

100 'Häftlingspersonalkarte' from Dachau concentration camp, ITS Arolsen 1.1.6.2/10144575; registry card from Dachau concentration camp, ITS Arolsen

1.1.6.7/10682438; 'Transportliste' from Dachau concentration camp, 26 July 1944, ITS Arolsen 1.1.6.1/9914105.

101 Spector, ed., *Jewish Life*, vol. II, pp. 604–7.

102 Miron, ed., *Ghettos*, vol. I, p. 291.

103 Vilna Gaon State Jewish Museum, *Holocaust Exhibition*, pp. 123–4.

104 Jürgen Matthäus, 'Kauen (Kaunas) – Stammlager', in Benz and Distel, eds., *Der Ort des Terrors*, vol. VIII, pp. 194–7; see also Sara Ginaite-Rubinson, *Resistance and Survival – The Jewish Community in Kaunas 1941–1944* (Oakville and Ontario 2005), pp. 45–80.

105 Vilna Gaon State Jewish Museum, ed., *Lithuanian Holocaust Atlas*, pp. 38–45.

106 Matthäus, 'Kauen', p. 189.

107 Ibid., pp. 197–208.

108 Vilna Gaon State Jewish Museum, *Holocaust Exhibition*, p. 158; see also Solly Ganor, *Das andere Leben – Kindheit im Holocaust*, 5th edition (Frankfurt am Main 2011), pp. 145–58.

109 Dr Anton Peretz, report, quoted from *Solidarität zu Kindern in den national-sozialistischen Ghettos* (Vienna 1984), p. 29.

110 Vilna Gaon State Jewish Museum, *Holocaust Exhibition*, p. 158.

111 Jerry Zalman Konvoj, testimony, Toronto, n.d. [2005].

112 Vilna Gaon State Jewish Museum, *Holocaust Exhibition*, p. 158.

113 Extract from transport lists from Stutthof concentration camp, n.d., ITS Arolsen 1.1.41.1/4404592.

114 Matthäus, 'Kauen', p. 202.

115 'Häftlingspersonalkarte' from Dachau concentration camp, ITS Arolsen 1.1.6.2/10144575; 'Überstellungsliste' from Dachau concentration camp, n.d., ITS Arolsen 1.1.6.1/9920501 and 1.1.6.1/9920759; 'Transportliste' from Dachau concentration camp, 26 July 1944, ITS Arolsen 1.1.6.1/9914105.

116 'Effektenkarte' from Buchenwald concentration camp, ITS Arolsen 1.1.5.3/6324622, and 'Arbeitskarte' from Buchenwald concentration camp, ITS Arolsen 1.1.5.3/6324624.

117 Helena Kubica, *From the Warsaw Uprising to Auschwitz* (Oświęcim, 2015), pp. 7–28.

118 Janusz Piekalkiewicz, *Kampf um Warschau – Stalins Verrat an der polnischen Heimatarmee 1944*, 2nd edition (Munich 2004), pp. 280–1.

119 Gutmann, *Holocaust*, vol. IV, p. 1633.

120 Heinrich Maier, 'Initiative Eckerwald setzt in Schömberg Zeichen – Neue KZ-Gedenkstätte führt Besucher in die Wüste', in *Gedenkstätten-Rundschau*, 2 (April 2009); Walter Looser-Heidger, '1774 Tote der KZ Dautermengen und

Schömberg erhalten ihre Namen wieder', in *Gedenkstätten-Rundschau*, 2 (April 2009).

121 Gerhard Lempp, 'Warschau – Auschwitz – Dautmergen – Schömberg – Mittenwald: Acht Monate aus dem Leben des ehemaligen. KZ-Häftlings Jerzy Sztanka aus Warschau (Teil II)', in *Gedenkstätten-Rundschau*, 6 (May 2011).

122 Federal Ministry of Justice and Consumer Protection, list of concentration camps and their satellite camps, p. 6, www.gesetze-im-internet.de/bundesrecht/ begdv_6/gesamt.pdf.

123 Jadwiga Matysiak, letter (excerpt), Warsaw, 8 October 1986.

124 Andrea Löw, 'Das Warschauer Ghetto', in *Das Warschauer Ghetto*, www. bpb.de/geschichte/nationalsozialismus/geheimsache-ghettofilm/141785/ das-warschauer-ghetto.

125 Hilberg, *Destruction*, vol. I, p. 221; Gutman, *Holocaust*, vol. IV, p. 1603; Gottwald and Schulle, 'Judendeportationen', esp. pp. 168, 188, 190, 193, 197.

126 Golczewski, 'Polen', p. 439.

127 Markus Roth and Andrea Löw, *Das Warschauer Ghetto – Alltag und Widerstand im Angesicht der Vernichtung* (Munich 2013), pp. 113–24.

128 Beate Kosmala, 'Ungleiche Opfer in extremer Situation – Die Schwierigkeiten der Solidarität im okkupierten Polen', in Benz et al., eds., *Solidarität*, vol. I (Berlin 1996), p. 39; Löw, 'Warschauer Ghetto'.

129 Wolfgang Benz, 'Treblinka', in Benz and Distel, eds., *Der Ort des Terrors*, vol. VIII, pp. 409–17.

130 Hilberg, *Destruction*, vol. II, pp. 510–12; Roth and Löw, *Warschauer Ghetto*, pp. 187–208.

131 Jochen August, 'Aufstand/Widerstand im Warschauer Ghetto – Emanuel Ringelblum und das Untergrundarchiv', in *Zeichen*, 1 (March 1983).

132 Report of the united underground organization of the Warsaw ghetto of 15 November 1942, in August, 'Aufstand/Widerstand'.

133 'Ringelblum – The Man and the Historian', https://yadvashem.org/yv/en/ exhibition/ringelblum/index.asp; Löw, 'Warschauer Ghetto'.

134 Gerhard Hirschfeld, 'Niederlande', in Benz, ed., *Dimension des Völkermords*, pp. 146–51, 153–7.

135 Gutman, *Holocaust*, vol. IV, p. 1645.

136 Angelika Königseder, 'Polizeihaftlager', in Benz and Distel, eds., *Der Ort des Terrors*, vol. IX, pp. 25–6; Hirschfeld, 'Niederlande', pp. 154, 162–5; see also Andreas Pflock, *Auf vergessenen Spuren – Ein Wegweiser zu Gedenkstätten in den Niederlanden, Belgien und Luxemburg* (Bonn 2006), p. 66.

137 Gerhard L. Durlacher, *Stripes in the Sky: A Wartime Memoir*, trans. Susan Massotty (London 1991), pp. 52–3.

138  Ibid., p. 51.
139  United Restitution Office (Frankfurt am Main) to ITS Arolsen, 5 October 1955, ITS Arolsen 6.3.3.2/100333270.
140  'Alphabetisches Verzeichnis zum Transport EK' from Theresienstadt with the name Wolfgang Wermuth, ITS Arolsen 1.1.42.1/4958817 und 1.1.42.1/4958841.
141  Certificate [Bescheinigung] dated 22 November 1958 for Channa Loewenstein (*née* Markowicz), ITS Arolsen, 6.3.3.2/102440057.

### Small Children, Mothers and Grandmothers

1   See, e.g., Anna Pawełczyńska, *Werte gegen Gewalt – Betrachtungen einer Soziologin über Auschwitz*, trans. from Polish by Jochen August (Oświęcim 2001), pp. 91–139.
2   Lucie Adelsberger, *Auschwitz – A Doctor's Story*, trans. Susan Ray (London 1996), pp. xiii–xvi.
3   Ibid., p. 100.
4   Simon Gotland, biographical details in writ of prosecution, Auschwitz Trial, pp. 2785–6, 43776.
5   Simon Gotland, statement in the writ of prosecution in the Auschwitz Trial, pp. 2786.
6   Magda Szabo, list of persons, Auschwitz Trial, p. 46355.
7   Magda Szabo, testimony, pp. 15584–6.
8   Michael John, 'Wien – Brüssel – St. Cyprien – Auschwitz, Erinnerungen eines Zeitzeugen (Norbert Lopper)', in *Auschwitz-Information*, 71 (Linz) (March 2006).
9   Norbert Lopper, statement, quoted from Margaretha Rebbeca Hopfner, 'Kinder in Auschwitz', dissertation, Vienna 1993, pp. 70–1.
10  Josef Glück, biographical details in writ of prosecution, Auschwitz Trial, p. 2897.
11  Josef Glück, statement in the writ of prosecution in the Auschwitz Trial, pp. 2898–900.
12  Klee, *Auschwitz*, pp. 162–3.
13  Kitty Hart, *Aber ich lebe* (Hamburg 1961), p. 68.
14  Rolf Weinstock, *Das wahre Gesicht Hitler-Deutschlands, Dachau – Auschwitz – Buchenwald* (Singen 1948), pp. 3, 5.
15  Ibid., p. 79.
16  Ibid., p. 80.
17  Hans-Jörg Jenne, 'Im Vorhof zur Hölle Auschwitz', *Badische Zeitung*, 22 October 2010.
18  Kateřina Čapková, 'The Testimony of Salmen [sometimes spelt Zalman]

Gradowski', in *Theresienstädter Studien und Dokumente 1999* (Prague 1999), p. 105.

19 Zalman Gradowski, 'The Manuscript' (translation edited), in Jadwiga Bezwińska and Danuta Czech (selection and editing), *Amidst a Nightmare of Crime: Manuscripts of Members of Sonderkommando* (Oświęcim 1973), pp. 93–5.

20 Otto Schwerdt and Mascha Schwerdt-Schneller, *Als Gott und die Welt schliefen*, 9th–11th edition (Viechtach 2002)), pp. 46–7.

21 Ibid., pp. 5–109.

22 Seweryna Szmaglewska, testimony, *Der Nürnberger Prozess – Das Protokoll des Prozesses gegen die Hauptkriegsverbrecher vor dem Internationalen Militärgerichtshof 14. November 1945 bis 1. Oktober 1946*, digital library 20, 2nd edition (Berlin 2004), p. 9124.

23 Ibid., p. 9129.

24 Czech, *Auschwitz Chronicle*, p. 652.

25 Henryk Szletynski, 'Erinnerung eines Freundes', in Maria Zarebinska-Broniewska, *Auschwitzer Erzählungen* (Potsdam 1949), pp. 5–11.

26 Ibid., pp. 45–6.

27 Bernd Steger and Günter Thiele, *Der dunkle Schatten – Leben mit Auschwitz, Erinnerungen an Orli Reichert-Wald* (Marburg 1989), pp. 12–84; Czech, *Auschwitz Chronicle*, p. 148.

28 Orli Reichert-Wald, 'Kinderwagenparade', in Steger and Thiele, *Der dunkle Schatten*, p. 108.

29 Grete Salus, *Eine Frau erzählt* (Bonn 1958), pp. 5, 14; Grete Salus at www.forumverlagleipzig.de/frame-inhalt/autoren/salus.htm.

30 Janda Weiß, 'Erlebnisse einer 15jährigen in Birkenau', in *Der Buchenwald-Report, Bericht über das Konzentrationslager Buchenwald bei Weimar*, 2nd edition (Munich 2010), trans. David A. Hackett as 'Experiences of a Fifteen-Year-Old in Birkenau', in *The Buchenwald Report* (Boulder, CO 1995), pp. 350–1.

31 Siegbert Löffler, testimony, Auschwitz Trial, pp. 27117–23.

32 Ibid., p. 27124.

33 Ibid., pp. 27124–5.

34 Simon Gotland, testimony, Auschwitz Trial, pp. 13319–20.

35 Dov Paisikovic, testimony, Auschwitz Trial, p. 21052.

36 Dov Paisikovic, in Vladimir Pozner, *Abstieg in die Hölle* (Berlin 1982), pp. 59–60.

37 Paisikovic, testimony, Auschwitz Trial, pp. 20973–4.

38 See Henryk Świebocki, 'The Resistance Movement', in Długoborski and Piper, eds., *Auschwitz 1940–1945*, vol. IV, pp. 552, 124–5.

39  Nina Gusiewa, 'Aufzeichnung', quoted from Hrabar et al., *Kriegsschicksale polnischer Kinder*, p. 66.

40  Gedalia Ben Zvi, testimony, Eichmann trial in Jerusalem, session 71, 8 June 1961, in https://collections.ushmn.org/search/catalog/irn1001718.

41  Ibid.

42  Dounia Zlata Wasserstrom, list of names, Auschwitz Trial, p. 46585.

43  Dounia Zlata Wasserstrom, testimony, Auschwitz Trial, transcript by associate judge, pp. 6495–6.

44  Ibid., quoted from Langbein, *People*, p. 123.

45  Zdzisław Soleski, in Hamburger Institut für Sozialforschung, ed., *Die Auschwitz-Hefte – Texte der polnischen Zeitschrift* Przegląd Lekarski *über historische, psychische und medizinische Aspekte des Lebens und Sterbens in Auschwitz*, vols. I and II (Weinheim and Basel 1987), vol. I, p. 315.

46  Piper, 'Mass Murder', pp. 41–52, 83–103; see also Pery Broad, 'Erinnerungen', in Jadwiga Bezwińska and Danuta Czech, eds., *Auschwitz in den Augen der SS – Höss, Broad, sec* (Katowice 1981), pp. 145–57.

47  Klee, *Auschwitz*, pp. 308–9.

48  Bolesław Zbozień, statement, quoted from Franciszek Piper, 'Ausrottung', in *Auschwitz – Nazi Death Camp* (Oświęcim 1996), pp. 113–14.

49  Franciszek Gulba, testimony and list of names, Auschwitz Trial, pp. 28943–6, 43849.

50  Franciszek Gulba, statement, quoted from Franciszek Piper, 'Direkte Methoden der Tötung von Häftlingen', in *Nationalsozialistisches Vernichtungslager*, p. 231.

51  Władysław Girsa, statement, quoted from Helena Kubica, *Man darf sie nie vergessen – Die jüngsten Opfer von Auschwitz* (Oświęcim 2002), p. 47.

52  Jan Szpalerski, testimony, Auschwitz Trial, transcript by associate judge, pp. 21723–33.

53  Jan Szpalerski, statement, quoted from Kubica, *Man darf sie nie vergessen*, p. 78.

54  Barbara Milewski, 'Krystyna Żywulska', in *Swarthmore College Bulletin* (July 2009).

55  Krystyna Żywulska, *I Survived Auschwitz* (Warsaw 2011), revised and expanded edition, pp. 229–31.

56  Kalman Bar On, in 'The Human Spirit in the Shadow of Death', www. yadvashem.org/yv/en/remembrance/2006/bar-on.asp#!prettyPhoto.

57  Kalman Bar On, statement, quoted from 'Schreie, die nie verhallen', in *Stern*, 14 February 1985.

58  Hermann Langbein, testimony, Auschwitz Trial, pp. 5501–3.

59  Hermann Langbein, list of names, Auschwitz Trial, p. 44836.

60 Hermann Langbein, *Die Stärkeren – Ein Bericht aus Auschwitz und anderen Konzentrationslagern*, 2nd revised edition (Cologne 1982), p. 225.

61 Szmaglewska, *Smoke over Birkenau*, pp. 286–7.

62 Otto Wolken, list of names, Auschwitz Trial, p. 46733.

63 Otto Wolken, testimony, Auschwitz Trial, pp. 5066–7; see also Inge Deutschkron, … *denn ihrer war die Hölle – Kinder in Ghettos und Lagern* (Cologne 1979), pp. 35–7.

64 Zywulska, *I Survived Auschwitz*, p. 241.

65 Ota Kraus and Erich Kulka, *The Death Factory*, trans. from Czech by Stephen Jolly (New York 1966), pp. 1–4.

66 Ibid., pp. 110–11.

67 Rudolf Höß, *Commandant of Auschwitz – The Autobiography of Höß*, trans. Constantine FitzGibbon (London 2000), pp. 128–9.

68 Ralph Gross and Werner Renz, eds., *Der Frankfurter Auschwitz-Prozess (1963–1965) – Kommentierte Quellenedition*, vol. I (Frankfurt am Main 2013), p. 1318, n. 105; see also Irmtraud Wojak, 'Der erste Frankfurter Auschwitz-Prozeß und die "Bewältigung" der NS-Vergangenheit', in Irmtraud Wojak, ed., for the Fritz Bauer Institute, *Auschwitz-Prozeß 4 Ks 2/63 Frankfurt am Main* (Cologne 2004), pp. 63–4.

69 Sehn, *Auschwitz-Birkenau*, pp. 157–60.

70 Marina Wolff, 'Persönliche Mitteilung', in Inge Deutschkron, … *denn ihrer war die Hölle*, pp. 105–6.

71 Josef Glück, testimony, Auschwitz Trial, pp. 15110–12.

72 Zywulska, *I Survived Auschwitz*, p. 272.

73 Szmaglewska, *Smoke over Birkenau*, p. 297.

74 Maria Zarębińska-Broniewska, *Auschwitzer Erzählungen* (Berlin and Potsdam 1949), pp. 5–11.

75 Ibid., pp. 44–5.

76 Ruth Bondy, 'Frauen in Theresienstadt und Auschwitz-Birkenau', in Barbara Distel, ed., *Frauen im Holocaust* (Gerlingen 2001), pp. 138–9; for the life of Ruth Bondy, see Nili Keren, 'Ruth Bondy', in http://jwa.org/encyclopedia/article/bondy-ruth.

### *'DI 600 Inglekh' and Other Manuscripts Found in Auschwitz*

1 Ya'akov Gabai, '"I'll Get Out of Here"', in Gideon Greif, *We Wept Without Tears: Testimonies of the Jewish Sonderkommando from Auschwitz* (New Haven, CT 2005), p. 205.

2 Ibid., pp. 181–214; Klee, *Auschwitz*, pp. 133–4.

3 Filip Müller, testimony, Auschwitz Trial, pp. 20458–768; see also Erich

Friedler, Barbara Siebert and Andreas Kilian, *Zeugen aus der Todeszone – Das jüdische Sonderkommando in Auschwitz* (Lüneburg 2002), pp. 44–50, 382.

4 Filip Müller, testimony, Auschwitz Trial, pp. 20679–80.

5 Ibid., pp. 20681–2.

6 Friedler et al., *Todeszone*, pp. 63–194, Sa 376.

7 Gotland, testimony, Auschwitz Trial, pp. 13297–8.

8 Jean-Claude Pressac with Robert-Jan van Pelt, 'The Machinery of Mass Murder at Auschwitz', in Gutman and Berenbaum, eds., *Anatomy of the Auschwitz Death Camp*, pp. 209–15; Piper, 'Mass Murder', pp. 134–43; Robert Jan van Pelt, 'Auschwitz', in Günther Morsch and Bertrand Perz, eds., *Neue Studien zu nationalsozialistischen Massentötungen durch Giftgas* (Berlin 2011), p. 207.

9 Friedler et al., *Todeszone*, pp. 76–194.

10 Ibid.; Piper, 'Mass Murder'.

11 Gabai, '"I'll Get Out of Here"', p. 193.

12 Höß, *Commandant*, p. 242.

13 Friedler et al., *Todeszone*, pp. 7, 307.

14 Krystyna Oleksy, 'Zalman Gradowski – ein Zeuge aus dem Sonderkommando', in *Theresienstädter Studien und Dokumente 1995* (Prague 1995), pp. 125–6.

15 Henryk Porębski, statement, quoted from ibid., p. 125.

16 Zalman Gradowski, 'Handschrift', in Jadwiga Bezwińska and Danuta Czech (selection and editing), *Inmitten des Grauenvollen Verbrechens – Handschriften von Mitgliedern des Sonderkommandos* (Oświęcim 1996), p. 138.

17 Greif, *We Wept Without Tears*, p. 165.

18 Bernard Mark, 'Über die Handschrift von Zalman Gradowski', in Bezwińska and Czech, eds., *Inmitten des grauenvollen Verbrechens*, pp. 133–6; see also Szlama Dragon, record of hearings on 10, 11 and 17 May 1945 in Oświęcim, in Piper, *Die Zahl der Opfer von Auschwitz*, pp. 203–25.

19 Mark, 'Über die Handschrift', p. 134.

20 Chaim Wolnerman, 'Introduction', in *Pro Memoria*, 25 (June 2006), pp. 31–3.

21 Zalman Gradowski, 'In harz fun gehinim', in *Theresienstädter Studien und Dokumente 1999*, trans. from Yiddish by Kateřina Čapková, pp. 112–40; Čapková, 'Testimony', p. 105.

22 Mark, 'Über die Handschrift', p. 135; Miron, ed., *Ghettos*, vol. I, pp. 434–5; see also Igor Bartosik, 'Zalman Gradowski – Ein Zeuge der Shoah', in Zalman Gradowski, *From the Heart of Hell: Manuscripts of a Sonderkommando Prisoner, Found in Auschwitz* (Oświęcim, 2017), pp. 7–15.

23 'Lunna-Wola During the Second World War and the Holocaust': http://kehilalinks.jewishgen.org/Lunna/Kelbasin.html.

24 Čapková, 'Testimony', p. 105.

25 Gradowski, 'Handschrift', p. 140.

26 Gradowski, 'In harz fun gehinem', p. 130; see also Czech, *Auschwitz Chronicle*, p. 595.

27 Gradowski, 'In harz fun gehinem', pp. 115, 118, 120, 123, 124, 126, 127.

28 Jadwiga Bezwińska and Danuta Czech, 'Vorwort', in *Hefte von Auschwitz 14* (Oświęcim 1973), pp. 5–11.

29 Ber Mark, *The Scrolls of Auschwitz* (Tel Aviv 1985), pp. 159–60; Ester Mark, 'Notes on the Identity of the "Anonymous" Author and on his Manuscript', in ibid., pp. 166–70.

30 Miron, ed., *Ghettos*, vol. I, pp. 450–1; 'Ghetto in Maków Mazowiecki', www.sztetl. org.pl/en/article/makow-mazowiecki/13,sites-of-martyrdom/10622,ghetto-in-makowmazowiecki.

31 Leib Langfus, 'Handschrift', trans. from Yiddish into Polish by Roman Pytel, from Polish into German by Herta Henschel (slightly revised version), in *Hefte von Auschwitz 14*, pp. 63–8.

32 Jadwiga Bezwińka and Danuta Czech, 'Über die Handschrift von Salmen Lewental', in Bezwińska and Czech, eds., *Inmitten des grauenvollen Verbrechens*, pp. 198–201.

33 Mark, *The Scrolls of Auschwitz*, pp. 159–60; Ester Mark, 'Notes', in ibid., pp. 166–70.

34 Probably the murder of 1,000 boys on 20 October 1944 in Auschwitz-Birkenau Crematorium III; Czech, *Auschwitz Chronicle*, p. 736.

35 Leib Langfus, 'Di 600 inglekh', in Bezwińska and Czech, eds., *Amidst a Nightmare of Crime*, pp. 12–13 [translation modified].

36 This was the 'Block of Death' in the Women's Camp at Birkenau. Female prisoners selected during such actions in the camp were put in this block. They were destined to die in gas chambers.

37 Leib Langfus, 'Di 3000 nakete', in Bezwińska and Czech, eds., *Amidst a Nightmare of Crime*, pp. 143–5.

## Births in Auschwitz

1 Irena Strzelecka, 'Women in the Auschwitz Concentration Camp', in Długoborski and Piper, eds., *Auschwitz 1940–1945*, vol. II, p. 172.

2 Janina Kościuszkowa, 'Kinder im Konzentrationslager Auschwitz', in *In der Hölle retteten sie die Würde des Menschen – Anthologie*, vol. II, part 2, published by the International Auschwitz Committee (Warsaw 1970), p. 208; Kubica, 'Children and Adolescents', in Długoborski and Piper, eds., *Auschwitz 1940–1945*, vol. II, p. 267.

3   Eugen Kogon, *Der SS-Staat – Das System der deutschen Konzentrationslager* (Frankfurt am Main 1961), pp. 262–3; Strzelecka, 'Women', pp. 172–3.

4   Jan Olbrycht, 'The Nazi Health Office Actively Participated with the SS Administration in Auschwitz', in *Auschwitz – Inhuman Medicine*, vol. I, part 1, published by the International Auschwitz Committee (Warsaw 1970), p. 187; see also Langbein, *People in Auschwitz*, p. 337.

5   Adelsberger, *Auschwitz*, p. 101.

6   Strzelecki, 'Große Entwesungs- und Desinfektionsanlage', pp. 11–26, 37–8.

7   Sima Vaisman, *A Jewish Doctor in Auschwitz: The Testimony of Sima Vaisman*, trans. Charlotte Mandell (New York 2005), p. xxx.

8   Alter Feinsilber, 'Aussage', in Bezwińska and Czech (eds.), *Inmitten des Grauenvollen Verbrechens*, pp. 23–38 and 40–1.

9   Simon Gotland, biographical details and testimony, Auschwitz Trial, pp. 2785, 13333–4.

10  Julian Niewiarowski, testimony, in Zdzisław Ryn and Stanisław Kłodzinski, 'Tod und Sterben im Konzentrationslager', in Hamburger Institut für Sozialforschung, ed., *Die Auschwitz-Hefte*, vol. I, p. 314.

11  Stanisława Leszczyńska, 'Bericht einer Geburtshelferin aus Auschwitz', in *In der Hölle*, vol. II, part 2, p. 180.

12  O. R., 'Geburt im KZ', in *Die Union*, 29 September 1946.

13  Margita Schwalbowá, *Elf Frauen – Leben in Wahrheit* (Annweiler and Essen 1994). The first edition of the book appeared in 1947 and was written by Margita Schwalbowá immediately after her liberation: p. 10.

14  Klee, *Auschwitz*, p. 370; for Block 25, see also Anna Palarczyk, testimony, Auschwitz Trial, pp. 21943–4; Vaisman, *In Auschwitz*, pp. 33–4.

15  For Tauber, see Kurt Knuth-Siebenlist, testimony, Hamburg, 3 December 1959, submitted to the Auschwitz Trial on 8 June 1964, pp. 10201, 10218; Klee, *Auschwitz*, pp. 399–400.

16  Judith Sternberg, 'Bericht', in Ernst Klee, *Auschwitz, die NS-Medizin und ihre Opfer*, 3rd edition (Frankfurt am Main 2004), p. 370; see also Adélaïde Hautval, *Medizin gegen die Menschlichkeit – Die Weigerung einer nach Auschwitz deportierten Ärztin an medizinischen Experimenten teilzunehmen* (Berlin 2008), pp. 52–3.

17  Langbein, *People in Auschwitz*, p. 233.

18  Julian Kiwała, 'An der Jahreswende 1942–1943', in *In der Hölle*, vol. II, part 2, pp. 167–8.

19  Kościuszkowa, 'Kinder im Konzentrationslager Auschwitz', p. 208; Hopfner, 'Kinder in Auschwitz', pp. 175–6.

20  Leszczyńska, 'Geburtshelferin', p. 181.

21 Anne Hunger, 'Der Weg einer Breslauer Antifaschistin – In Erinnerung an Irmgard Konrad 1915 bis 2003', in Cornelia Domaschke, Daniela Fuchs-Frotscher and Günter Wehner, eds., *Widerstand und Heimatverlust – Deutsche Antifaschisten in Schlesien* (Berlin 2012), pp. 154–5.

22 Irmgard Konrad, statement, in *Erinnern für Gegenwart und Zukunft – Überlebende des Holocaust berichten*, CD-ROM with accompanying booklet, Berlin 2000.

23 Kościuszkowa, 'Kinder im Konzentrationslager Auschwitz', p. 209; Kubica, 'Children and Adolescents', pp. 252, 268.

24 Kubica, *Pregnant Women*, pp. 9–10.

25 Johnnes-Dieter Steinert, *Deportation und Zwangsarbeit – Polnische und sowjetische Kinder im nationalsozialistischen Deutschland und im besetzten Osteuropa 1939–1945* (Essen 2013), pp. 234–47; Kubica, 'Children and Adolescents', p. 254.

26 'The Warsaw Uprising 1944' exhibition, Topography of Terror Berlin, 26 July – 15 October 2019, panel 'German Terror Policy'; see also Christoph Schwarz, *Geraubte Kinder – Vergessene Opfer, Exposé zur gleichnamigen Ausstellung*, 2nd edition (Freiburg 2016), p. 4.

27 Szmaglewska, testimony, *Der Nürnberger Prozess*, pp. 9.124–6. Seweryna Szmaglewska published *Dymy nad Birkenau* [*Smoke over Birkenau*], her impressive report on Auschwitz, in Poland in 1945. It was a major piece of evidence at all Nuremberg trials against leading representatives of the German Nazi state held until 14 April 1949. It has been compulsory reading for decades in Polish schools. It appeared in German in July 2020 under the title *Die Frauen von Birkenau*.

28 Marie-Claude Vaillant-Couturier, testimony, in *Der Nürnberger Prozess*, pp. 6397–406, 6419–20.

29 Leszczyńska, 'Geburtshelferin', pp. 174–5.

30 Vaillant-Couturier, testimony, p. 6410; Maria Nowakowska, 'Das "Frauen-Revier" in Birkenau', in *In der Hölle*, vol. II, part 2, p. 1445; Leszczyńska, 'Geburtshelferin', pp. 174–5.

31 Kárný, 'Theresienstädter Familienlager', pp. 174, 217–37.

32 Czech, *Auschwitz Chronicle*, pp. 648–9; Kubica, *Odebrane Dzieciństwo*, p. 17.

33 Elisabeth Guttenberger, 'Das Zigeunerlager', in H. G. Adler, Hermann Langbein and Ells Lingens-Reiner, *Auschwitz – Zeugnisse und Berichte*, 3rd revised edition (Frankfurt am Main 1984), p. 132.

34 Hermann Langbein, 'Im Zigeunerlager von Auschwitz', in Tilman Zülch, ed., *In Auschwitz vergast, bis heute vergessen – Zur Situation der Roma (Zigeuner) in Deutschland und Europa* (Reinbek bei Hamburg 1979), pp. 134–5.

35 Zimmermann, 'Die Deportation der Sinti und Roma', pp. 45–83; Kladivová, 'Sinti und Roma', p. 301; Kubica, *Odebrane Dzieciństwo*, p. 17; Central Council of German Sinti and Roma, ed., *European Roma Holocaust Memorial Day*, 2 August 2019, p. 16.

36 Piper, 'Mass Murder', p. 230.

37 Fritz Bauer Institut, ed., *Materialmappe: Das Konzentrationslager Buna Monowitz* (Frankfurt am Main), p. 6.

38 Hopfner, 'Kinder in Auschwitz', pp. 177–8.

39 Kubica, 'Children and Adolescents', pp. 268–72; Leszczyńska, 'Geburtshelferin', pp. 174–5; Kubica, *Pregnant Women*, pp. 11–12.

40 Kubica, 'Children and Adolescents', p. 240.

41 Strzelecka and Setkiewicz, 'Construction', pp. 98–100.

42 See Stefania Homik, statement, 5 April 1957, Archives of the Auschwitz-Birkenau State Museum; Anna Fefferling (married Gomez), affidavit, Paris, 5 April 1954, Archives of the Auschwitz-Birkenau State Museum, archive no. 25982.

43 Alina Cielemięcka-Naciążek, statement, Archives of the Auschwitz-Birkenau State Museum.

44 Leszczyńska, 'Geburtenhelferin', p. 179.

45 Kościuszkowa, 'Kinder im Konzentrationslager Auschwitz', pp. 209–10.

46 Leszczyńska, 'Geburtenhelferin', pp. 179, 181–2.

47 Kubica, *Pregnant Women*, p. 11.

48 Quoted from Dietrich Strothmann, 'Der Mörder mit dem Lächeln', in *Die Zeit*, 15 February 1985.

49 Ruth Elias (alias Ruth Iliav), 'Nur Gott und Dr. Mengele wissen es', in *Der Spiegel*, 5 August 1964; see also Elias, *Die Hoffnung erhielt mich am Leben – Mein Weg von Theresienstadt und Auschwitz nach Israel* (Munich 1988), pp. 178–91.

50 Lilli Segal, *Vom Widerspruch zum Widerstand – Erinnerungen einer Tochter aus guten Hause* (Berlin and Weimar 1986), pp. 196–216; Anni and Heinrich Sussmann, 'Macht's den Mund auf und red's', in Monika Horsky, ed., *Man muß darüber reden – Schüler fragen KZ-Häftlinge* (Vienna 1988), pp. 130–82.

51 Segal, *Vom Widerspruch*, pp. 196–210.

52 Hopfner, 'Kinder in Auschwitz', pp. 177–8; Kubica, 'Children and Adolescents', p. 272; Kubica, *Pregnant Women*, pp. 11–12.

53 Janina Kościuszkowa, 'Kinderschicksale im KZ-Lager Auschwitz', in *Przegląd Lekarski*, vol. XVIII, 2nd series (Kraków 1962), p. 37; see also Vaillant-Couturier, testimony, Nuremberg Trial, p. 6418.

54 Adelsberger, *Auschwitz*, pp. 100–1.

55  Nadine Brozan, 'Out of Death – A Zest for Life', in *The New York Times*, 15 November 1982.

56  Gisella Perl, statement, quoted from *Stern*, 14 February 1985.

57  Perl, statement in Langbein, *People in Auschwitz*, p. 235.

58  Gisela Perl, *I Was a Doctor in Auschwitz*, reprint of 1st edition, 1948 (North Stratford, NH 2009), pp. 71, 81–6.

59  Adelsberger, *Auschwitz*, p. 101; see also Anna Polshchikova, *Deti Osventsima* (Children of Auschwitz) (Yalta 1993), pp. 57–67.

60  Adelsberger, *Auschwitz*, p. 101.

61  Zywulska, *I Survived Auschwitz*, pp. 123–4.

62  Quoted from Jiří Fränkl, *Der brennende Himmel* (Prague 1995), p. 41.

63  Państwowe Muzeum Auschwitz-Birkenau et al., eds., *Kunst in Auschwitz 1940–1945*, pp. 382–3.

64  Zofia Stępień-Bator, statement, quoted from Kubica, *Man darf sie nie vergessen*, p. 328.

65  Interview with Erich Kulka, Jerusalem, 13–16 March 1988; see also Otto Dov Kulka, *Landschaften der Metropole des Todes – Auschwitz und die Grenzen der Erinnerung und Vorstellungskraft* (Munich 2013), pp. 15–114.

66  Erich Kulka, testimony, Auschwitz Trial, transcript by associate judge, pp. 6447–8.

67  Olga Lengyel: *Five Chimneys – A Woman Survivor's True Story of Auschwitz*, reprint (London 1984), pp. 5, 13–17, 110–13.

68  Kubica, *Pregnant Women*, p. 11.

69  Kubica, 'Children and Adolescents', p. 240.

70  Ibid., p. 276.

71  Knut Elstermann, *Gerdas Schweigen* (Berlin 2007), p. 157.

72  Polshchikova, *Deti Osventsima*, pp. 57–67.

73  Ibid.

74  Elstermann, *Gerdas Schweigen*, pp. 157–62.

75  Compare also Kubica, *Geraubte Kindheit*, p. 22; Kubica, *Pregnant Women*, p. 13.

76  *Sovyetskaya Sibir*, 26 September 1967; interview with Tadeusz Szymański, 1 December 1989; Edmund Polak, *Kim jesteś, Basiu?* [Who Are You, Basia?] (Kraków 1974); Kubica, *Man darf sie nie vergessen*, p. 332.

77  City of Vitebsk, certificate for Barbara Wesołowska, 20 August 1961.

78  Czech, *Auschwitz Chronicle*, p. 485.

79  Leszczyńska, 'Geburtshelferin', p. 180.

80  Steinert, *Deportation*, pp. 234–47.

81  Barbara Bromberger and Hans Mausbach, *Feinde des Lebens – NS-Verbrechen an Kindern* (Cologne 1987), p. 204.

82  Władysława Wesołowska, statement recorded by Izabela Smoleń in the Auschwitz-Birkenau Memorial and Museum, 28 July 1961; see also *Dziennik Zachodni*, 28, 8 March 1945.

83  Wesołowska, statement.

84  Theodore Lavi, ed., 'Sárospatak', *Encyclopedia of Jewish Communities in Hungary*: www.jewishgen.org/yizkor/pinkas_hungary/hun523.html; Ferenc Miller, Avraham Andi Goldstein, Ze'ev Spitzer and Yehudah Landau, eds., 'Sárospatak', www.jewishgen.org/yizkor/Sarospatak/sarospatak.html; Sandor Feinberg, 'Sárospatak': https://sanderfeinberg.com/sarospatak-history.

85  Hilberg, *Destruction*, vol. II, p. 859; Gerlach and Aly, *Das letzte Kapitel*, pp. 132–48.

86  See Robert Jay Lifton, *The Nazi Doctors: Medical Killing and the Psychology of Genocide* (New York 1986), pp. 270–84; Hans-Joachim Lang, *Die Frauen von Block 10 – Medizinische Versuche in Auschwitz*, revised version (Augsburg 2018), pp. 99–156.

87  Peter Huth, ed., *Die letzten Zeugen. Der Auschwitz-Prozess von Lüneburg 2015 – Eine Dokumentation* (Stuttgart 2015), pp. 9, 118–28.

88  Angela Orosz-Richt, Berlin, speech at the opening of the exhibition 'Geboren in Auschwitz', curator Alwin Meyer, on 23 January 2020 in Hotel Maritim and Gedenkstätte Deutscher Widerstand in Berlin.

## 'Twins! Where Are the Twins?'

1  Udo Benzenhöfer, 'Bemerkungen zum Lebenslauf von Josef Mengele unter besonderer Berücksichtigung seiner Frankfurter Zeit', in *Hessisches Ärzteblatt*, 4/2011.

2  Helena Kubica, 'Dr. Mengele und seine Verbrechen im KL Auschwitz-Birkenau', in *Hefte von Auschwitz 20* (Oświęcim 1997), pp. 376–455.

3  Lifton, *Doctors*, p. 342.

4  Ibid., pp. 337–83; Völklein, *Mengele – Der Arzt von Auschwitz*, pp. 111–86; Klee, *NS-Medizin*, pp. 449–91.

5  Klee, *NS-Medizin*, pp. 405–24; Barbara Huber, *Der Regensburger SS-Zahnarzt Dr. Willy Frank* (Würzburg 2009), pp. 108–29.

6  Völklein, *Mengele – Der Arzt von Auschwitz*, pp. 144–74; Lifton, *Doctors*, pp. 337–83.

7  Elżbieta Piekut-Warszawska, 'Kinder in Auschwitz – Erinnerungen einer Krankenschwester', in Hamburger Institut für Sozialforschung, ed., *Die Auschwitz-Hefte*, vol. 1, pp. 227–8.

8  Ibid.; Kubica, 'Mengele', pp. 384–90.

9  Piekut-Warszawska, 'Kinder in Auschwitz', p. 228.

10 Vera Alexander, list of persons, Auschwitz Trial, p. 42688.

11 Ibid., statement, quoted from *Stern*, 14 February 1985.

12 Klee, *NS-Medizin*, pp. 424–32; Lifton, *Doctors*, pp. 239–53.

13 Friedrich Herber, 'Der Lebensweg des Dr. Miklós Nyiszli', in Miklós Nyiszli, *Im Jenseits der Menschlichkeit – Ein Gerichtsmediziner in Auschwitz* (Berlin 1992), pp. 176–81.

14 Miklós Nyiszli, testimony on 28 July 1945, quoted from Klee, *Auschwitz*, p. 302.

15 Nyiszli, *Im Jenseits*, pp. 153–4.

16 Lifton, *Doctors*, pp. 357–60; Klee, *NS-Medizin*, pp. 488–9; see also Peter-Ferdinand Koch, *Menschenversuche – Die tödlichen Experiment deutscher Ärzte* (Munich and Zurich 1996), pp. 173–80.

17 Nyiszli, *Im Jenseits*, p. 46.

18 Nyiszli, quoted from Lifton, *Doctors*, p. 359.

19 Ella Lingens, testimony, quoted from Bernd Naumann, 'Lebende Kinder in die Flammen geworfen – Eine frühere Häftlingsärztin im Auschwitz-Prozeß', in *Frankfurter Allgemeine Zeitung*, 3 March 1964; see also Ella Lingens, *Gefangene der Angst – Ein Leben im Zeichen des Widerstandes* (Berlin 2005), pp. 155–6.

20 See transport list from Theresienstadt ghetto of 6 September 1943, ITS Arolsen 1.1.42.1/4957760.

21 See Auschwitz concentration camp inmate list, undated, ITS Arolsen 1.1.2.1/533065; Adler, *Theresienstadt*, p. 127.

22 Czech, *Auschwitz Chronicle*, p. 483.

23 Ibid., p. 635.

24 See extract from Auschwitz concentration camp inmate list, undated, p. 7, ITS Arolsen 1.1.2.1/533069.

25 Czech, *Auschwitz Chronicle*, pp. 628–9.

26 Lipscher, *Die Juden*, pp. 91, 116, 121, 179.

27 Ivan Kamenec, *Po stopach tragedie* (Bratislava 1991), pp. 267, 271.

28 List of liberated inmates with details of health and camp-related diseases, ITS Arolsen 1.1.2.1/534106 and 1.1.2.1/534107.

29 Susan Seiler, 'Das Mädchen im Käfig', memoirs recorded by Ernie Meyer, in *Die Woche*, 27 January 1995.

30 Lifton, *Doctors*, p. 362.

31 Vyjera Pavlovna, testimony, quoted from Kubica, *Man darf sie nie vergessen*, p. 323.

32 See, e.g., 'Zdzisław Ryn/Stanisław Kłodziński, Patologia sportu w obozie koncentracyjnym Oświęcim-Brzezinka' ['Pathology of Sport in Auschwitz-Birkenau Concentration Camp'], in *Przegląd Lekarski* 1 (Kraków) (1974), pp. 46–58.

33 Ondrichová, *Fredy Hirsch*, pp. 82–3.

34 Helena Kubica and Piotr Setkiewicz, 'The Last Stage of the Functioning of the *Zigeunerlager* in the Birkenau Camp (May–August 1944)', *Memoria*, 10 (2018), p. 15; Czech, *Auschwitz Chronicle*, p. 677.

### 'To Be Free at Last!'

1 Józef Marszałek, *Majdanek* (Reinbek bei Hamburg 1962), pp. 239–46, 248; Tomasz Kranz, 'Konzentrationslager Lublin-Majdanek', in Benz and Distel, eds., *Der Ort des Terrors*, vol. VII, pp. 51–3, 66–70; Daniel Blatman, *The Death Marches: The Final Phase of Nazi Genocide*, trans. Chaya Galai (Boston 2011), p. 17.

2 Andrzej Strzelecki, 'The Liquidation of the Camp', in Długoborski and Piper, eds., *Auschwitz 1940–1945*, vol. V, pp. 12–16, 41–8; Andrzej Strzelecki, 'Evakuierung, Auflösung und Befreiung des KL Auschwitz', in *Nationalsozialistisches Vernichtungslager*, pp. 400–13; Czech, *Auschwitz Chronicle*, p. 801.

3 See 'List of Survivors in Auschwitz, Birkenau and Monowitz', undated (probably drawn up at the end of January or in February 1945), ITS Arolsen 1.1.2.1/517488.

4 Strzelecki, 'Liquidation', pp. 31–3.

5 Czech, *Auschwitz Chronicle*, p. 786.

6 Ibid., p. 798.

7 Ibid., p. 800.

8 See photo on page 9 (bottom) of the second plate section, captioned 'Gabor Hirsch believed …'.

9 List of the health and camp-related illness of former inmates of Auschwitz, probably drawn up shortly after liberation. Gábor Hirsch is mentioned by name and with his inmate number, undated, ITS Arolsen 1.1.2.1/534726–534727.

10 Kubica, *Geraubte Kindheit*, pp. 17, 33, 59, 64; Kubica, *Pregnant Women*, p. 13.

11 Quoted from Czesław Pilichowski, *Es gibt keine Verjährung* (Warsaw 1980), p. 46.

### Transports, Death Marches and Other Camps

1 Blatman, *Death Marches*, pp. 88–9, 132–60.

2 Hans Ellger, 'Hamburg-Tiefstack', in Benz and Distel, eds., *Der Ort des Terrors*, vol. V, pp. 423–4.

3 Andrea Rudorff, 'Christianstadt (Krzystkowice)', in Benz and Distel, eds., *Der Ort des Terrors*, vol. VI, pp. 271–2.

4   Ibid., p. 273.

5   'Alphabetical list of EK transport, departed 28 September 1944', with the name of Wolfgang Wermuth, ITS Arolsen 1.1.42.1/4958817 und 1.1.42.1/4958841.

6   'Admissions book' of inmates at Dachau concentration camp, with the name of Wolfgang Wermuth, 10 October 1944, ITS Arolsen 1.1.6.1/9895716.

7   Edith Raim, 'Kaufering', in Benz and Distel, eds., *Der Ort des Terrors*, vol. II, pp. 360–73.

8   Georg Spitzlberger, 'Landshut', in Benz and Distel, eds., *Der Ort des Terrors*, vol. II, pp. 380–1.

9   William W. Wermuth, Hartford, CT, to the Generalstaatsanwalt bei dem Kammergericht Berlin, 7 May 1968.

10  Generalstaatsanwalt bei dem Kammergericht Berlin, Kouril, letter to William W. Wermuth, 10 May 1968.

11  List of the German Jews liberated from Camp Dachau, submitted by the World Jewish Congress (New York) with the name Wolfgang Wermuth, 13 June 1945, ITS Arolsen 1.1.6.1/993393.

12  Kaienburg, 'Sachsenhausen – Stammlager', pp. 17–67.

13  Ibid., p. 37.

14  Register of Ravensbrück concentration camp (Men's Camp) with the name of Herbert Adler, ITS Arolsen 1.1.35.1/3767395.

15  Harry Stein, 'Buchenwald – Stammlager', in Benz and Distel, eds., *Der Ort des Terrors*, vol. III, p. 316.

16  Ibid., pp. 329–31.

17  Czech, *Auschwitz Chronicle*, pp. 677–8.

18  Ibid., p. 677.

19  Kladivová, 'Sinti und Roma', pp. 314–15.

20  Adelsberger, *Auschwitz*, p. 89.

21  Rudolf Weisskopf, testimony, quoted from Kladivová, 'Sinti und Roma', p. 316.

22  Kubica and Setkiewicz, 'The Last Stage', p. 15.

23  Kladivová, 'Sinti und Roma', p. 317.

24  Vlastimila Kladivová, 'Tschechische Zigeuner-Kinder im KL Auschwitz 1943–44', manuscript, translated from Czech to German in 1985 by Marta Palczewska, p. 11.

25  Annette Leo, 'Ravensbrück – Stammlager', in Benz and Distel, eds., *Der Ort des Terrors*, vol. IV, pp. 478–84.

26  Mahn- und Gedenkstätte Ravensbrück / Stiftung Brandenburgische Gedenkstätten, ed., *Ravensbrück – Historischer Überblick und Lageplan* (Fürstenberg and Havel 2008).

27 Bernhard Strebel, 'Das Männerlager im KZ Ravenbrück 1941–1945', in *Dachauer Hefte 14* (Dachau 1998), pp. 146–54.

28 Mahn- und Gedenkstätte Ravensbrück, *Ravensbrück*.

29 Leo, 'Ravensbrück', pp. 501–14; Strebel, 'Männerlager', pp. 159–71.

30 Mahn- und Gedenkstätte Ravensbrück, *Ravensbrück*.

31 List of admissions on 20 September 1944 to Mauthausen concentration camp, with the names Géza and Zoltán Schein, ITS Arolsen 1.1.26.1/1319967 und 1.1.26.1/1319991.

32 Changes for 13 December 1944 in Mauthausen concentration camp, 'transferred to Gusen satellite camp', with the name Geza Schein, ITS Arolsen 1.1.26.1/1310109 and 1.1.26.1/1310111.

33 Bertrand Perz, 'Gusen I und II', in Benz and Distel, eds., *Der Ort des Terrors*, vol. IV, pp. 371–80.

34 Ibid., p. 374.

35 Janek Mandelbaum's name can be found on a list showing that he was evacuated from Bad Warmbrunn to Dörnhau on 14 April 1945, Muzeum Gross-Rosen, document 2330/DP.

36 Isabell Sprenger and Walter Kumpmann, 'Groß-Rosen – Stammlager', in Benz and Distel, eds., *Der Ort des Terrors*, vol. VI, pp. 195–221.

37 Wolbróm, www.yadvashem.org/yv/en/exhibitions/wolbrom/pdf/wolbrom. pdf; Maciej Przegonia, 'Wolbrom – Dedication', www.sztetl.org.pl/de/article/ wolbrom/16,erinnerungen/10715,dedication.

38 Barbara Sawicka, 'Bad Warmbrunn (Cieplice Zdrój)', in Benz and Distel, eds., *Der Ort des Terrors*, vol. VI, p. 227.

39 Dorota Sula, 'Dörnhau (Kolce)', in Benz and Distel, eds., *Der Ort des Terrors*, vol. VI, pp. 275–8.

40 Dachau concentration camp, registration form with the name Ede (Eduard) Kornfeld, admission date 29 September 1944, ITS Arolsen 1.1.6.2/ 10146355.

41 Stanislav Zámečnik, *Das war Dachau*, 2nd edition (Frankfurt am Main 2010), pp. 23, 303–5.

42 Raim, 'Kaufering', pp. 360–73; for the sequence of internments, see also Allied High Commission for Germany, International Tracing Service, internment certificate no. 51467 with the name Eduard Kornfeld, Arolsen, 29 April 1955, ITS Arolsen 6.3.3.2/99209067.

43 Edith Raim, 'Riederloh', in Benz and Distel, eds., *Der Ort des Terrors*, vol. II, pp. 470–2.

44 Ibid.

45 Mauerstetten municipal authority, abbreviated version of Mauerstetten

village chronicle, www.mauerstetten.de/freizeit-kultur/chronik-mauerstetten/kurzfassung.

46  Raim, 'Riederloh', p. 471; see also Allied High Commission, internment certificate (see n. 42).

47  Raim, 'Riederloh', p. 368.

48  Götz Aly, ed., *Aktion T4 1939–1945 – Die 'Euthanasie'-Zentrale in der Tiergartenstraße 4* (Berlin 1987), pp. 11–20; see also Ernst Klee, 'Von der "T4" zur Judenvernichtung', in ibid., pp. 147–52; Henry Friedlander, *Der Weg zum Genozid – Von der Euthanasie zur Endlösung* (Berlin 1997), p. 170.

49  Zámečnik, *Dachau*, pp. 390–400.

50  Stiftung Niedersächsische Gedenkstätten, ed., *Bergen-Belsen – Katalog zur Dauerausstellung* (Göttingen 2009), pp. 41–103, 145–295.

51  Thomas Rabe, 'Bergen-Belsen – Stammlager', in Benz and Distel, eds., *Der Ort des Terrors*, vol. VII, p. 187.

52  Eberhard Kolb, *Bergen-Belsen 1943–1945*, 2nd revised edition (Göttingen 1986), U4.

53  Rabe, 'Bergen-Belsen', p. 214.

54  Blatman, *Death Marches*, p. 89.

55  Inmate personnel file from Mauthausen concentration camp, with the name Heinz Kounio, ITS Arolsen 1.1.26.3/1570761.

56  Bertrand Perz, 'Melk', in Benz and Distel, eds., *Der Ort des Terrors*, vol. IV, pp. 405–8.

57  Kounio, *Ezisa*, pp. 127–8.

58  Perz, 'Melk', p. 407.

59  Inmate personnel file from Buchenwald concentration camp, with the name Robert Büchler, ITS Arolsen 1.1.5.3/5626863.

60  Harry Stein, *Buchenwald Concentration Camp 1937–1945: A Guide to the Permanent Historical Exhibition*, trans. Judith Rosenthal (Göttingen 2004), pp. 60–85, 104–29, 134–202, 218–53; Stein, 'Buchenwald – Stammlager', pp. 300–56; Buchenwald Concentration Camp 1937–1945, in www.buchenwald.de/en/72.

61  Dr Jonas Silber (Metz), 'Children in Buchenwald', in Hackett, *The Buchenwald Report*, p. 279.

62  Stein, *Buchenwald Concentration Camp*, p. 166.

63  Robert Büchler, 'Kinderblock 66 im KL Buchenwald', manuscript, undated, in the Moreshet Archives in Givat Haviva, Israel.

64  Stein, *Buchenwald Concentration Camp*, pp. 231–2.

65  Hans Maršálek, *Die Geschichte des Konzentrationslagers Mauthausen*, 4th edition (Vienna 2006), pp. 11–30, 45–62, 87–103, U4; Florian Freund and

Bertrand Perz, 'Mauthausen – Stammlager', in Benz and Distel, eds., *Der Ort des Terrors*, pp. 313–26.

66 Florian Freund, 'Gunskirchen (Wels I)', in Benz and Distel, eds., *Der Ort des Terrors*, pp. 368–70.

67 Kounio, *Liter of Soup*, pp. 139–64.

68 Freund, *KZ Ebensee — Außenlager von Mauthausen* (Vienna 1994) pp. 3–34; Verein Widerstandsmuseum Ebensee, ed., *Konzentrationslager Ebensee*, 2nd edition (Ebensee 2000), pp. 12–80; Freund, 'Ebensee' in Benz and Distel, eds., *Der Ort des Terrors*, vol. IV, pp. 354–60.

69 Kounio, *Liter of Soup*, pp. 142–64.

70 List of liberated inmates from the National Greek Committee at Ebensee – September 1945, with the names of Heinz and Salvator Kounio, pp. 1, 6, ITS Arolsen 1.1.26.1/1303843 and 1.1.26.1/1303848.

71 Freund, 'Ebensee', pp. 354–60; Freund, *KZ Ebensee*, pp. 31–48; Verein Widerstandsmuseum Ebensee, *KZ Ebensee*, p. 70.

72 Report by the director of UNRRA team 122, 1946, quoted from Verein Widerstandsmuseum Ebensee, *KZ Ebensee*, p. 89.

73 Inmate personnel file of Mauthausen concentration camp, with the name Jürgen Loewenstein, admission date 25 January 1945, ITS Arolsen 1.1.26.3/1595236.

74 Notification of change [at Mauthausen] for 24 February 1945 – Transferred to outside commando Vienna/Sauererwerke: (274 skilled workers) with the name Jürgen Loewenstein, ITS Arolsen 1.1.26.1/1310579 and 1.1.26.1/1310583.

75 Bertrand Perz, 'Wien (Saurerwerke)', in Benz and Distel, eds., *Der Ort des Terrors*, vol. IV, pp. 445–8.

76 List of 107 inmates transferred on 23 April 1945 from SS work camp Vienna XI, with the name Jürgen Loewenstein, ITS Arolsen 1.1.26.1/1317328 and 1.1.26.1/1317358.

77 Bertrand Perz, 'Steyr-Münichholz', in Benz and Distel, eds., *Der Ort des Terrors*, vol. IV, pp. 437–40.

## Dying? What's That?

1 See Emilia Klimczyk, statement recorded by Tadeusz Szymański, Jawiczowice, 2 August 1960, and Adam Klimczyk, statement recorded by Tadeusz Szymański, 27 August 1960, both in the archive of the Auschwitz-Birkenau State Museum.

2 Stanisława Jankowska, 'Chronicle of the Last Days of Auschwitz' (diary written in Auschwitz-Birkenau), 21–28 January 1945, archive of the Auschwitz-Birkenau State Museum.

3 Stanisław Krcz, statement recorded by Tadeusz Szymański, Oświęcim, 16 May 1963, archive of the Auschwitz-Birkenau State Museum.

NOTES TO PAGES 298–311

4 Karolina Krcz, statement recorded by Tadeusz Szymański, Oświęcim, 29 August 1960, archive of the Auschwitz-Birkenau State Museum.

5 Éva Krcz, statement recorded by Tadeusz Szymański, Oświęcim, 29 August 1960, archive of the Auschwitz-Birkenau State Museum.

6 Dinah Gottliebova survived Auschwitz. She lived in Felton, California, under the name Dina Babbitt until her death in July 2009.

7 Statements by Ryszard Rydzikowski and Bronisława Rydzikowska, recorded by Anna Zieba, Oświęcim, 4 November 1961, archive of the Auschwitz-Birkenau State Museum.

8 Lidia Rydzikowska, statement recorded by Tadeusz Szymański, Oświęcim, 27 December 1960, archive of the Auschwitz-Birkenau State Museum.

9 *Aufbau* (New York), 5 March 1948.

10 Recha Freier, *Let the Children Come – The Early History of Youth Aliyah* (London 1961), pp. 18–47, 79–80.

11 Freier, *Auf der Treppe* (Hamburg 1976), p. 62.

12 Freier, *Let the Children Come*, p. 61.

13 Lutz Kann, quoted from Gabrielle Goettle, 'Was ist Geld?! – Lutz Kann, ein jüdischer Remigrant' erzählt', in *die tageszeitung*, 29 July 2013.

14 Barbara Groneweg, 'Die Waisenkinder Israels – Ben Shemen, ein Dorf von internationalem Ruf', in *Frankfurter Rundschau*, 13 August 1960.

15 Mikhal Dekel, *Tehran Children – A Holocaust Refugee Odyssey* (New York 2019), esp. ch. 1, 'Each of Us Feels as if He Is Born Again' (Iran, August 1942), ch. 8, 'Polish and Jewish Nation Building in Tehran', and ch. 9, 'Hebrew Children: Kibbutz Ein Harod'; United States Holocaust Memorial Museum, 'Tehran Children', Tehran Children: The Holocaust Encyclopedia (ushmm. org); see also Henryk Grynberg, *Kinder Zions – Dokumentarische Erzählung* (Leipzig 1995), pp. 9–186.

16 Interview with Richard Levinsohn, Ben Shemen, 14 March 1988.

17 Aryeh Simon, '… die Gegenwart junger Menschen', in *Zeichen*, 1 (March 1987).

18 Interview with Richard Levinsohn.

## *Alive Again!*

1 Nelly Wolffheim, 'Kinder aus Konzentrationslagern – Mitteilungen über die Nachwirkungen des KZ-Aufenthaltes auf Kinder und Jugendliche', part I, in *Praxis der Kinderpsychologie und Kinderpsychiatrie*, 11/12 (November/December 1958), pp. 302–12; part II, 1 (January 1959), pp. 20–7; part III (conclusion), 2 (February/March 1959), pp. 59–71.

2 Jewish History | About Us | World Jewish Relief: The Boys – Child Holocaust

Survivors | World Jewish Relief; see also Martin Gilbert, *The Boys: The Story of 732 Young Holocaust Survivors* (Berlin 2007), pp. 11–14, 329–411.

3 Wolffheim, 'Kinder aus Konzentrationslagern', part III, p. 61, and part II, pp. 59–71.

4 Ibid., part III.

5 Mick Zwirek, '45 Aid Society.

6 Harry Olmer, in World Jewish Relief: The Boys.

7 Quoted from Wanda Półtawska, Andrzej Jakubik, Józef Sarnecki and Julian Gątarski, 'Ergebnisse der Untersuchungen der in den nazistischen Konzentrationslagern geboren oder in den Kinderjahren inhaftierten Personen', in *In der Hölle retteten sie die Würde des Menschen — Anthologie*, vol. II, part 3, published by the International Auschwitz Committee (Warsaw 1970), pp. 57–9.

8 See Herbert Diercks, ed., *Verschleppt nach Deutschland! – Jugendliche Häftlinge des KZ Neuengamme aus der Sowjetunion erinnern sich* (Bremen 2000), pp. 161, 168–77; Alla Tumanova (Reif ), *Šag vlevo, šag vpravo* [One Step to the Left, One to the Right] (Moscow 1995), p. 120; 'Many were branded for ever with the number from Auschwitz on their arms ... and the number of the Soviet camp on the back of their fufaika': Verena Buser, Überleben von Kindern und Jugendlichen in den Konzentrationslagern Sachsenhausen, Auschwitz und Bergen-Belsen (Berlin 2011), p. 281, n. 33: Howard Margol tells of a boy deported from Kaunas to Auschwitz, who was interned for two years after the war in a Siberian camp because he had set off to look for members of his family: Howard Margol, 'Finding a Holocaust Survivor after 63 Years'; Schura Terletska, 'Es gab Berge von Haaren – Man hat uns geschoren', in Senatsverwaltung für Arbeit, Berufliche Bildung und Frauen, ed., *Frauenkonzentrationslager Ravensbrück – Auschwitz Chronicles 2000* (Berlin 1999); Anne Applebaum, *Der Gulag* (Munich 2005), pp. 447–68; Jörg Osterloh, *Sowjetische Kriegsgefangene 1941–1945 im Spiegel nationaler und internationaler Untersuchungen* (Dresden 1996), pp. 38–54, 93–6; Diana Siebert, 'Zur Geschichte der Belarus und der dortigen Geschichtspflege seit 1944', in Projektgruppe Belarus, ed., *'Dann kam die deutsche'*, pp. 191–2.

9 Nadezhda Tkacheva, statement in Projektgruppe Belarus, *'Dann kam die deutsche Macht'*, pp. 69–72.

10 Julia Gerra, *Narisovavshiye smert – ot Osventsima do Noyengamme* [Painting Death – from Auschwitz to Neuengamme], documentary film, Russia 2012.

11 See Detlef Garbe, 'Neuengamme – Stammlager', in Benz and Distel, eds., *Der Ort des Terrors*, vol. V, pp. 330–9.

12 Carl Lutz, 'Die Judenverfolgungen unter Hitler in Ungarn', in *Neue Zürcher*

*Zeitung*, 30 June 1961; Agnes Hirschi, 'Carl Lutz und der Jüdische Widerstand in Ungarn', in *Neue Zürcher Zeitung*, 13 May 2005.

13  Tom Segev, *The Seventh Million – The Israelis and the Holocaust*, trans. Haim Watzman (London 2000), pp. 178–83.

14  29th General British Hospital in Bergen-Belsen, patient list of 5 July 1945, with the name Helene (Channa) Markowicz, ITS Arolsen 3.1.1.2/81968899.

15  UK Ministry of Defence, ed., *The Liberation of the Death and Concentration Camps, Europe, June 1944 – May 1945*, Second World War 60th Anniversary, Booklet No. 9 (London 2005), pp. 10–13.

16  'Displaced Persons Leaving on … Ingrid', list of 7 July 1945, with the name Helena (Channa) Markowicz, ITS Arolsen 3.1.1.2/82009607.

17  Vienna Jewish Community (IKG), 'List of Practising Jews Living in Vienna 1946', with the name Jürgen Rolf Loewenstein, pp. 1, 51, ITS Arolsen 3.1.1.3/78805412 und 3.1.1.3/78805439.

18  'Jews in Vienna – 1st List of Returnees from Concentration Camps', with the name Jürgen Loewenstein, *Aufbau*, 12.9, 1 March 1946, p. 21.

19  *Hannah Senesh: Her Life & Diary*, Introduction by Abba Eban (New York 1973), pp. 80–7, 164–7; Catherine Senesh, 'Memories of Hannah's Childhood', pp. 5–12, and Reuven Dafne, 'The Last Border', pp. 170–9, in ibid.; John Oppenheimer, *Lexikon des Judentums*, 2nd edition (Gütersloh 1971), p. 790.

20  *Senesh: Her Life & Diary*, p. 256.

21  Czech, *Auschwitz Chronicle*, p. 283.

22  The name Dagmar Fantlová is in list 1979 of 1 June 1945 of those repatriated from Bergen-Belsen to Czechoslovakia, ITS Arolsen 3.1.1.2/81967838.

23  See also the Czech list of orphans with the name Dagmar Lieblová, undated, address: Kutná Hora, Husova 125 (the street still exists today), ITS Arolsen 3.1.1.3/78783152.

24  Lothar Martin, 'Vor 60 Jahren: Industriestadt Ostrava wird vom Westen her befreit', www.radio.cz/de/rubrik/tagesecho/vor-60-jahren-industriestadt-ostrau-wirdvom-westen-her-befreit.

25  Registration card from Steyr DP camp with the name Eduard Kornfeld and the comment: 'Left for Switzerland Nov. 49', ITS Arolsen 3.1.1.1/67776356.

26  Gutman, *Holocaust*, vol. I, p. 377.

27  Schoeps, ed., *Lexikon des Judentums*, pp. 46–7.

28  See Janos Hauszmann, *Ungarn – Vom Mittelalter bis zur Gegenwart* (Regensburg 2004), pp. 259–63.

29  Tibor Schaechner, biography: Schaechner, Tibor – El Paso Holocaust Museum, ttps://elpasoholocaustmuseum.org/tibor-schaechner.

30 Agnes Schaechner (*née* Klein), biography: Schaechner, Agnes – El Paso Holocaust Museum.

31 Hans Ellger, 'Salzwedel', in Benz and Distel, eds., *Der Ort des Terrors*, vol. V, pp. 514–16.

32 Agnes (Klein) Schaechner, *Reflections*, video, part 8, Agnes (Klein) Schaechner – El Paso Holocaust Museum.

33 Spector, *Jewish Life*, vol. I, p. 481.

34 Helmut Braun, 'Viersprachenlieder erfüllen die Luft – Die Stadt in der Erinnerung der Dichterinnen und Dichter', in Braun, ed., *Czernowitz – Die Geschichte einer untergegangenen Kulturmetropole* (Berlin 2005), pp. 85–106; Spector, *Jewish Life*, vol. I, pp. 237–8; Daniel Fuhrhop, 'Heute das Damals suchen', in *die tageszeitung*, 21 April 2012.

35 Rose Ausländer, quoted from Braun, 'Viersprachenlieder', p. 94.

36 Hauszmann, *Ungarn*, pp. 259–63.

37 Ibid., pp. 264–7.

38 'Liste von Mutters Transport von Auschwitz nach Stutthof, 4501 Frauen, am 27. September 1944', in Hirsch, *Als 14-jähriger durch Auschwitz-Birkenau*, including CD with photos and documents.

39 List dated 30 June 1945 of former inmates from Hungary and Romania housed in the Alpenjäger barracks in Wels, with the name Gesa (Géza) Schein, ITS Arolsen 3.1.1.2/82048362.

40 The names Olga, Vera and Sari (their mother) Grossmann appear on the following list dated 18 April 1945: 'List No. 1 Czechoslovak People Freed in Oswięcim', submitted by the Relief Committee of Jews from Czechoslovakia – 'At the beginning of March there were in OSWIECIM the following CZECHOSLOVAK Citizens', ITS Arolsen 3.1.1.3/78786329.

41 Olga and Vera Grossmann appear in the following list from July 1946 with Košice as their place of abode: 'List of Children in Kosice, Slovakia, C.S.R. – Submitted by the World Jewish Congress, 1834 Broadway, New York 23, N.Y.', ITS Arolsen 3.1.1.3/78784317 and 3.1.1.3/78784318.

42 Spector, *Jewish Life*, vol. III, p. 1252; Melody Amsel, *Between Galicia and Hungary: The Jews of Stropkov* (New Haven, CT 2002).

43 The names Olga and Vera Grossmann appear in the following list dated 22 April 1948: 'List of Children Who Arrived in England from Czechoslovakia on 22nd April, 1948', ITS Arolsen 3.3.2.1/87427687 and 3.3.2.1/87427688.

44 Reference written by Rabbi S. Schonfeld, London, 28 November 1952.

45 The name Wolfgang Wermuth can be found in an Outer Camp Hospital Dachau list dated 9 June 1945, ITS Arolsen 1.1.6.1/9935071.

46 List of names of the Regensburg Jewish community, with the name of

Wolfgang Wermuth, address: Denzingerstrasse 5, 22 May 1947, ITS Arolsen 3.1.1.2/82024757 and 3.1.1.2/82024776.

47  US Maritime Commission Passenger Manifest Form, with the name of Wolfgang Wermuth, sailing date 21 February 1947, ITS Arolsen 3.1.3.2/81650577.

48  Robert Büchler's name is listed in the Register of all persons saved from anti-Jewish persecution in Slovakia, issued on 15 October 1945, with the address Bratislava, Listova 9, ITS Arolsen 3.1.1.3/78817785 and 3.1.1.3/78817830.

49  Yahil, *The Holocaust*, p. 493; Gutman, *Holocaust*, vol. III, p. 1250.

50  Givat Haviva Institute, ed., *The Givat Haviva Institute*, n.d.

51  See also Yehuda Bacon, affidavit, Jerusalem, in February 1954, ITS Arolsen, 6.3.3.2/99461792 and 6.3.3.2/99461793.

52  Přemsyl Pitter, *Unter dem Rad der Geschichte* (Zurich and Stuttgart 1970), pp. 88–120.

53  H. G. Adler, 'Yehuda Bacons Weg in die Freiheit', in *Yehuda Bacon*, exhibition catalogue, n.d.

54  Ibid.

55  David Gat, 'Ich habe meinen Namen gewechselt, sooft es nötig war', in Pavel Kohn, *Schlösser der Hoffnung – Die geretteten Kinder des Přemsyl Pitter erinnern sich* (Munich 2001), pp. 67–8.

56  See, for example, Lizzie Doron, *Warum bist du nicht schon vor dem Krieg gekommen?* (Frankfurt am Main 2006), or Ruth Bondy, 'Überleben', in *Theresienstädter Studien und Dokumente 1998*, pp. 277–87.

57  Tom Segev, 'Die zwei Gesichter des Eichmann-Prozesses', in *Le Monde diplomatique / die tageszeitung* (April 2001), pp. 14–15.

58  Gedenk- und Bildungsstätte Haus der Wannsee-Konferenz / Stiftung Topographie des Terrors / Stiftung Denkmal für die ermordeten Juden Europas, eds., *Der Prozess – Adolf Eichmann vor Gericht* (Berlin 2011), pp. 140–2.

59  Gutman, *Holocaust*, vol. II, p. 432; Segev, *The Seventh Million*, pp. 476–83.

60  Werner Renz, 'Anmerkungen zur Geschichte des Auschwitz-Prozeßes', in Friedrich-Martin Balzer and Werner Renz, eds., *Das Urteil im Frankfurter Auschwitz-Prozess* (Bonn 2004), pp. 28–31.

61  Wojak, ed., for the Fritz Bauer Institute, *Auschwitz-Prozeß 4 Ks 2/63*, pp. 275–611.

62  Preliminary remarks on the criminal charge against Mulka et al., *Auschwitz-Prozeß*, p. 46.

63  Yehuda Bacon, testimony, *Auschwitz-Prozeß*, p. 23187.

64  Wojak, ed., for the Fritz Bauer Institute, *Auschwitz-Prozeß*, pp. 637–813.

65 Bernd Naumann, *Auschwitz – Berichte über die Strafsache Mulka u.a. vor dem Schwurgericht Frankfurt* (Berlin 2004).

66 Hermann Langbein, *Der Auschwitz-Prozess – Eine Dokumentation*, unrevised reprint of the first edition from 1965, vols. I and II (Frankfurt am Main 1995), pp. 7–8, 903–9.

67 Micha Brumlik, 'Die Deutschen und der Auschwitz-Prozess', in *Frankfurter Rundschau*, 27 September 2002.

68 Balzer and Renz, eds., *Das Urteil*, pp. 33–7.

69 Jim G. Tobias and Nicola Schlichting, *Heimat auf Zeit – Jüdische Kinder in Rosenheim 1946–47* (Nuremberg 2006), p. 7.

70 Kristina Dietrich, '"… ich wundere mich, dass ich überlebt habe" – Pädagogik in den DP Children's Centers und Kindergärten der jüdischen Nachkriegsgeden 1945–1948', in *nurist – Beiträge zur deutschen und jüdischen Geschichte*, vol. V (Nuremberg 2010), pp. 26–33.

71 Jim G. Tobias, *Zeilsheim – Eine jüdische Stadt in Frankfurt* (Nuremberg 2011), pp. 47–127.

72 Museum of the History of Polish Jews, 'History of the Jewish Community in Gdynia'.

73 Spector, *Jewish Life*, vol. I, p. 350.

74 Ibid., vol. III, p. 1200.

75 Robert Kuwalek, Bełżec, in Benz and Distel, eds., *Der Ort des Terrors*, vol. VIII, pp. 331–71.

76 Zygmunt Klukowski, *Diary from the Years of Occupation 1939–44*, trans. George Klukowski (Urbana, IL 1993), p. 219.

77 Drozd, *Whirlwind of War*, pp. 418, 452.

78 Freund, 'Ebensee', pp. 356, 358.

79 Angelika Meyer, 'Malchow', in Benz and Distel, eds., *Der Ort des Terrors*, vol. IV, pp. 569–71.

80 Kounio-Amariglo, *Thessaloniki*, p. 141.

81 Hans-Joachim Lang, *Die Namen der Nummern – Wie es gelang, die 86 Opfer eines NS-Verbrechens zu identifizieren* (Frankfurt am Main 2007), pp. 160–86, 271–301.

82 Hella Kounio, 'A Report for My Relatives and Friends of My Trip to the Old Hometown and to Auschwitz', Thessaloniki, 3 October 1987.

83 Ibid.

84 Ibid.

85 *Jerusalem of Lithuania*, 3–4 (134–5) (April–June 2004).

86 The name Joschna (Josif) Konvoj appears in the Dachau admissions book, ITS Arolsen 1.1.6.1/9895194.

87 Jerry Zalman Konvoj, testimony, Toronto, n.d. (2005).

88 Certificate of Oslavany city administration of 3 December 1993.

89 Energotrust Brno – Elektrána Oslavany, reference for the period 16 September 1946 to 9 November 1948, 1 December 1955.

## Who Am I?

1 Interview with Tadeusz Szymański, Berlin, 30 January 1983.

2 Interview with Tadeusz Szymański, Oświęcim, 17 November 1984.

3 Hanka Paszko, biography, 17 November 1986; interview with Tadeusz Szymański, Lankum, 1 December 1989.

4 Interview with Tadeusz Szymański, 1 December 1989.

5 Paszko, biography, 17 November 1986; Szymański, interview, 1 December 1989.

6 Nina Gusieva, 'O tym zapomnieć nie wolno' ['This Must Not Be Forgotten'], in *Zeszyty Oświęcimskie 5* (Oświęcim 1961), pp. 133–40.

7 Paszko, biography, 1986; Szymański, interview, 1 December 1989; see also Ewa Wanacka, 'Daslze losy dzieci Oświęcimskich' (2) ['The Fate of the Auschwitz Children'], in *Trybuna Robotnicza*, 27/28 October 1962; and Kubica, *Man darf sie nie vergessen*, p. 330.

8 Czech, *Auschwitz Chronicle*, p. 612; Paszko, biography, 1986.

9 Szymański, interview, 1 December 1989; Paszko, biography, 1986; see also Wanacka, 'Daslze losy dzieci Oświęcimskich', in *Nowiny Gliwickie*, 21 May 1962.

10 See letter from the German Red Cross to the Arolsen International Tracing Service of 17 May 1960, ITS Arolsen 6.3.3./105550935.

11 Hanka Paszko, letter to Kola Klimczyk from Vitebsk, 21 August 1962.

12 This is the number in Mikołaj Klimczyk's first ID from the Polish Association of Former Political Prisoners from Auschwitz, issued on 17 June 1948.

13 Czech, *Auschwitz Chronicle*, pp. 609–12; Kubica, *Man darf sie nie vergessen*, p. 331.

14 Letter to the German Red Cross, 17 May 1960.

15 Gala Kozlova (married name Strukova), letter, 21 May 1962.

16 Marusya Kozlova (remarried name Kieslakova) and Galina (Gala) Strukova (Kozlova), letter of 15 June 1962.

17 Marusya Kieslakova (Kozlova), undated letter, probably written in winter 1962.

18 Gala Strukova (Kozlova), undated letter, probably written in winter 1962.

19 Gala Strukova (Kozlova), letter, 18 December 1962.

20 Ibid., undated letter, probably written in 1963.

21 István Gyenes, 'Üzenet Az Elöknek' ['Message to the Living'], in *Nök Lpja*, 14 April 1973.

22 Deutsches Rotes Kreuz – Suchdienst Hamburg, letter to Lidia Rydzikowska of 15 January 1962.

23 Anna Bocharova, telegram, 14 February 1962.

24 Lidia Rydzikowska, letter, 14 or 15 February 1962.

25 Anna Bocharova, letter, February 1962.

26 Czech, *Auschwitz Chronicle*, p. 629.

27 Kecskemeti György, 'A kis Eva az Uj Elet ütjän keresi szüleit, akiktöl Auschwitzben szakitottäk el' ['Little Eva Seeks Through *The New Life* Her Parents from Whom She Was Separated in Auschwitz'], in *Uj Elet*, 1 November 1962.

28 Kecskemeti György, 'Nem illüziö' ['No Illusion'], in *Uj Elet*, 1 January 1963; Päl Geszti, 'Az A 5116 rejtelye' ['The Mystery of A 5116'], in *Ndpszabadsäg*, 18 July 1963; Jerzy Iwanowski, 'Najmiodsza b. wieiniarka Ogwieimia' ['The Youngest Inmate in Auschwitz'], in *Express Wieczorny*, 24 August 1963.

29 Magyar Vöröskereszt (Hungarian Red Cross), letter of 14 March 1963 to Ewa Krcz.

30 S. Ökrös, 'Daktyloskopische Untersuchungen zur Feststellung der Abstammung', in L. Breitenecker, ed., *Beiträge zur gerichtlichen Medizin*, vol. XXII (Vienna, n.d.).

### '... The Other Train Is Always There'

1 Półtawska et al., 'Ergebnisse der Untersuchungen', pp. 41–7; see also, e.g., Antoni Kępinski, 'Das sogenannte KZ-Syndrom – Versuch einer Synthese', in Hamburger Institut für Sozialforschung, ed., *Die Auschwitz-Hefte*, vol. II, pp. 7–13; Wanda Półtawska, *Und ich fürchte meine Träume*, 2nd edition, trans. from Polish by Eva Luhn-Geiger (Abendsberg 1994, Polish 1962); Wanda Półtawska, 'Die "Kinder von Auschwitz" – Das Syndrom der paroxysmalen Hyperamnesie', in Carole Sachse, ed., *Die Verbindung nach Auschwitz – Biowissenschaften und Menschenversuche an Kaiser-Wilhelm-Instituten*, symposium documentation (Göttingen 2003, Polish 1965, 1967), pp. 285–305.

2 Półtawska et al., 'Ergebnisse der Untersuchungen', pp. 57–64.

3 Ibid., pp. 80–4.

4 Ibid., pp. 85–8.

5 Ibid., pp. 114–15.

6 Thomas Buergenthal, *Ein Glückskind: Wie ein kleiner Junge zwei Ghettos, Auschwitz und den Todesmarsch überlebte und ein neues Leben fand* (Frankfurt am Main 2000), pp. 82–106.

7   Thomas Buergenthal, 'Meine KZ-Nummer ist wie eine Medaille', in *Der Tagesspiegel*, 14 May 2007.

8   To protect the desired and promised anonymity, no precise source or file reference is provided here.

9   Leo Eitinger, 'Die Traumatisierungen der KZ-Gefangenen und deren heutige Probleme', in Beratungsstelle für NS-Verfolgte und deren Kinder, ed., *Spätfolgen bei NS-Verfolgten und deren Kindern* (Berlin 1991), p. 20; Stanisław Kłodziński, 'Das KZ-Syndrom', in Długoborski and Piper, eds., *Auschwitz 1940–1945*, vol. V, pp. 70–86.

10  See, e.g., Eitinger, 'Die Traumatisierungen', pp. 16–21.

11  Christian Pross, *Wiedergutmachung – Der Kleinkrieg gegen die Opfer* (Frankfurt am Main 1988), pp. 187–90.

12  Ibid., p. 120.

13  Raul Teitelbaum, *Die biologische Lösung – Wie die Schoah 'wiedergutgemacht' wurde* (Springe 2008), pp. 45–7, 328, 350; Pross, *Wiedergutmachung*, pp. 286–90, 341–6.

14  Association of Former Child Inmates in Nazi Concentration Camps, letter, Warsaw, 15 October 1990.

15  Hans Günter Hockerts, 'Die Entschädigung für NS-Verfolgte in West- und Osteuropa', in Hans Günter Hockerts, Claudia Moisel and Tobias Winstel, eds., *Grenzen der Wiedergutmachung – Die Entschädigung für NS-Verfolgte in West- und Osteuropa 1945–2000* (Göttingen 2006), pp. 7–58.

16  Deutsche Rentenversicherung Nord (Neubrandenburg), pension decision of 29 August 2011.

17  Bruno Bettelheim, *Erziehung zum Überleben – Zur Psychologie der Extremsituation, 2. Auflage* (Munich 1985), pp. 34–9.

18  Yoram Bark, Dov Aizenberg, Henry Szor, Marnina Swartz, Rachel Maor and Haim Knobler, 'Increased Risk of Attempted Suicide among Aging Holocaust Survivors', in *American Journal of Geriatric Psychiatry*, 13 (August 2005), pp. 701–4. The study by these Israeli psychiatrists concludes that the risk of Holocaust survivors attempting to commit suicide triples in old age.

19  Stella Müller-Madej, *Das Mädchen von der Schindler-Liste, Aufzeichnungen einer KZ-Überlebenden, 3. Aufl.* (Augsburg 1994), pp. 180–221.

20  Interview with Stella Müller-Madej by Jörg Thunecke, 'Wer leben will, stirb und wer tot zu sein wünscht, muss leben', in Viktoria Hertling, ed., *Mit den Augen eines Kindes* (Amsterdam and Atlanta 1998), p. 36.

21  Martin Buber, *The Way of Man: According to the Teaching of Hasidism* (London 2002).

22  Interview with Halina Birenbaum, Berlin, 13 June 1989; see also Birenbaum,

*Hope Is the Last to Die*; Halina Birenbaum, *Rückkehr in das Land der Väter* (Frankfurt am Main 1998).

23  Yaakov Gilad in Orna Ben-Dor Niv, *Biglal Ha'Milchama Hahi* (*Because of That War*), biographical film, Israel 1988.

24  Halina Birenbaum in Ben-Dor Niv, *Because of That War*; see also interview with Halina Birenbaum, Berlin, 13 June 1989.

25  Yaakov Gilad in Ben-Dor Niv, *Because of That War*.

26  Interview with Halina Birenbaum, 13 June 1989.

27  The author was asked not to mention the family's name.

28  Günther Schwarberg, *Der SS-Arzt und die Kinder vom Bullenhuser Damm* (Göttingen 1998), pp. 38–110, 169–70.

29  'Gedenkstätte Todesmarsch im Belower Wald', in www.stiftung-bg.de/below (see also Carmen Lange, 'Gedenkstätte Todesmarsch im Belower Wald nach umfassender Neugestaltung wieder eröffnet', in *Gedenkstättenrundbrief* 156, 1 August 2010, pp. 3–13).

30  Patronka transport list of 4 June 1942 containing the names Simon (born 1898), Rosalia (born 1905), Matilda (born 1930), Jozef (born 1932), Alexander (born 1934) and Renata [Rachel] (born 1937) Kornfeld, ITS Arolsen 1.1.47.1/5166943 and 1.1.47.1/5166955.

31  'Bratislava during the Holocaust – Deportations', www.yadvashem.org/yv/en/exhibitions/communities/bratislava/deportations.asp.

32  Martin Gilbert, *Never Again: A History of the Holocaust* (New York 2015), p. xviii.

33  'Conscripted Slaves: Hungarian Jewish Forced Labourers on the Eastern Front during World War II', https://yadvashem.org/articles/general/conscripted-slaves-hungarian-jewish-forced-laborers.html.

34  For the history of the Jewish community in Bilky, see Moshe Avital, *Not to Forget – Impossible to Forgive* (Jerusalem 2004), pp. 61–72, 103–26; Jelinek, *The Carpathian Diaspora*, pp. 4–24, 241–321.

35  Raz Segal, *Days of Ruin – The Jews of Munkács during the Holocaust* (Jerusalem 2013), pp. 73–110, 133–6.

36  Rena Molho, *Der Holocaust der griechischen Juden – Studien zur Geschichte und Erinnerung* (Bonn 2016), p. 50.

# Index